"This book is a global 'enactment' of the rebirth of systemic therapy to heal families and communities in the 21st century – a must-read for all interested in true human, relational and societal transformation."

Silvia M. Kaminsky, *M.S.Ed., LMFT, American Association for Marriage and Family Therapy (AAMFT) President (Jan. 2023–Dec. 2024)*

"A comprehensive systems framework that inspires both trainees and seasoned practitioners to use creative interventions, nurturing family resilience through various life stages and bridging cultural and national divides."

Joel Elizur, *Professor (Emeritus), Clinical Child and Educational Psychology Program, The Hebrew University of Jerusalem*

"What a tour de force! Andolfi's book captures the spirit of his Assisi conference and its Manifesto: Valuing our children, couples, our resiliencies and diversities. It's a must-read!"

Rob Garfield, *M.D. clinical faculty, Department of Psychiatry, University of Pennsylvania*

INTERNATIONAL FAMILY SYSTEMS THERAPY

Detailing a wide range of systemic approaches to mental health and relational issues, this essential guide demonstrates the power of family systems therapy as a means of fostering genuine human, relational, and societal transformation.

With contributions from more than 50 internationally recognized family therapy scholars and practitioners, this text illustrates how family systems therapy can provide a comprehensive, effective, and more humane approach to the dominant paradigm of mental health treatment. The book offers an integrative approach that blends action-oriented techniques with multigenerational and multicultural insights, and provides an understanding of children and adolescents' issues, couple crises, and losses and life adversities, and shares stories of resilience from families all over the world. Chapters explore how family and couple therapy can be used to address a variety of challenges, such as engaging children's voices in sessions, couples in which a partner suffers from a chronic illness or disability, strengthening family healing and resilience, teens at risk of suicide, the intricacies of power dynamics in couples, infertility, and much more.

This text is essential reading for mental health and human service practitioners, researchers, and policymakers, as well as graduate-level trainees in all mental health disciplines.

Maurizio Andolfi, MD, is an internationally renowned child psychiatrist, Director of the Family Therapy Academy in Rome, Italy, and Editor-in-Chief of Italian journal *Terapia Familiare*. He is also Director of the Perth Circle for the Advancement of Family Therapy in Western Australia.

Antonello D'Elia, MD, is a psychiatrist, trainer, and supervisor of the Family Therapy Academy, Italy, and Deputy Editor of Italian journal *Terapia Familiare*. He is also President of Società Italiana di Psichiatria Democratica.

Peter Fraenkel, PhD, is an associate professor in the Department of Psychology at the City College of New York and a former faculty member of the Ackerman Institute for the Family.

INTERNATIONAL FAMILY SYSTEMS THERAPY

Global Perspectives on the Healing Power of Families

Edited by Maurizio Andolfi, Peter Fraenkel, and Antonello D'Elia

Routledge
Taylor & Francis Group
NEW YORK AND LONDON

Designed cover image: A-Digit © Getty Images

First published in English 2026 by Routledge
605 Third Avenue, New York, NY 10158

and by Routledge
4 Park Square, Milton Park, Abingdon, Oxon, OX14 4RN

Routledge is an imprint of the Taylor & Francis Group, an informa business

ISBN: 978-1-032-88233-8 (hbk)
ISBN: 978-1-032-87008-3 (pbk)
ISBN: 978-1-003-53676-5 (ebk)

DOI: 10.4324/9781003536765

Typeset in Times New Roman
by Apex CoVantage, LLC

CONTENTS

ACKNOWLEDGMENTS

First and foremost, we extend our deepest gratitude to the Family Therapy Academy (FTA), the new international branch of the Italian Accademia di Psicoterapia della Famiglia. Without the FTA's unwavering support at every level, the Assisi Conference, the Assisi Manifesto, and now this book would not have been possible. A special thanks goes to Dr. Pierina Zavagni, Head of Administration, and Dr. Francesca Ferraguzzi, Deputy Director of FTA, for their steadfast support of this book project from its inception.

This is truly an international volume – of the 37 chapters, only 10 are authored by native English speakers. The first languages of the remaining authors include Arabic, Brazilian Portuguese, Chinese, French, Hebrew, Italian, Japanese, Malay, and Spanish. This multicultural dimension adds a unique richness to the book.

We also extend our sincere appreciation to the professional translators and to Vincenzo Di Nicola, MD; Tazuko Shibusawa, PhD, and her husband, James Runsdorf, PhD; and Mustafa Qossoqsi, PhD, for their professional and generous contributions to the editing process.

Finally, we would like to recognize the dedicated staff in Rome, who worked tirelessly to review references, format chapters, and coordinate with authors and editors to meet the publisher's deadlines. Among them, we extend special thanks to Dr. Laura Bruno, who has been Maurizio Andolfi's assistant for more than 30 years, and to Lucia Porcedda, PhD, an expert in academic editing and the editorial secretary of the journal *Terapia Familiare*.

Our heartfelt thanks also go to Mary Hotvedt, PhD, for her beautifully written preface, and to Julia Giordano, Editor at Taylor & Francis, for her patience and warm collaboration throughout this process.

PREFACE

What a pleasure to introduce you to this very new, very exciting family therapy book, the work of so many practitioners from five continents. New compendia in the field of family therapy are scarce. There are recent textbooks and some works aimed at a particular treatment approach or a specific problem. This volume takes you, the reader/therapist, through the field as it stands today as an antidote to the pervasive treatment model of individual psychotherapy for every age group and every problem.

The works within this volume came out of the Assisi Conference, in July 2023, chaired by Maurizio Andolfi, MD. This beautiful event, at which all of these authors and others presented, was attended by more than 1,000 practitioners of family therapy, representing 50 countries. It is difficult to recreate in a book the excitement this gathering of like-minded people generated. Still, I hope you will share some of the curiosity and enthusiasm of that event as you delve into these chapters.

Family therapy is alive and well. The field started more than 70 years ago in the US and Europe as a movement, founded mostly by psychiatrists and social workers, who questioned the standard models of treatment. Those pioneers, as with the writers presenting in Assisi, saw the interrelated nature of humans, as existing in families and communities. Now we call such a perspective *ecosystemic*. That perspective is apparent throughout the book, and it is highlighted in the last section.

International Family Systems Therapy: Global Perspectives on the Healing Power of Families is new in its strong international perspective and breadth. New centers for the work have sprung up in many parts of Asia and South America, and some now in Africa. These are areas where emphasis is still very strong on "family" as opposed to individualism and the individualistic method of treatment, which has had priority in the West for the past several decades.

What ties these authors' thinking together? The ecosystemic view is one thing. Another is a shared philosophy that resources exist in the same context as pain. That is, families have the capacity to contribute to healing much of their distress. The role of the therapist is to give voice to all the members of a family and to help activate those resources. In this shared thinking, the voices of children and adolescents – often overshadowed or seen as a privileged conversation just with the child therapist – are given emphasis in the context of the family session.

There is much practice-based research in this book. Many authors outline approaches and outcomes that can be useful to the reader. Yet, one could argue that these chapters are not rooted in statistical analysis of methodology and traditional outcome research. Rather, there is a strong connection to humanism and humanity in this work. The therapist is expert in the field in general, but not the instrument of healing. The clinician is more like a conductor, eliciting connection and compassion. To achieve this synthesis of knowledge and comfort in working with whole family groups, the therapist must know their own history and the ways in which that history may impact their work. This is best done in group consultation with other therapists, often using the genogram as a starting point for insight. In a sense, the ongoing training of the clinician, finding their own dilemmas and resources, parallels the family's work.

A part of this book focuses on the larger systems that affect therapy today, themes such as migration, gender roles, and climate change. The authors argue that therapists need not only to be aware of such issues but also to actively engage with their clients on them because they are so impactful. In this way, new writers are echoing the social and economic concerns of the founders of family therapy.

So, welcome to this book. Whether you are an experienced practitioner who wants to be excited in your work, or a new student of the field, you will find fresh ideas and new approaches that build on the work of the founders of family therapy. What the authors would hope is that you will be encouraged to work with whole families and to use the resources they bring, along with their dilemmas.

Mary E. Hotvedt, PhD
Co-chair, Assisi Conference, July 2023
Chair, Advisory Board, Family Therapy Academy, Italy

CONTRIBUTORS

Elisa Agostinelli – PhD, clinical psychologist, family psychotherapist, teacher and director of counseling post-graduate master, Department of Psychology, University of Southern Queensland (Australia)

Maurizio Andolfi – MD, child psychiatrist, director of the Accademia di Psicoterapia della Famiglia and Family Therapy Academy, editor-in-chief of the Italian journal *Terapia Familiare* (Italy)

Alejandro Astorga – clinical psychologist, family psychotherapist, deputy and technical director of Corporación OPCION, director of the Centro Intervención Multigeneracional (Chile)

Dominique Bardou – MD, psychiatrist, child and adolescence psychiatrist, multigenerational family therapist, trainer, and supervisor, Université de Psychologie di Nantes (France)

José Barrera – clinical psychologist, family psychotherapist, Unidad de Salud Mental Infanto Juvenil, Hospital de Valme, Seville (Spain)

Tiziana Bufacchi – clinical psychologist, psychotherapist, Open Up, Mental and Health Care Amsterdam (Italy)

Carmen Calatayud Lliso – MD, PhD, co-director, Centro de Reproducción Asistida (CREA) Valencia (Spain)

Lorena Cavalieri – clinical psychologist, family psychotherapist, director – Silvano Andolfi Foundation (Italy)

Bawany Chinapan – counselor, family psychotherapist, deputy president – Malaysian Marriage and Family Therapy Association (MyMFT), clinical director – Andolfi Family Therapy Centre in Kuala Lumpur (Malaysia)

Alicia Cruzat – clinical psychologist, family psychotherapist, director of the post-lauream Diploma in Therapy and Multigenerational Psychosocial Intervention, Director – Centro Intervención Multigeneracional (Chile)

Salvatore D'Amore – PhD, clinical psychologist, psychotherapist, professor of child, adolescence and parental clinical psychology, Université Libre de Bruxelles (Belgium)

Antonello D'Elia – MD, psychiatrist, psychotherapist, trainer – Accademia di Psicoterapia della Famiglia (Rome), Deputy Director of the Italian journal *Terapia Familiare*, president – Società Italiana di Psichiatria Democratica (Italy)

Ivy Daure – PhD, clinical psychologist, lecturer, Université de Bordeaux, director of the Art de la Psychothérapie Collection (France)

Wai Eng Ding – clinical psychologist, counselor, founder – Ding Psychology Center (Malaysia)

Vincenzo Di Nicola – MD, MPhil, PhD, child psychiatrist, family psychotherapist, philosopher, professor – Université de Montréal, President – World Association of Social Psychiatry (WASP) (Canada)

Fatou Waly Diop – psychologist, family psychotherapist, psycho traumatologist, co-founder – Centre de Thérapie KIRAAY (Senegal)

Enrique Falceto de Barros – MD, professor – University FEEVALE/RS, member – Planetary Health Brazilian Group, University of São Paulo, coordinator of the Policy Briefs for Brazilian Stakeholders of the Lancet Countdown, member – The Lancet Commission on Sustainable Healthcare (Brazil)

Luisa Falceto de Barros – psychologist, family and group psychotherapist (Brazil)

Olga Garcia Falceto – MD, PhD, professor of adolescent and child psychiatry, Universidade Federal do Rio Grande do Sul (UFRGS), family psychotherapist, curator Planetary Health Panel – Latin American Advanced Studies Institute, coordination group, Planetary Health Brazilian Ambassadors Program, Advanced Studies Institute – University of São Paulo (Brazil)

John Farnsworth – PhD, sociologist, psychotherapist, member – Australian and New Zealand Psychodrama Association, founding member – New Zealand Film and Media Studies (New Zealand)

Isabelle Feijo – MD, child and adolescent psychiatrist and psychotherapist, director – Walker Adolescent Unit, Concord Centre for Mental Health, Sydney (Australia)

Francesca Ferraguzzi – clinical psychologist, family psychotherapist, deputy director and trainer – Accademia di Psicoterapia della Famiglia (Italy)

Peter Fraenkel – PhD, associate professor – City College of the City University of New York, board member – American Family Therapy Academy, Couple, Family, and Individual Therapy (USA)

Breno Irigoyen de Freitas – clinical psychologist, teacher of mindfulness and social emotional learning (Brazil)

Eva Gerino – PhD, psychologist, family psychotherapist (Italy)

Laura Gorla – PhD, clinical psychologist, postdoctoral associate – Center for Child and Family Policy, Duke University (USA)

Shulamit Graber – clinical psychologist, couple and family psychotherapist, founder and coordinator of PTSD services (Mexico)

Klaus Iglesias Hensel – social psychologist, teacher of social emotional learning (Brazil)

Michael C. LaSala – PhD, LCSW, social worker, family psychotherapist, Dean – Simmons School of Social Work, professor emeritus – Rutgers University (USA)

Wai Yung Lee – PhD, clinical director – Asian Academy of Family Therapy and Shanghai Aitia Family Institute (Hong Kong)

Camillo Loriedo – MD, psychiatrist, director – Istituto Italiano di Psicoterapia Relazionale and Scuola Italiana di Ipnosi e Psicoterapia Ericksoniana, President – Società Italiana di Psicoterapia (SIPSIC) (Italy)

Anna Mascellani – clinical psychologist, family psychotherapist, professor – Salesian Pontifical University (Italy)

Noga Nabarro – PhD, clinical psychologist, president, co-founder and director –Institute for Systemic Studies, Family & Personal Change (SHINUI), Herzliya (Israel)

Shinichi Nakamura – MD, psychiatrist, family psychotherapist, Director – Nakamura Psychotherapy Institute, past president – Japanese Association of Family Therapy and Family Studies (Japan)

Takeyoshi Nozue – MA, psychologist, family psychotherapist, professor, Department of Psychology – Meiji Gakuin University, Director – Institute for Psychotherapy Integration, Past President – Japanese Family Psychology Association (Japan)

Noriko Odagiri – PhD, psychologist, Professor, Department of Sociology – Tokyo International University, mediator – International Family Alternative Dispute Resolution (ADR), registered with the Tokyo Bar Association (Japan)

Mami Onishi – PhD, psychologist, lecturer, Faculty of Health Sciences, Department of Clinical Psychology, Kyorin University, international committee member – Japanese Association of Family Therapy (Japan)

Giulia Pace – MD, child psychiatrist, director of Touchstone Service – Child Adolescent Mental Health Service (CAMHS), Perth (Australia)

Natividad Perez Álvarez – clinical psychologist, family psychotherapist – Centro de Reproducción Asistida (CREA), Valencia (Spain)

Patrizia Petiva – clinical psychologist, psychotherapist, founder of Family Gender Team – Turin, member of the editorial committee, Italian journal *Terapia Familiare* (Italy)

Geneviève Platteau – psychologist, professor – Université Libre, Brussels, member – Institut d'Estudies de la Famille et des Systems Humains in Senegal (Belgium)

Mustafa Qossoqsi – PhD, clinical psychologist, supervisor, family psychotherapist, poet, former chief – English Hospital of Nazareth (Palestine, Israel)

Lisiane Milhoranza Rech – clinical psychologist, teacher of social emotional learning, systemic family psychotherapist (Brazil)

Peter Rober – PhD, clinical psychologist, professor of family therapy – Institute for Family and Sexuality Studies (KU Leuven), family therapist, supervisor, and trainer – Context, Center for Marital and Family Therapy – UPC KU Leuven (Belgium)

John S. Rolland – MD, MPH, professor of psychiatry and behavioral sciences – Northwestern University Feinberg School of Medicine, co-founder and executive co-director – Chicago Center for Family Health (USA)

Raffaella Salvo – clinical psychologist, senior lecturer – Edith Cowan University (Australia)

Alessandra Santona – PhD, psychologist, family psychotherapist, associate professor – Department of Psychology, Bicocca University of Milan, trainer – Accademia di Psicoterapia della Famiglia (Italy)

Christine Senediak – clinical psychologist, director of the clinical supervision services – Sydney Family Therapy Training Institute (Australia)

Tazuko Shibusawa – PhD, social worker, family psychotherapist, executive director – Shibusawa Eiichi Memorial Foundation (Japan)

Rossella Siragusa – psychologist, relational-systemic psychotherapist, member – Tourin Family Gender Team (Italy)

Arianne Struik – clinical psychologist, founder and director – Institute for Chronically Traumatized Children (ICTC) – (Australia)

Brian Sullivan – PhD, CEO, Red Rose Foundation, founder of SICURA, domestic violence intervention, education, and training (Australia)

Umberta Telfener – clinical psychologist, systemic psychotherapist, president – European Family Therapy Association (EFTA), trainer – Centro Milanese di Terapia della Famiglia (Italy)

José Ovídio Copstein Waldemar – MD, child and adolescent psychiatrist – Instituto da familia de Porto Alegre (Brazil)

Froma Walsh – PhD, clinical psychologist, co-founder and co-director – Chicago Center for Family Health, distinguished professor emerita – University of Chicago (USA)

Michele Zappella – MD, child psychiatrist, scientific editor of the Italian journal *Autismo e Disturbi del Neurosviluppo*, former director, Child Psychiatry Department – Hospital of Siena (Italy)

INTERNATIONAL FAMILY SYSTEMS THERAPY

Global perspective on the healing power of families

Editors Maurizio Andolfi, Peter Fraenkel, and Antonello D'Elia

Introduction

This introduction chapter presents a broad overview of innovative and creative practices designed to elevate and strengthen the field of family systems therapy around the world. Originating in the United States in the 1960s, family systems therapy quickly gained recognition as a revolutionary approach to mental health. By the mid-1970s, it had spread across Europe and beyond. Unlike traditional individual psychotherapy, which focuses on the person experiencing anxiety, depression, substance use disorders, schizophrenia, anorexia, or serious adolescent behavioral issues, family systems therapy introduced a fundamental systemic perspective. This "lens" recognized that these challenges were often caused, maintained, or exacerbated by dysfunctional interaction patterns among couples and families. In contrast to dominant pathology-centered approaches of the time, family systems therapy addressed problems by also identifying and mobilizing the inherent but often underutilized strengths of families and their social context. Additionally, family therapy offered healing not only to the person with the presenting problem but also to other members of the family, making it an efficient approach to improving the mental health and well-being of all concerned.

Yet, despite the demonstrated effectiveness of family systems therapy, including in carefully conducted randomized clinical trials, various social, educational, economic, institutional, and political forces have kept the individualistic approach to mental health as the reigning form of treatment. The power of the medical establishment and its diagnostic system, in concert with the pharmacological and medical insurance industries, have continued to promote individual treatment and, especially, medication as the dominant approach – despite repeated outcome studies indicating that these medications are often ineffective and have serious side effects. Additionally, many graduate programs in mental health disciplines continue to emphasize individual forms of treatment.

More broadly, worldwide social media such as YouTube, TikTok, and Instagram, as well as some "pop/self-help" books, have fed what can be termed "the Glorification of the Individual" – the belief that a person's success stems solely from individual talent, charm, luck, and perseverance, and that struggles and failures are attributable solely to individual "deficits" or pathologies. A concerning trend has emerged in which recent young social media influencers grappling with anxiety, depression,

DOI: 10.4324/9781003536765-1

ADHD, trauma, and other mental health issues have incorporated these disorders and their diagnoses into their glorified self-image – some wearing clothing that displays their diagnosis and prescribed medications. Missing from these narratives are the well-documented social, cultural, and economic factors that contribute to mental health challenges. Equally absent are stories of seeking relationally based therapy or explorations of support from family, community, or broader social networks, reinforcing the notion that healing is a solitary endeavor rather than a relational one.

All of these factors, along with the isolation experienced during the COVID-19 pandemic, have contributed to the breakdown of couples, families, and communities. They have also reinforced a growing tendency to blame individuals for their struggles rather than recognizing these difficulties as often stemming from treatable relationship issues or responses to broader systemic oppressions, such as racism, ethnic discrimination, classism, poverty, violence against marginalized communities, religious persecution, homophobia, transphobia, and anti-Queer attitudes. In contrast, family systems therapy considers a more holistic context of a person's life to identify the root causes of mental health challenges. Rather than focusing solely on the individual, it emphasizes necessary changes within both personal relationships and broader societal structures to foster healing and well-being.

Despite the dominant paradigm of mental health treatment being individually and medically focused, family systems therapists across the globe have persisted, learning from their own early mistakes and developing innovative and alternative approaches that highlight the healing power of human relationships. One of the most profound transformations in the field came from the Feminist Family Therapy movement, which challenged traditional family therapy models rooted in patriarchal values. By bringing to light issues of power, gender, and systemic inequality within family dynamics, this movement reshaped family therapy, making it more inclusive and attuned to the complexities of relational dynamics.

This book advocates for a Second Systemic "Revolution" – or to put it more gently, a "Renaissance" of systemic therapy in the field of mental health. Its origins may be traced back to a powerful gathering in Assisi, Italy, in July 2023, where leading family systems theorists and therapists from around the world convened. Many of us have attended numerous international conferences over the years, yet the consensus was clear: "This gathering is different!" There was a heightened sense of energy and a strong feeling of a community of mental health practitioners united with a shared mission: to collect and integrate our international therapeutic experiences and clinical and research achievements in the field to promote family systems therapy as the treatment of choice. The conference culminated in the *Assisi Manifesto*, a declaration emphasizing the interconnection among individuals, families, communities, and societies. It calls for the integration of family therapy as a key approach to assessing resilience and fostering healing (Andolfi and the International Faculty, 2023).

The 56 authors of this book form an international network of scholars and family experts, all of whom presented their work in Assisi. They explore alternative research and practices that emphasize the healing power of human relationships. United by sharing the same multigenerational and multicultural principles, they embrace the *humanistic sciences* as the foundation for understanding family and community life. Moving beyond the rigid categorizations of the medical-psychiatric model, they illustrate how psychology, cultural anthropology, sociology, traditional values, and spiritual and artistic expressions offer deeper dimensions to respond to people and life's adversities. By shifting the focus from pathology to resilience, they highlight the importance of community support in fostering healing.

This book is divided into five parts, beginning with the trajectory of family development and adverse life events, including losses and trauma, and culminating in a section addressing social inequality and cultural discrimination.

Part 1 – Get rid of labels and pills: Empowering children as an invaluable resource

Readers of this book will discover how much children have been neglected in family therapy, often excluded from family sessions altogether. This volume presents a very innovative and transformative approach, demonstrating how children can be actively included in therapy as *experts* in their own family dynamics. By shifting from a stance of needing to protect children to one of respecting children's knowledge and integrity, therapists can unlock their valuable perspectives. Valuing children's voices does not mean blaming parents, who are often overwhelmed by life's challenges. Instead, it seeks to restore parental confidence and competence, particularly in navigating difficult transitions in life, one such example being divorce, which can have such a devastating impact on the life of children.

The authors emphasize the significance of integrating children's memories – including those from the perinatal period – into therapeutic interventions for pre-verbal childhood trauma. They advocate for transcending diagnostic labels and biases when addressing relational challenges faced by children on the autism spectrum or those with learning difficulties. Additionally, the authors emphasize the importance of open and authentic communication in adoptive families and stress the need for family-centered approaches in treating somatic conditions such as childhood diabetes or early eating disorders. This systemic perspective becomes even more critical in broader social contexts, particularly in marginalized schools where bullying and exclusion are prevalent.

Part 2 – Adolescents at high risk: How to listen to their voice

Adolescents seek to be themselves, to express their individuality, and to enjoy the freedom to define who they are. Yet, the challenge is that, more often than not, they do not yet *know* who they are. They crave exploration and discovery, but in the process, they may lose their way due to complex family dynamics and societal pressures. Some withdraw, some become violent or self-destructive, and others use their bodies as a means of expressing deep distress – even to the point of risking their own lives. Too often, as experts, we rush to diagnose and label them. The great danger is that these labels can harden into identities, becoming a shadow they carry throughout their lives. In today's fragmented and often toxic society – marked by family disintegration, single parenthood, and absent fathers – adolescents face increasing risks.

The authors in this section explore universal challenges encountered by youth, such as suicide attempts, self-harm, social withdrawal, eating disorders, gender identity issues, and violent responses to marginalization and dehumanizing environments. Intergenerational conflicts, social marginalization, and the harmful effects of social media further compromise adolescent development, resulting in symptoms that risk becoming permanent. Through clinical examples and innovative practices, the authors highlight the critical importance of truly *listening* to adolescents in both family therapy and peer group settings. Whether through defiance, cryptic messages, or even silence, adolescents communicate an urgent need for care, understanding, and recognition.

Part 3 – Family and social dimensions of couple crises and divorce

Couple crises, hostile separations, issues around racism, ethnocentrism, gender inequity, gender identity conflicts, and domestic violence are not just private battles and struggles within a relationship. These challenges must be understood and addressed within the broader context of family and society, using appropriate and specific interventions that set limits on them. Research and clinical experience strongly suggest that individual therapy alone is often unproductive for couples in crisis.

This section explores the complexities of couple crises, which frequently destabilize family relationships and have a profound impact on children's well-being. The authors examine various social and therapeutic scenarios, including working with hostile couples contemplating separation, same-sex couples, couples navigating assisted reproduction or physical disabilities, and intercultural relationships. Despite the uniqueness of each situation, the authors emphasize the interplay between marital crises and the larger family system. By guiding couples to revisit their personal histories and unresolved family-of-origin issues, therapists can help foster resilience and healing through a multigenerational lens.

Part 4 – Trauma, loss, and resilience: The healing power of the extended family and community

Death is a universal human experience, yet the grieving process is deeply shaped by cultural traditions, religious beliefs, and spiritual practices. It cannot be defined as simply "*healthy*" or "*pathological*" based on individual experiences or psychiatric criteria alone. All cultures around the world recognize that grief is not meant to be endured in isolation. Healing is a relational process – our ability to grieve, recover, and build resilience depends on our closest bonds, our extended families, social support systems, and the broader community.

A central theme of this section is the impact of traumatic losses caused by violence, war, and forced migration, crises unfolding today on an unprecedented global scale. The authors emphasize that healing from trauma requires the inclusion of extended family and community as essential resources. By integrating collective support, individuals can process, reframe, and transform trauma into an opportunity for growth, reconnection, and even forgiveness. Throughout these contributions, the healing power of memory emerges vividly, carried through the voices of extended families and communities, reinforcing the importance of shared narratives in the journey toward resilience.

Part 5 – Cultural diversity, migration, and social discrimination

"The migrant has become the political figure of our time." American philosopher Thomas Nail (2015) argues that migration is the rule, not the exception, in human history and calls for a new psychology and politics of movement – a *kinopsychology* and *kinopolitics.* The phenomenon of immigration has long been a defining aspect of human existence, with entire communities forced to move in search of better living conditions. In recent times, however, this natural movement has been met with resistance, as wealthier nations erect "walls" – both literal and figurative – against those seeking refuge. Forced migration is one of the greatest wounds of our time, with millions of people displaced each year by violence and destruction. The journey toward a dignified life is perilous, often marked by exploitation and met with harsh immigration policies from host countries that are either unwilling or unprepared to provide sanctuary. At the core of this crisis is global inequality and political injustice, which privilege some while severely disadvantaging others based on geography, race, or social status.

Despite these challenges, the authors highlight the immense value of cultural diversity as a powerful resource in family therapy, particularly in an increasingly multicultural world. They explore how therapists can support those in need by respecting their values and recognizing their extraordinary resilience in the face of adversity. Migration is not just a physical transition; we must also be aware of the process of emotional investments, losses, ruptures, and discoveries. As migrants adjust to their new country, differences in values and lifestyle can heighten intergenerational conflicts. Therapists play a crucial role in helping families navigate these challenges and establish a new family culture that integrates elements of both their heritage and their new environment.

Conclusion

Throughout this final section – and indeed the entire volume – a call to action emerges: mental health professionals are urged to adopt courageous, countercultural positions and build networks that promote social justice, inclusion, and human rights. This appeal also extends to humanity's relationship with the environment, a vital yet often neglected aspect of existence. Such a shift demands a profound transformation in the training of family therapists and mental health professionals. Beyond learning techniques or fixing people's problems, they must broaden their understanding of the profession – one that, in many ways, can be considered a *mission* by embracing diversity, fostering resilience, and advocating for systemic change to create a more just and equitable world.

This book provides guidelines on the cognitive and/or affective qualities required for therapists to enter with compassion and empathy into the most difficult and complex painful family issues without judgment or attitudes shaped by cultural stereotypes. Therapists must learn how to work collaboratively, utilizing their own emotional resonance to establish meaningful connections with family members. They need to facilitate new relationships, mend past emotional disconnections, and engage actively in social change – working "at the edge" to address systemic issues. Beyond professional competence, creativity, humanity, love, and genuine care for clients are among the most powerful therapeutic tools. By attuning themselves to both the pain and despair expressed by families in therapy, as well as their underlying vitality and hope, therapists can help transform these emotions into sources of strength and change. The book seeks to reenergize the family therapy movement and foster connections among English-speaking professionals and students worldwide who work with families and communities. This book also aims to equip family systems therapists – whether in mental health service organizations (inpatient and outpatient clinics, private practices), universities, training programs, or professional associations – with the knowledge and inspiration needed to advance their work and strengthen this global network.

References

Andolfi, M., Hotvedt, M., LaSala, M., Astorga, A., Chinapan, B., Daure, I., Elizur, J., Espaillat, V., Falceto, O., Qossoqsi, M., Senediak, C., Shibusawa, T., Spligaer, G., & Waldemar, J. O. (2023). *The Assisi manifesto*. Website Family Therapy Academy.

Nail, T. (2015). *The figure of the migrant*. Stanford University Press.

PART 1

Get rid of labels and pills

Empowering children as an invaluable resource

1

FROM CHILD PROBLEMS TO FAMILY RESOURCES

A healing process

Maurizio Andolfi

1.1 At the start, the child was a significant presence in family therapy

The history of family therapy is slightly confused, and there is no full agreement about who started to work with families first. Nathan Ackerman, renowned psychiatrist and psychoanalyst, is often identified as the grandfather of this field, even though social workers had a vital role in the development of family therapy, starting with Jane Addams and Mary Richmond from the early 1900s (Beels, 2002). Ackerman's clinical work with children and their families in New York started when he was 29 years old, just before the Second World War, and continued long after. His large body of writings is encapsulated in several publications (Ackerman, 1938, 1958, 1966; Ackerman & Naubaurer, 1947), but sadly, he was largely forgotten after his death, even within the Family Institute that he founded in 1960 and that was later renamed the Ackerman Institute for the Family after his premature death in 1971. This lack of recognition is probably because Ackerman was ahead of his time and the explosion of family therapy that occurred in the 1970s–1980s.

He introduced ideas that even today are still mostly valid, like his definition of the family as a social and emotional unit that is influenced by social transformation. In therapy, he focused on intergenerational relationships and conflicts, placing the child at the center of the therapeutic scenario and outlining the importance of shared authority between parents. His description of the child as the *scapegoat* in marital conflicts and his intervention model was active and provocative, based on movement and physical contact.

I remember that he was everywhere when I visited him for a month in March 1970, moving back and forth from his Institute to Columbia University. He would supervise a therapist staying in the same room with the family (at his Institute) and eventually call him out for a short time to instruct him. Or he would conduct a more formal supervision with a one-way mirror at Columbia University, assembling the family, the therapist, and the trainees in the same room for general feedback at the end of a session.

Ten years after his death, the book *The Strength of Family Therapy* was published (Bloch & Simon, 1982), which included Ackerman's selected papers, demonstrating his significant contribution to the field. Lyman Wynne, a prominent early family systems researcher and theorist, reviewed this book and mentioned his brief encounter with Ackerman in New York ten years earlier, just two days before his sudden death in 1971 (Wynne, 1984). He wrote:

> This man, whose personal strength and feistiness had long energized the family therapy movement, was now strangely quiet and subdued. . . He asked me whether I thought there was still a

DOI: 10.4324/9781003536765-3

place for him and his style of therapy, nationally or even at the Family Institute that later would be renamed to honor him.

(p. 279)

The question Ackerman raised about his place in the field of family therapy has never satisfactorily been answered. and he has been wrongfully neglected. Did the field of family therapy simply move on, leaving the significant contributions of Ackerman behind? And a more crucial question arises: *Did the field of family therapy leave the child behind?*

1.2 The founding innovators of family therapy: Where is the child?

Historically, placing the child at the center of the newly born "family therapy movement" was not the main interest of systemic therapists, nor was the child included in the mainstream thinking of psychodynamic family therapists.

Systems theorists, guided by outstanding figures such as Bateson and Don Jackson, brought significant innovations in the field, outlining the principles and the axioms of Human Communication (Watzlawick et al., 1967), which became the foundation of systemic therapy all over the world. However, they were focusing on the *here and now*, by observing the interactions of family members in the session. Their interest in the child was abstract and only present in their description of the "double bind theory." In fact, the child was considered the victim of a double bind, caused by a main actor (the double binder) who was a significant adult, usually the mother. For this reason, and by the fact that this theory was only based on a dyadic interaction, it was later dismissed and abandoned officially at the conference called *Beyond the Double Bind Theory* (Berger, 1978).

The studies and research of the innovators coming from a psychodynamic background were concentrated mainly on the *adult*. Therefore, they focused on his process of differentiation from the family of origin (Bowen, 1978; Williamson, 1991), the invisible loyalties that are transmitted from generation to generation (Boszormenyi-Nagy & Spark, 1973), and on couple therapy from an intergenerational perspective (Framo, 1992). For them, the child was of indirect interest. Furthermore, the child as a therapeutic resource or, at the very least, as a significant presence in therapy was absolutely absent in the majority of their studies and in their clinical activity. However, the child was present in Carl Whitaker's thinking, as he tended to broaden the family system by including children just as much as the older people in his sessions (Napier & Whitaker, 1977). Virginia Satir (1967) introduced a Gestalt approach centered on emotions into family therapy, and children were included in her experimental work.

The most significant contribution to working with families by engaging actively the child was made by Salvador Minuchin, who broadly dealt with children within their disadvantaged or multi-problematic families and communities. Minuchin studied as a child psychiatrist in New York and followed the teachings of Nathan Ackerman. Inspired by Ackerman's direct and provocative interventions, Minuchin developed the idea of "a therapy of challenge," in which individuals are challenged to change. Notably, the child was at the center of his therapeutic model and of the clinical work at the Philadelphia Child Guidance Clinic, which became the Mecca of family therapy in the 70s and 80s (Minuchin, 1974).

The innovative path traced by Minuchin in focusing on children in family therapy and utilizing them as a resource was followed by several therapists and authors up to the present day (Minuchin, 1974, 2009, 2017; Andolfi, 1979a; Byng-Hall, 1995; Everett Bailey, 2000; Combrinck-Graham, 1989; Sori, 2006; Gil, 2016; Lee, 2019; Omer, 2003; Forougue, 2018). Criteria of the efficacy and effectiveness in family-based treatment for children's issues were also developed in order to be considered practice evidence based (Carr, 2009, 2025; Andolfi et al., 2001; Sheidow et al., 2022; Babinski & Sibley, 2022; Kaminski et al., 2022).

However, all of these aforementioned authors, as well as therapists and counselors who work in child mental health services and hospitals all over the world, have commonly found strong resistance and bias from the medical-psychiatric dominant system to include the child in therapy *as a resource and not just as a problem*, as well as to consider *the family as an expert* in child observation and treatment.

Children's extraordinary relational resources have been largely ignored or underestimated and their voices mostly unheard. The reason for this has been the failure to see the child as a complete person, rather than as a "young, fragile, incomplete creature" and a bearer of problems who mostly needs protection in the process of growth. Instead of respecting children's creative abilities and authenticity by enlarging the focus on the relational meaning of their symptoms, the main direction has typically been the labeling of the child, following manualized techniques and protocols. Narrowing the interventions to "fixing the problem" was the best way to deny that the ill-being signals and suffering children carry in their bodies or appearing in their behaviors are a litmus test of an increasingly alienated and violent society and of families becoming more fragile and disunited (Minuchin, 2009; Zappella, 2021; Maté, 2022; Andolfi, 2016, 2024).

1.3 The bottom-up approach in multigenerational family therapy: The child as the therapist's consultant

Seeing the problem child as a consultant is an idea I developed beginning in the 90s, and it is well described in the book *Please Help Me with This Family* (Andolfi, 1994). To establish this special alliance with the child, it is first necessary to reframe his symptoms instead of labeling them and to find a relational meaning for his problems as soon as possible. Second, therapists discover that once the child is appreciated for his expertise, he can become a special guide to enter into his family's emotional world, and with his genuine help can explore relevant family events (losses, hostile divorces, betrayals, secrets, abuses, cut-offs, forced migrations, chronic diseases, gambling, addictions, and more). The genogram is the *map of the family world*, which provides a wonderful platform to start this therapeutic journey (McGoldrick & Gerson, 1985). Instead of exploring the family life cycle (Carter & Mc Goldrick, 1980) from the older generation down to the younger ones, we can explore family development "upside down" – from the bottom-up (Andolfi, 2022, 2024).

To bring the genogram more to life and to elicit even more evocative memories, families can be invited to bring along family photos that are particularly significant to illustrate aspects of their development (de Bernart & Senatore, 2016). Entering in their genogram with respect and curiosity is like a *home visit* and creates a context of intimacy and closeness, reducing distance between those who help and those who come for help (Andolfi, 2017).

From the present, we can look at the past and, in the presence of the family, we can ask the child "intergenerational questions" directly, which refer to adversities experienced by parents or grandparents in their history. The result of this intimate journey with the family is a real transformation of family emotional bonds and the disappearance of children's problems, which always represent the tip of the iceberg, while painful family issues and open wounds represent the submerged greater part of the iceberg (Andolfi, 2022, 2024).

Moving away from the medical-psychiatric model allowed the therapist to embrace Humanistic Sciences as the main source of knowledge about family and community life. Psychology, cultural anthropology, sociology, traditional values, and spiritual and artistic expressions provide much deeper dimensions to encounter people on the essence of their life's adversities and to encourage their resilience and community support (Andolfi, 2022, 2024).

1.4 The art of reframing

The art of reframing has been greatly elaborated in family therapy and centers on shifting the focus from individual issues to relational dynamics. Reframing the problem and shifting the context of the encounter to a family exploration can have a number of advantages (Andolfi, 1979b; Andolfi & Zwerling, 1980; Keeney, 1983; Andolfi, 2022). It eases the child from the negative implications of being labeled and elicits trust and curiosity towards the therapist, who is asking for his help. This might implicitly encourage collaboration from parents, who see a therapist eager to look at their child's problems in a positive way. Therefore, children's symptoms can be reframed and transformed from individual symptoms to relational indicators, by using metaphors and symbolic and playful language. The following case is a good example of reframing.

1.4.1 Case illustration: Chiara and the ritual of love

Chiara, a 10-year-old girl, presented an obsessive ritual of routinely touching her mother's hands up and down in a certain way. After amplifying her rituals, and playing with her behavior in the session, I asked the girl to "teach" the younger sister to do the same. This action created curiosity and fun and was possible to transform it into a "ritual of love," which included also the parents, who were invited to repeat the ritual of touching their hands up and down. The context of the session transformed and gave the opportunity to move to an area of deep pain suffered by both parents as children. The lack of physical expression of care and recognition in their own families was still an open wound and was replicated in their own marital relationship, which was very dry: they could not show any affection among themselves and never say *bravo* to each other. Now, Chiara is happy to be at the center of the stage and to change her controlling behavior for a higher goal – the love between her parents – and she feels proud of herself now that her obsessive rituals have been changed into a ritual of love. From this moment, therapy shifted from Chiara's problems to the exploration of open wounds from the past in order to produce a transformation in the marital relationship.

1.5 The world map in the session

Sometimes, especially when the therapist wants to explore cultural values and issues of family migration, the use of the *world map* in the session can be very productive. A child or other significant family members can be asked to pinpoint specific countries, villages, mountains, and rivers that have a particular meaning for the parents or for the older generation. If the child does not know about all this, he can consult with the parents, who are happy to inform him about their relevant memories. Once a mother started to sob as soon as her young son indicated on the map the city of Casablanca in Morocco, because she had migrated to France a long time before and missed the town where she had grown up and her family tremendously. Another time during a session, I opened a very small map attached to my diary and asked an angry man who had migrated from Algeria many years before to indicate with a pencil the village where he was born in Algeria. He took the pencil and, with great emotion, marked the "exact point" where his village was in the middle of the Algerian mountains and finally smiled.

1.5.1 Case illustration: Marco and the Croatian grandmother

Marco, a 12-year-old boy, came to a family session in Rome with a hat pulled down over his eyes covered by large dark glasses, so as to avoid his father's gaze, and toward whom he conveyed all his anger. His paternal grandmother, whom Marco grew up with, also attended the session and was seated next to Marco in the therapy room. I learnt that she was the only person in the family who was able to understand and make Marco feel relaxed. His mother was too busy and preoccupied with taking care of his disabled younger sister, and his father was described by Marco as a "man without balls."

The emotional climate of the session, which had been very tense from the start, changed a great deal when I asked Marco to talk about his grandmother's migration from Croatia after the loss of her husband in the atrocious Balkan war. As Marco went about showing where Croatia was on the world map and which village his grandmother had come from, his grandma was visibly moved by the sad memories this stirred up for her. This exercise of visibly pinpointing Croatia on the world map paved the way to connect the boy's angry feelings to a painful piece of a family history and to intervene with the use of relational questioning.

> Therapist: Do you know what happened in the Balkans before you were born? Does your anger come from there, and how do we make it disappear? Maybe grandma can tell you about her terrible experiences back then and you will be able to understand the value of peace.

Once a vital piece of history had been recanted and connected to the present situation, the tension in the room palpably dissipated. Before ending the session, it was possible to suggest for Marco to exchange his hat with that of his father and for his father to put on Marco's dark glasses so they could try to put themselves in the other's shoes.

For sure, an advantage of a *multigenerational family therapy method* – and in particular of a *bottom-up approach* (Andolfi, 2024) – is that it allows parents to lower their resistance while their child is engaged in a therapeutic dialogue. It also allows for a shift in the emotional context of the session, as greater authenticity and a sense of togetherness can be elicited by the recanting of painful family history. The child revels being at the center of the stage and is happy to be considered as a guide (Marco showing where his grandmother's village is on the map) and as a reliable person (therapist encouraging the grandmother to tell him about her terrible experience). Moving away from the presenting issue (Marco's anger toward his father) and relating the boy's anger to the greater destructive anger of a war, facilitated a positive move between father and son, amplified by the concrete actions of exchanging hats in order to promote greater empathy for each other.

1.6 From child protection to respecting child knowledge and integrity

Training programs for family therapists, although lengthy and inclusive of theories and clinical applications, only rarely include specific modules to learn about child development and child communicational skills based on verbal and nonverbal language. Therapists, who are guided by "adult thinking," logical reflections, complex models, and careful questioning, often feel uncomfortable to connect with children, who instead use creative words, body language, and eye signals, as well as playful and metaphoric expressions and are generally direct and authentic. Moreover, children move a lot while therapists tend to keep still, steady, and serious. These are some of the reasons that bring therapists to ignore or exclude children from the session, thinking it is far more useful to work with the parents to help the children. If the presenting problems are issues of child abuse or marital conflicts, even more children are excluded with the general reasoning of "protecting them" from the risk of being overexposed.

My lifelong experience of working with children in therapy has taught me to trust children and to respect their knowledge and integrity all the time. Then, it will be easy for me to see *two worlds* in a session and to position myself as a mediator between the two languages, the expression of pain of the parents and the language and the emotional responses of children, without ignoring either one.

Asking a 6-year-old child in a session: "Which of your parents will suffer the most after their separation?" or "Which one will most need your affection and support?" is equally pertinent as asking the same questions to the parents regarding their children.

Asking a little boy in a session: "Who is more in need: you of dad or dad of you?" And soon later: "Is helping your father your mission?" and finally: "Can you show how you embrace him? As a child or as a caring old man?"

The boy's responses to these three questions are very moving and direct. "Dad of me" and then "Yes, yes." And the last one (before embracing him): "When I embrace him, I almost suffocate him."

Asking a 4-year-old girl in a session: "How can you console your mother now that she feels so lonely? Can you show me how to make her stop crying? Which is your trick to make your mum smile?"

All these relational questions asked directly to children in front of their parents provoke very moving affective responses from them and indirectly from the adults, who can experience how much their children love them. All of this is solid proof that children develop a *special sense of care and protection* towards their parents from a very young age and use very refined strategies to provide affection and console their parents in adverse life situations, such as the loss of an important family member, a parent's or grandparent's chronic disease, or forced migration, and other circumstances of disruption and loss. After all, they do it for their own sake as well, because if they support their parents, in return, the parents will be able to help them grow and love them more. This behavior comes absolutely naturally to children, even if it can provoke embarrassment or a sense of guilt in parents, who could be brought to ask themselves: "Where have we gone wrong, if it is our child who has to take care of us?"

On the other hand, if a child learns to please his caregivers all the time, he might lose his own authenticity and start to develop a "false self." Maté has described well the tension between attachment (safety needs) and authenticity (a true sense of yourself) and the child's dilemma between satisfying what parents expect from him and connecting to his real feelings (Maté, 2022).

In today's society, the concept of the *secure base* (Bowlby, 1988) provided by parents, where children can come home safely after having explored the world, transforms into a *fragile base*, whereby security is substituted by mechanisms of hyper-protection and control or other times, of neglect. Parents are often divided on matters regarding education and spare time and do not have a common voice or shared authority about their children. All of this leads to an increase in triangulations or manipulations, to the extent that it becomes unclear "who must protect whom."

In clinical terms, there is a greater presence of *parental children*, whereby they play a parental role in the family to compensate for the immaturity of one or both parents. But instead of blaming parents for being the source of children's problems, we try to transform dysfunctional roles by eliciting multigenerational resources, and the problem child can become a family guide in the process of change (Andolfi, 2024).

1.7 Secrets and lies and the lack of trust in children

Lying about family issues and keeping secrets are a very common way in which parents and other significant relatives tend to overprotect children, with the idea that they are too young or fragile to know the truth.

In general, we can affirm that the truth, spoken with care, is better than the best, most well-intentioned lie. Parents can show love for their children through disclosure of the truth, rather than trying to protect children with a fake lie. In this way, they shift from *protecting their children* to *respecting them*. However, to produce a positive result, disclosing a painful truth requires the right timing, a condition of mutual trust, and a context of safety. Therapy is often a good place to make these revelations to foster a healing process.

Case illustration: Mimi's anger and the secret of divorce

In the extended example that follows, it is possible to see how parents can move from keeping a very damaging secret to finding the courage to disclose it in front of Mimi, their 11-year-old daughter, and the incredible results of this revelation followed by the complete healing of Mimi's presenting problems and a transformation of family relationships (Andolfi & Mascellani, 2023).

An Asian family contacted me for a consultation to be held in Perth. The couple have one daughter, Mimi, who was 11 years old at the time. The mother is a schoolteacher and sent an email, saying that the main problem was Mimi being withdrawn and being very aggressive with the father. She often refused to talk to him when he rang from another city, where he works as an architect. The father would come home on weekends with expensive gifts for his daughter, but the daughter was always very displeased with the gifts and would reject them. She explained that the daughter was the most important thing in the world for the father.

At the end of the email, she added that they would come with their daughter, on the stipulation that I would not disclose the fact that she and her husband had been separated since Mimi was 4 years old and had officially been divorced for the past three years. The father lived and worked outside of their hometown and returned to the family home on the weekends to stay with Mimi.

I agreed to see the family, assured the mother that I would not divulge any secrets, and proposed to see the family for two long sessions. During the first session, the girl, very tall, looked older than her age. She was wearing a hoodie and had an angry countenance. She sat between her parents, kept silent, and it was apparent that she was not happy to attend the session.

I placed the genogram that the parents had prepared on the table. When the exploration moved to the grandparents, the girl became more animated and involved in giving information about spending time with them when she was younger. Then, I asked Mimi to draw her family to elicit more collaboration from her. She chose a black marker and drew her mother and maternal grandparents on one side and her paternal grandparents and her father on the other and herself in the middle with her puppy. In the background, she drew another solitary figure in green that she labelled "father"; her father was thus drawn in two different places. At this point, she suddenly seemed to become very angry. I asked Mimi if she trusted me and did not mind if I saw her parents alone for the next hour and she agreed.

Once she left, my goal was to help the father become aware that no matter how much he loved his daughter and tried to show that to her (with his regular phone calls, visiting home each weekend, and bringing her expensive presents), his love for her was enveloped in a very big lie. I thus opened the conversation by speaking to the parents about other families that I have been working with, where secrets had been kept to protect children.

I described a family in which the father of two young boys had hidden for four years the fact that their mother had been mentally unwell and had in fact committed suicide. The boys had merely been told that their mother had been unwell and died. I spoke of how the distance and issues in family were healed when the father found the courage to tell his sons the truth and how this brought the father and sons closer, as they were finally able to join with their pain and sorrow.

Then, I brought up another case of a man who had been in prison for many years for his criminal actions and had met a woman for the first time while she was performing in a show inside the prison. Then, they got to know each other, fell in love, and eventually had a child. The father, for good behavior, was allowed to work outside the prison during the day, and he could meet and play with his son before going back to prison at night. Now the child was 6 years old, and the parents and the maternal grandmother consulted with me, as they did not know how best to handle the situation, whether to wait a few more years or to tell the child the truth. So far, the child was told that the father was working at night in the prison system.

I asked them to carefully consider the effects of keeping the truth from the child as the great danger was that the longer they withheld the truth, the greater the possibility that their son would hate his parents for lying to him for so long. I spoke to them about the resilience of children and encouraged them to have the courage to be honest and authentic with their son. In the next session, which included the child, the father embraced his son tenderly and in a tone that conveyed how deeply moved he was, he told his son the truth, and his son responded by kissing and embracing him very warmly.

When the parents and Mimi returned the next day for the second session, the father greeted me with such a firm handshake that signaled that he was ready to tell the truth to his daughter. After the pleasantries had been spoken, the father moved his chair towards his daughter and, deeply moved, he looked into his daughter's eyes and started to explain the whole truth about the situation: the separation, the divorce, his new life, which also included a new partner who lives with him in a nearby town. He added that he had made the decision never to have any more children, as Mimi was the only child he loved and had cherished deeply since the day she had been born. The daughter was staring at her father hypnotized by his words, as if she did not want to miss a single thing he was saying. The father said that he had made a big mistake by protecting her and depriving her of the truth and respect she deserved. He explained that his trips back and forth over the years were the proof of how much he loved her and how scared he had been of hurting her. The mother appeared relieved and almost surprised by the father's speech, which hinted that the parents had not discussed telling their daughter the truth that day.

I congratulated the father for the courage he had shown by taking full responsibility to establish a climate of respect and authentic love in the family. I also thanked the daughter for allowing me to talk with the parents alone the day before and for listening to her father so attentively. Then, I asked the daughter if she would like to show gratitude to her father for giving respect back to her. The daughter stood up and embraced the father for a long time, and then she turned to her mother and also embraced her tenderly!

In order to enhance the family transformation, I suggested that they prepare an *award*, to present to their daughter to honor the move from protection to respect, and to give this to her on a special occasion. Two weeks later, I received an email, which included a picture of the award they had given their daughter and a new drawing of the family. The mother said that, after the second session, she noticed that Mimi had appeared much lighter and less angry. Her behavior toward her father had changed dramatically; she chatted openly to him, sat close to him at mealtimes, and often embraced him. The mother reported that Mimi had maintained these changes in her behavior with the father for the two weeks since the session. She said Mimi often spoke of Andolfi and mentioned that she was happy she had met him. The mother said that Mimi's behavior towards her had also changed a lot. Mimi was happier at home, talked openly about her thoughts and feelings, and asked how she felt about the father building a new relationship.

The mother included a picture of the award, which reads:

> *To our beloved daughter,*
>
> *This is a special card that we did for our daughter in order to remember a special day in Perth where we had a family session in which we transformed our love for you from protection to respect, once we shared the truth with you.*

In the card were also two pictures of each parent embracing their daughter. There was a drawing of a red heart inscribed with the words: "A special day to remember in Perth (with the date of the meeting)." It was signed, with love forever, mum and dad.

The mother reported that Mimi had been so happy to receive the special award and had said how much she would like to receive many more awards like this in the future. Mimi also wrote a brief message to me: "Hi Professor Andolfi, I'm feeling very happy. My family is ok." She also included a picture of her family using figures from the Little Pet Shop Collection, and she even included me in the picture as the raccoon.

Four months later, I received another email from the mother. Mimi was more affectionate and tender with them and wanted to know more about the divorce. She seemed to be able to connect different episodes of her life when she was younger and had remarked that she was putting together the missing pieces of the puzzle. The mother also said that she believed her daughter would need time to process and accept the pain of the separation and divorce now that she knew the truth. The mother also poignantly acknowledged that she would need time to accept the situation and that she did not want her daughter to continue to protect her.

1.8 Conclusion

In this chapter, the main concepts of Multigenerational Family Therapy and the bottom-up approach have been described. Several clinical examples illustrate how to build a solid therapeutic alliance with the family through the active collaboration of the problem child, who is a special bridge to enter into the family and to explore the nodal points in family development. The presenting problem becomes the doorway to the family's world and the child becomes a privileged guide in the exploration of still-open wounds and broken emotional bonds.

The model of therapy described is *experiential*, a special personal/professional encounter shared by therapist and family in a safe and active context. For this to happen, it is necessary for the therapist to keep in mind a multigenerational map of the family, a kind of living genogram, where active resources and open healing pathways can be accessed, with the curiosity of an explorer who launches with enthusiasm into an unknown world.

The chapter also highlights the cognitive and affective qualities required by therapists to enter with passion and empathy into the most difficult and painful issues of the family without a judgmental or culturally stereotyped attitude. Therapists should be able to use themselves and their affective resonances, approaching and establishing physical contact with this or that family member, facilitating new connections, and mending the emotional disconnections of the past (Whitaker, 1989). Creativity, humanity, love and care for clients, besides professional competence, are the most effective therapeutic instruments to make direct and authentic contact with each person. By attuning to the pain and despair expressed by families, as well as highlighting implicit aspects of vitality and hope, therapists can transform sources of suffering into elements of strength and change (Andolfi, 2022).

References

Ackerman, N. W. (1938). The unit of the family. *Archives of Paediatrics, 55*, 51–62.

Ackerman, N. W. (1958). *The psychodynamics of family life*. Basic Books.

Ackerman, N. W. (1966). *Treating the troubled family*. Basic Books.

Ackerman, N. W., & Naubaurer, P. B. (1947). Failures in the psychotherapy of children. In P. H. Hoch (Ed.), *Failures in the psychiatric treatment*. Grune & Stratton. https://doi.org/10.1037/11208-006

Andolfi, M. (1979a). *Family therapy: An interactional approach*. Plenum Press.

Andolfi, M. (1979b). Redefinition in family therapy. *The American Journal of Family Therapy, 7*(1), 5–15. https://doi.org/10.1080/01926187908250297

Andolfi, M. (1994). The child as consultant. In M. Andolfi & R. Haber (Eds.), *Please help me with this family* (pp. 73–89). Taylor and Francis.

Andolfi, M. (2016). How to give voices to children in family therapy. In M. Borcsa & P. Stratton (Eds.), *Origin and originality in family therapy and systemic practices*. EFTA Series (pp. 143–168). Springer. https://doi.org/10.1007/978-3-319-39061-1_10

Andolfi, M. (2017). *Multigenerational family therapy: Tools and resources for the therapist*. Routledge.

Andolfi, M. (2022). *The gift of truth*. Accademia Press.
Andolfi, M. (2024). The bottom-up approach in multigenerational family therapy: The child as a family guide. *Journal of Marital and Family Therapy*, *50*(4), 1026–1037. https://doi.org/10.1111/jmft.12730
Andolfi, M., Angelo, C., & D'Atena, P. (2001). *La terapia narrata dalle famiglie*. Raffaello Cortina.
Andolfi, M., & Mascellani, A. (2023). *Teen voices: Tales of family therapy*. Accademia Press.
Andolfi, M., & Zwerling, I. (Eds.). (1980). *Dimensions of family therapy*. Guilford Press.
Babinski, D. E., & Sibley, M. H. (2022). Family-based treatments for attention-deficit/hyperactive disorder: A review of family functioning outcomes in randomized controlled trials from 2010 to 2019. *Journal of Marital and Family Therapy*, *48*(1), 83–106. https://doi.org/10.1111/jmft.12572
Beels, C. C. (2002). Notes for a cultural history of family therapy. *Family Process*, *4*(1), 67–82. https://doi.org/10.1111/j.1545-5300.2002.40102000067.x
Berger, M. M. (1978). *Beyond the double bind theory: Communication and family system, theory and techniques with schizophrenics*. Brunner/Mazel.
Bloch, D. A., & Simon, R. (Eds.). (1982). *The strength of family therapy: Selected papers of Nathan W. Ackerman*. Brunner/Mazel.
Boszormenyi-Nagy, I., & Spark, G. (1973). *Invisible loyalties*. Harper & Row.
Bowen, M. (1978). *Family therapy in clinical practice*. Jason Aronson.
Bowlby, J. (1988). *A secure base: Parent-child attachment and healthy human development*. Routledge.
Byng-Hall, J. (1995). *Rewriting family scripts*. Guilford Press.
Carr, A. (2009). The effectiveness of family therapy and systemic interventions for child-focused problems. *Journal of Family Therapy*, *31*(1), 3–45. https://doi.org/10.1111/j.1467-6427.2008.00451.x
Carr, A. (2025). Family therapy and systemic interventions for child focused problems: The evidence base. *Journal of Family Therapy*, *47*(1), 153–213. https://doi.org/10.1111/1467-6427.12476
Carter, B. A., & Mc Goldrick, M. (Eds.). (1980). *The family life cycle: Framework for family therapy*. Gardner.
Combrinck-Graham, L. (Ed.). (1989). *Children in family context*. Guilford Press.
De Bernart, R., & Senatore, I. (2016). *Cinema e terapia familiare*. Franco Angeli.
Everett Bailey, C. (2000). *Children in therapy: Using the family as a resource*. W.W. Norton & Company.
Forougue, M. (2018). *Emotions focused therapy with children and caregivers*. Routledge. https://doi.org/10.4324/9781315161105
Framo, J. (1992). *Family of origin therapy: An intergenerational approach*. Routledge.
Gil, E. (2016). *Play family therapy*. Guilford Press.
Kaminski, J. W., Robinson, L. R., Hutchins, H. J., Newsome, K. B., & Barry, C. M. (2022). Evidence based review of couple and family-based interventions to promote infant and early childhood mental health, 2010–2019. *Journal of Marital and Family Therapy*, *48*(1), 23–55. https://doi.org/10.1111/jmft.12570
Keeney, B. P. (1983). *The aesthetic of change*. Guilford Press.
Lee, W. Y. (2019). Working trans-generationally: A clinical discussion on family dynamics and treatment. *Journal of Family Therapy*, *42*(2), 1–19. https://doi.org/10.1111/1467-6427.12286
Maté, G. (2022). *The myth of normal: Trauma, illness & healing in a toxic culture*. Penguin Random.
McGoldrick, M., & Gerson, L. (1985). *Genograms in family assessment*. W.W. Norton & Company.
Minuchin, S. (1974). *Families and family therapy*. Harvard University Press.
Minuchin, S. (2009). *Key note speech at the evolution of psychotherapy conference*, Anaheim, CA.
Minuchin, S. (2017). Salvador Minuchin at 95 reflects on his life. *The Psychotherapy Networker*, *1*, 1–4.
Napier, A. Y., & Whitaker, C. A. (1977). *The family crucible*. Harper-Collins.
Omer, H. (2003). *Non-violent resistance*. Cambridge University Press.
Satir, V. (1967). *Conjoint family therapy: A guide to theory and techniques*. Science & Behavioral Books.
Sheidow, A. J., McCart, M. R., & Drazdowski, T. K. (2022). Family-based treatments for disruptive behavior problems in children and adolescents: An update review of rigorous studies. *Journal of Marital and Family Therapy*, *48*(1), 56–82. https://doi.org/10.1111/jmft.12567
Sori, C. F. (Ed.). (2006). *Engaging children in family therapy*. Routledge.
Watzlawick, P., Beavin, J. H., & Jackson, D. D. (1967). *Pragmatic of human communication*. W.W. Norton & Company.
Whitaker, C. (1989). *Midnight Musings*. W.W. Norton & Company.
Williamson, D. S. (1991). *The intimate paradox*. Guilford Press.
Wynne, L. (1984). Review of "The strength of family therapy: Selected papers of Nathan Ackerman" by Bloch, D., & Simon, R. *Family Process*, *23*(2), 279–280.
Zappella, M. (2021). *Bambini con l'etichetta*. Feltrinelli.

2

AMPLIFYING CHILDREN'S VOICES

Empowering distressed children as family healers

Wai Yung Lee

2.1 Introduction

Children's voices have traditionally been suppressed, even within the field of family therapy. The Philadelphia child guidance movement of the late 1960s and 1970s, which propelled family therapy to its peak, ironically silenced children's voices in favor of parental hierarchy. Even Sal Minuchin, one of the pioneers of the movement, acknowledged that the subsystem of children within the family system had been notably underexplored (Lee, 2017).

As professionals, we have often shielded children from exposure to familial conflicts, missing out on their direct expressions and feedback on family dynamics. Although a vast body of literature explores how children are affected by interparental tension (Harold & Sellers, 2018; Cummings & Davies, 2010), few studies exist on the interface between parents and children in real family situations.

In my work with children facing mental health issues, I have discovered that when given the opportunity to express their views and feelings on interparental dynamics, children can provide compelling insights. Their narratives can often shift our understanding of their presenting symptoms, from seeing them as individual mental illness to stress generated from interparental conflicts. Amplifying children's voices in conjoint family therapy sessions not only promotes their own healing but also has a profound impact on the healing of the parental relationship, especially in high-conflict situations.

2.2 How it began

It all began when we were asked to provide a consultation for an 8-year-old boy described as "emotionally and behaviorally unstable for no apparent reason." During the family assessment, we struggled to find a logical explanation for the child's behavior. The boy spent most of the time hiding his face on the couch and refused to engage with the therapist. However, the mother recounted an incident at a parent-teacher gathering where her son scolded her for not asking any questions in response to the teacher's invitation. He said, "If you don't work on your problems, how can you expect us to work on ours?"

This information indicated that the child had been closely observing his mother, and we suspected that his behavior might be a reaction to her internal turmoil (Stevenson-Hinde et al., 2007). Building upon numerous studies that had shown children's physiological reactions to parental conflict (Cummings & Davies, 2002), we devised a protocol in which the parents were invited to engage in a

DOI: 10.4324/9781003536765-4

discussion about their differences in the presence of their child, while monitoring the child's physiological changes using a biofeedback program.

During the exercise, the couple's conversation seemed relatively calm, with minimal signs of conflict. The mother discussed her challenges with disciplining the child, but her underlying message conveyed a complaint about the lack of support from her husband. The husband remained unresponsive, dismissing her complaints as her own problem of setting unattainable expectations. While the boy sat quietly without displaying any reactions, the biofeedback machine recorded internal upheavals that would otherwise have gone unnoticed. His heart rate and skin conductance displayed significant deviations from the baseline, particularly during moments when his parents failed to respond to each other.

In the subsequent debriefing session, the child suddenly became animated and outspoken, providing feedback to his parents akin to that of a seasoned therapist. He told them that they were like "water and oil that cannot be mixed." He advised his father to be more expressive and not to keep things bottled up, while suggesting to his mother that she should allow others more time to respond instead of "pouring her heart out relentlessly." He also recommended that they communicate with each other more, preferably in the morning when their minds are fresh and better able to remember things.

The child's remarkable level of verbal sophistication took us all by surprise. It became evident that the protocol, originally designed to capture the child's physiological arousal, could also serve as a valuable clinical tool in the therapeutic process.

2.3 Family Biofeedback Assessment protocol

Over the past decade, our clinical team has been dedicated to refining and improving the Family Biofeedback Assessment© protocol while applying it to children with different presenting problems. The protocol serves two primary purposes: (1) to investigate whether the child's presenting problem is related to the family relationship and, if so, (2) to understand the specific ways in which the family dynamics contribute to the issue.

2.3.1 The protocol consists of two parts

1. *Physiological measurement*: Initially, parents are asked to engage in a 30-minute discussion focusing on unresolved issues, while the child is seated within full visibility of the parents at the other end of the room. A technician utilizes the Biograph Infiniti Software to measure the child's physiological responses, including skin conductance, peripheral temperature, and heart rate. An arousal is defined when at least one of the aforementioned physiological responses exceeds or falls below two standard deviations from the child's baseline, which is established before the assessment.
2. *Debriefing*: Immediately following the physiological measurement, the therapist convenes with the entire family to review the child's arousal patterns. For each arousal score, the therapist asks the child questions such as, "When your mother said this (quoting the exact words and tones), and your father responded with that (quoting the exact words and tones), your heart rate increased to 150 bpm (or your skin conductance increased by fourfold) from the baseline. What were you reacting to?" or "What were you experiencing at that moment?" By revisiting each episode within the parental discussion that triggered the child's arousals, the therapist guides the child in expressing his/her thoughts on the specific issues within the interparental dynamic. The goal is to encourage the parents to listen and to promote dialogue among all family members (Lee, 2017, 2019; Lee et al., 2010).

Table 2.1 Family biofeedback assessment

First part	Second part	New Family Story
Depicted arousal point: Gut language *(What is the body telling you?)*	Translate arousal point(s) to verbal/nonverbal expression *(What are you telling us?)*	
first arousal point ______ →	1. ____	______
second arousal point ______ →	2. ____	______
third arousal point ______ →	3. ____	______
fourth arousal point ______ →	4. ____	
fifth arousal point ______ →	5. ____	

2.3.2 The interface between the two parts of the protocol

The therapist's role is to facilitate the transformation of the physiological score (what we call the gut language) obtained in the physiological measurement into verbal and nonverbal communication during the debriefing process. Starting with the inner self of the child and moving toward the child's perception of the parents, the therapist encourages the child to open up to the parents. Significant exchanges between the parent and child are anticipated in this process, creating a new experience that may lead to a shift in the understanding of the presenting problem and create new possibilities for treatment:

Self → Self and Others → Commenting on parental relationship → Significant exchange

Researchers have extensively examined responses such as vagal tone, skin conductance, cortisol activation, and the autonomic nervous system as mechanisms underlying children's adaptation to hostile interparental conflict (El-Sheikh et al., 2009; Porges, 2009; Zemp et al., 2014). In our protocol, we focused on heart rate, skin conductance, and peripheral temperature, as these measures provide instantaneous results, enabling the therapist to tap into the child's fresh memory of the parental experience, making it easier for the children to express their emotions more spontaneously.

2.4 First illustration

In the case of a 14-year-old boy diagnosed with somatization disorder, he presented with various somatic symptoms such as abdominal cramps, dizziness, and headaches since primary school, leading to frequent school absences. Despite multiple physical examinations, no apparent organic pathology was found. During the 30-minute parental discussion that was part of the Family Biofeedback Assessment©, the boy became highly anxious. His heart rate increased from his baseline of 74 bpm to 106 bpm when his parents argued about his behavior. However, his heart rate spiked up to 185 bpm when his parents fell silent after a heated argument.

During the debriefing section, the therapist asked the boy, "I can understand why you experienced high arousal when your parents were arguing with each other, but then they were just sitting there without even talking to each other. What were you responding to?"

Boy: In my family, silence is deadly. Each time when there is silence, something bad will happen. . . . They will explode, mom will cry, and dad will run away. I have to stay to comfort her. I can't run away, can I? I have studied very hard to please her for the past eight years, but it's of no use. And I become easily irritated . . .
Therapist: Then how do you deal with your own share of anxiety?
Boy: I just swallow it . . . Or it goes to my head.
Therapist: That's why you have headaches and stomach pains?
Boy: Yes.

In a simple statement, the boy was able to connect his physical symptoms to parental conflict. This revelation had an immense impact on the parents, and they began to see the need to deal with their own marital difficulties. After the assessment, the boy enrolled himself in a boarding school in the UK. He told the therapist in private that because of the difference in time zone between the UK and Hong Kong, his parents could not easily contact him.

2.5 Second illustration

A 13-year-old girl was diagnosed with somatic pain disorder and depression. Her 10-year-old brother accompanied her to the Family Biofeedback Assessment©. In contrast to the previous case, where the boy's arousal scores increased when the parents became silent, this girl's arousal scores decreased significantly but her somatic symptoms increased.

During the 30-minute parental discussion, the parents engaged in a highly conflictual argument about their marital relationship, which transitioned into silent tension. In the beginning, the girl displayed high arousal scores, with her heart rate ranging between 35 bpm and 194 bpm from her baseline of 107.85 bpm. However, when her parents fell into silence, her heart rate dropped dramatically to 35 bpm. It was at this point that her abdominal pain emerged, causing her great discomfort. Her younger brother, who was seated next to her, looked very worried and immediately passed her a hot water bottle to provide comfort.

During the debriefing section, she talked about her distress in relation to her family situation:

Girl: Many years ago, I asked my mother to run away with me one night. I don't know why I did that. It wasn't cause of just one particular thing, but many things added together. . . . I think a lot, and people often said that I think like an adult. I have to protect my family and I have to hide my feelings from them. . . . I may appear to be very normal on the outside but even at school, people don't know why I would suddenly become very upset. . . . I often burst into tears just thinking about my parents' relationship. . . . My brother is still very young and innocent. I hope to keep him away from these things until he gets older. . . . If it weren't for my brother, I would have left this home already.

Although she did not explicitly connect her symptoms and the parental conflict, the way in which her abdominal pain occurred clearly indicated that her symptoms are generated by the conflict. On the other hand, although her younger brother did not come with a diagnosis, he appeared to be very sad throughout the assessment. When asked for his feedback, he answered quietly, "It's like my family is falling apart, and no one is there to fix it."

The sense of hopelessness conveyed by the siblings was deeply disturbing to their parents and the professionals involved in the assessment. As a result of the experience, the parents began to recognize the importance of attending to their children's emotions instead of being consumed by their own animosity toward each other. Unlike the first case, in which there was only a single child, in this case, the support and comfort the siblings provided to each other at times of distress showed their resilience in mitigating their stress and offering solace.

2.6 Custodial cases

Among the various interparental difficulties, we have observed that prolonged custody battles between parents can have the most damaging impact on children. Unfortunately, the trauma experienced by these children is often overlooked. Through intensive therapy, a 9-year-old girl was finally able to express her experience of being forcibly separated from her mother due to the custody arrangement. The separation caused her nightmares and other somatic problems, and despite her father's sincere efforts to repair his relationship with his daughter, she could never fully accept him. She told her father, "You think you're the victim. What about me? You snatched me from my mother's arms when I was a baby, leaving me crying and screaming. I think I'm the victim." Amid the family battle, everyone is victimized, but as I have noted, children are often not given a chance to describe their suffering when parents are in conflict.

Parents who are engaged in child custody battles can become so consumed by their own conflict that they fail to recognize the suffering their children endure. When parents fight, some children exhibit psychosomatic symptoms such as vomiting and diarrhea, while others scream at the top of their lungs or simply gaze tearfully into the distance in silence.

A 6-year-old pleaded with his parents, saying, "Please don't fight. Excuse me. Get me out of here!" He suffered from anxiety attacks.

An 8-year-old asked, "My parents split up because they said they were unhappy. But it's been four years, and they're still not happy. Why did they split up then?" Every night, the boy pondered this question without finding an answer, which led to insomnia.

A teenage girl told her parents, "I'm like the padding inside your boxing gloves, trying to soften each blow as you hit each other." As a result, every emotional blow landed on her.

Some children were born amidst the court battle, with their parents fighting for custody in court every year until the children reached adulthood. Think of the impact this can have on a child growing up in such a hostile and bitter atmosphere (Lee, 2023).

When we shared these children's stories with a 9-year-old whose parents were similarly fighting about their custodial arrangement, she could easily relate to their feelings, and drew us a picture of herself being fried in a frying pan alongside an egg (Figure 2.1).

In another picture (Figure 2.2), she showed us that it was her parents' hands turning up the heat.

It is not our intention to blame the parents, as they are clearly traumatized by their own losses and stress. However, it is crucial for parents to hear and acknowledge their children's voices, as this may help them empathize with each other, attune to their children's emotional needs at critical moments, and attempt to resolve custody disputes more quickly and with less conflict for the sake of their children. In fact, after listening to the children's pleas, many parents admitted that going to court has also been a traumatic experience for them, and they decided to work things out between themselves and stop going to court altogether.

In their post-session written feedback, most children indicated that the best part of the experience was an opportunity to express their thoughts in front of the adults. As for the parents, they were mostly surprised to find their children to be so observant. The information on the children's "gut language" added a new dimension to the parents' understanding of their children's internal processes. Many parents have found it instrumental in shifting their focus from conflict to conflict resolution. Because the body cannot lie, the gut response speaks louder than words for children who do not express themselves verbally.

Figure 2.1

Figure 2.2 Drawing by the child patient

2.7 Clinical observation

We have applied this protocol to more than 500 cases involving children aged 4 to 20 years, as well as to some adults, who presented with various mental health issues such as Attention Deficit-Hyperactivity Disorder (ADHD), anxiety disorders, depression, and eating disorders. The protocol is particularly valuable for children struggling with mental health issues, as it helps determine whether their problems are purely biological or relational in nature.

In our transgenerational project, the protocol is applied twice: first to measure the connection between children and their parents, and then between the parents and their own parents. This approach provides insight into the emotional linkage among the three generations, forming the basis for treatment planning. With a grant from the Hong Kong Jockey Club Charities Trust, we are able to conduct a systemic analysis of the data obtained from this protocol.

2.8 The gut language

As stated in the Assisi Manifesto, it is the children's right to have their voices heard. The design of our assessment protocol is to elicit not only verbal language but also the "gut language" to facilitate an in-depth exploration of the children's experiences in relation to interparental distress.

In general, the physiological arousal patterns observed in the children indicated a high level of vigilance toward their parental relationship, regardless of their specific issue in diagnosis. It appears that the intensity of the parental conflict may correlate with the number of arousal points measured. As was noted earlier, these arousal patterns are primarily manifested through increased heart rate, sometimes exceeding 190 bpm, and heightened skin conductance, often three to four times higher than their baseline. These patterns indicate that children feel compelled to engage in the parental conflict. Some children exhibit decreased skin conductance and heart rate, occasionally dropping to dangerously low levels of 30 bpm, indicating that the situation is too critical for their bodies, leading to a state of dissociation.

According to the Polyvagal Theory (Porges, 2009), the autonomic nervous system would kick in to regulate the body's gut responses, ranging from fight-or-flight to even shut down ("freeze"), in times of overwhelming disaster, when one cannot escape a situation nor effectively fight it. It was alarming to find that interparental conflict has a similar impact on children's physiology as that of a natural disaster or catastrophe.

It is also important to note that children experience equal or even heightened arousal when their parents fall into silent tension, as compared to open arguments. This suggests that children are highly perceptive of interparental tension, regardless of their parents' attempts to conceal it. Even though some children verbally deny caring about their parents' conflicts, their gut responses indicate otherwise.

2.9 Debriefing contents

The initial half-hour discussion is crucial as it often reveals clear interpersonal patterns between parents as well as the nature of their disagreements. When this information is combined with the child's arousal points, it provides a solid context for therapists to explore the family dynamics with the child. After quietly observing their parents' conversation for half an hour, children often have much to say during the debriefing. Their remarks, and sometimes criticisms, had tremendous impact on the parents. Furthermore, it has the effect of transforming highly distressed children into "parent experts," challenging the validity of the medical labels that they were diagnosed with.

Contrary to the usual practice in the field of family therapy, which tends to create a hierarchy with the parental system taking precedence and with the children's subsystem ignored or hidden, our protocol places children in the role of parent experts, allowing them to comment on and criticize their parents' behaviors (Lee, 2017). Evan Imber-Black (2014) described this attempt as "turning ideas of Structural Family Therapy upside down" (p. 374), but she also found it necessary for the new generations to build on what has come before and create innovative methods that suit the current context.

2.10 Discussion

We have found the protocol to be highly effective in enabling therapists to elicit the children's voices in the face of interparental conflict, and to amplify these voices for therapeutic intervention.

The protocol is not intended to be problem-oriented, but rather, it aims to draw upon the strengths of both parents and the child to navigate the seemingly helpless relational impasse and create new possibilities. To successfully follow these procedures, the therapist must deal with interpersonal conflict with respect and empathy while being willing to explore intense emotions in sometimes highly conflictual situations. The therapist must also be spontaneous like a Tai Chi master, flowing with the child's energy and not blocking it.

Utilizing children's comments on their parents' relationship is undoubtedly the most powerful technique for raising awareness among parents, but it can also be the most challenging intervention for therapists. In addition to the common belief that only parents have the right to criticize their children, especially in certain cultures, not all therapists are experienced in treating children within the family context. Training and supervision are required in carrying out the procedure. In any case, the biofeedback measure serves as a tool to navigate the clinical process. An experienced therapist would likely perform the procedure even without the tool, but this tool comes in handy, particularly in working with highly resistant families.

2.11 Limitation

The protocol is a clinical attempt to elicit children's physiological and verbal expressions to initiate conjoint family sessions. As our focus is on exploring the children's subsystem, our observations may be biased by our team's clinical orientation. The families in the study were predominantly Asian Chinese. Although we believe that children's physiological reactions to interparental conflicts are universal, there is currently no existing data to compare the nuances of children's voices in different cultures. We are currently undertaking a cross-regional study involving several countries from both Eastern and Western cultures in the hope of shedding new light and enabling cultural comparisons.

Our analysis of the "gut language" obtained from the assessment protocol is still at a preliminary stage. To fully comprehend the link between an individual's physiology and their family relationship, a more systematic analysis of the data would be required.

2.12 Conclusion

Based on the initial analysis of our clinical data, there is a strong indication that within each troubled child there is a "family healer" who is trying desperately to sustain and repair the broken family. We have discovered that many of the children's presenting problems, when seen individually, align with the criteria of the diagnostic manuals, but when seen in the context of the family, they are just normal reactions to highly stressful family situations.

In conclusion, the children's subsystem within the family system remains an unexplored territory and an untapped resource. More therapists (Andolfi, 2016; Walters & Friedlander, 2016; Lee, 2017) are calling for the field to recognize children as an invaluable resource in the process of change in family therapy. Our work is just beginning.

References

Andolfi, M. (2016). How to give voice to children in family therapy. In M. Borcsa & P. Stratton (Eds.), *Origins and originality in family therapy and systemic practice* (pp. 143–168). Springer. https://doi.org/10.1007/978-3-319-39061-1_10

Cummings, E. M., & Davies, P. T. (2002). Effects of marital conflict on children: Recent advances and emerging themes in process-oriented research. *Journal of Child Psychology and Psychiatry*, *43*(1), 31–63. https://doi.org/10.1111/1469-7610.00003

Cummings, E. M., & Davies, P. T. (2010). *Marital conflict and children: An emotional security perspective*. Guilford Press. https://doi.org/10.1037/0033-2909.116.3.387

El-Sheikh, M., Kouros, C. D., Erath, S., Cummings, E. M., Keller, P., & Staton, L. (2009). Marital conflict and children's externalizing behavior: Interactions between parasympathetic and sympathetic nervous system activity. *Monographs of the Society for Research in Child Development*, *74*(1), 1–79. https://doi.org/10.1111/j.1540-5834.2009.00501.x

Harold, G. T., & Sellers, R. (2018). Annual research review: Interparental conflict and youth psychopathology: An evidence review and practice focused update. *The Journal of Child Psychology and Psychiatry*, *59*(4), 374–402. https://doi.org/10.1111/jcpp.12893

Imber-Black, E. (2014). Eschewing certainties: The creation of family therapists in the 21st century. *Family Process*, *53*(3), 371–379. https://doi.org/10.1111/famp.12091

Lee, W. Y. (2017). An unexplored subsystem – young children as healers: Dialogue with Sal Minuchin. *Journal of Systemic Therapies*, *36*(4), 35–45. https://doi.org/10.1521/jsyt.2017.36.4.35

Lee, W. Y. (2019). Working transgenerationally: A clinical discussion on family dynamics and treatment. *Journal of Family Therapy*, *42*, 499–517.

Lee, W. Y. (2023, July 6). *Listen to the children's voices*. International Conference Family Therapy: The Road That Connects Individual and Social Resources, Family Therapy Academy, Assisi, Italy.

Lee, W. Y., Ng, M. L., Cheung, B. K., & Yung, J. W. (2010). Capturing children's response to parental conflict and making use of it. *Family Process*, *49*(1), 43–58. https://doi.org/10.1111/j.1545-5300.2010.01307.x.

Porges, S. W. (2009). The polyvagal theory: New insights into adaptive reactions of the autonomic nervous system. *Cleveland Clinic Journal of Medicine*, *76*(2), 86–90.

Stevenson-Hinde, J., Curley, J. P., Chicot, R., & Johannsson, C. (2007). Anxiety within families: Interrelations, consistency, and change. *Family Process*, *46(4)*, 543–556. https://doi.org/10.1111/j.1545-5300.2007.00231.x

Walters, M. G., & Friedlander, S. (2016). When a child rejects a parent: Working with the intractable resist/refuse dynamic. *Family Court Review*, *54(3)*, 424–445. https://doi.org/10.1111/fcre.12238

Zemp, M., Bodenmann, G. M., & Cummings, E. M. (2014). The role of skin conductance level reactivity in the impact of children's exposure to interparental conflict on their attention performance. *Journal of Experimental Child Psychology*, *118*, 1–12. https://doi.org/10.1016/j.jecp.2013.09.007

3

IMAGINATION AND CREATIVITY IN FAMILY THERAPY WITH CHILDREN LABELED WITH AUTISM SPECTRUM DISORDER

Michele Zappella

3.1 Introduction

Family interventions have evolved over time, reflecting shifts in focus on mental health, diagnosis, and treatment. For example, in Italy in the 1950s and 1960s, several family therapists questioned the use of certain mental tests. These tests were often employed to place many children of Southern Italian immigrants – who had moved to work in the North – into special and segregated classes. These children, many of whom spoke dialects and lived in poverty in homes without any newspapers or books, faced the risk of being unfairly marginalized and inaccurately labeled as "mentally retarded." At the time, many of us fought to integrate these children into regular classes and campaigned for legislation that segregated classes altogether. Thankfully, a law was passed in 1977.

Today, a similar phenomenon is emerging on a much larger scale, affecting numerous countries worldwide. There has been a significant proliferation of precise labels, increasing by 70 to 80 times compared to just a few years ago. Labeling often leads to an "internalization of difference" in a totalizing manner that affects individuals – whether boys or girls – and their parents and teachers. This process is further driven by mental health institutions and insurance companies (Zappella, 2021). The contexts contributing to new forms of exclusion are diverse, encompassing dyslexia, other learning disorders, bullying, and, most notably, Autism Spectrum Disorders (ASD). The term ASD broadens and blurs the definition of "autism," which is otherwise classified as a specific pathological category (F84) in the *International Classification of Diseases* (ICD-10).

Although the biological basis of some childhood difficulties – such as impairments in cortical areas of the left hemisphere, parietal-temporal, or occipital-temporal regions, and genetic factors – cannot be denied, the transformation of diagnoses into labels carries significant scientific, cultural, and social implications. The expanded criteria for ASD have widened the scope of the autistic spectrum. However, the prevalence of diagnosed cases does not align with an actual increase in affected children, resulting in a notable bias. The prevalence of the number of patients who have been diagnosed does not match the real increase in children who are affected, which in turn creates an impressive bias. In the 1960s and 1970s, autism diagnoses had a prevalence of 4 in 10,000 worldwide (Lotter, 1967; Gillberg et al., 1991). Since the 1980s and 1990s, the increase in the use of ASD diagnoses has been accompanied by a large increase in the prevalence rates, often driven by false-positive diagnoses. Studies have shown false-positive rates of 34% (Greene et al., 2022) and 29% (Hong et al., 2022), further highlighting the need for critical evaluation of diagnostic practices (Salari et al., 2022).

DOI: 10.4324/9781003536765-5

The increase in ASD has coincided with a cultural shift that began in the last two decades of the 20th century. The adoption of the diagnostic processes has, in some cases, devalued the role of possible hypersensitivity in a child during an evaluation or testing. In their 1993 book, Baron-Cohen and Bolton explain how to make a diagnosis and "how to assess children with developmental problems" (Baron-Cohen & Bolton, 1993). The authors emphasize that the clinical setting provides a "standardized" context in which to observe the child's difficulties. Although parents may feel exasperated by their child's behavior in this setting, the authors argue that this environment allows for comparisons among children. For example, if a child cries and screams during the evaluation, this behavior is not considered problematic but rather one of the factors contributing to the diagnosis. Fortunately today, we possess a more comprehensive understanding of the overlapping symptoms between autistic behaviors and other neurodevelopmental disorders, as well as nuances of behavioral patterns exhibited by children.

This approach suggests that ignoring the child's feelings is considered the appropriate path to ensuring objectivity, although the exact opposite is true. The widespread use of semi-structured tests such as the Autistic Diagnostic Observation Schedule-2 (ADOS-2), which frequently evaluates how a child responds to specific requests, has contributed to a rapid increase in diagnoses. For instance, in Sweden, diagnoses reached 246 per 10,000 in 2011 (Idring et al., 2015), and shortly after, the United States reported rates of 250 per 10,000 (Kogan et al., 2018). By comparison, slightly lower rates, below 1% of examined cases, were reported in England (Brugha et al., 2011), Spain (Morales-Hidalgo et al., 2018), and Italy (Narzisi et al., 2018). However, significantly lower rates (less than 40 per 10,000) are observed in France (van Bakel et al., 2015), Germany (Bachmann et al., 2018), Pomerania (Skonieczna-Żydecka et al., 2017), and China (Wang et al., 2018). In these regions, diagnoses are primarily based on criteria defining autism as a disorder category (as indicated by the ICD-10, code F84). These criteria are often supplemented by evaluations using the Childhood Autism Rating Scale (CARS), which is largely observational, straightforward to implement, and involves a few simple tests with the child, alongside additional information gathered from parents.

In my current professional practice, I predominantly work with children aged 2–4 years old, where communication often takes on a unique character. These children and their families come from various parts of Italy, typically following a suggested diagnosis of "autism spectrum disorder," often accompanied by a prognosis of incurability. However, many of these children exhibit delays in language development, often paired with social anxiety, which can make it challenging for them to engage during evaluations (Thurm et al., 2018). This challenge is further intensified by the distress of parents' experience when bringing their child to yet another specialist.

The first element of this label is often a misdiagnosis, influenced by a complex web of factors. In many cases, families and schools may come to accept the label, inadvertently constructing a self-image around the child that can be difficult to overcome. To better understand and assess the abilities and potential difficulties of these children, I take care to structure the evaluation process in a way that includes extended family members such as siblings and grandparents.

3.2 Communicating with very young children

When communicating with 2- or 3-year-old children, there are at least two key aspects to consider. First and foremost, it is important for the child to understand who you are. Are you someone they can trust – someone "of their family or one of their own" – or a stranger wearing a white coat, who might do things that frighten them, like touch them, give them injections, or look in their mouth with a tongue depressor? That said, talking to a new person can also be enjoyable for the child if a free and imaginative communication is created, both from their side and ours. Second, there is a third, often overlooked, aspect that plays a key role in building a therapeutic alliance with the child: "What are we doing in this room that resembles a toy store?" While the child explores the room full of toys scattered all over the place, the adults can talk freely to each other. Playing is what the child loves, and creating an environment full of fascinating games is a natural way to get to know them. To achieve this goal, the visit must be prepared in advance. The room should be organized in advance with toys placed in appropriate places. Additionally, it is important to know the child's name and greet them warmly at the door, ensuring that they feel expected and welcome. This warm welcome to the child is even more crucial when considering the emotional state of the child's parents. They often arrive worried and distressed – especially mothers – after receiving a dramatic diagnosis. They are anxious to know if their child has a severe disorder, whether the child is autistic, and if the condition is incurable. I anticipate meeting a family burdened by heavy worries, with the child sensing this tension as they embark on what feels like a new and potentially intimidating experience.

When I was a young doctor working in Washington, the person leading the discussions about the children we treated gave us a piece of advice that has stayed with me throughout my career: "When a child comes to see you, they should feel like you were waiting for them." This applies even to children who have been seen before.

3.3 How to welcome a child during the first visit

There are many ways to warmly welcome a child during their first session, and my approach has evolved over the years. One of the simplest and most effective methods is to begin the session by immediately addressing the child directly. Some of my ideas have come to me through interactions with families, including customs I've observed of Neapolitan families whose humanity and emotional richness are often overflowing. These families often have a family friend whom they call "Uncle," and over time, they started calling me "Uncle Michele." In some cases, I even became "Grandpa Michele." I used to introduce myself as "Uncle Michele" with new children and families that visited me.

When my clients ring the office doorbell, I go to the door, and the first person I see is the child exiting the elevator, staring at me. I begin with a compliment: "What a beautiful T-shirt, you look so elegant!" Then I go add, "Well done, Giovanni, you have come to see me. Come in, have a seat. Let's go into this room where you'll find your puppet friends." Meeting a young child is meeting with their imagination, and it is through this that the first bond is formed. After a short break, during which I leave the family alone, I return and resume talking to the child, who is now likely interacting with the stuffed toys they've found. I might say, "Look how happy the elephant is! He's so glad that you're holding him." If it's a little girl, it's also good to start with a compliment: "What a beautiful little girl! Such lovely hair and such a bright look in your eyes. And those red shoes are so fashionable."

At this point, the family members, starting with the mother and grandmother (often the grandparents come along with the parents), usually smile and relax. I then guide the family into the therapy room, pointing out the toys to the child. The room is large, with two wide windows offering scenic views of Siena. A long, white wooden table divides the space into two parts, each with a window in the background. The room is thoughtfully organized with different areas dedicated to play. There is a basket filled with stuffed animals including small cows. Along the edge of the bookshelf is a sequence of toy trains, a palm tree, little houses, and a wide-open-mouth crocodile showing off its white teeth. Nearby are the Seven Dwarfs and Snow White, Pinocchio, Geppetto, and Jiminy Cricket. On a large table beneath the window, there are puzzles, sheets of paper, pencils, and building blocks. Off to the side, but still in a clear view, is a small table with plastic cups, cutlery, and little chairs. And of course, there are also dolls in a stroller.

I begin by bringing the child into the room first, saying aloud, "Now, Giovanni is the master of the games, and he can do whatever he wants." This immediately sets a playful and welcoming tone.

Meanwhile, the adults – myself and the child's parents – stand on the other side of the room, where I start talking to the child's parents about their journey and listen to their story. They tell me their child's story, their major concerns, and the reasons they've sought therapy. Observation forms the foundation of listening. At this point, the little boy often spontaneously approaches his parents, holding a toy in his hand. When this happens, I gently call him over, take his small hands in mine, and guide him to give me a little pat. As he looks at me and allows this interaction, it creates a moment of trust. With the mother's help, as she holds him on her lap, I encourage him to engage in activities such as building a tower or a train with blocks or even drawing a picture. My immediate response is a cheerful, *"High five, you are so good!"* This informal interaction not only builds rapport but also serves as a way to assess the child's manual skills and motor praxis.

Many children who come to me do not speak or say very few words. They often have social anxiety, which can manifest as shyness but also as moments of aggression. These children may prefer to communicate through gestures or engage more easily with older or younger children (Zappella, 2002). With these children, communication becomes easier with them if I use exaggerated facial expressions and if I use elements of the special language often used with young children (baby talk). This includes sounds and fragments of words. If I happen to hum a tune, the child frequently looks at me with curiosity and amusement – and sometimes even follows along, imitating me. These interactions create a shared space of connection and help facilitate communication.

The neurological exam begins in this playful setting, but only I am aware that it is an exam. For the child and his family, it feels like a continuation of the game. I might ask his mother: "Can you try putting your tongue out at him, moving it from one side of your mouth to the other, and see if he copies you?" This helps assess whether there is verbal dyspraxia, a difficulty coordinating mouth movements. I also check if the child can give a loud kiss, blow air, or produce sounds using lip syllables, which might indicate a simple speech sound disorder. To investigate manual skills, I use various activities such as asking the child to build a small construction or observing how they fold a fork. These tasks help evaluate their ability to use their hands and check for signs of manual dyspraxia.

Some very young children respond especially well to humor and playful, slightly transgressive actions. For example, I might sit the child on their mother's lap, or sit in front of the child and pretend to take off their shoe. I might then hold the shoe under my nose, making a disgusted face, and muttering words like "that stinks!" before placing it under the child's nose for their reaction. These playful movements often elicit laughter and engagement. I will never forget Edoardo, a 4 1/2-year-old boy with severe verbal dyspraxia. He laughed uncontrollably during one such game and became so relaxed that he happily stood up. His father then pointed to my small hammer and asked "What's this?" Edoardo replied clearly, "It's a hammer," leaving us all astounded. This boy, previously considered mute due to his dyspraxia, had just pronounced a full sentence with distinct words. This is a powerful example of how engaging the child through play and humor can create the right environment for them to express themselves, especially when they struggle to get words out. Another example is the following case study.

3.3.1 Case illustration

Ludovico is a 2-year and 5-month-old boy. After normal development during his first year and a half, he experienced a regression at 18 months: He began moving objects aimlessly and showed no interest in people. He never spoke, was unable to blow, but demonstrated an ability to use a fork competently. When Ludovico walked into the therapy room, he moved around restlessly, picking up toys and immediately dropping them, seemingly unsure of how to use them. He then picked up a bowling pin and repeatedly banged it against the wall.

The situation changed dramatically when I began humming music from *The Magic Flute.* In an instant, Ludovico's face lit up. He looked at me, smiled, and began imitating my gestures, including some exaggerated, playful dance moves. He laughed and seemed to enjoy himself. I took his hand, encouraged him to run, and then placed him on his mother's lap, instructing her to provide manual guidance to help him build a tower with blocks. After stacking two or three blocks with his mother's help, Ludovico continued on his own, building a tower 13 blocks high – a feat he had never achieved before. When I saw him again two months later, no formal therapy had been initiated in the interim. Nevertheless, Ludovico had made notable progress: He showed more interest in games, stacked rings onto a wooden stick, and paid attention to a puppet placed in front of him. While he picked up the bowling pin again, this time he banged it against the wall only once before dropping it. Guided by his parents as before, he successfully drew vertical lines on a piece of paper. He also began saying "mummy" and "daddy."

If, during the first visit, I had limited myself to simply observing him during his first session, the diagnosis could have easily leaned towards behavior resembling autism, which would have been a serious mistake. Ludovico had dyspraxia of the mouth and hands. He was able to move his mouth and hands, but he did not know how to use them. This is why he took a bowling pin and kept banging it against the wall repeatedly.

This example, along with many others, demonstrate that assessing general movements (general praxia) often requires strategies that are only effective if the diagnostician enters the child's world. For a 3- to 4-year-old child, the Bergés-Lézine imitation test, which evaluates motor skills and body schema, can be introduced in a playful way: "Let's do some exercises together – you, your little sister (or brother, if there is a younger sibling), and your Daddy. That way, we can put on a good show for Mummy." Framing the activity in this way makes it unexpected, fun, and inclusive, involving part of the family rather than solely focusing on the child.

For younger children who refuse to cooperate, the father can take the lead. He might hold the child's hand and run back and forth with them, then carry the child on his shoulders and play a "fly-fly" game. The running and playful interaction are meant to make the child laugh and feel joyful. Once the child is in a happy and engaged state, the father can place them on the mother's lap. The mother then gently guides the child's hands to stack blocks, creating a tower, or to place blocks one behind the other to form a toy train. She might also guide the child to draw vertical lines on a piece of paper. Gradually, the mother reduces her manual assistance, encouraging the child to build towers, bridges, and cube trains or draw lines independently. If the child is less interested in running and playing with the father, the mother can take the lead. She might scoop the child up, lay them across her lap, and engage them with playful phrases like, "I've caught you! I'm going to eat you!" as she tickles and teases, making the child laugh uncontrollably. She then sits the child on her knees, facing her, and gently touches their nose, saying, "I'll take it away!" She might follow this by saying, "Now grab my nose," guiding the child's hand to her nose if necessary. This playful interaction can extend to other parts of the body, such as the forehead or ears, alternating with tickles to keep the child engaged and laughing. Once the child is fully attuned to the mother, she introduces simple, short words such as "mum, mummy, dad, daddy!" to encourage verbal interaction. Later, she helps the child stand, guides them to a small desk, and encourages them to draw, build, or engage in other activities that they may have previously refused to attempt. Through these strategies, the child gradually begins to participate more actively, developing motor and verbal skills in a way that feels natural and enjoyable.

Sometimes, these approaches are not immediately successful. For example, a 2 ½-year-old toddler might feel annoyed by physical closeness but be perfectly content standing on a chair, laughing with their father. The father, lowering himself to the child's level with a cheerful expression, playfully murmurs, *"Ba, bab-ba, ba . . ."* to engage the child in a way that feels comfortable and fun. Similarly, consider the case of a 3-year-old with verbal and manual dyspraxia who resists many suggestions. However, when his grandmother takes him by the hand and runs with him while singing a playful song like *"One, two, three: star!"* he becomes captivated. As she introduces something new – such as guiding him to draw lines with a pencil – the child takes the lead, moving the pencil in the correct direction.

3.4 The dysmaturity syndrome

Among the many children I see, there are those with unique developmental pathways. After an initial period of normal development – walking and saying a few words around their first year – these children experience a regression in the months that follow, often around 18 months of age. This regression is characterized by the loss of language, play, smiles, attention, and responsiveness to others, resulting in autistic-like behavior that can persist for several months. Gradually, the child begins to regain interest in both play and social interaction. Over time, communication returns, first through gestures and then with a few words, and the autistic behaviors fade. By around 2½ years of age, the family's response to these developmental abnormalities becomes a crucial factor in the child's future progress.

If, based on recommendations from teachers or specialists, the child is labeled as "unrecoverable" or permanently autistic, this often triggers emotional collapse in the parents. In turn, the child may cease making progress and withdraw further into themselves. Conversely, if the parents are given genuine hope – typically through accurate information about the characteristics of this condition – and are encouraged to actively support their child's development, significant progress can be made. In such cases, parents, with the aid of therapists and structured therapeutic methods such as the Portage method, take the lead in fostering their child's growth. During the third and fourth years, progress continues, albeit slowly, although the child may display oppositional behaviors. It is essential to explain to parents that this oppositional behavior is a symptom of the disorder and part of the recovery process. Understanding this can empower parents and bolster their determination to support their child. For the child, therapeutic interventions align with the principles discussed earlier, emphasizing engagement, play, and family involvement. Over time, most children show significant improvement, and in many cases, a complete recovery is achieved. This recovery is often remarkable, particularly in intellectual abilities (Zappella, 2002, 2010, 2020).

3.5 Listening to parents and offering support

The way parents – particularly mothers – process their child's diagnosis is profoundly influenced by their child's condition, which becomes the central focus of their emotions. It is worth noting that many mothers – approximately four out of five – experience depression within days of receiving an autism diagnosis for their child. When reassessed 18 months later, a significant proportion remain depressed (Taylor & Warren, 2012). The diagnosis, or even the mere suspicion of it, often delivers a devastating emotional blow, leading to depression frequently accompanied by heightened anxiety. For fathers, stress and anxiety tend to escalate when the child's condition is severe, with their pain sometimes reaching levels comparable to grief. Interestingly, there is often a balancing dynamic between parents: when the mother is depressed, the father may cope better, and vice versa; when the mother displays resilience, the father may become more emotionally affected. When mothers are deeply alarmed by their child's diagnosis, their predominant emotion is concern for their child, and addressing this concern becomes a priority. At the same time, it is important to explore the broader aspects of their anxiety and depressive state, assess how they are coping, and explain that these feelings stem from a mother's natural sensitivity. Offering appropriate treatments, which may include medication or relational interventions, can help address these emotions and improve other areas of their life. Empowering mothers by giving them a sense of control and competence in managing their child's challenges provides them with a renewed sense of satisfaction and energy. This, in turn, improves their quality of life as well as that of their child. Professionals play a key role in fostering and reinforcing this sense of capability. Similarly, for fathers, successfully handling difficult situations often enhances their confidence and effectiveness. It is equally important to recognize that fathers, too, frequently need to be listened to and supported as they navigate the emotional and practical challenges of their child's condition.

3.5.1 Case illustration

In the following paragraphs, I present a mother who recuperated following her son's optimal progress.

I meet Dario, a client of mine from many years ago. He is now an adult in his mid-40s, but he looks at least twenty years younger. We are at a café in Siena, where he is passing through the town with his mother. Both are smiling and affectionate. Dario is tall, sturdy, and well-dressed in a t-shirt and jeans. He has a warm, lovely smile, and his face is remarkably smooth, free of wrinkles or lines, radiating sweetness and kindness. He looks at me, but does not try to interpret what I might be thinking. When I ask him questions, he answers briefly but does not initiate conversation. His mother is quite the opposite: Her face is full of energy, and she looks me straight in the eye. She moves effortlessly from one topic to another. She recalls how, when Dario was just a few years old, she brought him to see me at the hospital. She tells me how I helped ease her anxiety and gave her the confidence to believe that she could help her son build a life for himself. "I am your student!" she tells me with a big smile. She is accompanied by Dario's father, uncle, and aunt. As we talk, I comment on Dario's strengths and weaknesses – traits that, of course, we all share. Smiling, the aunt chimes in: "Speaking of repetitive behavior, just think of how repetitive so many elderly people are!"

This case is exemplary. For a number of favorable reasons, Dario did not suffer the devastation that so often accompanies the label of autism – an "incurable condition that prevents communication." His mother did not fall into depression, and her anxiety reactions were successfully managed. The school, often a challenging environment where bullying can dominate, supported Dario. Later at age 18, he was fortunate to find a job tailored to his abilities, which also helped him develop skills, such as using a computer. Dario was listened to, supported in his strengths, and was given space and trust to grow. As he leaves, he smiles at me warmly.

3.6 Reframing, trust, and the power of individualised diagnosis

Normally, at the end of the first session with the child and their family, I share my conclusions. The focus is always on the child, who is acknowledged and valued first. I begin with positive initial comments, which are not part of the written report but are delivered with some emphasis: *"I met Antonietta, and I found her to be beautiful, elegant, cheerful, and quick to joke,"* or *"Giuseppe is a handsome young man, tall and friendly."* These remarks capture a fragment of truth that resonates with both the child and the parents, illuminating qualities they already recognize but appreciate hearing articulated. These comments also extend to the parents, who are visibly pleased to hear compliments that affirm their child's uniqueness. Once this reframing is done, I move on in a softer, calmer tone to address the difficulties, challenges, and practical advice for managing them better, focusing on the specific issues at hand. Starting with positive reframing helps clarify the real situation without discouraging the entire family. It sets a constructive tone and provides a balanced view of both the child's strengths and the areas that need support.

A young child, or even an older one, who is not met with trust is often frightened, and this can significantly alter their behavior. For example, the results of certain ADOS-2 tests, such as the "doll party," may vary greatly depending on the child's level of comfort with the therapist. A child may successfully complete the test with a familiar and trusted therapist, but often fails when the test is administered in the unfamiliar setting of a hospital evaluation.

In one of my studies, I examined 127 young children who had been referred to me to assess whether they were autistic, as this had been their prior diagnosis (Zappella, 2020). I assessed them using the methods described earlier, keeping in mind that autism-like symptoms can also be observed in typical children experiencing anxiety reactions and in various developmental disorders, such as social phobias, language disorders, partial or complete deafness, reactive attachment disorders, dyspraxias, and others. Additionally, I considered frequent comorbidities, such as ADHD with autism or autism with Gilles de la Tourette syndrome (GTS), where aggressive behaviors that hinder social interaction can stem from either condition. These children received a diagnosis and therapy consistent with the approaches previously outlined, including the Portage method (Zappella, 2001). In this approach, parents often became the primary agents in addressing deficits across various areas (cognitive, autonomy, social, etc.). In all cases, the children lost their autism-like behaviors. This demonstrates how systemic therapy intersects with pediatric neurology, which plays a critical role in distinguishing between GTS and autism. Accurate diagnosis and a tailored therapeutic approach can transform the child's developmental trajectory, highlighting the importance of trust and individualized care in the evaluation process.

All of this confirms that today, a young child who comes for a visit should be welcomed as a dear companion. Their unique way of expressing themselves should be met with a reciprocal response from us. This exchange opens the door to shared imagination and creativity, fostering an alliance with both the child and their family to identify and address any potential difficulties. When approached in this way, family therapy can effectively uncover false labels, reveal the true nature of the child and their challenges, and empower parents and family members to take an active role in managing much of the child's activities, with the participation and support of the school. In many cases, this approach helps guide the child out of pathology.

3.7 The child is not a label

The labels assigned to children or adolescents often stem from a culture deeply rooted in certain aspects of today's consumer society, where diagnoses of disabilities can become opportunities for profit. The label of "different" often begins in school and is disproportionately applied to difficulties related to the skills most in demand in today's job market. These diagnoses are frequently followed by costly therapeutic interventions, while others marginalize children and young people due to characteristics deemed inadequate, reducing their existence and potential to a single label.

Too often, these labels are used carelessly, with little regard for confidentiality – a demeaning "stamp" that erases both the true nature of a person's challenges and their strengths.

Psychiatry, across all ages, must be recognized as both a human science – subject to societal influences such as trends, economic interests, and cultural models – and a natural biological science (Borgna, 2019). If we ignore its human dimension, we risk misusing evaluation tools in ways that foster exclusion and labeling. On the other hand, neglecting its biological dimension may lead to underestimating the needs of patients, particularly those with severe conditions.

For those who do not require an accurate diagnosis – such as schoolmates, parents, and family friends – it is far more beneficial to understand a child or adolescent's strengths and weaknesses rather than fixating on their diagnosis. Freeing ourselves from the confines of labels and from the systemic violence present in educational settings paves the way for a more democratic society – one that begins in schools and continues throughout life.

References

Bachmann, C. J., Gerste, B., & Hoffmann, F. (2018). Diagnoses of autism spectrum disorders in Germany: Time trends in administrative prevalence and diagnostic stability. *Autism*, *22*(3), 283–290. https://doi.org/10.1177/1362361316673977

Baron-Cohen, S., & Bolton, P. (1993). *Autism: The facts*. Oxford University Press.

Borgna, E. (2019). *La follia che è anche in noi*. Einaudi.

Brugha, T. S., McManus, S., Bankart, J., Scott, F., Purdon, S., Smith, J., Bebbington, P., Jenkins, R., & Meltzer, H. (2011). Epidemiology of autism spectrum disorders in adults in the community in England. *Archives of General Psychiatry*, *68*(5), 459–65. https://doi.org/10.1001/archgenpsychiatry

Gillberg, C., Steffenburg, S., & Schaumann, H. (1991). Is autism more common now than ten years ago? *British Journal of Psychiatry*, *158*, 403–409. https://doi.org/10.1192/bjp.158.3.403

Greene, R. K., Vasile, I., Bradbury, K. R., Olsen, A., & Duvall, S. W. (2022). Autism diagnostic observation schedule (ADOS-2) elevations in a clinical sample of children and adolescents who do not have autism: Phenotypic profiles of false positives. *Clinical Neuropsychology*, *36*(5), 943–959. https://doi.org/10.1080/13854046.2021.1942220

Hong, J. S., Singh, V., Kalb, L., Reetzke, R., Ludwig, N. N., Pfeiffer, D., Holingue, C., Menon, D., Lu, Q., Ashkar, A., & Landa, R. (2022). Replication study for ADOS-2 cut-offs to assist evaluation of autism spectrum disorder. *Autism Research*, *15*(11), 2181–2191. https://doi.org/10.1002/aur.2801

Idring, S., Lundberg, M., Sturm, H., Dalman, C., Gumpert, C., Rai, D., Lee, B. K., & Magnusson, C. (2015). Changes in prevalence of autism spectrum disorders in 2001–2011: Findings from the Stockholm youth cohort. *Journal of Autism and Developmental Disorders*, *45*(6), 1766–1773. https://doi.org/10.1007/s10803-014-2336-y

Kogan, M. D., Vladutiu, C. J., Schieve, L. A., Ghandour, R. M., Blumberg, S. J., Zablotsky, B., Perrin, J. M., Shattuck, P., Kuhlthau, K. A., Harwood, R. L., & Lu, M. C. (2018). The prevalence of parent-reported autism spectrum disorder among US children. *Pediatrics*, *142*(6), e20174161. https://doi.org/10.1542/peds.2017-4161

Lotter, V. (1967). Epidemiology of autistic conditions in young children. *Social Psychiatry*, *1*, 163–173. https://doi.org/10.1007/BF00578950

Morales-Hidalgo, P., Roigé-Castellví, J., Hernández-Martínez, C., Voltas, N., & Canals, J. (2018). Prevalence and characteristics of autism spectrum disorder among Spanish school-age children. *Journal of Autism and Developmental Disorders*, *48*(9), 3176–3190. https://doi.org/10.1007/s10803-018-3581-2

Narzisi, A., Posada, M., Barbieri, F., Chericoni, N., Ciuffolini, D., Pinzino, M., Romano, R., Scattoni, M. L., Tancredi, R., Calderoni, S., & Muratori, F. (2018). Prevalence of autism spectrum disorder in a large Italian catchment area: A school-based population study within the ASDEU project. *Epidemiology and Psychiatric Sciences*, *6*(29), e5. https://doi.org/10.1017/S2045796018000483

Salari, N., Rasoulpoor, S., Rasoulpoor, S., Shohaimi, S., Jafarpour, S., Abdoli, N., Khaledi-Paveh, B., & Mohammadi, M. (2022). The global prevalence of autism spectrum disorder: A comprehensive systematic review and meta-analysis. *Italian Journal of Pediatrics*, *48*(1), 112. https://doi.org/10.1186/s13052-022-01310-w

Skonieczna-Żydecka, K., Gorzkowska, I., Pierzak-Sominka, J., & Adler, G. (2017). The prevalence of autism spectrum disorders in West Pomeranian and Pomeranian regions of Poland. *Journal of Applied Research in Intellectual Disabilities*, *30*(2), 283–289. https://doi.org/10.1111/jar.12238

Taylor, J. L., & Warren, Z. E. (2012). Maternal depressive symptoms following autism spectrum diagnosis. *Journal of Autism and Developmental Disorders*, *42*(7), 1411–1418. https://doi.org/10.1007/s10803-011-1375-x

Thurm, A., Manwaring, S. S., Cardozo Jimenez, C., Swineford, L., Farmer, C., Gallo, R., & Maeda, M. (2018). Socioemotional and behavioral problems in toddlers with language delay. *Infant Mental Health Journal*, *39*(5), 569–580. https://doi.org/10.1002/imhj.21735

van Bakel, M. M., Delobel-Ayoub, M., Cans, C., Assouline, B., Jouk, P. S., Raynaud, J. P., & Arnaud, C. (2015). Low but increasing prevalence of autism spectrum disorders in a French area from register-based data. *Journal of Autism and Developmental Disorders*, *45*(10), 3255–3261. https://doi.org/10.1007/s10803-015-2486-6

Wang, F., Lu, L., Wang, S. B., Zhang, L., Ng, C. H., Ungvari, G. S., Cao, X. L., Lu, J. P., Hou, C. L., Jia, F. J., & Xiang, Y. T. (2018). The prevalence of autism spectrum disorders in China: A comprehensive meta-analysis. *International Journal of Biological Sciences*, *14*(7), 717–725. https://doi.org/10.7150/ijbs.24063

Zappella, M. (2001). *Il metodo portage: Guida pratica per l'educazione veloce*. Edizioni Omega.

Zappella, M. (2002). Early-onset Tourette syndrome with reversible autistic behaviour: A dysmaturational disorder. *European Child & Adolescent Psychiatry*, *11*(1), 18–23. https://doi.org/10.1007/s007870200003. PMID: 11942423.

Zappella, M. (2010). Autistic regression with and without EEG abnormalities followed by favourable outcome. *Brain & Development*, *32*(9), 739–745. https://doi.org/10.1016/j.braindev.2010.05.004

Zappella, M. (2020). Sintomi simil-autistici nei disturbi del neurosviluppo. *Autismo e disturbi del neurosviluppo*, *18*(3), 309–330. https://doi.org/10.14605/AUT1832004

Zappella, M. (2021). *Bambini con l'etichetta. Dislessici, autistici, iperattivi: Cattive diagnosi ed esclusione*. Feltrinelli.

4

EXPLORING THE PSYCHOLOGICAL LANDSCAPE OF CHILDREN WITH TYPE 1 DIABETES

A family approach

Tiziana Bufacchi

4.1 Introduction

Type 1 diabetes is a chronic condition that requires lifelong management of blood glucose levels, insulin injections, diet, exercise, and problem-solving skills. When a child is diagnosed, usually at least three or four other family members are affected. Diabetes is therefore a disease that affects the whole family (Anderson et al., 1981).

Diabetes management is a constant and often overwhelming daily task for the whole family. It involves frequent decision-making, can be stressful and uncomfortable, and even when a patient does everything he is "supposed to" do, diabetes can be unpredictable and frustrating. Emotional pitfalls are common. Feelings of anxiety, anger, guilt, and hopelessness are powerful and prevalent. These feelings can have a huge effect on behavior, affect relationships, and lead to cyclical deterioration. People living with diabetes are at increased risk of being diagnosed with depression, anxiety, and eating disorders. Even those who don't necessarily meet the criteria for a mental health diagnosis will likely face behavioral, emotional, and relationship issues at some point during their diabetes journey.

Diabetes burnout or diabetes distress is considered separate from major depressive disorder and is the result of the nature of suboptimal self-management behaviors, with zero "vacations" or moments of respite (Delamater et al., 2018). In addition to feeling overwhelmed, distress can also manifest as lingering worries about the possibility of future complications, both for children and especially for parents. Eating disorders are common in adolescents with diabetes, who use the disease to control weight, often skipping insulin at meals (Young et al., 2013).

Studies have also shown that there is a two-way relationship between psychological state and metabolic control of type 1 diabetes. Poor metabolic control can increase psychological difficulties and vice versa (American Diabetes Association, 2020). It follows that living with a chronic disease, such as type 1 diabetes, requires not only constant management of the disease but also a complex and constant psychological adaptation, both for children and their families.

This chapter delves into the complex psychological aspects of children with type 1 diabetes and their families, highlighting the critical role of multigenerational family therapy in alleviating the

DOI: 10.4324/9781003536765-6

associated psychological burdens and making the family stronger. More attention will be given to the child than to the adolescent, who will be discussed but less extensively given the space limitations for this chapter.

A clinical case from the clinical practice of the author, who has been working for years in the role of clinical psychologist specialized in diabetes, will be discussed.

4.2 The psychological impact on children

4.2.1 Self-esteem, self-efficacy, and sense of identity

A chronic disease that arises during a child's early development weighs on emotional development and is one of the risk factors for personality difficulties and an impaired sense of identity and self-esteem. Children with type 1 diabetes often struggle with the formation of their own identity.

Constant demands on health management can lead to feelings of difference from one's peers, affecting self-esteem and sense of self-efficacy (Grey et al., 2000).

4.2.2 Anxiety and fear

The unpredictability of diabetes management promotes anxiety and fear in children. Concerns about hypoglycemia and long-term complications contribute to increased stress levels (American Diabetes Association, 2020).

4.2.3 Depression and emotional well-being

The chronic nature of type 1 diabetes can lead to depression in some children. The emotional cost of daily routine and fear of consequences affect overall emotional well-being (Hilliard et al., 2016).

4.3 Family dynamics

Studies have demonstrated the role of family dynamics in the management of diabetes by the child and in the more or less optimal adherence to therapy. High levels of family cohesion and an attitude of support and problem-solving (rather than blaming) within the family correlate with a higher degree of adherence to therapy and better glycemic control of the child or adolescent and with improved relationships among family members. On the contrary, a high degree of internal conflict and poor glycemic monitoring by parents becomes a risk factor that can lead to poor glycemic control of the person with diabetes, causing further stress in the family (Wysocki et al., 2001, 1995). These research findings have implications for family therapy in the context of pediatric diabetes. Therapeutic interventions can address communication patterns, distribute responsibilities, and improve parental collaboration to create a more supportive and effective family environment for diabetes management.

4.3.1 Parenting stress

Following the onset of their child's type 1 diabetes, parents typically supervise all aspects of their child's complete regimen, often experiencing severe discomfort due to the great responsibility, which can sometimes generate a negative emotional response to their child's management of therapy, both during the first few months following the child's diagnosis and afterward. Many parents report having difficulty returning to normal after their child is diagnosed with diabetes, due to feeling "always on guard" and hesitancy to trust other caregivers to manage their child's diabetes regimen. Mothers often report greater distress than fathers immediately after their child's diabetes diagnosis (Streisand & Monaghan, 2014).

Social support during the period of initial diagnosis may be essential for parents and is associated with decreased stress. A recent study found that greater family support predicts less stress in mothers, and more support from the partner predicts less stress in fathers (Wang et al., 2021). The constant vigilance required for the well-being of one's children, coupled with the fear of complications, can contribute to parental burnout (Monaghan et al., 2009).

4.3.2 Sibling dynamics

Siblings may feel neglected or burdened by the attention given to the child with diabetes. Understanding and addressing the potential impacts on sibling relationships is critical to maintaining a supportive family environment (Wysocki & Gavin, 2006).

4.4 Family therapy

Among the psychological and behavioral interventions (individual or group) generally used in diabetes support, solution-focused therapy, cognitive behavioral therapy, training to develop coping skills in diabetes, motivational interviewing, and family therapy have been showed to be effective.

Distressed families of child patients with diabetes are often characterized by excessive rigidity, failure to resolve conflicts, overprotectiveness, and entanglement. Family therapy takes a systemic approach, recognizing the interconnectedness of the family members and addressing problematic interactional patterns (Minuchin & Fishman, 1981). It addresses not only the needs of the child but also the family dynamics that contribute to the psychological burden (Minuchin et al., 1975).

Family therapy and systemic thinking more generally also provide a platform to educate the family about type 1 diabetes, to understand the emotional impact on the child, and to develop effective support strategies (Anderson & Coyne, 1991). Family therapists work with families to develop coping strategies that improve resilience and overall family functioning. Stress management techniques, effective communication skills, and problem-solving approaches are crucial components of family intervention (Pinquart & Teubert, 2012). In general, family-centered interventions can help families of children with type 1 diabetes cope with the emotional and practical challenges of diabetes management, improve their family relationships, and improve their quality of life.

Effectiveness results on adolescent adherence to therapy have been found with interventions that integrate some "diabetes-specific components" within a structured family therapy intervention. These components center on resolving problems specifically related to diabetes, training for more effective communication in the family, cognitive restructuring, and functional-structural family therapy (Wysocki et al., 2001). Other family-based interventions have sought to improve patient and family self-management by identifying and exploring patterns of family communication that hinder or support positive clinical outcomes (Solowiejczyk, 2004).

4.5 The use of multigenerational family therapy in diabetes

The multigenerational family therapy of Maurizio Andolfi (Andolfi, 2017) is widely used and adapted by family therapists all over the world. It provides a comprehensive framework for understanding the complexities of family systems and offers interventions to promote positive change in the context of a family's history and relationships. This approach allows the therapist to explore and address problems within a family by exploring patterns of behavior and communication that are passed down from generation to generation.

Integrating the principles of Andolfi's multigenerational family therapy into the broader context of family therapy for type 1 diabetes allows the therapist to address not only the immediate challenges but also the deeper systemic issues that can affect family dynamics. By examining intergenerational patterns and fostering emotional expression, therapists can contribute to a more complete and lasting impact on the well-being of both the child and the entire family. The behavioral and communicative patterns that are passed on from generation to generation are explored by multigenerational family therapy to understand problematic family interactional patterns, beliefs, and emotions, with the aim of discovering and addressing unresolved issues that may contribute to present family difficulties. The family functions as a system whose members interact and influence each other, grow together, and as a single organism face the challenges of life.

This becomes of particular importance in a context such as that of the family experiencing the chronic illness of the child. In the face of illness, the family tends to organize itself in ways that may not be functional to the well-being of individuals and of the entire family system (see John S. Rolland's chapter on serious illness and disability in this book). Especially at the beginning of therapy, the therapist is encouraged to thoroughly explore the history of the patient and their family and previous generations. Any medical and psychological problems, events, and traumas that have characterized the history of the family are explored and, above all, how the family reacted to the communication of the diagnosis.

Highlighting how beliefs and coping strategies are passed down through generations can shed light on family reactions to their child's diabetes diagnosis. The information about the disease is often not distributed equally between husband and wife. The mother often takes on many management responsibilities, and this leads to an increase in family stress, especially interparental conflict, and frequently, triangulation of the child in the family.

Through the multigenerational family approach, it is possible to understand how this information is actually used or how it is shared among family members. This can help to redistribute responsibilities and to understand how emotions are expressed with respect to the condition or particular emergency situations, such as nocturnal hypoglycemia or hyperglycemia.

In dealing with a disease as complex as diabetes, priority is initially given to the assimilation of educational content regarding how to "manage" diabetes. However, at the same time, emotions such as anxiety, anger, fear, and guilt may remain and impair quality of life of all members, as well as interfere with healthy behaviors and routines needed to manage diabetes. These emotional experiences can be explored with multigenerational family therapy, considering family members' emotional responses to the disease and the resources the family can use to react. In the initial sessions, the family therapist seeks to create a collaborative therapeutic alliance to promote openness and trust, resulting in the creation of a safe space where all family members can openly express and process difficult (and sometimes suppressed) emotions related to diabetes.

These general guidelines and the associated case report (names and identifying details have been changed to maintain family anonymity) is drawn from my clinical experience working with children and adolescents with type 1 diabetes and their families over the past 15 years. It offers a brief guide on how to transfer and utilize multigenerational family therapy (Andolfi, 2017) in the context of type 1 diabetes. Additionally, it provides insights for the medical team to evaluate family functioning in relation to the management of and adherence to medical treatment. This work outlines key questions to engage the family in effective communication about diabetes and foster new family coping strategies.

Furthermore, it emphasizes the importance of understanding family dynamics, such as intergenerational patterns of caregiving and conflict, which may influence the family's ability to support the individual with diabetes. By addressing these dynamics, it seeks to enhance collaboration between family members and healthcare providers, ultimately promoting better outcomes for both physical and emotional well-being.

4.6 Case illustration: Not an easy diagnosis, or rather two!

4.6.1 Background

The Calitri family, living in a sunny coastal town in Australia, faced an unexpected challenge when both daughters, 11-year-old Isabella and 9-year-old Sofia, were diagnosed with type 1 diabetes within a few months of each other.

The parents, Davide and Emma, come from different cultural backgrounds: Davide is Italian and moved to Australia for love of Emma in the early 2000s. Emma was born and raised in Australia; her parents immigrated to Australia from Germany in the late 1980s and now live only a few suburbs away from her. Davide finds it very difficult to emotionally distance himself from his family of origin, who live in Italy and with whom he shares a close bond. In contrast, Emma does not have a particularly deep relationship with her parents and prefers not to ask them for help, especially in managing the girls' diabetes. This is partly because her parents lead busy work lives, are older, and have not yet received diabetes education, making them afraid of making mistakes.

This initially led to the exclusion of her family from important holidays such as Christmas because the maternal grandparents did not know how to manage the girls' dietary needs during holidays, social lunches, and other events involving meals or snacks. As a result, Emma organized a small Christmas lunch for Davide and the girls, planning to join the extended family and grandparents later in the afternoon to exchange presents. However, Davide, Sofia, and Isabella were unhappy with this arrangement. The girls felt "excluded" and "isolated," while Davide believed the maternal grandparents had not made sufficient effort to accommodate the girls' dietary needs.

The shock of the diabetes diagnosis for both girls, along with Sofia's aggressive attitude toward her illness, prompted the family to seek psychological support – initially for Sofia – through their local diabetes service, which subsequently referred them to me.

After the first evaluation meetings, I proposed family therapy so as to negotiate the challenging terrain of this journey together.

4.6.2 Presentation of the problem

The Calitri family learned the news of Isabella's diagnosis in a state of disbelief and anguish. No one in either of the parents' families had ever suffered from chronic diseases in general, or from diabetes specifically. Isabella, being the eldest sister, felt a sense of responsibility for Sofia's well-being and at the same time found it "unfair" that she herself had diabetes.

Sofia struggled to comprehend the abrupt changes that had taken place in her daily life. Davide and Emma were overwhelmed by the emotional and practical implications of managing diabetes in the family and could not manage the youngest's angry and upset emotions.

Within a few months of Isabella's diagnosis, Sofia had begun to show the same symptoms as her sister. Isabella took a glycemic test at home, and Emma administered the test to Sofia as well, confirming her fear that Sofia also had diabetes. The shock of both daughters having diabetes was enormous for all the members of the family.

During the routine diabetes check-ups, the doctors began to see noticeable differences in Sofia's management of diabetes, especially compared to her older sister. Glycemic control was precise and stable for Isabella, but not optimal in Sofia's case. Sofia also began to express troubling behaviors in class, such as sudden crying, anger, and difficulty in following lessons.

Not surprisingly given her behavior, when I began working with the Calitri family, the parents' and older sister's concern was only for Sofia, who somehow came to "carry" the family emotions and adjustment to the shock of the diagnoses. At the request of the girls, despite their mother's negative feelings for her, the maternal grandmother was invited to participate in the family sessions. She was hesitant at first, but continued to come regularly thereafter.

4.6.3 Exploration of family history

I thought of this family, especially in regard to their respective families and cultures of origin, somewhat poetically – as "a family halfway between the Italian hills and the Australian deserts."

I asked the girls to help me observe the history of their family through the genogram, a tool for visual representation of family relationships over generations, useful for highlighting the roles and shifts of the family, highlighting emotional cut-offs, possible traumas and dependencies in each of the parents' families of origin, and in the current core and extended family. Through the genogram, I was able to identify the Calitris' alliances between members, important beliefs, especially regarding illness in general and diabetes, and their communication patterns, which were both described and demonstrated spontaneously as we explored their histories.

Introduction of this exercise brought movement and lightness to the sessions, and by my asking the girls for help as "guides in the exploration of family dynamics," their moods improved and they were energized.

A difficulty that was evident from the outset was the position of the girls' father, Davide, with respect to his life in Australia. Davide was a very "present" man and engaged husband, a loving father, and a caring son. Davide had left his entire large family (four siblings and elderly parents) in Italy to be with Emma and the girls.

A close-knit family, Davide missed them terribly. Moreover, since the diabetes diagnosis, he had been unable to visit them because Emma was worried that organizing the long-distance flight with all the diabetes equipment would be difficult. She was also concerned about handling diabetes emergencies abroad and preferred local holiday destinations, closer to the city.

Isabella and Sofia felt sad and angry when they were told they wouldn't be visiting their paternal grandparents and cousins in Italy anytime soon, especially after spending so much time at school learning Italian to interact with them once there. On the other hand, despite having her parents nearby, Emma felt the need to remain independent and avoid burdening them with the management of her daughters' diabetes. She was an incredibly strong and determined young mother, trying to manage this complex situation as best she could without asking for help from family or friends, although secretly hoping they would offer support.

Another reason Emma eschewed the help of her parents was that her father had also been ill for some time, and this made Emma reluctant to ask her mother for help. She thought she could handle everything on her own, but often she found herself feeling overwhelmed and hopeless. Davide helped her at night, but he was at work all day.

4.6.4 Unspoken emotions

The use of metaphor allowed me to reframe the symptom and problems associated with the disease, allowing each family member to put themselves in the other's shoes.

The family expressed their grief, shock, and anger about the diabetes, both through specific conversations and by drawing a picture of what diabetes means and what emotions were associated with it for each family member. The girls immediately asked to be able to draw their responses to my questions on the board.

I used relational questions, especially between Emma and maternal grandmother Inga, to help them openly express their most difficult emotions.

> "*Inga, how do you think Emma feels when you don't offer your help?*"
> "*Emma, what might change in your relationship with your mum if you started expressing your needs more openly?*"

Emma was able to tell Inga that she was angry with her because, since diabetes had entered their lives, she had not felt supported and sometimes felt excluded from family traditions. She wanted her mother to offer help, even without being asked.

Inga cried and explained to her daughter that she would like to help her granddaughters more, but she was afraid that it would worsen their condition, because she didn't really understand what to do, and managing the pump or feeding her granddaughters terrified her. She also told Emma that it was difficult to understand her needs at times and that she felt heavily criticized for her approach to disciplining her granddaughters when she tried to spend time with them.

For example, on one occasion, she preferred the girls to stay at home rather than go to the park because she was afraid of the potential consequences of hypoglycemia if they ran or played too much. Her fear stemmed from not knowing how to manage a hypoglycemic episode, highlighting the need for more diabetes education and clearer communication about how to safely handle such situations.

The expression of these unspoken emotions brought mother and daughter closer together and allowed them to arrange a special meeting for the grandmother with their local diabetes educator, to provide her with more skills in managing the disease.

I also used family members' positions in space (moving closer, moving to be more distant) to bring a kinesthetic, movement dimension into therapy. This further aided the family members to express difficult emotions to one another, fostering greater closeness.

> "*Isabella, go to your mom and ask her what your diabetes means to her.*"
> "*Sofia, now move close to Dad and give him a hug.*"

As noted earlier, the girls played the fundamental role of "co-therapists" by helping me to explore family difficulties and history, and this demonstrated to the parents the relational resources that were already available. Getting the girls so active in the therapy helped the family develop more functional strategies together for adjusting more successfully and improving their quality of life.

One example is that we came up with a plan to allow the girls to return to sports, as these activities were very important to them before they were diagnosed with diabetes. It also showed that despite their chronic illness, they could live a pleasurable, full life and enjoy their otherwise healthy, vigorous bodies. This realization boded well for reducing the impact of diabetes on their identities and self-esteem.

In this way, the therapy sessions became a space for shared understanding and support and for strengthening resilience, in which the Calitri family (including grandmother) participated assiduously. Their participation was high despite the logistical challenges of accommodating the girls' after-school sports activities and attending therapy.

4.6.5 Dynamics between sisters and family roles

One of the goals of multigenerational family therapy involves understanding how roles are assigned within the family. I observed and commented on the interactions between the sisters and encouraged each to express her feelings about it.

Isabella: "Sofia always does what she wants, she's the youngest and mum protects her."
Sofia: "You (the parents) love her more because she's good at everything!"

The vocalization of these feelings, and my use of triadic and temporal questions, fostered a sense of collaboration between the girls rather than competition.

"Sofia, how do you think your mother feels when you and Isabella argue?"
"Isabella, how did your relationship with Sofia change after your diabetes diagnosis?"

In particular, Sofia was able to tell her parents that she felt like the "black sheep," because unlike her older sister, she had not accepted the diagnosis of diabetes and was not able to manage it as well as her sister did. Isabella explained to her little sister that she never wanted Sofia to have diabetes too, and that she partly felt guilty because she had it first and, who knows, maybe somehow, she had passed it on to her.

4.6.6 Parental roles and cultural influence

Given the family's cross-cultural background, I explored how Davide and Emma's cultural differences might affect their parenting styles and responses to the diabetes diagnoses. Davide, being Italian, came from a culture that often values close-knit family bonds and collective decision-making, while Emma, raised in Australia, leaned toward a more independent and self-reliant approach. These differences sometimes led to misunderstandings in how they managed the challenges of their daughters' diabetes.

Much attention was given to metaphorically understanding "where" the parents were emotionally when they felt sad or hopeless – especially Davide, who often felt torn between emotionally being "in" Italy, connected to his family, and physically "in" Australia, facing the reality of their daily life. I worked with both parents to explore "how" they could support each other instead of feeling psychologically isolated on two different continents.

Strategies were employed to integrate both cultural perspectives, ensuring a holistic approach to the girls' care. The parents were therefore guided to develop a unified parenting plan and also worked on improving communication through active listening and non-defensive dialogue to bridge gaps in their approaches.

4.6.7 Reorganization of the family in the face of illness: Exploration of intergenerational coping models

How did Davide and Emma reorganize themselves in the face of the disease? As they did previously with other difficulties? Or differently?

What coping legacies could they discover and utilize from their families of origin?

These questions were posed around consolidating all the resilience-building work we had done over a period of months. I explored with them patterns of reactions to other traumatizing events experienced by their parents, grandparents, and previous generations, to develop awareness of the resources and strategies available to the present-day Calitri family. We also identified and disrupted potentially harmful patterns.

4.6.8 Results and considerations

Over the course of therapy, the Calitri family reported experiencing positive transformations. Isabella and Sofia had developed a strong alliance and collaborated in their diabetes management, supporting each other especially at school, when the parents were not available.

Davide and Emma, through the expression of difficult emotions about diabetes, particularly anger, guilt, sadness, and fear, and the integration of different cultural perspectives, had become a more cohesive parenting team. Sofia's worrisome behaviors at school decreased, and the girls were also able to sleep and eat at their grandmother's house.

The family had learned to meet the challenge of diabetes by drawing on the strengths of their multigenerational history.

4.6.9 Follow-up

Continuous follow-ups with Sofia and Isabella's diabetes team were recommended to monitor their progress and address any emerging issues. The family was encouraged to engage with community resources and support groups to strengthen their care network.

By exploring family history, coping roles, and patterns, multigenerational family therapy facilitated a more resilient family dynamic, ultimately contributing to the well-being of both Isabella and Sofia, their parents, and the extended family as a whole.

4.7 Conclusion

Families of children with diabetes need ongoing support from their diabetes team and to use family-centered interventions that promote responsible diabetes management behaviors, effective emotional coping, and new ways of communicating. Problems of management and adherence to therapy in young patients and their families must be seen in a broader perspective than the simplistic and reductionist "non-compliance" of the child or adolescent, using a holistic perspective that puts the family and its resources at the center. The most recent guidelines from the International Society for Pediatric and Adolescent Diabetes (ISPAD) also attest that "the interdisciplinary team should provide preventive interventions at key moments of development, especially after diagnosis and before adolescence, emphasizing appropriate family involvement and support and realistic expectations" (de Wit et al., 2022, pp. 1373–1389). A useful support in this regard can come from the use of multigenerational family therapy, because it can help the family to deal with the diagnosis of diabetes and the course of the disease over time, observing intergenerational and cultural influences and promoting collaboration among family members, to promote optimal management of diabetes by the patient and a better psychological adjustment of the family unit.

References

American Diabetes Association. (2020). Standards of medical care in diabetes – 2020. *Diabetes Care, 43* (Suppl 1), S1–S212.

Anderson, B. J., & Coyne, J. C. (1991). Family context and compliance behavior in chronically ill children. *Children's Health Care, 20*(1), 7–17.

Anderson, B. J., Miller, J. P., Auslander, W. F., & Santiago, J. V. (1981). Family characteristics of diabetic adolescents: Relationship to metabolic control. *Diabetes Care*, *4*(6), 586–593. https://doi.org/10.2337/diacare.4.6.586

Andolfi, M. (2017). *Multi-generational family therapy: Tools and resources for the therapist*. Routledge.

Delamater, A. M., de Wit, M., McDarby, V., Malik, J. A., Hilliard, M. A., Northam, E., & Acerini, C. L. (2018). ISPAD clinical practice consensus guidelines 2018: Psychological care of children and adolescents with type 1 diabetes. *Pediatric Diabetes*, *19*(Suppl 27), 237–249. https://doi.org/10.1111/pedi.12736

de Wit, M., Gajewska, K. A., Goethals, E. R., McDarby, V., Zhao, X., Hapunda, G., Delamater, A. M., & DiMeglio, L. A. (2022). ISPAD clinical practice consensus guidelines 2022: Psychological care of children, adolescents and young adults with diabetes. *Pediatric Diabetes*, *23*(8), 1373–1389. https://doi.org/10.1111/pedi.13428

Grey, M., Boland, E. A., Davidson, M., & Li, J. (2000). Coping skills training for youth with diabetes mellitus has long-lasting effects on metabolic control and quality of life. *Journal of Pediatrics*, *137*(1), 107–113. https://doi.org/10.1067/mpd.2000.106568

Hilliard, M. E., Powell, P. W., Anderson, B. J., & Evidence Review Group. (2016). Evidence-based behavioral interventions to promote diabetes management in children, adolescents, and families. *American Psychologist*, *71*(7), 590–601. https://doi.org/10.1037/a0040359

Minuchin, S., Baker, L, Rosman, B., Liebman, R., Milman, L., & Todd, T. C. (1975). A conceptual model of psychosomatic illness in children. *Archives of General Psychiatry*, *32*(8), 1031–1038. https://doi.org/10.1001/archpsyc.1975.01760260095008

Minuchin, S., & Fishman, C. (1981). *Family therapy techniques*. Harvard University Press.

Monaghan, M. C., Hilliard, M. E., Cogen, F. R., & Streisand, R. (2009). Nighttime caregiving behaviors among parents of young children with type 1 diabetes: Associations with illness characteristics and parent functioning. *Family Systems & Health*, *27*(1), 28–38. https://doi.org/10.1037/a0014770

Solowiejczyk, J. (2004). The family approach to diabetes management: Theory into practice toward the development of a new paradigm. *Diabetes Spectrum*, *17*(1), 31–37. https://doi.org/10.2337/diaspect.17.1.31

Streisand, R., & Monaghan, M. (2014). Young children with type 1 diabetes: Challenges, research, and future directions. *Current Diabetes Reports*, *14*(9), 520. https://doi.org/520.10.1007/s11892-014-0520-2

Pinquart, M., & Teubert, D. (2012). Academic, physical, and social functioning of children and adolescents with chronic physical illness: A meta-analysis. *Journal of Pediatric Psychology*, *37*(4), 376–389. https://doi.org/10.1093/jpepsy/jsr106

Wang, C. H., Tully, C., Monaghan, M., Hilliard, M. E., & Streisand, R. (2021). Source-specific social support and psychosocial stress among mothers and fathers during initial diagnosis of type 1 diabetes in young children. *Family Systems & Health*, *39*(2), 358–362. https://doi.org/10.1037/fsh0000610

Wysocki, T., & Gavin, L. (2006). Paternal involvement in the management of pediatric chronic diseases: Associations with adherence, quality of life, and health status. *Journal of Pediatric Psychology*, *31*(5), 501–511. https://doi.org/10.1093/jpepsy/jsj042

Wysocki, T., Greco, P., Harris, M., Bubb, J., & White, N. (2001). Behavior therapy for families of adolescents with diabetes: Maintenance of treatment effects. *Diabetes Care*, *24*(3), 441–446. https://doi.org/10.2337/diacare.24.3.441

Wysocki, T., White, N. H., Bubb, J., Harris, M. A., & Greco, P. (1995). Family adaptation to diabetes: A model for intervention research. In J. L. Wallander & L. J. Siegel (Eds.), *Adolescent health problems: Behavioral perspectives* (pp. 289–304). Guilford Press.

Young, V., Eiser, C., Johnson, B., Brierley, S., Epton, T., Elliott, J., & Heller, S. (2013). Eating problems in adolescents with type 1 diabetes: A systematic review with meta-analysis. *Diabetes Medicine*, *30*(2), 189–198. https://doi.org/10.1111/j.1464-5491.2012.03771.x

5

THE COMMUNITY PROJECT IN THE SCHOOLS OF THE FAMILY INSTITUTE OF PORTO ALEGRE, BRAZIL

Description and purpose

José Ovídio Copstein Waldemar, Breno Irigoyen de Freitas, Klaus Iglesias Hensel, and Lisiane Milhoranza Rech

5.1 Introduction

Family therapy began in the sociopolitical context of the success of many national liberation movements and the decline of the colonial powers (Waldemar & Falceto, 1986). In the United States, there were large mobilizations for civil rights, and in France the protests of May 1968. At the same time, there was the presence of community psychiatry in the US (Community Mental Health Centers Act, 1963), and both in the US and England appeared innovative inpatient therapeutic communities, where staff and psychiatric patients lived in close proximity (Barnes & Berke, 1972).

Many of the pioneers of family therapy were progressive people, who believed that scientific and social advances could take humanity to a higher level of evolution. Bateson, with the theory of the double bind in schizophrenia, denounced the "no way out" situation of the psychotic patient. Minuchin in *Families of the Slums* described the indigence, the disorganization, and at the same time signaled the resources that the poorest had; later with his team, he continued working with the neediest families and the agencies that managed their destinies. Don Bloch, president of the Ackerman Institute, raised the red flag of nuclear destruction and lobbied for the elimination of atomic weapons, having witnessed the Soviet missile crisis in Cuba. Antipsychiatry contributed much to the view that individual illness was connected to family dysfunction and family dysfunction to a larger social dysfunction.

Together, these pioneers proposed a therapeutic approach that took into account the political and sociocultural dimensions as the larger context of individual and family dramas. My impression of my family therapy training colleagues at that time was that they also were a progressive group. The end of the 20th century brought many advances in social justice, more democracy, racial and gender equality, sexual freedom, respect for the LGBT community, and mechanisms of social protection such as free health and education in many countries. However, these advances are very recent, and there is a permanent tension between the progressive and the conservative forces. Democracy and the trend towards gender equality still only exists maybe in half the nations of the world. In the 1970s, pioneering research by the Lewis group showed that the healthy Western family is a flexible group, with shared power, dialogue, and tolerance for differences (Lewis et al., 1989).

DOI: 10.4324/9781003536765-7

Another well-known model, Olson's Circumplex (Olson et al., 1989), emphasized the importance in the family of the balance between the forces of cohesion and autonomy for the well-being of the individual and the family. These values of freedom, gender equality, sexual diversity, and tolerance began to be achieved in the late 20th century, through the struggle and social mobilization of millions of people in many countries. For these nascent achievements to continue to develop and become established, there is a need to develop a cultural and political context that supports them.

Indeed, starting in the last decade or so, many of these developments and rights have been under threat of being blocked and dismantled. Opposite values including authoritarianism, hate language, violence, inequality, and exclusion are on the rise. In most countries, the rich are getting richer and the poor are getting poorer. The latest data reveals that the combined wealth of the 26 richest people in the world is equal to the total financial holdings of half of the world's population! We are already observing in many countries a real setback of civilization and democratic values, with human and social rights being attacked. In the Middle East, radical groups have returned, and all over the world the migrant crisis continues to be politically manipulated to strengthen social hate and exclusion, and to play upon the dominant group's fears of becoming culturally and economically displaced – all in part to garnish votes.

Recent wars in Europe, the Middle East, and Africa have highlighted some of the worst that humankind has to offer. Our colleagues from sociology and social psychiatry have already shown us in countless papers that poverty, abandonment, and abuse in childhood are associated with long-term serious psychopathologies and criminality. Other studies associate unemployment with depression and suicide, especially in the poor. We know that unemployment is higher among young people; for instance, in Brazil young psychologists are mostly underemployed. It is very clear that the rules of dysfunctional major systems increasingly condition the dysfunction of the minor subsystems – for example, with nationalism and individualism reinforcing each other.

We suggest that the systemic therapist is in a privileged position to understand and contribute to the maintenance of the civilizational advances and to resist the present conservative wave. Much of what happens in the political arena is not that different from what we see, for example, in dysfunctional couples who blame each other, cannot listen, speak with hate language, and hold rigid stances. If we want things to be different, experience shows that social changes, without parallel individual, family, and cultural changes, do not contribute to new sustainable societies. The family therapy field has grown a lot, and today in large university centers and clinics it's not hard to find well-trained family therapists and training (Fraenkel, 2005, 2022a). In private practices, it is even easier. Therefore, more than simply continuing to train psychotherapists, we have the strong opinion that together with our colleagues in the mental health field, we need to assemble and take a stand about the main issues in the field, such as the fragility of public mental health policies, the influence of "Big Pharma" in the medicalization of psychiatry, and the limits and fees of private health plans.

We propose that systems thinkers, as conscious and coherent citizens, should join the more general effort against these regressive tendencies, supporting the values that promote the formation of healthy families and communities. This new appreciation of social and political issues, the *macrosystem*, it is very important in the systemic vision. We already observe that the common scientific fragmentation in science in general is also occurring in our field. Journals and books, as well as conferences, offer a plethora of different family therapy theories and techniques, although there is also a strong trend towards integration (Fraenkel, 2017, 2022a, 2022b). As the well-known metaphor states, we have to make an effort not to lose sight of the forest while looking at the trees. If not, even when we talk about the systemic vision, we run the risk of looking at family therapy as a technique and not as a way of thinking, as we believe the pioneers tried to teach us.

When we say that the systemic thinker has to be a social activist, we are not saying that we have to jump to join political parties, but rather that we need to get out of our comfort zone (including the four walls of our offices) and find practical ways to support movements that promote the values we believe in and that now are being fiercely attacked. One of the best ways to try to build a better society is to teach kids in school the skills of emotional intelligence: self-awareness, self-regulation, and how to create good interpersonal relationships with cooperation, empathy, and responsibility. This chapter describes our effort to get out of our comfort zone, as teachers and students of psychotherapy.

5.2 Overview

This chapter describes how a school of systemic psychotherapy (INFAPA) developed a program that has been at the cutting edge of the educational field. It starts by describing the first 12 years of a mindfulness and socioemotional learning (M-SEL) program called SENTE. Then it presents the last four years during which SENTE initiated a collaboration with the Instituto Cidade Segura (ICS), an NGO that offers an evidence-based systemic consultancy on how to diminish urban violence. SENTE had long-time experience in public schools, had developed its own approach based on evidence, but it was staffed with volunteers and had limited reach. ICS already had many years of experience developing public policies at the request of several middle-size cities, but it did not offer a socioemotional learning (SEL) program. The association of these two provided a more comprehensive and effective community-based intervention.

5.3 The first phase

In Porto Alegre, Brazil, in 2007, a combined M-SEL program began to develop, sponsored by the Instituto da Familia de Porto Alegre (INFAPA), a postgraduate school for psychotherapists with a systemic orientation. It was initiated by the first author, a child psychiatrist and mindfulness teacher associated with Zen Peacemaker International and the Porto Alegre group Viazen. It started when the first author (JOCW), as a member of Zen Peacemakers International, was looking for a new social project with an underserved population. Being a child psychiatrist, Zen meditator, and familiar with the basics of emotional intelligence (Goleman, 1995), he was able to start the project, initially in a single classroom.

The volunteers for the school interventions were young psychologists undertaking psychotherapy training, most having recently graduated, who had free time to spare and an interest in learning the intervention. This was possible due to the social mission of INFAPA and the inspiration of Bernie Glassman, founder of the Zen Peacemakers, who motivated Waldemar (first author) to use the ingredients that you have, with the people who need it the most (Glassman & Field, 1996). The psychologists volunteered four hours a week of their time in exchange for weekly supervision in learning and developing the new method. Twenty-five different professionals participated over those 12 years, six of them having now at least five years of experience with the method. To foster cohesion, each group supervision started with an initial check-in with the psychologists, and brief moments of mindful meditation started and ended each meeting. In this approach to teaching and supervising the volunteer instructors, we used practices of emotional intelligence to "teach-the-teachers" of emotional intelligence. Gatherings also facilitated fun and friendship building among the instructors.

Another key aspect of conducting the program was tolerating "not knowing" if the program would have continuity the following year. Being staffed with volunteers, it meant we needed new ones each year, because most stayed only one year. As an incentive to build a permanent team, INFAPA developed a four-year educational track where the trainees initially received diplomas as teachers of M-SEL after two years and then as trainers of teachers of M-SEL after four years. Six psychologists finished the four-year training, and ten completed the two-year training. Small donations provided additional international online courses for the trainees.

As the young psychologist/trainees and experienced trainers alike discovered, working in poor communities is not an easy task. We often think, "we don't know, we can't, it will not work." These feelings can paralyze us. Our experience with SENTE taught us that, quoting Saint Francis of Assisi, "If you start doing what is needed, then what is possible, all of a sudden you may be doing the impossible." Or said in a different way: "If you do today what is possible today, tomorrow you will be doing what was not possible today."

5.4 The development of SEL and mindfulness in schools

Thirty years ago, a group of educators, including Daniel Goleman, who popularized the concept of emotional intelligence, came together and created CASEL (2020), an organization with the goal of promoting SEL in schools. Research shows that beyond cognitive intelligence (IQ), SEL skills are fundamental to a happy life and should ideally be taught in schools. Today this is already a reality in some schools in many countries, where various evidence-based programs certified by CASEL are taught alongside the traditional subjects. A recent paper (Durlak et al., 2022) reviewed 12 meta-analyses and presented findings from 24 countries, with about one million students in 523 studies. Compared to controls, SEL participants demonstrated significantly improved socioemotional skills, attitudes, behavior, and academic performance. According to CASEL (2020):

> SEL is an integral part of education and human development. SEL is the process through which young people and adults acquire and apply the knowledge, skills, and attitudes to develop healthy identities, manage emotions and achieve personal and collective goals, feel and show empathy for others, establish and maintain supportive relationships, and make responsible and caring decisions. SEL advances educational equity and excellence through authentic school-family-community partnerships to establish learning environments and experiences that feature trusting and collaborative relationships, rigorous and meaningful curriculum and instruction, and ongoing evaluation. SEL can help address various forms of inequity and empower young people and adults to co-create thriving schools and contribute to safe, healthy, and just communities.

According to The Mindfulness Initiative (2021), a group dedicated to implementing mindfulness in schools:

> Mindfulness means intentionally paying attention to present-moment experience, inside ourselves, our minds and bodies, and in our environment, with an attitude of openness, curiosity, kindness and care. Mindfulness is a natural human capacity, cultivated by ancient wisdom traditions, that has long been valued as underlying authentic happiness, coping with difficulty, and the ability to live an ethical life. In modern times mindfulness practices have been combined with psychological and wellbeing theories and developed into secular teachings. Modern mindfulness has been the subject of many scientific trials and has shown clear and beneficial outcomes for human flourishing.
>
> *(Weare & Bethune, 2021)*

These skills can be developed from exercises that use focusing on breathing and surrounding sounds; observing thoughts, emotions, sensations; and paying attention to external objects and body movements. Mindfulness also facilitates an alignment of behavior with our deepest values, bringing a greater sense of subjective coherence. We added to the curriculum the Council Method of the Ojai Foundation (Zimmerman & Coyle, 1996) to develop positive relationships. To teach how to deal constructively with conflict, we taught principles of nonviolent communication (Rosenberg, 2003), adapted for the students' age range. Thus, in the comprehensive SENTE program, mindfulness practices reinforce the development of skills related to socioemotional education, council, and nonviolent communication.

5.5 The method in practice

In Brazil, 86.1% of elementary school students attend public schools (Censo da Educação Básica, 2022). The middle to upper classes try to avoid the public schools because they are underfunded and the teachers are poorly paid. Many teachers work 60-hour schedules to make ends meet, and students generally attend classes either in the AM or PM, to make room for all of them. Many of the students come from disorganized single-mother families, and several fathers in our sample were in jail or involved with drugs. Also, almost 15% of the students lived in group homes.

Initially, the schools asked fifth graders to be the participants in the intervention because this is the last grade for which they have only one teacher for all the disciplines, and therefore feel less fragmented and disjointed than they do in sixth grade and beyond. Sixth-grade teachers usually complain that the sixth graders show difficulty adapting to having so many new teachers. The school expected that the program would lead to more collaborative and cooperative students once they entered the sixth grade. This indeed occurred.

In the final years of the SENTE intervention, we were able to work with kindergarten children and late adolescents.

The method followed the basic general orientation of CASEL. Each classroom received up to 12 sessions to teach the five basic CASEL skills: (1) self-awareness, (2) self-management, (3) social awareness, (4) relationship skills, and (5) responsible decision-making. Usually, the five skills were presented in this order, but priority was always given to any urgent issue brought by the students having to do with problems in school, at home, or with peers. The interventions usually started and finished with exercises focused on mindful breathing. Between these exercises, we interspersed reflexive and playful activities, as well as informal mindfulness exercises.

The interventions were usually delivered by a pair of facilitators, matching a new and a more experienced facilitator. Each intervention was planned ahead and the results reviewed in group supervision, when the next intervention was planned (de Freitas & Marin, 2022).

We will try to give a general idea about what happens in the classroom, but needless to say, what actually happened over the 12 years and 30 classrooms in which we carried out the program was varied, complex, and responsive to the particular youths and their unique circumstances. In the beginning, we like to enter the classroom and ask the students: "You learn math, history, Portuguese, and music, but who teaches you how to feel well?" The students looked at the teacher with curiosity with facial expressions indicating, "What kind of question is this?" They often said that they never imagined such a topic could be discussed in class! The teacher explains that we are psychologists, and this is one of the themes that psychologists talk about with young people. We explain that we are going to have a series of weekly meetings with them to talk about this subject. We ask the students to give examples of situations in which they feel good and others in which they feel bad. They usually say that they feel bad when criticized, when parents do not pay attention to them, when they are ridiculed, bullied, or have to do something they don't want to do. And what makes them feel good? The opposite: when they are praised, receive attention, don't have fights at home, or are doing something they like.

Next the program instructor says: "So, if we all avoid criticizing and try to praise instead, if we respect and pay attention to people, avoid fights, and try to do the things we like we are going to feel better, right?" Of course, we were in this way introducing the "Golden Rule": "Treat others like you want to be treated." The students generally agree with this but come to the conclusion that they don't have the patience to act the way they would like (we all know very well how it is much easier said than done). Again, we tell them: "Right! You don't have patience, but has anyone taught you how to *have patience*? Of course not, so we have to learn how to *be patient*!" At this moment, they are ready to start learning the mindful breathing exercise. We explain that for each three minutes of exercise, we build up a three-minute reservoir of patience that can be used when we most need it, much the same way physical exercise will help us when we need that extra muscular effort.

Following are some examples of how we teach the five SEL competencies.

Self-Awareness: We start by teaching how to recognize, name, and express feelings, both positive and negative. One exercise involves giving colors to the emotions students are experiencing. We also use the "Deck of Cards with All the Emotions" (Caminha & Caminha, 2008). Each student draws a card and tells a story about that emotion. One girl picked the sadness card and started to cry, saying she felt bad about being called a derogatory nickname. A peer expressed his surprise at her reaction, saying he had called her by the nickname because he did not know how bad she felt about it. He promised not to do it again.

There is an exercise in which each student writes an emotional problem and puts the paper in a box. Another reads aloud the problem, and many peers share experiences and opinions about how they would handle the situation. We tell students to avoid saying what to do, but instead, to share similar experiences. One day we were asking the group about how they were feeling, and a girl started to tell how sad she was because her parents were divorcing. She started crying and some of her friends came close to embrace and console her. After she calmed down, the group talked about how that has happened to others, how difficult it is, and that bad feelings will eventually pass.

Self-Management: We use the mindfulness of the breath exercise for teaching how to "stay calm and be patient." We emphasize the effort and not the results, suggesting that just keeping quiet is a very good outcome. We explain that the combination of alertness and relaxation that comes with the breathing exercise can be used to compete in the well-known "Simon Says" game, which they love to play. They also use this skill to play the game of "staring at each other" without bursting out laughing. We also use silent meals (mindful eating) to teach about self-management and truly appreciating the flavor of foods. We were told the following story by a student: One teacher came into the fourth-grade classroom very agitated and anxious because she had little time to give the test, so one of the students raises her hand and when she catches the teacher's attention, she says: "Please breathe deeply teacher, breathe deeply!" Both the teacher and the classroom quickly recovered with the aid of the humor.

Relationship Skills and Social Awareness: We frequently employ the fishbowl technique, with the following Council (Zimmerman & Coyle, 1996) structure: (1) *Deep Listening*: we taught them to use mindfulness of breath "to listen deeply," with the "whole body." We liked to say that the ear is too small for good listening. They also understood that listening mindfully is an effective way to become more patient, a quality they accepted as highly desirable. (2) Only the person who has *the talking piece* may talk, because otherwise we can't listen mindfully! With time, they get more skilled at raising their hand and waiting their turn. (3) *Using "I" statements*, expressing our needs and opinions in the first person, rather than criticizing others' thoughts and feelings. We called this "to speak in favor and not against something." (4) *Talking from the Heart*: express the feelings and experiences that led to certain ideas, trying to describe why you think you got to where you are in your thinking. (5) *To be as brief as possible*, so more people have a chance to speak, and nobody speaks again before everybody has a chance to participate.

Example: Fifth-grade students wanted to talk about gender tensions, the usual routine of boys complaining about girls and vice versa. In this fishbowl exercise, first the boys sit inside and talk about what annoys them in the girls, while the girls listen quietly outside. Then the girls go inside and the boys listen from the outside. Afterwards, everyone sits in a circle and comments about what they have learned from "deep listening" to each other. The consensus was that it helped a lot in understanding and getting along with each other.

Some more vignettes:

1. We were organizing one more fishbowl when a girl said that she did not need to participate anymore because she took home the exercise of taking turns to listen to each other, and now she and her mother are getting along much better.
2. Another student follows suit and tells that at home his father and sister liked the exercise, but he is sorry the mother doesn't have the time to participate.
3. With late adolescents, we have experimented with a briefer approach, teaching mindfulness and holding the fishbowl circles, with the psychologists/volunteers being the first in the middle and the teens joining later. Many students participated actively. The experience was very rewarding. Some of the issues initiated by the students were about sexuality, absent or intrusive parents, and questions about mental health.

Responsible Decision-Making: One day we arrive and are told by the teacher that a former 13-year-old classmate had been murdered. His older brother had involved him in the war between drug gangs. One boy starts by saying that this classmate was violent and that he had suffered at his hands: "He got what he deserved!" Another one said that it was true he was rough, but that he had ups and downs and had also helped him in a number of situations. A third one who had attended the funeral made similar comments and described how the boy's family was completely devastated. After many other students expressed their feelings, the boy who initially spoke asked to speak again, apologized for what he had said, explaining that listening to his colleagues he was able to also see good aspects in the boy: "He sure needed to learn a lesson, but it was very wrong to kill him, and I am really sorry for his family!"

5.6 Outcome research and program dissemination

The research was possible because the SENTE program became part of a wider intervention in schools, sponsored by the Department of Family and Community Medicine of the Federal University of Rio Grande do Sul, one of the most prestigious universities in Brazil. This research was conducted when we had five years of experience with the method. The study examined the impact of the mindfulness and socioemotional learning (M-SEL) program on mental health issues and quality of life (QoL) among fifth-grade students (n = 132) in public elementary schools. The participants, consisting of 64 students, underwent up to 12 M-SEL sessions over a period of five months, and their outcomes were compared to 68 students in a control group. In comparison to the control group, M-SEL participants demonstrated *modest* but significant improvements in various mental health domains, including emotional, conduct, relationship, and prosocial behavior, as well as in QoL scores.

Looking back, there certainly have been many roadblocks in the implementation of the program, but a democratic leadership and a weekly meeting that now includes representatives from all the schools involved in the wider school program have been of fundamental importance to tolerate and overcome the normal periods of uncertainty and confusion that eventually lead to creative and positive outcomes (Glassman & Field, 1996). During the COVID-19 pandemic, an online course was delivered to 40 program teachers all over Brazil, with 12 having had more advanced training in the intervention. It is important to emphasize that our efforts affected the participating youths, the school cultures where the intervention took place, and also served as excellent post-graduate training in community-based socioemotional programs and mindfulness-based techniques. The psychologists who implemented the intervention benefited the more than 40 homeroom teachers who were present with the students. Of the more than 30 psychologists who delivered our courses, our impression is that at least half of them are involved in paid or voluntary work where they apply the skills they have learned (Waldemar & Freitas, 2024).

5.7 Emotional intelligence training to decrease urban violence

Urban violence is a complex, multidetermined phenomena. Brazil is one of the more economically unequal and violent countries in the world. Close to 50,000 people are murdered every year. Like in other countries, the dead are mostly young poor people. Brazilian prisons are under the control of criminal organizations, whose leaders frequently give orders from inside the prison to eliminate their drug trafficking rivals. This explains most periods of peak or quiet in the number of murders.

The Instituto Cidade Segura (ICS) is an NGO that has many years of experience consulting cities on evidence-based methods to diminish violence (Kopittke, 2023). The ICS approach is to coordinate the police and justice departments with the other social agencies in the city government, building an integrated evidence-based platform that is essential to the task of diminishing violence.

Before the partnership with SENTE, ICS had a very successful experience with Niterói and Pelotas, two middle-sized cities in Brazil. In four years in Pelotas, homicides declined by 62%. In Niteroi, the number of car thefts and other police incidents diminished sharply. ICS is now an internationally recognized organization in the field, with its head, for many years, a consultant on police issues to the World Bank. ICS was looking for a program to promote mental health in schools when it came across SENTE (de Freitas & Marin, 2022; Waldemar & Falceto, 2015). When it started its partnership with ICS, senior psychologists of SENTE were assigned the task of developing a manual for teachers and another for students, with 20 lessons for each grade, from the first to ninth grade. This manual received the name of SEJA and has already been in use for four years in the schools. It is now being rewritten based on the feedback received from the teachers. In the last three years, elementary and middle school teachers of Lajeado, a city of 150,000 people; Santa Cruz, with 220,000; and Rio Grande, 300,000, were trained to deliver the program.

The decision to implement the program in cities comes top down from the mayor's office, usually without asking the teachers if they are interested. All of the teachers from elementary and middle school are now required to take this initial training of 12 hours and then apply the manual with the help of weekly online supervision. The big challenge now that the program has become a public policy is that many teachers feel they do not have enough training or are not motivated enough for the task. They are also not given a special time for the weekly online supervision, having to use part of their own free time. There is a big contrast between the training offered previously by SENTE, which was intensive and with motivated colleagues, to what is now possible to offer under the present contract between ICS and the cities. We still don't have numbers on how many teachers that were trained through the partnership with ICS are currently implementing parts of the program that was taught.

Our suggestion to overcome this obstacle in future interventions is to train more intensively only the teachers who are motivated to learn the program, who will then get more extensive supervision and time allotted for it, so that later they can train their colleagues in the method. This approach is supported by CASEL findings (Durlak et al., 2022, 2010, 2011; Taylor et al., 2017). The politicians who decide about implementing the program will have to be convinced this is the best thing to do. In 2024, SENTE will resume its program with volunteers in the original catchment area where it all started.

References

Barnes, M., & Berke, J. H. (1972). *Mary Barnes: Two accounts of a journey through madness*. Harcourt Brace Jovanovich.

Caminha, R., & Caminha, M. (2008). *The deck of emotions*. Sinopsys Editora.

CASEL – Collaborative for Academic, Social, and Emotional Learning. (2020). *CASEL's framework: What are the core competence areas and where are they promoted?* https://casel.org/casel-sel-framework-11-2020/

de Freitas, B. I., & Marin, A. H. (2022). Experiências e reflexões sobre intervenções baseadas em aprendizagem socioemocional e atenção plena no Brasil. In B. I. de Freitas & A. H. Marin (Eds.), *Aprendizagem socioemocional e atenção plena no contexto escolar brasileiro* (2nd ed., pp. 210–241). Editora Gênese.

Durlak, J. A., Mahoney, J. L., & Boyle, A. E. (2022). What we know, and what we need to find out about universal, school-based social and emotional learning programs for children and adolescents: A review of meta-analyses and directions for future research. *Psychological Bulletin, 148*(11–12), 765–782. https://doi.org/10.1037/bul0000383

Durlak, J. A., Weissberg, R. P., Dymnicki, A. B., Taylor, R. D., & Schellinger, K. B. (2011). The impact of enhancing students' social and emotional learning: A meta-analysis of school-based universal interventions. *Child Development, 82*(1), 405–432. https://doi.org/10.1111/j.1467-8624.2010.01564.x

Durlak, J. A., Weissberg, R. P., & Pachan, M. (2010). A meta-analysis of after-school programs that seek to promote personal and social skills in children and adolescents. *American Journal of Community Psychology, 45*(3–4), 294–309. https://doi.org/10.1007/s10464-010-9300-6

Fraenkel, P. (2005). Whatever happened to family therapy? *Psychotherapy Networker, 29*, 30–39.

Fraenkel, P. (2017). Integration in couple and family therapy. In J. Lebow, A. Chambers, & D. Breunlin (Eds.), *Encyclopedia of couple and family therapy* (Vol. 3, pp. 1501–1506). Springer International Publishing. https://doi.org/10.1007/978-3-319-15877-8_534-1

Fraenkel, P. (2022a). Whatever happened to family therapy? Today's renaissance in systems thinking. *Psychotherapy Networker, 46*, 20–26.

Fraenkel, P. (2022b). Therapeutic palette integrative couple therapy. In J. L. Lebow & D. K. Snyder (Eds.), *Clinical handbook of couple therapy* (6th ed., pp. 339–361). Guilford Press.

Glassman, B., & Field, R. (1996). *Instructions to the cook*. Bell Tower.

Goleman, D. (1995). *Emotional intelligence: Why it can matter more than IQ*. Random House.

Instituto Nacional de Estudos e Pesquisas Educacionais Anísio Teixeira. (2022). *Censo da educação básica 2022*. https://download.inep.gov.br/areas_de_atuacao/notas_estatisticas_censo_da_educacao_basica_2022.pdf

Kopittke, A. (2023). *Manual de segurança pública baseada em evidências: O que funciona e o que não funciona na prevenção à violência*. Conhecer.

Lewis, J. M., Beavers, W. R., Gossett, J. T., & Phillips, V. A. (1989). *No single thread: Psychological health in family systems*. Brunner/Mazel.

Olson, D., Russell, C. S., & Sprenkle, D. H. (1989). *Circumplex model: Systemic assessment and treatment of families* (1st ed.). Routledge. https://doi.org/10.4324/9781315804132

Rosenberg, M. (2003). *Nonviolent communication: A language of life*. PuddleDancer Press.

Taylor, R. D., Oberle, E., Durlak, J. A., & Weissberg, R. P. (2017). Promoting positive youth development through school-based social and emotional learning interventions: A meta-analysis of follow-up effects. *Child Development, 88*(4), 1156–1171. https://doi.org/10.1111/cdev.12864

Waldemar, J. O. C., & Falceto, O. (1986). Terapia de família: Escola norte-americana. In L. C. Osório (Ed.), *Grupoterapia hoje* (pp. 192–202). Artes Médicas.

Waldemar, J. O. C., & Falceto, O. (2015). Multiprofessional school consultation lead by "Estratégia de Saúde da Família": A model for Brazil. *Nova Perspectiva Sistêmica, 51*, 25–36.

Waldemar, J. O. C., & Freitas, B. I. (2024). The role of mindfulness and social-emotional learning within a systemic multidimensional approach to diminish violence in cities in Brazil. *World Social Psychiatry, 6*(1), 53–56. https://doi.org/10.4103/wsp.wsp_66_23

Weare, K., & Bethune, A. (2021). *Implementing mindfulness in schools: An evidence-based guide*. Mindfulness Initiative. www.themindfulnessinitiative.org/implementing-mindfulness-in-schools-an-evidence-based-guide

Zimmerman, J. M., & Coyle, V. (1996). *The way of council*. Bramble Books.

6

"TELL ME A STORY . . . MINE!"

Children and parents talk about adoption

Alessandra Santona and Laura Gorla

6.1 Introduction

"*Where do I come from? Why was I abandoned? And why did you want me?*"

These are just some of the many questions that adopted children ask their adoptive parents to explore and try to understand their story. These questions refer to three important themes: origins ("Where do I come from?"), the reasons behind abandonment ("Why was I abandoned?"), and those concerning the formation of the adoptive family ("Why did you want me?"). It is clear that the content of the questions and possible answers that adoptive parents provide does not end in sharing information but refers to a deep dimension of the self (Colaner & Soliz, 2017): children ask because they desire to understand their past and to construct a thinkable representation of what happened. Very frequently, however, children do not address their history directly through questions; they usually do so disguisedly, recounting vague memories, idealizing their past, or enacting behaviors more or less connected to exploring past experiences. Just as frequently, they implement strategies that enable them to avoid approaching anything related to the experience of loss and abandonment.

In general, the questions that children ask and the behaviors they act out can be particularly difficult for adoptive parents to manage because they touch on aspects that are dense with meaning and require the ability to understand the child's needs and tune in to his or her emotions and needs (Brodzinsky, 2011; Harrigan, 2013; Wrobel et al., 2003). The presence of this competence could enable the establishment of a continuous and dynamic communication process related to the child's history. Several studies have, in fact, pointed out that communicating openly regarding adoption means structuring a path of progressive unraveling and sharing of experiences, information, emotions, and meanings. The importance of sharing within the adoptive family the information and aspects related to the adoption itself and the child's history is, finally, emphasized not only by research and clinical practice but also by the Italian law itself, which, formerly Article 28 of Law 184/1983 and with Law 149/2001, states the right of the adopted child to be informed about his or her origins by the adoptive parents.

But how can adoption-related communication within the adoptive family be conceptually defined?

DOI: 10.4324/9781003536765-8

6.2 The family adoption communication model

Theoretically, we talk about communicative openness when referring to adoption-related communications within the family (Brodzinsky, 2006; Jones & Hackett, 2007). There are two levels of openness: structural and communicative (Brodzinsky, 2005). The first term refers to aspects of the family structure, such as the level of contact between its members and how information is shared, while the second one refers to how adoption-related issues and emotions are explored, managed, and shared within the family.

Considering the second type, communicative openness, the primary reference in the current theoretical framework is the Family Adoption Communication Model (FACM) proposed by Wrobel and colleagues (2003). According to this model, communicative openness is a dynamic, evolving process and follows the child's development because, depending on the stage of the life cycle and the developmental tasks that the adopted child is going through, how parents communicate the child's story to him or her changes. Moreover, according to this model, communication of the adoption story is usually marked by three moments characterized by great flexibility. Each family can progress or retrogress between the stages, overlap, skip, or place one before the other.

The three phases are as follows:

Phase 1: The adoption story. In the first phase, the parents decide on the content, timing, and modality of telling the child his or her adoption story since the child does not habitually take an active role in asking and starting the communication process.

Phase 2: The child's questions. Although the adoptive parents still have high control over the information and modality of communication, the child is now a more active interlocutor and asks the parents for more information about his or her history, coming to understand it more than in the previous phase.

Phase 3: The child searches for information. In this phase, the child, usually an adolescent or young adult, independently searches for information. This is a sensitive phase where the child may also seek direct contact with the family of origin.

It becomes clear that communicating one's story to the adopted child is considered a dynamic, flexible process (Barbosa-Ducharne & Soares, 2016; Colaner & Soliz, 2017), changing over time, also depending on the child's age, cognitive skills, and the relationship created with the adoptive parents. In particular, a study by Brodzinsky (2011) showed that children between the ages of 3 and 5 cannot really understand what being adopted means and implies, but they learn the language of adoption. They learn to talk about adoption and biological and adoptive parents. However, they do not arrive at a deep understanding of what these terms mean. In the period between the ages of 6 and 12, however, new cognitive skills lead to greater curiosity about their origins and enable children to understand that they have been abandoned due to the responsibility of their biological parents. Understanding the decision behind their abandonment often leads children to address the issue with their adoptive parents. Thus, they question them about their biological parents' behavior ("Was I ever wanted by my biological parents? Did they regret their decision to give me up for adoption?").

With the onset of adolescence and the cognitive maturation associated with it, the adopted child builds a more realistic picture of his or her story and is more able to identify him or herself with the biological parents, thinking about and imagining the motivations that led to the adoption. The adolescent also revisits and redefines his or her personal identity in the process of separation and differentiation, both from the adoptive parents and biological parents, who are imagined but always symbolically present. This path leads the adolescent to begin a journey into the past and deal more with his origins and may also push him or her to seek contact with his biological parents (Andolfi, 2017).

6.3 The importance of talking about the adoption story

Knowing one's history and the significant events that characterized it allows for an adequate psychological growth of the person. To have the possibility of living an evolutionary and coherent developmental experience, individuals must give a logic of continuity to their own experience. Individuals need to be aware of the effects of certain events on their lives, the relevant characteristics of their personality, and the strengths and weaknesses that come from the past. On the contrary, if one cannot attribute an origin to experiences, emotions, and thoughts, these may seem threatening or foreign, thus becoming a source of sufferings (Chistolini, 2010).

Moreover, two levels are always present in the long process of searching for the origins: knowing the significant events in one's life and attributing meaning and significance to them. In the case of adoption, moreover, such events are often painful and refer to abandonment, directly affecting the person's self-image as a subject worthy of love, affection, and care. The presence of abandonment in one's past leads to questioning one's existence, with important consequences on self-esteem, security, and the ability to tolerate frustrations and build positive relationships with others (Balenzano et al., 2018).

Several researchers have investigated the topic and have focused on the effects that telling the adoption story has on the adopted child: in particular, it has been shown that adequate communicative openness in the family seems to increase the child's self-esteem, improve his or her ability to handle emotions correctly, thus experiencing fewer emotional and behavioral problems and increasing the feeling of security in one's family (Brodzinsky, 2006; Jones, 2016; Von Korff & Grotevant, 2011).

Moreover, for children, talking about adoption means integrating past and present, perceiving their family as a safe place where they can express their emotions and have their past experiences acknowledged (Soares et al., 2017), and, finally, building a more integrated sense of identity (Chistolini, 2010; Horstman et al., 2016). Through encounters with affectively significant people, the child will be able to reread his or her self-image, transforming the one shaped by experiences of abandonment and going on to create a new circuit of meanings and experiences. Only through a new representation of his or her past and what happened to him or her will the child be able to start a process of resilience (Cyrulnik, 2004) and tell his or her history.

The narrative capacity, defined as the ability to tell one's story, is crucial for processing grief and defining one's role within the context of constructing one's own family novel as a child of the adoptive couple.

However, often, the adopted child cannot independently attribute proper meaning to what happened in his or her past and needs help in understanding his or her experience. Therefore, building the child's narrative capacity will be a joint task of the child and his or her adoptive parents. Both must, in fact, accept and process their own histories, as well as each other's, to weave them into a shared narrative that aligns with the intergenerational continuity of the new family. If unaccompanied in the process of re-signifying his past, the child may experience widespread discomfort, often without understanding its causes.

This discomfort is then expressed with a range of negative emotions such as anger, grief, despair, and guilt. The acceptance of the fact that he has not been biologically born to his adoptive parents, along with the freedom from the need to blame his biological parents for abandoning him (but seen as always ready to take him back), will allow the child an untroubled narrative of his story within the family. Accompanying the child in the process of discovering and integrating his past with his present is not an easy task. Adoptive parents must be prepared to acknowledge and tolerate the emotional baggage of the child's history and integrate it only through a deep process of elaboration. For this reason, the presence of a strong feeling of love in the adoptive parents is not enough; it is equally necessary that they adopt an attitude of deep listening to the child's needs, which are characterized by specificities that must be recognized.

Chistolini (2010) pointed out that certain criteria would be appropriate to follow when communicating with adopted children. These criteria set the rules for the dimension of knowledge, meaning that they direct the sharing of the information in the child's story. The criteria are as follows:

The relevance or involvement criterion: Only events that directly affect or involve the child should be told.

The relevancy criterion: Parents need to tell the child about events that are considered important to his or her story.

The congruence criterion: The child must receive information congruent with each other, without contradictory, confusing, or secret aspects.

The sustainability criterion: The story told to the child must be emotionally sustainable for him.

Following these criteria, alongside the narrative capacity, adoptive parents should pay special attention to the dimension of understanding, not focusing exclusively on the specific facts that happened to the child, but they should provide an interpretive key that helps him or her to make sense of these facts, allowing for a coherent meaning to his or her story. The delicacy of storytelling construction can be frightening for parents, who wonder when to talk, what information to share, and how to answer their child's questions (Harrigan, 2010; Colaner & Soliz, 2017).

Adoptive parents also may find themselves in the situation of lacking information about the child's past or feeling unable to address certain issues with the child. Research on the topic has shown that adoptive parents feel that talking to their child about adoption involves reflecting on the very nature of the adoptive bond (Greco, 2014). Telling about their child's adoption, in fact, also means addressing how they came to adopt, and if the adoption was the consequence of a diagnosis of infertility or the impossibility of having a biological child, the telling of the adoptive story would also have to include the reworking of that experience. Being an adoptive parent also refers to not being the biological parents of that child.

Thus, the "imaginary child" reemerges, that is, a highly idealized child conceived in the minds of the spouses and extended family that must be integrated into the experience and self-image of the individual partners to direct the necessary affective investments toward an authentic desire for parenthood, concretized in the adoptive action (Santona, 2003). Here, then, is an understanding of how each story told is not only the child's story but an interweaving of stories. The protagonists are multiple: the child, the family of origin, the adoptive family, and any other people who may have accompanied the child (social workers, foster family, professional workers, and staff working at the child's institution) on his or her journey between abandonment and adoption. The child's story becomes the story of his or her family, in an interconnection of choices and events that led to that child being adoptable and the prospective adoptive parents waiting for a child to be welcomed.

6.4 How to tell an adoption story to the child: Guidelines and tools for parents

Starting from the attachment and identity development theories, several studies in the literature have examined the topic of "life story work," which focuses on the adopted child's history, defined as a dynamic and flexible process of continuous communication about the child's past and personal history.

Underlying such research is the idea that the child has a right to access any information relative to his or her history (to the extent that such information is known to adoptive parents) and that only by knowing his or her history and integrating his or her past with the present can he or she develop a coherent sense of self (Ryan & Walker, 2007; Treacher & Katz, 2000; Livingston Smith, 2010; Watson et al., 2015). An important study on the topic (Harrigan, 2010) explored the adoptive parents' experience in the process of building and sharing history with their children.

The first aspect that all parents highlighted was that communication and storytelling occurred interactively, involving the child from the beginning, and often changed over time, adapting to how the child coped and responded emotionally. Despite the dynamism inherent in storytelling, the interviewed parents highlighted that they never changed the story's content and information but added more details as they felt the children were ready. The most frequently used mode of storytelling was spoken word, direct dialogue, which was accompanied by fairy tales, songs written specifically to tell their child's story, or life story books (i.e., books containing photos, drawings, and stories about the child's life from birth to arrival in the adoptive family). All parents used physical objects to accompany their stories: most used photographs depicting some of the key places in the child's life (such as a hospital, the institution, and the child's country of birth). Others used a globe to illustrate their family's journey and to talk about their family coming together from different parts of the world before reuniting. Others chose to share with their children objects that recalled their country of birth, such as flags or coins.

When asked about the content expressed in the story, the adoptive parents pointed out that the topics they dealt with the most were as follows:

The biological parents' decision to give up the child for adoption: In the communication with the child, adoptive parents tried to convey a positive image of the intentions behind the decision to give up the child for adoption, saying that the biological parents acted with the child's best interests in mind, because they wanted a better life for him or her and were aware that they could not offer it. However, the positive image of the biological parents provided to the child rarely corresponds to the real motivation that led to his abandonment. In fact, adoptive parents wish to sweeten what happened, both because of the difficulty of touching sensitive issues and for fear of hurting the child further. What often escapes their notice is that for the child to maintain an unrealistic view of his or her birth parents, as already pointed out, is not conducive to the processing path and can negatively impact the child's well-being.

The adoptive parents' strong desire to have a child: Parents conveyed the idea that the decision to adopt was not impulsive or quick but was particularly thought out, anticipated, and desired.

The long process that led the adoptive parents to meet their child: Adoptive parents often described the adoption process as lengthy and guided by institutional professionals who facilitated the meeting between the parents and the child. The judge, social workers, and people who cared for the child in his or her country of birth are often mentioned as helping the family.

The permanence and enduring strength of the family bond: Adoptive parents described their family as permanent and everlasting, emphasizing that they will accompany the child throughout his or her life to reassure him or her about their bond.

The special qualities the child possesses: Adoptive parents wanted to convey that the child was wanted and loved precisely as he or she is and for the characteristics he or she possesses. Underneath this action, there is the desire to make the child understand that the decision to adopt him or her and not another child was not accidental but that the adoptive parents would not have wanted any other child.

The modalities and themes described are not only reported in the study of Harrigan and colleagues but also represent a common thread in the adoption-related narrative between adoptive parents and their children. Even in clinical practice, it is not unusual for adoptive parents to ask for support from local services to prepare the story and themselves for the narrative. Equally common is the use of some of the operational tools mentioned by Harrigan, such as photographs, fairy tales, and picture books. These, in fact, help parents talk to the child about his or her prior experience and facilitate the child's elaboration (Greco, 2014; Miliotti, 2015; Watson et al., 2019). Thanks to objects, photos, and drawings, the child can symbolize essential moments in his past, rediscover thoughts, emotions, and memories, and connect the factual dimension of the information received about his history to a more emotional and more profound dimension. It is, therefore, not so much the object that takes on the importance for the child as everything that object represents: the child's past, their place of origin, and the journey that led them to a family where they could feel safe and secure. By sharing such objects and the narratives that flow from them with parents, the child maximizes the possibility of constructing a coherent narrative of his or her experiences, even the negative ones (Watson et al., 2019).

6.5 The life story books

One of the most widely used tools by adoptive families to talk about adoption with their children is life story books. These books tell the child's story through photos, information, and meaningful stories that hold relevance. For example, they often contain drawings and photos of the child's country of birth, the institution or foster family, medical information about the child's birth, photos of the adoptive parents taken before knowing the child and while waiting for the child's arrival, greeting cards from other relatives for the newly created family, and more. Life story books are usually used to support the child in contacting the experiences associated with separation from the birth family and his or her emotions (Hanney & Kozlowska, 2002) and in attributing appropriate meaning to what happened (Atwool, 2017; Watson et al., 2015).

The frequency of use of life story books is also evidenced by the availability of numerous online guides designed to help parents create them. Although adoptive families use such tools in everyday practice, from the standpoint of scientific research on the topic, there seems to be a paucity of research that has studied life story books' effects on children's well-being, their understanding of their history, and the overall value of such items (Gallagher & Green, 2012; Watson et al., 2015). On the other hand, some studies have focused on the characteristics that life story books must have to facilitate open communication in the family and have highlighted how important it is for parents to be guided by professionals in their construction. Adoptive parents may, in fact, make some mistakes, such as withholding some information from the child for fear of his or her reactions, not being able to answer the child's questions, or conveying too precise or technical information about the adoption journey with the risk of confusing the child; and finally, focusing too much on their feelings of expectation for the child while leaving out the child's specific experiences (Watson et al., 2015).

Other research has emphasized that life story books should be constructed by parents in conjunction with the child (Atwool, 2017; O'Malley, 2000) to create an opportunity to explore different issues together, sharing information and emotions related to adoption (Harrigan, 2010). It is also essential that life story books are neither overly focused on the informational dimension nor on a collection of photographs and pictures without salient information for the child (Brookfield et al., 2008) but also touch on the emotional aspect of adoption.

Finally, it should be remembered that life story books should touch on the central themes of adoption-related communication, as highlighted in Table 6.1.

6.6 Conclusion

Talking about adoption and everything related to it is not an easy task for either the child or the adoptive parents. However, this experience can be lighter if the adoptive parents establish a communication process that considers the specific characteristics of the topic and the child's characteristics. Adoptive parents are the ones who will have to guide the child through a long, progressive, and emotionally intense discovery: the discovery of him or herself, their roots, and their history. Leading

Table 6.1 Themes to include in the construction of the Life Story Books

Parents' history
- Information related to the family of origin and the adoptive couple
- Parenthood desire, decision to adopt, and waiting for the adoption
- Emotions felt before meeting the child and during the first meeting with him or her
- Expectations and representations about the child, the parenthood, the birth family in the past, present, and future

Child's history
- Past life experiences
- Information about the child's life in his birth country, birth family, and institute
- Preparation of meeting with the adoptive family
- Emotions experienced in the institute and foster family
- Experiences related to the first meeting with adoptive parents
- Self-representations and construction of meaning related to the personal experiences
- Emotions, needs, and doubts about present and future

the child on this journey means first being there for the child: it is essential that there be a common construction of the story in which the listening and recognition of the child's skills have adequate space. Rethinking and understanding one's own story can be possible if concern for touching on the painful issues and the emotional, familial, and social realities that marked the developmental trajectory of the child and his or her adult caregivers does not prevail. Narrative truth can become a glue, the beginning of a path of repair and construction of new affective, relational, and social belonging that allows children and their adoptive parents to experience a sense of continuity, a new precursor to epistemic trust (Gergely & Unoka, 2008). Then, the continuity of affection, of feeling family, becomes a compass that integrates past and present and allows momentum into the future without too many evolutionary stumbles.

References

Andolfi, M. (2017). The adolescence crisis in adoptive families. In M. Andolfi, M. Chistolini, & A. D'Andrea (Eds.), *The adoptive family between crisis and development* (pp. 168–192). Franco Angeli.

Atwool, N. (2017). Life story work: Optional extra or fundamental entitlement? *Child Care in Practice*, *23*(1), 64–76. https://doi.org/10.1080/13575279.2015.1126228

Balenzano, C., Coppola, G., Cassibba, R., & Moro, G. (2018). Pre-adoption adversities and adoptees' outcomes: The protective role of post-adoption variables in an Italian experience of domestic open adoption. *Children and Youth Services Review*, *85*, 307–318. https://doi.org/10.1016/j.childyouth.2018.01.012

Barbosa-Ducharne, M. A., & Soares, J. (2016). Process of adoption communication openness in adoptive families: Adopters' perspective. *Psicologia: Reflexão e Crítica*, *29*(9). https://doi.org/10.1186/s41155-016-0024-x

Brodzinsky, D. M. (2005). Re-conceptualizing openness in adoption: Implications for theory, research and practice. In D. Brodzinsky & J. Palacios (Eds.), *Psychological issues in adoption: Research and practice*. Greenwood.

Brodzinsky, D. M. (2006). Family structural openness and communication openness as predictors in the adjustment of adopted children. *Adoption Quarterly*, *9*(4), 1–18. https://doi.org/10.1300/J145v09n04_01

Brodzinsky, D. M. (2011). Children's understanding of adoption: Developmental and clinical implications. *Professional Psychology: Research and Practice*, *42*(2), 200. https://doi.org/10.1037/a0022415

Brookfield, H., Brown, S. D., & Reavey, P. (2008). Vicarious and post-memory practices in adopting families: The re-production of the past through photography and narrative. *Journal of Community & Applied Social Psychology*, *18*(5), 474–491. https://doi.org/10.1002/casp.960

Chistolini, M. (2010). *The adoptive family. How accompanying and support it*. Franco Angeli.

Cyrulnik, B. (2004). *Il coraggio di crescere. Gli adolescenti e la ricerca della propria identità*. Frassinelli.

Colaner, C. W., & Soliz, J. (2017). A communication-based approach to adoptive identity: Theoretical and empirical support. *Communication Research, 44*(5), 611–637. https://doi.org/10.1177/0093650215577860
Gallagher, B., & Green, A. (2012). In, out and after care: Young adults' views on their lives, as children, in a therapeutic residential establishment. *Children and Youth Services Review, 34*, 437–450. https://doi.org/10.1016/j.childyouth.2011.11.014
Gergely, G., & Unoka, Z. (2008). The development of the unreflective self. In F. N. Busch (Ed.), *Mentalization: Theoretical considerations, research findings and clinical implications* (pp. 57–102). Taylor and Francis Group.
Greco, O. (2014). Telling the adoption: The reference to the origins in Italian books about international adoption. *Familia: Revista de ciencias y orientación familiar, 48*, 47. https://hdl.handle.net/10807/56470
Hanney, L., & Kozlowska, K. (2002). Healing traumatized children: Creating illustrated storybooks in family therapy. *Family Process, 41*(1), 37–65. https://doi.org/10.1111/j.1545-5300.2002.40102000037.x
Harrigan, M. M. (2010). Exploring the narrative process: An analysis of the adoption stories mothers tell their internationally adopted children. *Journal of Family Communication, 10*(1), 24–39. https://doi.org/10.1080/15267430903385875
Harrigan, M. M. (2013). Exploring the narrative process: An analysis of the adoption stories mothers tell their internationally adopted children. In J. K. Kellas (Ed.), *Family storytelling* (pp. 17–32). Routledge.
Horstman, H. K., Colaner, C. W., & Rittenour, C. E. (2016). Contributing factors of adult adoptees' identity work and self-esteem: Family communication patterns and adoption-specific communication. *Journal of Family Communication, 16*(3), 263–276. https://doi.org/10.1080/15267431.2016.1181069
Jones, C. (2016). Openness in adoption: Challenging the narrative of historical progress. *Child & Family Social Work, 21*(1), 85–93. https://doi.org/10.1111/cfs.12113
Jones, C., & Hackett, S. (2007). Communicative openness within adoptive families: Adoptive parents' narrative accounts of the challenges of adoption talk and the approaches used to manage these challenges. *Adoption Quarterly, 10*(3–4), 157–178. https://doi.org/10.1080/10926750802163238
Livingston Smith, S. (2010). *Keeping the promise: The case for adoption support and preservation.* The Donaldson Adoption Institute.
Miliotti, A. G. (2015). *Fairy tales to talk about adoption.* Franco Angeli.
O'Malley, B. (2000). *Lifebooks: Creating a treasure for the adopted child.* Adoption-Works.
Ryan, T., & Walker, R. (2007). *Life story work: A practical guide to helping children understand their past.* BAAF. https://doi.org/10.1111/j.1365-2206.2007.00504.x
Santona, A. M. (2003). Trasformazione della coppia nel percorso verso la genitorialità adottiva. *Minori giustizia, 1*, 1000–1012.
Soares, J., Barbosa Ducharne, M., Palacios González, J., & Pacheco, A. (2017). Adopted children's emotion regulation: The role of parental attitudes and communication about adoption. *Psicothema, 29*(1), 49–54. https://doi.org/10.7334/psicothema2016.71
Treacher, A., & Katz, I. D. (2000). *The dynamics of adoption – social and personal perspectives.* Jessica Kingsley Publishers Ltd.
Von Korff, L., & Grotevant, H. D. (2011). Contact in adoption and adoptive identity formation: The mediating role of family conversation. *Journal of Family Psychology, 25*(3), 393. https://psycnet.apa.org/doi/10.1037/a0023388
Watson, D., Hahn, R., & Staines, J. (2019). Storying special objects: Material culture, narrative identity and life story work for children in care. *Qualitative Social Work, 19*(4), 701–718. https://doi.org/10.1177/1473325019850616
Watson, D. L., Latter, S., & Bellew, R. (2015). Adopters views on their children's life story books. *Adoption and Fostering, 39*(2), 119–134. https://doi.org/10.1177/0308575915588723
Wrobel, G. M., Kohler, J. K., Grotevant, H. D., & McRoy, R. G. (2003). The family adoption communication (FAC) model: Identifying pathways of adoption-related communication. *Adoption Quarterly, 7*(2). https://psycnet.apa.org/doi/10.1300/J145v07

PART 2

Adolescents at high risk

How to listen to their voice

7
THE SILENT ADOLESCENT IN THE FAMILY THERAPY SESSION

Peter Rober

It is the first session with the Sels family, and mother and father are eager to tell their story. Their daughter An (14 years old) avoids eye contact and is hiding behind her long hair. There are serious concerns about An. The referring psychiatrist wrote that she is depressed and may be suicidal. He also mentioned that she self-harms and possibly has an eating disorder.

I look at An, but I can't make eye contact as she hides behind a curtain of hair. She radiates that she doesn't want to be here and that I should leave her be. I realize that it will not be easy to connect with her, and indeed after a few moments of small talk, I notice that I'm speaking with her parents, while An remains silent. I ask myself: *How can I start a therapeutic process with this family?*

Research strongly suggests that the therapeutic alliance is a crucial therapeutic factor (Crits-Christoph & Connolly Gibbons, 2021). The quality of the alliance is one of the strongest and most robust predictors of successful psychotherapy (Norcross & Lambert, 2019). In family therapy, the alliance may even be more important than in individual therapy (Friedlander et al., 2018). In family therapy, the alliance is more complex than in individual therapy as the conjoint context of the sessions is challenging for family members, as well as for the therapist (Escudero & Friedlander, 2017).

7.1 The complex alliance in family therapy and the silent adolescent

The challenge of the complex alliance takes a typical shape when the identified patient in the family is an adolescent (Escudero & Friedlander, 2017). The adolescent who is the focus of the concern of the parents is often reluctant to talk together in the session. The parents have taken the initiative to start the therapy. They are what Byng-Hall (1995) called *the doorkeepers*, as they have taken the initiative to invite the therapist inside the privacy of family life. The adolescent often does not want therapy, but he/she comes along. The adolescent may be what Friedlander and colleagues (2006) have called *the therapy hostage*: Although he/she does not agree with the parents about the need for therapy and about the way they describe the problem, he/she feels forced to come to the session. The parents often talk about the problem as something that objectively exists and that in some way relates to their son or daughter. The adolescent opposes such ideas and claims not to be the problem.

DOI: 10.4324/9781003536765-10

For adolescents, it is important to have the autonomy to be themselves. At the same time, they don't really know who they are and are exploring who they are. So, the central adagio of the adolescent might be "let me be myself, while I'm trying to find out who I am." What is clear for the adolescent and what he/she wants to demonstrate is that his/her world consists of his/her peers, and that he/she is not dependent on his/her parents for his/her personal identity.

If the parents then decide that there is a problem with him/her and that family therapy might contribute to a solution, the adolescent's guard is up, as it feels like the therapy is forced on him/her. It might be the intention of the family therapist to create a dialogical context of collaboration and empathy; for the adolescent (at least at the start of the therapy), the therapist may be part of the parents' strategy to make him/her give in to their norms and expectations. Rather than a place for caring and nurturing, the adolescent often experiences therapy as a place of coercion and parental control. The most common strategy adolescents use to deal with what they experience as a threatening trap is being silent and keeping not only their parents at a safe distance, but also the therapist.

7.2 Establishing a good alliance

It is the first task of the family therapist to have a good alliance with each of the family members (Rober, 2024). The family therapist must be empathic to each family member's worries and pain. Furthermore, he/she must see each family member's resources and what is his/her contribution to make life together better in the family. Establishing a good alliance with each family member means that each family member feels heard and understood. This is not easy in a polarized context like the one that often exists at the start of family therapy with a silent adolescent.

In my way of working with families (Rober, 2017), I refrain from using the word "problem," as well as the word "solution." Also, I avoid speaking of "diagnosis," "symptoms," "treatment," and "interventions," except when family members use such words. Then I curiously ask them what they mean exactly. I might, for instance, say: "You say your son is autistic. Yes, ok, but can you help me to understand what that means? There are so many kinds of autism, what kind of autism characterizes him? What does he do that makes you say he is autistic?"

In the case of the Sels family that I will discuss in this chapter, An said she was "depressed." From her account, I understood that the word "depressed" seemed to refer to a *reactive depression*: a depressive reaction to some kind of setback in her life. This made me ask questions about its source: *what triggered it?* This is the way I work: When family members talk about diagnoses, I try to connect these labels with experiences and with life events. My response is always empathic and warm, as I have learned that people who use words like diagnoses, symptoms, and treatment usually are genuinely worried, and have tried many different things to face their worries but to no avail. They feel powerless.

So rather than framing family therapy as treatment of a disorder, or as a way to find a solution for a problem, I prefer to frame family therapy as "talking together as a family about your worries." Rather than focusing therapy on treatment or intervention, the focus is on dialogue about worries. I talk about "worries" in plural because there usually is no unanimity among the family members about what is going on (Friedlander et al., 2006). In that sense, the statement that therapy revolves around *worries*, rather than around *the problem*, makes a big difference for those family members who are not convinced that there is a problem, or that the description of *the problem* provided by the family member who worries most is an accurate representation of the family's struggles. Focusing on worries is helpful in dealing with the complex alliance: the therapist can identify with the doorkeepers by empathically listening to their worries, and at the same time he/she can connect with the hostage by avoiding characterizing these worries as *the problem* or as disorders and refraining from legitimizing them with scientifically based psychiatric labels.

Another typical aspect of my way of working with families is to postpone the discussion of the worries in the family, and to make room first for each family member to introduce themselves, without referring to worries (Rober, 2017). This allows me to connect briefly with each family member in his/her preferred identity and in things they are proud of about themselves. This opens space for a first verbal exchange with the silent adolescent, usually rather brief, in which we can talk about hobbies, music, dance, friends, sports, and so on. Most often this is a good start to carefully connect with the adolescent, at least if the therapist is authentic in his/her responses and questions. If you say, "how interesting," this must be genuine, or else the adolescent will not trust you.

The Sels family: The first session

I listen to the family members' introductions of themselves. Although her reluctance to talk is obvious, An briefly mentions her hobby of playing football (known as "soccer" in the US). I can easily be enthusiastic, as I played football myself, and as I'm still following what happens in the world of football nationally as well as internationally. But still no eye contact. I feel a bit uncertain. Then father says, "She is still young, but she really has talent. She plays midfield and she is like the conductor of her team." Father sounds proud.

I look at An and wonder how she would accept this praise of her father's. It surprised me, but it did not seem to affect her at all. She seemed indifferent, as if father had been talking about somebody else.

The parents are worried about An's depression: "She sometimes talks about suicide, but most of the time she is silent. That is most worrisome," mother says with teary eyes.

"She is not open at all about what she experiences," father says. "She wants us to mind our own business, but she doesn't seem to realize that *she* is our business. Or would she want us not to care about her?" It is meant as a rhetorical question, but I cannot help but hearing father's desperation and maybe also his anger. Yes, I think I could understand his anger, as An's silence seems to radiate hostility and blame.

I try to connect with An, but she seems bored with me as she sighs, and I start to doubt myself and wonder why I keep on asking the wrong questions. Only later I will realize that these feelings of impotence and self-criticism that are evoked in my inner dialogue mirror what the parents experience in dealing with their daughter.

I neglect what I'm feeling, I decide to try one more time, and I say: "So An you are depressed. Do you have any idea where your depression comes from? What sparked it?"

An shrugs. I turn to the parents and say: "So An is depressed. Do you parents have any experience with depression? Did you come across depression in your growing up or in your adult life?" Mother shakes her head, but father says: "I have been depressed. I was 32 years old, and I burned out at my job. I was depressed and I stayed at home for a year. Then I started my own company – we manage football players, athletes, professional cyclists, and so on. My company saved me."

I turn to An and I ask: "Your father has been depressed too, but now he's better. His depression was triggered by things at his job. Do you have any idea what triggered your depression?"

An shrugs.

I decide to try something else, and I say: "A few weeks ago, I was talking to this girl who was a bit older than you. She was depressed, and she told me that she became depressed after she had been raped. So she knew where her depression started. Do you have any idea what started your depression?"

An hesitates a moment and then she says: "I need to go to the bathroom. Can I go?"

"Yes, of course," I say a bit surprised by her unexpected question.

I point her the way to the bathroom, and I assure her that we will be quiet, and we won't talk about her behind her back.

An goes out the door, and the parents and me stay in the room in silence. We wait for a minute, two minutes, three minutes, four minutes. . . . I'm becoming nervous as I start to contemplate my question with the reference to the other girl's rape. In my mind's eye, I see images that An is leaving the building and going to the train tracks. . . . *She was described as suicidal*, I remind myself, . . . Then I notice that the parents are anxious too. I look at mother and that is her cue:

"Can I go and look for An?" she says.

"Yes," I say somewhat relieved.

Mother gets up and walks to the door, but at that moment An enters the room.

Mother and An sit down again.

I decide to be more careful and refrain from asking questions about rape and trauma.

The parents elaborate on their experience of powerlessness ("How can we help her? It is as if we are always saying the wrong things.") and their feeling of disconnection ("It seems that she keeps us at a distance."). They also talk about their worries and fears about An's suicidality. As I'm listening to them, I start to realize that their experiences are very similar to what I experienced in the session until now: feeling powerless, not being able to connect, blaming myself for being a bad therapist. . . . It seems that my experiences in the session reflect the parents' experiences at home. This is in a sense reassuring, I realize, but on the other hand it indicates that I succeeded in connecting with the parents, but that I failed in my most challenging task for the first session: connecting with the silent adolescent.

"It is the end of the session," I announce. Then I address the three family members, and I ask: "Anything that needs to be said before we end the session?"

I'm surprised as An says, "There are other things, that my parents don't know about. But I cannot talk about it."

I notice the parents are as baffled as I am. I have plenty of questions about this enigmatic utterance of An's, but it is the end of the session.

I say to An: "That's ok, An. It is typical that in the first session of family therapy the most important things are not said."

I distribute the feedback questionnaire to the three family members for them to fill out.

7.3 Feedback questionnaire

I use the Dialogical Feedback Questionnaire (DFQ) (Rober & Van Tricht, 2023; see attachment). The main aim of the DFQ is to open space in the session to the family members' experiences in the session. In the questionnaire, family members are asked to what extent they were able to talk about the things that they wanted to talk about (question 1). They are also asked if they felt understood by the therapist (question 2) and by the other family members (question 3). Furthermore, they are asked what surprised them in the session (question 4). This question often leads to client answers with hopeful prospects and opportunities to move towards growth or connection. Finally, the questionnaire explores what moved the family members in the session (question 5). Answering this question, family members often refer to what happened between them and other family members in the session. This question often gives the family members the chance to express appreciation or recognition towards the other (e.g., "I was moved when my wife told me how proud she was about my achievements as an entrepreneur" or, "I was moved when my father explicitly said he loved me for the first time.").

Feedback-oriented work in family therapy is more than collecting information (Rober, 2017, 2024). Rather, it is in essence a process of self-reflection and dialogue. The process begins with the family members filling out the questionnaires at the end of the session. At that moment, they are invited to reflect on the way they experienced the session. There is time for each family member to focus on his/her experiences and to find the words to express how they felt about the session. In a second moment, the feedback from the family members is used by the therapist to reflect on the therapeutic process in preparation for the next session. The feedback of the Sels family was particularly interesting for the preparation of the next session.

The Sels family: Feedback about the first session

On the DFQ, An did not write much. One thing she wrote was: "I did not feel understood, but I felt respected." This strangely reassured me. It was as if An opened the door for me a little bit, so the first session wasn't a complete failure. So maybe my reference to rape had not been as destructive as I had feared. Furthermore, she wrote, "I don't want to say," as an answer to the fifth question ("What moved you most during the session?). The silent adolescent again.

In response to the fourth question ("What surprised you during the session?") both parents refer to An's silence about important issues. Mother wrote: "There are important things she doesn't talk about." Father wrote: "It strikes me that there are other things we don't know about."

While the feedback of An was reassuring, the feedback of the parents worried me when I prepared for the second session. I was afraid that in the second session there would be a polarization between An and her parents, with An insisting on her right to be silent and not to speak, and her parents putting pressure on her to speak because they are understandably worried. So I thought of a way for the parents to address the issue of being silent and not confiding in the parents, on the one hand, and respecting An in her wish not to share certain important things.

7.4 Working intergenerationally

When confronted with the typical family dynamic with parents who are worried and a silent adolescent, an intergenerational perspective is often enriching. What I often do is ask the parents to discuss their life growing up in a family, and I focus on the theme at hand in the relationship with the adolescent. In the case of the Sels family, as an adolescent keeping something important from sharing it with your parents. The idea is that the parents are the doorkeepers, and they have taken the initiative to go in therapy. Probably they are more open to talking than their adolescent son/daughter. So I invite them to talk about their own experiences as an adolescent, and I invite the adolescent to listen. While the parents are talking, I listen to them with an ear for aspects of their story that could be meaningful for the adolescent and that might contribute to some kind of emotional connection (however brittle) between the parents and the adolescent. In the case of the Sels family, when I was reading their responses to the DFQ in preparation for the second session, it seemed to me it was worth trying this approach.

The Sels family: The second session

Mother starts the session with "I'm glad we can talk today," and she glances at An, who, as in the first session, is hiding behind her hair.

"Yes," father says, "because I must say, I have been worrying all week about what An didn't tell us."

He addresses An and says, "My dear, here in the session you can talk freely . . ."

An avoids his stare, safe behind the curtain of her hair.

I realize that the polarization between the silent adolescent and the parents insisting on talking is on the verge of escalating.

I feel I must do something to make the dialogue fruitful, rather than frustrating and pointless.

I address the parents: "When you were 14 years old, like An is now, did you tell everything to your parents?" My question surprises the parents. I proceed: "What did you not talk about with your parents?" The parents look at each other and, after a moment of silence, father starts to talk about his struggles with himself and his loneliness when he was 14.

He says, "I was also – even though I was only 14 – into experimenting with drugs." "And you didn't talk about it with your parents?" I ask. "No, it would not have helped, I think. Furthermore, I guess

I was ashamed, as I wanted to prove that I did not need them anymore." He casts his eyes down as if in shame.

Then I look at mother, and I notice she was poised to start to tell her story.

"My turn," mother says almost gaily. She seems to be eager to tell her story. She turns her chair to face her daughter. I notice that An is surprised and intrigued. She peers through her hair at her mother who explicitly addressed her. "Dear, when I was growing up, I was quite popular with the girls of my class. We were a cool band of sisters. But then when I was about 14 years old, my body started to change as I became a woman. And one of the things, I had big boobs, and I became the laughingstock of my class. It is as if I fell from grace with the cool girls with smaller breasts. I remember me in the bathroom standing naked in front of the mirror. I looked at myself and I was ashamed of my body."

I notice that An is listening intently.

I ask mother: ". . . and you did not talk with your parents about this?" "No, although I had a good relationship with my parents – I still do – I didn't dare to talk about it. I was too ashamed."

At the end of the session, I asked the family members to fill out the feedback questionnaire.

The family members filled out the feedback questionnaire sparsely. An only wrote: "I didn't want to say anything, and I didn't" (answer to question 1) but she also wrote "the emotions of my parents" as an answer to the question of what had moved her in the session. So there had been an emotional connection between An and her parents. Mother left everything blank, but indicated that she felt understood by the therapist, and by her husband and daughter. Father also felt understood, but in addition he wrote: "Not discussing An's biggest problem is tricky."

The Sels family: The third session

The family members enter the room, and everybody chooses a seat. An is the last to sit down. I notice that she does not hide behind her hair and that we even make eye contact for a brief moment. I address nobody when I ask, "What is useful to talk about today?"

Surprisingly, An says, "Let's talk about the hot potato today." There is silence for a moment, and then An starts to talk about her worries and her doubts. First, she mentions the tensions between her parents in which she tries to play a balancing role. Then she moves on to talk about the apprehension about wanting to be a good daughter to her parents and the fear that she might disappoint them.

The Sels family: The follow-up session

The therapy with the Sels family lasted almost two years. Over this period, we had six family sessions and four sessions with the parents. Then we ended the therapy; about two years after the first session, we had a follow-up session.

In that session, they reported that the depression experienced by An is much better, and she is attending school again. Therapy had done her good, but what was more important was her falling in love with a boy named Bert, whom she felt good with. She was still playing football, and her father was still very proud of her performance: "She is like a female Kevin De Bruyne," he said.

An beamed and cast her eyes down. As I usually do, I also asked the family members which moment of the therapy in retrospect had been the most important. Both the parents and An said the first two sessions. The parents described how in the first session they were scared and desperate because of An's depression. "We also were afraid that you were going to tell us that we were bad parents. We had tried so hard to help her, but we felt impotent."

I asked An how she had experienced the first session. She said: "I was confused. I was angry because they seemed to blame me for being a bad daughter. But I was also scared because I disappointed them. I could only be silent. My silence was my shame as well as my protection."

7.5 Discussion

Different family members have different perspectives on therapy, and in working with adolescents in family therapy, the therapist will often encounter adolescents who are reluctant to talk. A focus on the different worries (plural) in the family, rather than on the presenting problem (singular), can be helpful in dealing with the silent adolescent – especially when the therapist establishes that the parents are worried about something and the adolescent is not (or at least is reluctant to talk about the worries). The therapist not only establishes this, but he/she also accepts the adolescents' hesitations and his/her discomfort with being the center of the therapy. The therapist tries to connect with the adolescent on domains of his/her positive identity: *What do you like to do? What is important for you? What are you proud of?* The focus on these domains will not immediately open up the adolescent necessarily, but it can be a beginning as the adolescent starts to understand that the therapist is not blaming him/her or trying to convince him/her to engage in the therapy. Rather, the therapist is curious about who he/she is apart from or alongside the worries. Furthermore, by using the concept of *worry*, the therapist does not endorse the parents' perspective as an objective truth, but rather as *their perspective*.

Moreover, worrying implies caring. A focus on the worries in the family creates a warmer atmosphere in the session and automatically invites dialogue, as the differences between the family members are framed within this context. The therapist makes it clear to all who are present that he/she wants to listen to each of the family members' voices and perspectives: those who worry a lot, those who do not share the same worries, and those who have no worries at all.

7.6 The feedback questionnaire

Furthermore, the therapist is interested in all the family members' experiences in the session, not only in the parents' view. This is made plain by the invitation to all family members to fill out a feedback questionnaire, the Dialogical Feedback Questionnaire (DFQ).

The DFQ is different from other feedback tools in a lot of respects, as it was not conceived as a measuring instrument. A measuring instrument is intended to obtain quantitative information about one or more variables. The psychometric properties of a measuring instrument can be calculated. The information generated by a measuring instrument can form the basis of graphic and software applications. The DFQ is not a measuring instrument and was designed with a different objective, i.e., for use as a *conversational tool* (Sundet, 2014).

Questionnaires as conversational tools are not intended to give answers, but rather to raise interesting questions and topics to talk about in the session. For example, in the case of the Sels family, the answers provided by An and her parents on the DFQ sparked the therapist's reflection. The therapist after the first session could catch a glimpse of what was hidden in An's silence when she wrote that she felt respected by the therapist. And after the second session, she confided to the therapist that she had been moved by her parents' emotions. Such answers helped the therapist to get a sense of where the silent adolescent is in the process. Used in this way, questionnaires as conversational tools can contribute to a better attunement between therapist and family members, in terms of trust, goals, themes, tempo, and so on. Such attunement is important because of its direct link with the quality of the therapeutic alliance.

7.7 The family dynamic in which the silent adolescent makes sense

As a family therapist is confronted with the complex alliances in a family with a silent adolescent, the therapist can observe the parents as the doorkeepers, insisting on the need for therapy, while they voice their worries by complaining about problem behaviors that alarm them. There might be anger or rejection in their tone. The adolescent reacts with silence and indifference, loaded maybe with

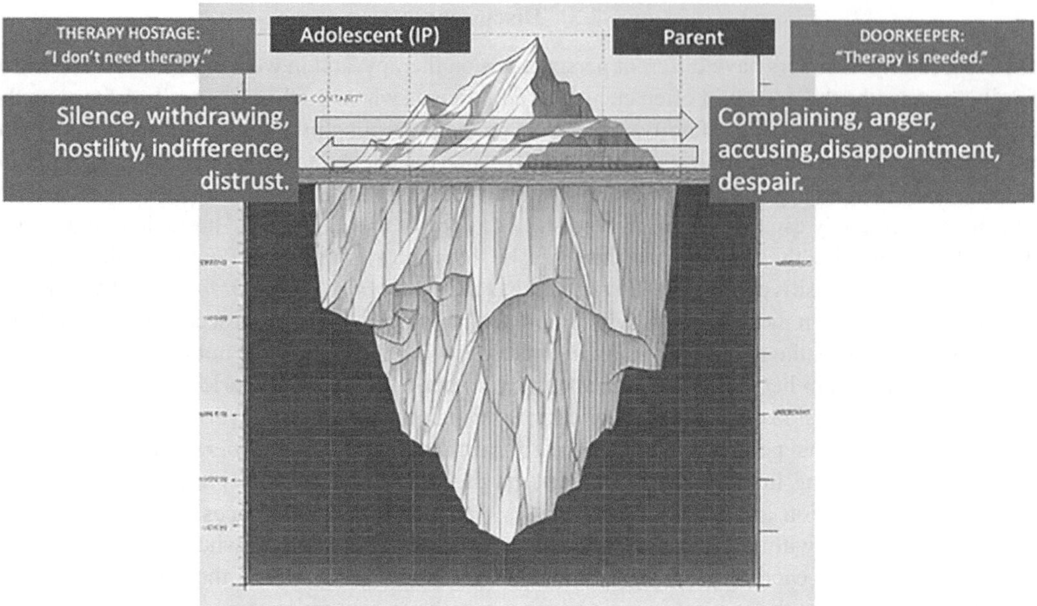

Figure 7.1

irritated sighs and hostile one-liners. He/she did not want therapy but is forced to be present in the session: he/she is the therapy hostage.

The therapist can also observe how both parents and adolescent seem inadvertently to invite the others' response: The complaining leads to indifferent silence, and the indifferent silence leads to more complaining, in circular, reciprocal fashion (Figure 7.1).

Underneath this dynamic between the parents and the silent adolescent, there are experiences that cannot be expressed in the session; but, as in the case of the follow-up session of the Sels family, they sometimes can be described, and associated feelings can be expressed retrospectively. Parents fear that they are bad parents. They feel guilty, ashamed, powerless, scared. The silent adolescent fears that he/she is an unworthy child. He/she is confused, ashamed, desperate. The therapist must hold on to the belief that both the parents and the adolescent have a deep need to feel respected and connected. Although experience has taught me that this belief may not be warranted in all cases, in most cases believing in such a need seems to be necessary to help the family out of the polarizing dynamics that fuels their distrust and drives them apart.

On a more theoretical level, the dynamic between the parents and the silent adolescent can be better understood when links are made between the behavior of the parents and the unexpressed experience of the adolescent, as well as between the adolescent's behavior and the unexpressed experience of the parents (Figure 7.2). The parents' desperate complaining fuels the adolescent's shame, confusion, and despair, with which he/she copes with a protective shield of indifferent silence. The adolescent's silence in turn fuels the parents' fear of being a bad parent and their feelings of guilt and powerlessness. The parents don't express these feelings, as they are too vulnerable to share them with their seemingly indifferent son/daughter. They translate their unexpressed experiences into accusing complaints. The unexpressed experiences of the parents are sometimes evoked in the therapist's experiences when he/she is trying to connect with the adolescent in the session (this happened several times in the sessions with the Sels family, when the therapist doubted his actions and felt like a bad

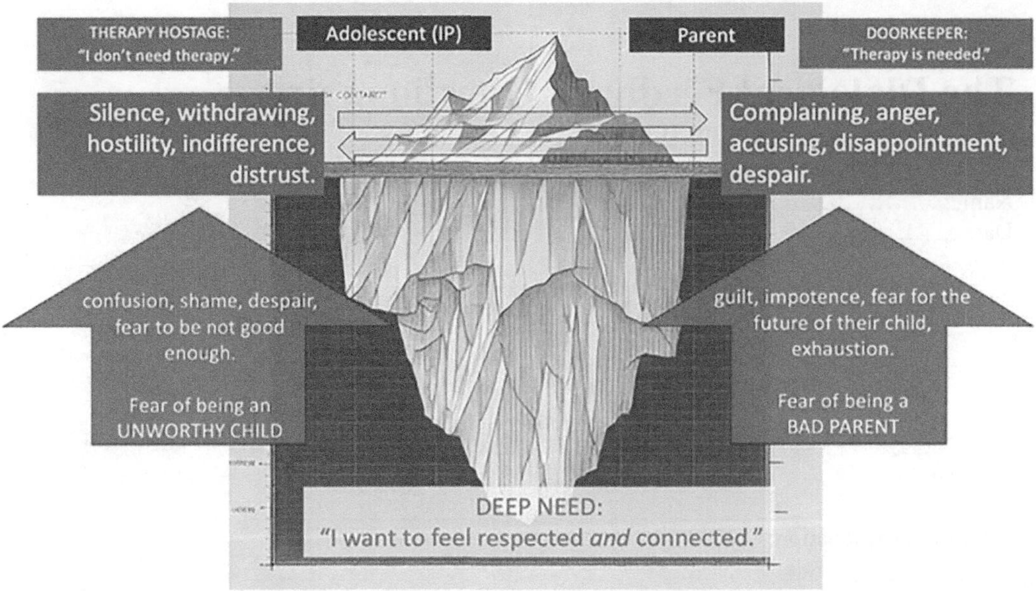

Figure 7.2

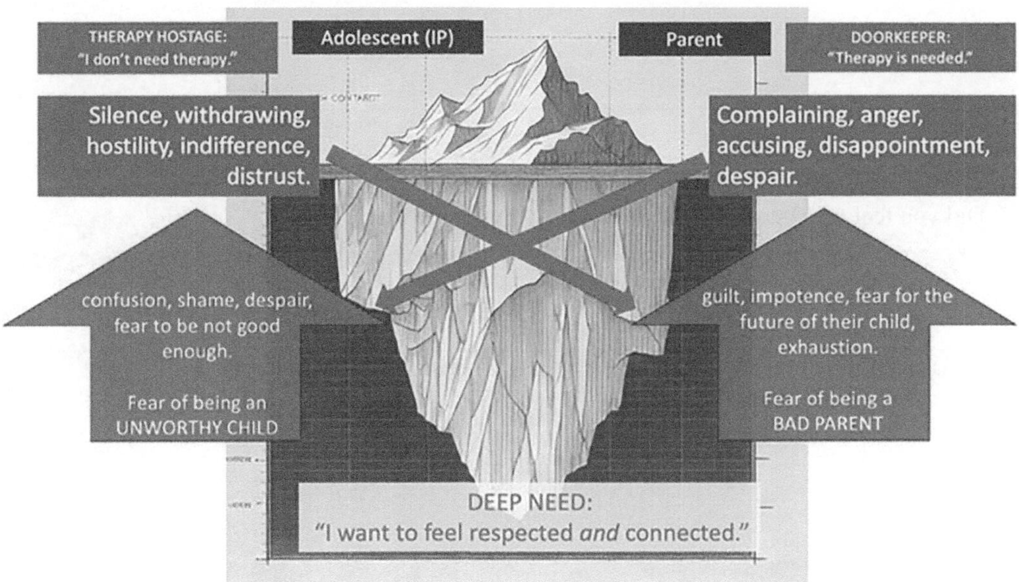

Figure 7.3

therapist), just as at other moments the adolescent's unexpressed experiences may be evoked in the session when he/she engages with the parents (in the session with the Sels family, this did not happen). In cases in which the unexpressed emotions of the adolescent are evoked in the therapist, the therapist will feel the urge to protect the adolescent against the parents, who are experienced as toxic or insensitive towards the adolescent (Figure 7.3).

The Dialogical Feedback Questionnaire

(DFQ - Rober & Van Tricht, 2015)

Name: ....
Date: ....

1. Were you able to talk about what you wanted in the session?

0	1	2	3	4	5	6	7	8	9	10

Not at all *Totally*

A word of explanation:

2. Did you feel understood by the therapist(s) during the session?

0	1	2	3	4	5	6	7	8	9	10

Not at all *Totally*

In this area I didn't feel understood:	In this area I felt understood:

(DFQ p.1/2)

Figure 7.4

3. Did you feel understood by your partner / the other family members during the session?

0	1	2	3	4	5	6	7	8	9	10

Not at all … *Totally*

In this area I didn't feel understood:	In this area I felt understood:

4. What *surprised* you most during the session?

5. What *moved* you most during the session?

(DFQ p.2/2)

Figure 7.5

While the family dynamics that I sketched here implies the presence of unexpressed experiences of both the parents and the adolescent, I would not recommend the therapist to try to dig up such experiences in the first sessions. Rather, it is important for the therapist to hear these silent voices and to attune to them cautiously. He/she must realize that beneath the parents' complaining there is fear, guilt, and shame, and he/she must also realize that the context in the session is probably not safe enough for the expression of such vulnerable emotions. The same holds true for the adolescent: beneath his/her silence and indifference, there are probably feelings like confusion, despair, and shame, which as yet are too vulnerable to be expressed in a session in which the parents are complaining about him/her. The adolescent feels like an unworthy child as it is.

7.8 Conclusion

Based on the case story of the Sels family, I have tried to outline a family dynamic that a family therapist can expect at the start of therapy with a silent adolescent. Of course, every family is different, and in each family this dynamic will take its unique shape. What these different families will probably have in common is a certain observable dynamic in which the adolescent's silence can be understood in the context of the parents' complaints and their insistence on the importance of therapy. Furthermore, within parents as well as within the adolescent, a dynamic can be deduced in which the parents' complaining and their pressure on their child makes sense, but in which also the adolescents' silence makes sense. Furthermore, the unexpressed experiences of both parents and adolescent may be evoked in the therapist and can help him/her to empathize with the family members and attune to them in the session.

7.9 Attachment

This questionnaire can be downloaded for free via the website: www.intherapytogether.com

References

Byng-Hall, J. (1995). *Rewriting family scripts: Improvisation and systems change*. Guilford Press.

Crits-Christoph, P., & Connolly Gibbons, M. B. (2021). Psychotherapy process – outcome research: Advances in understanding causal connections. In M. Barkham, W. Lutz, & L. G. Castonguay (Eds.), *Bergin and Garfield's handbook of psychotherapy and behavior change* (pp. 263–295). Wiley.

Escudero, V., & Friedlander, M. J. (2017). *Therapeutic alliances with families: Empowering clients in challenging cases*. Springer.

Friedlander, M. L., Escudero, V., & Heatherington, L. (2006). *Therapeutic alliances in couple and family therapy*. American Psychological Association.

Friedlander, M. L., Escudero, V., Wilmers-van de Poll, M. J., & Heatherington, L. (2018). Meta-analysis of the alliance – outcome relation in couple and family therapy. *Psychotherapy*, *55*(4), 356–371. https://doi.org/10.1037/pst0000161

Norcross, J. C., & Lambert, M. J. (2019). What works in the psychotherapy relationship. In J. C. Norcross & M. J. Lambert (Eds.), *Psychotherapy relationships that work: Evidence-based therapist responsiveness* (Vol. 1, 3rd ed., pp. 631–646). Oxford University Press. https://doi.org/10.1093/med-psych/9780190843953.003.0018

Rober, P. (2017). *In therapy together: Family therapy as a dialogue*. Palgrave Macmillan.

Rober, P. (2024). *Becoming an effective family therapist: Research, practice, and case stories*. Routledge.

Rober, P., & Van Tricht, K. (2023). Using questionnaires as conversational tools to bolster the therapeutic alliance in family therapy practice. *Family Process*, *62*, 1346–1361. https://doi.org/10.1111/famp.12936

Sundet, R. (2014). Patient-focused research supported practices in an intensive family therapy unit. *Journal of Family Therapy*, *36*, 195–216. https://doi.org/10.1111/j.1467-6427.2012.00613.x

8

CONFRONTATIVE INTERVENTION IN FAMILY THERAPY WITH SUICIDAL ADOLESCENTS

Noga Nabarro

8.1 Introduction

Dealing with seriously suicidal adolescents and their families is a complicated challenge. It is like navigating the high seas, sometimes battling the waves, and other times, being caught in a whirlpool. It is a mix of perplexing, disturbing challenges and, at times, rewarding or even exciting ones. Therapists often become overly cautious, afraid to escalate the adolescent's distress. Thus, they avoid crucial confrontations with the parents, siblings, or adolescents themselves.

This chapter shares thoughts and strategies for effective confrontative interventions based on more than 40 years of clinical experience at Shinui: Israel Institute for Systemic Studies, teaching internationally, and the field of family therapy. This chapter focuses on the initial and most critical phase of family therapy with severely suicidal adolescents.

8.2 Families of suicidal adolescents

Adolescent suicidality stems from complex causes. Family interactions and harmful family dynamics play a crucial role in adolescent suicidality (Aldridge, 1984; Richman, 1986; Adams et al., 1994; Walcott, 1995; Slaby & Garfinkel, 1996; Frey & Cerel, 2015). Despite appearing impulsive, an adolescent's suicide attempt usually follows longstanding issues, indicated by their behavior and communication.

8.3 Patterns of families of severely suicidal adolescents

Harmful family dynamics, particularly destructive interactional patterns, significantly impact the risk of severe suicide attempts (Shinui Project, 2012–2024). These patterns commonly include confusing or harmful messages, sometimes disguised as concern, which can profoundly and negatively impact the adolescent's mental state. Families of severely suicidal adolescents tend to show emotional disengagement, obliviousness, lack of support and care (Richman, 1986), and toxic patterns, which may be explicit or implicit. These include destructive messages, rejection, scapegoating, secretiveness, sexual or physical abuse, and unhealthy alliances, especially in times of need. As will be demonstrated, these negative qualities can lead to a misinterpreting of the suicidal and distressed behavior as rebellious or manipulative rather than as a desperate cry for help. These behaviors contribute to

DOI: 10.4324/9781003536765-11

the adolescent's sense of isolation and despair. As shall be demonstrated, families often conceal and deny problems due to shame, exacerbating the adolescent's feelings of loneliness and disconnection. However, families can be central to prevention and recovery.

8.4 The process of therapy: Reversing the suicidality vector

The immediate goal is reducing suicide risk and initiating family healing (Richman, 1986). Shifting the suicidality vector to that of hope and a renewed desire to live is crucial. By the end of this phase, adolescents should move beyond reluctant discussions about suicide to exploring fresh avenues and possibilities for life. A feeling of significant change must commence in the first session, as this usually instills greater hope, motivation, and therapeutic collaboration (Nabarro-Rubinstein, 1994; Shinui Project, 2012–2024).

The initial sessions are emphasized as crisis intervention, with longer sessions and therapist availability. Friends, extended family, and school counselors often may join as support systems (Nabarro-Rubinstein, 1994; Andolfi, 2017).

From the start, the family's involvement is essential, with therapy aiming to reintegrate the adolescent into family life quickly. It is better to start the first session by engaging parents and siblings first before focusing on the suicidal adolescent (IP), thus reducing anxiety and promoting a family approach. This strategy tends to encourage cooperation from the IP.

Five essential questions to be answered in the initial phase are as follows:

1. Why does the adolescent view death as preferable to life?
2. How do family dynamics discourage the adolescent from valuing life?
3. What external factors, such as social pressures or unbearable binds, push the adolescent towards escaping from life?
4. What imperative changes should be made in the family to shift the motivational vector to the desire to live?
5. How can the family's unique resources be utilized in therapy?

8.5 Major guidelines and interventions

Nine major guidelines are crucial in the first phase. These are expanded on later and demonstrated in the verbatim section (and further expanded upon in my upcoming book to be published in 2026).

1. Utilize confrontative interventions to challenge and activate the family system towards immediate and crucial changes, fostering healthier interactions in the present moment.
2. Clarify implicit issues, including suicidal motivations and destructive communication.
3. Directly confront harmful messages, behaviors, and assumptions.
4. Use the "open check" approach, involving a commitment to as many meetings as are necessary and essential in the first phase.
5. Highlight and address suggestive, hidden messages for suicidal ideation within the family context.
6. Intervene to strengthen cohesion and interconnectedness (i.e., face-to-face communication, sharing, touch).
7. Improve healthy, coherent, and consistent communication and personal responsibility.
8. Ritualize the "Family Commitment Process" as expanded upon later.
9. Develop flexible coping strategies in the family.

Given space limitations, I will focus on the three most important interventions.

8.5.1 Confrontative interventions

Confrontative interventions are essential for addressing and changing the harmful dynamics of the family. These interventions are utilized to halt destructive implicit or explicit messages, transform unhealthy alliances, and change interactional messages such as denials, disqualifications, double binds, and scapegoating (Watzlawick et al., 1967; Zanor, 1974; Kutz, 2023). Their primary role is to mobilize the system to initiate immediate vital changes within the "here-and-now" of the session.

In the first phase, well-designed, empathic confrontative interventions convey professionalism and seriousness to the family. They provide reassurance, especially to adolescents whose concerns were previously disregarded or silenced. For confrontative interventions to be effective, they must adhere to these guidelines:

a. Obtain consent to confront, for example, asking, "Is it OK if I tell you something challenging but crucial?" This approach reduces resistance and fosters acceptance of the intervention.
b. Adopt a supportive and empathic approach rather than one of criticism.
c. Be sensitive and accurate with timing and content to enable immediate responses to harmful dynamics or messages.

8.5.2 Confrontative systemic questions about the suicidal motivation

These very challenging groups of questions can be powerful illuminators when strong denial or destructive implicit messages exist.

Although usually delivered to the IP, participation from other members is always beneficial.

1. Who in the family will suffer most or would be most upset or angry if you killed yourself? What would life look like without you?
2. Whose life do you think would be better or easier if you weren't around?
3. What do you think will be the effects of killing yourself and not being in the family and with friends anymore? What do you imagine things will be like two years, five years, or ten years from now?
4. What if things could really change very soon – ask your mother (father, sister, brother) if they are willing to do whatever is necessary so that you can live better and with less suffering and with a family that supports you.
5. What would make it worthwhile for you to live and *not* kill yourself?

8.5.3 The family commitment process

Establishing a sincere commitment process or ritual as early as the first session is highly beneficial to instilling hope for positive change (Nabarro-Rubinstein, 2023; Shinui Project, 2012–2024). At the end of the first session, all family members make five fundamental commitments together:

1. Safeguarding the suicidal adolescent from self-destructive actions is a responsibility shared by all, including the adolescent themselves.
2. Pledge to transform any harmful family legacies, like suicide, insisting it does not have to "run in the family."
3. Commit to the well-being of all family members, emphasizing mutual support and responsibility.
4. Dedicate to the family's development, fostering transparent, honest, and constructive communication, and eliminating fear and harmful secrets.
5. Commit to ongoing efforts to enhance family unity, problem-solving skills, flexibility, affection, and authoritative guidance.

8.6 Case illustration: Family of Lalli

This verbatim family session illustrates the process, development, and utilizations of confrontative interventions in a case of a serious suicide attempt, focusing on the shift from denials and destructive interactions to acknowledgment and commitment to change. Dr. Noga Nabarro is the therapist (Th) in the case. All possible identifying data has been totally changed or removed. Commentaries in the verbatim excerpts are in parentheses and italicized.

Present are the two parents (M&F) in their late 50s, and two daughters: Lalli, 16 – the suicidal IP, and Dalia, 20 – the older sister. The younger sister (10) is at home. Note that the serious suicide attempt is not disclosed until the middle of the session. This verbatim section starts after general joining with each person. Lalli sits withdrawn and guarded most of the session.

Th: So please tell me how I can be of help; why are you here?

F: I'll tell you . . . we're here because we're worried. And I'm worried about her (points to Lalli) endless need for attention. Can take us to the worst places.

Th: So . . . you're here because you're worried about Lalli's endless need for attention?

F: Yes! I think her need for attention takes her to the lowest places and we don't know why.

Th: Like what?

F: Like everything . . . from how she talks to drinking, drugs, and the way she relates to everything. Sometimes, I come home, and I can smell the alcohol on her breath . . . and it's my feeling that she's doing this on purpose so that we'll smell it . . . all sorts of things. . . . And somehow, the attention is never enough for her . . . she's the classic middle child.

Th: How is your youngest?

M: She's our greatest gift! It's always best to be the youngest.

F: Like in the books – the middle child has all the problems.

(These are the first signs of scapegoating and unhealthy alliances in the family.)

Th→Lalli: So, it pays to be the third child, and worth being the first . . . but it's really not worth being the middle child?

Lalli: (cynically): That's what they say and that's how it is.

Th→Lalli: Wow, so you didn't have such good luck!

Lalli: Correct!

Dalia: It's not exactly so! What Dad's saying . . .

Th: What's not so?

(Dalia takes it upon herself to disclose the secret and the truth.)

Dalia: (emotionally): The truth is we're here because two weeks ago, she drank liquid bleach. Our parents weren't home. I arrived early just by chance, and found her in the bathroom, and the bottle was on the floor, and she was unconscious. . . . They didn't even know about this . . . it completely freaked me out . . . and I called an ambulance immediately . . . we raced off to the hospital. The hospital called my parents . . . So we're here because of that!! (angrily) . . . Not because . . . seeking attention or her drinking.

M: I think it's also about the attention!

F: I think it is, too . . . !

(This is a good example of harmful denial and scapegoating that must be challenged.)

Th→ F & M: No, no, wait! . . . We'll discuss the interpretation later. But, I just want to understand, OK? So, what Dalia is saying . . . actually happened, right? It happened?

F (in a low voice): Yes, it happened.

(The following is the first confrontative intervention; the therapist challenge their assumption.)

Th→F: If she had succeeded and died, would you still call it attention-seeking?

M: You make my heart race. I'm sorry, I can't even imagine it happening, and . . . it brings tears to my eyes. . . . My heart's thumping, I can't think (looks distressed).

F: The one who'll end up dying here, is her mother . . . from all these stories and troubles. (F scapegoats Lalli again and evades the disturbing question.)

Th→M: You can't think what would've happened if she had succeeded and died? (confronting M)

M: I can't imagine what could happen if she would do such a thing to us!

Th→M: You can't imagine how she could do such a thing to <u>you</u>?

M: Of course! We're her parents, <u>we gave her our entire lives</u>!!

(The implicit message is that Lalli is eternally ungrateful. Even her "suicide" is ungrateful. This, again, calls for a confrontation to make the implicit messages explicit, thus possible to handle therapeutically.)

Th→M: I'd just like to understand: you cannot imagine it if she would have succeeded? . . . Or you can't think of the idea that she is doing this to <u>you</u>? . . . Or are you interested in <u>why she'd do this to herself</u>?

M: (silent)

(Now is the time to obtain permission for the confrontative interventions that will open the way for the important therapeutic work, and to start forming the therapeutic contract. Note that in this case, the therapist is the first one to make the commitment in order to increase serious motivation and sense of safety on the family's part.)

Th→F&M: Sorry for being hard on you in our first meeting. . . . I know it isn't easy, but what just came up here isn't easy! . . . You asked for help, right? . . . I want you to understand that I'll do my very best to give you the help you need so this won't happen again. <u>But I need your agreement and permission for me to say what I feel must be said</u> without sweeping matters under the rug. <u>Are you willing to accept that</u>?

F: That's why we're here!

Th: I just want to clarify and make sure it's OK with you that I do my work in the manner that I – professionally – believe I should, and I won't be sweeping things under the rug or covering anything up, because we need to do the utmost so that Lalli will not want to kill herself again. Since you're her parents, you have the responsibility.

F: . . . For sure, we agree . . . we're not people who sweep things aside; ever since they were little, they told us everything.

(The girls look at each other with ironic smiles. This is the pseudo-mutuality myth of openness in the family. It is important the parents take clear and explicit responsibility in front of the daughters.)

M: Of course, it's no problem for us, we're used to everything being open . . . that's why she shocked us so much, because we don't understand.

(M persists with the "open family" myth.)

F→Th: It's clear that . . . things should be open here.

Th→F&M: So, it's OK with both of you?

F&M: Yes!

(Now the road is open for some serious confrontations related to the disturbed dynamics and the big secret.)

Th→F&M: I'd like to understand: your daughter seriously attempted suicide and almost killed herself.

F: Yes, it's hard to admit, but yes . . . it's difficult to say that, Doc, but we need to face a new reality because we never imagined she'd do such a thing to us, but we realize now that it comes from her distress, and we're here to solve it.

M: My heart is pounding . . . I feel very unwell.

Th→F&M: Did you discuss it in the family?

F: My wife and I did. Like I said, this need for attention can lead to the worst . . .
(The denial continues and calls for a more powerful confrontation.)

Th: So, your daughter drank bleach and caused damage that could destroy her esophagus and stomach and even kill her, only for the sake of attention?

M: I can't fathom it all.
(In the following part, the therapist leads the family into a more complex emotional terrain. Gaining their previous permission and confidence clears the way to further explore and confront the harmful parental interactional patterns and disclose the actual circumstances behind the suicidal act. The therapist pushes the family to make explicit what was, destructively, kept secret.)

Th→family: Now, I need all of you to help me understand something very significant! I'm aware that we don't really know each other yet. Is it OK? . . .
(Parents and daughters affirm their readiness.)

Th→F&M: What happened that made your 16-year-old daughter need attention so terribly that she needed to "scream it out" in such a destructive way that it could have caused her death? (looking at Lalli) I assume there are other issues?

M: Doctor, if we had the answer we wouldn't be here. That's just it!

F: Personally, I think it has to do with the wonders of genetics and the "sandwich child" situation. A mix of those two.
(F tries to enlist another myth for the denial.)

Th: (confronting) So . . . genetics makes her seek attention and show it in her willingness to kill herself? Or, at least to cause herself such serious damage for its sake?

F: Uh . . . yes. I think her dramatic side came through very strongly and she certainly didn't realize there would be such damage. . . . I don't believe she thought she could kill herself that way.

M: It's so difficult for me to sit here now . . .

Th→F&M: So, I need to know if you truly want to discover why your daughter needed to scream so loudly for you to hear her?

M: I see she's dissatisfied. I see she's very angry with me.

Th →M: I see despair.

M: (pointing at Lalli, yelling): She's acting! You said you see that she's in despair – but we're the ones in despair!

F: Very much so . . . nothing can be done with her! We give her our lives, and I think we give even more than our lives – everything we possibly can . . .

(This interaction exemplifies the obliviousness and "turning one's back" characteristics spoken about earlier in the chapter. Lalli can't get out of the scapegoated, IP position, and the double bind situations further push her to suicidal ideation. Continuous confrontative interventions for the truth eventually prompt Dalia to force her parents to disclose and deal openly with the toxic secret which they chose to ignore for so long.)

Dalia→F: How can you say you don't know!? She left you crumbs, like Hansel and Gretel, and you didn't see them! She even cut herself (shows them) and you didn't see it!

M: Many teens try cutting themselves a bit. She'll do anything to get attention.

Th→F&M: You know, again and again I come back to the question: Dalia says that Lalli leaves you crumbs, and you don't see them. I don't know what the crumbs are, but I do wonder again what might have happened if she'd succeeded in killing herself. How would your lives be?

M: She would ruin our lives. Simply ruins our lives.

Th: So, you're saying that she, Lalli, ruins your lives when she's alive and she'd ruin your life if she dies. So, in any event, she'd be ruining your lives?

M: Yes. That's why we're here! That's why we're here.

(This is a complicated and difficult situation for a therapist. On the one hand, it is clear Lalli's parents want her to live and the family to be well. On the other hand, they send conflicting and destructive messages that must be firmly, yet empathically, dismantled. It is apparent that neither parent is aware of the harmful effects of their doings. This is a situation where confrontative intervention is vital for changing the suicidality vector.)

Th→M&F: Wow! . . . So, what I've just heard from you is that Lalli ruins your life when she is alive, and if, God forbid, she would have died, she would ruin your lives then, too. So, I'm asking you: <u>what option does she have</u>? Would you like her to swap families?

M: No!!! Of course not!

Th: Or to leave the family and perhaps end her life? . . . Or do you want her to stay with your family? I'm asking these tough questions because I listen well to what you're saying . . . and it sounds terrible!

M&F: Of course we want her to live!! Of course! Of course!

M: Yes, we want her happy and lively, not flopped down somewhere drunk on some street bench (M begins to cry, and F is very sad).

(The confrontative intervention must continue with firmness, yet with empathy, until the parents are willing to truly acknowledge the seriousness of the situation.)

Th (softly, leaning forward gently): So, what other thoughts do you have on what your daughter needs to scream so hard about, other than just needing attention? And I need to understand what she needs to call your attention to . . . not just why, but for what? <u>What is she holding inside</u>?

Th→Dalia: Dalia, please help me understand this situation from <u>your</u> perspective because you are older.

Dalia: Well, I experience our parents a little differently. Nothing's ever good enough for them. . . . She's never enough, she gets excellent grades, she's a fantastic dancer, and so on. She has friends and everything. But at home, it's not seen; none of it is seen. So, it was really lucky that I got home early, because they do not see!! They only see what they want to see. <u>It's terrible what she went through</u>. It's terrible, her experience.

Th→Dalia: What do you think she needs their attention for in such a painful and dangerous way?

Dalia: I don't think it's her need for attention! I think it's what you said earlier – a scream! . . . Because they don't see! They don't know everything, not at all. They don't know everything and don't see everything; they see only what they want!

M: What don't we see?

Dalia →Th: My father has a brother who comes to visit us quite a lot, and Lalli is the prettiest, and he would sit her on him and touch her and do all kinds of things that shouldn't be done, for years, it was called getting "special attention," and they saw but ignored it. They didn't do anything about it . . .

Th: Is it still going on?

Dalia: It's still going on.

M: Oh!!! . . . That's terrible!

Dalia: I am sure it's still happening at every family get-together.

F: I need to hear this from our Lalli. I need to hear this!

M: It's terrible, just terrible, what she's going through.

F: If it's true. That's like dropping a brick on Joe!! You don't get it!! . . . He has a wife and children . . .

(F now sends Lalli a message that her life is less important. This is probably not what he truly means and is unaware that this is his message, but this needs to be clarified.)

Dalia: I told them plenty of times; it's nothing new to them! I told them, and they ignored it like always . . .

F: I didn't think it was so serious!

Lalli: (Lalli speaks for the first time, bursting out emotionally and angrily) I told him!! I told you, Dad! . . . And you saw me . . . I begged not to go there, and you wouldn't agree, because what's important to you is what they will say? . . . And what's important to you is that he is your brother. . . . And that you know him because you raised him as a child, all these years. . . . And what will outsiders think? And that's it. . . . I have nothing more to say.

F: I didn't think it was so serious. . . . What actually happened there?

(Here again are the characteristics of obliviousness and "turning one's back on" mentioned earlier.)

Dalia: What is "serious"? You have no clue what's happening! He did things to her! That's why she tried to commit suicide – because he touched her!

F: I didn't think it was so serious. I thought she was exaggerating like she was being dramatic . . . And how do you know it's serious?

Dalia (shouting): Look at her! She is pale as death! Does she have to die, Dad, before you and Mom understand it's serious and that he harmed her? . . . I don't understand why I need to be the responsible adult here? We've been hinting at this for years!

(The system is now catalyzed to change. Dalia is determined to disclose destructive patterns, demanding that her parents deal with their denials, take responsibility, and rearrange family roles more healthily.)

M: You're not the responsible adult. We're here for her . . .

Dalia→M: Did you hear what Dad said? It's his brother and he's got a family and kids . . . but I am asking you who's more important?

M: My daughter.

Dalia: No, that's what you are saying. It's not what Dad is saying.

F: I also mean it . . . I agree . . . the children are always more important.

Dalia (confronting her father to own his claims): It doesn't look that way.

F→Th: Yes, my daughters are always more important! . . . But it's so hard for me to believe that Joe would do such a thing. . . . It is difficult to comprehend . . . my own brother. (on the verge of tears)

Th: I know it's so hard to understand and believe, but let's say, OK . . . let us just say, for a moment, that it is true.

(At this point, the therapist leads a conversation disclosing the details of the abuse since Lalli was a young child. This is a challenging experience for all. In this first session and first phase of the therapy, it is most important to focus on creating a situation that will allow Lalli to "come back" to her family rather than focus on the punishment of that uncle. The parents need to "digest" the situation in order to begin a process of healing with their daughters and reduce the risk of another suicide attempt.)

Th→F: Assuming that it's true, what does it mean to you? What do you think? Or feel?

F: . . . My first thought is that it's hard for me to imagine that Joe did this.

I cared for him from the day he was born. I was the first to see him walk. We lived in another country. It was a difficult time. Our father abandoned us when Joe was a baby, and Mother died shortly after. So, as a child, I took care of him. I know him, and it is hard to imagine. He is my only brother.

(It is clear F will need to deal with several complicated personal issues, like guilt, anger, loss, and a tremendous amount of pain and grief. However, since the tendency to doubt is still there, the confrontation must empathically continue.)

Th →F (continues confronting): Yes . . . I understand. . . . But you also know Lalli from the day she was born, and even so, she went and did something super drastic, which almost cost her her life, and yet you did not see that coming at all.

(Everyone has long moments of emotional silence. M cries silently, Lalli and Dalia are withdrawn into themselves, and F looks distressed and lost.)

Th→F: How are you feeling now, with all of this?

F: It's the end of the world for me . . . to think that my brother is like that. Wow, it's too much for me. It's terrible!

Th: It's too much for you.

F: Firstly, to think that my daughter went through this! And by my own brother, whom I have known since his birth! . . . And that we didn't believe her. . . . We thought it was all drama. We didn't understand that it was true (said with much pain, gasping for air).

(It is time now to create a change in the session towards direct, personal interaction and take a step towards acknowledgment and acceptance.)

Th→F (said with lots of compassion): Can you please look at your daughter Lalli for a moment and tell her, "When I think about what you have been through, I feel . . ." And then go on and tell Lalli what you feel . . .

F: How do I feel . . . ? It's like the end of the world for me.

Th→Lalli: (moving to sit next to her and put a hand on her arm, with her permission) Can you look at your dad here, for a moment? . . . I know it might be really, really hard, and you can hold on to me, but I invite you to look at him. I want your dad to really feel how it is to say these things to you . . . OK?

F→Lalli (with much pain): What I'm saying is that . . . it's the end of the world, for me. End of the world.

Th→F: So maybe you're not willing to give Lalli up as quickly as it sounded earlier.

F: I'd never be willing to give up on her. I don't have another daughter like her. Each of my daughters is a unique world, and she's a whole world, and I'd never give up on her.

TH: Yes! But you didn't say that. Maybe that's what Lalli needed to hear, "My daughter, I'm not willing to give you up, and even if it hurts and tears me apart, I'm not willing to give up on you!" Can you say that in a way that comes from your heart? I promise to deal later with your pain over your brother. But now it is the pain over your daughter.

(Lalli cries quietly.)

F→Lalli (looking at each other): OK. I'm certain, sweetie, that I'm not willing to ever give up on you, on who you are, what you are, all your special qualities! It's important for me that you understand that <u>we could not hear you. . . . I think because it was too painful to hear and to think about . . .</u> not just because of Joe, but really, also because of you!

Th→F&M: You are saying that you couldn't hear Lalli or Dalia because the thought was so painful, so you chose to close your ears and eyes and your heart. That is precisely what Lalli felt, <u>so she needed to scream so drastically</u>. She did indeed seek your attention but for a very painfully important reason.

Ending the Session and Moving Forward

Now it is the time to enter the "ritual of the five commitments." The therapist explains this to the family, who agree to follow up and check on it during every session. The five commitments are as follows:

1. To keep Lalli alive and well by changing the relationship with her to a healthier one.
2. To release Dalia from her role as the "protector" and "the responsible adult."
3. Parents will listen more attentively to their daughters and get to know them better.
4. Each will learn to recognize "their own and the other's pain and what it does to them."
5. As parents: "We will assist you, Lalli, to appreciate yourself, support you in your pain and distress, and do what is necessary for you to develop a will for life and blossom."

The parents have to claim their commitments until Lalli experiences them as authentic and earnest. She, too, commits to working conjointly with her family and individually and never again giving up on her life. The following course of therapy has to deal with helping the parents discover the factors in their own life experiences and psychodynamics that prevent them from "hearing" and "seeing," therefore causing the creation of such harmful interactions. It is also necessary to release feelings of guilt on all sides and turn guilt into responsibility.

8.7 Conclusion

The particular reasons and dynamics behind severe adolescent suicidality are varied, often elusive, and not clear-cut. Therefore, therapists should not try to adhere to a particular protocol. The therapist must quickly understand systemic-personal situations and be brave, observant, determined, and creative enough to confront, modify, and improvise interventions. Helping suicidal adolescents cherish life is incredibly rewarding and heartwarming work.

8.8 Acknowledgments

I am deeply indebted to my colleagues and our trainees at Shinui: Israel Institute for Systemic Studies. Their relentless pursuit of solutions, their first-hand understanding, and their excellence in preventing adolescent suicides has helped many families come together in the successful pursuit of healthy development. Their success has been phenomenal and is worth noting.

The formal clinical research project drawn upon here is still underway and will be published within the next two years.

References

Adams, D. M., Overholser, J. C., & Lehnert, K. L. (1994). Perceived family functioning and adolescent suicidal behavior. *Journal of the American Academy of Child and Adolescent Psychiatry*, *33*(4), 498–507. https://doi.org/10.1097/00004583-199405000-00008

Aldridge, D. (1984). Family interaction and suicidal behaviour: A brief review. *Journal of Family Therapy*, *6*(3), 309–322. https://doi.org/10.1046/j.1467-6427.1984.00652.x

Andolfi, M. (2017). *Multi-generational family therapy: Tools and resources for the therapist*. Routledge.

Frey, L. M., & Cerel, J. (2015). Risk for suicide and the role of family: A narrative review. *Journal of Family Issues*, *36*(6), 716–736. https://doi.org/10.1177/0192513X13515885

Kutz, A. (2023). *Double bind-communication as a cause of burnout: A proposal for a theory on the effects of toxic communication in organisations*. Springer Nature.

Nabarro-Rubinstein, N. (1994). Sequential preventive meta-consultation (SPMC): A model of collegial consultation in systems therapy. In M. Andolfi & R. Haber (Eds.), *Please help me with this family: Using consultants as resources in family therapy* (pp. 197–218). Routledge.

Nabarro-Rubinstein, N. (2023, July 6–8). *Change-focused family therapy with suicidal adolescents*. International Conference of Family Therapy: The Road That Connects Individual and Social Resources, Assisi, Italy.

Nabarro-Rubinstein, N. (in press). *Shinui institute project: Family therapy with suicidal adolescents 2012–2014*. Shinui Institute for Systemic Studies.

Richman, J. (1986). *Family therapy for suicidal people*. Springer Publishing Company.

Slaby, A. E., & Garfinkel, L. F. (1996). *No one saw my pain: Why teens kill themselves*. W.W. Norton & Company.

Walcott, R. I. (1995). *Adolescent suicide: Contributions of the family*. McGill University.

Watzlawick, P., Beavin, J. A. B., & Jackson, D. (1967). *Pragmatics of human communication*. W.W. Norton & Company.

Zanor, G. B. (1974). *Disqualification: An implicit verbal communication pattern and its relationship to avoiding or accepting personal responsibility for behavior, locus of responsibility, and sex of the subject* [Doctoral dissertation, University of Massachusetts].

9

ADOLESCENT FAMILY THERAPY

Consideration of systemic and developmental lenses

Christine Senediak and Isabelle Feijo

Adolescence is a time of change where the young person establishes autonomy and identity. Many challenges are often identified in the literature about how to interact with the parents of a symptomatic young person. It is not uncommon for parents and caregivers to seek the outsourcing of the healing process. The therapist, in this instance, is asked on referral to "fix my child." Historically, children and adolescents seen individually was the preferred intervention, and this still is often the way many therapists choose to work rather than by engaging the whole family in therapy.

The "problem adolescent" is seen as the one who needs changing, rather than exploring the experiences of the young person within their family and what might be contributing to their difficulties. Seeing a family can be messy, emotion laden, and at times chaotic. However, this can be a snapshot of what is really happening within the family and is an effective way to look for and use the resources, however small, within the family.

The adolescent years are recognized as an important period of growth and as a transition from dependence on family to independence. This is particularly true within Western-based societies and in accordance with the cultural expectations of the environment. During this period of growth and development, the relationship between child and parent changes, with the young person hopefully moving to interdependence with parents, allowing for incorporation of wider social systems including friends, partners, and others. This often requires tolerance of difference of opinions, values, behaviors, and expectations. Meeting as a family in therapy can help this process and aid communication.

It is important that therapists work with the whole family: the adolescent, siblings, parents/caregivers, and relevant others to both understand the nature of mental illness and concerns for the identified patient and for those impacted. By engaging in meaningful therapeutic conversation, both the therapist and family can properly understand the developmental and transgenerational familial history. By seeking the family narrative across multi-generations (i.e., grandparents, parents, and young person/siblings), the therapist can better understand and help the family understand how their problems may have developed and are being maintained. This is not to find fault or blame, but rather to use the history of the family to find strengths in how adversity has been, and how it can be managed moving forward. Family meetings also allow for greater cultural and systemic exploration and opportunities to look for resources.

Pioneers of family therapy were adamant about the need to include all family members in family therapy sessions. In the 1960s, Nathan Ackerman, a pioneer of family therapy, introduced a shift from individual pathology to a wider consideration of the influence of family dynamics. He believed

DOI: 10.4324/9781003536765-12

understanding and using family interactions and family relations was crucial for effective therapy. He also highlighted the importance of a systemic lens and considering multiple generations, believing that issues and patterns were passed down through generations and that it was important to consider these dynamics alongside current family life cycle challenges (Ackerman, 1966).

Salvador Minuchin, another influential pioneer in family therapy, laid the foundation for many contemporary family therapy approaches. He developed ideas to look at boundaries, subsystems, hierarchy, and power dynamics within the family and a historical/multigenerational perspective. Minuchin used this information in the session to better understand, enhance communication, and help the family to make change (Minuchin, 1974; Minuchin et al., 2013).

9.1 A developmental-systemic lens

Robinson et al. (2011) noted that parents play a crucial role in adolescent mental health and treatment, extending beyond just the young person. Including parents and siblings should always be considered. Within a developmental, attachment, and systemic frame, a therapist should explore the emotional links between family relationship systems and the development and maintenance of symptoms. It is helpful to explore the parents' capacity to be attuned to the needs of the adolescent and how they provide guidance towards self-regulation (Allan & Power, 2011). Cognitive, emotional, and behavioral processes are expressed and best understood when examining and working with the family system (Brown, 2020).

It is important for family therapists to be committed to the integrity and well-being of families, in whatever form they take, and across all communities. Families are the cornerstones of society in small as well as global communities. Families are a major resource to deal with isolation and loss of connectedness (Andolfi et al., 2023). Within the literature, there is widespread acknowledgement that it is helpful to engage all family members in the therapeutic process (Andolfi, 1979, 1994; Allan & Power, 2011; Carr, 2016; Larner, 2009).

This is not to say that individual work should not also take place, but involvement with the family is required to foster and sustain change. Treatment outcome is determined by the multiple interactions of adolescent, parent/carer, family and contextual factors (e.g., social, political and cultural), and working with these various systems in which the young person lives, learns, and relates is essential (Larner, 2004).

Carr (2016), in his review of research-based family therapy interventions, notes there is clear evidence that a number of models of family therapy have been developed and work effectively for a range of adolescent problems. From a research-informed perspective, there is evidence that supports Brief Strategic Family Therapy (BSFT) (Szapocznik et al., 2015), Functional Family Therapy (FFT) (Sexton, 2011), Multisystemic Therapy (MST) (Henggeler et al., 2002), and Attachment-Based Family Therapy (ABFT) (Diamond et al., 2014). There is also widespread evidence in the literature for the Maudsley model of family therapy for young people with eating disorders (Lock, 2011), for those with first episode psychosis (McFarlane, 2002), and for drug misuse using Multidimensional Family Therapy (MDFT) (Liddle, 2015).

The role of parents in an adolescent's life is important as they offer many family-related protective factors. These include providing a secure base, connectedness, and making the adolescent feel valued, supported, and providing a sense of belonging (Ulrich et al., 2012). Conversely, when a family does not have the resources to or is unable to provide this security, it is important to help the family alongside the young person to make positive changes. Characteristics of such family environments may include abuse (physical, emotional, or sexual), neglect, family conflict and violence, attachment problems, parental drug and alcohol misuse, and mental illness and stress. Social issues and where young people are impacted by external stressors (e.g., political tensions, war) will of course add additional immediate risk for the young person and their family, which necessitates that physiological and safety needs to be addressed in the first instance (Silwal et al., 2023).

Within the contemporary application of family therapy with young people, there needs to be an interface between the individual and their relational context. Today, family therapy is an integrative ecosystemic approach that needs to consider the complexity of biological, emotional, social, multi-generational family, cultural, political, and neuroscience influences (Hawks et al., 2015). As Andolfi (2013) notes, "a positive therapeutic result is achieved not only by the resolution of a presenting problem . . . but also by the transformation of the family in terms of personal and relational well-being" (p. 184).

9.2 Practice issues and considerations

Several issues must be addressed in conducting family therapy with adolescents, as well as for clinical institutions in training and supervision, and integration of family therapy with other treatment modalities. These issues are discussed as follows.

Involving young people in family therapy. In family therapy, the individual adolescent can be at risk of becoming invisible, ignored, silenced, or excluded. This is complicated by the challenging behaviors young people often display in the therapy room by being sullen, unresponsive, angry, loud, or arrogant. Looking behind these expressions of distress is a young person's desperate need for care, understanding, and help. The Assisi Manifesto (Andolfi et al., 2023) proclaims that the therapist must look beyond just psychiatric diagnoses and labels, seeing the individual both holistically and relationally. It is not uncommon that the designated patient is "silenced" with medication, ostensibly to reduce symptomatology, but with the "relational side effect" of diminishing the adolescent's voice about problematic aspects of family interaction and its culture. Then the family feels no need to engage in family therapy to understand the function of the adolescent's symptom(s). However, family therapy is important as it helps with the acceptance that everyone must change in order for there to be lasting improvement in the adolescent's psychological state and behavior.

A young person's voice can be invited into therapy by the initial question: "How can I help your family?" (Andolfi, 1979; Andolfi & Mascellani, 2013). By inviting the adolescent to create a perspective for family change rather than individual change, this helps to broaden the lens from which the problem is seen, again drawing on the resources that exist within and for the family. An example in therapy demonstrating the use of this questioning was with a 13-year-old who was self-harming. When asked this question, they said "why does it matter . . . no one listens to me?" This took the parents by surprise, who stated that their child seemed not to want to speak to them anymore. A conversation ensued in the session guided by the therapist. What became clear was that the young person was worried that the parents were going to split, based on the obvious tensions experienced between the parents. This was news to the parents, who were able to reassure their child that they were not going to split, but indeed that the father was experiencing his own mental health issues, which were impacting the marital relationship. The recommendation was for the father to seek his own individual therapy alongside couple therapy and family therapy. Family sessions helped to support the young person to express their emotions and learn ways to manage their distress.

Issues around training and supervision. A challenge for many therapists is a lack of training in family therapy. Many therapists are most comfortable seeing the young person alone or with a brief parent "catch-up" at the end of a session. Also, many psychiatrists do not have the training in family therapy and feel uncomfortable with the unpredictability of being part of a changing, interacting family system. They often prefer to stick to prescribing medication despite the lack of clear evidence for many pharmacological indications in psychiatry.

In addition, working with children and adolescents is often seen as a specialty area of human development – once again, requiring training and supervision beyond therapists' dominant training in adult individual psychotherapy. There has been a growing literature emerging on how to work with young people using art, drawing, and play techniques, therapeutic stories, experiential approaches, and narrative therapy (van Doornik, 2023; Nielsen et al., 2021). More of this work needs to become part of everyday therapeutic practice, allowing young people the freedom to be expressive in the therapy room, often with resulting greater insight about their situation. Involving parents and siblings in these creative therapeutic processes can also facilitate greater understanding and connection.

Integrating family therapy into adolescent mental health practice. Over the past few decades, alongside managed care and the growth of evidence-based practice, family therapists are applying a more integrative stance in the way they work with young people, by applying a biopsychosocial framework. As Larner states, it is important to integrate family therapy based on an "ethic of hospitality," being open to different discourses of therapy (Larner, 2003). This involves an integrative, multimodal approach, combining the use of cognitive, narrative, art, music, groupwork, and family therapy to help the adolescent presenting with mental health concerns. This may also include pharmacotherapy in the case of severe mental illness or distress. An integrative stance invites the application of family therapy in adolescent services, aligning it to best mental health practice and collaborative multidisciplinary practice.

Risk factors within the family (e.g., mental illness) will influence outcomes for adolescents. Therefore, it makes sense that the family therapy should be seen as an essential part of any treatment plan. Although individuation, autonomy, and confidentiality are important considerations when working with young people and their families, involvement of the family remains critical for both individual and systemic change.

Family therapy as evidence-based practice. As noted earlier, working conjointly with families and young people is a logical response to the outcomes of research-based interventions (Carr, 2016). The following are identified as features of family interventions with young people that are effective agents for change:

1. Improving communication skills
2. Ensuring that the adolescent client has a voice in therapy that is heard and understood
3. Promotion of systemic family-based problem-solving
4. Using nonverbal techniques that allow for alternative ways to understand concerns and to promote communication
5. Promoting attachment
6. Reducing negative and critical interactions
7. Building resilience and hope

For Andolfi (1979), using the adolescent client as "consultant" provides a bridge for the family to connect with the therapist and receive help. Inside the symptom, the problem is the solution – the flip side of the coin. What is the meaning of the symptom in relation to the development of the family in time? Andolfi writes that

> often a child is the best indicator of the affective situation of a family at a given moment. A child is able to express openly feelings and tensions that the parents are experiencing but are reluctant to reveal. . . . And he frequently indicates to the therapist the direction to take in therapy.
>
> *(p. 87)*

Family therapy as part of multidisciplinary inpatient care for adolescents with severe, unremitting, and treatment-resistant mental illness. The families of adolescents who present with a severe and chronic mental illness despite adequate outpatient and/or acute inpatient interventions benefit from an intensive family therapy approach. An example is an adolescent presenting with a diagnosis of treatment-resistant schizophrenia. This presentation is typically severe in nature, and there can be lack of change despite multiple medication trials. A holistic approach including verbal and nonverbal therapies for the adolescent and the family is of extreme importance, with family therapy being aimed at improving family relationships, achieved in part through psychoeducation of parents and other family members about the illness and about interactional styles that best prevent relapse and rehospitalization (McFarlane, 2002). An aim of therapy is to help the adolescent stabilize and gain enough functionality to remain living with the family (Miklowitz et al., 2014). The family system needs help to "grieve" their earlier image of the "ideal child," and needs a lot of support to accept the adolescent in their process of recovery. In these cases, art therapy has proven to be a powerful tool for families to connect and express themselves via a nonverbal process.

In those cases where everything has been tried and nothing has worked, families usually feel helpless, guilty, and exhausted. Some families will have tried different types of family therapy and others might have focused the treatment on the identified patient (the adolescent). When consideration is taken to admit an adolescent to a longer-stay inpatient setting, it is important to prepare the family before the admission to make sure they understand the necessity to engage in at least weekly family therapy sessions. This requires a big time and emotional commitment. However, when families do not see any other solution, they will agree to family therapy. The best outcome is achieved when all important family members participate consistently throughout the admission, where the family members have reflective capacity, and where the change achieved in hospital can be applied to the home environment during leave and after discharge.

In the clinical service of the second author, towards the end of the admission, the outpatient treating team of clinicians is invited to meet the family and to participate in the family therapy session in order to facilitate a smooth transition and ensure continuation of the goals achieved during the admission (Sarmiento & Feijo, 2022). The family therapy sessions are held at the same time and day every week and attended by the family, the adolescent, the treating psychiatrist, a co-therapist from the allied health team, the allocated doctor in training, and the allocated nurse. Where indicated, the family or part of the family group will be referred for art or music family therapy sessions, which are in addition to the weekly family therapy sessions.

There are many examples of adolescents with a trauma history and a diagnosis of complex post-traumatic stress disorder (cPTSD) with severe self-harm/suicidality, where the positive change only happened once all members of the family were committed to intensive systemic family therapy. In these cases, it is not uncommon that not only the designated patient benefits from the therapy but also all of the siblings living in the same family home, as they have often been exposed to the same traumatic events or have been traumatized by witnessing the designated patient being dysregulated due to witnessed or unwitnessed abuse (Winley et al., 2016).

9.3 Conclusion

The adolescent is part of the family system, and it is imperative that the family be included in the treatment of the adolescent. Through family therapy, the practitioners, the adolescent, the family, and the wider system gain an understanding of the context and the contributing and maintaining factors of the mental illness or the psychological and behavioral symptoms. Only by working together is it possible to achieve positive outcomes and lasting change – not only for the adolescent but also for the whole family system.

References

Ackerman, N. (1966). *Treating the troubled family*. Basic Books.
Allan, D., & Power, L. (2011). Family therapy with adolescents: Key ideas and their application. In A. Wallis, K. James, & P. Rhodes (Eds.), *A practical guide to family therapy: Structured guidelines and key skills* (2nd ed., pp. 148–178). Routledge.
Andolfi, M. (1979). *Family therapy: An interactional approach*. Plenum Press.
Andolfi, M. (1994). The child as consultant. In M. Andolfi & R. Haber (Eds.), *Please help me with this family: Using consultant as resources in family therapy* (pp. 73–89) Brunner/Mazel.
Andolfi, M. (2013). Engaging fathers in family therapy with violent adolescents. *Australian and New Zealand Journal of Family Therapy*, *34*, 172–185. https://doi.org/10.1002/anzf.1015
Andolfi, M., & Mascellani, A. (2013). *Teen voices: Tales from family therapy*. Wisdom Moon Publishing (Original work published 2010).
Andolfi, M., & The International Faculty. (2023). *Assisi manifesto*. https://europeanfamilytherapy.eu/assisi-manifesto-2023/
Brown, J. (2020). Engaging with parents in child and adolescent mental health services. *Australian and New Zealand Journal of Family Therapy*, *41*, 145–160.
Carr, A. (2016). Family therapy for adolescents: A research-informed perspective. *Australian and New Zealand Journal of Family Therapy*, *37*, 467–479. https://doi.org/10.1002/anzf.1409
Diamond, G. S., Diamond, G. M., & Levy, S. A. (2014). *Attachment-based family therapy for depressed adolescents*. American Psychological Association. https://doi.org/10.1037/14296-000
Hawks, J. M., Parker, T. S., Werner-Wilson, R., Huff, N., & Lianekhammy, J. (2015). Adolescents' and parents' expression of empathy: A social neuroscience perspective. *Contemporary Family Therapy: An International Journal*, *37*(2), 142–152. https://doi.org/10.1007/s10591-015-9334-x
Henggeler, S., Clingempeel, G., Brondino, M., & Pickrel, S. (2002). Four-year follow up of multisystemic therapy with substance-dependent juvenile offenders. *Journal of the American Academy of Child and Adolescent Psychiatry*, *41*, 868–874.
Larner, G. (2003). Integrating family therapy in child and adolescent mental health practice: An ethic of hospitality. *Australian and New Zealand Journal of Family Therapy*, *24*, 211–219. https://doi.org/10.1002/j.1467-8438.2003.tb00563.x
Larner, G. (2004). Family therapy and the politics of evidence. *Journal of Family Therapy*, *26*, 17–39. https://doi.org/10.1111/j.1467-6427.2004.00265.x
Larner, G. (2009). Integrating family therapy in adolescent depression: An ethical stance, *Journal of Family Therapy*, *31*, 213–232. https://doi.org/10.1111/j.1467-6427.2009.00468.x
Liddle, H. (2015). Multidimensional family therapy. In T. Sexton & J. Lebow (Eds.), *Handbook of family therapy* (4th ed., pp. 231–249). Routledge.
Lock, J. (2011). Evaluation of family treatment models for eating disorders. *Current Opinion in Psychiatry*, *24*, 274–279. https://doi.org/279.10.1097/YCO.0b013e328346f71e
McFarlane, W. (2002). *Multifamily groups in the treatment of severe psychiatric disorders*. Guilford Press.
Miklowitz, D., O'Brien, M., Schlosser, D., Addington, J., Canda, K., Marshall, C., Domingues, I., Walsh, B., Zinberg, J., De Silva, S., Friedman-Yakoobian, M., & Cannon, T. (2014). Family-focused treatment for adolescents and young adults at high risk for psychosis: Results of a randomized trial. *Journal of the American Academy of Child and Adolescent Psychiatry*, *53*, 848–858. https://doi.org/10.1016/j.jaac.2014.04.020
Minuchin, S. (1974). *Families and family therapy*. Harvard University Press.
Minuchin, S., Reiter, M., & Borda, C. (2013). *The craft of family therapy: Challenging certainties*. Routledge.
Nielsen, F., Feijo, I., Renshall, K., & Starling, J. (2021). Family art therapy: A contribution to mental health treatment in an adolescent inpatient setting. *Australian and New Zealand Journal of Family Therapy*, *42*, 145–159. https://doi.org/10.1002/anzf.1449
Robinson, E., Power, L., & Allan, D. (2011). What works with adolescents? Family connections and involvement in interventions for adolescent problem behaviours. *Family Matters*, *88*, 57–64.
Sarmiento, K., & Feijo, I. (2022). *Longer-term psychiatric inpatient care for adolescents*. Palgrave Macmillan. https://doi.org/10.1007/978-981-19-1950-3
Sexton, T. (2011). *Functional family therapy in clinical practice*. Routledge.
Silwal, S., Bohdanova, T., Hodes, M., & Skokauskas, N. (2023). Impact of the Russian invasion on mental health of adolescents in Ukraine. *Journal of the American Academy of Child & Adolescent Psychiatry*, *62*, 335–243. https://doi.org/10.1016/j.jaac.2022.07.845

Szapocznik, J., Muir, J., Seth, D., & Brown, C. H. (2015). Brief strategic family therapy: Implementing evidence-based models in community settings. *Psychotherapy Research*, *25*, 121–123. https://doi.org/10.1080/10503307.2013.856044

Ulrich, O., Robins, R., & Widaman, K. (2012). Life-span development of self-esteem and its effects on important life outcomes. *Journal of Personality and Social Psychology*, *102*, 1271–1288.

Van Doornik, A. (2023). *An extra language: A handbook for systemic work with figures*. Acco Uitgeverji, Westvlietweg.

Winley, D., Ogbaselase, F., Kodish, T., Okunrounmu, E., & Rauthamer Ewing, E. S. (2016). Attachment-based family therapy for teen suicidality complicated by a history of sexual trauma. *Australian and New Zealand Journal of Family Therapy*, *37*, 177–189. https://doi.org/10.1002/anzf.1150

10

DE CORPORIS MOMENTUM

The importance of the body in family therapy

Dominique Bardou

10.1 Introduction

In this chapter, I discuss the role of the body in human psychological and behavioral functioning and in family interaction. I describe how interventions that directly address the body as the initial change entry point in intrapsychic and relational systems that also include cognitions (the "mind") and emotions (the "heart") can be effective in family therapy for trauma. These conceptualizations are illustrated by short case examples that demonstrate innovative techniques that engage persons' bodies.

10.2 The role of the body in human functioning and in trauma-centered family therapy

Momentum translates from Latin as "importance, influence, weight" and "movement, impulse." Thus, *corporis momentum* means both "importance of the body" and "movement of the body." Stern (2004) teaches us that action and movement are the real path to knowledge. Therefore, the body's mobilization allows access to a form of awareness, perception, and representation.

In most personal or family situations of loss or trauma, the story is engraved in the bodies of the people who experience it (Van der Kolk, 2014). Patients, through their symptoms, suffer in the body or bring it to the forefront: extreme thinness, dissociation, self-harm, suicide attempts, vomiting, inhalation or ingestion or injection of various drugs, and psychosomatic manifestations. Their family members also suffer in their bodies: anxiety, depression, anger, as well as psychosomatic symptoms.

Human biopsychobehavioral functioning and experience are composed of three aspects, which have corresponding centers in the brain and autonomic nervous system: (1) the "mind," our thought patterns, beliefs, perceptions, reflections, and values; (2) what we often still refer poetically to as the "heart," our emotions and broader levels of arousal (Gross, 2015); and (3) the body, our actions, movements, postures, and sensations. When all goes well, these three aspects communicate, exchange information, and react to each other in a fluid, congruent, and relevant way, working together to regulate or "modulate" (Jurist, 2018) one another and restore a sense of body/mind well-being. For example, a sudden encounter with a lion causes the mind to perceive danger, the "heart" to feel fear, and the body to mobilize for escape. Once our mind perceives ourselves to be safe, the "heart" starts to calm, and the body can become still and relax, sending further physiological signals from the

DOI: 10.4324/9781003536765-13

limbs through the autonomic nervous system to the emotion and cognitive centers of the brain in a circular, systemic fashion. Similar conceptualizations have been long described by Ogden (Ogden & Fischer, 2015; Ogden et al., 2006) in her groundbreaking sensorimotor therapy; by Porges (2017) in his highly influential polyvagal theory; by Dana (2018) in her popular and practical application of Porges' theory; and by Armstrong (2019), among others.

Unfortunately, many experiences of trauma, bereavement, or loss cause us to lose this fluidity in the circulation of information or can lead to inadequate or even pathological reactions. For example, the mind may allow a behavior to continue despite it being identified as self- or other-destructive; the heart may not identify the correct emotion or express anger instead of sadness or fear – or suppress appropriate anger due to overconcern with the emotional state and safety of a trauma perpetrator; and the body can freeze and no longer react, thereby exposing a person to further danger instead of escaping it.

Therefore, the bodily dimension is often central to the problems patients and their families bring to therapy, but it is often neglected or avoided by therapists (Argyle, 1988; Dana, 2018; Ekman & Friesen, 1972; Ogden & Fischer, 2015; Scheflen, 1972; van der Kolk, 2014). Yet, a focus on the body can be an extraordinary tool for change, as long as the therapist helps reconnect it to the minds and hearts of patients and their families.

Family therapists' reservations can likely be explained by the fact that the body (including the face), although objectively more readily exposed than a person's feelings and thoughts, is often viewed as more "private" and not comfortably available or appropriate for therapeutic commentary. Furthermore, the body is the ultimate domain of sexual intimacy, and therapists may be reluctant to comment on a patient's body for fear that such comments might be interpreted as a sexual advance – a serious ethical violation that can lead a patient to report the therapist to licensing bureaus and revocation of the therapist's professional license. It is a not uncommon experience among therapists that comments to a patient about their overall appearance, their weight, height, style of dress, posture, gestures, and facial expressions may be met with surprise, alarm, and discomfort, as therapy is generally viewed among the public as an activity that focuses only on verbalized thoughts and feelings.

Therefore, therapists generally prefer to avoid delving into this territory during individual or family sessions. Based on the absence of body-centered theory and techniques in the voluminous therapy training literature, it can be assumed that training programs in psychotherapy and family therapy worldwide rarely teach students how to talk with patients and families about their bodies and their nonverbal, physical expressions of thoughts and emotions. It should be noted that there has been greater development and implementation of body-based therapies for treatment of individual patients suffering from trauma than for working with families – for instance, popular techniques such as sensorimotor psychotherapy (Ogden & Fischer, 2015; Ogden et al., 2006); somatic experiencing (Levine, 1997), Dana's (2018), application of Porges's (2017) influential polyvagal theory, Shapiro's (2018) eye movement desensitization and reprocessing (EMDR) therapy, among others (Armstrong, 2019).

Of course, the therapist must introduce discussion about patients' bodies and interventions centering on their bodies with respect and ethical caution, gauging whether to pursue these interventions based on the patients' expressed openness and receptiveness to the therapist's initial foray into the domain of the body through tentatively posed questions and comments. However, as I will show, I and my colleagues have found repeatedly that therapists can encourage bodily experiences in their work with families. Such body-centered interventions in family therapy can help overcome the trials the bodies have been subjected to and the self-destruction inflicted by patients, and can alleviate the physical and psychological suffering of the family members (Andolfi, 2016).

10.3 Family-centered, body-based therapeutic practices

So, how can bodies be involved, activated, and set in motion to serve change? I will describe the significant benefits of experiential activation, drawing on my and my colleagues' extensive clinical experiences developed over time in various hospital and outpatient intervention settings. The proposed tools are designed to put the bodies into action and activate emotional sharing among family members and therapists.

They should be adapted to the particular family and culture the family inhabits, not necessarily replicated identically as described. As in all therapies, it is necessary first to establish a strong, trusting therapeutic alliance with the patient and the family, and to explore transgenerational issues and stories to understand the symptoms in the historical context that gives them relational meaning. From there, body-based interventions will encourage novel, transformative reflections, emotions, and bodily experiences for the patient and their family members.

To activate this process, the familiar practice of attending to the "self of the therapist" (Hardy & Bobes, 2016) – usually construed solely in terms of one's here-and-now thoughts and feelings along with one's personal family histories and social locational identities that contribute to potential countertransference – must include being in touch with one's own bodily sensations, feelings, and evaluations of one's body. For instance, if the therapist has held negative views of their own body and worked through them, this can potentially provide a source of empathy and hope for a patient who hates or is otherwise dissatisfied with or rejecting of their body. In contrast, if the therapist is unaware of their past or *current* dissatisfaction with their own body, this could problematically influence their view of the patient's experience of their body or the family members' views of the patient's body.

10.4 Case illustration: Working with the mirror

Lea, a white, French, Jewish, 25-year-old woman, was brought by her parents to our clinic, presenting with severe anorexia that had developed over ten years. Starting at age 14, she had benefited from various specialized therapies in different clinics, but her denial of the disorders and their consequences persisted.

In our work with her and her family, two moments were extremely powerful turning points. During a family session, we discussed Lea's early childhood. Her mother vividly recounted how Lea particularly loved dressing up, putting on impromptu shows that amused everyone, dancing and acting, and how she involved her two younger sisters in these shows. We suggested that, for our next session, the mother bring the children's clothes from that period, which she had kept in a chest. Two weeks later, the family arrived with a bag full of clothes and various items that Lea had used in these song and dance performances. We asked the girls to choose their favorite outfits. Without hesitation, Lea picked up a tiny, straight, bright yellow skirt, saying with a look of fond reminiscence, "I *loved* this skirt when I was six!" The family members confirmed she always wore it. She was visibly delighted about this journey into her early years. With a calm, encouraging smile and voice tone, I said, "Try it." "But it is impossible! I wore it when I was six! I am 25 now!" With a look of irritation and defiant cooperation (her facial grimace, narrowed eyes, and gestures essentially expressing, "Fine! OK! Be that way! I'll prove it's impossible!"), Lea quickly and a bit roughly pulled the yellow skirt over her pants. It fit loosely on her: She had to hold it up, as otherwise it would have slipped past her shapeless hips. Lea was shocked. She fell silent and stopped smiling. She burst into tears, something she had not done in years. Through this kinetic, tactile experience, she realized directly with her body her distorted self-perceptions and extreme thinness.

To take her profound change about the state of her body even further, we proposed a session of mirror work. This therapeutic technique works on body image. Lacan (1938) spoke of the "joyful assumption of the specular image" of the unified self to discuss a phase of child development. The child, after experiencing himself as fragmented in the early months of life, due to seeing only separate parts of his body (hands, feet . . .), suddenly realizes, upon seeing his whole image in the mirror, that these different parts form a whole – a child – and that the child he is looking at is none other than himself. This is Lacan's theory of how an infant begins to form a sense of "self." This results in a joyful state in him, often with great excitement in front of the mirror. However, he cannot do this psychic work alone. He must have his parents around him, who confirm: "Yes, sweetheart, it is you, the person you see."

In clinical settings, there appear to be an increasing number of young patients who present with a distorted body image, which can escalate to full-blown body dysmorphia (Himanshu et al., 2020). They perceive their bodies as deformed, large, and shapeless. They focus on specific parts that they perceive as monstrous (abdomen, thighs, buttocks, nose, cheeks), and they often insist on the veracity of their gross physical imperfections, which are completely undetectable to others. They desperately wish to transform their bodies with an obsessive extremism that is never satisfied and out of touch with reality. These symptoms are often found in persons who have experienced trauma, where the body's boundaries and safety have been violated by the abuser. These patients no longer accurately see their image in the mirror: They cognitively construct these misperceptions – in other words, they *think* their body rather than seeing it. They no longer use their eyes but rather their mind to represent and describe their body (Baltazar et al., 2014). This was the case with Lea.

The technique of mirror work involves having patients look at themselves in the mirror, accompanied by two therapists, who comment on what they see. The therapists' corrective gaze and comments provide emotional containment and a related "holding environment" similar to what parents do in the early months of life – if the parents are indeed loving and affirming of the child's physicality and emerging sense of self.

We developed four variations of this technique:

1. Asking the patient to wear a mask covering their face. This changes the experience because they no longer recognize themselves. This helps them focus their gaze on the body and its parts as if they belong to a stranger. The description becomes more accessible and objective.
2. Using a one-way mirror. A therapist positioned behind the mirror can play the role of the one in Snow White: "Mirror, mirror, on the wall, what do you see?" Through the intercom, the mirror starts to speak, and an often-intense dialogue is established between the patient questioning their reflection and the mirror responding. For the patient, it is no longer a therapist speaking (with their subjectivity) but an inanimate, neutral, and objective object.
3. Using this technique with a peer group in therapeutic or educational settings, with each member of the peer group taking turns in front of the mirror and receiving corrective feedback from their peers. The group format engages at least three of Irving Yalom's (Yalom & Leszcz, 2020) therapeutic factors of group psychotherapy – that of universality (seeing that other people struggle with the same or similar issues as you do), cohesion (connectedness and emotional support), and new information, the power of feedback from other patients or students. The group format allows peer members to feel less shame and stigma, by seeing others struggling with similar issues. It is akin to the technique of sculpting (Papp et al., 2013) in the intensity of emotions experienced and the potency to stimulate change.
4. Utilizing this technique not with two therapists in the role of parents, but with the actual parents and possibly siblings (as we did with Lea and her family), observing and commenting on what they see. In a family-based approach, the effect is amplified by family members, who often share intense emotions and perspectives different from those of the identified patient.

We proposed doing mirror work with Lea and her family in the session following the session with the yellow skirt. We asked her to stand in front of the mirror, at the distance she preferred, surrounded by her parents and sisters. Initially, she remained quite distant from the mirror, framed by a parent on each side and by her sisters standing behind them. The sisters initially seemed somewhat emotionally disengaged from the therapeutic process. However, as the session began, only the sisters timidly offered their thoughts about Lea's thinness. The eldest sister dared to offer the following evocative perception: "You look like you came out of a concentration camp." This sentence created an emotional explosion. To maintain the intensity, we asked the family to approach the mirror, and we circulated photos on a smartphone of Holocaust survivors at the moment of their liberation from those famous camps. The mother looked at Lea, started to cry, and spoke about her pain in seeing her daughter inflict such torment on herself.

The father then, as if stunned, sat down, and for the first time, told his daughters the story of his father, who was a partisan (helping the resistance against the Nazis). In 1942, this man was deported, along with his brother (the girls' great-uncle). In the Nazi camp where they were deported, the grandfather made a promise to his dying brother "on his deathbed" – a French expression meaning "on the verge of death" – that he would keep his memory alive after his death. So, only the girls' grandfather returned to France from that camp in 1945, weighing 32 kilograms.

Having witnessed his brother's death from starvation and hardship, the grandfather developed a special relationship with food. This relationship with food became the central theme and axis of his life, both professionally (he was a butcher and delicatessen owner and caterer) and personally. He regularly organized large banquets for the extended family in addition to weekly Sunday meals that lasted all day, with family gathered around the table. Lea's father inherited this emphasis on food and pressured his daughters to eat a lot.

Moreover, the father chose Lea's name in memory of his uncle, a resistance hero. Indeed, this great-uncle was named Leon, and Lea was given her similar name to honor his memory. The father spoke with great emotion during this session, saying he now realized how he had unwittingly imposed the tragedy of his father's and uncle's story onto his current family, especially Lea. He took Lea in his arms and gave her a long and intense embrace. He apologized to Lea and stated his new intention to release Lea from the narrative of food scarcity and the death of her great-uncle 65 years earlier. He stated his wish that this might allow Lea to recover and forge her own, healthy relationship with food and create a meaningful life. The father's revealing of this story, the family's resulting shared emotions, the therapeutic mobilization of Lea's body, and her father's strong physical embrace greatly alleviated Lea's symptoms, and she embarked on the path towards her own self-defined life. As an adult, she went on to work with children and has opened an association to help groups of people develop creativity and self-confidence and to stimulate the joy of living.

10.5 The family pack

The pack, or packing, is a hydrotherapy body technique that emerged in the 18th century. It involves a wet and cold wrap of the entire body, including the head with a hood. The main indications for use of this unusual and somewhat "old-fashioned" therapeutic technique are acute psychotic crises and chronic disorders of body schema (e.g., body dysmorphic disorder or dysmorphia) (Anzieux, 1989; Chanoit et al., 1988; Delion, 2014). The aim is to give the patient a concrete, tactile stimulus to reorganize the patient's body schema and to control their self-destructive and aggressive tendencies, without alienating them through treatments or isolation ("isolation" is to put a patient into an isolated and closed room in an hospital. It's an old "prison technique"). Water promotes a sense of security and containment while providing a sensation of movement, resulting in enhanced awareness of the body's existence and, due to the feeling of safety and intimacy, it fosters the relationship with the caregivers around the patient. Furthermore, patients often regain the capacity to put feelings into words, allowing them to share significant psychic material that can be processed in psychotherapy.

The classical packing technique involves wrapping the patient with layers of different materials, akin to swaddling a newborn or mummifying. The room should be quiet, with dim and soft lighting. The patient wears underwear. The first layer in contact with the skin is a damp and cold sheet. The second layer is a plastic sheet. The third layer is a thick blanket. The bandaging is carried out by two therapists, ideally a man and a woman, as substitutes for the parents. In addition to the initial wrapping, they have the task of massaging the patient, upon request, to warm him up at the beginning of the session, helping him to become aware of and verbalize bodily sensations through physical pressure. The treatment ends with therapists providing assistance to the patient as he "exits" the packing by removing the wrappings, and to help dry himself. The patient's first sensation is the cold that runs through the body, followed very quickly by a sensation of pleasant, sometimes intense, heat that spreads throughout the body. The therapists encourage the patient to express in words his physical sensations and mental images. The procedure takes about an hour. Usually, the sessions are weekly over five to ten weeks.

We have created and clinically tested a family-based version of this ancient individual treatment technique. We engage parents as co-therapists alongside the actual therapists for a single session. The therapists always perform the wrapping while the parents wait outside the room. Once the wrapping is done, the parents enter the room, replacing the therapists/parental substitutes, and resume their parental roles. They perform various gestures, guided by the therapist. If necessary, the parents also warm up their child through massage and assist the patient to express themselves in verbal and nonverbal emotional exchanges.

At the end of the session, particular attention is paid to the process of exiting from the wrapping pack. This moment is symbolic and metaphorical, harkening back to the parents' earliest contact with their newborn, who is now a teen or adult. In addition to drying and the final, often emotionally regressive warming process, recalling the care offered to a newborn when he is removed from the bath, parents can also help their child to emerge from the "bandages" of this mummification to move towards "liberation," or take off the "diapers" to "grow."

10.6 Case illustration: Becoming free of "presences" and psychological dysfunction

Jules was a white, cisgender, 20-year-old French man. He had to interrupt his university studies about a year and a half before coming for treatment, due to sudden onset of delusions and hallucinations. He reported a constant sensation of "presences" surrounding him, who knew what he was thinking, who communicated with him, who told him what to do, and who were very intrusive. He was haunted by voices that spoke to him and commented on his every move. He felt spied on at home, followed on the street. Initiation of a neuroleptic medication led to rapid improvement in symptoms. However, Jules stopped taking the meds due to unpleasant side effects, until he relapsed and had to restart the medicine. This improvement/relapse sequence occurred three more times, always following treatment discontinuation.

With the fifth crisis, he was sent to my institute, which specialized in the care of adolescents and young adults and that included the family. During this hospitalization, Jules had some classic pack sessions, which calmed his anxieties and helped him become more organized psychologically and became more grounded in reality-based perceptions.

The highlight of the treatment was the family pack session. In the first few minutes of the session, the family sat silently and somewhat cold and distant from one another. Jules was wrapped in three layers for several minutes. He kept motionless and impassive like a mummy. We encouraged the parents to approach Jules to warm him up, which they did gently and quietly. In this confined, safe atmosphere, with soft light, the family members were encouraged to concentrate on themselves.

The father spoke first, revealing for the first time to his family that for years, when alone in a quiet room such as his bedroom, the living room, or his office at work, he also experienced "presences" visiting him, such as his deceased parents and other deceased family members. In addition to his parents, he said that he strongly felt the presence of his brother, a grandfather, and one of his best friends – all of whom died relatively young. He reported that he talked to them in his mind about trivial things, or confided his deepest thoughts and challenges, and asked them for advice. In contrast to the negative, critical tone of the voices Jules heard, the father said he felt much goodwill from them and viewed them as supporting and protecting him. It is noteworthy that the father was not psychotic and functioned well in his work and personal life.

An interaction between father and son then unfolded naturally, allowing Jules to feel deeply affected by what he had heard. There were strong similarities between the father's and son's respective narratives of the "presences." Observing their conversation, we hoped it might transform the emotional quality and meaning of his presences. This is indeed what happened: Hearing his father's gentler experience with presences led Jules to shift his sense of them as spying on and judging him, and he considered viewing them as ancestors that surrounded and protected him. Although aware that what he feels or perceives around him remains a hallucination, he never again felt spied on, commented on, and judged. The treatment dosage for his neuroleptics was reduced by one-third and that for anxiolytics was discontinued. In a follow-up with Jules 12 years later, he had not been rehospitalized.

10.7 Case illustration: Simultaneous treatment of a daughter and her mother for eating disorders

Cloe, a 17-year-old, white, cisgender female, suffered from several eating disorders. She had mistreated her body for almost six years, alternating between periods of severe food restriction (anorexia) and others in which she ingested considerable amounts of food, followed by vomiting (bulimia). During the preliminary visit to our clinic, where her daughter was to be hospitalized, the mother fainted upon entering the intensive therapy unit (ITU) reserved for the most challenging patients: psychotic individuals in delusional crisis, depressed patients with intense suicidal ideation, and those with significant somatic alterations due to eating disorders. This fainting spell interrupted the visit, as she anxiously insisted on leaving immediately. She said that her daughter's planned hospitalization was difficult to face, as she perceived it as a personal failure as a mother. However, she said she understood they had no choice, in light of Cloe's deteriorating health condition. Cloe was subsequently admitted to the unit.

In a subsequent family session, the mother told her children and husband that she too had been hospitalized in that same clinic, practically at the same age as her daughter, also for anorexia nervosa. That period had been traumatic for her and her parents. Her stay in that ITU almost 20 years earlier was a prison-like experience. She was largely confined to her room, with practically no contact with the outside world (her family, the other young people in the institute), and she was forced to eat by staff. She left the ITU against medical advice and subsequently refused any kind of treatment. She struggled alone to overcome her anorexia, frightened by the idea of being hospitalized again one day, and maintained a fraught relationship with food her entire life. Consequently, as a mother, control over meals quickly became an issue with her partner and children.

She revealed in this painful session that she had never told her husband and children or anyone else about her history with anorexia. We explored her "transgenerational institutional history" with this institution. We discussed how treatment for eating disorders had evolved in the ensuing decades from quite forceful, even brutal interventions in asylum-like conditions to a much more collaborative and compassionate approach.

Subsequently, a family pack was proposed with a dual objective: to simultaneously treat both Cloe and her mother. To achieve this, we first helped Cloe, who had now been in the ITU for a few weeks, explain to her mother how, in 20 years, the treatment at the ITU had changed and no longer resembled the prison-like environment her mother had experienced. Even the physical spaces in the unit had changed, including a beautiful common room that viewed a forest through large windows, nicely decorated patient rooms, and freedom of movement within the unit and towards the outside and the rest of the institution. Patients went to groups providing a sense of cohesion and mutual support (Yalom & Leszcz, 2020). With her husband's support, the mother agreed to go to Cloe's room for the special pack session.

In the pack session, the father played a supporting role for his wife and significantly strengthened his bond with his daughter. The most significant moment was Cloe's exit from the wrapping carried out by the two parents, who finally united in supporting their daughter, who literally let herself go. She appeared to experience "intense emotional nourishment" in this moment of shared affection. When Cloe was "sated," warmed, dried, and then dressed, we proposed to her: "You have occupied your parents' minds for a long time. You received all the care and attention you deserved today, with which they will now nourish you. However, you still have one last task to do: Can you help your parents hold each other's arms so that they support each other and show them the way out of the ITU so that you can all resume the course of your lives together?" The look of complicity with us that Cloe gave us made us understand that it was a done deal!

When she was discharged from the hospital three months later, the parents warmly thanked their daughter for having raised them; the father spoke of the awareness he had acquired about his role as an indispensable support for his wife and children and how much he now loves spending time with them. The mother spoke of that "exit from the ITU," which was for her a "liberation from all those dark years," adding: "For me, a weight was lifted, and I could breathe deeply as soon as I walked through that door that finally opened twenty years later. Even eating with my family became a pleasure for the first time in my life!"

10.8 Case illustration: Dramatizing the traumas

Marc is a white, gay, 20-year-old French man. As some people do, he understood why he was struggling. These persons can identify the reasons for their suffering. However, despite this awareness, they are unable to change. They continue to suffer and, at times, to self-destruct. This shows that intellectual understanding is not enough: a somatic approach is necessary to initiate real change. This is what we will illustrate for Marc.

He interrupted his life five years ago, dropping out of school and quitting sports. It all started with a school phobia at the age of 13; during this time, he experienced school refusal until he ultimately dropped out of school at the age of 15.

After that, his anxiety and dysfunctional behavior worsened to the point of having an increasingly disabling social phobia, reaching the point of hardly leaving the house. He also suffered from excruciating migraines, for which he was being treated with opioids, to which he became addicted.

Marc's symptoms seemed to be a response to his parents' very contentious separation. For years, he had been the "hostage" in their conflict and the parents' focus when disagreeing. Although his older sister was held to the same expectations from the parents (success in studies, wise behavior), Marc was engaged to be the triangulated, symptomatic child.

As a child, Marc was considered "fragile," and his parents required frequent doctors' visits for any nonserious common childhood illnesses, such as fevers and abdominal pain, which were psychosomatic, related to his school refusal and anxiety being the focuses of the parents' conflicts.

Marc discovered early in childhood that he could exercise control over his parents as soon as he reported feeling "sick," especially with his migraines. His father had a diagnosis of bipolar disorder and suffered from the same symptoms (migraines).

The father's symptomatology and its apparent effects on Marc caused a big tension between Marc's parents, with the mother frequently blaming the father for Marc's symptoms.

Marc noted that once his migraines developed, the father's painful migraines became much less frequent. The reproaches the mother used to give to the husband were shifted to Marc. Marc even acknowledged that he deliberately simulated or exaggerated migraine attacks to divert his parents' tension and attention onto him.

Despite all his efforts and sacrifices, these failed to avert the parents' separation. He felt a deep sense of failure in his "mission" to keep them together, albeit unhappily. Now feeling useless and incompetent, he sabotaged all his activities and learning through his severe anxiety and phobia.

The parents' separation caused another drama, as the family split up, with each child choosing which parent to live with. The daughter went with the mother out of fear that the mother's depression might otherwise worsen, including losing her zest for life (anhedonia). The mother frequently said that when her daughter finished her university studies, she will have fulfilled her duty and can "disappear," which came across as an emotional/relational threat that created anxiety in the adult children. Marc decided to stay with his father for the same reasons: As noted earlier, the father was bipolar and had already made several suicide attempts. Both children, therefore, feared leaving their parents alone. From that moment on, each parent deeply resented the children's choices of which parent to live with and actually severed their relationship with the child who chose the other parent (father cutting off daughter, mother cutting off Marc).

In summary, Marc was clearly aware from a young age of relational and individual challenges presented to him by his parents and how he attempted to stabilize the parents' marriage through his psychosomatic symptoms in a classic example of Murray Bowen's concept of triangulation. Despite his awareness, he remained stuck in his problems and unable to grow.

During this therapy, we ensured that the two children were present (almost) every time together, alternating with each of their parents. However, these sessions did not result in improvement between each parent and the children, and not at all in the parents' relationship (although brother and sister grew closer), so we decided to offer a unique session with the simultaneous presence of both parents. The sister was "not able" to attend this session, of course raising questions about how Marc alone was triangulated, and the daughter wished to avoid the same fate. The parents accepted the idea despite the animosity between them even five years after separation. At the beginning of the session, parents and Marc were asked to stand up. We asked Marc to come to the center of the room and to spread out his arms. The parents were then asked to take one of their son's hands and pull as hard as possible to bring him close to them. Quickly, the situation became unbearable, both for Marc, who felt torn apart, causing him a lot of physical pain (he even said he feared, at one point, being "ripped apart") and for his parents, who could not bear to hurt him so much.

We paused this sculpting activity to allow their bodies to rest for a while and to discuss the experience. Then, it was suggested that this "sculpture" be resumed. When everyone had resumed their position, and the bodies were tensed again, we suggested the following: "What is the smallest movement that each one could start to make to move towards a more comfortable position?" We intended this changed version of the activity to amplify this small physical change in bodies and tension as a moving metaphor for changes in their respective "relational postures." We hoped that this kinesthetic exercise would lead them to adopt an attitude that is comfortable for all of them simultaneously. In this way, each person becomes responsible for the actions and gestures that might lead them to evolve in a more positive, less conflictual manner. Of course, none of them had any faith that the others would change. And yet, what was extraordinary was the synchronicity of the parents' movements: Both stopped pulling the son towards them simultaneously and moved closer to him until they were almost touching him (and therefore, only about a meter apart from one another). At this moment, Marc spontaneously released each of the parents' hands and grabbed them by their waists. These gestures elicited many emotions from all three of them. As the session moved towards ending, each parent stated that they now understood "firsthand" (notice the allusion to their bodies/hands) the painful, destructive position they had put Marc in, for years. In this sculpting activity, rather than pushing away their son – which made everyone suffer – they first had to move towards him. The parents' newly stated understanding was reassuring for Marc, who in subsequent weeks expressed affection for both parents without feeling like he was betraying the other one. He felt supported, rather than torn apart, by a strong presence and closeness with each parent that was no longer threatening. The final task was for each of the three to call or visit the daughter/sister to share with her what happened, and to invite her into a similar activity designed to eliminate the effects of the ongoing conflict between the parents on her.

10.9 Case illustration: The black eagle

Michèle was a 22-year-old white female. Her story has been previously described in several books (Andolfi, 2022, 2023; Bardou, 2023). Here, we talk about a moment of the care she received that has not been described elsewhere. During childhood, Michèle was the victim of physical assaults and sexual abuse (incest) within her family. There was a transgenerational history of violence on the maternal side and incest on the paternal side. Michèle began to manifest a restrictive anorexia nervosa in adolescence. During her first hospitalization and a first series of family therapies when she was still a teenager, the violent acts perpetrated by her two older brothers on her, the mother's violence directed at her two sons, and the maternal grandfather's violence directed towards the two adult daughters (the mother and the mother's sister, Michèle's aunt) were all addressed. Michèle's two brothers each acknowledged their violence, as well as its consequences on their sister, and sincerely asked for her forgiveness. Their mother did the same with her sons, framing these events in a multigenerational perspective (as she was, in fact, repeating the physical violence she had suffered from her own father). This acknowledgment of the facts and their impacts, of course, did not undo what Michèle had endured, but it brought her significant relief. This treatment led to temporary remission of Michèle's symptoms. However, a few months later, Michèle had a severe relapse with many self-harming acts: massive alcoholism; cuts on the arms, inside the thighs, and abdomen; and dramatic forms of suicidal ideation. This led to a second admission, where she revealed the sexual abuse suffered by her paternal grandfather. Her parents believed her account and supported her. Her father was especially supportive: He confronted his father in an intense session, before accompanying his daughter to file charges against his father

Following this revelation, Michèle's behavior worsened, with multiple acts of self-harm: cuts on her face and breasts, vomiting, and several suicide attempts. Her behavior continued for some years, despite various hospitalizations and specialized treatments.

In these "years of lead" (metaphor used by Michèle to describe the violence she inflicted on herself during all those years), a common thread persisted in some meetings in person or via video between Michèle, her family, and Dr. Andolfi. During a session, Andolfi proposed a final hospitalization with the sole objective of "returning to life," after Michèle responded to Andolfi's warmly delivered but evocative question: "Will this be a fast suicide or a slow suicide?" to which she responded, with a subtle smile, "a slow suicide." She accepted the idea of returning to life but was not yet ready to give up her symptoms despite all her suffering.

Subsequently, an extraordinary meeting occurred via video during the lockdown period linked to COVID-19. Attending the meeting were about 50 people invited by Michèle, all over the world (all parts of France, Australia, Sicily, Rome). The session duration was approximately three hours. All of the people attending expressed a lot of love and support (these sessions are described in Andolfi [2022, 2023]).

Shortly after this meeting, Michèle asked and, indeed, insisted on being admitted: "I am ready!" Probably, what helped Michèle decide to ask for this ultimate hospitalization is precisely all this love sent to her by her friends and her family, and the constant support from Dr. Andolfi and me for five years, and also the trust she had in us.

However, despite a clear commitment on her part and from her loved ones, despite an excellent elaboration of her story and her traumas, despite the access to her feelings that she no longer represses, she could not soothe her psychic suffering without hurting herself physically. "I always have visual and sensory flashes of abuse scenes, with physical sensations of my aggressions." Her traumas are etched into her flesh. She literally senses them (see Van der Kolk, 2014, on the ways in which "the body keeps the score after severe trauma").

Michèle was offered a particular exercise, similar to sculpting (Satir, 1967, 1988), a technique inspired by the famous song "L'Aigle Noir" by the French singer Barbara (1970). The song uses the image of a threatening black eagle that ends up landing on her as a metaphor for the incest suffered by the singer and perpetrated by her father. Michèle knows this song and often mentions it. Since she perceives these "sensory flashes" inside and on her skin, she was offered to lie down on a bed while the two health professionals placed over her a heavy punching bag covered by a large black cloak, a symbolic representation of that black eagle. She initially felt crushed and paralyzed by that sense of helplessness. However, encouraged by health workers who believed in her ability to act, she gradually freed herself, forcefully rejecting the "stalker eagle" out of the bed. She stood up and symbolically dominated that black mass at her feet. Although she hesitated to react violently by kicking it, she found the strength to speak to that representation of her aggressor, affirming her strength, the absence of fear, and her victory over him. As a sign of dominance, she stepped on the punching bag. The situation had now reversed. Michèle dominated her black eagle, her aggressor. There is no violence, only serenity and a deep sense of relief and liberation. She was able to free herself from her trauma and make her sensory flashes disappear. This visual metaphor allowed her to regain a sense of control and domination over her painful past. Tired but unable to sleep, she later created a design representing this experience and visually expressing her resilience (Figure 10.1).

10.10 Conclusion

In most personal or familial situations of loss or trauma, the story is engraved in the bodies of the people who experience them, and these bodies speak and suffer. Cognitive, verbal interventions such as developing awareness of self-destructive thoughts and behaviors, changes in how the patient makes meaning of the trauma, elaboration and verbal expression of psychic or relational patterns, explanations of the patient's psychopathological symptoms, and tracing the transgenerational patterns of disorders are not always sufficient to solve problems. Many patients and families "understand" why they are sick, but they continue to suffer and self-destruct. In other words, the mind alone is not enough. It is often necessary to involve the body and bodily experience. As we have shown, the therapist can facilitate bodily experiences during work with families to help overcome the trials that bodies have

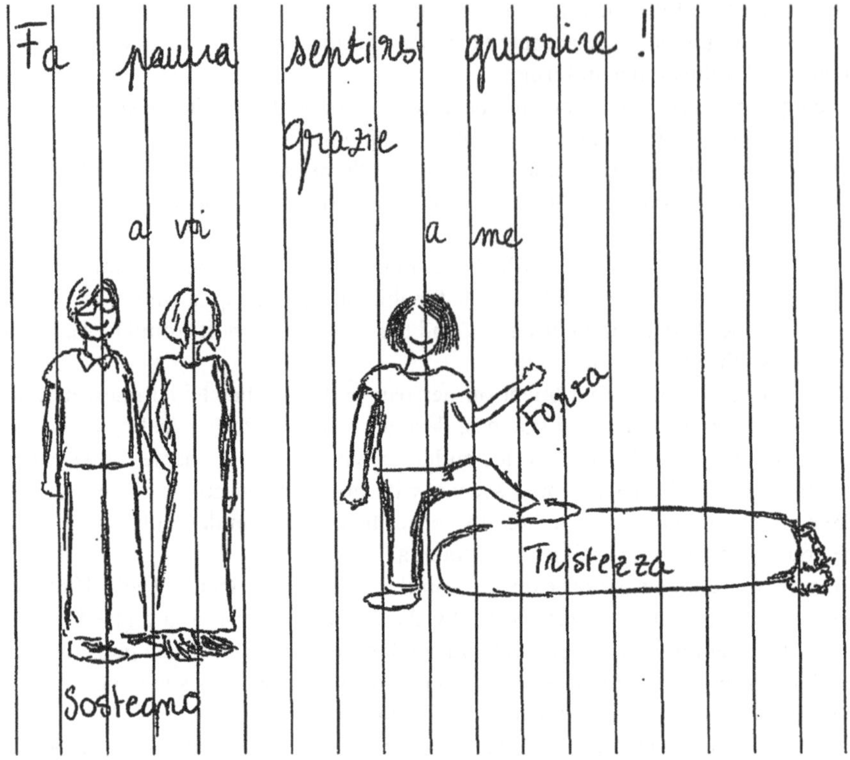

Figure 10.1

been subjected to or that patients inflict upon themselves and to alleviate the physical and psychological suffering of all members of the system.

In all of the situations described here, the bodies that have been mistreated, violated, or abused should not be "protected" (meaning that the therapist, in a position of authority, decides not to allow patients to experience these events because they might consider them too fragile or incapable), but "respected" (meaning that the therapist relies on and adapts to the resources and timing of their patients, allowing them to develop resilience [Cyrulnik, 2009] by experiencing these new bodily and emotional experiences in a safe environment).

To activate this process, the therapist must be able to engage and mobilize their own body, as well as their emotions and reflections, to allow patients to experience these often intense and transformative experiences.

References

Andolfi, M. (2016). *Multi-generational family therapy*. Routledge.
Andolfi, M. (2022). *The gift of truth*. Accademia Press.
Andolfi, M. (2023). *Dal suicidio lento al ritorno alla vita*. Family Therapy Master Series. Multimedia Library APF.
Anzieux, D. (1989). *The skin-ego*. Yale University Press. https://doi.org/10.4324/9780429483202
Argyle, M. (1988). *Bodily communication*. Methuen.
Armstrong, C. (2019). *Rethinking trauma treatment: Attachment, memory reconsolidation, and resilience*. W.W. Norton & Company.

Baltazar, M., Hazem, N., Vilarem, E., Beaucousin, V., Picq, J. L., & Conty, L. (2014). Eye contact elicits bodily self-awareness in human adults. *Cognition, 133*, 120–127. https://doi.org/10.1016/j.cognition.2014.06.009

Barbara. (1970). *L'Aigle Noir*. Philips.

Bardou, D. (2023). *La douleur indolore: De la profondeur noire des abysses à la lumière dans les grands arbres*. International Conference of Family Therapy, The Road That Connects Individual and Social Resources, Assisi.

Chanoit, P. F., Garrabé, J., & Zana, J. P. (1988). *Techniques corporelles en thérapeutique psychiatrique* (Psychiatrie, 37870 A10, 11-1988, p. 9). EMC.

Cyrulnik, B. (2009). *Resilience*. Penguin.

Dana, D. (2018). *The polyvagal theory in therapy: Engaging the rhythm of regulation*. W.W. Norton & Company.

Delion, P. (2014). *Le packing*. Eres.

Ekman, P., & Friesen, W. V. (1972). Hand movements. *Journal of Communication, 22*, 353–374.

Gross, J. J. (Ed.). (2015). *Handbook of emotion regulation* (2nd ed.). Guilford Press.

Hardy, K. V., & Bobes, T. (2016). *Culturally sensitive supervision and training: Diverse perspectives and practical applications*. Routledge. https://doi.org/10.4324/9781315648064

Himanshu, A. K., Kaur, A., & Singla, G. (2020). Rising dysmorphia among adolescents: A cause for concern. *Journal of Family Medicine and Primary Care, 9*(2), 567–570. https://doi.org/10.4103/jfmpc.jfmpc_738_19

Jurist, E. (2018). *Minding emotions: Cultivating mentalization in psychotherapy*. Guilford Press. https://doi.org/10.1177/000306511989726

Lacan, J. (1938). *Le Stade du Miroir: Puissance Seconde de l'Image du Miroir. Structure Narcissique du Moi* (Tome VIII (sous la direction de Wallon, H.), La Vie Mentale, Encyclopédie Française). La Famille.

Levine, P. (1997). *Walking the tiger: Healing trauma*. North Atlantic Books.

Ogden, P., & Fischer, J. (2015). *Sensorimotor psychotherapy: Interventions for trauma and attachment*. W.W. Norton & Company.

Ogden, P., Minton, K., & Pain, C. (2006). *Trauma and the body: A sensorimotor approach to psychotherapy*. W.W. Norton & Company.

Papp, P., Scheinkman, M., & Malpas, J. (2013). Breaking the mold: Sculpting impasses in couples' therapy. *Family Process, 52*, 33–45. https://doi.org/10.1111/famp.12022

Porges, S. W. (2017). *The pocket guide to the polyvagal theory: The transformative power of feeling safe*. W.W. Norton & Company.

Satir, V. (1967). *Conjoint family therapy: A guide to theory and technique*. Science and Behavior Books.

Satir, V. (1988). *The new people making*. Science and Behavior Books.

Scheflen, A. E. (1972). *Body language and the social order*. Prentice-Hall.

Shapiro, F. (2018). *Eye movement desensitization and reprocessing (EMDR) therapy* (3rd ed.). Guilford Press.

Stern, D. (2004). *The present moment in psychotherapy and everyday life*. W.W. Norton & Company. https://doi.org/10.1176/appi.ajp.162.3.642

Van der Kolk, B. (2014). *The body keeps the score: Brain, mind, and body in the healing of trauma*. Penguin Books.

Yalom, I. D., & Leszcz, M. (2020). *The theory and practice of group psychotherapy* (6th ed.) Basic Books.

11

SUICIDE ATTEMPTS IN ADOLESCENCE

The line where life and death meet

Maurizio Andolfi

11.1 Introduction

The rates of self-injury and suicide attempts in adolescence have been increasing dramatically in the last decade. According to the World Health Organization (WHO, 2024), suicide is the second highest cause of death for adolescents and young adults, immediately following road accidents. After COVID, calls for help from teenagers contemplating suicide increased by 55%. If we examine this worrying phenomenon through a systemic lens, these suicidal behaviors seem to be a strong sign of existential malaise and bewilderment the new generation is experiencing, as they face the upheavals of our entire planet and their very uncertain future. COVID-19 and its social and family consequences, increasingly brutal wars endangering the very essence of our human condition and resulting in the decline of moral values and mass exodus, and climate change are just some of the challenges families and communities are having to deal with. Children and adolescents are paying the highest price.

A teenager's threat of suicide is not only a warning sign for his or her family, but it should prompt mental health institutions, schools, and the entire community to create a solidarity and support network. This can only happen if we overcome the social stigma associated with a child's suicidal behavior, a stigma based on people's mistrust and fear of disquieting behavior that is deemed socially unacceptable, nurtured through blame and guilt. All of this leads families to disguise or "deny" a child's suicide attempt once it has not turned into a real suicide.

> He leaned too far out from the balcony and fell over; he accidentally took his mum's medication; he was playing with a rope and got caught up in it; they poured something into her cocktail; he lost control of his car and fell from an overpass.

These are just some of the many lies that families try to convince themselves of out of fear of acknowledging the truthfulness of their own child's self-injurious behavior with the resulting anguish over the fear of its social implications. Thus, once one's child has escaped danger, you would like things to go back to the way they were before, you stop talking about the "accident" at home, as if naming death were dangerous and could increase the risk of new attempts and, even more so, raise the family's levels of anxiety and bewilderment. During hospitalization for attempted suicide, the tendency is to create a cocoon-like safety environment where everything must be under control, avoiding as much as possible rising anxiety and worry levels. For the same reasons, it is preferable to avoid the

DOI: 10.4324/9781003536765-14

presence of family members who might "stress" both the young person and healthcare professionals, who often adopt a corporate attitude and activate a series of defensive strategies due to being faced with the risk of being reported for malpractice.

Much has been written in the systemic literature about the usefulness of family therapy in dealing with suicide attempts in adolescence (Carr, 2009; Cha et al., 2017; Asarnow & Mehlum, 2019). In particular, research has demonstrated the effectiveness of dialectical behavior therapy (Mehlum et al., 2014; Gøtzsche & Gøtzsche, 2017), cognitive-behavioral family treatment (Asarnow et al., 2017), and attachment-based family therapy (Diamond et al., 2010; Barnes, 2011). However, all of this research focuses on the adolescent's individual change supported by his or her family members. Little attention is given to changes in family relationships as a primary goal.

This chapter presents a systemic intervention based on a multigenerational developmental model, with a special focus on the cultural and social dimensions of the family, in addressing the issue of suicidal behavior in adolescence (Andolfi, 2017, 2007). The family members, peer group, and the community at large can become the main players for treatment starting from hospitalization until the later stages when the adolescent returns home. Utilizing their support and resources, the intention is to break the vicious cycle between the adolescent's low self-esteem, fragile identity, and feelings of shame (*I'm not worth anything*) and the negative connotations often reinforced by family, school, and peer group (*You are not worth anything*). Extended family therapy and network interventions can become the safest and most effective setting to encourage deep transformations in an adolescent's identity and interpersonal world. Affection, love, and solidarity shared among family members, friends, and neighbors are wonderful opportunities for an at-risk adolescent to reconsider the value of life and are equally important for the family to carry out deep transformations within it as well as in the broader social context (Andolfi et al., 1977; Barreto & Camarotti, 2021).

For this to happen, therapists should embrace a profoundly humanistic approach based on self-knowledge, acquisition of an inner balance, and a therapeutic serenity in attuning to people's suffering (Satir, 1967; Yalom, 1980; Andolfi, 2022). Once these special skills are learnt, the therapist will then be able to move from the *comfort zone of life defense* to meet suicidal young persons in that *liminal space* between life and death and engage families and communities in an extraordinary healing project. At the same time, psychotherapists should open the door of their professional offices and look for social resources, making their voices heard even at the political level where decisions are made about the orientation of mental health services and their practices, as described in the Assisi Manifesto (Andolfi et al., 2023).

11.2 Risk factors associated with suicidal behavior

Several researchers have been describing risk factors functioning at various levels – individual, family, and social – in order to understand and possibly prevent suicidal behavior in adolescence (Asarnow & Mehlum, 2019; Carr, 2009; Erdem & Safi, 2018; Bilsen, 2018; Apter & Wasserman, 2006; Brent & Mann, 2006; Cheng et al., 2000; Biddle et al., 2008). In this section, we summarized a few of them, useful to reflect on the multigenerational-systemic approach in dealing with adolescents at risk.

11.2.1 Individual risk factors

These are the adolescent's own thoughts, phrases, signals, and behaviors. The very first risk factor is having already attempted suicide or exhibited self-injurious behaviors, such as cutting oneself, banging one's head on the wall, breaking a glass window with one's fist, or getting involved in serious road accidents. Suicidal ideation, quite common in adolescence and not only in adolescence, in itself is a generic signal, but when accompanied by its verbalization in the family with the implication that the family would be better off without the teen ("I must get out of the way," "the day I leave home will be a liberation for everyone"), and extreme changes in mood or persistent states of sadness and isolation at home, it could become a serious indicator of a possible transition to suicidal action. In addition to behaviors unrelated to pre-existing forms of psychopathology, which may be partly new and unforeseen, the presence of mental illness (psychosis, bipolar or personality disorders, and others), drug addiction, alcohol abuse, or compulsive gambling, to name only the most common, should be considered as relevant suicide risk factors.

11.2.2 Familial risk factors

If we consider suicide not as an isolated individual choice but rather as an extreme form of interpersonal communication, the family's relational difficulties may represent a strong element of suicidal risk in adolescence. At the same time, the family may be the most relevant protective factor in the growth of the adolescent (Wagner et al., 2003; Andolfi, 2007). So, for better or worse, the family plays an extraordinarily important role.

The most serious risk factor amongst them all is repeated sexual abuse within the family, a devastating event in the construction of personality in childhood and adolescence with serious repercussions on the child's mental health and emotional stability. The most relevant consequence of sexual abuse is the betrayal of trust developed because of the abuse being denied by the very people who should be the source of primary care and protection, such as parents, grandparents, and siblings, that you would never expect betrayal from. Sheinberg and Fraenkel (2001) and Fraenkel (2019) coined the term "relational trauma" to capture the most inevitable effect of incest – the fracturing of relationships that the child expected to be safe and protective. Incest can result in a condition of suffering and shame that continues for years and that can lead to a series of psychopathological events of which the suicide attempt, repeated over time, represents only one component, and that is generally represented as a form of slow suicide – thoroughly described by a former client named Chantal – which we shall be discussing later.

Physical abuse and extreme forms of domestic violence may equally represent other family-based risk factors for suicide in adolescence. The strong emotional impact of one parent's acts of violence against the other parent on a young child and on his or her fragile identity is underestimated far too often by professionals. A family sculpture was used in therapy by a 17-year-old boy after an unsuccessful suicide attempt to show how he used his body as a shield to defend his mother from his father's brutal behavior. As he wept while reliving that condition, he kept repeating to himself: "I couldn't take it anymore, I couldn't take it anymore."

Hostile parental separations and divorces with severe triangulation of the children in the couple's conflict, as well as the feeling of being rejected or neglected by the parents, may be other triggering elements (Asarnow & Mehlum, 2019).

11.2.3 Case illustration

Marta, 18 years old, swallowed 150 tablets of Tegretol (an anti-epileptic drug) and was still alive after a miraculous hospitalization in the intensive care unit. After two months, in the first family therapy session with her parents present, Marta said she has never felt loved or wanted, especially by her father. The parents had been divorced for many years and were still in strong conflict. Her grandmother verbally confirmed Marta's sense of not being wanted in one of the subsequent meetings with the mother's family: Marta was born because her grandmother had stopped her daughter from having an abortion. To learn the full story of Marta and her therapy with the family, please refer to previous works (Andolfi & Mascellani, 2023; Andolfi, 2007).

Marta's candor towards her parents taught me that in family therapy you should always ask an adolescent if he or she felt wanted and loved by his/her parents. This question may seem inappropriate or too direct, like asking a sad young person in session if he has ever thought about committing suicide, but it is definitely liberating. These kinds of direct questions, if asked casually and empathetically, can lead to gaining vast knowledge and understanding of family dynamics. These sorts of questions also facilitate a strong therapeutic alliance with an adolescent at risk, who then feels the therapist is genuinely interested in tuning into his or her anxieties (Andolfi, 2017; Lancini, 2019).

Other risk factors are the loss of special people in the emotional balance of a family or in the emotional well-being of a teenager who has grown up with the love and care of a special grandparent (the grandparents that on more than one occasion we have described as beacons) and cannot accept the idea of losing him/her forever. "I want to join him/her!"

Pressures emanating from the larger society's expectations can also be risk factors. These expectations are magnified in social media, extensive use of which has been found to be associated with depression and anxiety in teens. In modern society, the prevailing family and educational models focus on image, high success, and appearance, and children are forced into early adulthood from a very young age. This means that any sort of failure, such as a bad grade at school or romantic rejection, may not be accepted, and if you do not live up to expectations, it's better to "disappear."

11.2.4 Social risk factors

School, peer groups, and neighborhoods can be risk factors, especially in severely degraded social and environmental settings, which are sometimes veritable ghettos on the outskirts of large urban agglomerations. Although school represents the greatest socialization agency for childhood and adolescence, when placed in violent and deprived contexts, it can become a training ground for bullying and social anger that needs to find its victims among the most fragile and defenseless children. Verbal violence and denigration can reach the highest point through social media. Cyberbullying, sexting, and revenge porn, with the exposure and dissemination of intimate material online, can lead to unbearable feelings of shame, frequently accompanied by suicidal behavior, experienced as the only way out of a situation of distress that is becoming increasingly unbearable.

At the root of suicidal behavior lies the vicious circle described earlier where the low self-esteem and fragile identity of so many young people are strengthened by broken families, lacking affection and financial resources, and by strongly judgmental and authoritarian schools located in poor and run-down neighborhoods, acting as a negative reinforcement to the destructive or irresponsible behavior of adolescents. If the value of life is perceived as so uncertain or even nonexistent with no positive role models capable of providing stable emotional support, it is easy to take action and directly or indirectly put one's life at risk.

11.3 Case illustration: Demonstrative suicide attempts

Believing demonstrative gestures should not be taken too seriously is a mistake, for prior suicide attempts are one of the best predictors of future attempts. Even a guy who says he attempted suicide with two tablets of Panadol should be taken seriously. It is always better to accept and never dumb down the communicative significance of a gesture that often replaces words to and seeks the attention and care of parents or other important caregivers (Lancini, 2021).

Jerry, a 15-year-old boy whom I met in therapy, used to go and lie along the tracks of a closed-down train station every day. This was seen as a sign of the boy's mental imbalance by his parents – both of whom were doctors – and they were extremely worried about it. What they failed to grasp was the meaning of this behavior as a desperate plea for love and care from a son who wanted to be noticed.

For this desired attention, he felt he had to "lie along the railway tracks" waiting for a train to make him disappear from this world, a train that ironically would never pass.

Another younger boy, Gregory, would devise the most bizarre forms of suicide attempts. He would jump off the roof of his very low, one-story home while his father drove his car into the backyard or would pretend to hang himself with a string in the bathroom next to his father's study to be, in his words, "seen and saved." Like the previously described boy, in this case the boy had been brought to therapy by a parent who was seriously concerned he might be suffering from some serious mental disorder. The father, who was torn with anguish, was unable to understand his son's message: a dramatic cry to be seen and cared for.

11.4 Case illustration: The liminal space between life and death

Maggie was 21 years old when I started seeing her in therapy, and she had suffered from anorexia since she was 12. Over the years it had developed into a chronic form, a condition that can lead to death due to severe kidney, heart, and skeletal impairment. The clinical picture was exacerbated by a condition of isolation due to a desire to avoid negative remarks and other behaviors based on strong social stigma (Robinson, 2018). As a result of her anorexia, Maggie was physically very frail and emaciated, had difficulty showering, and even completing simple actions such as going shopping and tidying up her room because everything was extremely strenuous. When I first met her, the girl lived alone in her own room separated from her parents' house, but her mother assisted her in everything. In addition to the anorexic disorder, she suffered from a persistent state of anxiety and a severe obsessive-compulsive disorder that enslaved her life, forcing her into constant rituals, and not being able to fall asleep before 3:30 in the morning.

Building the alliance with Maggie was a crucial and definitely difficult step. Maggie had never trusted her family, let alone the various doctors and psychiatrists she had had to deal with for nine years. In particular, Maggie remembered a long period she had to spend in hospital because of her starvation as the worst experience of her life, from which she said she came out of severely traumatized. The amount of time I spent talking about her strong desires to die, never mentioning food or pushing her to eat, was a key point in gaining her trust and entering her complex inner world. Therapy was conducted both in person and online. Skype connections allowed me to enter her narrow living space, a small room with a darkened window and dim light illuminating a giant chair where Maggie, with her slim, emaciated little body, seemed to sink. It appeared more like a tomb than the room of a young woman barely out of her teens. Yet she had trusted me to enter this space between life and death, and I had not been afraid to do so.

During our sessions, we spoke about many different things, including this tyranny of being unable to fall asleep before 3:30 a.m., which for many would be absolutely impossible without going crazy. The second basic element in building the alliance with Maggie was introducing the idea that there was a "tyrant" forcing her into these inhuman rhythms of sleep and wake up and that together we would have to kill him, which surprised and amused her. By externalizing the symptom (White & Epston, 1989), the tyrant thus became the third party in our relationship, and we could reach a therapeutic understanding and share the same goals. The first success came when Maggie admitted that she had fallen asleep at 3:15 a.m., as the result of a superhuman struggle! Our sessions also ranged over other topics: her family and my professional and personal life that Maggie seemed very interested in. She liked the idea that at 80 years old I still had the curiosity and pleasure to explore her life, her illness, and her growth processes. Maggie had a keen introspective capacity and artistic culture, so I encouraged her to write short stories about her life as a child, which she described as her only happy time, and later, stories about her illness.

These improvements went hand in hand with family therapy, where we were able to relativize Maggie's problems and enter her family's many old and new unresolved conflicts. Maggie was born shortly after the dramatic ending of an unhappy marriage, in which her mother had suffered repeated domestic violence from her husband and had suddenly run away from home with two small children. Maggie was born with the burden of a very violent past and with two older siblings whose emotional growth was seriously damaged. She could have been a happy child from her mother's second marriage, but unfortunately her mother's new partner had an extremely violent family history, got drunk and aggressive as well, and even during the session he was totally rejected and attacked by Maggie's eldest sister, who simply wanted to protect her mother from another violent man. These issues were addressed in therapy during sessions that sometimes got overheated, and Maggie often acted as co-therapist in delving into family stories and wounds that were still open and painful. I have often wondered how it is possible that children so tried by life as to look like "living skeletons," while bearing visible signs on their bodies of a condition of extreme fragility and total surrender of their lives, at the same time are like "treasure troves of knowledge and relational sensitivity." The effects of family therapy and the beginning of positive transformations in the family went hand in hand with some changes in Maggie's: behavior—first of all, her return home to a brighter room and a commitment to sit at the dinner table with her parents, partially modifying her diet and moving out of her total isolation.

Maggie and I exchanged many emails, but I would like to include a few that seem like real "essays" in understanding the liminal space between life and death. Interestingly, Maggie sent me these emails at the time she was gradually moving into the space of life. I have extracted and quoted some sentences from them.

> My last year of online University classes gave me the chance to describe my liminal space. This space is neither here nor there. From a physical point of view these spaces may be airports, churches, cemeteries; on a more essential level it could be the murky gray matter that lies between black and white. I think I exist in a state of liminality, in the space between life and death. It is like a waiting room allowing one or the other possibility to take shape. Maurizio, I have told you several times in our meetings that I do not wish to die, but nor do I like to live. I do not fear death as much as I fear life. I live in a gray space where I don't need to be anything.

A few months later, during waking hours she wrote:

> I'm so tired of everyone in the family worrying about me, whether I want to live or die. I have decided that I have reached rock bottom, things can't get worse than this. My life is small, I admit it, but from now on it can become bigger and that is what I'm going to do. The first step is finding renewed pleasure in life. I am lost and I want to find myself again. I want to go out for a coffee with my sister, watch the sunset, write, read, paint. I want passion and happiness back into my life.

Almost one year later, she wrote:

> Dear Maurizio, I am learning to be patient and self-tolerant. I have to remind myself not to go back to my old beliefs based on guilt, shame and self-punishment. I am tired of the many lies that my Eating Disorders have betrayed me with! The last few months I have gone against my illness and made big changes. I am eating a wider variety of food. I get up in the morning! I am spending time with my family and have dinner with my parents. I am learning to feel my emotions and not chase them away. My parents and sister have been an amazing support in my rebirth. And then Andrea arrived (her brother's son), he is a baby, fragile and new and each of us has to take on our new role.

11.5 When the community heals

Within the family therapy movement, which originated in the US, network therapy (Speck & Attneave, 1973), home visits and crisis interventions (Ackerman et al., 1982), and more generally systemic work in the community, including schools and marginal neighborhoods, had been developing since the 1960s–70s in parallel with the process of deinstitutionalization of mental illness. In this regard, Zwerling (Andolfi & Zwerling, 1980) was an innovator in the US by opening the doors of Bronx State Hospital, following the leads of the European psychiatric renewal movement promoted by Laing (1960) in the UK, Basaglia (1973) in Italy, and Guattari in France (1984). The mental health professionals of that time worked in communities and were trained in urban ghettos. There, families and adolescents at risk were met (Minuchin et al., 1967), and network therapy was born. From 1987 on, it was further developed by Barreto in the favelas of Brazil, thanks to his model of integrative community therapy (Barreto & Camarotti, 2021).

In line with these developments, I would like to briefly mention two very significant personal experiences, the first in the South Bronx in the 1970s in the climate of social engagement described earlier; the second, much later, in the Australian Aboriginal communities. Both experiences, although very different from each other, addressed the same issues of social exclusion and injustice and subsequent suicidal behavior in adolescence.

11.5.1 The South Bronx project

In the systemic work project we conducted in the South Bronx (Andolfi et al., 1977) at a neighborhood middle school attended by very angry and violent African American and Puerto Rican teenagers, who inevitably were destined for criminal careers, we practitioners were often confronted with the suicide risk of 15-year-old young persons. The "extreme sport" of the time was jumping from one downhill elevator to another uphill elevator outside dilapidated neighborhood buildings. The consequence was often that of getting crushed between the two elevators.

The project, designed together with the local Community Mental Health Center, was to work on a systemic approach to reduce the high level of interpersonal violence inside the school. At the same time, we were encouraging positive resources in the classroom peer group, the teacher group, and with the "family members" (who were often mothers and sometimes concerned neighbors rather than actual family) present in the community. Class group meetings allowed the youths to understand the full sense of their feeling of "emptiness" and to talk about how the underlying question "Who am I?" distressed them. Without a core identity, it is difficult to answer the question "Who am I?" and have a purpose in life, which seems to have very little value to those who intend to take their own life, as well as to those adults who are supposed to take care of that teen and his life. Disappearing altogether then became the best solution these youths could hold in mind to prevent them from sinking into further anguish and avoiding a criminal career.

11.5.2 Teenagers' suicide attempts in the Australian aboriginal communities

I have been living in Australia for many years and have encountered the reality of Aboriginal communities, where the phenomenon of suicide among young people is truly terrifying and is the leading cause of death in adolescence. Intergenerational trauma and extreme poverty of entire communities is associated with a wide variety of mental illnesses, dramatic forms of sexual abuse, and excessive use of drugs. All of this is reinforced by an ancient and unresolved feeling of social exclusion and by a complete lack of an acceptable future, notwithstanding the spiritual values and ancient conceptions of the Universe, the creative symbolism about ancestors, and the values of the land that is home to human beings, which are so well represented in the extraordinary paintings of native Australians (Andolfi & Cavalieri, 2008).

Once again, the lack of identity and lack of an emotional support social network and real social inclusion prevents healthy growth and drives suicidal behavior. I was given a good lesson in "leaping over prejudices" when I met Chris Sarra, a great Aboriginal educator, in the Cherbourg (Queensland) community, who had managed to "work wonders" by turning an Aboriginal school into a school of excellence. He was convinced that only school could change the direction of many children's lives and save them. For this reason, he had the words *Strong, Smart and Deadly* printed on their school uniforms. The strong belief conveyed to the pupils that they were *Strong, Smart and Deadly* had enabled a true identity shift. The feeling of pride in recognizing themselves as different from the stereotype depicting Aboriginal peoples as stupid and lacking vital energy had produced a radical transformation (Sarra, 2013). The same approach later adopted in so many schools across the continent has fostered a strong and positive view of what it means to be Aboriginal in Australia's contemporary society.

11.6 Case illustration: How to seek resources in the social network

The story of Chantal, an 18-year-old French girl, helps us understand how the community can become part of care even today, to the extent that we are able to break out of the dominant psychiatric culture. I met Chantal in my first consultation session in Paris with her entire family and with Dominique, the psychiatrist and family therapist who has been following the girl for her self-injurious behavior, repeated suicide attempts, and severe eating disorders in a Residential Institute for Difficult Adolescents. In the session, I learned that during her childhood, Chantal suffered repeated sexual abuse by her paternal grandfather. Ever since the abuse was revealed, her father's relationship with his entire family of origin was abruptly severed due to the defensive wall erected by his family, which had resolutely denied the facts. There was a long history of physical violence in her mother's family too, and in Chantal's growing up, repeated quarrels and disagreements occurred between her two brothers and her father, who was often away for work.

Chantal's story is reported extensively in previous works (Andolfi, 2022); the purpose here is to focus exclusively on the positive effects produced by a network meeting suggested to Chantal after several months of therapy. Recently, before this meeting, the girl had relapsed into a severe state of depression with constant thoughts of death and severe anorexic symptoms. She felt dirty and ashamed, she perceived herself as a nobody and a real burden to everyone, stating that hers was a "slow and inevitable suicide." For these reasons, she had been rushed into a psychiatric ward in the local hospital. The proposal for a network meeting was made to Chantal when she was in the hospital, while her parents were connected through Zoom from home. I told Chantal the story of Bianca, a teenager I previously worked with for severe anorexia. She had the same death thoughts and was so weak and emaciated that every night her mother had to check whether she was still breathing or whether she was dead. I told Chantal about the proposal I made to Bianca to invite for a special session all the people who loved her and who would go to her funeral, which perhaps could be avoided if they attended this meeting. Chantal came to life, especially when she heard that 23 people had attended this meeting and had restored Bianca's faith in life through their love and solidarity (Andolfi, 2022).

This made it easier to give substance to the proposal of inviting to a Zoom session all family members, schoolmates, guests of the Institute for Adolescents – in short, all the people who loved and cared for Chantal. The meeting was proposed to occur only if she was going back to the Institute for the period required to "come back to life." Chantal's immediate response was, "No one will come for me." Two weeks later, Dominique informed me that approximately 40 people were to be present at the meeting, including about 30 family members, friends, and schoolmates, with the other ten being guests of the Institute of Adolescents The meeting lasted three hours with the active participation of many of the attendees. It is impossible to recap the full content of that reunion and even more difficult to fully capture the intimate context of the session, in which everybody wanted to make their care and concern for Chantal heard. Her parents, her brothers, and a special granny who raised Chantal since she was a little child, peers and friends from primary and high school, adolescents who shared the same program at the juvenile institution, talked with great emotions. Words, memories, tears, and personal anecdotes were intertwined together, offering a live testimony to the therapeutic power of love. The networking meeting broke the halo of stigma and prejudice against a family raised in shame and guilt and laid the foundation for a great transformation in family relationships. Chantal's healing process began from the love and solidarity shown by 40 people at this special meeting, and it ended almost one year later.

This is a summary of the letter Chantal sent me after the meeting:

> This Zoom consultation produced strong emotions in me and in everyone else. I was able to talk openly about my suffering and my idea of slow suicide. I saw how saddened my parents were, but they were also very close and supportive. The best idea was to bring together all the people who love me and whom I love, and the second was going back to the Institute for Adolescents as a life project. I felt a strong friendship and goodwill toward my family. I was touched to discover that no one wanted me to fail! This encounter seemed a gift to me, since I no longer believed in anything.

Chantal spent about six months back at the Institute for Adolescents. A few days before Christmas of that year, I received another email from Chantal, which she intitled "The proclamation of healing," together with pictures she had drawn and photos. Here are a few lines from her long email:

> Today I go back home and say goodbye to the Institution! I say goodbye to psychiatry and in particular to my life as a psychiatrist case. Now I can say I'm healed. My disease has become a fragility full of strength. Now more than ever I feel myself alive. I'm alive because I can smile and I can cry and my life is full of colors, from the brightest to the darkest shade.

11.7 Conclusion

I would like to end this chapter with a sentence from the Assisi Manifesto (Andolfi et al., 2023). It states the need to recognize the interconnection of individuals, families, communities, and societies, thus having a truly systematic view of families, of their cultural values and resources. Suicidal ideation and attempts are among the most isolating behaviors a person can engage in, never mind a teenager who is at a life stage often dominated by the desire for connection with peers and for working on gaining independence from parents, as well as the stage in which the young person begins to plan the next steps of their life. Systemic therapy is ideally suited to address suicidality in teens, as it emphasizes the centrality of relationships in mental health and illness and provides the perspectives and tools to heal and strengthen those relationships.

References

Ackerman, N., Bloch, D., & Simon, R. (1982). *The strength of family therapy: Selected papers of Nathan W. Ackerman*. Brunner/Mazel.

Andolfi, M. (2007). Tentativi di suicidio e morti traumatiche in adolescenza. In M. Andolfi & A. D'Elia (Eds.), *Le perdite e le risorse della famiglia* (1st ed., pp. 99–133). Raffaello Cortina.

Andolfi, M. (2017). *Multigenerational family therapy*. Routledge.

Andolfi, M. (2022). *The gift of truth*. Accademia Press.

Andolfi, M., & Cavalieri, L. (2008). Viaggio all'interno della realtà aborigena in Australia. *Terapia Familiare, 88*(3), 5–25.

Andolfi, M., & The International Faculty. (2023). *The Assisi manifesto*. Family Therapy Academy.

Andolfi, M., & Mascellani, A. (2023). *Teen voices: Tales of family therapy*. Accademia Press.

Andolfi, M., Stein., D., & Skinner, J. (1977). A system approach to the child, school, family and community in an urban area. *The American Journal of Community Psychology, 5*(1), 33–43. https://doi.org/10.1007/BF00884783

Andolfi, M., & Zwerling, I. (1980). *Dimensions of family therapy*. Guilford Press.

Apter, A., & Wasserman, D. (2006). Adolescent attempted suicide. In R. King & A. Apter (Eds.), *Suicide in children and adolescents* (pp. 1–40). Cambridge University Press.

Asarnow, J. R., Hughes, J. L., Babeva, K. N., & Sugar, C. A. (2017). Cognitive-behavioural family treatment for suicide attempt prevention: A randomized controlled trial. *Journal of the American Academy of Child & Adolescent Psychiatry, 56*(6), 506–514. https://doi.org/10.1016/j.jaac.2017.03.015

Asarnow, J. R., & Mehlum, L. (2019). Treatment for suicidal and self-harming adolescents-advances in suicide prevention care. *Journal of Child Psychology and Psychiatry, 60*(10), 1046–1054. https://doi.org/10.1176/appi.focus.23021005

Barnes, A. J. (2011). Attachment-based family therapy reduces suicidal ideation in adolescents. *Evidence-Based Mental Health, 14*(1), 1. https://doi.org/10.1136/ebmh.14.1.8

Barreto, A., & Camarotti, H. (2021). *Integrative community therapy*. Springer.

Basaglia, F. (Ed.). (1973). *L'istituzione negata*. Einaudi.

Biddle, L., Donovan, J., Hawton, K., Kapur, N., & Gunnel, D. (2008). Suicide and the internet. *BMJ, 336*, 800–802. https//doi.org/10.11336/bmj.39525.442674.AD

Bilsen, J. (2018). Suicide and youth: Risk factors. *Frontiers in Psychiatry, 9*, 1–5. https//doi.org/10.3389/fpsyt.2018.00540

Brent, D., & Mann, J. (2006). Familiar factors in adolescent suicide behaviour. In R. King & A. Apter (Eds.), *Suicide in children and adolescents* (pp. 86–117). Cambridge University Press.

Carr, A. (2009). The effectiveness of family therapy and systemic interventions for child-focused problems. *Journal of Family Therapy, 31*(1), 46–74. https://doi.org/10.1111/j.1467-6427.2008.00451.x

Cha, C. B., Franz, P. J., Guzman, E., Glenn, C. R., Kleiman, E. M., & Nock, M. K. (2017). Annual research review: Suicide among youth-epidemiology, aetiology and treatment. *Journal of Child Psychology and Psychiatry, 59*(4), 460–482. https://doi.org/10.1111/jcpp.12831

Cheng, A., Chen., T., Chen, T., & Jenkins, R. (2000). Psychosocial and psychiatric risk factors for suicide. *British Journal of Psychiatry, 177*, 360–365. https://doi.org/10.1192/bjp.177.4.360

Diamond, G. S., Wintersteen, M. B., Brown, G. K., Diamong, G. M., Gallop, R., Shefel, K., & Levy, S. (2010). Attachment based family therapy for adolescents with suicidal ideation: A randomized controlled trial. *Journal American Academy Child Adolescent Psychiatry, 49*(2), 122–131. https://doi.org/10.1097/00004583-201002000-00006

Erdem, G., & Safi, O. A. (2018). The cultural lens approach to Bowen family system theory: Contribution of family change theory. *Journal of Family Theory and Review, 10*(2), 469–483. https://doi.org/10.1111/jftr.12258

Fraenkel, P. (2019). Incest and relational trauma: The systemic narrative feminist model. In P. Pitta & C. Datchi (Eds.), *Integrative couple and family therapies: Treatment models for complex clinical issues* (pp. 47–70). American Psychological Association Press. https://dx.doi.org/10.1037/0000151-003

Gøtzsche, P. C., & Gøtzsche, P. K. (2017). Cognitive behavioral therapy halves the risk of repeated suicide attempts: Systematic review. *Journal of the Royal Society of Medicine, 110*(10), 404–410. https://doi.org/10.1177/0141076817731904

Guattari, F. (1984). *Molecular revolution: Psychiatry and politics*. Penguin.

Laing, R. D. (1960). *The divided self*. Pelican Books.

Lancini, M. (2019). *Il ritiro sociale degli adolescenti*. Raffaello Cortina.

Lancini, M. (2021). *L'età tradita*. Raffaello Cortina.

Mehlum, L., Tørmoen, A., Ramberg, M., Haga, E., Diep, L. M., Laberg, S., Larsson, B. S., Stanley, B. H., Miller, A. L., Sund, A. M., & Grøholt, B. (2014). Dialectical behavior therapy for adolescents with repeated suicidal and self-harming behavior: A randomized trial. *Journal American Academy Child Adolescent Psychiatry, 53*(10), 1082–1091. https://doi.org/10.1016/j.jaac.2014.07.003

Minuchin, S., Montalvo, B., Guerney, B., Rosman, B. L., & Schumer, F. (1967). *Families of the slums*. Basic Books.

Robinson, P. (2018). Severe and enduring disorders: Recognition and management. *Advance in Psychiatric Treatment*, *20*(6), 392–401. http://dx.doi.org/10.1192/apt.bp.113.011841
Sarra, C. (2013). *Good morning Mr. Sarra*. University of Queensland Press.
Satir, V. (1967). *Conjoint family therapy: A guide to theory and technique*. Science and Behavioural Books.
Sheinberg, M., & Fraenkel, P. (2001). *The relational trauma of incest: A family-based approach to treatment*. Guilford Press.
Speck, R. V., & Attneave, C. L. (1973). *Family networks*. Pantheon Books.
Wagner, B. M., Silverman, M. A., & Martin, C. E. (2003). Family factors in youth suicidal behaviour. *American Behavioural Scientist*, *46*(9), 1171–1191. https://doi.org/10.1177/0002764202250661
White, M., & Epston, D. (1989). *Literate means to therapeutic ends*. Dulwich Centre Publications.
WHO. (2024). *Adolescent and young adult health (online)*. World Health Organization.
Yalom, I. (1980). *Existential psychotherapy*. Basic Books.

12

WORKING WITH HIGH-RISK ADOLESCENTS IN COMBINED GROUP AND FAMILY THERAPY

José Barrera

12.1 Introduction

Public mental health is a context that serves a wide range of disorders, ranging from serious situations that significantly affect the capacity to adapt to stressors, compromising individual development to the point of hindering processes of individuation and socialization enormously. The unit in which I have worked for more than ten years receives a high percentage of patients who are severely affected. The patients are children and adolescents, with a more intense level of problems compared to the other community units dealing with mental health, serving people of all age groups. It is important to give a therapeutic response consistent with serious problems that are present with minors, trying to open possibilities that allow them to achieve the functioning necessary to face the challenges of life, and thus be able to experience a satisfactory life.

I began to conduct family therapy at the end of the 1980s, and then I began doing group therapy at the end of the 1990s. This background has allowed me to integrate enough experience to combine both approaches in the treatment of problems that manifest in the adolescent stage, which sometimes represent a huge obstacle in the evolution of the person and the family, and is accompanied by severe pain and suffering. My experience as a psychotherapist encompasses clinical problems of every age group, but in the last ten years I have started focusing mainly on children and adolescents and their families, although it is easy to imagine, I do not always encounter a single patient identified as younger than 18, but it is also possible that another sibling may be affected, as well as the parents. However, therapeutic work is based on an initial demand formulated around the figure of the minor.

In 1988, I took care of a family in mental health with adolescents suffering from tics. The following year, I had the good fortune to have a consultation with Dr. Maurizio Andolfi. Although I had previously begun to be interested in training as a family therapist, that occasion marked the true awakening to systematic practices and transgenerational lenses in therapy, as well as the boarding of problems that present themselves during adolescence. Since then, my clinical journey has been developed and guided by family therapy as the focus in addressing problems for which the consultants asked for help, whether they were individuals, families, or institutions.

At the end of the 1990s and at the start of the 2000s, I started working with groups maintaining a relational and interpersonal vision, initially with adult patients. It was not until the following decade that I started working with adolescents in groups. My task with the child and juvenile mental health unit began after the summer of 2012 with the design of a therapeutic device that integrated the group

DOI: 10.4324/9781003536765-15

approach with various adolescents and their parents, defining a group therapy space for the children and another for the parents, as well as an art therapy space for both. The design also included multi-family sessions configured as the place of intersection of other spaces to integrate experiences (Barrera & Gómez, 2016). Ever since, I maintain group activity along with family therapy, which is my approach of choice.

12.2 Combining family and group therapy

Some of the teenagers that are in group therapy also attend family therapy with me. That is, they receive family and group therapy. The rest are cared for by colleagues from the unit according to their respective approaches or reference schemes. Therefore, not all the adolescents that participate in group therapy have family therapy in their plan.

The decision about a treatment plan that covers both frames is made after an initial evaluation based on what is supposed to respond to the need of the case. I propose to start group therapy for patients I have started to treat according to the relational approach and that I attend in family therapy. Something similar happens with the other patients who are referred internally to the unit's group therapy program; the difference is that these other patients are not previously treated with family therapy, but in accordance with the approach of the respective physicians. In any case, group therapy is a complementary approach.

Being able to see the evolution of the adolescents in both settings – family and group – I found it revealing because in addition to giving a more intensive character to the treatment, various facets could be seen, as well as observing functioning of two different and complementary systems.

12.3 Therapeutic approach

I can affirm that psychotherapeutic work is articulated around two axes, described as follows:

- The *axis of the family*, with family therapy sessions with an average interval between them of four weeks. Each session lasts one hour. The process varies in duration, depending on the evolution and achievement of objectives. In general, it lasts no more than 15 sessions or two years. Throughout the process, we tend to invite members of the family of origin of one or both parents.
- The *axis of equals*, strange in principle, as is usual and necessary in group therapy, and which is reflected in biweekly sessions, an hour and a half in duration. The treatment lasts one to two years, interrupted by the summer months, and in the second year, new additions often occur. The process usually lasts two years. The number of members in a group ranges from six to ten young people.

In the 2022–2023 edition of the groups formed, added complementary activity was added: we offered, from the initiative of a clinical psychologist colleague to the parents of the adolescents a parallel group, being led by the parent and the occupational therapist. We defined this group as supportive for parents, and we established a monthly frequency. Likewise, we are organizing two multi-family meetings, at the beginning and at the end of the annual edition. In the current edition, there are three multi-family meetings throughout the process, at the beginning, at the halfway point, and at the end.

In my therapist role, I oversee conducting the group sessions with the children and the family sessions with a portion of them. Clinical or psychiatric psychology residents usually accompany me, as observers who transcribe the sessions, or have the task of intervening with 15–20 minutes remaining at the end of each session to highlight those signs that seem relevant to them. It could be objected that my work as a coordinator of both spaces entails framing difficulties, but even recognizing the complexity, it has its advantages. Synthetically, the position I adopt in family therapies is that of exploration with curiosity (Cecchin, 1987), while in group sessions it is to facilitate cohesion (Yalom, 2005; Rodríguez-Zafra & García, 2022), without losing sight that each member comes from a system with its own values, beliefs, and worldviews (Serebrinsky, 2012), therefore considering the similarities and difficulties. In both frames, the common posture is to orient oneself in the fluctuating attention towards the singularity. It can be argued whether it would not be better to act as a therapist in one space and as a co-therapist in another, and that may be the case, although I like to think I have greater maneuverability. I think that the self-referential bias can be used for therapeutic purposes, since I can amplify some elements considering the relevance that I attribute to its appearance in one space or another. Perhaps it would be complicated if all the patients in the group were treated by me in family therapy, but that is not the case.

12.4 Guiding ideas

The first would be the purpose of accelerating or enhancing the recovery process of the adolescent and his or her family. I have met very damaged and isolated adolescents who, by participating in both therapeutic experiences, could feel better supported, as well as more hopeful about the future.

The other idea that guides our work is that the adolescent transition had to be dealt with, helping to achieve progressive separation, reduce the individuation deficit (Bowen, 1978), facilitate co-individuation, and advance in facing the identity crisis of this period. I consider that group also has the connotation of transitional space (Winnicott, 1953), a space between fantasy and reality, between inside and outside, that provides emotional support to accommodate deep existential anguish and facilitate the achievement of the experience of emotional independence. So, the idea of transition has a double reading and acquires the value of an analogy about adolescence and therapy.

12.5 Adolescent problems that were treated

Patients treated in family therapy and group therapy are considered high risk, and they present various problems that include self-harming behaviors, threats and self-harm attempts, high levels of anxiety and recurrent anxiety attacks, emotional instability, traumatic experiences and dissociative symptoms, depressive states, eating disorders, social withdrawal, school absenteeism, and high-risk mental states.

12.6 The family therapy framework

The main framework is the multigenerational family therapy approach (Andolfi, 2016, 2022; Andolfi & Mascellani, 2013), contemplating the adolescent as the family member who allows access to the system and is configured as an aid to the therapist. This means that throughout the family treatment, members of the extended family and significant others will be involved, and that they will be invited at some point in the process to look for possibilities and resources with which to face problems and suffering. The adolescent often collaborates in the exploration of difficult and adverse family stories that allude to events and developments that have been marginalized, denying its validity or importance in fruitless attempts to keep at bay the chronic anguish that parents carry since before building their procreative family, and that inevitably reappears when a problem emerges in one of their children, when going through the adolescent stage.

So, we connect the young person's risky adolescence with stories and with experiences, from difficult family members or those who are adverse to the therapeutic task, which seeks to mobilize resources to dissolve the evolutionary blockage that imposes the problem and the response that is given to it, always counting on the adolescent as the person who will help in the exploration and facilitate the transformation process. Presumably, in this process, the young person will free himself or herself from emotional and vital constraints, to give way to a joint development of individuation that opens the possibilities of growth in the family group.

Among the pioneers, I recognize the influence of Bowen's work (1978) on my perspective on the functioning of the family and the constitution of the individual. However, as everyone knows, any therapist is exposed to multiple theoretical and experiential influences. To name some of them, I would highlight family therapy and the narrative practice of Michael White (1983, 2007; White & Epston, 1990). It is interesting to note that at the beginning, White reported the use of the transgenerational perspective for the understanding and family therapy of anorexia nervosa (White, 1983). Externalizing problems can be integrated with the multigenerational approach. In this line, new stories can be generated that represent the evolution of the family over time when they are freed from the restrictions imposed by problems, discovering that when they can recognize denied aspects this enriches the emotional connection while making it possible to conquer one's own individuality.

I also recognize the influence of the contributions of Marcelo Pakman with his critical-poetic approach in psychotherapy (Pakman, 2011, 2014, 2018, 2022). The therapist's posture with his receptivity to singular elements in the therapeutic encounter, being able to attend to the emergence of events, leads to new coping experiences facing marginalized aspects, placing people in a new state of consciousness and relational and emotional integration.

12.7 The group therapy model

Under the systemic umbrella, I integrate various approaches, such as the interpersonal existential vision of Irvin Yalom (1989, 2005), the operational group with the notion of emergent and the theory of the link of Enrique Pichón-Rivière (1975), as well as psychodramatic techniques (Población & López, 1997, 2000; Moreno, 1987).

The systemic conception of the group is due to Yvon Agazarian (1989, 2011), with his system-centered group theory and the theory of the invisible group. This author uses purely systemic concepts to understand group functioning and the interface between the individual and the group, assuming isomorphism among the group, the subgroup, and the individual, so that the individual is contextualized in the subsystem and the individual is contextualized in the group. Using the notion of subgrouping to work on conflicts in group dynamics as a means for evolution of the group and its members, helps to facilitate the emergence of functional subgroups, capable of addressing conflicts that will make the group and, therefore, the individuals grow. The work is done with the subgroups that would be the constituents of the group, not the individuals. This innovation makes it easier to work with adolescents, avoiding personalism, since the self is not placed at the center of the world or the scene. Thus, a certain problem or personal aspect can be seen as something like that of other members of the group, and the person is experienced as connected to another member within a subgroup and, at the same time, different from other members who constitute another subgroup.

In connection with these contributions, the idea of circulating information among group members is central to the conduct of the sessions, favoring cohesion and relational glue. We must help participation become balanced, linking significant elements between the members due to similarities or differences.

Finally, I must recognize the influence of various currents of systemic and narrative therapy, where work with generations and resonance (Elkaïm, 1990) is not lost sight of. The relationship among the various approaches is recursive and gives rise to their integration.

12.8 Configuration of therapeutic groups

The composition is not made by grouping clinical diagnoses; therefore, in this sense, the groups are heterogeneous. What they have in common is precisely the life stage they are going through, sharing the existential problems and evolutionary tasks typical of that stage. Two age ranges are distinguished. Based on an evaluation and preparatory interview, groups of boys and girls are formed in two ranges: between 13 and 15 years old, and between 15 and 17 years old. The groups integrate participants who demonstrate both internalizing (inhibited or "acting in") and externalizing (disruptive or "acting out") behavior.

For the selection of patients, reasons for rejection are considered, such as lack of motivation, previous failure in group therapy, hostile rejection of group therapy, unrealistic expectations (such as "to make friends"), or very deviant behavior (extreme negativism, self-marginalization). The predisposition to the group task is also assessed, to the extent that the young person perceives himself or herself as capable of speaking in front of strangers and adjusts to the objectives and tasks of the group.

12.9 Assumptions

It is assumed that combining family and group therapy implies that the emerging phenomena in both approaches constitute information that circulates recursively between both levels of experience, producing therapeutic effects. This dual process is directed towards increasing differentiation and individuation, in coherence with a state of better integration-connection of the adolescent with the family and with the group. I can affirm that combined therapeutic work helps with the definition of identity, which is shaped to the extent that individuals can achieve greater autonomy within a connected system.

The recursive interaction between the two approaches alludes to a dynamic process of inclusion-exclusion consistent with a stable self-organizing system that facilitates adolescent separation, preventing rupture or fusion (Figure 12.1).

The feedback between both approaches constitutes a potential help to achieve a series of therapeutic goals that point to several possibilities, as illustrated in Figure 12.2.

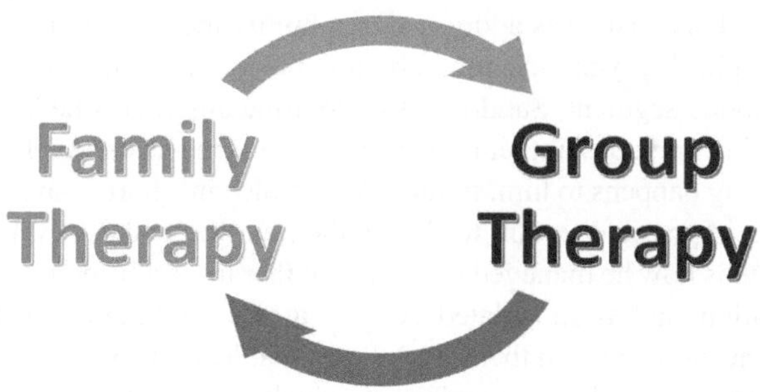

Figure 12.1

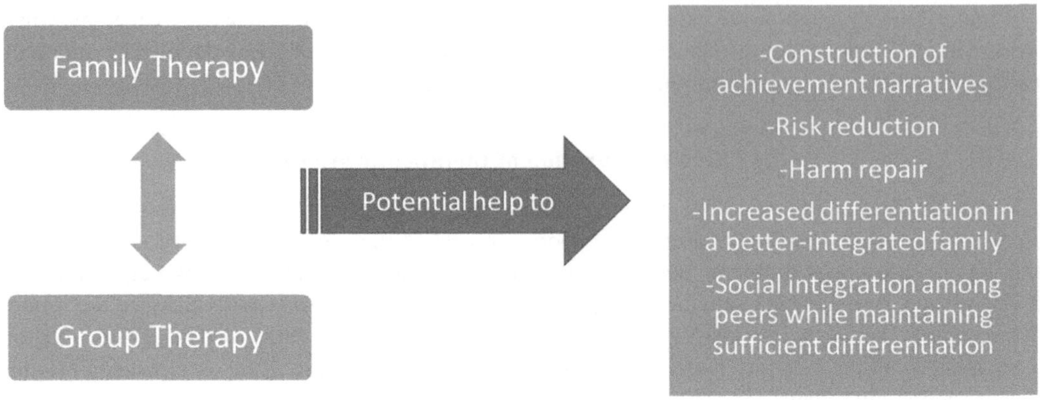

Figure 12.2

12.10 Case illustrations

1. Session number 5 of a group made up of six teenagers: three girls and three boys, one of them trans. One of the girls is absent from the session.

   In the session's initial segment, the difficulty that some boys have in their relationship with their respective mothers is addressed. Of the five adolescents who participate in the session, a verbal interaction occurs between the trans boy (Axel) and the other two boys (Sandro and Ander), while the two girls do not intervene.

   To contextualize, it must be said that Axel has had an open story since 2021, after carrying out an autolytic attempt by precipitation, which left him lame in one leg, while fighting to "come out of the closet," announcing that he was changing his name. He had a severed relationship with his father, but his father's presence in the hospital has generated some hope in him, since his father told him that he had always wanted to have a son (he has two older daughters from a previous relationship), and there has been rapprochement, even with the father returning home stably. However, Axel's hope does not take long to fade, since his relationship with his father is quite frustrating with communications of rejection and disqualification. It is also confirmed that the parental couple has separated.

   Axel has overcome a period of intense conflict with his mother, which had led him to show a recurrence of altered states with restlessness, high anxiety, and despair, considering making a new suicide attempt. This crisis was addressed in a family therapy session in which he demanded admission to the hospital's psychiatric unit, about ten days before the group session.

   In the aforementioned segment, Sandro talks about the arguments he has with his mother, who gets upset, yells at him, and does not let him speak. With some haste, Axel intervenes to communicate that the same thing happens to him. In turn, Ander, also in a hurry, says the same thing happens to him and that it is impossible to talk to the mother, and he makes several interventions in that sense. In turn, Axel tells how he managed to get his mother to start listening to him and both manage to have "a conversation" not as an isolated event, but as something that is being maintained over time, creating a connection between them. He relates that he took as a model the dialogue between the two of them with me in a family session, in which I asked: "Can I speak?" and he refers to speaking using the same formula. Reiterate the message and the expression "and it works!" It thus conveys that mother and son can now have "a conversation." At this point, I ask how the group can help Sandro have a conversation with his own mother, and the group's task focuses on this point.

It can be seen from this fragment that the therapeutic work of a family session, in which a mother-child conflict and the associated alterations are addressed, together with the question of identity, gives rise to a positive result after the sessions by developing an emotional encounter between both, experiencing recognition from the mother. That event, of which there is news in the group session, based on the singular event that took place in the preceding family session, constitutes itself as an act of repair of the bond, which acts not only by sharing the achievement but also making present the group hope. In turn, it responds to a similar element (conflictive mother-child relationship) through the emotional resonance that emerges between various members of the group, introducing new coping possibilities.

As additional information, we can point out that the quality of mother-child relationships in the children of the group has progressively improved, reducing the influence of conflict and emotional reactivity, and therefore an interpersonal encounter with greater differentiation of the selves.

2. Session 14 of a group composed of eight adolescents: one boy, five girls, and two gender-fluid adolescents, one of them with a male name. One of the girls is missing.

Rania, 14 years old, says that her parents, her sister, and she took a trip for the first time in a long time, in which there was an incident between her father and her while they were eating in a restaurant. She explains that, for no apparent reason, she received verbal attacks from her father, feeling very hurt and ashamed, so she left the restaurant sobbing. She described the father as angry, venting his anger frequently, and the mother as fearful of the father, as is the sister. Another girl, Karen, intervenes to propose that perhaps Rania is protecting her mother and her sister by becoming the target of her father's anger. Rania, in reaction to Karen's comment, talks about how conflicts are avoided in the family and submitted to the father, and emotionally she opens more.

To contextualize this exchange, in May 2022, Karen had been hospitalized for four days due to attempted suicide, persistent suicidal thoughts, and dysregulation with behavioral alterations. A crisis intervention was performed and, upon discharge, she began receiving therapy with the family. The animosity towards her father was in the foreground, along with his non-contingent response. The father is a man in conflict with his family of origin, with emotional cuts from everyone except for his brother. He suffers from an anxiety disorder, sometimes has explosive reactions, and drinks to calm his anxiety. In turn, the mother shows intense concern for her daughter. She is a very dedicated mother of two daughters. Her role in the family is that of appeaser. This mother lives geographically very far from her family of origin and does not acknowledge being affected by it, maintaining contact during the summer or Christmas and whenever she can. Her mother (Karen's grandmother) died in 2018, an event that preceded the first community mental health consultation.

Meanwhile, two other girls, who join a stereotypical subgrouping for several sessions, appear intrusive and anxious, with blunt interventions, giving advice about the story of Rania's stressful experience. One of these two girls is an only child and has received various family therapy sessions, notably reducing confrontation with her mother and the self-destructive behaviors for which she consults. She is proud of her achievements and tries to help the group with an attitude of superiority as if she were "back from everything," although as the sessions progressed it would moderate.

In this case, what we observe is first a reformulation made by one of the girls, Karen, to another, Rania, regarding the story of a painful experience on a family trip and which gives an account of the type of relationships that are sustained inside their family. What happens next is a greater openness, not just from the girl targeted, Rania, but from the group. Again, as in the previous case, similar elements produce resonance and allow us to initiate or activate a process of coping with painful and harmful experiences related to significant ties, opening possibilities for repair in the future. Unlike the previous vignette, Karen's intervention, although also inspired by her own experience of family therapy, represents a different movement from communicating an achievement since, rather, it has to do with the incorporation of a relational vision of the conflicts and attitudes and the pain they produce.

12.11 Results

Since no tests have been administered, the results are observational and clinical, resulting in the following achievements:

- Resume studies in cases of absenteeism and abandonment
- Prosocial initiatives and establishing connections between peers
- Reduction of clinical symptoms, for example, reduction/disappearance of self-harming ideation or actions, reduction of anxiety levels, self-regulation, reduction/disappearance of self-harm
- Family conflict management
- Increased parental collaboration
- Change in parental attitudes

12.12 Reflections

While the professionals of the unit generally agree on the benefits of implementing group psychotherapy regardless of the clinical approach that is being applied (clinical follow-up, psychopharmacological, individual therapy, guidance), in my experience, family psychotherapy together with group psychotherapy resonates at the relational level, exerting greater therapeutic influence.

The use of both approaches takes on greater meaning in the adolescent stage than in any other life stage, with the representation of two differentiated spaces. The interplay and transition between the two spaces helps face the identity crisis of this vital phase and recognize the desire for exploration and discovery, along with the need for the supportive presence of parents. It is common for the group sessions' theme to be organized family relationships. The echo of family therapy on group therapy is evident, generating a more complex level of interaction.

Regarding the role of parents in parallel groups, in the evaluations made by the participants we found very positive responses in general, with descriptions of what they learned in the sessions.

As for multifamily meetings, it must be said that they constitute common spaces of integration and socialization, not only for young people and their families, but also for therapists and their interventions, where it is possible to participate in another way, everyone in common, also being articulated as a ritual meeting of the beginning, midpoint, and end of the process.

References

Agazarian, Y. M. (1989). The invisible group: An integrational theory of group as a whole. *Group Analysis, 22*(4), 355–369. https://doi.org/10.1177/0533316489224001

Agazarian, Y. M. (2011). *Systems-centred theory and practice: The contribution of Yvonne Agazarian*. Routledge.

Andolfi, M. (2016). *Multi-generational family therapy: Tools and resources for the therapist*. Routledge.

Andolfi, M. (2022). *The gift of truth: The inner journey of the therapist*. Accademia Press.

Andolfi, M., & Mascellani, A. (2013). *Teen voices: Tales from family therapy*. Wisdom Moon Publishing.

Barrera, J., & Gómez, M. D. (2016). Intervenciones psicoterapéuticas con familias. *Cuadernos de Psiquiatría y Psicoterapia del Niño y del Adolescente, 61*, 65–72.

Bowen, M. (1978). *Family therapy in clinical practice*. Jason Aronson, Inc.

Cecchin, G. (1987). Hypothesizing, circularity, and neutrality revisited: An invitation to curiosity. *Family Process, 26*, 405–413. https://doi.org/10.1111/j.1545-5300.1987.00405.x

Elkaïm, M. (1990). *If you love me, don't love me: Constructions and reality and change in family therapy*. Basic Books.

Moreno, J. L. (1987). *The essential Moreno: Writings on psychodrama, group method, and spontaneity*. Springer Publishing Company.

Pakman, M. (2011). *Palabras que permanecen, palabras por venir. Micropolítica y poética en psicoterapia*. Editorial Gedisa.

Pakman, M. (2014). *Texturas de la imaginación*. Editorial Gedisa.

Pakman, M. (2018). *El sentido de lo justo*. Editorial Gedisa.

Pakman, M. (2022). *El exilio del Mesías*. Editorial Gedisa.

Pichón-Rivière, E. (1975). *El proceso grupal*. Nueva Visión.

Población, P., & López, E. (1997). *La escultura y otras técnicas psicodramáticas aplicadas en psicoterapia*. Editorial Paidós.

Población, P., & López, E. (2000). *Introducción al role-playing pedagógico*. Editorial Desclée de Brouwer.

Rodríguez-Zafra, M., & García, L. (2022). La cohesión grupal: Factor terapéutico y requisito para la creación de un grupo de terapia. *Revista de Psicoterapia*, *33*(121),71–84. https://doi.org/10.33898/rdp.v33i121.1122

Serebrinsky, H. (2012). Psicoterapia de Grupo. *Ajayu (Online)*, *10*(2), 132–155. www.scielo.org.bo/scielo.php?script=sci_arttext&pid=S2077216120120002000001&lng=es&nrm=iso

White, M. (1983). "Anorexia Nervosa": A transgenerational system perspective. *Family Process*, *22*(3), 255–273. https://doi.org/10.1111/j.1545-5300.1983.00255.x

White, M. (2007). *Maps of narrative practice*. W.W. Norton & Company.

White, M., & Epston, D. (1990). *Narrative means to therapeutic ends*. W.W. Norton & Company.

Winnicott, D. W. (1953). Transitional objects and transitional phenomena. *International Journal of Psycho-Analysis*, *34*, 89–97.

Yalom, I. (2005). *Theory and practice of group psychotherapy* (5th ed.). Basic Books.

Yalom, I. D. (1989). *Love's executioner: And other tales of psychotherapy*. Basic Books/Hachette Book Group.

13
GENDER VARIANCE IN ADOLESCENCE

Patrizia Petiva, Eva Gerino, and Rossella Siragusa

13.1 Introduction

The growing number of adolescents who do not identify with the biological sex assigned to them at birth, or who do not conform with the social rules that such assignment expects, is a phenomenon of increasing significance. The new forms of expression of sexuality and identities in adolescents raise questions for clinicians and families that are not easy to resolve, since the new "gender expressions" challenge entrenched positions both in the scientific and social fields.

The health system data provided by the *Standards of Care, Version 8* guidelines, developed by the World Professional Association for Transgender Health (Coleman et al., 2022), show that the proportion of people who identify as transgender worldwide is between 0.3% and 0.5% in adults and between 1.2% and 2.7% among minors.

Tavistock & Portman's Gender Identity Development Service (GIDS) in London, the only referral center for minors with gender variance in the UK up until 2023, received more than 5,000 patients in 2021, compared to 250 in 2011.

There is no research in Italy showing the number of minors diagnosed with gender dysphoria or who define themselves as transgender. Because there is a lack of formal research on the epidemiology of gender dysphoria in childhood, some studies report percentages around 2–3%, which may be underestimated. As far as adolescents are concerned, Ferrara and colleagues (2021) write:

> Studies on clinical groups indicate a prevalence between 1 in 7,400 and 1 in 100,000 for males and between 1 in 30,400 and 1 in 400,000 for females, but in this case too, actual figures may be higher because surveys are based only on people accessing specialized centers.
>
> *(Ferrara et al., 2021)*

According to the Italian National Observatory on Gender Identity (ONIG), the number of individuals accessing specialized centers in Italy in 2018 was 250, a figure that is progressively increasing, especially after Covid lockdown (Caldarera et al., 2019).

The concrete and emotional repercussions produced by the pandemic have had a significant impact on the entire population, especially in some of the most marginalized groups. In adolescents, lockdown – and the drastic reduction of social life reaching the point of forced isolation, the closure of schools, meeting and recreational spaces – increased stress-related symptoms. According to

DOI: 10.4324/9781003536765-16

UNICEF's research study conducted in Italy, the issues that united adolescents were characterized by the perception of experiencing an abnormal adolescence, with emotional and relational fallout not fully recognized by adults. Some specific groups with significant problems, such as unaccompanied foreign minors (MSNAs) and youth who identify as LGBTQI+, seem to have spent more time within their own group, mixing less with other peers. LGBTQI+ youth "already involved on a journey seeking their own sexual orientation and gender identity, have remained even longer within their closed circle of friends, those who understand and respect them" (Viola et al., 2021, p. 3).

Another interesting element, also according to the *Standards of Care, Version 8*, concerns a significant increase in the number of Assigned Female at Birth (AFAB) persons requiring gender transitioning. This increase is between 2.5 and 7.1 times higher than for Assigned Male at Birth (AMAB) persons. Lemma (2022), in her most recent book, questions the function of social roles in the increase of female-to-male transition requests. According to some research, the overrepresentation of AFAB people could be an effect of misogyny and of the difficulty and dangers of declaring oneself a lesbian in certain cultural contexts (Kaltiala-Heino et al., 2015) – a hypothesis involving the political, social, and cultural spheres.

Although there is no consensus on the reasons for the increase in people identifying as transgender, we can speculate that this is the result of a multiplicity of factors. One important factor is the vaster amount of information available online about transgender identity and use of the social media that encourages acknowledging one's gender identity. There is also information and guidance about the subsequent coming-out process, which is often challenging but, in the end, can be exhilarating and freeing. Another factor is the progressive depathologizing of the transgender identity, which has led to a reduction in stigma and an increase in access to specialized centers to undertake the transitioning process.

In previous articles (Petiva & Spirito, 2015, 2020), we approached the journey of adolescents diagnosed with gender dysphoria from a perspective that privileged the role of the family in relation to how attachment processes affect overcoming a developmental crisis that involves all members of the system. Little research has been focused on the attachment styles of transgender children, adolescents, or adults. The relationship between caregivers and gender-nonconforming children after the coming-out process is often characterized by a state of confusion and parental rejection (Amodeo et al., 2015). Working with the family system reduces the risk of internalizing social stigma and transphobia. After the adolescent verbalizes his/her gender variance, the whole family is emotionally and concretely involved and can represent a fundamental resource of competences, comprehension, and resilience – or its opposite! The value of family intervention comes from the awareness that for the adolescent it is important to receive a sign of comprehension and acceptance of his/her path. This is only possible if the family share part of the path.

In accordance with Asen and Fonagy's (2015) and Asen and Scholtz's (2010) approach to fostering greater mentalization in work with the parent and sibling subsystems, we supported the mirroring/mentalizing process among members of the family system at the most critical developmental moment after adolescents' coming out.

We assess the change in relational dynamics inside and outside the family system, and the change in personal experiences of each member after the coming out. Within this time frame, all the members need to redefine themselves in relation to other systems (parents, siblings, friends, school, society, etc.) as well as consider its internal dimension. During this phase, the therapeutic work is finalized to help persons expressing and giving meaning to their emotional approach to particular events. For example: Who do I want to share my coming out with?

Being under stress makes it difficult to control and evaluate one's mental states, and this causes huge mistakes in "reading" others and attributing feelings, desires, etc. Our work with the families is intended to help them develop family members' capacity to recognize others' thoughts and feelings and respect their perspective. This allows the family to lessen prejudices and preconceptions.

More recently, the variety of gender-related expressions among adolescents has confronted us with clinical situations in which the binarism of the young person with gender dysphoria, described in our earlier work, no longer corresponded to a complex, unstable self-perception, often characterized more by exclusionary statements like "I am not . . . , I don't feel like . . ." than by positive definitions of self (e.g., "I am . . ."). In this clinical setting, it is important to keep in mind the individual's evolutionary moment, being aware that the expressions of sexual fluidity expressed by the adolescent cannot be derived from gender identities of an adult, which are generally marked by greater stability. For this reason, developmental age is particularly controversial in terms of the clinical responses that can be provided, both in the psychological and medical fields, in a stage during their life cycle "with its rapid fluctuations in the assumption and abandonment of identities that characterize this phase of development" (Lemma, 2022, p. 24).

Dealing with the fluidity of nonbinary youth represents a continuous challenge for therapists that often begins in seeking a common language, e.g., how the youth's often-shifting identity is to be named in a manner that feels correct to the youth, even if confusing or distressing to the family. Indeed, conflict between the youth and their family often centers on this issue of the language a nonbinary youth chooses to describe themselves. The issue of the fluid and nonbinary experience of gender identity is discussed in more detail as follows.

13.2 Fluidity and nonbinary identity in adolescence

If, in our and in many other cultures, gender is conceived according to a binary model,[1] then for many transgender people, gender can be experienced and can express itself outside of the binary gender categorization. It is intuitive that a binary conception is of little use in understanding the issue of transgenderism, as it tends to polarize and oppose identities, an attitude we find in both academic debates and public discussions.

It is essential to remember that we are not referring to a homogeneous population and that there are different ways of expressing one's gender, multiple pathways and routes that do not necessarily lead solely to a turn in a male or female direction or that involve significant suffering, impaired functioning, or resorting to specific hormonal (masculinizing or feminizing) or surgical treatments. In recent years, in fact, the scientific community has increasingly looked at gender not necessarily as a dichotomous variable – male or female – but rather as characterized by a much broader and more complex range of intermediate shades and tones (Crapanzano et al., 2021). Coleman and colleagues (2022) write:

> While our ability to understand the development of gender identity in adolescence is constantly evolving, it is equally important to know what is still unknown. In the developmental years, there is no certainty about the outcomes of the subject's self-reported identity: while for some, the declaration of one's gender identity as not conforming to the sex assigned at birth is early and stable over time, in other cases, the statement of non-conformity occurs only during the onset of pubertal development or during adolescence.
>
> *(Coleman et al., 2022)*

For these reasons, there is no single path suitable for all. If the adolescent's request is to be helped through psychotherapy, then the therapist's task will be to safeguard their search for self-expression, avoiding any affirmative or corrective position of the adolescent's recognized identity. Because psychotherapy gives the opportunity to explore the unconscious aspects of one's choices, but also the doubts and resistance related to the choice, the ethical responsibility we take on as therapists is to stand by the adolescent without judgment.

13.3 Families of adolescents with nonbinary identity

Sexuality is developed and gender identity is strengthened during adolescence. Acceptance by the family is crucial, as we have seen repeatedly in work with adolescents. Families who are involved and have accepted and supported their child's journey to transition have encouraged their achievement of better stability and existential balance.

The emergence of nonbinary gender identity in adolescence is linked to a developmental stage characterized by the physical and psychological changes typical of the onset of adulthood. The adolescent, while experiencing the possible definitions of his/her gender identity, challenges the known, reassuring (to parents and others), and clear representation the parent had of their child's identity. Being the close, caring adult capable of guiding and reassuring, without imposing any choices towards the preferred identity direction, is a challenge for the family.

To illustrate the process and challenges both for the transgender youth and their family, we present two cases. In the first case, Viola/Purple is a girl who in childhood found herself angrily sustaining her gender as she was constantly mistaken for a male, but who during adolescence asserts the need to identify as neither male nor female. In Simon's case, on the other hand, previous work with the family allowed the therapist to explore the parents' gender expectations, their ways of relating to their child's body, and how much these reverberate in his perceived conformity or nonconformity to parental desires and adherence to the expectations in the parents' minds formed before his birth. In his case, being able to express himself using his preferred name, Simon, represents the achievement of a laboriously pursued goal. For this reason, the therapists used only his initials (S.) during the period when Simon could not yet assert his male identity.

The use of the specific pronoun in the two following clinical cases underscores the subjectivity of the perception of one's own or others' gender.

13.4 Case illustration

13.4.1 Viola/Purple

The parents of 16-year-old Viola discovered her self-inflicted cuts and contacted a psychotherapist, who met with her for several months. These individual sessions were discontinued at the girl's request, due to the therapist's inexperience in gender identity issues. The following year, she began psychotherapy with a new female therapist, chosen by her parents for her expertise with gender-variant adolescents, since Viola had started to express doubts over her gender identity to her family. The dialogue with the new therapist started on the issue of her self-injury. The symbolic significance of the self-destructive gesture became apparent. What did she want to cut away? She said, first of all, her own name. She explained that her name is connected to the female gender never fully recognized. Purple, the name by which she asked to be called during the session, is the name of a manga character, a warrior full of contradictions, sometimes brave and resolute, sometimes wimpy and dependent. She came to the sessions dressed in a loose, black jumpsuit and T-shirt, her hair colored purple.

Purple reported that she had neither "good nor bad" childhood memories. When asked by the therapist to find some pictures of herself as a child, she brought a couple with her brother; they were dressed and their hair was combed in almost the same way, in dull, neutral-colored clothes, almost like a photograph in black-and-white. The mother recalls that Viola, as a child, was often mistaken for a boy, and she would reply angrily, shouting, "My name is Viola and I am a girl!"

The conversation with Viola/Purple takes a completely different turn from that of the manga she favors: no twists and turns, but exhausting stories – "I have nothing to say today," said to avoid topics that aroused negative emotions. Only the therapist's patient listening slowly gives meaning to this journey.

13.4.2 Viola's family

Besides her name, another thing Viola's cutting represents is her desire to "cut away" the sometimes oppressive and silent family atmosphere. The mother comes across as a woman with a resolute and hasty manner, unwilling to talk about herself but ready to define her daughter in a one-dimensional and unempathetic way.

She describes Viola as "the one who makes big decisions hastily. . . ." The mother is concerned that Viola might embark on the transition path without the necessary awareness and understanding of what this path will entail. On the other hand, the mother acknowledges that, as a child, Viola did not like to dress as a girl and preferred to play with boys.

It is during the first pandemic lockdown that Purple, in the connections she initiated on the Internet with other teenagers, acknowledged herself, in the alternating self-definitions of her virtual friends. She felt these new friends seemed better able to describe the way she feels, than were her parents.

"You have given me a girl's name, but I don't feel like that!" she told her parents. Her mother replied, "I'm sure you don't have a binary identity, but I don't think you're transgender." This initial response to their daughter's declaration about herself seemed to reflect the mother's mantra about being efficient and effective all the time. Her mother uttered, "if you fail it's because you haven't tried hard enough," rather than being empathic and caring towards her daughter.

When lockdown was over, the parents immediately searched for the telephone number of the regional public health facility dealing with gender identity and that of a private psychotherapist, leaving it up to Viola to decide who to contact and whether to do so.

Purple described her father as capable of greater physical and emotional closeness than the mother. He seemed to be able to listen to his daughter's distress but unable to express support for her. And Purple remains Viola, never undergoing treatment to become more male.

The nature of Purple's relationship with her brother Piero, who is two years older, and her understanding of the relationship's effects on her, became clearer across therapy sessions. Although the mother claimed her children did not get on with each other, and Piero "could never stand his sister who instead admired him," Purple says that it is the brother who was jealous of her. Despite this, Purple reports that there was a good relationship between them, even though they "spoke little." Only later did Purple acknowledge feeling jealous of Piero, whom she feels receives more attention from their parents and whose demands are satisfied, especially by the father.

In general, a family picture emerged from Purple's narratives that they appeared solid and efficient to others in their world, but inside the family they were divided and isolated. The impression the therapist got is that of four planets revolving in space, occasionally coming together at conventional times such as dinner time, but with great difficulty in communication. The mother appeared to be the main planet, often in conflict with her children. The father stayed in the background, but Purple said that when their mother was absent, he sought the children's complicity, saying "without her we are just fine!" while in her presence he conformed to her critical ways.

13.4.3 The course of Purple's therapy and her relationship to cutting

Purple started self-cutting in the ninth grade, after concluding that high school was too hard for her. However, this led to her feeling guilty for being unproductive and not knowing what to do in life. This feeling of loss of life purpose and direction was exacerbated later with her isolation during lockdown and by a suicide committed by a boy from her school. She did not know the boy personally, but she projected onto his death her own emotions of intense loneliness and despair. She said, "If I committed suicide, no one would miss me. I think about it sometimes . . . I don't know why. . . ."

As therapy continued, Purple alternated between times when she injured herself and others when she traced the scars with a marker, because she doesn't want to cut herself anymore, but "if they (parents) don't see any marks, they'll think I'm fine, and I'm not," she explained.

At the end of the second year of high school, Purple decided to change schools, and in the new, smaller, and more sheltered environment, Purple immediately came across as male.

Her self-definitions regarding gender identity changed over time. At the beginning of therapy, she talked about herself as a male, but in more recent sessions she has sometimes defined herself as a female, and the gender expressions are also more female-oriented. She has taken up dancing and films herself, and the image shown to the therapist in the videos is of a supple, female body. Whereas in the most critical period of her teen years, Viola was extremely isolated and never left the house except to go to school, today she has a girlfriend and a group of friends. Recently, in class she declared herself a nonbinary girl, who is dating another nonbinary girl.

In the first period of individual therapy, it emerged that the family seem to be chasing the alternating identities and gender expressions that Purple proposes to them, and they use a confusing and confounding alternation of male and female pronouns, provoking Purple's anger. Purple expressed her anger in the therapy room because she doesn't feel authorized to ask her parents for anything, due to her guilt at having disappointed them.

She gradually became more objective and less critical towards her parents, recognizing both the father's weaknesses and the positive sides of the mother. This was aided by her mother welcoming both her girlfriend and her friends into the house.

Overall, the feeling is that Purple's behavior was meant to challenge a rigid family system with parents (especially the mother) incapable of showing affection and closeness except in a more practical and concrete way. She challenged her parents with a demand for acknowledgement of Purple as a person not categorized in a binary way.

The stages of therapy are marked by discontinuous but important steps: Purple's need to create bonds, at first virtual, then real; the increasing ability to make friends, at first limited to the queer world alone, then extended to school and dance class mates; experimenting different affective relationships, where belonging and identifying with one gender rather than another seems to be the least of the problems; and finally, recovering a less critical and judgmental attitude toward the parents, who are certainly struggling and often, as Purple describes them to the therapist, find themselves in a solitary rotation in the family space.

In this clinical case, there was no parent availability for family therapy. The individual therapy focused on Purple's sense of guilt and her fears of being rejected. She has become more active and confident in the relationships inside and outside the family.

Viola's/Purple's challenge is to be acknowledged and accepted in her/his dimension of being a teenager who is still seeking a personal vital ground, where changes and contradictions are part of her/his journey of growth and self-acceptance.

13.5 Case illustration

13.5.1 Simon

Before describing S.'s case, we believe it is necessary to point out that we will focus mainly on the elements inherent to the gender variance. The therapist used only the initials (S.) during the period when Simon could not yet assert his male identity.

S. is a 20-year-old AFAB person, who is currently going through the gender-affirming pathway. At the age of 14, together with his parents, he was followed for about a year and a half by our family therapy team in agreement with the local Hospital Center that specialized in gender variance in children and adolescents. The interventions had been agreed upon with the center and the family as a first step to assess the diagnosis of gender dysphoria and accompany and support both the adolescent and his parents during the assessment process.

13.5.2 Simon's family

S. was born in Italy, where his parents have lived for more than 20 years after moving from an Eastern European country. The first impression of this family was positive: They looked like a close family, in which the parents were caring, understanding, and affectionate with each other and with S., their only daughter.

S. was a high school student at the time therapy began and showed a profound state of distress during our initial sessions, marked by a peculiar posture: She sat between her mother and father, spoke in low monotones, sitting closed in on herself and curled up, her face in her hands, while her parents stroked her shoulders in a comforting way. The predominant theme was school. During the sessions, she worried constantly about time taken away from studying, and she didn't want our appointments to interfere with the need to "do [her] homework, review math and physics," as if this was the only real problem.

Difficulty in talking about herself, coupled with a demand for her parents' presence, her refusal to share with her mother and father the name she had chosen to correspond to her experienced gender, and anxiety about school performance, which she expressed obsessively, were all part of the complex relationship with her parents. Fear of letting them down and being rejected was accompanied by a protective attitude toward them "that they should not suffer" because of her/him, coupled with a self-perception marked by deep feelings of shame, self-denigration, and the belief that she/he was not worthy of being recognized and loved for her/his own characteristics.

Halfway through our sessions with the family, S., who has increasingly confirmed male self-perception, asks the therapists' help in coming out in the school setting, the place where most of all other life contexts generated a state of anxiety and discomfort for him. For example, in the school there aren't any nongender bathrooms or gym locker rooms. At the same time, S. has been receiving support from the pediatric endocrinologist, who together with him has considered the future possibility of undertaking hormone treatment (starting with full parental consent as he was still a minor).

After about a year and a half of monthly sessions with the family, toward the end of the process of assessment and psychological support to the family system, the team recommended individual therapy, for which the adolescent is now ready and motivated.

13.5.3 Individual therapy

Many issues addressed in the sessions with the family have been the focus of individual sessions as well. In particular, during the middle phase of the support process carried out with the family system, Simon expressed more and more clearly the discomfort caused by the evidence of female somatic features by tracing their psychological and relational impact during the course of development. Therefore, the major theme of the therapy, both in family and in individual sessions with Simon, was his evolving gender identity. Simon said he suffered from the discrepancy between his perceived gender and his birth gender from an early age, narrating episodes of intense pain and withdrawal into himself. Simon explains that he couldn't share his suffering with his parents. We explored Simon's relationship with his gender identity, becoming aware of identifying predominantly with the male gender, but without a clear exclusion of female elements. Both of the therapeutic settings helped Simon and his family inhabit the uncertainty of his own identity and express the pain of being assigned to a gender he did not identify with.

First in the therapeutic setting, then progressively in the family and then, again, in the social context, Simon found the courage to talk about himself. He explained that he had been confused from childhood about his gender. For a long time, he had not been able to understand what was happening to him, and it was only in his teens, thanks to information found on the web, that he was able to realize he was transgender. After reaching this awareness, Simon told his parents that he thought he was transgender, a declaration that was apparently well-understood by them. The mother, solely concerned with Simon's well-being and success in life, apparently supported Simon's request to begin the transition process without any hesitation.

According to the parents, all of Simon's life transitions and goals, including gender affirmation, must be "executed on time and in the best possible way"; this is because Simon represents the social redemption of the family and, therefore, is overloaded with grandiose expectations. The main concern reported by the mother for Simon was regarding the discrimination that her son might encounter in life. Another fear of hers was that the path she was facing would prevent Simon from concentrating on developmental tasks that are important for children his age, especially studying. The role of parental expectations on his well-being has been discussed in therapy at length. Simon was also able to understand the weight of the other's expectations on himself. Progressively, he was confronted with his emotional pain, confusion, and the complexity of constructing a Self, an identity independent of multigenerational mandates.

Simon's main experience was that of being emotionally uncontained, poorly understood and accepted by his parents beyond the formal level. Indeed, although in initial family sessions the parents seem warm and close to Simon, in individual sessions Simon revealed this was not the case, and that he experienced little warmth from his mother. In particular, the stiffness in his mother's body movements has been observed during our family sessions when dealing with issues that were difficult for her. The attitude is confirmed by the lack of warmth that Simon recounts that he encountered in his mother from childhood when he did not adhere to her expectations. Nonverbal communication showed an ambivalence for Simon, disoriented by two opposing images of the mother figure. Parallel, and equally significant, beyond appearances, deepening his description of the father, Simon reveals he was sometimes hypermasculine and overbearing in the family. These parents had difficulty managing Simon's separation-individuation transitions, causing confusion and disorientation in their son.

During the family sessions, it had become evident that they were struggling to support their son's attempts to be autonomous. On the one hand, they were urging him to make adult choices; on the other hand, they were making him childish with their caregiving patterns. In fact, they come to acknowledge that they did not treat Simon as an emerging young adult. They were present and distant in the parental relationship, unclear and rigid, in other words, ambivalent towards Simon. As a result, during individual sessions he recounts his confusion and difficulty in understanding what his real abilities, desires, and expectations are. He often shows himself scared, but also eager to have new experiences and choose for himself who to be.

Simon's family immigrated from another country, and metaphorically, he described himself as a "lifelong stranger in his own body." He wanted a male/masculine body that would exemplify the stereotypical image of maleness that he also criticizes: a muscular and athletic body that expresses strength, a full beard, hairy skin, pectorals and no breasts, and a low, deep voice; when describing these characteristics, he recognizes that they are part of a glossy image of a man and feels uncomfortable adhering to such a stereotype, which divides the human world into idealized binary categories. He ideally advocates the possibility of "being what we are," a female "all flowery" and a male wearing his "boxing gloves." Simon's position seems to defer to an ideal of non-categorization rather than a personal aspiration. As he comes into contact with the pain associated with his feeling male in a female body, he expresses revulsion for the secondary characteristics of women's bodies, such as menstruation, or graceful attitudes and elegant clothes.

Simon's emotional experiences are often undefined, sometimes oscillating between being impulsive and explosive in times of difficulty, sometimes childlike and chaotic. His main relationships are with his parents primarily, and more recently, with a few friends. He seeks to maintain himself in a protective environment that mitigates his anxiety and defends him from a world he perceives as dangerous and disorienting. This way of relating to the world stems partly from his family experience and partly from his fear of being rejected, judged, and attacked for both his sexual orientation and gender identity. We think that therapeutic work has helped Simon to better understand how much these anxious aspects are related to his primary experiences and how much to his being transgender. As the therapeutic work progressed, in fact, the anxiety component became more evident and the main object of the work with him. In synergy with this, he felt more confident in being able to face some complex challenges for him. For example, recently he has taken steps toward potentially mature behaviors, such as enrolling in the course to get his driver's license, attending a course in the performing arts (far from what his parents accomplished careerwise and desired for him), and taking a short vacation with friends without mum and dad.

Simon's sexuality path is still evolving, marked more by uncertainties rather than by defined or rigidly characterized aspects. Although he declares being attracted to male partners, he has never been involved in a romantic relationship or has physically approached anybody. The very thought makes him nervous, and he prefers to avoid these experiences until the surgical journey of gender affirmation is completed. Simon seems to be clear about his sexual orientation, but he fears that his body, especially his female genitals and breasts, might cause confusion and revulsion in a male partner. He also has not developed confidence with proper body dimension, having found it repulsive from an early age. He is certain he wants to have his breasts removed, which make him feel so embarrassed – because they are difficult to contain with chest-compressing bands and are not concealable with male loose-fitting clothes – but he has doubts over whether to transform his genitals from female to male.

The factors that seem to have affected Simon's psychic evolution most have been the recognition and expression of his own suffering; increased ability to name emotions; the experience of increasingly embodying and allowing an evolving self to be known, putting up with the oscillating back-and-forth movements in his evolution; and the coexistence in his identity of gender fluidity and binary gender. This includes the complexity of the journey, the difficulty in understanding himself, the fatigue of suspending judgment and the need for clarity and categorization, and his ongoing and sometimes difficult process of reflection about his relationships. This process is still ongoing. Listening and empathetically accepting his doubts, uncertainties, and pain seems to have helped Simon understand that closeness of the other is possible and not dangerous.

Often, and especially in the early stages of therapy with Simon, the therapist went through the disorienting sensation of feeling both important and insignificant, experiencing Simon's dependence on the therapist and then at times devaluing their relationship. During individual sessions, it was important to seek, together with Simon, a dynamic balance between closeness and distance that would foster his integration between the drive for autonomy and the need for dependence. This has been and still is in part an important therapeutic issue, involving both the boy and the therapist. The individual drives that Simon perceives more and more clearly are welcomed and supported in the therapeutic setting, seeking integration with the emotional experiences – especially the uncertainty and fear – that these entail.

In conclusion, family therapy was fundamental in the evaluation of relational dynamics, understanding, acceptance, and support of one's gender nonconformity. However, we believe that it was fundamental in helping the family system to maintain a functional attitude toward the transition process of Simon. Although Simon's therapeutic path has not yet finished, some important steps have been taken on the individual, family, and social levels. For example, the therapists worked so that he could talk first with us and then with his parents and friends about his gender affirmation journey. The work with the family and the individual sessions helped Simon to better understand his fears and try to experiment with a more autonomous self. In this, self-efficacy and self-esteem have been two important areas of work.

The therapists discussed the topic of motivation and the therapeutic alliance several times. In the first family sessions he had adhered to his mother's desire to make quick transitions, to quickly reach the goal of starting the gender affirmation process, without hesitation and uncertainty. Gradually, both he and the family opened up to complexity, abandoning the rationalizing and defensive attitude that had made them resistant to accepting each other's difficulties and supporting each other as a team.

The authors believe that the main result was to amplify their ability to mentalize and exercise the reflective function. We think that this happened because we were the first to exercise this function towards them, proposing experiences that amplified this relational position and giving them clear information on the issues connected to gender variance.

13.6 Conclusion

In these two cases, the therapeutic process kept the therapists for a long time in contact with uncertainty and indefiniteness where it was difficult to remain, to not intervene by shaping the identity process or rejecting the less defined parts of the patients. In other words, avoiding similar family dynamics. One possible key to interpreting the stories of Simon and Purple, and an interesting reflection on the deep dynamics involved in the two cases, is the concept of *embodiment*.

From a developmental viewpoint, this perspective connects the intersubjective mirroring process and bodily states in primary relationships. In particular, Lemma (2022) described the experiences of some transgender people as experiences of being noticed or not being noticed, of being held or not held in the other person's mind in response to the embodied experience of self. According to the author, this is related to four recurring themes: (1) sense of incongruity between the given body and the body identified as the proper bodily "home" for the self; (2) difficulty in communicating this incongruity to attachment figures in childhood and adolescence; (3) experience of being noticed connected to a sense of rejection and shame; and finally (4) urgency of investing in the surgical transition with a focus on the concrete and material dimension of the body, a transition that is perceived as particularly urgent in cases experiencing rejection, hostility, or non-tuning of attachment figures in response to the experience of incongruity between body and gender identification.

Simon, like other transgender people, describes his own experience of feeling like a stranger inside his own body as a feeling of discontinuity in the subjective perception and search for a new bodily dimension offering relief from this intolerable experience (Lemma, 2012, 2022). In inhabiting one's body during transition, it is as if Simon were seeking and chasing a mythicized body, an idealized embodiment that can never be embodied. It is a body that is seen in the mirror but does not seem to have been mirrored by *caregivers* and, therefore, remains largely foreign land. As a result, sexuality, which by its very nature exposes others and requires coming to terms with a physicality far from the ideal, frightens Simon and as such risks becoming neglected.

On the other hand, Purple's identity research tells us about a body that claims its fluidity, its non-categorization, its non-belonging to any one category. In both cases, the dimensions of the self are ultimately seeking a shared narrative, becoming a presence in the session and in the relationship with the therapist in the individual space. Therapy is the opportunity to experience acceptance by another on our own who gets closer and is interested and respectful, is curious and welcoming, attentive to the complex dynamics of mentalization.

Sometimes the most difficult challenge in work with transgender youth occurs with family, especially the parents, who have been seen as more distant and inaccessible by the adolescent. The parents' willingness to be engaged in uncertainty, while preserving the commitment of one's closeness and love toward the child, may occur spontaneously for some, but for others it is an impossible task. Anger, disappointment, and grief that are impossible to process toward a child you feel betrayed by is a painful possibility that lots of transgender people have had to face.

Not surprisingly, the *Standards of Care V8* stress the critical involvement of parents or caregivers during assessment and treatment. As family therapists, we are in agreement with this recommendation and with the others included in the SOC-V8.

Note

1 Binary model means that it is classified through a dichotomous variable: male/female, man/woman.

References

Amodeo, A. L., Vitelli, R., Scandurra, C., Picariello, S., & Valerio, P. (2015). Adult attachment and transgender identity in the Italian context: Clinical implications and suggestions for further research. *International Journal of Transgenderism, 16*(1), 49–61. https://doi.org/10.1080/15532739.2015.1022680

Asen, E., & Fonagy, P. (2015). Interventi basati sulla mentalizzazione in terapia familiare. *Terapia Familiare, 106*, 5–39. https://doi.org/10.3280/TF2014-106001

Asen, E., & Scholtz, M. (2010). *Multi-family therapy*. Routledge.

Caldarera, A., Baietto, C., Castellini, G., Dalle Luche, C., Delli Veneri, A., Di Grazia, M., Fisher, A. D., Lavaggi, M., Lavorato, E., Mazzilli, V., Mosconi, M., Nadalin, D. A., Pace, V., Palleschi, L., Quagliarella, L., Ristori, J., Sanfelici, A. P., Santamaria, F., Stella, P., . . . Massara, D. (2019). Children and adolescents referred to an Italian network of specialised gender clinics: Gender presentation and psychological features. In *Book of abstracts: 3rd biennal EPATH conference inside matters. On law, ethics and religion* (pp. 51–52). Iris.

Coleman, E., Radix, A. E., Bouman, W. P., Brown, G. R., De Vries, A. L. C., Deutsch, M. B., Ettner, R., Fraser, L., Goodman, M., Green, J., Hancock, A. B., Johnson, T. W., Karasic, D. H., Knudson, G. A., Leibowitz, S. F., Meyer-Bahlburg, H. F. L., Monstrey, S. J., Motmans, J., Nahata, L., & Arcelus, J. (2022). Standards of care for the health of transgender and gender diverse people, version 8. *International Journal of Transgender Health, 23*, S1–S259. https://doi.org/10.1080/26895269.2022.2100644

Crapanzano, A., Carpiniello, B., & Pinna, F. (2021). Approccio alla persona con disforia di genere: Dal modello psichiatrico italiano al modello emergente basato sul consenso informato. *Rivista di Psichiatria, 56*(2), 120–128. https://doi.org/10.1708/3594.35771

Ferrara, P., Di Sipio Morgia, C., & Sacco, R. (2021). Primo Piano: Disforia di genere quello che il pediatra deve sapere. *Pediatria, 10–11*, 8–12.

Kaltiala-Heino, R., Sumia, M., Työläjärvi, M., & Lindberg, N. (2015). Two years of gender identity service for minors: Overrepresentation of natal girls with severe problems in adolescent developments. *Child and Adolescent Psychiatry and Mental Health, 9*, 1–9. https://doi.org/10.1186/s13034-015-0042-y

Lemma, A. (2012). Research of the couch: Re-visiting the transsexual conundrum. *Psychoanalytic Psychotherapy, 26*(4), 263–281. https://doi.org/10.1080/02668734.2012.732104

Lemma, A. (2022). *Transgender identities: A contemporary introduction*. Routledge.

Petiva, P., & Spirito, M. (2015). Generi di prima necessità: Terapia familiare di adolescenti con disforia di genere. *Terapia Familiare, 109*, 5–20. https://doi.org/10.3280/TF2015-109001

Petiva, P., & Spirito, M. (2020). "Cose tra fratelli . . ." L'impatto del coming-out nella relazione tra siblings. *Terapia Familiare, 122*, 7–23. https://doi.org/10.3280/TF2020-122002

Viola, F., Centrone, M. R., & Rees, G. (2021). *Vite a Colori, Esperienze, percezioni e opinioni di bambinə e ragazzə sulla pandemia di Covid-19*. Centro di Ricerca UNICEF Innocenti, UNICEF Office of Research.

14

MULTIGENERATIONAL THERAPY AND VIOLENCE AGAINST CHILDREN

Alejandro Astorga and Alicia Cruzat

This chapter describes the main components of a multigenerational intervention model used in clinical settings where family violence, neglect, and sexual abuse are experienced by children and adolescents. The model's components are derived from our professional experience of more than 25 years of clinical efforts to develop an integrated working model of a multigenerational psychosocial and psychotherapeutic intervention that constitutes an alternative model to traditional individual approaches and to systemic models that do not consider the evolutionary and historical dimensions of families.

14.1 The family as a multigenerational emotional unit

Although systemic intervention models focus on describing the family as a "system," few of them focus on what drives it. Addressing the dynamics of violence, abuse, or neglect within the family requires the therapist to adopt a viewpoint that considers the family as an emotional unit (Smith, 2023). The consideration of the family as a "natural" system is the great legacy of the natural systems theory or Bowen family systems theory proposed by Murray Bowen (Bowen, 1978). This consideration opens an important explanatory framework for understanding the emotional processes related to violence within families. Placing the evolutionary context as a foundation for understanding human functioning, and how the forces that guide its functioning are the same that move the rest of the living process, allows us to observe the human family as a relational system mobilized to a large extent by automatic or semi-automatic tendencies anchored in its phylogenetic history on a large scale, and by multigenerational tendencies that shape its emotional manifestation (Bowen & Kerr, 1988).

Understanding the human family as an emotional unit invites us to observe how it possesses a natural engine that shapes relationships and moves it to be in a permanent adaptive interplay between togetherness and individuality or emotional autonomy depending on the level of anxiety in the environment (McCullough, 2006). Through togetherness, members are compelled to stay in the group, needing each other, depending on the other to do or stop doing such things to be well, making the others responsible for their own well-being. Through individuality, members are driven by their own goals or interests without depending on what the other does or does not do to stay oriented in life, focused on their own growth while remaining in close and meaningful connection with others. That is to say, depending on how demanding the external or internal context is for that unit, it will activate levels of anxiety that will mobilize in it those semi-automatic forces expressed in predictable

DOI: 10.4324/9781003536765-17

movements among its members oriented to adaptation, even if this implies the appearance of impairment of the functioning of some of its members (Rodríguez & Martínez, 2015).

Understanding the human family as an emotional unit allows us to observe how its evolution is fundamentally determined by processes that the family activates trying to adapt to internal or external changes that demand accommodation and adjustment. For example, the dynamics of aggression among family members usually appear when the family deals with external or internal contextual challenges (loss of employment, diagnosis of serious illness, death of a member of the extended family, onset of adolescence in one of the children, etc.) and the consequences or threats of these changes on the stability of the relational dynamics within the family (distance of a child, loss of relationship with a parent, increased emotional demands on the partner due to the birth of a daughter, etc.).

The multigenerational perspective invites us to recognize how the challenges faced by the nuclear family experiencing abuse or violence are often in emotional connection and resonance with those stories that each adult brings from his or her own family of origin and that, most often and much to their regret, are repeated in current emotional and relational dynamics (Framo, 1992). Although it is evident that these resonances or connections do not "cause" the current dynamics of aggression, they do provide us with a comprehensive contextual framework of great value for generating processes of change (Smith, 2023).

14.2 Symptoms as expressions of the family emotional process

One of the major consequences of understanding the family as a multigenerational emotional unit is the therapist's recognition that families and the way they function are not so different from the way his or her own family functions (Titelman, 1987). In our experience as supervisors of psychologists and social workers, each year we continue to be surprised how after students understand the human family as a natural organism moved by our historical-evolutionary design, they instill a deep and real sense of humility and respect for the clients. They are able to observe how the human relational process is universal and that possible differences among families are only quantitative and not qualitative. The multigenerational approach puts us in our real place as therapists working in contexts of vulnerability: the same semi-automatic tendencies that move the families we work with are also present in our own families.

Violence towards children is part of the automatic responses of the human family to cope with anxiety and its adaptive challenges. It is therefore key to recognize that it is present to a greater or lesser extent in every human family unit. Just as we must humbly acknowledge that violence is part of our neurobiological design activated by a series of internal and external contextual conditioning factors, we must also assume that one of the ways families stabilize their functioning is through aggression and violence directed at their children.

In the professional and academic world, aggression, abuse, and violence are often described as a "phenomenon" alluding to an anomalous, unexpected, or rare occurrence. From this point of view, violence is given an aspect that positions it as an exception, something incomprehensible, a pathological and unusual manifestation that needs to be addressed, condemned, and eradicated. From a multigenerational point of view, violence, abuse, and child maltreatment are considered part of a larger family emotional process and not an isolated "phenomenon." This means, at a minimum, considering violence to be:

(a) as part of the possible coping responses in family systems to internal or external demands that exceed a family's adaptive resources,

(b) as a manifestation of shifting family relationships, not just individual behavior, and
(c) as one form of family aggression and violence that coexists with forms, like gender-based violence in couples, aggression towards the elderly or members with disabilities or handicaps, violence between siblings, etc.

14.3 The child as protagonist of the intervention process with his or her family

One of the great challenges for professionals working with children who have experienced violence is their emotional resonance with their own histories and the very frequent temptation to observe and treat the child as a victim to be protected from his or her own family and adverse context. It is evident that seeing the child as a fragile, incompetent subject, without resources, and at the mercy of what others do is a frequent mistake that shows how the psychosocial intervenor and the protection system itself fail to respect him or her (Andolfi, 2022). Child maturation best occurs in nuclear and extended family. Many professionals recognize that the primary parent and child bond is influenced by other family members and family relationships. For example, a father and grandmother's relationships with the primary parent and child shape the outcomes of child maturation (Fivaz-Despeursinge & Corboz-Warnery, 1999; Titelman, 2008).

The relational triangle is the minimum unit of observation and intervention in emotional processes of abuse and violence. A caregiver who engages in aggressive behavior towards one of his or her children is always in relation to at least one third party. The relationship with his or her own mother, for example, becomes the main context for understanding the challenges he or she has to face as a caregiver of his or her own children. In working with child sexual abuse and maltreatment, it is very common to observe that such fundamental triangles are multigenerational. The abuse or maltreatment keeps active old episodes or patterns of abusive relationships between the older generations with the newer ones. Although this opens up a world of painful experiences in these adults, it also opens up the possibility of healing not only current but also past relationships.

Intervention work in the dynamics of violence directed towards children therefore requires a relational and family approach. What every child needs and deserves is a loving and available relational space that respects his or her value as a subject. The same requires our therapeutic and psychosocial approach. Most of the children who enter the child welfare system through the courts seem to ask for the same type of help; if we manage to open our ears to listen to what they want to tell us, we will be able to hear: help my family! It is common to observe how most of the children who are immersed in dynamics of aggression and violence quickly activate their intention to help, contain, protect, or distract adults from the great pains they carry in their own history as children and in the challenges that adult life has forced them to deal with.

14.4 The symptom as a metaphor of the historical and current process of the family

The emotional, physical, or social symptomatology manifested by children who have lived experiences of violence in their families is diverse. Each of these symptomatic manifestations of that child not only reflects the experience of suffering and affectation of his or her body and subjectivity, but also reflects the emotional process of the entire family.

Andolfi's invitation to recognize in the child's symptom a real and metaphorical manifestation of the relational and historical process of the family forces us to recognize both its fragilities and pains, as well as its strengths and resources (Andolfi & Ackermans, 1990). The symptom, therefore, shown by that child not only accounts for his or her individual processes, but also reflects the main historical emotional processes of his or her family. A child's rebelliousness towards one of his parents communicates how much tension there is in that relationship, but it can also account for how much tension there has been between his father's relationships with his own father, among other tri-generational triangles. Thus, the child's symptom is not only a gateway to his subjective world and the world of his relationship with his parent, but also offers access to the multigenerational emotional process of which the child is a part.

14.5 Participation of children in intervention processes

Traditionally, the model of intervention in the work with children who have suffered experiences of violence and child abuse considers the participation of psychologists, social workers, and lawyers. Therefore, a psycho-socio-legal intervention is configured, where the main objectives of the work are the interruption of the abuse by applying judicial measures (such as the removal of the aggressor) and psychosocial measures (support to protective adults, addressing emotional damage and strengthening the family's resources).

However, we frequently observe that the psychotherapeutic work carried out, once the abuse has ceased, is characterized by the psychologist working with the child individually and the social worker working with the parents (usually the mother or grandmother in charge) to guide or psycho-educate their parenting practices. This model is very frequent not only in the work with violence, but it usually extends throughout the entire therapeutic practice with children. If we visit the office of a child psychologist or psychiatrist, we will see parents and adults sitting in the room with the secretary waiting for the session between the child and the professional to end. Of course, from time to time these professionals also invite parents into the session to tell them about their progress and to gather more elements that may be useful in their therapeutic work with the child.

We consider that these practices reflect premises that do not consider the family as an emotional unit, that do not consider the role played by the child's symptoms within the family process and of the consideration of the child as a holder of human rights. On the contrary, a multigenerational model considers the child as a subject of respect and resources (Andolfi, 2017). Andolfi considers that the child should not only become a member who must be present in the family intervention process whatever the difficulty faced, but must also become the protagonist of the process. The child becomes the one who guides the exploration of the family processes and becomes a key co-therapist in accompanying the family in its challenge to deal with the current symptom and what it brings from the histories with the families of origin of each parent.

We have observed an interesting progression that practitioners make when including a child in the session with his or her family, as they begin to accept multigenerational premises in their work:

1. They start by asking themselves a series of questions to make sure that incorporating the child into conversations with adults will not harm the child or make things worse.
2. They decide to participate in the conversations with the parents, keeping the children as observers of the conversations.
3. They decide to generate a working space with the adults, consulting and involving the child in some moments of the therapeutic encounter.
4. They encourage sessions with the children and their families, developing a therapeutic alliance with the child, and together with the child, they explore and elaborate current and past family processes.

Each of these steps shows progress towards therapeutic intervention from a multigenerational perspective with violence against children within families:

(a) *Bringing the child into conversations with adults is not harmful to the child and will not make things worse.*

One of the fears professionals have when working with children who have lived abusive experiences in their own words is "re-traumatizing" or "re-victimizing" them. Knowing the painful accounts behind the stories of children who have been severely mistreated, neglected, or abused activates all our human sensitivity, so it is understandable that professionals are especially cautious in technical decisions about how to work with them.

Talking about abuse in session, even in the presence of protective adults, is often seen as an experience that could re-victimize the child and therefore tends to be avoided.

Our experience has shown us that by coaching intervention teams and connecting professionals' fears with their clients with their own experiences as children in their families of origin, it soon encourages them to try to incorporate the children into the conversations. It is not uncommon to hear their reports of surprise and excitement as they observe the turn the work takes in terms of becoming more creative, honest, and meaningful for all participants, including the therapist.

(b) *Engage in conversations with adults while keeping children as observers of those conversations.*

The move toward incorporating children into conversations about issues that concern them is a big step on the road toward incorporating multigenerational ideas into psychosocial work. As the therapist focuses on dialogue between "adults," at least he or she has overcome the fear that the presence of the child, listening to family issues from the adult voice, exposes the child to harm.

It is common when observing video recordings of this type of session, or in the reports of the interveners, how the children remain attentive to the conversation while playing and from time to time interrupt by asking something that has not been made clear to them (for example, if the mother says a word that the child does not understand, the child approaches her in the middle of the mother's conversation with the therapist and asks her, "what does that mean, mom?"). Another common observation is how, in the child's play while the adults "work," the child develops an overt representation that accounts for the conversation taking place between "the adults."

Gradually, the therapist realizes that even the youngest children are in full connection with the therapeutic process taking place with their parents and that it is therefore absurd not to incorporate them more proactively into the work. Children's participation in therapy with adults communicates something fundamental: the child has the experience of being present when being talked about, and someone is "taking care of their parents or caregivers," which makes it easier for them to start taking care of their own issues, such as playing, exploring, and growing.

(c) *Therapy primarily with adults, consulting and involving the child at certain moments.*

Having overcome the initial fear, and observing that the child actively wants to participate and have a say in the conversation between adults, the therapist seems more encouraged to ask the child directly about some issues and to consider him or her as a valid interlocutor in this important conversation between "adults" about "serious" family issues. It is not uncommon to observe the surprised reactions to the sincere, direct, and wise opinions that children often develop in response to the intervener's questions. Moreover, it is very common to observe that these participations easily instill relaxation, humor, and a playful space in the conversation carried out between the therapist and the adults of the family.

The participation of the children in the therapy with the adults, sometimes being the protagonists, communicates something fundamental: it allows them to have the experience of being someone competent within the system, contributing ideas and relevant observations to the work.

(d) *Family therapy, developing a therapeutic alliance with the child, and together with him or her explore and elaborate current and past family processes.*

Once the previous stages have been overcome, and the therapist's fears have been overcome, the therapist can begin the work process, taking advantage of the child's resources to enter into the family's emotional process. The therapist summons the significant system of the child, who has lived through abusive situations and quickly allies with them to explore with their guidance what issues have mobilized the process in their family and how their experience is often not so "original." With the help of the construction of the family diagram, we visualize how the child's experience is connected to current and past processes and relationships that now have the possibility of being visible.

The child's participation in therapy together with the adults, being the gateway to the system, allows him to visualize himself as the main collaborator of the therapist in the task of overcoming the experience of abuse and to have the experience of being a subject of respect and not an object of adult protection.

14.6 The family genogram in child abuse

The family genogram is a graphic representation of the family in at least three generations considering its structure and main emotional and relational processes (Harrison, 2018; McGoldrick et al., 2020).

After years of working with the family genogram and despite being a widely extended tool in psychosocial intervention (Astorga, 2018), the main challenge is still how to put the family genogram at the service of the family.

14.7 Case illustration

The family of Carlos, a 14-year-old boy, consults for behavioral maladjustments at school. The mother also refers significant episodes of aggression from Carlos towards her. Both parents are lawyers, and they separated a few months after Carlos was born. The father reported feeling overwhelmed and decided to leave home at that time. In response, the mother developed a major depressive episode that lasted for at least the first four years of Carlos's life. Meanwhile, the couple's second child (Pedro), now 12 years old, was born. The pregnancy occurred in an effort by the couple to get the situation back on track. The parents now have joint custody of Carlos and his brother. As the mother points out, there is a "cordial" relationship with her ex-husband.

During the first session, there is a great deal of silent tension between the parents and Carlos, when asked by the intervener, usually replies "I don't know." The intervener takes the blackboard and places it in front of the family. On it, he draws the nuclear family (both parents and both children) and then asks Carlos: "Tell me, what do you know about the degree of aggression in your parents' family of origin?" Carlos indicates that he does not know much and is invited to ask his parents. A process then begins, led by the adolescent, in which the family explores how aggressiveness has been present in each parent's life in a significant way and how, much to their regret, it has manifested in the nuclear family. The mother becomes emotional, and each child has the experience of visualizing how he is part of a family fabric and the historical challenges of their family system as an emotional unit. After exploring and mapping the relationships each parent has had with their own parents, each child is invited to draw the relationship with each parent. It is then that Carlos points out that there have been significant episodes of verbal abuse by his mother and father towards him. The family then allows the possibility of talking about what is important in a climate of respect but also of courage. Carlos opens the door.

14.8 The experiential dimension of family therapy

Working with abuse exposes the adults in the family to important feelings of guilt and shame. Even if they are not the direct perpetrators of the violence, having been part of the relational process makes them feel insecure and judged. It is to be expected that the therapist's effort to develop meaningful conversations with them will be difficult. Professionals often describe these adults as resistant, rigid, or intransigent.

In supervising therapists where the symptom is violence toward children, the therapist is often a main source of rigidity that decreases the effectiveness of treatment. The therapist's rigidities are often associated with identification with the child's pain, a desire to protect the child, a fear of harming him or her again and, above all, unresolved issues with his or her own parents and other adults in their family of origin. If a therapist gets upset when faced with a parent who says that he does not wish to attend any more sessions and who insists that the treatment is of no use to him, supervision often reveals the therapist will find in his own history resonances of his own relationship with his father and/or grandfather with whom he was "impossible to talk to." In our experience, the therapist making this simple observation and connection allows the therapist to be freer and more creative in future clinical sessions.

To summarize, we can point out that working with violence from a multigenerational point of view should focus on highlighting the historical process that underlies the experiences of abuse in the family nucleus. Some orientations behind this general purpose are:

1. Help the family (adults and children) to visualize themselves as part of a history involving several generations where aggression and violence have been present.
2. Recognize that the current effort to overcome abusive experiences and interrupt abusive relationships is not only an individual effort but also a relational one.
3. Accept that past histories had their own determinants or facilitating contexts and recognize which of those factors are similar to current ones and which are different.
4. Identify those unresolved issues and proceed to address them in the original.
5. Develop not only "good conversations" where we talk about what has not been previously talked about but also activate analogical and nonverbal interactions that allow us to re-signify not through words but in the "experience."
6. Facilitate family experiences where play, metaphors, and the use of the body are part of the intervention developed within the therapeutic system.
7. Progressively advance to consider the child as a protagonist and competent subject in the work that addresses the violence that he or she and his or her family system have experienced.

14.9 Conclusion

Psychosocial and psychotherapeutic intervention with children, adolescents, and their families in contexts of violence, neglect, and sexual abuse requires a theoretical and practical approach based on a multigenerational systemic perspective. It is possible to address the different situations of violence experienced by children, giving them a leading role to address not only their own experiences, but also to contextualize them in a tri-generational framework, where violence has often already been present in the family. In this way, a family system that has generated pain and suffering can become a resource for change and protection.

The experience of training and supervising professional psychologists and social workers has allowed us to understand that to the extent that each of them has addressed their own unresolved issues with their own family of origin, building their own family genogram and developing personal work, they can become an effective facilitator of family processes, even when dealing with complex issues. Likewise, the construction of genuine and flexible therapeutic systems, as well as their supervision, are fundamental for respectful and effective clinical work.

References

Andolfi, M. (2017). *Multigenerational family therapy: Tools and resources for the therapist*. Routledge (Original work published 2015).

Andolfi, M. (2022). La traición de la terapia familiar hacia el niño. *De Familias y Terapias*, *52*, 35–49.

Andolfi, M., & Ackermans, A. (1990). *La Creación del Sistema Terapéutico*. Editorial Paidós.

Astorga, A. (2018). Guía para la construcción y análisis del diagrama familiar centrado en la situación del niño, niña y adolescente desde una mirada de derechos y con miras a su presentación en reunión técnica. In *Intervención en Infancia y Adolescencia desde un enfoque de Derechos Humanos* (pp. 78–113). Gráfica LOM.

Bowen, M. (1978). *Family therapy in clinical practice*. Jason Aronson.

Bowen, M., & Kerr, M. (1988). *Family evaluation*. W.W. Norton & Company.

Fivaz-Despeursinge, E., & Corboz-Warnery, A. (1999). *The primary triangle*. Basic Behavioral Science.

Framo, J. (1992). *Family of origin: An intergenerational approach*. Routledge.

Harrison, V. (2018). *The family diagram & family research: An illustrated guide to tools for working on differentiation of self in one's family*. Center for the Study of Natural Systems and the Family.

McCullough, P. (2006). Implicaciones Clínicas de la Teoría de Bowen. In A. Roizblatt (Ed.), *Terapia Familiar y de Pareja* (pp. 270–284). Mediterráneo.

McGoldrick, M., Gerson, R., & Petry, S. (2020). *Genograms: Assessment and intervention*. W.W. Norton & Company.

Rodríguez, M., & Martínez, M. (2015). *Teoría Familiar Sistémica de Bowen. Avances y Aplicación Terapéutica*. Mc Graw Hill Interamericana S.L.

Smith, W. (2023). Abuso infantil en el proceso emocional familiar. *De Familias y Terapias*, *34*, 118–141.

Titelman, P. (1987). *The therapists own family: Toward the differentiation of self.* Jason Aronson.

Titelman, P. (2008). *Triangles: Bowen family systems theory perspectives*. The Haworth Press.

15
SOCIAL WITHDRAWAL IN ADOLESCENCE

Francesca Ferraguzzi

15.1 Introduction

It is increasingly common to receive a "cry for help" from parents who feel they cannot cope with their teenage children's distress. Teenagers who seem to have lost all interest in life, in others, in themselves, who stop dreaming about their future, shut themselves away in their rooms, locked in a silence that seems impenetrable, deadly. Sadness, alongside feelings of emptiness and fear, brings about a setback to their developmental pathways.

For parents, this experience often feels incomprehensible. The domestic walls become the place where you can breathe anger and anguish, where suffering is screamed out loud but has no chance of being expressed, signified, and acknowledged. Dropping out of school, using their room as a refuge that is perceived as a protected and safe place, become defensive mechanisms for adolescents who feel unequipped to face the outside world.

In an increasingly individualistic and performance-driven society, it is difficult to find a dimension that is consistent with self-expression and with the construction of one's own identity, even more so in adolescence, the time of metamorphosis, as Andreoli (2006) describes it. Changes occurring in the body, in social contexts, in family and intergenerational relationships, cause distress, simultaneously pushing adolescents toward the development of a new identity while also evoking insecurities and fears that can lead to withdrawal and a desire to escape.

Becoming an adult can be experienced with great anxiety, as adolescents must come to terms with transformations, the collapse of childhood ideals, and the confrontation with peers. This can trigger an active withdrawal, starting with absence from school, then from social relationships, and eventually leading on to outright self-isolation.

In the interplay of adolescent acquisition and loss (Andolfi & Mascellani, 2023), there is a strong desire to become increasingly autonomous from one's family of origin, as well as feeling a sense of belonging to the family as a basis for experiencing oneself outside, in a delicate balance between belonging and separation (Bowen, 1979).

15.2 Social withdrawal: A global phenomenon

Social withdrawal has become an increasingly prevalent way for adolescents to express distress. The emergence of this phenomenon dates to the 1980s when in Japan, psychiatrist Tamaki Saito

DOI: 10.4324/9781003536765-18

coined the term *Hikikomori*, which means "social withdrawal." Over time, the number of recognized cases has grown significantly, so much so that it has created a great deal of social alarms. Saito (2013) described its peculiarities, such as social withdrawal, school phobia, reversal of circadian rhythm, avoidance of social relationships, agoraphobia, self-mysophobia, anthropophobia, persecution mania, obsessive-compulsive symptoms, depressed mood, apathy, lethargy, suicidal thoughts, and violent behavior toward family (Aguglia et al., 2010; Saito, 2013; Kato et al., 2019).

Among the various sociocultural and family-related risk factors, several studies have highlighted the presence of high expectations of success in school by parents, resulting in a loss of confidence on the part of children in their own abilities (Li & Wong, 2015). The same experience can be triggered by aggressive or rejecting attitudes acted out by peers toward those who do not excel or appear introverted or fragile. Another risk factor is the sharp distinction between gender roles characteristic of the Japanese family. The emotional and physical absence of the father figure, with almost total delegation of child-rearing to the mother, can become breeding grounds for bonding between mother and child that is destined to continue beyond the childhood period.

Currently, *hikikomori* does not fall within a rigid diagnostic category, but it is described as a particular state, influenced by various environmental factors, affecting the expected developmental process. Numerous data confirm that there is no disorder associated with the phenomenon, to the point that a split is made between "primary *hikikomori*," referring to a condition that does not originate from any pre-existing disorder, and "secondary *hikikomori*," indicating the presence of an associated disorder (Suwa & Suzuki, 2013). One of the major contributions to the formulation of criteria for assessing *hikikomori* stems from the bio-psycho-socio-cultural model, developed by Kato (Kato et al., 2019), who emphasized its multidimensional nature starting with the identification of three specific diagnostic criteria: (1) marked social isolation in one's home, lasting for at least six months, (2) significant impairment in functioning, and (3) perceived distress related to isolation. Additional specific elements are used to assess its severity and guide the type of intervention, such as the presence of the feeling of loneliness, comorbidity with psychiatric disorders, family characteristics of overparenting or underparenting, and absence of real social interactions or replaced with virtual ones (Kato et al., 2019).

Initially identified in Japan, this phenomenon appears to be widespread globally, as shown by several epidemiological surveys indicating its presence across many countries (Aguglia et al., 2010; Lancini, 2019).

In Italy, in 2013, about 240,000 cases of social withdrawal were reported in surveys from the Italian Federation of the Orders of Doctors and Dental Surgeons (FNOMCeO) and the Istituto Minotauro in Milan (Lancini, 2019). The Italian and Japanese phenomena are similar first of all in terms of prevalence in the male sex and onset between 11 and 15 years of age (Lancini, 2019; Crepaldi, 2019; Santona et al., 2023). The same is true for the characteristics of families, regarding both the symbiotic parent-child relationship that continues into adulthood, delaying the process of separation and identification from the family of origin, and the narcissistic investments in an idealized child (Lancini, 2019; Aguglia et al., 2010). In addition to the type of bonding with adult figures of reference, school phobia, interest in virtual reality, and social phobia represent traits that share the experience of *Hikikomori* with Italian withdrawn children (Spiniello et al., 2015). School phobia can escalate to intense physical symptoms such as nausea, stomachache, migraines, states of anxiety, and panic attacks. We often report an escalation of associated behaviors: initially, students are late for school or leave early, experiencing strong mental and physical distress, then absence from school increases until they stop going altogether. Being aware that they cannot perform daily life activities like everyone else and the resulting sense of shame is one of the reasons why withdrawn children tend to reverse their circadian rhythm, going to bed at dawn and waking up in the afternoon. This allows them to minimize the comparison with activities normally performed by peers but increases their belief of being losers and feeling socially inadequate (Pietropolli Charmet, 2013). Only a handful spend time on the web. Heavy media use, including video game addiction, contributes to the illusion of stopping time and denies their need to be in touch with the outside world. Failure and distress are related to confrontation with their peers, failing parents' expectations, and body shame. The process of body mentalization is challenging, with self-representation often shaped by narcissistic ideals reinforced by society, resulting in a strong sense of inadequacy (Fiorin et al., 2015).

The Web allows you to interact without the body (Tonioni, 2013) and experience intense emotions through the creation of an avatar they can relate to through an ideal virtual identity. This is referred to as gaze aversion (Lancini, 2019), especially towards their peers, since they can expose intellectual, bodily, and relational inadequacy. Lack of self-confidence causes anxiety about having to address performance, associated with social anxiety and depressive states. Social withdrawal can therefore become the immediate solution required to mitigate suffering, alongside the illusion of regaining control over one's life.

15.3 Clinical interventions in social withdrawal

Therapeutic interventions require a high level of adaptation and flexibility. In my clinical experience, when an adolescent comes to me in person, he or she does so with great difficulty and is forced by his or her parents. The biggest challenge is to make contact and establish a therapeutic alliance. Usually, the first contact is with the child's parents since it is not possible to go to the meeting with the teenager; planning home visits represents a preferred route to reach out to the teen in his place of withdrawal, to earn his trust and offer him a way to voice his suffering and feel less lonely.

In my therapeutic work, I refer to the multigenerational family therapy model (Andolfi, 2017) by following its basic steps: the primary goal is to access the teenager's pain, respecting his time and suffering, entering his places and history, to understand his behavioral signals, which are sometimes extreme. Addressing the blocks, the distance, the emotional cuts that have developed within the family's evolutionary history, is the first step toward reconnecting generations, opening communication, and bringing the experiences of parents and children closer.

The teenager acts as a family expert sending out warning signals that need to be understood, acknowledged, and reinterpreted: his suffering reflects his needs, desires, and fears, while simultaneously turning into a weapon uncovering conflicts and unresolved events belonging to family history. One of the main goals of therapy is to make everyone capable of moving away from their position and putting themselves in the shoes of others, through an intense experience, which can reach deeper authentic emotional connections.

15.4 The cry for help

Social withdrawal represents a block and a cry for help; the urge to step out of the family environment is transformed into a movement going in the opposite direction, leading to self-exclusion. Frequently, this cry for help does not occur when the first symptoms appear, but at a more advanced stage. Parents initially notice irregular school attendance, progressive indifference towards friends, and a decline in participation in sports and other extracurricular activities. As soon as the first signs of withdrawal appear, parents often resort to medical examinations to investigate the nature of their child's physical symptoms, such as migraines, abdominal pain, nausea, and stomachache. In other cases, difficulties are attributed to laziness, apathy, fear of facing life's challenges, or the seduction of the virtual world. Anguish, frustration, and helplessness are the feelings experienced by parents asking for help after having tried out different options to persuade their child to overcome their state of isolation, shifting between expulsive and excessive caregiving styles.

15.5 Case illustration

Lorenzo is a 17-year-old boy who has not attended school for three months. He is in the fourth year of scientific high school and has always achieved good results even in sports, such as karate. At the beginning of the year, he had been experiencing physical symptoms, such as headaches and severe abdominal pain, that often forced him to arrive to school late or miss it entirely. As time went on, attendance became more and more irregular, until he stopped going to school altogether. To help the boy avoid failing his academic year and reduce his anxiety level, the headmaster suggested planning scheduled tests, following an agreement on the topics to be studied. However, the boy refused, believing this would further worsen both his self-perception and how others viewed him.

The parents' cry for help came three months after Lorenzo had stopped going to school, he had given up all sports activities, and spent his time locked up in his room sleeping most of the day and staying up all night on his computer. His parents were extremely worried, and communication with their son declined, leaving only a few shared moments between them.

They felt they had tried everything, even to the point of physical confrontation, and the family atmosphere had become very tense: there were moments when Lorenzo alternated between toddler-like tantrums, complaining of physical discomfort and feelings of diversity and worthlessness, reminding his mother of her caring role, and others when he is oppositional, refuses help and reacts with anger and aggression, especially toward his father, toward whom he is dismissive and critical. During the initial phone consultation with Lorenzo's parents, we considered the possibility of a first meeting in person with the whole family.

15.5.1 The therapeutic alliance

When we talk about the construction of the therapeutic alliance (Andolfi, 2017), we do not only refer to the adolescent but also to the process involving the entire family. The alliance with the family is achieved through the adolescent, and it is through him or her that we may enter the family emotional-relational dynamics. A fundamental step in this process is to highlight his/her relational skills, starting precisely from what is positive in him/her and approaching his/her reality with genuine curiosity.

When Lorenzo turns up for the session with the whole family, he is very annoyed. He sits with his arms folded without even taking off his jacket and covers his face by lowering his hat to eye level. He looks in pain and only gives one-word answers expressing his anger against his parents who forced him out. A slight opening is possible when we ask him how he spends his time in his room and about his karate skills. His achievements in school, sports, and social activities with his peers seem to have created expectations that are currently an unbearable burden. While his parents describe him as the model son, he feels incompetent and good for nothing. He cries, and gradually anger gives way to sadness and disappointment. Lack of communication in the family emerges early on. He resists any intervention to bring him out of isolation with anger, shouting and shutting himself away in his room. An escalation is described in which a circuit of aggression is developed over time. After an initial phase in which his parents had tried to convince him through dialogue, the son's constant refusal led to stronger and more aggressive actions, such as breaking into his room, dragging him out of bed, cutting off his Internet access, up to physical confrontation. His room has turned into a protected place from the threats of the outside world and his family, thus intensifying the state of isolation.

Giving the adolescent a voice by becoming curious about him and his activities facilitates the creation of a trusting relationship that goes through the therapist's communication of implicit messages: *I am more interested in you than in your problems, I am not only here for you, but for your whole family*. To approach his world and forge a therapeutic alliance, it is essential to show respect for his problems, his time, his silence, and his function within the family.

How is it possible to move from the state of immobility sustained by withdrawal to a more active position when the family is stuck in a state of pain and helplessness? The description of this clinical situation makes it possible to highlight some basic tools to get in touch with the withdrawn teenager and restore the family resources within a system marked by rigid positions, lack of communication, and emotional distance.

15.5.2 Home visits: Reaching the adolescent in his or her place of withdrawal

Home visit is a valuable intervention tool turning the teenager's room into a meeting space and no longer just a place of solitude. It is important to assess the degree of severity of his withdrawal early on to understand whether there is a chance of getting the child to the therapist. In cases where this is unfeasible, it is essential to plan home-based interventions to establish initial contact with the adolescent while respecting his or her own pace. In other cases, as in the one described in the case illustration, the home visit represents a modality of intervention that fits into the therapeutic path to facilitate the construction of a therapeutic alliance and family communication. Agreed upon during the family sessions, it represents an elective way of entering the adolescent's private space, connecting to his or her vital areas, enhancing his or her skills, and facilitating the creation of a shared space between parents and children, with the therapist playing a bridging role between generations. Entering the home makes the place of the relationship more intimate and the experience of boundary more human and emotional. This makes it possible to establish a trusting relationship, starting with sharing the adolescent's activities in his or her room. For example, when the main activity is using the Web, the therapist can ask to be guided through his/her virtual world, bringing out his experiences and emotions through the only channel that keeps him/her in close contact with the outside world. Parents can get closer to their child, tuning into his fear of showing up and his/her desire to become invisible.

During the home visit following the first family session, I meet Lorenzo and his parents in the living room, we have coffee, and then head off to his room. The atmosphere is tense; Lorenzo is of few words. We review pictures hanging on the walls of Lorenzo as a small child and in karate competitions. He tells me that karate is a martial art you fight bare-handed, and it trains mind and body and teaches you how to protect yourself from outside aggression. This allows me to enter an initial area of distress where Lorenzo says that at some point he felt that he was no longer making any progress in that discipline and that he was afraid of losing a fight: "If you are not strong in the head, you cannot be strong in the body either, and others are stronger and braver than I am." For Lorenzo, losing became intolerable, just like the gaze and judgment of others. We discuss loneliness and the fear of not standing in comparison with his peers, but words are not enough to overcome the closed state of mind; it is essential to start doing things and being together, while putting up with long moments of silence.

Learning about the virtual world of online games is the key to enter on the next visit, into the most profound depths of his existence. He describes his strong and high-performance avatar that allows him to play and talk to others without fear, giving vent to all his emotions. He talks about his anger, sadness, aggressiveness, and not feeling understood by his parents. Together, we agree to introduce his parents to this world, inviting them into his room. Thus, a meeting based on an agreement of trust is planned: listening to each other without criticism and prejudice, laying down the hatchet. Sitting in the child's room and sharing their child's activities allows parents to find a point of connection, tune in to the retreat, and allow Lorenzo to feel welcomed and reassured, seen for what he can express at that moment. Physical and verbal confrontation, acted out on both sides, are resignified as extreme acts of powerlessness, suffering, and lack of communication. Getting to know the "tribe" of kids connected on social media, with whom Lorenzo is in touch, provides a new key to openness to the outside world, quite different from the demonization and forced suspension of Internet by his parents.

As Haim Omer (Omer & Weinblatt, 2005) suggests, in describing some strategies supporting parents of aggressive or self-destructive teens, one must not enter the vicious cycle of self-feeding behavior. Parental submission increases the demands of the child, who comes to the certainty of getting what he wants through threat and hostile behavior, while the more one tries to impose his authority by threatening, shouting, and punishing, the more the adolescent will be inclined to react with even more aggressive attitudes: hostility creates hostility. The child's behavior can be interrupted through *nonviolent resistance*, in which parental authority is exercised without resorting to physical or verbal attacks but based on a determination to resolve the situation by remaining present in his or her life (Omer & Weinblatt, 2005). The meeting in the room conveys a signal of openness and willingness, but also assertiveness in clearly communicating that one intends to emerge from isolation. This isolation often extends beyond the adolescent, reflecting a broader family dynamic, as the family may attempt to conceal the child's distress out of shame.

And it is precisely by sharing the common sense of failure and shame, experienced by the family, that one can move on to a fundamental phase of therapy, giving a different connotation to symptoms, reinterpreted and redefined in light of family development.

Already during the first visit, Lorenzo was able to express his fear of having disappointed his parents. He shared his deep concern about being perceived as a burden, particularly to his mother, who had sacrificed her career for the family. The anger at his father, accused of being absent from family life because of his job, could finally be expressed. That phrase "You are the little man of the house," which made him feel grown up and important in the past, now stirs Lorenzo's anger. Now he feels little and is afraid of being a bluff, that he will no longer be able to achieve the results he hoped for, not even that of passing his high school graduation exam. He doesn't know if the studies he has undertaken are suitable, he can't cope with school tests, and he is terrified by the idea that others might make fun of him.

15.5.3 The adolescent as co-therapist

"Help me get in, guide me through the family history": this is the request for the adolescent during the therapeutic session, making him a central figure and protagonist in a new way, by recognizing his relational skills. A movement that is also represented by the body, asking him to move his chair next to the therapist.

I ask Lorenzo to sit next to me and help me explore the family history. The narrative reveals the loneliness of his mother, unnoticed child of a deeply depressed mother and a father who died early, who learned to step aside and take care of the other since childhood. The same feeling of loneliness marks the story of the father, a man totally focused on a sense of duty and performance. Growing up in the shadow of a brother who was considered a genius, he strove to prove to his parents that, despite everything and everyone, he would make it on his own. Two examples of resistance to life's challenges, where surrender and failures are unthinkable. Lorenzo represented the son of redemption from a history of invisibility. They felt like better parents than their own by projecting their expectations onto him. The son's social withdrawal becomes a narcissistic wound that carries huge pain, while for the boy it is a way to detach himself from his parents from which he felt the implicit demand to be perfect. The fear of failure has become paralyzing, leading to the abandonment of all attempts of identification. Sharing the story allows the parents and the child to tune into the suffering. No one is invincible; everyone's soul has been wounded by a form of injustice suffered. Expectations can be reinterpreted as a desire to provide different opportunities for growth, while suffering and imperfection are shared experiences crossing generations. During our sessions, pain has greater possibilities to express itself and takes on a new meaning. It is possible to address the fragility of the marital couple stiffened in roles played inside and outside the family, determining a strong physical and emotional distance between them. Individual islands of loneliness were reinterpreted within their own story and called upon to confront the past through their child's suffering.

Helping the adolescent become a competent subject is a fundamental step. When he sits next to the therapist who guides him into family exploration, he gains a more adult position than when the focus is exclusively on him and on his symptoms, keeping him in a childlike position. The genogram tool is often used, which is useful to identify significant persons, traumatic events, losses, and situations that have had an impact on family relationships, creating a developmental block. Unspoken secrets may emerge, clarified by his parents' narrative, and these help the adolescent feel respected, less protected, and acquire new meanings with respect to his family history. A new language, shared by all, can be spoken: the language of emotions and a sense of belonging gained by feeling part of the same story.

15.5.4 Networking

Alongside the work done with the family, leading to a relationship of trust through the acceptance of suffering and its redefinition within the family history, it is essential to set up a proper network-based intervention. This involves opening up to other systems and subsystems related to the person's life. Particularly in cases of severe social withdrawal, the figure of the educator is crucial in helping the adolescent to re-enter the outside world in small steps through concrete proposals for resocialization. Parents can be supported in dealing with their child's moments of crisis daily and be consistent in the way they intervene. Networking should also be established with the school in order to gradually reconnect with the educational activity: identifying alternative learning situations could be a way to decrease the sense of failure vis-à-vis his peers. The goal is to allow the adolescent, through a gradual and protected experience, to reclaim his or her life outside the home.

The transition from an idealized family to the sharing of each person's experiences of loneliness has allowed them to contact their own areas of suffering to meet the other, and restarting a development process anew was supported by networking. The boy was assisted by an educator from the local services, who helped him reconnect with the outside world: having breakfast in a café, going for a walk in the park, choosing a book in the silence of a library, all small actions supported by the presence of a person who can make him feel safe in restarting a body accustomed to perceiving himself within his own room or idealized through virtual experience. This resocialization program was carried out at home, as well by reactivating collaborative behaviors within the family. Even with Internet, new channels of openness and sharing were activated up to access to an online educational platform, which made it possible not to lose a whole school year. All steps were discussed in the multidisciplinary network involving the family, social services, therapist, and teachers, with the common goal of implementing agreed modes of intervention and getting Lorenzo back to life.

15.6 Conclusions

The multigenerational family therapy model highlights the basic ingredients to succeed in approaching and giving meaning to the pain experienced by families. The goal is to reconnect individuals to their own history by taking a three-generational perspective where the adolescent becomes a special guide on this journey. The transformative process is brought about by shifting the focus from the symptom to the relationship, and the therapist assumes the role of a mediator: builds connections, connects generations, and activates social and network resources. Clinical intervention related to social withdrawal in adolescence is an opportunity to question ourselves as therapists about our identity and how we think of therapy. Rigid adherence to models that allow us to move skillfully and safely within our settings can limit the therapeutic experience if not proportional to the true needs of the family. Flexibility, putting ourselves and our professional identity at stake, alongside the courage to contact aspects of humanity and authenticity that belong to us, are a breeding ground to break away from immobility and access areas of distress. This is the only way the therapeutic relationship can be transformed into a true encounter with the family – one capable of recognizing the skills and activating the resources present inside.

References

Aguglia, E., Signorelli, M. S., Pollicino, C., Arcidiacono, E., & Petralia, A. (2010). Il fenomeno dell'Hikikomori: Cultural bound o quadro psicopatologico emergente? *Giornale Italiano di Psicopatologia, 16*, 157–164.

Andolfi, M. (2017). *Multi-generational family therapy: Tools and resources for the therapist.* Routledge (Original work published 2015).

Andolfi, M., & Mascellani, A. (2023). *Teen voices*. Accademia Press (Original work published 2010).

Andreoli, V. (2006). La violenza della metamorfosi. *Terapia familiare, 81*, 5–15.

Bowen, M. (1979). *Dalla Famiglia all'individuo: La differenziazione del sé nel sistema familiare*. Astrolabio.

Crepaldi, M. (2019). *Hikikomori. I giovani che non escono di casa.* Alpes.

Fiorin, M. C., Cappellini, M., & Comazzi, D. (2015). Il sostegno al ruolo genitoriale. In R. Spiniello, A. Piotti, & D. Comazzi (Eds.), *Il corpo in una stanza. Adolescenti ritirati che vivono di computer*. Franco Angeli.

Kato, T. A., Kanba, S., & Teo, A. R. (2019). Hikikomori: Multidimensional understanding, assessment, and future international perspectives. *Psychiatry and Clinical Neurosciences, 73*, 427–440. https://doi.org/10.1111/pcn.12895

Lancini, M. (2019). *Il ritiro sociale negli adolescenti*. Raffaello Cortina.

Li, T. M. H., & Wong, P. (2015). Youth social withdrawal behavior (hikikomori): A systematic review of qualitative and quantitative studies. *Australian & New Zealand Journal of Psychiatry, 49*, 595–609. https://doi.org/10.1177/0004867415581179

Omer, H., & Weinblatt, U. (2005). Résistance non violente: Guide pour les parents d'adolescents présentant des comportements violents ou autodestructeurs. *Cahiers critiques de thérapie familiale et de pratiques de réseaux, 1*(34), 77–105. https://doi.org/10.3917/ctf.034.0077

Pietropolli Charmet, G. (2013). *La paura di essere brutti: Gli adolescenti e il corpo.* Raffaello Cortina.

Saito, T. (2013). *Hikikomori: Adolescence without end.* University of Minnesota Press (Original work published 1992).

Santona, A., Lionetti, F., Tognasso, G., Fusco, C., Maccagnano, G., Barreca, D., & Gorla, L. (2023). Sensitivity and attachment in an Italian sample of Hikikomori adolescents and young adults. *International Journal of Environmental Research and Public Health, 20*(12), 6148. https://doi.org/10.3390/ijerph20126148

Spiniello, R., Piotti, A., & Comazzi, D. (2015). *Il corpo in una stanza: Adolescenti ritirati che vivono di computer*. Franco Angeli.

Suwa, M., & Suzuki, K. (2013). The phenomenon of "Hikikomori" (social withdrawal) and the socio-cultural situation in Japan today. *Giornale Italiano di Psicopatologia, 19*, 191–198.

Tonioni, F. (2013). *Psicopatologia web-mediata: Dipendenza da internet e nuovi fenomeni dissociativi.* Springer.

16

SILENT EMOTIONS

Embodied metaphors in early-onset eating disorders in adolescence and pre-adolescence

Camillo Loriedo

16.1 Introduction

Anorexia and bulimia nervosa are generally known as disorders whose onset occurs mainly during adolescence. However, in the last 20 years, we have witnessed a progressive tendency of these disorders to appear in increasingly earlier periods of life (under 12 years of age), with a concomitant proportional increase in their incidence over time (Holland et al., 2016; Nicholls et al., 2011). Especially in anorexia nervosa, the early onset of the disorder in pre-adolescence or even childhood can no longer be considered an exceptional event (van Son et al., 2006; Favaro et al., 2009). The increasingly frequent confirmations of this trend became over time a good reason to investigate the clinical consequences of early-onset eating disorders. Questions have been raised as to whether these forms are more or less severe than those that have the typical adolescence onset and whether their course has a shorter or longer duration than the others.

To clarify these aspects, Jenkins et al. (2020) explored some important variables of early-onset anorexia nervosa and concluded that these types of forms result in a significantly longer duration of the disorder than both the group with typical adolescence onset and that with late-onset anorexia nervosa. In addition, significantly reduced cognitive flexibility, such as increased tendency towards *body dissatisfaction* and other symptoms of the eating disorders spectrum, are significantly more severe than those present in the other two control groups.

The data indicating a longer disorder duration and a higher severity that accompany an early onset explain why clinicians who deal with anorexia and bulimia nervosa tend to monitor with increasing attention the phases that precede the development of symptoms, as well as the first signs that anticipate the actual disorder onset.

What we know today is that most of these early signs are mainly related to the *emotional component* capable of activating a peculiar communicative and interactive modality that precedes the disorder onset, but that tends in time to consolidate into a solid barrier that is increasingly difficult to overcome.

This emotional barrier surrounds not only the symptom-bearer adolescent but also the entire family system, which consequently tends to acquire interactive patterns that facilitate the early onset of the disorder.

DOI: 10.4324/9781003536765-19

16.2 Silent emotions and bodily metaphors

The early indicators preceding the onset of the full-blown disorder largely belong to the emotional world of the adolescent and his or her family. It is a particular form of what Nemiah and Sifneos (1970) have termed *alexithymia*. Typical features of this construct include:

(a) difficulty identifying one's own feelings (DIF)
(b) difficulty describing one's own feelings (DDF)
(c) an externally oriented thinking style (EOT)

Although alexithymia has been found primarily in subjects with psychosomatic disorders, its highest levels have been confirmed especially in the eating disorders population, where it can reach 68% (Schmidt et al., 1993; Taylor et al., 1997). These levels are much higher than those of the general population, where the incidence of alexithymia barely reaches 10% (Parker et al., 1989), but also significantly higher than that found in all other known disorders.

If in eating disorders alexithymia incidence is particularly high, on the other hand, the factors that allow its early recognition mainly depend on a few predominant characteristics of food alexithymia that make it unique in its kind. It consists first in a *concrete and material verbalization*, which concerns almost exclusively body shape, food, and physical fitness (Treasure, 2012). Every small communicative space is meticulously filled with these verbalizations. These types of concrete verbalizations appear to serve as a sort of protection against emotional communication, aimed at maintaining oneself as long as possible on topics that do not arouse significant affective reactions.

However, careful observation reveals that the loss of emotional meanings, so carefully avoided, is only apparent because rather than being completely eliminated, they are transformed into *silent emotions* taking the form of *embodied metaphors* (Loriedo, 2018).

So, from the adolescent voice, even before the diagnostic criteria of the disorder can be established, we could hear phrases such as:

(a) "I feel a weight on my belly that is unbearable for me and that prevents me from thinking about anything else."
(b) "I can't swallow the things I once wanted with all my heart."
(c) "I feel exhausted, but my body needs to move."

These words apparently seem to indicate only bodily sensations, but when we connect them to the pre-adolescent or adolescent relational world, we can easily discover some metaphoric meaning that can't be openly expressed by verbal communication. For example, these phrases could be read as:

(a) "I have a heavy secret that I can't bear and that prevents me from thinking about anything else."
(b) "There are things (or behaviors) that I used to want with all my heart, but that now I can no longer accept."
(c) "This situation makes me feel exhausted, but I can only get my body moving."

16.3 Early indicators

There are several early indicators of presence of these silent, metaphorically expressed emotions.

Exaggerated Verbal Production. The *verbal volume* of families with an eating disorder is particularly high, and even for the therapists working with these families, sometimes it can be difficult to find enough space for any back-and-forth verbal communication. I will never forget the family who for three sessions in a row left me only the opportunity to introduce myself and say goodbye, apologizing at the end of each session for not leaving me enough space to have my say, but always expressing their desire to listen to my comments in the next session.

If this crowded communication style, often worsened by frequent verbal overlaps among family members, is accompanied by a consistent poverty of content, as is typically observed (these families rarely go beyond the few allowed areas – body, food, and physical fitness), one has the feeling of being in front of a solid defensive wall that prevents emotional experiences and expression.

Another interesting indicator is demonstrated, regardless of the family educational and cultural level, by a high linguistic competence supported by a very wide repertoire of words. Consequently, although the content is limited and often even repetitive, family members can keep the conversation going for a long time on the tracks of what we have called *pleasant stereotypy*.

Immersed in this forest of words, the adolescent or pre-adolescent is unable to access the most important form of communication, the one with the most intense affective color, which in these families is not conveyed through words, but tends to be expressed by assuming a bodily form.

A 12-year-old girl, with restrictive eating habits that seemed to be a prelude to anorexia, effectively described her family by saying: "Talking is always very important to us, but very important things cannot be talked about."

The Curtain of Silence. The alexithymia form that is peculiar in eating disorders can be achieved through a completely different or even diametrically opposite path, leading nevertheless to the same result. Barriers based on impenetrable walls of words can be followed from time to time by tension-laden silences that alternate with the flood of words and make it difficult to access the most significant components of the intense emotions experienced by the adolescent. In cases where an emotional content becomes an unbearable burden, the verbal wall can give way and a heavy *curtain of silence* can take its place.

In such situations, unexpectedly, silence can be broken by *dramatic revelations of secrets*, of which the adolescent is often the bearer, which can jeopardize the apparent solidity of the family structure, as well as collapse the very scaffolding of alexithymia. The following case also shows that such eventuality could pave the way for a possible positive development.

16.3.1 Case illustration: Family A

In Family A's previous sessions of family therapy, Aurora, Beatrice's older sister, often complained about the excessive attention paid to her sister, both in the special diet that has always been reserved for her and in the higher costs of clothing incurred only for her, along with other privileges she was granted from an early age.

Even though none of the family members admits the existence of real privileges and all of them verbally deny the validity of her complaints, in fact no one seems to care about Aurora and her claims. On the other hand, Aurora fails to adequately argue her grievances and to present herself in such a way as to draw the attention of those present to herself when she speaks.

On the contrary, despite her 15 years of age, Beatrice succeeds in being considered by everyone with great attention, and every time she starts to speak, her parents seem to hang on every word that passes from her lips. This is also the case when, at the beginning of the fifth session, Beatrice announces that she wants to reveal separately to the therapist an important secret.

The therapist immediately replies that to avoid unbalanced situations within the family relationships, it would be preferable to tell the secret in front of everyone. The parents also much prefer the secret be revealed in the presence of the other family members and encourage her to reveal everything, regardless of the consequences, "come what may." Aurora herself urges Beatrice, who seems very hesitant, to move on, saying, "It is always good to speak openly: In a family you must always be able to tell each other everything."

Beatrice, pressured from all sides, declares that at this point she is forced to reveal her secret, because it is too heavy, and she can no longer bear it on her own. In the end, she steels herself and reveals that, for a few years now, Aurora's husband has been secretly courting her. He secretly picks her up from school and tells her that, since he met her, he is no longer interested in his wife.

Aurora's first reaction seems reassuring. She says with exhibited ease: "You see, nothing happened. You spoke and nothing happened. You were right to speak up. You must talk. We always have to be able to tell each other everything." Then, as she continues to utter her reassuring words, suddenly, she faints. The mother tries to help her and shakes her forcefully, telling her: "Nothing has happened, nothing has happened," as Aurora herself had said a few moments before. But as soon as she begins to recover, Aurora finally responds to her mother's words, with all the anger she has in her body: "What the fuck are you talking about! How can you say it is nothing? My sister has always taken everything away from me: First, all the things I liked, she also took my parents, then my friends, and now she's taking my husband away from me too. And you say it is nothing! But it goes . . ."

After Beatrice's dramatic revelation, the family's relationships suffer a profound positive change: Aurora has finally managed to make herself heard, and her parents are starting to take care of her. In addition, Beatrice has lost her primacy over her sister and, in the face of the marital drama that will lead Aurora to a bitter divorce, the privileged space she held within the family has been abruptly reduced. But the change that took place within the family allowed Beatrice to finally start moving in search of some external space for herself.

16.4 Emotional reactions to family member's physical appearance and health

When listening to the voices of adolescents in the phases preceding the onset of the eating disorder, it is possible to identify a series of emotional reactions of adolescents in response to the health and appearance of what we can define as the "family body," anticipating the contents that will later be represented by eating symptoms.

For example, here is a family in which a pre-symptomatic daughter was preoccupied with a family member's health condition.

16.4.1 Case illustration: Family B

In the case of Family B, it is difficult to reconstruct the period that preceded the onset of anorexia nervosa in Carla, Dario and Emilia's 14-year-old daughter. What emerges, between admissions and contradictions, is that about two years earlier Dario had had a myocardial infarction that had put his survival at serious risk. The event had been related above all to Dario's severe overweight (around 150 kg), which had led the doctors to suggest bariatric surgery or, at least, to prescribe a particularly strict diet for him. The situation had caused critical concern in his wife Emilia, but especially in the young daughter Carla, who had begun to neglect her schoolwork to devote herself almost exclusively to her informal, auto-didactic study of medicine.

Claiming to have the right based on her acquired knowledge, she forced her father into a grueling ritual every night in which he had to tell her everything he had eaten in the office, and then she forced him to allow her to measure his heart rate and blood pressure. The results of this "doctor's game," as her exhausted mother called it, had been particularly disappointing, and the father had now decided that he would no longer accept the torment of that ritual. Only then did Carla give up continuing with her "doctor's visits" to her father, but a few months later, she began to gradually reduce her food intake, without any apparent reason.

Emotional reactions to family members' body appearance can also take the form of *concern about the physical appearance of family members* other than the teen who will eventually develop an eating disorder.

16.4.2 Case illustration: Family C

In Family C, the signs of an incipient eating disorder in 17-year-old Francesca arise long before the onset of the disorder and are centered on the physical appearance of her mother Giovanna. Francesca considers her mother sloppy and unkempt, and incapable of looking sexy and attractive. She calls her "the invisible woman," mocks her for her scruffy attire, and takes every opportunity to give her provocative and sensual undergarments, forcing her to wear them.

Giovanna is embarrassed by her daughter's demands and can only partially satisfy them. She does not feel comfortable in a conspicuous lifestyle, which would not be consonant with her identity. But Francesca is not satisfied with her mother's slow progress. To convince her finally to become "a visible woman," she insinuates the suspicion that her husband may decide to cheat on her with a more attractive woman. Francesca even decides to pay for some beauty treatments for her mother with her own money as well as a membership for fitness classes. Once again, Giovanna only does a small part of what her daughter has arranged for her.

A year later, Francesca discovers that her father has a mistress and, while the mother takes the news with a restrained reaction, Francesca's anger is unleashed, and she breaks several precious objects that had always been religiously guarded in the home. Within a few days, her first bulimic crisis accompanied by self-induced vomiting began, but her parents did not notice it until six months later and, after another three months, they asked for family therapy.

The adolescent may also respond to parental conflict and separation by *alternating between ways in which they treat their body*, such that their behavior with food communicates two different messages.

16.4.3 Case illustration: Ilaria

At the beginning of her adolescence after an early childhood that she described as happy, Ilaria senses the presence of strong conflict and growing tension between her parents. The mother reacts to this tension through an obsessive commitment to cleaning the house and meticulously preparing food. Her mother's enrolling in a cooking school further intensified her focus on food.

For his part, Ilaria's father responds to conflict with his wife by expanding his professional commitments and extending his working hours until late in the evening. This results in a substantial increase in income (which he uses as the justification for his increased hours) but also to a drastically reduced amount of free time, meaning that he was largely absent from the family, thereby avoiding his wife and spending little time with Ilaria.

Ilaria's dissatisfaction with her parents' conflict and choices about how to spend their time reaches its peak when her parents tell her that they are separating. The separation agreement provides that the "family body" will be divided into two parts: the father will live on his own in a new rented house, while the mother will keep the family home and Ilaria will have to transition from one house to the other every other week.

Some weeks later, Ilaria's symptoms begin, and her eating behavior alternates in its style between one home and the other. When she is at home with her mother, Ilaria is rigidly restrictive and resolutely refuses the food that her mother makes available to her with meticulous care. In contrast, when

Ilaria is with her father – who provides her with money yet no time together – she spends substantial sums on food, which she devours during enormous binges that lead to her systematically vomiting into the toilet. Two different symptoms, two ways of physically communicating her feelings about the parents' split, commensurate with each of the two parts of the divided family body.

16.5 Emotion expression through embodied metaphors

Crucial to understanding and adequately intervening in the onset and course of eating disorders is a series of actions and behaviors by adolescents, and often also by their family members, that depicts peculiar emotional conditions, especially anger. These emotional conditions are not explicitly declared but can be recognized by examining the embodied metaphors through which they are expressed. This is an area of assessment that has received little clinical attention, and yet is critical to ascertaining the silenced emotions of the adolescent.

A powerful example of this process is the violent binge eating that characterizes bulimia nervosa or other impulsive actions (e.g., self-injuries) that can also be present in bulimia and anorexia nervosa. Here we consider some that have predictive value in the onset of the disorder.

The presence of abnormal eating practices during meals is currently considered one of the most reliable predictors of the onset of eating disorders (Monaco et al., 2011) and, with great probability, also a good predictor of possible relapse (Sala et al., 2023), despite initial symptoms remission.

Abnormal eating behaviors during mealtime, such as discarding substantial amounts of food and meticulous shredding of food in the plate, have been documented for a long time (Abraham et al., 1983), but these aspects have not been paid enough attention as a form of metaphoric communication and, especially, expression of emotions.

Here is a list of the most frequent behaviors that can be observed during meals of those who will later develop an eating disorder. The adolescent often continues to enact these behaviors during the course of disorder, and often even after the florid state of the disorder has subsided. In addition to their pervasive presence, these abnormal eating behaviors indirectly reveal intense negative emotions, such as anger and disgust. These emotions give rise to the gestures that are made during the meal and the quality of a daily *battle against food*:

- Discarding substantial amounts of the meal contents
- Repeated food inspection
- Repeated food selection
- Repeated seasoning scraping
- Meticulous food shredding
- Bite preparation by reducing it to minimal quantities
- Arranging a series of tiny amounts of food in rows
- Using cutlery that is not suitable for a specific type of food (this will hinder consumption)
- Alternating intake of food from different courses
- Concealment of uneaten food
- Nonverbal expressions of anger and disgust towards food
- Keeping a significant distance from the plate, even if this makes feeding uncomfortable
- Negative verbalizations (sometimes, even insults) towards food during the meal
- Repeated and ostensibly unmotivated movement of the food in the plate
- Frequently touching objects on the table without using them
- Looking at the watch repeatedly
- Often staring into space
- Fidgeting relentlessly in the chair

- Repeatedly getting up from the table without any reason
- Crying
- Stretching
- Tidying up clothes
- Repeatedly fixing own hair
- Excessively slow or excessively fast meal
- Particularly prolonged chewing or ingestion without chewing
- Intake of disproportionate amounts of fluids compared to food
- Ritual activities in both the arrangement and intake of food
- Excessive nor related to food activity during the meal
- Inability to maintain conversation during a meal

This is far from an exhaustive list of behaviors that reveal a strong and persistent hostility towards food, which is perceived as an unspoken, powerful enemy. In this way, the emotions that the adolescent and her family cannot express explicitly spill over into the food area and everything it metaphorically represents.

16.6 Self-harm

The adolescent's anger, fear, and disgust are emotions that can be directed toward food, but that can often be directed as well towards oneself, with behaviors that can damage both one's health in general and some parts of one's body. In addition, some adolescents with eating disorders, especially those who have gone through traumatic experiences, can develop dissociative conditions that could completely erase emotions and perceptions. In these cases, self-injurious behavior (especially cutting) may result from a desperate attempt to regain some form of feeling that others allow themselves to feel freely and naturally.

In other cases, the feeble, self-censored voice of these adolescents cannot be expressed through common emotional language and can only be accessed through means of *embodied emotions*, which gain their salience through being connected to a special meaning.

16.6.1 Case illustration: Lucia

Lucia is hospitalized in a condition of severe malnutrition. She is emaciated due to undereating and has also reduced her fluid intake. Many of the clinical parameters of health have begun to deteriorate. To make matters worse, after a few days she uses a particularly sharp pen to make some cuts on her left arm.

After carefully examining the wound, we notice the cut has a particular shape which, albeit in a rudimentary way, represents the number 30. When asked to explain the meaning of the incision she has made on herself, Lucia simply replies that she can only talk about it in a confidential interview. Shortly after, alone with the doctor, she explains that on the 30th day of the month before her hospitalization, after a furious quarrel that took place inside the house between her parents, her father first tried to physically suppress her mother. Then he left and never came home. From that day on, the number 30 has become and will always be an enemy for her.

16.7 The advantages of early intervention

If it is possible to identify the indicators that we have described before the symptoms drastically arise and reduce all the "doors of access" to the adolescent's emotions, the heart of the adolescent's beginning discomfort will still be available for successful interventions. Helping the teen identify and articulate in words how they feel, how they see their families, and how they view themselves may even prevent the onset of an eating disorder.

This is also the right time to awaken the family and help them listen to the adolescent's or pre-adolescent's voices, before the eruption of the uncontrolled emotional explosions (either in affective words or in symbolic, metaphoric behavioral analogues of emotions) that the family will have enormous difficulty containing. The presence of these early indicators is certainly valuable for structuring an effective therapeutic intervention for eating disorders. Among many other challenges, the challenge that these disorders present to the therapist is to discern silent emotions expressed through physical metaphors. This requires a keen, empathic mind, clinical experience, and some degree of creative, even poetic sensibility in order to develop a hunch, to then be explored with the teen, about what they might be trying to "say" about their feelings and thoughts through bodily means.

References

Abraham, S. F., Mira, M., Beumont, P. J., Sowerbutts, T. D., & Llewellyn-Jones, D. (1983). Eating behaviours among young women. *Medical Journal of Australia, 3*, 225–228. https://doi.org/10.5694/j.1326-5377.1983.tb122429.x

Favaro, A., Caregaro, L., Tenconi, E., Bosello, R., & Santonastaso, P. (2009). Time trends in age at onset of anorexia nervosa and bulimia nervosa. *Journal of Clinical Psychiatry, 70*, 715–21. https://doi.org/10.4088/JCP.09m05176blu

Holland, J., Hall, N., Yeates, D. G., & Goldacre, M. (2016). Trends in hospital admission rates for anorexia nervosa in Oxford (1968–2011) and England (1990–2011): Database studies. *Journal of the Royal Society of Medicine, 109*, 59–66. https://doi.org/10.1177/0141076815617651

Jenkins, Z. M., Chait, L. M., Cistullo, L., & Castle, D. J. (2020). A comparison of eating disorder symptomatology, psychological distress and psychosocial function between early, typical and later onset anorexia nervosa. *Journal of Eating Disorders, 8*, 56. https://doi.org/10.1186/s40337-020-00337-w

Loriedo, C. (2018). Embodied metaphors: La comunicazione silenziosa del corpo familiare nell'anoressia nervosa. In M. L. Manca (Ed.), *Amore e psiche: La dimensione corporea in psicoterapia* (pp. 83–91). Alpes.

Monaco, L., Torti, M. C., & Loriedo, C. (2011). Rilevamento e valutazione di anomalie comportamentali durante il pasto in pazienti affette da Disturbi dell'Alimentazione: Implicazioni diagnostiche e terapeutiche. In M. Biondi & C. Loriedo (Eds.), *Disturbi di Personalità: Identità conflitti in una società in trasformazione* (pp. 164–184). Franco Angeli.

Nemiah, J. C., & Sifneos, P. E. (1970). Psychosomatic illness: A problem in communication. *Psychotherapy and Psychosomatics, 18*, 154–160. https://doi.org/10.1159/000286074

Nicholls, D. E., Lynn, R., & Viner, R. M. (2011). Childhood eating disorders: British national surveillance study. *British Journal of Psychiatry, 198*, 295–301. https://doi.org/10.1192/bjp.bp.110.081356

Parker, J. D. A., Taylor, G. J., & Bagby, R. M. (1989). The alexithymia construct: Relationship with sociodemographic variables and intelligence. *Comprehensive Psychiatry, 30*, 434–41. https://doi.org/10.1016/0010-440x(89)90009-6

Sala, M., Keshishian, A., Song, S., & Moskowitz, R. (2023). Predictors of relapse in eating disorders: A meta-analysis. *Journal of Psychiatric Research*, 158, 1879–1379. https://doi.org/10.1016/j.jpsychires.2023.01.002

Schmidt, U., Jiwany, A., & Treasure, J. (1993). A controlled study of alexithymia in eating disorders, *Comprehensive Psychiatry, 34*, 54–59. https://doi.org/10.1016/0010-440X(93)90036-4

Taylor, G. J., Bagby, R. M., & Parker, J. D. A. (1997). *Disorders of affect regulation: Alexithymia in medical and psychiatric illness*. Cambridge University Press. https://doi.org/10.1017/CBO9780511526831

Treasure, J. (2012). Emotion in eating disorders. *European Eating Disorders Review, 20*, 429–430. https://doi.org/10.1002/erv.2211

van Son, G. E., van Hoeken, D., Bartelds, A. I. M., van Furth, E. F., & Hoek, H. W. (2006). Time trends in the incidence of eating disorders: A primary care study in the Netherlands. *International Journal of Eating Disorders, 39*, 565–569. https://doi.org/10.1002/eat.20316

17

THERAPEUTIC WORK WITH FAMILIES AND ADOLESCENTS AT RISK IN A WESTERN AUSTRALIAN MENTAL HEALTH SERVICE

Giulia Pace

17.1 Introduction

This chapter reflects the experience of the work conducted at Touchstone, a public mental health service for children and adolescents located in Perth, Western Australia. Touchstone offers an innovative model for working with families in which an adolescent is at risk of suicide. The service aspires not only to decrease risk but also to use crisis as an opportunity to create personal transformation. This chapter will describe the underlying theoretical approaches of the service, the Touchstone journey, and a real-life example that highlights the service and its intervention in action.

17.2 The target of intervention

Touchstone has been operational since 2015 and was created with the aim of reducing emergency department presentations and hospital admissions for young people between the ages of 12 and 18, with a history of repeated self-harm, chronic suicidal ideation, and attempted suicides. The young people referred to this service are generally socially isolated and disengaged from the school environment or not yet part of a working environment. Their social and family context is usually quite compromised, and a high percentage have experienced abuse and other trauma. From a psychiatric perspective, the cohort have diagnoses such as depressive and anxiety disorders, post-traumatic stress disorders, eating disorders, substance use disorders, gender identity disorders, and in rare cases previous psychotic episodes. A large number have learning, attention, or socio-communicative disorders. However, the main diagnosis at the time of referral is personality disorder, predominantly borderline. In many cases, marked avoidant or narcissistic traits are also evident.

Given the high degree of psychiatric dysfunction among young people attending the service, most, prior to their entry into the Touchstone program, have accessed treatment in an acute or community setting during which they received psychological and, where necessary, pharmacological intervention. Adolescents are often treated, in various combinations, with antipsychotics, antidepressants, anxiolytics, stimulants, and in rare cases mood stabilizers. The aim of pharmacotherapy is to reduce impulsivity, anxiety, or depressed mood; however, in most cases, medications offer limited benefits.

DOI: 10.4324/9781003536765-20

17.3 Guiding theoretical approaches

The Touchstone model of care integrates three distinct theoretical frameworks with many common and complementary aspects. These are mentalization-based therapy (MBT) (Bateman & Fonagy, 2016), the multigenerational family therapy model (Andolfi, 2017), and principles of therapeutic communities (Royal College of Psychiatrists' Centre for Quality Improvement, 2008).

MBT focuses on strengthening mentalizing and improving social learning and has been successfully adopted in day programs for adults with borderline pathology since the 1990s (Bales et al., 2015; Bateman & Fonagy, 2010). Allen and Fonagy (2006) define mentalizing as "the imaginative mental activity that enables us to perceive and interpret human behavior in terms of intentional mental states (e.g. needs, desires, feelings, beliefs, goals, purposes and reasons)." Mentalizing is a process as natural as it is complex. It is not a static, unitary skill or trait. Mentalizing is influenced by stress and arousal, particularly in the context of specific attachment relationships. The ability to mentalize in such circumstances enables better capacity to regulate emotions, impulses, and greater interpersonal functioning. Behavioral disorders associated with personality dysfunction, in particular the borderline type, are associated with inhibited mentalizing and the reemergence of more immature representations of internal states, called non-mentalizing modes (Bateman & Fonagy, 2016).

Although there is growing evidence that supports the use and effectiveness of MBT in adolescents (Bo et al., 2017; Byrne et al., 2020; Jørgensen et al., 2021; Rossouw & Fonagy, 2012), clinical studies in this area are still scarce, particularly regarding day program services for adolescents with personality disorders.

Touchstone was developed as a day program within a therapeutic community context (Royal College of Psychiatrists' Centre for Quality Improvement, 2008) as adolescents have a unique sensitivity to social pressures and can thrive when immersed in a supportive peer culture.

Caregivers and family also play a crucial role for this age group. In adolescence, more than in any other stage of life, needs for separateness and belonging co-exist. It is therefore essential to balance the engagement of families so that they can actively be present to respond to attachment needs, but not intrusive. The multigenerational family therapy approach (Andolfi, 2017) offers a framework for this developmental challenge.

17.4 Guiding theoretical approaches in practice

One of the starting points of the work at Touchstone is considering that the young person's presenting behaviors are a response to underlying mental states that can be explored and understood. By centering the approach on this assumption, from the first moment and entirety of the adolescent's therapeutic journey at Touchstone, the clinician relates to the adolescent and their family in a neutral, non-judgmental manner, free of presumption and aiming at curiosity and discovery. This way of positioning oneself in the therapeutic encounter is defined in MBT as the "not-knowing stance" (Bateman et al., 2023).

During initial conversations and regular therapy sessions, the clinician aims to join or connect with all members of the family, especially the adolescent. The exploration of facts is explicitly oriented towards understanding any events the family narrates from the personal perspective of each family member. The collection of information occurs in a natural and spontaneous dialogue, which aims to create a sense of trust in each family member and real interest on the part of the clinician. The clinician presents themselves as humble and aware of their own limits, but eager to understand and get closer to each family member's emotional experience. This generates a sense of "epistemic trust," a term utilized by Peter Fonagy to describe "an individual's willingness to consider new knowledge from another person as trustworthy, generalizable and relevant to the self" (Fonagy & Allison, 2014).

This state of trust is required for any change to take place because, in its absence, anything even the most expert of therapists has to offer runs the risk of being rejected as not relevant to the specific needs of the individual. This way of relating helps to approach, without fear or preconceived ideas, the suffering that exists underneath the developmental stalls or regressions of the adolescent. In addition, it serves as an opening into the pain of those around the young person.

This is also what Maurizio Andolfi teaches (Andolfi & Mascellani, 2023). Andolfi describes not only the suffering of the identified patient but also that of members of their relational context, observing how this resonates within the group, whether it be the family, the peers, and/or the surrounding community (Andolfi & Mascellani, 2023). The adolescent is engaged in therapeutic work by valuing their role within the family, reading their symptoms as a key to entering the family's history and their distress as a strong push for everyone to change. The adolescent therefore becomes a co-therapist, encouraged to use their knowledge as an expert on their family and to guide the clinician in exploring the needs of all members of the family group (Andolfi, 2017; Andolfi & Haber, 1994).

In Touchstone, this approach is essential, because in most cases the families who come to the service don't hold clear motivation or confidence in their ability to change family dynamics. The parents are often afraid to approach their child, with whom they are frequently in severe conflict. If in meetings with the family the focus is on current conflict, more often than not, the tension between the adolescent and the parents worsens, to the point that the distance between them becomes unmanageable. By shifting the focus outside the current conflict between parents and children, and relocating it within the history of the family, the multigenerational model helps to navigate these tumultuous waters, exploring the generations preceding that of the adolescent and making time leaps that help to stimulate reflectiveness, understanding, and connection among family members (Andolfi, 2017). Relatives and members of the extended family are identified and potentially included in the consultations, with the aim to develop a support network that the family so desperately needs.

It is in thinking about the network of support for young people and families that Touchstone integrated into its foundations the principles of therapeutic communities (Royal College of Psychiatrists' Centre for Quality Improvement, 2008). Touchstone follows the typical organization of therapeutic communities at "low dosage," i.e., a non-residential structure with non-daily attendance of its clients. Therapeutic communities are based on the principles of commonality, reciprocity, and shared responsibility (Pearce et al., 2017; Shuker, 2010), and value the co-construction of the entire treatment path (Middleton, 2017). In Touchstone's therapeutic community, young people are placed in several group activities together (e.g., creative therapies, occupational therapy groups) and are encouraged to take initiative in looking after one another and establishing a safe and constructive culture. Staff members work alongside young people both in ecological interactions as well as in planned whole-community meetings and interventions.

The active participation of young people in all the groups and meetings at Touchstone promotes a sense of belonging in them and at the same time encourages young people to use their internal resources to take responsibility for their treatment, which in turn promotes increased life skills and competence. From this point of view, the prosocial function of the group at Touchstone is central and represents one of the major attractions of the program. Young people who attend the program have often expressed feeling marginalized by their peers and intrinsically inadequate. Feeling part of a community of people who are experiencing similar difficulties and who can understand each other, as well as being immersed into a strength-focused culture, provides opportunity for a more positive view of self to emerge. Moreover, the desire to be a part of a group that strives for change, so physiological for this phase of development, acts as a powerful engine. However, the group has the potential to influence both positively and negatively. Therefore, the formation of a milieu that inspires mutual support and a desire for functional change is crucial in minimizing the negative influence and potential "contagion" in the use of dysfunctional behaviors. It isn't unusual for adolescents who want to fit in to emulate self-destructive behaviors (such as self-harm or food restriction) displayed by their peers or shown through the online world. A positive peer culture can act as an antidote to this and in contrast model the development of self-enhancing behaviours.

The service also places emphasis on having a structured timetable, which functions as a solid support for young people without routine, helping them to re-establish order in their lives. Individual and group sessions are allocated set times and are intertwined with regular interactions with the allocated care coordinator. The care coordinator offers the adolescents support with their daily needs, and the psychiatrist keeps a thread among the various therapeutic interventions. Families are also invited to attend the program at set times. This approach (1) aims to keep families consistently active and involved in their child's therapeutic journey, and (2) also provides families with the ability to set aside some personal space. The need to self-sacrifice while reorganizing a big part of their lives around their child's care is a commonly expressed sentiment of family members.

17.5 The Touchstone journey

Touchstone offers a wraparound service that is family inclusive and involves three layers of intervention that can be undertaken either consecutively or as stand-alone, depending on what the family opts in to. The clinical team consists of a multidisciplinary group that includes psychologists, social workers, nurses, occupational therapists, and psychiatrists.

The first intervention offered is a diagnostic and therapeutic evaluation, after which young people and their family can elect to attend an introductory psychoeducational group followed by an intensive day program of six months duration. During the day program, young people attend Touchstone three times a week.

The diagnostic evaluation is offered to all young people referred to the program. It takes place over four sessions, and one of the outcomes of this process is to generate a formulation, also referred to as a "relational passport" (Grove & Smith, 2022). The relational passport captures patterns of relating within the young person's family as well as more specifically, an understanding of the way in which the adolescent perceives themselves and others, their attachment patterns to family members and peers, and the dominant non-mentalizing modes they tend to get into when under stress. Once these initial hypotheses and intuitions are understood by clinicians, they are then discussed with the young people and their family to collaboratively define the goals of the intervention and put them in writing. The family is then supported in their decision making about whether they want to continue engaging with Touchstone for further therapeutic work on their relational passport or take it with them to begin this work in a different context or at a different time in their life.

If the adolescent and their family decide to continue their journey at Touchstone and are motivated to continue group-based work, they progress into the second stage of treatment: a psychoeducational group. The sessions occur twice a week and are based on the MBT-Introductory group (MBT-I) with some adaptations specific to adolescence. The MBT-I aims to provide information, prepare patients for long-term treatment, increase motivation, elicit more detail about their mentalizing capacities, and confirm impressions from the initial assessment (Bateman et al., 2023). The Touchstone psychoeducation group focuses on recognizing the loss of mentalizing and learning how to recover it, the impact that adolescence and attachment have on the ability to mentalize, the meaning and approach to chronic suicidality and self-harm, and the understanding of personality.

In keeping with research in personality pathology in adolescence, which highlights the long-term benefits of early recognition and treatment (Bozzatello et al., 2019; Chanen et al., 2008, 2020), the concept of personality disorder is discussed during the psychoeducation sessions. This is done in a non-stigmatizing way and with emphasis on how personality function exists along a continuum, as described in the DSM-5 alternative model of personality disorder (*Diagnostic and Statistical Manual of Mental Disorders*, 5th ed., 2013). In addition to this educational component, the sessions are focused on an experiential component and are carried out in an interactive manner, in which the facilitators and participants explore together experiences related to the topics discussed. Caregivers and extended family members are invited to participate in the first and last of these sessions. At the conclusion of the psychoeducation group, each family meets with clinicians to evaluate how they found the experience of being in a group with others and to determine whether they will complete their engagement with Touchstone there or progress to the third stage: the day program.

The day program is organized into groups, and entry occurs at intervals of approximately three months, to create a regular incoming and outgoing flow. This "set cohort" model (rather than an open group model in which adolescents and families are added to ongoing groups) allows the young people to take on different roles in the community, depending on the phase of the program they are in. For example, those who have been in the program the longest are in charge of orienting new members and chairing, with the support of staff, some group meetings.

The program is a structured multimodal intervention that includes individual, group, and family psychotherapy, music therapy and other creative therapies (for example, stop-motion animation), occupational therapy, school lessons, psychiatric reviews, and the presence of a care coordinator. The interactions between patients and clinicians are continuous and spontaneous but are also formalized in the context of twice-weekly community meetings. These meetings have the function of managing the day-to-day needs (i.e., what group activities to organize or food to order), as well as discussing ways to regularly uphold the existing community guidelines, aimed at maintaining a healthy community, based on respect and reciprocal support. Twice a month, young people and staff organize recreational or relaxation activities in which they discover or rediscover their ability to play and express themselves through art and nonverbal means. At pre-specified junctures in the treatment process, caregivers and relatives are invited to participate or observe what the young people create during the program. With the aim of providing a model for families on how to mark moments of transition, the beginning and end of the day program are celebrated with welcome and conclusion ceremonies. Once discharged, young people are invited to a Leavers group, which takes place once a month, to reconnect with team members or ex-consumers.

17.6 Addressing self-harm and suicidality

Dealing with an adolescent's suicide attempt, given its emotional resonance, deserves specific attention. Suicide is generally approached with the main goal of preventing it, but an excessive focus on avoiding the suicidal act often limits the opportunity to understand its meaning. In general, a young person's suicide attempt represents an action that allows the adolescent to escape from the experience of emotional suffering in which they feel trapped. Helping adolescents to get in touch with their emotions is therefore one of the essential and most complex therapeutic challenges.

It is important to consider how alexithymia – the inability to identify discrete emotions and verbalize them internally and in speech – is often part of an adolescent's struggles, especially for those with insecure attachment, deficits in mentalization, and personality and behavioral disorders (Taylor et al., 1997). Asking a troubled, alexithymic young person to describe their feelings may be perceived by the adolescent as a threat or an insurmountable challenge. However, if the adolescent can describe their feelings, these may be so intense and chaotic that the clinician may find themselves sucked into the young person's emotional turmoil. When this happens, the clinician is at risk of relating vicariously to the experience of the young person, rather than with empathy, and offer unmentalized responses that can be harmful both for the patient and the clinician (Paulus et al., 2013). The therapist must find the courage to go deep inside the emotional states of the young person and sit closely with the adolescent's emotional wound. However, the therapist must also keep themselves outside to observe with an open mind the transitory nature of this experience and hold in mind different perspectives from which this experience can be understood. This effort to see the young person's experience through their eyes while remaining open and curious is what enables the therapist to maintain a sense of hope, towards which the clinician can lead the young person to, as soon as they are ready. The therapeutic relationship is put to the test when exploring the emotional experiences of a volatile suicidal adolescent, as the therapist must tolerate moments of distancing that replicate the young person's attachment instability and ruptures, followed by repair and rapprochement. If the therapist can sustain the tension and weather the emotional storms gripping the adolescent, this can truly become a transformative experience for the young person.

Similarly to what the therapist-patient must face, the family also needs support to find the strength to tolerate the adolescent's emotions and not respond to the suicidal act with unprocessed actions. If it is difficult for the therapist to get in touch with and hold the adolescent's suffering, then for the family this often seems impossible. Feeling the pain of a son or a daughter who suffers to the point of wanting to die can immediately arouse protective mechanisms that aim to create distance from the family's own pain and the pain of their child. The role of the clinician is to accompany parents and extended family members in the brave exploration of what the adolescent experiences, addressing the topic of death openly, creating a dialogue aimed at understanding how these experiences are woven from the thread of family history and in turn have an impact on the living tapestry of today. Through this, the family can learn that they do not have to be a protective shield against the adolescent's distress, and to not feel alone while going through that experience. The challenge for parents is to persist, until they discover that accompanying the young person in their experience has itself a containing and organizing function for them. If the parents can contact their child's pain but at the same time find inner strength not to collapse or explode and can see a way forward, the young person will feel supported and carried forward towards that future. It is therefore central to work with the family so that parents feel able to provide support to their child, receive support themselves and find the resources, both internal to them and in their external environment, to feel solid and clear in the pathway to take.

For this to happen, it is necessary that the same emphasis that is placed on creating space to get to know the young person's internal world is extended to the exploration of the parents' internal world, helping them to get in touch with their own emotions, learning to distinguish what is theirs from what belongs to their child's experience. By showing their interest in looking within themselves and within the history of the family, parents provide the adolescent with inspiration, drive, motivation, and a concrete model of exploration. Clinical work aims to create a connection among family members rather than supporting adolescents in an isolated manner separately from the parents. Through this process, the therapist acts as a pillar and bridge, activating in everyone a desire to consolidate the foundations of these renewed bonds. It is also important that the clinician does not become the only active participant in the treatment process and that they are aware of how getting in touch with strong experiences of deprivation, loss, desire, and fear, to name a few, often tends to generate an impulse to take on the emotional burden of the adolescent and/or family and rescue them from their feelings. Instead, it is essential to instigate autonomy and competence in the young person and family, thus activating them to be authors of their narrative of change.

For the therapist to achieve this delicate balance of empathizing and aiding but not saving, it is essential to structure regular times for clinical supervision and reflection. There must be a culture of accepting therapists' and other treatment personnel's struggles in staying present during this difficult work, a culture that creates the opportunity to reveal and process the loss of this balance between care and healthy emotional distance. Andolfi (Andolfi, 2017) emphasizes the importance of the work that the therapist must undertake with themselves and the willingness to explore honestly their personal "handicaps." He encourages therapists to extrapolate recurring themes from the blocks encountered in therapy and connect them to possible areas of personal challenges that these themes activate, so that the parallels between the therapist's personal issues and professional challenges can emerge into awareness. Similarly, studies on the identification of key areas for the treatment of personality disorders in adolescence (Project Air Strategy, 2018) highlight how one of the essential components of this work is the use of colleagues and dedicated supervisors with the aim of understanding and managing countertransference experiences in the best possible way.

Touchstone offers group supervision on clinical work and regular reflection groups that aim to recognize how the emerging dynamics in therapeutic work impact clinical team members and activate emotional reactions in individuals and in the group. With this understanding of dynamics, clinicians are prevented from acting counter-therapeutically and in ways that are not conducive to team collaboration. Clinical group meetings for staff enable therapists to recognize a potential pull to act as rescuers for highly distressed adolescents and families or to lose empathy when they appear difficult to engage. Furthermore, this space offers the opportunity to acknowledge how direct contact with the experiences of young people and their families, as they travel along their transformative paths, provides inspiration and drive for personal, team, and agency growth and change.

17.7 Case illustration: Luna's story

Luna arrived at Touchstone at the age of 15, following a recommendation from the Inpatient Unit in Perth, where she had spent almost the entire year prior to her referral. She had a diagnosis of depressive disorder and borderline personality disorder and had been prescribed two antipsychotics and two antidepressants. She was seeking every possible opportunity to take her own life, resorting to various methods such as drug overdoses, ingestion of toxic solvents, jumping from high floors, and recently she had started ingesting small lithium batteries. These gestures took place suddenly and left her parents, brothers, and clinicians shocked and highly distressed. Luna could not describe what gave rise to these acts, but she spoke about feeling a constant state of emotional distress, centered around a self-concept of being unworthy and profoundly insufficient.

Her marked decline in mood had occurred in the two years prior to Luna's arrival at Touchstone and was associated with a parallel functional decline. Luna had stopped going to school and had progressively lost contact with friends both at school and from the musical band she had been a part. She expressed also feeling distant from her family, especially because of her prolonged hospital stays. Her mother, father, and 18-year-old and 11-year-old brothers had progressively isolated themselves from friends and leisure activities, maintaining only essential activities, to dedicate themselves as much as possible to Luna's mental health.

When Luna and her family arrived for their first set of sessions at Touchstone, they were in a state of utter desperation, having no sense of what to do to address Luna's dramatic self-destructiveness, and they felt lost and scared. In the first psychoeducation group session with other young people, Luna broke the ice by highlighting the state of apprehension she sensed the group was in, all being in a new, unknown relational context. She admitted openly her own worries about commencing these group sessions and encouraged her peers to open up and express their anxieties. However, when she entered the day program and began her individual therapy, she was very reluctant to openly share how her internal world was painted entirely black; Luna was living minute by minute and was unable to imagine herself outside the hospital walls or without being at the mercy of suicidal thoughts. The idea of sharing a part of her mind with others, particularly to those of a similar age, terrified her, for fear of overwhelming them and being perceived as "too much."

Colleagues who had previously treated Luna on the ward or as a client of outpatient services thought of Luna as a girl to be feared, given her unpredictability and the high level of risk of her conduct. She was viewed as a patient who could not be trusted to make decisions in her best interests and to stay safe with herself. Despite these concerns, Luna was immediately appealing due to her liveliness. She was smart and enterprising, with an incredible capacity to observe what was happening around her and to intuit others' feelings. Despite her extremely serious self-destructive impulses and low sense of self-esteem, she, as well as her family, evinced a strong sense of humor, although they sometimes seemed to hide behind it.

Over time, once immersed in the culture of the therapeutic community, Luna had several opportunities to rediscover a sense of competency. In peer interactions, she often took on leadership roles, acted as a spokesperson for the group's needs, and appeared encouraging with others and charismatic. She had great knowledge and talent in music, having played trumpet in a musical band several years prior, which allowed her to find common ground with her peers. She was thoughtful and, when the other members of the community were willing to express their feelings, even if in small doses, Luna tried to be empathically present with them. She started to understand that the core of the work was to try and explore internal mental states and to share them to the best of her abilities. This realization seemed to lift to a degree the internal pressure she had been putting on herself and to allow her to view her attempts and her new desire to share with others as signs of inner strength that she had forgotten she possessed. With the gradual realization that this was the transformational process that Touchstone wished to encourage in her, Luna found new motivation. It seemed as if she sensed that, with effort, she could look within herself in a different way than how she had before, and she could desire to be listened to, just as she lent herself to listen to others. However, this positive drive still existed in an embryonic and fluctuating state, and her self-harming gestures continued to proceed in ups and downs.

About two months after the start of the day program, Luna began to question her need for medications and requested to stop them. With initial apprehension, her parents accepted and supported her decision and, following a pharmacological plan established together, she gradually stopped all the drugs that she had arrived at Touchstone with. Luna expressed that this path required her total presence and that by aiming to get in touch with her emotions, she no longer wanted to feel shielded from them through medications.

Unexpectedly, about halfway through her treatment, Luna attempted to hang herself while participating in the day program at Touchstone. Her gesture was a real shock for the clinical team. Luna's contradictory nature of being sincere and driven, but also out of control and unaware of the impact she had on other people, was truly alarming. Her gesture activated an intensity of the emotions in the Touchstone staff that allowed clinicians to understand more deeply the experience of this young person and that of her parents who, like the clinical team, regularly found themselves lost in trying to understand the underlying meaning of those gestures and how to deal with them. By making sense of the various states of mind of team members, it became possible to imagine the parallel experience going on for the parents at the time. This understanding enabled clinicians to empathically validate the experience of the family and provide them with a concrete model that would guide them to understand how to face Luna's gesture without fear but with curiosity. This model involved first, attending to her necessary medical care, then taking an interest, as soon as possible, in understanding Luna's underlying mental states, staying focused on the process of exploration and maintaining awareness that the mind is opaque, and nobody can ever know with certainty what is on someone's mind. These principles represent the general strategies that are used in MBT, where after having stabilized the high-risk behaviors, clinicians use supportive and empathic validation to reduce the level of arousal and enable mentalizing, followed by clarification and elaboration to identify affective experiences and contextualize them, with the ultimate goal of enabling an exploration of alternative perspectives (to the suicidal gesture, for example) (Bateman et al., 2023).

Through family therapy meetings, it came to light that the family had, for a long time, experienced an internal urge to act but avoided getting in touch with painful emotions. This tendency to avoid feelings and engage in pure coping action had many sources. Luna's mother had moved away from her family of origin to remove herself from difficult dynamics linked to a traumatic past. Luna's father had also left behind his family of origin, losing closeness to them. Both parents had emigrated from another country and arrived in Australia without having any connections, possibly enacting unprocessed urges to get away from difficult feelings without examining and addressing them. By becoming aware of these parts of the family's history, Luna and her two brothers understood how their parents had attempted to protect themselves and their children from the suffering that tied them to their families and their homeland and had simultaneously created a very strong bond between the five of them, focusing every desire and expectation on their immediate family unit. This exploration of their story helped Luna and her family understand how their union was both a blessing and a curse. They lived for the family and were also ready to sacrifice everything for the family. In a way, Luna preferred to die, rather than exist in a state of constant, unthinkable distress that she knew impacted negatively on her loved ones, inflaming even more her deeply negative view of herself. Similarly, family members felt so intimately connected with Luna that they had become one thing with her distress and could not imagine exploring what this sufferance was made of.

By creating some space to reflect in family sessions, all family members consciously decided to stop running away from the pain of their past and present and face the topic of Luna's potential death. Only when her parents and siblings were able to talk and express their feelings when imagining Luna's absence could she understand firsthand the pain of her parents and brothers. Likewise, her parents discovered the importance of listening, without the expectation of solving anything, and with the confidence that "being with" was what they needed to do with Luna. It was not Luna, the parents, or the siblings alone who had to do something new to change the course of events. Instead, they had found each other united, on the same page, ready to imagine themselves capable of implementing change.

Upon completion of the day program, the suicide attempts stopped and, shortly thereafter, Luna enrolled in a new course of study and re-established a social life. About a year after the conclusion of her time at Touchstone, Luna was continuing with her studies, had made new friends and felt good, confident in herself and her opportunities. She was aware that what she had developed at Touchstone was a new way of being curious about her own experiences, and she had learned, with her family, to explore these together. Luna's journey highlights the social learning that MBT aims to foster. Being mentalized by another person generates a sense of epistemic trust, unblocks social isolation, and reactivates the capacity to learn and grow in contexts of relationships outside of therapy. The renewed capacity for thinking about mental states enables the person to use their environment in a different way, which in turn improves the level of functioning (Bateman et al., 2023).

Six years later, Luna and her mother visited the service again, talking about the opportunities and difficulties that life had presented them. They gave several examples of how Luna had bravely faced some complex moments and how, given the difficult circumstances, the family had feared she would relapse into her self-destructive behaviours. Luna, speaking metaphorically, explained how the seeds planted many years before at Touchstone had given life to shrubs that were still strong and thriving. These "shrubs" supported her in the awareness that she was not alone in facing anger and pain, and that by giving it a voice she could partly free herself from it and partly get help in taking care of it. Both Luna and her family wanted to be spokespersons for Touchstone, based on the arduous path they had traversed, thus hoping to be a source of inspiration for other young people and other families who, like them six years earlier, were still desperately looking for direction.

17.8 Conclusion

Touchstone is a service run by a multidisciplinary team that offers a comprehensive set of interventions, using a variety of therapeutic modalities. Various components of the service and the level of intensity of the day program are potentially difficult to apply to daily outpatient work with adolescents and families. In any case, it is hoped that the principles illustrated in the chapter can be considered relevant and potentially implementable in small doses, in any therapeutic context with adolescent and family distress, particularly when manifested in self-harming behavior.

17.9 Acknowledgments

A heartfelt thank you to the Touchstone multidisciplinary team for their dedication to the daily running of this service and to Sandra Louise for her support with the writing of this manuscript. Special thanks to Luna (pseudonym) and her family for agreeing to share their story.

References

Allen, J. G., & Fonagy, P. (2006). *The handbook of mentalization-based treatment*. John Wiley & Sons, Inc. https://doi.org/10.1002/9780470712986

Andolfi, M. (2017). *Multi-generational family therapy tools and resources for the therapist*. Routledge. https://doi.org/10.4324/9781315545592

Andolfi, M., & Haber, R. (1994). *Please help me with this family: Using consultants as resources in family therapy*. Brunner/Mazel. https://doi.org/10.4324/9780203727461

Andolfi, M., & Mascellani, A. (2023). *Teen voices: A book on adolescent problems and family resources*. Accademia Press.

APA. (2013). *DSM-5: Diagnostic and statistical manual of mental disorders* (5th ed.). American Psychiatric Association. https://doi.org/10.1176/appi.books.9780890425596

Bales, D. L., Timman, R., Andrea, H., Busschbach, J. J. V., Verheul, R., & Kamphuis, J. H. (2015). Effectiveness of day hospital mentalization-based treatment for patients with severe borderline personality disorder: A matched control study. *Clinical Psychology and Psychotherapy, 22*(5), 409–417. https://doi.org/10.1002/cpp.1914

Bateman, A., & Fonagy, P. (2010). Mentalization based treatment for borderline personality disorder. *World Psychiatry, 9*(1), 11–15. https://doi.org/10.1002/j.2051-5545.2010.tb00255.x

Bateman, A., & Fonagy, P. (2016). *Mentalization-based treatment for personality disorders: A practical guide*. Oxford University Press. https://doi.org/10.1093/med:psych/9780199680375.001.0001

Bateman, A., Fonagy, P., Campbell, C., Luyten, P., & Debbane, M. (2023). *Cambridge guide to mentalization-based treatment (MBT)*. Cambridge University Press. https://doi.org/10.1017/9781108896054

Bo, S., Sharp, C., Beck, E., Pedersen, J., Gondan, M., & Simonsen, E. (2017). First empirical evaluation of outcomes for mentalization-based group therapy for adolescents with BPD. *Personality Disorders: Theory, Research, and Treatment, 8*(4), 396. https://doi.org/10.1037/per0000210

Bozzatello, P., Bellino, S., Bosia, M., & Rocca, P. (2019). Early detection and outcome in borderline personality disorder. *Frontiers in Psychiatry, 10*, 710. https://doi.org/10.3389/fpsyt.2019.00710

Byrne, G., Murphy, S., & Connon, G. (2020). Mentalization-based treatments with children and families: A systematic review of the literature. *Clinical Child Psychology and Psychiatry, 25*(4), 1022–1048. https://doi.org/10.1177/1359104520920689

Chanen, A. M., Jovev, M., McCutcheon, L., Jackson, H., & McGorry, P. (2008). Borderline personality disorder in young people and the prospects for prevention and early intervention. *Current Psychiatry Reviews, 4*(1), 48–57. https://doi.org/10.2174/157340008783743820

Chanen, A. M., Nicol, K., Betts, J. K., & Thompson, K. N. (2020). Diagnosis and treatment of borderline personality disorder in young people. *Current Psychiatry Reports, 22*(5), 25. https://doi.org/10.1007/s11920-020-01144-5

Fonagy, P., & Allison, E. (2014). The role of mentalizing and epistemic trust in the therapeutic relationship. *Psychotherapy, 51*(3), 372–380. https://doi.org/10.1037/a0036505

Grove, P., & Smith, E. (2022). A framework for MBT formulations: The narrative formulation and MBT passport. *Journal of Contemporary Psychotherapy*, *52*(3), 199–206. https://doi.org/10.1007/s10879-022-09531-0

Jørgensen, M. S., Storebø, O. J., Bo, S., Poulsen, S., Gondan, M., Beck, E., Chanen, A. M., Bateman, A., Pedersen, J., & Simonsen, E. (2021). Mentalization-based treatment in groups for adolescents with borderline personality disorder: 3- and 12-month follow-up of a randomized controlled trial. *European Child & Adolescent Psychiatry*, *30*(5), 699–710. https://doi.org/10.1007/s00787-020-01551-2

Middleton, H. (2017). More focused attention upon relationship; another call for paradigm shift in psychiatry. *European Journal of Psychotherapy & Counselling*, *19*(3), 252–266. https://doi.org/10.1080/13642537.2017.1348374

Paulus, F. M., Müller-Pinzler, L., Westermann, S., & Krach, S. (2013, May). On the distinction of empathic and vicarious emotions. *Frontiers in Human Neuroscience*, *7*, 196–196. https://doi.org/10.3389/fnhum.2013.00196

Pearce, S., Scott, L., Attwood, G., Saunders, K., Dean, M., De Ridder, R., Galea, D., Konstantinidou, H., & Crawford, M. (2017). Democratic therapeutic community treatment for personality disorder: Randomised controlled trial. *British Journal of Psychiatry*, *210*(2), 149–156. https://doi.org/10.1192/bjp.bp.116.184366

Project Air Strategy. (2018). *Adolescent intervention: Guide for clinicians*. https://documents.uow.edu.au/content/groups/public/@web/@project-air/documents/doc/uow261710.pdf

Rossouw, T. I. M. R. C. P., & Fonagy, P. P. D. F. B. A. (2012). Mentalization-based treatment for self-harm in adolescents: A randomized controlled trial. *Journal of the American Academy of Child and Adolescent Psychiatry*, *51*(12), 1304–1313.e1303. https://doi.org/10.1016/j.jaac.2012.09.018

Royal College of Psychiatrists' Centre for Quality Improvement. (2008). *The development of core standards and core values for therapeutic communities*. Retrieved January 3, 2023, from www.rcpsych.ac.uk/docs/default-source/improving-care/ccqi/quality-networks/therapeutic-communities-c-of-c/coc-cscv-final-briefing-paper.pdf?sfvrsn=1bb2f2f_2

Shuker, R. (2010). Personality disorder: Using therapeutic communities as an integrative approach to address risk. In R. Shuker & E. Sullivan (Eds.), *Grendon and the emergence of forensic therapeutic communities: Developments in research and practice* (pp. 115–136). Wiley Blackwell. https://doi.org/10.1002/9780470661444.ch7

Taylor, G. J., Bagby, R. M., & Parker, J. D. A. (1997). *Disorders of affect regulation alexithymia in medical and psychiatric illness*. Cambridge University Press. https://doi.org/10.1017/CBO9780511526831

PART 3

Family and social dimensions of couple crises and divorce

18

RESOLVING POWER STRUGGLES IN LAST-CHANCE COUPLE THERAPY

Peter Fraenkel

18.1 Introduction

This chapter addresses the many ways in which "last-chance couples" – those in which one or both partners are strongly considering dissolving the relationship – engage in repetitive, rigid power struggles. Many of these struggles are quite explicit and readily identified by the partners – for instance, the couple in which each partner vigorously asserts their respective and differing accounts of a troubling event, or the correctness of opinions on all manner of common issues, such as finances, domestic chores, parenting, and daily schedules. Other exertions of power are more subtle and may not initially be identified as such – for instance, the power derived from having a mental health issue that the partner uses to justify underfunctioning or irresponsible behavior, or the power of a partner's physical attractiveness or sexual desirability to intimidate a partner into acquiescing to demands.

Systemic therapists encountering a couple that presents with these repetitive power struggles often describe such couples as engaging in "vicious spirals." Although early family systems theory (Watzlawick et al., 1974) utilized this term simply to describe the problematic negative circularity of partners' relationships without reference to the emotional quality of the interaction, it is noteworthy that some of the sixty-six synonyms for "vicious" listed in Google (based on Oxford Languages dictionary) include "remorseless," "heartless," "harsh," "spiteful," "acrimonious" "hate-filled," "nasty," "catty," "bitchy," and "slanderous." Indeed, partners presenting with relentless vicious cycles often use just these sorts of words to describe one another. Other synonyms – "ferocious," "brutal," "dangerous," and "violent" – capture the ways in which such power struggles can set the stage for interpersonal violence (Fraenkel et al., 2022).

Effective resolution of these power struggles requires an integrative approach that provides couples with new skills for communicating and resolving problems equitably, for revealing vulnerable emotions and engaging in intimacy, and that encourages insight about family- and culture-of-origin-based beliefs and experiences that lead to reactivity and the desire to protect self-interest (Fraenkel, 2022). Most broadly, partners need encouragement to identify the constellation of relational values they wish to guide their lives together. They also need assistance to shift from a "You vs. Me" transactional model of relationship to one in which they experience themselves as part of a "We" – a joint identity and consciousness that does not subsume each partner's needs and identity, but that modifies how they define themselves (Fraenkel, 2023).

DOI: 10.4324/9781003536765-22

18.2 History of the study of power in couples

The role of power in couple distress has been well-documented in research and clinical theory. It was feminist family therapists who first highlighted power inequities between men and women in cisgender heterosexual couples (Goldner, 1985, 1988; Hare-Mustin, 1978; Walters et al., 1988). This focus included the more extreme instances that appear in domestic violence (Goldner, 1998; Goldner et al., 1990), more recently renamed "interpersonal violence" (see Fraenkel et al., 2022 for a review). In many of these clinical theoretical descriptions, men borrow a sense of entitlement to greater power from the larger patriarchal beliefs that suffuse most cultures around the world and use it to force women to accept their decisions about money, time, and other common aspects of couple and family life (Knudson-Martin & Mahoney, 2009).

However, some of these early descriptions of men powering over women reveal greater psychological complexity. For instance, Goldner et al. (1990) describe how in many cases of violence, men come from homes in which they witnessed their fathers being intimidating or violent to their mothers and, as boys, felt emotionally vulnerable and wanted to protect their mothers but could not. Emotional vulnerability thus becomes associated with being "feminine," and in an attempt to identify with their fathers, these boys reject their feelings of vulnerability. In addition, the violence and instability of the home results in an anxious-insecure sense of attachment. In their adult intimate relationships, when their female partner criticizes them or voices any form of displeasure, or threatens to leave them, these men feel emotionally vulnerable; these feelings are unacceptable because they are associated with being "feminine" or "not male"; in an attempt to restore their sense of masculine identity and to make sure their partner doesn't leave them, they become controlling, threatening, and violent. This trenchant analysis reveals an important theme that explains many instances of partners' attempts to power over one another: At the base of these attempts often lie feelings of vulnerability, fear, and potential loss of identity garnered from being in the relationship.

In addition, as greater documentation of interpersonal violence within same-sex and queer couples has emerged, it has become clear that not all instances of one partner powering over another are due to these patriarchal beliefs. For instance, in queer couples in which one partner is a cisgender lesbian and the other is a trans man or woman, the greater social acceptance of lesbian women over trans persons may facilitate a lesbian partner exerting power over her trans partner through threats to "out" the trans partner (Fraenkel et al., 2022). Similarly, study of biracial couples in which one partner is white and the other a person of color has found that the greater privileges generally afforded to white people irrespective of gender can contribute to those partners' sense of entitlement to assert greater power in the relationship (Killian, 2013).

The same sorts of power dynamics can characterize relationships (a) in which partners come from different socioeconomic class backgrounds or have greater and lesser financial resources or earning power; (b) where one has attained a higher level of education; (c) where one is a citizen and the other a first-generation immigrant from a struggling country, where the latter may be less fluent in the majority language; or (d) where one is able-bodied and the other has a disability. In such couples, the recruitment of their greater societal status to power over the partner with less status may simply be a strategy to get their way. But in many cases, the dynamic may be far more complex: The partner who avails themselves of their location in a higher-status group may do so because they feel vulnerable due to something their partner said or did (usually because they also feel vulnerable), and this mutual vulnerability needs to be identified, understood, and managed in order for the couple to resist the temptations to utilize the power-over strategies available to them.

In some sense, this is a way to reinterpret the phrase, "the personal is political." The personal is not inherently political, but rather "the personal *becomes* political" when "politics" is utilized as a strategy or tool to manage the "personal," when it is advantageous for partners to access the higher status afforded them by the broader society to manage (or avoid altogether, through silencing the other) the difficult emotions that arise in moment-to-moment intimate interactions. Therapy must assist the partners to reveal to one another how they hurt one another, to learn new, compassionate ways to speak to one another about differences and feelings, to find compromise or accommodations to one another, to engage in apologies, and to repair.

18.3 What is relational power?

Before examining the moments in which power becomes a problem in couples, it is important to look more broadly at the phenomenon of relational power. A potentially useful definition is behavior by one partner, intentional or unintentional, exerted with awareness or without unawareness, that influences the actions, decisions, thoughts, feelings, and arousal levels of the other partner. Is relational power always a problem? Or is it inevitable and often non-problematic? It can be argued that it is inevitable and, indeed, often represents a useful exchange of energy in relationships. As early systemic communication theorists Watzlawick et al. (1967) noted, all communications, verbal or nonverbal, have a pragmatic/influencing intended or unintended impact. A useful demonstration of this principle is to say the words "come here" with different tones that express different desired effects or requests: for obedience, sexual connection, urgent assistance; for an opportunity to apologize, or to engage a very young child or pet. Aside from the request for obedience, all the other versions of "come here" are not attempts to dominate someone, but to have them respond in one way or another.

Research further normalizes the appropriate exchange of power. Gottman and colleagues (Driver et al., 2012) have documented that partners' willingness to "take influence" from each other is an important predictor of relationship quality and stability. Attempts to "get a partner" to try something that might help them solve a problem or relieve suffering can be one of the most loving gestures made by a partner. Of course, when a partner becomes too insistent in their attempt to help (for instance, to get a partner to speak more firmly to a difficult boss or colleague, to confront a difficult parent, sibling, or friend, to lose weight, exercise, or relax), the attempt to help can be experienced as oppressive nagging. But to avoid any attempt to influence a distressed partner can be experienced as a lack of care.

Likewise, trying to get a partner to join oneself in a source of pleasure that they are reluctant or anxious about (e.g., a sport, dancing, form of music, new type of food) can open the door to new experiences for the partner. Providing energy, support, encouragement, and enlivenment to a partner is a loving gesture, but the partner exerting power or influence in these positively intended ways must be attuned to the other's signals that they really don't want that help or that new experience, and know when to cease efforts to influence them.

A musical analogy is helpful. The role of a drummer in a jazz group is to provide a steady tempo and energy that drives the other musicians forward. It is also to introduce energy when a soloist seems to be stuck and needs some inspiration. A drummer does this through various musical techniques: varying the feel to intensify the groove (for instance, shifting from a regular jazz beat to a driving shuffle), changing the dynamics (from soft to louder, or the reverse), adding accents that the soloist responds to, or creating a new repetitive rhythmic theme within the beat that the soloist can play along with. One story from the present author's drumming experience shows what happens when the drummer refrains too much from providing this influence. He was a young white drummer playing with an older group of accomplished Black musicians. In an attempt to be respectful, the drummer kept his playing lowkey. At one point, the tenor sax player, a tall, imposing man and distinguished musician, turned around and said firmly to the drummer, "Kick my ass!" The drummer anxiously began to play more actively, sending accents to the sax player. After one chorus, the sax player turned around again, and with a big smile, said, "Yeah! That's it!"

In couples, vigorous lively debate and dialogue leading to mutual influence makes for a good team in coping with life's challenges and in making relationships intellectually interesting. Thus, the goal of therapy with a couple that is entrenched in destructive power exchanges is not to move to a relationship in which both partners avoid any attempt to extend influence. Rather, it is to create a relational culture in which partners equally share power and avoid force. Power becomes a problem when one person (or both) violates the healthy/ethical circular/relational pattern of respectful mutual influence/dialogue by asserting linear/dominating influence: Powering Over, rather than Powering With.

18.4 Problematic power

In this section, the various forms of problematic power are described.

18.4.1 The connection between power and closeness

Wood (1985) provided an elegant theory of two major "orthogonal" or independent dimensions of family functioning: proximity and hierarchy. These echoed dimensions were described in Minuchin's (1974) structural family therapy: power or hierarchy, and closeness or connectedness, with the latter dimension varying from enmeshment to disengagement. Fraenkel (2022) adapted these formulations to remove the assumption of dysfunction at either end of the closeness dimension, changing them to "high" vs. "low," and described the continuum of hierarchy or power as varying from symmetrical to asymmetrical. As Wood suggests, from a research perspective, couple partners can be highly symmetrical in power and anywhere on the closeness continuum (from high to low) or asymmetrical in power, and again, anywhere on the closeness continuum. This is the meaning of the dimensions being "orthogonal" or independent.

However, in couples' interactions, these two dimensions are often experientially highly connected. For instance, the classic circular pattern of "distancer/pursuer" or "demand/withdraw" (Christensen & Heavey, 1990) may arise because one partner attempts (in a nonconflictual manner) to get the other partner's attention – what Gottman and Gottman (2018) call making a "bid for attention." This bid can be for various reasons – to make a plan or address a practical need (scheduling a child's doctor's appointment, calling the plumber, discussing an upcoming vacation), to address a problem or concern about the relationship (to talk about "what happened last night at the party," to discuss one partner's frustration with the lack of sexual intimacy), or to garner some emotional support from the partner ("Can I tell you about what happened today at work?" "Oh, you'll never believe what my mother said to me today!"). If the other responds by "turning away" (Gottman & Gottman, 2018), this can lead the other partner to intensify her or his efforts to get the other's attention, which then results in further withdrawal by the other, and they launch into a destructive conflict, in which one exerts power by insistently approaching and the other exerts power by relentlessly avoiding. But underlying the attempt by one partner to forcefully get the attention of the other is a desire or need for connection. Likewise, engaging in this power struggle around connectedness is likely to diminish both partners' desire for further connection.

Another common scenario demonstrating the connection between these two dimensions is that in which one partner tends to dominate – talking without allowing the other to speak, insisting decisions go her or his way, demanding that weekend plans follow her or his needs. The other partner gets turned off emotionally and loses interest in any form of intimacy, which the dominant partner notices and complains about, which leads the other to feel even less desire for intimacy.

In a variant of this pattern, one partner requests sex at a frequency that the other feels uncomfortable with, and that partner makes various excuses to avoid it; the requesting partner feels rejected, states that the other is exerting the power to withhold sex, and intensifies his or her demands for sex in an increasingly aggressive tone, leading the other to feel increasingly uncomfortable with the prospect of sexual intimacy being demanded in such a forceful manner.

In yet another intertwining of desire for closeness and power, one partner frequently presents as emotionally troubled, even hinting at engaging in self-harming action unless the other partner provides attention. Initially, the other partner may enjoy the role of soother and rescuer, but over time, comes to resent these requests and feels manipulated by the other's distress. This leads the distressed partner to amplify her or his distress, either by becoming more vocal or by withdrawing but in a provocative manner ("it's ok, if something happens to me, it's probably better for you, you can find someone healthier than me"), and this behavior feels like yet another manipulative power move to obtain attention.

In sum, although the dimensions of power and closeness are empirically orthogonal and couples can appear in many different combinations of their place on them, in the lives of couples they are often quite connected.

18.4.2 Subtle covert forms of power

As noted earlier, a great deal of attention has been paid in the literature to the ways in which partners' differing intersectional social locations – of gender, gender identity, sexual orientation, race and skin tone, ethnicity, culture of origin, social class, economic status, education, age, citizenship status, ability/disability, and other dimensions – can result in power inequities and struggles between partners (McDowell et al., 2022). It is important in work with couples to identify and discuss the ways in which these social locations afford one partner greater or lesser power and to encourage the more powerful partner to resist the temptation to recruit their location(s) as a means to dominate the other partner.

For instance, in one couple, the woman, a fiction writer, was white, well-educated in private schools, and from an upper-middle-class politically and socially liberal family in the American South. The man was African American and Latino, born and raised in a low-income family in the Bronx, but had managed to go to law school and was now a successful criminal prosecutor. Their bright, assertive, biracial 8-year-old daughter had corrected her teacher on some aspect of history being taught, which the teacher found rude, and the daughter was sent to the principal's office for discipline. When the father heard about this, he sat his daughter down and firmly admonished her about "talking back" to the teacher, noting that he did not want her to get in trouble. The mother thought her husband was too harsh with the daughter and quite matter-of-factly said that if he spoke to her again like that, she would call the police (even though she acknowledged there was nothing "abusive" in how her husband had spoken to their daughter). The husband was astounded, hurt, angry, and alarmed, noting what the consequences might be for his career as a city prosecutor if she were to make such a call. The therapist had to help the wife understand that her white privilege and assumed superior stance about parenting styles led her to be ignorant of the reality of children of color in schools being singled out for disciplinary treatment more than white students, and that her privilege led her to ignore the possible effects of her intended behavior on her African American/Latino husband.

However, relatively little attention has been paid in the literature to a whole host of other personal attributes, behavioral styles, and beliefs that can lead to or be utilized in power struggles. The following sections briefly identify some of these factors.

18.4.3 Speech styles

Partners often differ in the pace of their speech (fast to slow), the typical volume or loudness with which they speak, and their verbosity and fluency (even when both partners are adept at the language in which they speak). Partners' struggles around particular issues (child-rearing, finances, domestic chores, sex) can be undergirded by persistent differences in *how* they talk about these issues. In one couple, the female partner's fast, loud, verbose speech was met by the male partner's slow, quiet, minimal utterances, which frustrated the female partner and led her to assume he was not listening or didn't care about her feelings and point of view, which lead her to intensify her speech style. Likewise, the female partner's verbal delivery felt pressuring and overwhelming to the male partner, and although he wanted to respond, he felt shut down. Their conflict was as much or more about *how* they spoke to each other as about the issues about which they disagreed.

It was only when the therapist noted the nature of their paralinguistic (nonverbal) exchanges that they were willing to embrace a different style of communication that provided each an opportunity to speak. The therapist did this by suggesting to the woman, who happened to be a musician (like the therapist), that it was like she was playing her violin at triple fortissimo (extremely loud) and 200 beats per minute, and her husband could not keep up, so his only way to protect himself was to become quiet and shut down his listening receptors. In turn, the therapist noted that we had to find a way for the husband to speak so that the wife did not feel anxious and angry when he was silent (Fraenkel, 2020).

18.4.4 Physical attractiveness and sexual desirability

Decades of research shows that people who are judged physically attractive tend to be viewed as more desirable, intelligent, "competent, confident, and socially skilled than the unattractive . . . more likely to be hired, promoted, and to earn higher salaries than unattractive individuals . . . compared with unattractive adults, they have more dating and more sexual experience" (Gupta et al., 2016, p. 1314). They also tend to be more powerful in attaining their goals. Gupta et al. (2016) write, "Attractive people are more likely to win arguments, persuade others to change their opinions, and be offered assistance" (p. 1314). Li (2022) notes that a wife's degree of physical attractiveness is positively associated with her "intra-household bargaining power" (p. 1).

In cisgender heterosexual intimate relationships, differences in physical attractiveness between wives and husbands work in different ways. When wives are more attractive than their husbands, both partners behave in more positive ways, but when husbands are more attractive than their wives, interactions are more negative (McNulty et al., 2008). What research has not yet documented is what happens when these differences in physical attraction exist within a highly distressed couple.

Nevertheless, these findings suggest that if one partner is more physically attractive than the other and deemed the more sexually desirable partner, this can lead the physically attractive partner to capitalize on her or his beauty to exert power over the other partner, whose power may be due to other factors such as wealth, occupational status, age, or other factors. One hypothetical way to conceptualize this dynamic is that beauty elicits desire, desire elicits longing for contact, and longing for contact elicits anxiety about possible rejection, which can lead the less attractive, desiring partner to "give in" to the attractive partner's requests even when he or she does not want to do so.

In one couple, the husband was an older, successful, pleasant-but-unremarkable-looking lawyer, and the wife was an internationally successful model, 20 years younger than her husband. Although she had the power of her beauty and was quite intelligent, she had only completed high school and often felt intimidated by her husband's intellect and career achievements. When she did not agree with his ideas or requests, she would anxiously withdraw from his gaze and his touch, which triggered anxiety in him, leading him to assert himself more firmly, leading her to withdraw even more, refusing to have sex with him. The husband, extremely anxious about the loss of connection with her, countered by escalating his threats (for instance, to cut her off financially) and, in one serious incident, dragged her across the floor and threw her out of the apartment. The therapist commented on how each of them held a type of power, and each of them felt insecure in relation to the sources of power the other possessed. By providing them with some concrete tools to speak more calmly and equitably about the decisions they needed to make on a day-to-day basis, and by helping them to communicate to one another early on when they were feeling anxious about their perspective or wishes being diminished, they were able to avoid further instances of power struggles.

18.4.5 Recruitment of cultural/societal norms of health and optimal functioning

Another source of power partners may access during conflict are cultural and societal norms about health and optimal functioning. The norms depend on the particular culture in which the partners live; in most Western, "global north" societies, the following sample of norms are generally endorsed by the majority culture:

- Punctuality
- Pace (doing things faster seen as better, more efficient)
- Future Focus (planning, saving money) vs. Present Focus (live for the moment) vs. Past Focus
- Gentle, emotion-centered parenting versus stricter, punishment-oriented parenting
- Work resulting in economic gain more valuable than work that does not earn money
- Beliefs about optimal emotional and relational health:
  - Be in touch with and express your feelings.
  - It's always important to talk about issues – not to let any issue pass without discussion.
  - Love is best shown through words (not all "Love Languages" are equal in status).
  - Investment in and assertion of certain emotions and physiological arousal levels as norms imposed on partner: the importance of experiencing and expressing sadness, anger, the valuing of high arousal or low arousal, of attaining joy, peacefulness, and happiness as constant states of being.
  - Beliefs in the value of critical perspectives vs. "positive" perspectives on events in the world as well as in the relationship.

Many couples argue about these issues (see Fraenkel, 2023, for a detailed discussion of conflicts that occur around temporal factors such as punctuality, time perspective, regularity of daily rhythms, pace). Gottman and Gottman (2018) have discussed how persons may differ in terms of what they call "meta-emotions," or beliefs and feelings about the role of emotion and emotion expression. The present author views these as "emotion ideologies," and in the heat of an argument, a partner who endorses these beliefs may reference these as accepted, inviolable norms and quote data accessed through the internet or from self-help books and podcasts by psychologists and other psychotherapists. The partner who differs on these beliefs then feels silenced by "normative knowledge."

18.4.6 The power of passivity: The underfunctioning/overfunctioning pattern

Along with the pursuer/withdrawer pattern, one of the classic vicious spirals long identified by systemic theory is that of underfunctioning/overfunctioning. In this pattern, one partner develops a difficulty, such as depression, anxiety disorder, trauma, or substance overuse, or comes to believe (sometimes through psychotherapy) that they have a disorder that has not previously been diagnosed, such as OCD or ADHD, and initially, the other partner responds with care and compassion and takes over some of the troubled partner's responsibilities.

However, relieved of their responsibilities, the troubled partner then becomes even more disabled and passive, leading the other partner to take on even more responsibilities. Eventually, the overfunctioning partner comes to resent the underfunctioning partner and tries to mobilize them through increasingly insistent strategies: heartfelt pleas, cajoling, demands, and eventually, threats of negative consequences (such as ending the marriage). The underfunctioning partner responds by deepening their passivity, and the couple is at a deadlock. The underfunctioning partner will often recruit their diagnosis and their therapist as a support for their behavior: "I'm too depressed (or ADD) to do (or remember to do) the dishes, pick up our son on time from school, remember to take the key out of the front door" (these are all actual examples from couples seen by the author). Sometimes the underfunctioning partner will claim family-of-origin-based ineptitude, even with simple tasks that they could readily learn as an adult: "My parents were messy, so I am messy, I can't help that," or "I never learned to wash dishes as a kid – sorry!"

The therapeutic strategy for disrupting this power struggle begins by sharing the concept of underfunctioning/overfunctioning with the couple and suggesting to the underfunctioning partner that, as powerless as they may feel, their passivity is a form of power. The therapist then needs to challenge that partner to reflect on the unfairness of this pattern and to examine the negative emotional effects it is having on their partner and also on themselves and their identity. The therapist should note that people are not responsible for having a psychological condition, but they are responsible for managing it in a manner that does not affect their loved ones and their colleagues. If the underfunctioning partner is not in individual treatment, a referral for therapy or medication is warranted; if they are in treatment, a referral for a second opinion or different form of therapy is recommended (for instance, if they are in a talk-based therapy and are struggling with OCD, depression, anxiety, trauma, or ADHD, a more skills-based therapy with demonstrated effectiveness should be recommended). If these interventions have even a slight impact, the therapist should then gradually have the overfunctioning partner stop filling in for the underfunctioning partner, and the latter partner must take on a responsibility that they had relinquished.

18.4.7 Time as power

In a previous section, the ways in which normative beliefs about time – punctuality, a fast efficient pace, a dominant focus on the future versus the present or past – are often recruited by a partner to attempt to change the other partner's behavior around these temporal behaviors. On a broader level, time is often used by one partner to control the other partner. It's useful to think about the relationship between time and power from the perspective of the associative principle of mathematics, wherein A = B, B = C, and therefore, A = C:

Time = Money
Money = Power
Therefore . . .
Time = Power
The partner who controls the time controls the relationship.

Partners may use temporal demands to control the other partner's work schedules, sleep-wake schedules, times of expected arrival home, and the regularity and frequency of intimacy. The control of time by one partner is often a feature of relationships edging towards or already engaged in interpersonal violence.

18.5 An integrative approach to disrupting power struggles

The fundamental psycho-relational pattern that underlies most power struggles in couples, last chance or otherwise, is as follows: An issue comes up about which partners differ in their beliefs, needs, or desires. Each partner feels anxious about not getting their way. They lack an approach to talking calmly and compassionately with one another about their respective points of view, or they have such an approach but decide that the issue is too important for them to engage this approach, so they elect not to use it and engage in conflict in which each attempts to convince the other of the correctness or necessity of their desired outcome. They recruit any "power tool" available to them: their respective social locations, their speech styles, beliefs that align with cultural norms (including those supplied by the mental health and psychological well-being professions), their attractiveness, and if all else fails, emotional or physical threats or acts of aggression or violence. From a social psychological perspective, the "power tools" are termed "affordances" (Good, 2007), opportunities within an ecology to adapt and thrive.

An integrative approach (Fraenkel, 2022) to disrupting power struggles must do the following:

- Ascertain and describe to the couple the circular nature of the power struggle and the ways each of them has accessed certain affordances or strategies to power over their partner.
- Ask how they feel just as a power struggle is about to start, and name the vulnerability (anxiety, fear) each is feeling about not having the conversation result in their desired outcome. Ask, what would be the ramifications/effects of *not* getting their way? Note that this anxiety drives each of them to engage in the power struggle.
- Explore each partner's family-of-origin experiences regarding how parents and other elders handled differences, and explore each partner's respective family- and culture-of-origin to understand the beliefs each holds about the issues they conflict over, as well as beliefs that may exist about the "rights" of persons of certain locations to get their way and to hold more power – beliefs based on gender, race, ethnicity, class, and so on.
- Teach the couple research-supported communication and problem-solving skills and emotion modulation (mindfulness) skills, and coach them in these skills (see Fraenkel, 2023 for a detailed guide). Emphasize the importance of taking a "time out" if they are too negatively aroused, explaining that the autonomic nervous system's sympathetic "fight or flight" arousal interferes with the higher, prefrontal cortical functioning necessary for judgement and empathy (Fishbane, 2013).
- Suggest that in moments of high negative arousal they embrace the beauty of silence and of darkness as a quiet space in which to calm down. Taoism suggests that before the creation of differences that led to the planet and all its life, the Tao was a place of darkness and infinite potential. This idea often intrigues and "inspirits" couples. Introduce the Taoist practice of "Wei Wu Wei" – "doing not doing." This practice suggests that when faced with a challenge that is negatively arousing, the best first step is to do nothing, calm down, and reflect on whether anything needs to be said or done. Introduce the term "deemergencizing," suggesting that the notion of an "emotional emergency" is an oxymoron – strong feelings should not be confused with an actual emergency like a fire in the kitchen.
- Using the narrative therapy practice of externalizing, encourage the couple to give the problem of power struggles a name, as if it is a creature or being or force that takes them over and leads them to interact in destructive ways. Suggest that at the slightest hint of an emerging power struggle, they state the creative name they've assigned and redouble their intentions to remain "side by side" against whatever challenge they are facing, rather than going "head to head" into conflict, and to use the communication skills to have a thoughtful, respectful dialogue that leads to a compromise solution.

In some, generally less-distressed couples, this set of interventions will result in a marked decrease in power struggles. But clinical experience with last-chance, highly distressed couples reveals that most do not use the insights and techniques immediately. What is required next are the following interventions.

18.6 The relational values constellation

When after a few sessions it is clear that the couple has not engaged the skills, ask them to reflect on the values they want to guide their relationship. Say: "Imagine that the sky is full of stars, and each star is a value you want to have shining down on you and your relationship, day and night. What values would you like to place in that constellation?" Experience with this technique reveals that couples repeatedly name many of the following values: respect, kindness, love, support, patience, compassion, fairness, grace, cherishment and adoration, loyalty, awe, generosity, self-awareness (of thoughts, feelings/physiological arousal, behavior), responsiveness and responsibility, conscientiousness, maintaining and repairing connections (partners, in-laws, friends, community), honesty, presence, courage, adventuresomeness.

The concept of a "constellation of values" is drawn from the moral philosopher J. N. Findlay (1970, 1980), who asserted that the philosophic project of attempting to deduce the core values by which humans should live is redundant with history and unnecessary – that these values are readily apparent from cross-cultural examination and across generations. More important was to engage people to discuss what is already clearly available in terms of how we should live our lives with one another. Fishbane (2023) has recently emphasized that the practice of couple therapy needs to engage couples to examine and utilize their values.

18.7 Changing the relationship paradigm

In highly distressed couples, partners often have constructed the relationship from a "You + Me" paradigm. This means the partners see the relationship as a place in which they retain all their goals and desires unmitigated by the fact that they are sharing a life with someone else. Such relationships remain transactional: "I'll do this for you if you do this for me," and "If this relationship does not fulfill my needs, it needs to change fully in the direction I want, or I leave." In other words, the "You + Me" form of relationship readily becomes "You vs. Me," setting the stage for unremitting power struggles.

Instead, healthy long-term relationships require partners to co-construct a sense of the "We" – who they are as a couple. The "We" is a sense of shared identity that does not subsume the individual identities of each partner but adds another conjoint layer to the couple that modifies what each partner can expect in life. Some new things are added to the life through participating in the relationship, and some need to be released or reduced by each partner in order for them to get along. Research shows that couples who narrate their relationship story with a preponderance of the word "we" do better over time (are more stable and satisfied) than those that narrate their story in terms of "you" and "me" (Buehlman et al., 1992).

Attaining a sense of We-ness requires each partner to get to know the other's mind – a process termed "mentalization" (Asen & Fonagy, 2012, 2021; Jurist, 2018). Knowing one another's minds – including how the partner views oneself – provides the space to find areas of commonality that become central to the We identity, along with acceptance of differences, which can also be part of the broader sense of We (as in, "we are similar in these ways, we are different in these other ways, and we accept those differences"). A related process is attaining a degree of intersubjectivity (Benjamin, 2017), wherein shared understandings and feelings form the basis of the relationship, which then recursively reshape each individual's intrapsychic life, such that each partner's individual identity is reconstructed to include being part of a We.

The notion of the development of We as a combination of identifying shared and different aspects of identity is at the base of all theories of couples and couple therapy: psychodynamic, CBCT, integrative behavioral couple therapy (IBCT)/acceptance therapy, Bowenian intergenerational therapy, EFCT, and narrative therapy. From an existential psychology perspective, love and intimacy require "social courage . . . the courage to relate to other human beings, the capacity to risk one's self in the hope of achieving meaningful intimacy" (May, 1975, p. 17). Partners need to continue to attend to the quality of the relationship and put energy into it. May (1975) writes, "It is the courage to invest one's self over a period of time in a relationship that will demand an increasing openness" (p. 17).

18.8 Conclusion

This chapter has presented an orientation to the wide range of ways that couples engage in power struggles and a set of techniques that can be useful to disrupt those struggles. One more reframe is offered here that is useful to inspirit partners to view each other as full "Others," persons with their needs, feelings, desires, hopes, and dreams that need to be acknowledged and considered in creating a conjoint life. In music, harmony requires at least two different notes, played simultaneously. If there is only one note, the result is monoTONy – monotone – which if spoken differently, is moNOTony, which means boredom. Partners select each other in part for the ways the other is different from themselves, to complement themselves, to be enlivened, and to learn from each other. But when couples descend into repeated acrimonious conflict and power struggles, they are essentially trying to silence the other's "notes." A successful, thriving relationship requires space and time for each other's "song," for each other's "notes," and with patience and attention to one another's different notes, the couple can bring those notes into harmony and play beautiful music together.

A less delicate and poetic suggestion, more typical of the author's hard-edged New York City and Boston upbringing, is: "If you want to be married to a *mirror*, get divorced, go to the store, and buy yourself a full-length mirror; they're on sale right now for $19.99 plus tax, and you can look at it and talk to yourself all day." Couples laugh when they hear this pointed but humorous suggestion, delivered in the appropriate regional accent. Sometimes, it inspires them to change.

References

Asen, E., & Fonagy, P. (2012). Mentalization-based therapeutic interventions for families. *Journal of Family Therapy*, *34*, 347–370. https://doi.org/10.1111/j.1467-6427.2011.00552.x

Asen, E., & Fonagy, P. (2021). *Mentalization-based treatment with families*. Guilford Press.

Benjamin, J. (2017). *Beyond doer and done to: Recognition theory, intersubjectivity and the Third*. Routledge.

Buehlman, K. T., Gottman, J. M., & Fainsilber Katz, L. (1992). How a couple views their past predicts their future: Predicting divorce from an oral history interview. *Journal of Family Psychology*, *5*, 295–318. https://doi.org/10.1037/0893-3200.5.3-4.295

Christensen, A., & Heavey, C. L. (1990). Gender and social structure in the demand/withdraw pattern of marital conflict. *Journal of Personality and Social Psychology*, *59*, 73–81. https://doi.org/10.1037//0022-3514.59.1.73

Driver, J., Tabares, A., Shapiro, A. F., & Gottman, J. M. (2012). Couple interaction in happy and unhappy marriages: Gottman laboratory studies. In F. Walsh (Ed.), *Normal family processes: Growing diversity and complexity* (4th ed., pp. 57–77). Guilford Press.

Findlay, J. N. (1970). *Axiological ethics*. St. Martin's Press.

Findlay, J. N. (1980). *Ethics as an art*. University Lecture, Boston University. The Trustees of Boston University.

Fishbane, M. D. (2013). *Loving with the brain in mind: Neurobiology and couple therapy*. W.W. Norton & Company.

Fishbane, M. D. (2023). Couple relational ethics: From theory to lived practice. *Family Process*, *62*, 446–468. https://doi.org/10.1111/famp.12861

Fraenkel, P. (2020). Integrating music into couple therapy theory and practice. *Clinical Social Work Journal, 48*, 319–333. https://doi.org/10.1007/s10615-020-00755-y; https://link-springer-com.ccny-proxy1.libr.ccny.cuny.edu/article/10.1007/s10615-020-00755-y
Fraenkel, P. (2022). Therapeutic palette integrative couple therapy. In J. L. Lebow & D. K. Snyder (Eds.), *Clinical handbook of couple therapy* (6th ed., pp. 339–361). Guilford Press.
Fraenkel, P. (2023). *Last chance couple therapy: Bringing couples back from the brink*. W.W. Norton & Company.
Fraenkel, P., Benson, K., St. James, C., & Bowen, M. (2022). Intimate partner violence: A focus on queer families, families and substance use, and military couples: Clinical applications. In S. Browning & B. van Eeden-Moorefield (Eds.), *Treating contemporary families: Toward a more inclusive clinical practice* (pp. 93–126). American Psychological Association.
Goldner, V. (1985). Feminism and family therapy. *Family Process, 24*, 31–47. https://doi.org/10.1111/j.1545-5300.1985.00031.x
Goldner, V. (1988). Generation and gender: Normative and covert hierarchies. *Family Process, 27*, 17–31. https://doi.org/10.1111/j.1545-5300.1988.00017.x
Goldner, V. (1998). The treatment of violence and victimization in intimate relationships. *Family Process, 37*, 263–286. https://doi.org/10.1111/j.1545-5300.1998.00263.x
Goldner, V., Penn, P., Sheinberg, M., & Walker, G. (1990). Love and violence: Gender paradoxes in volatile attachments. *Family Process, 29*, 343–364. https://doi.org/10.1111/j.1545-5300.1990.00343.x
Good, J. M. M. (2007). The affordances for social psychology of the ecological approach to social knowing. *Theory & Psychology, 17*, 265–295. https://doi.org/10.1177/0959354307075046
Gottman, J. M., & Gottman, J. S. (2018). *The science of couples and family therapy: Behind the scenes at the love lab*. W.W. Norton & Company.
Gupta, N. D., Etcoff, N. L., & Jaeger, M. M. (2016). Beauty in mind: The effects of physical attractiveness on psychological well-being and distress. *Journal of Happiness Studies, 17*, 1313–1325. https://doi.org/10.1007/s10902-015-9644-6
Hare-Mustin, R. T. (1978). A feminist approach to family therapy. *Family Process, 17*, 181–194. https://doi.org/10.1111/j.1545-5300.1978.00181.x
Jurist, E. (2018). *Minding emotions: Cultivating mentalization in psychotherapy*. Guilford Press.
Killian, K. D. (2013). *Interracial couples, intimacy, and therapy: Crossing racial borders*. Columbia University Press.
Knudson-Martin, C., & Mahoney, A. (Eds.). (2009). *Couples, gender, and power: Creating change in intimate relationships*. Springer.
Li, Z. (2022). Physical attractiveness and women's intra-household bargaining power. *Frontiers in Psychology, 13*, 853083. https://doi.org/10.3389/fpsyg.2022.853083
May, R. (1975). *The courage to create*. W.W. Norton & Company.
McDowell, T., Knudson-Martin, C., & Bermudez, J. M. (2022). *Socioculturally attuned family therapy: Guidelines for equitable theory and practice* (2nd ed.). Routledge.
McNulty, J. K., Neff, L. A., & Karney, B. R. (2008). Beyond initial attraction: Physical attractiveness in newlywed marriage. *Journal of Family Psychology, 22*, 135–143. https://doi.org/10.1037/0893-3200.22.1.135
Minuchin, S. (1974). *Families and family therapy*. Harvard University Press.
Walters, M., Carter, B., Papp, P., & Silverstein, O. (1988). *The invisible web: Gender patterns in family relationships*. Guilford Press.
Watzlawick, P., Beavin-Bavelas, J. T., & Jackson, D. D. (1967). *The pragmatics of human communication: A study of interactional patterns, paradoxes, and pathologies*. W.W. Norton & Company.
Watzlawick, P., Weakland, P. H., & Fisch, R. (1974). *Change: Principles of problem formation and problem resolution*. W.W. Norton & Company.
Wood, B. (1985). Proximity and hierarchy: Orthogonal dimensions of family interconnectedness. *Family Process, 24*, 487–507. https://doi.org/10.1111/j.1545-5300.1985.00487.x

19

TREATING SAME-SEX COUPLES

Harnessing the power of love

Michael C. LaSala

Paul and José entered my office in a fog of weary defeat. Both in their early 40s and together for 12 years, one of the few things they could agree on was that arguing was their only connection. Which of their difficulties were common to all couples seeking help, and which were a result of the stresses and strains of being a same-sex male couple?

In this chapter, I hope to begin to address this important question. Most major theories of mental health and couples therapy are thought to apply universally to *all couples* (Kerr & Bowen, 2009; Minuchin & Fishman, 1981) and, when developed, social and cultural issues were not taken into consideration. However, in time, several scholars called attention to issues of difference and power. McGoldrick and her colleagues underscored the previously overlooked effects of sexism on families and family therapy (McGoldrick et al., 1991). For Black families in the US, Nancy Boyd-Franklin (2013) (among others) asserted that we must view these families through a lens of racism and its consequential discrimination and violence. Gay and lesbian individuals and couples must cope with societal disapproval, so the usual boundaries considered functional for heterosexuals might not apply as they seek to protect their unions from the impacts of a hostile and even rejecting society that can include extended family members (LaSala, 2002). If, as therapists, we uncritically rely on existing theory in its purist form, we risk missing out and/or pathologizing client variations, cultural practices, and in the case of oppressed people, healthy protective mechanisms. In my many years of practice with marginalized peoples, I have found that unless I ask about the impacts of oppression on their lives and relationships, the topic goes unspoken. It is not advised that we abandon our theories as they are our roadmaps. However, they must be modified, and this chapter is written in that spirit.

19.1 Stigma

No discussion of gay and lesbian couples would be complete without an acknowledgement of the impacts of discrimination and marginalization. Imagine first learning of a particular stigma at the hands of childhood bullies and then later finding oneself bearing it. By the time a person realizes they are gay or lesbian, they have grown up in a culture that designates them as sick, perverted, and therefore unworthy of respect, civil rights, and even love (LaSala, 2010). Thus, as a person realizes their sexual

DOI: 10.4324/9781003536765-23

orientation, they could develop a devalued self-image that bodes poorly for their mental health and their ability to maintain long-term intimate relationships (Meyer, 2003).

> *When asked about his childhood, Paul discussed how he had been bullied as a young boy, called homophobic slurs due to his feminine gender expression. José, mindful of how taboo homosexuality was in his Guatemalan culture, kept his sexual orientation and resultant shame hidden throughout his youth into adulthood. No doubt, these formative experiences play a role in their current relationship difficulties. How could they not?*

On June 26, 2015, the US Supreme Court reached a decision to recognize same-sex marriage, thus granting all federal benefits to such couples (*Obergefell v. Hodges*, 2015). While this is undeniable progress in the advancement of lesbian and gay rights, there is still a ways to go in eliminating anti-gay oppression (NeJaime, 2015). Currently in the US, no federal laws prohibit discrimination in housing or employment. The current rightward shift of the US Supreme Court casts a shadow on hope for progress in the foreseeable future or even that current gains will be maintained. Nevertheless, unsurprisingly, the legal recognition of same-sex marriage has a direct impact on the lives of gay and lesbian couples, not the least of which is the right to be covered under a spouse's health insurance, to make hospital visits and health decisions for each other, and to access their government benefits such as social security. Relatedly, marriage may also contribute to couple longevity for same-sex couples (Rosenfeld, 2014). When it comes to physical and mental health, repeated findings indicate that marriage is a protective factor for those in heterosexual couples and their same-sex counterparts (Wight et al., 2013). Thus, happy same-sex marriages can potentially heal the ravages of anti-gay stigma. It is worth noting that one of the myths about same-sex couples is that they are not real or do not last. There is no evidence to support this notion; however, this idea, like a foul odor, remains in the air and can lead gay men and lesbians in troubled couples to feel particularly pained.

19.2 Stigma and parental relationships

> *Before emigrating to the US, José was born and raised in Guatemala, a culture in which open homosexuality was taboo and thus kept underground. José's mother Maria was initially shocked to learn her son was gay and, subsequently, her discussion of the topic over the years amounted to a few disapproving quips and a refusal to acknowledge José's relationship. When she came to stay with the couple for six months out of each year, Maria's silent but obvious disapproval made Paul angry, especially at his husband for fostering this arrangement.*

Although many couples argue about in-laws, this is a potential minefield for gay and lesbian unions. One of their most feared and painful challenges is parental rejection, and lesbian women and gay men utilize a variety of methods, some good and some not so good, to cope. Harsh parental disapproval can damage a child's mental health and may be related to sexual behavior that is at high risk for HIV/AIDS (Ryan et al., 2009). Additionally, parental negativity can significantly interfere with their ability to form healthy adult relationships. Previous studies suggest gay men rely more on distancing to protect their relationships, while lesbian couples seek closeness, resolution, and connection (LaSala, 2002, 2007). Such methods of coping can backfire, as we see with Julie's partner:

> On Mother's Day I bug her all day to call her mother, and by the afternoon she does it. By the end of the call, she is so upset, she's saying, "Why do I subject myself to this?" And then she blames me and we have a couple of days of tension.

And Robert:

> Anytime my husband wants to see them, which is frequent, we have this conversation about whether I should or shouldn't go. If they were accepting, there would be no friction.

Boszormenyi-Nagy and Spark (2014) describe the importance of prioritizing *horizontal* or couple relationships over those that are *vertical* – namely, those with parents – however, for same-sex couples, fear of upsetting parents could weaken their resolve to do so. A careful assessment of intergenerational relationships, including tensions across boundaries and their impacts, is called for when working with these couples. Relatedly, it is important to assess the *multigenerational transmission process* (Kerr & Bowen, 2009) to get an impression of the historic influences on the couple's difficulties. It became clear that José became his mother's caretaker at age 13 after his parents divorced, and that he comes from a long line of unstable, unhappy marriages, consisting of distant and cheating men, and women who appeared weak and helpless. Paul's parents rarely argued, but there was an unacknowledged strain of hostility that crackled like electricity throughout his family of origin. Such backgrounds understandably can leave a couple with poor conflict-resolution skills.

19.3 Nonmonogamy

When working with gay male couples, it is important to understand that a large proportion might be consensually, sexually nonmonogamous (Levine et al., 2018) with few if any negative consequences for their relationships (LaSala, 2004a; Stults, 2019). As described by this 49-year-old gay male research respondent:

> We've discussed at length the difference between sex and love and not counting on one person to meet all of your needs, desires, and interests. I mean Sam is the number one person for all of my emotional needs. He is the man I am connected to at the heart, bank account, day-to-day living and he is the only man I will ever make love to. We have monogamy of the heart and not the genitals.
>
> *(LaSala, 2004b)*

Like Sam, some gay men can separate sex from a loving commitment with their partners. However, it is important to acknowledge that this might not be the case for all such couples and to distinguish when sexual nonmonogamy does not work, as is often the case when either the couple has committed to monogamy or has not discussed their extradyadic agreements.

> *One night at a party, José walked in on Paul engaged in a sex act with another guest in the hosts' bedroom. While José did not consider this occasion grounds for a breakup as it might be for a heterosexual couple, both men saw this incident as a sign among a string of others that the relationship was in trouble.*

19.4 Sex roles

> *Recently, my barber asked a friend of mine whether I was the man or the woman in my relationship. He was confused whereby I did not appear gay and seemed "normal."*

Our ideas about gender roles in relationships remain so deeply engrained that it is hard for some people to imagine a successful relationship in which these roles are not clearly scripted. One prevailing myth about same-sex couples is that each partner enacts the role of either female or male. For example, people – including some gay men and lesbian women themselves – wonder who is "the man," the "top," or the one who plays the inserter role in sexual intercourse. Some find it impossible to understand how such a couple could exist without the assumed functional complementarity that exists between a man and a woman. People may misperceive that a masculine or "butch" woman takes on a traditionally male sex role in her relationship. She might do so, but simply because a woman acts in a way that could be interpreted as cross-gendered or has supposedly masculine interests does not mean that she takes on masculine roles in the relationship, sexually or otherwise (Wilson, 2009).

Who mows the lawn, who does the cooking and cleaning? Although some couples may choose to divide housework in a gendered way, research findings suggest that gay couples do not necessarily view housekeeping as feminine or masculine, and they divide these chores based on partner preferences (Barrett, 2015). Some gay men prefer exclusively bottom or top sexual positions, but very few engage in one position all the time (Moskowitz & Hart, 2011). Potential freedom from gender roles is a benefit of being in a same-sex couple. However, without clear agreement about guidelines, sex and housework may be areas of conflict for gay male and lesbian couples, and therapists must use their skills to help them negotiate mutually agreed upon arrangements.

Both José and Paul were career oriented. However, José's work as a hospital administrator required long hours, leaving the bulk of housework to Paul. Unsurprisingly, this left him feeling resentful, yet another area of conflict for the couple.

19.5 Treatment

19.5.1 Joining

For gay and lesbian couples, the joining process begins before they enter your office. Because they are sensitive to disapproval, they will do their homework, asking their networks about your reputation ("Do they work well with gay people?") and perusing your website. If you want to work with these couples, there should be a nondiscrimination statement on your website as well as mention of your expertise in working with these couples. It is also advised that therapists inspect their offices and waiting rooms. Lesbian and gay clients will want to see something of themselves in the physical surroundings. An easy addition is a prominently featured rainbow flag, an international symbol of lesbian, gay, bisexual, and transgender (LGBT) welcome. Other possibilities are magazines or brochures targeting the LGBT community. Such symbols are not only reassuring to same-sex couples, but they also help heal the impacts of growing up and living in a hostile world.

Just like for all couples, one must start by getting to know each member, collecting basic information such as where the person works, how many children they have, etc. It is also a good idea for the therapist to notice and acknowledge strengths:

Therapist: How long have you guys been together?
José: 14 years.
Therapist: Wow, despite what I am sure are the difficulties you guys are facing, that's a good amount of time. I am guessing that there is still some connection and resilience there.

Praising a same-sex couple for longevity is particularly important considering the prevailing myths about them. Once this introductory phase is completed, my favorite opening question is:

People come to see me because they want to change something in their lives; what is it you would like to change?

The beauty of this question is that, right from the start, it dismantles the expectation that the therapist is going to apply magic that will change the client or their relationship. I believe this question is relevant to all clients no matter what their culture, ethnicity, or sexual orientation. Like other troubled couples, José and Paul want to improve communication – but what that looks like can be idiosyncratic to the couple and must be followed with an invitation to be more specific:

Therapist: OK, a good place to start. Communication, of course, is essential in a relationship. What would be happening that isn't happening now, that would tell you that your communication has improved?

Paul: We would be fighting less, there would be more trust. He is angry all of the time.

Therapist: So, it sounds pretty unhappy at home.

Paul: Yes, absolutely.

Therapist: *(To José)* What would you say?

José: I am not sure I want to stay in this relationship. I need help to figure that out.

Therapist: Wow, I can see that things are really at a breaking point.

This unleashes a litany of complaints. José sees Paul as not fully understanding of the burden he carries with his family and at work. Paul believes that José, a hospital administrator, is a workaholic and is irritated that he is never home, including when his mother comes to stay, leaving him alone with her. These complaints seem like what one might find in a troubled heterosexual couple; being gay does not make them unique, but the fact that she disapproves of their homosexuality does. Although there are numerous problems to cover, the mother issue becomes focal, particularly since her next six-month visit is imminent.

19.5.2 Focal problem

Therapist: OK, out of all of the problems you have mentioned, what is the most difficult for you guys?

Paul: I would say his mother coming to live with us for six months. You know, she doesn't even accept our relationship – and having her here feels intrusive.

José: He really does not get it! I have been taking care of my mother since I was 13, when my Dad left us. It is *my* job to look after her, and I must be grateful for all she has done for me and my siblings. I can't *not* let her come and stay here!

It is important to recognize that cultural factors can complicate matters for a same-sex couple, so they must be acknowledged:

Therapist: I am guessing there is a cultural issue here as well, no? What about that? In the US, it is not always expected that children will remain close to their parents once they become adults. But I take it that in your culture, José, the expectation is different.

José: Yes, that is absolutely true. To be honest, Americans and their families always seem cold to me for this reason. However, in my country, people are less accepting of gay people, which is why I moved here. So, it's really a mixed bag.

19.5.3 Enactment

Enactment is a classic family therapy intervention in which the therapist gets family members to discuss a problem in their presence, giving them a sense of how the couple communicates, where things go wrong, and what corrections are needed (Minuchin & Fishman, 1981; Nichols, 2016). Again, this is used for all types of couples, including those that are same-sex, although the content of these discussions could vary:

Therapist: OK, I can see that there is some disagreement here. Now, I am going to have you do something that you might not have expected. I want the two of you to talk to each other while I just sit here and listen. *(Therapist gets up from his seat to help them move the chairs so that Paul and José face each other.)* OK, so right now, I would like you to talk to each other about this problem in front of me, and I will be sitting here, hearing everything.

Paul: He knows how difficult it is for me to have his mother visit us for such a long time.

Therapist: *(redirecting)* OK, Paul, but tell your husband, not me – I will hear you.

José: I don't see what the problem is *(addressing Paul)*. She's very quiet, barely talks, and she is not much trouble.

Paul: When she is here for so long, I feel like she is in the way. She sits in the living room all day; she makes subtle anti-gay comments. I can't be comfortable knowing how disapproving she is. Not only do we have to host and entertain her while she is here, I feel like we have to hide parts of ourselves – getting rid of our gay art and magazines and not having certain friends over.

Hiding is a sensitive issue for LGBT people as they are often invisible and need to "come out" to others in their lives, including family members, friends, and coworkers, to make themselves known. Further, in many cultures, like that of José's, there is a taboo around same-sex relationships, so they are not discussed, leaving gay people feeling isolated and alone, particularly before they come out. Many, including lawmakers, medical professionals, and clergy, maintain homophobic and heterocentric views because they have not had their prejudices challenged by knowing openly gay people. Finally, recent LGBT book banning in the US and attempts to outlaw drag queens (gay men who dress and perform in flamboyant women's attire) are additional ways to invisibilize LGBT people, so it is understandable why gay men like Paul might be particularly sensitive to this issue. However, it also must be understood that José is caught between conflicting loyalties to his family and Paul.

José: You need to understand, Paul, she is my mother. I cannot just make her stay in a hotel when she is here. I think you are making too much of all of this. She really is no trouble, and I think you are blowing things way out of proportion.

Paul: You never understand me when I am talking. Now you are minimizing the issue, per usual. Jesus!

José: And you are so stubborn; we have been through this over and over again!

After this short interchange, both José and Paul encountered a stalemate and, in exasperation, turned their gaze to the therapist.

Therapist: So, is this how it goes at home when you discuss this issue?

Paul and José nod their heads.

Therapist: OK, I think I can see how things get bogged down.

Through enactments, the clinician can coach couple members to have new, more productive interactions.

Therapist: Paul, can you understand where José is coming from? What did you hear him say?
Paul: Yes, that he feels some obligation to his mother, but per usual, this seems to override my own feelings and preferences – what *I* want.
Therapist: Ask your husband if you got that right. Just the part about obligations for now.
José *(jumps in)*: Yes, I feel responsible to be a good son to my mother, but I don't agree that I don't understand or care about your feelings.

The therapist often must invite the couple to discuss the issue of stigma as a factor. If not, it might never come up.

Therapist: We gay men often have to put up with a lot of discrimination and bullying at some point. This can make us very sensitive to any signs of rejection or even disapproval from the very people we love. Does this resonate for you, Paul?

A therapist who is not gay can begin the last statement with "I understand gay men often . . ." "Do I have that correct?"

Paul: Yes, my parents are very old school. When I grew up, homosexuality was not acceptable, and even though the kids teased me and called me faggot, I had to hide myself in order to get along. So, I do not want to do that in my own home.
Therapist: Do you think José understands that?
Paul: I don't know. We never really talk about those type of things.

(Which of course, might be related to the tendency for two men to distance in silence rather than confront a potentially volatile issue.)

Here is where the clinician can introduce elements of the couple problem that relate specifically to a gay couple, and offer empathy as well as normalization.

Therapist: It is not uncommon, particularly with families from other cultures, for them to struggle with a child's gay sexual orientation, leaving children to wonder how to negotiate their identities and relationships with love but also loyalty to disapproving parents.

It is always a good idea to check in with the clients after making such a pronouncement.

Therapist: Does that sound about right?
(*Paul and José nod.*)
Therapist: Painful, for sure, but in that way you two are not unique. However, as gay men, it is important to come together to decide how you will deal with this difficult dilemma. Some gay male couples set firmer boundaries and guidelines with their parents to protect their unions. Others distance altogether, while still others acquiesce to their parents' demands and stay silent, which is not healthy for themselves or their partnerships. What troubles me about you two is that there does not seem to have been much communication about this arrangement. It looks like, José, you decided this issue unilaterally and, Paul, you just resentfully went along. To resolve this, you are going to have to find an arrangement that prioritizes your couple while maintaining family connections.

This issue is complex, but as therapy continued and they were able to clearly state their positions, they began to understand each other's feelings, which had a ripple effect on the other troubled areas of their relationship, including housework.

In keeping with the family therapy tradition of getting everybody in the room, a meaningful addition to the therapy was to include José's mother, Maria. Up until now, she was seen as a burdensome obligation to both José and Paul, despite their different opinions about how to deal with her. Including Maria in therapy could reframe her role in ways that would help not only her son and his husband but also herself. For sure, if she could communicate acceptance to the couple, it could be yet another pathway for Paul and José to resolve the conflict surrounding her visit. Maria spoke very little English, but fortunately the therapist knew enough Spanish to understand and speak with her.

Therapist: *(translated into English)* Maria, thank you for coming in today. It is a pleasure to meet you. I know you and your son share a close connection, which, in my mind, is a tribute to your mothering.
Maria: (*smiled*)
Therapist: Do you know why I asked for you to come in today?
Maria: Not sure.
Therapist: Well, I am working with your son and Paul and trying to help them improve their relationship. You are clearly a very important person in this family, and therefore, I wanted to get your perspective and your help.
Maria: Well, I am not sure how I can help, but I do see they fight a lot.
Therapist: Any ideas as to why?
Maria: I am not sure. My son works very hard, long hours, and Paul yells a lot. (*Paul rolls his eyes in silence.*)
José: *(to Paul)* See, that attitude doesn't make things better!
Paul: José, you don't understand my feelings! She doesn't respect us or our relationship, and we are forced to live with her.
Therapist to Maria: Is that true? Can you tell us honestly what you think about their relationship?
Maria: I am not sure I can. I don't want to . . . insult you . . .

If, as in this case, the therapist happens to be LGBT, parents of LGBT children might be reluctant to discuss their disapproval, out of a desire to be sensitive to the therapist's feelings. However, as we all know, hiding feelings during a therapy session is never a good idea. When working with families with rejecting parents, it is important to initially "tolerate the intolerance." The therapist needs to find a way to give permission or invite parents to express their fears and other negative reactions:

Therapist: It is ok. I have heard all sorts of things from parents. When I first told my parents that I was gay, they stated that they rather I tell them I was a murderer. However, they eventually came around. So, there is nothing you can say that will shock me.
Maria: Wow, good heavens! That's awful! That's something a mother must never say!
Therapist: I appreciate that. Clearly, you are a caring mother, Maria.
Maria: For me, I am more worried about José. Maybe I did something wrong when he was a baby, or maybe it was because his father left us when José was young, I don't know. But I worry that life is harder for him, especially if he doesn't get married and have children.
Therapist: Maria, when was the last time you and your son talked about this topic?
José: I can't remember. (*Maria shrugs.*)

Therapist: Paul and José know how I like to get people to talk to each other in front of me. How about if you, José, and your mother do so right now? Why don't you start by addressing her concerns? Paul, I know you have a lot of feelings about what is happening, but, as you know, this is something they need to work out. So, let's you and I just sit back, relax, and listen for right now.

José: Mom, I am a grown man now; I need to make my own decisions and live my life.

Therapist: OK, good, now tell your mother what you need from her.

José: I need you to respect me and respect my relationship.

Maria remains silent and expressionless.

Therapist: Maria, what do you think of what José is asking? Can you respond to him?

Maria: *(after much prompting and a long pause)* I am worried that I did something wrong – maybe it is because your father left us when you were so young.

Therapist: Wow. These must be incredibly painful thoughts to have as a mother. However, you should know that the idea that a parent causes a child to be gay is outdated and lacks scientific proof. So, you have no reason to feel guilty, Maria. I am wondering if José can respond to you.

José: Yes, Mother, you did nothing wrong. This is the way I am, and the way God created me. I want you to see that. Though Paul and I are having some difficulties, I am happy with who I am.

It is notable that what belies worry for a gay or lesbian child is a lack of understanding of their resilience. By the time a gay or lesbian person becomes an adult, they have survived bullying, living in a rejecting world, and coming to terms with sexual and romantic feelings that are outside the norm. This resilience is often overlooked.

Therapist: It is not uncommon for parents and children to go through this when a child comes out as gay. I am also thinking that culture might have something to do with it.

José: *(to me)* Yes, in Guatemala, there is more disapproval of gay men. Men are supposed to be macho, and being gay is very taboo. But, Mom, I am happy with who I am.

Therapist to Maria: So, some of this might be related to culture shock, no?

Maria: Yes.

Therapist to Maria and José: I really get that, Maria, but I think it will very much help your relationship with Paul if you both can come to terms with José being gay. It will also help their relationship with each other. In that way, you can be my co-therapist.

Framing Maria as a co-therapist helped engage her and also elevate her beyond the role of a passively interfering in-law who needed to be obstructed or ignored.

Family adjustment is rarely quick, often taking weeks, months, even years. For Maria, it took ongoing sessions over several weeks, but eventually, through continued discussion, Maria, while never fully approving, came to slowly accept her son and his relationship. Once this started to happen, the therapist prescribed that Maria and Paul have alone time, going for a ride or for coffee so they could get to know each other better. The more Paul is humanized in Maria's eyes, the better she will feel about her son's sexual orientation. After several such outings, the therapist brought Maria back into the couples' session.

Therapist: Maria, I am wondering, as a mature person who has seen a lot in her life, if you could give José and Paul one piece of advice as a couple, what would it be – can you tell them this right now, while I sit back and listen?

After years of being considered a "burden" and a "bother" to this couple, it was important to further help her step out of this role in this way and see her, even with her history of disapproval, as a potential resource for the couple:

Maria: I think you both argue and even yell a lot at each other and do not listen. I know you are both hot-headed, but that doesn't help you. You need to talk more calmly and respectfully to each other.

Therapist: That sounds very wise, Maria. I completely agree. Keep that up and I am going to hire you!

As time progressed, José and Maria continued to discuss his sexual orientation and how it clashed with his family's cultural and religious values. Improving the relationships between Maria and the couple lowered the flame of couple conflict and, as a result, they were able to work out several agreements, including a tentative plan to turn a section of the home into a private apartment for Maria and an agreement for her to knock or call before entering each other's living quarters. On a separate issue, the therapist raised the issue of monogamy, normalizing several options, including allowing for outside sexual partners. Paul and José decided that they would reaffirm their monogamous commitment but that if either wanted to have sex outside the relationship, they would communicate that to each other beforehand. Along the way, they learned to express their feelings, listen to each other better, and as a result their relationship improved.

19.6 Conclusions and lessons learned

As stated previously, when working with same-sex couples, one must assess and address intergenerational boundaries, extradyadic sexual agreements, sex roles, and the impacts of discrimination and oppression. For female couples, the challenges are similar, although the boundaries around the couple might be more diffuse, allowing for more intergenerational interference, particularly if the parents are disapproving, which can have a deleterious impact on the couple (LaSala, 2002). This might be because women in general are more likely to prize connection both within their couples and also intergenerationally. It is a good idea for all gay and lesbian couples to determine what role societal disapproval plays in their relationships, how they protect their relationships from this threat, and how to strengthen their coping mechanisms.

Culture must also be taken into consideration. LGBT rights movements have taken place in largely Western contexts, where the importance of individual happiness and self-actualization is a priority over allegiance to one's family or community. Even for some cultures in the US, such as Asian or African cultures, the idea that an individual would claim an identity and thus put their own needs over those of their family or tribe is unimaginable. In other cultures (such as African American, Latino/a or Hispanic cultures), the emphasis on sex roles and particularly the expectation that men be masculine or even hypermasculine can fuel hatred and disapproval toward gay and lesbian people (LaSala & Frierson, 2012). Finally, even with the advancement of gay rights and legalization of same-sex marriage in some countries, the role of stigma on not only individual well-being and couple and family dynamics cannot be underestimated. However, neither can the healing power of a strong same-sex union. Same-sex couples but also families have something to offer to the field of couples therapy, namely, exemplars of how, even under the toughest of circumstances, it is possible to create strong family and couple relationships. In doing so, they demonstrate and reflect back to us the importance of following one's heart and accessing the healing power of love.

References

Barrett, C. (2015). Queering the home: The domestic labor of lesbian and gay couples in contemporary England. *Home Cultures, 12*(2), 193–211. https://doi.org/10.1080/17406315.2015.1046298

Boszormenyi-Nagy, I., & Spark, G. M. (2014). *Invisible loyalties*. Routledge.

Boyd-Franklin, N. (2013). *Black families in therapy: Understanding the African American experience*. Guilford Press.

Kerr, M. E., & Bowen, M. (2009). *Family evaluation*. W.W. Norton & Company.

LaSala, M. C. (2002). Walls and bridges: How coupled gay men and lesbians manage their intergenerational relationships. *Journal of Marital and Family Therapy, 28*, 327–338. https://doi.org/10.1111/j.1752-0606.2002.tb01190.x

LaSala, M. C. (2004a). Extradyadic sex and gay male couples: Comparing monogamous and nonmonogamous relationships. *Families in Society, 85*(3), 405–412. https://doi.org/10.1606/1044-3894.1502

LaSala, M. C. (2004b). Monogamy of the heart: A qualitative study of gay male couples. *Journal of Gay and Lesbian Social Services, 17*(3), 1–24. https://doi.org/10.1300/J041v17n03_01

LaSala, M. C. (2007). Parental influence, gay youth, and safer sex. *Health and Social Work, 32*, 49–55. https://doi.org/10.1093/hsw/32.1.49

LaSala, M. C. (2010). *Coming out, coming home: Helping families adjust to a gay or lesbian child*. Columbia University Press.

LaSala, M. C., & Frierson, D. (2012). African American gay youth and their families: Redefining masculinity, coping with racism and homophobia. *Gay, Lesbian, Bisexual, Transgender Family Studies, 8*, 428–445. https://doi.org/10.1080/1550428X.2012.729948

Levine, E. C., Herbenick, D., Martinez, O., Fu, T. C., & Dodge, B. (2018). Open relationships, nonconsensual nonmonogamy, and monogamy among US adults: Findings from the 2012 national survey of sexual health and behavior. *Archives of Sexual Behavior, 47*(5), 1439–1450. https://doi.org/10.1007/s10508-018-1178-7

McGoldrick, M., Anderson, C. M., & Walsh, F. (Eds.). (1991). *Women in families: A framework for family therapy*. W.W. Norton & Company.

Meyer, I. H. (2003). Prejudice, social stress, and mental health in LGB populations: Conceptual issues and research evidence. *Psychological Bulletin, 129*, 674–697. https://doi.org/10.1037/0033-2909.129.5.674

Minuchin, S., & Fishman, H. C. (1981). *Family therapy techniques*. Harvard University Press.

Moskowitz, D. A., & Hart, T. A. (2011). The influence of physical body traits and masculinity on anal sex roles in gay and bisexual men. *Archives of Sexual Behavior, 40*(4), 835–841. https://doi.org/10.1007/s10508-011-9754-0

NeJaime, D. (2015, June 26). With ruling on marriage equality, fight for gay families is next. *Los Angeles Times*. www.latimes.com/opinion/op-ed/la-oe-nejaime-gay-marriage-decision-does-not-solve-everything-20150628-story.html

Nichols, M. P. (2016). *Family therapy: Concepts and methods* (11th ed.). Pearson.

Obergefell v. Hodges, 576 U.S. 644 (2015).

Rosenfeld, M. J. (2014). Couple longevity in the era of same-sex marriage in the United States. *Journal of Marriage and Family, 76*(5), 905–918. https://doi.org/10.1111/jomf.12141

Ryan, C., Huebner, D., Diaz, R. M., & Sanchez, J. (2009). Family rejection as a predictor of negative health outcomes in white and Latino lesbian, gay, and bisexual young adults. *Pediatrics, 123*, 346–362. https://doi.org/10.1542/peds.2007-3524

Stults, C. B. (2019). Relationship quality among young gay and bisexual men in consensual nonmonogamous relationships. *Journal of Social and Personal Relationships, 36*(10), 3037–3056. https://doi.org/10.1177/0265407518809530

Wight, R. G., LeBlanc, A. J., & Lee Badgett, M. V. (2013). Same-sex legal marriage and psychological well-being: Findings from the California health interview survey. *American Journal of Public Health, 103*(2), 339–346. https://doi.org/10.2105/AJPH.2012.301113

Wilson, B. D. M. (2009). Black lesbian sexual culture and lesbian gender: Celebration and resistance. *Culture, Health, & Sexuality, 11*, 297–313. https://doi.org/10.1080/13691050802676876

20

INTERGENERATIONAL COUPLE THERAPY

Maurizio Andolfi and Anna Mascellani

20.1 Models of couple therapy compared

Systemically based couple therapy began to emerge as a specific treatment independent of family therapy only in the early 1980s. Before that for several decades, there was the field of couple counseling that was not based in systems theory (Gurman & Fraenkel, 2002). In recent decades, three methodologies have developed significantly: cognitive-behavioral couple therapy (Dattilio, 2010; Baucom & Epstein, 1990; Gottman & Gottman, 2015), psychoanalytic couple therapy (Sharf & Sharff, 2003; Bartholomey & Horowitz, 1991), and emotion-focused couple therapy, based upon the integration of Gestalt, systemic, and attachment theories (Johnson, 2020). Another trend that began in the early 1980s and became significant in the 1990s is integrative couple therapy, in which different theories and their associated practices are combined in a systematic manner (Fraenkel, 2017, 2022; Lebow, 1987, 1997; Pinsof, 1995; Scheinkman, 2008). All of these integrative approaches combine techniques that increase couple members' insight about how their family-of-origin experiences and unconscious issues and beliefs contribute to feelings and behaviors in the current relationship, as well as action-oriented techniques designed to change dysfunctional interaction patterns and to improve communication. All of these therapeutic methods seem effective in modifying dysfunctional couple dynamics and problematic communication patterns, or in focusing on revealing and expressing vulnerable emotions. However, although some of them examine partners' family-of-origin reactivity and beliefs about relationships, these models ignore or discard the possibility of broadening the picture to include other significant members of the family, inviting to the session members of both partners' families of origin, their children, and in some cases their friends (Andolfi, 1999; Andolfi et al., 2022).

In the book *Intergenerational Couple Therapy* (2021), Andolfi and Mascellani present a model of couple therapy that follows Bowen's pioneering ideas on differentiation of self (1978), Williamson's approach on the process of intergenerational intimidation (1982), Boszormenyi-Nagy and Spark's invisible loyalties (1973), and especially Framo's ideas on forgiveness and repairing intergenerational ties (1992). Our intervention model expands the *multigenerational* dimension and also reaches downwards, drawing resources from the children, who are included as special consultants/guides in the exploration of the family world. This has been described as the *bottom-up approach* in multigenerational family therapy (Andolfi, 2022, 2024).

Couple crises include a wide range of difficulties that threaten to alter the stability and harmony of all relationships. These crises are often considered as private quarrels, although they are both a

DOI: 10.4324/9781003536765-24

symptom and a cause of the problems noted in the broader family system. Consequently, exploring the couple relationship requires entering the most vulnerable area of the entire family structure, which is often burdened by intergenerational collisions and incomplete or partial separations from their respective families of origin. Partners in a couple are in an intimate relationship with each other, and, at the same time, they are children vis-à-vis their parents, with whom they may still have loose ends or unresolved conflicts. The couple partners may have problematic relationships with siblings, and these difficulties may affect the couple functioning.

Once they have built their own family, the partners have become parents, and we know how the presence of children can unite and increase harmony or, on the contrary, become a destabilizing event in the life of the couple. This complex network of functions and roles is structured on two dimensions. The vertical dimension includes the various hierarchical levels –grandparents, parents, children – and is crucial for observing and assessing the quality of intergenerational ties. The horizontal dimension outlines the quality and strength of the couple as a unit, which we define the *We space*, as well as the sibling alliance and friendship system. The main ingredients of this special bond, based on an implicit pact (couple alliance), are mutual respect, trust, and intimacy, which seem to disappear when a couple is undergoing a deep crisis or is close to hostile separation. Restoring respect, increasing trust, and rediscovering intimacy are the main goals of every couple therapist, regardless of his/her orientation.

20.2 Exploring the developmental history of the couple

In our experience, we have realized that the more we broaden the field of observation, the more we help the couple overcome their difficulties. In many years of clinical work, we have learned to appreciate and use the *symbolic presence* of the family of origin (parents and siblings) in the session, presences often introduced by one or the other partner from the very beginning of our therapy. We have often observed the centrality of children, often triangulated or engaged in the couple's problems. Instead of considering these presences as intrusive or inappropriate, we have redefined them, made them visible, and valued them as special resources available in therapy. We extensively used the *as if* language and space as a metaphor for relationships. This "as if" technique is illustrated below:

> *If your mother were here, what would she say to make me understand her suffering? If your father were here in the session (he passed away recently), what would you want to tell him that you couldn't when he was still alive? If your son were present in the session, where would he be sitting? Between the two of you, on one side, far away? And if so, what would he advise me to do to help you? Can you show me some pictures of your children? Who do they most resemble in character, to the mother's family or to the father's family?*

The construction and discussion of the genogram during the session is like a roadmap that orients the therapeutic process. It allows us to explore the developmental history and major events in each partner's family setting so as to understand and assess their family's functioning, the family's resilience towards life's adversities, and the sources of their individual identity and personality traits. We are also able to observe and assess each partner's respect for each other's developmental storytelling and their ability to listen without interfering. We know all too well that when two partners want to attack each other, the hardest blow occurs by saying very mean things about the other partner's family. Couples often come to therapy full of anger or experiencing relational tension and would like their "burning issues" to be the immediate focus of attention. In this case, asking them to draw the genogram has the advantage of momentarily "freezing" the couple's conflicts, giving each partner the chance to describe the most significant events of his or her personal growth, without any intrusion or criticism from the other. In our clinical experience, a couple has never felt the therapist's request to get to know their families better before getting to the heart of their current difficulties as being offensive or unnecessary. If anything, the difficulty might be with a therapist who is "dragged" into these burning issues, lacking the ability to draw boundaries and point to an alternative path. Giving a feeling of individual autonomy back to each partner and marking a "boundary between you and me" is the first step in restoring mutual respect and appreciation of each other's life experiences, as well as representing *a context mark* (Andolfi, 2017).

20.3 Case illustration: A cocktail of anger and anxiety with a couple in crisis

An Italian couple, Laura and Luca, living in Australia recently visited me (Andolfi) for therapy. Prior to the meeting, I received a short email from Laura saying she needed couple therapy because of Luca's problem with verbal violence (perhaps not only verbal), which had become unbearable. The only information about the family was that they have two school-age children. Before meeting them, with the little information offered thus far, I had drawn the genogram diagram on a flipchart, including symbols and names of the parents and the children. The two partners look surprised when they enter the therapy room and find their names already written on a paperboard, as if they were already present in that space. After introductions were made and the choice of the preferred language was selected, the therapist showed the draft genogram and asked them: "Shall we complete it so I can get to know you better before we get into the heart of your problems? Who wants to start? You can each use a different color marker."

The husband, Luca, was the first to answer. This was surprising, as he was the partner who had come to the session reluctantly and only because he had been pushed by his wife to do so. He approached the flipchart, wrote down the names of his parents and his sister, and started to talk about the history of his father's physical and verbal violence towards his two children. Apparently, only the maternal grandmother protected them as children. Upon the recent death of his father, the two women (Luca's mother and sister) agreed to exclude Luca from the will. The anger at his family, with whom he had broken off all relations, at his job where he had debts, at his wife who "keeps moving his papers all over the place and makes him furious," and at the world at large was palpable. Only his children, whose photos were gladly shown at the beginning of the meeting, seemed to be a healthy, peaceful relational territory for him, not yet invaded by his anger. Anger therefore seemed to be his identity card.

Laura's story was diametrically opposite to Luca's. She talked about her close-knit family, where love and care are the key elements. As she talked about this, tears came to her eyes because she missed everyone so much, since she is the only one who left Italy and immigrated to Australia. She studied languages and then started traveling. This is how she met Luca, who had been traveling for work to many countries, and she fell in love with him and then they got their residency in Australia. Laura has a part-time job as a secretary, is very anxious, and seems to be a perfectionist. "Everything in the house has to be tidy, otherwise I go crazy."

In the second part of the session, I invited them to describe the qualities that each partner recognized in the other and write them on the flipchart. Based on what they have written down, they seemed to be a solid couple, and both love their children very much. However, it takes very little for negativity to take over, virtually every day. At the end of the session, I asked them to think about whether to return a second time. However, I told them I was willing to see them again only on condition that there was no longer one pushing and the other following. I stressed the fact that the description of Luca's anger as a motive for therapy was a valid reason for Laura, but it was only one part of a therapeutic project, which must get both of them involved in their commitment to change. His anger and her anxiety were just the emerging problems in their relationship as a couple. But to enter their lives, we needed to go much deeper than that, even if part of the agreement was first for Luca to stop his verbal violence at home in order to move on.

This therapeutic attitude and message allowed Laura and Luca's positions to be rebalanced, and the couple returned to therapy because both partners wanted to change. Once a joint motivation was built, in a few sessions we started to explore the transmission of intergenerational anger in Luca's family, starting from his paternal grandfather and continuing with his father, who never believed in him and punished him all the time. For these reasons, he had to leave his own family and his small town at a very young age. With great pain, Luca described him being labeled as the "black sheep" of the family and bullied in school at the point to interrupt his studies and start travelling far away from his country. This is how he described the lack of care while he was growing up: "My mother never defended me, she cared only for my younger sister. . . . My grandma was good with me when I was very little, then she died and nobody cared for me." Later on in the therapy, taking about what each of them got from the other, Luca candidly admits that Laura has been the most important woman in his life – once free from mutual blame, competition, and criticism. He doesn't want to lose her for any reason.

A few sessions later, I asked the couple to invite their children to see what good parents they are and how Luca has been able to learn from his children to become a good father with them. In the session, it was visible how Luca tried very hard to be a "different father," one who is able to play and have fun with his children. His older daughter, Lisa, was curious to know about her father's childhood. She was very moved and jumped onto her father's lap, when Luca described how tough it was for him growing up with no love and a lot of physical punishment. The session with the children was very productive and brought more lightness and positive feelings inside the couple.

Laura could explore now more freely her own long story of anxiety and perfectionism, and we could explore the family roots of her anxiety, following the female side from grandmother down through the generations. Her anxiety was also increased by her sense of solitude because of the great physical distance from her family members, all living very close to each other in the south of Italy.

For this reason, Laura was invited to bring along some of the objects, pictures, drawings, and mementos that she carefully keeps at home to be in touch with her family when she is missing them. Laura was greatly relieved by the proposal to have a special session online with her family members. From what has been described so far, it is easy to understand how useful it is to make family explorations, retelling important family events, and including the children as resources in order to help couples in crisis to gain more trust and benevolence in their relationship. Moving upstairs first into family history allows the couple to come back in the present to the couple's realities, freer from mutual blame, competition, and criticism.

As in the case of Laura and Luca, concrete and metaphorical objects, pictures, and drawings are tangible and concrete, highly evocative tools that introduce curiosity and reduce competition and conflict. For example, both partners can be asked to bring to therapy the most important family pictures of their childhood, or even personal items, such as a pendant, a bag, or a musical instrument, reminding them of the great affection for a parent who has passed or a beloved grandparent or faraway sibling. It is like introducing a parallel process into couple therapy so that, along with addressing their conflicts and dysfunctional patterns, each partner can learn something about the other that is very meaningful, and often painful, in a collaborative way, allowing both to share an intimate moment. Once the family is symbolically present in the session, through imagery, metaphorical objects, and intergenerational questions (Andolfi, 2017), it will be easier for both the therapist and the couple to ask the families of origin to come for joint consultation.

20.4 The family of origin in session

The presence of each partner's family of origin for a special session is prepared for thoroughly and is proposed only once a relationship of mutual trust has been established between the therapist and couple pair. The meeting is presented as a great opportunity for each partner "to ask for help" once from their parents and siblings, who are invited as consultants for a special session in which their development through the presence and the words of the parents and siblings will be explored. Couple conflicts and presenting issues will not be addressed in this meeting, and they will be coached by the therapist as to how to invite their families, making clear that this meeting aims to look at the positive resources of the family and is not meant to be a forum for critiquing the parents or siblings. The presence of the other partner as an attentive observer and listener is encouraged in order to learn more in depth the other partner's early experiences in life and to support him or her empathically.

Once the session begins, their storytelling will make it possible to go back to some key moments of the past, heal open wounds, and forgive long-standing conditions of neglect or abandonment, as well as to look at the strength and positive resources of the family unit. During these sessions, each person will be able to retrace, together with his or her family members, a journey into the past all the way back to childhood when the emotional bonds of care and primary attachment are built (or not). They will be able to compare different and sometimes discordant descriptions of reality between parents and children, learn new and unexpected things, in an authentic and respectful atmosphere. The therapist's task is to lead the session, to ask relational questions and broaden the positive aspects, avoiding conflicts or judgmental situations. Parents are very sensitive to blame, and sometimes they come to the session with mixed feelings and may easily "feel guilty" about any mistakes or sense of failure towards their children. The therapist can lower the risk of these feelings emerging by greeting the family members warmly, thanking them for attending the session, and setting the frame of the session as a chance to explore different experiences and points of view, and that it is not meant to be a "parent-blaming" session.

What is even more important is to find the strength and courage to ask faraway or absent parents to attend. Discussing the possibility of making this request allows therapist and couple partners to discuss their anticipation that their parents or other family members will reject the invitation, and to prepare emotionally if indeed the request is rejected. "He will never come and help me; he has never done it all the years we lived together in the same house!" This is a typical example of the often-justified reluctance of an adult to reopen dialogue with an uncaring or even abusive parent. Rather than being stuck in some sort of an emotional limbo or chronic anger over past rejection, we encourage the adult to make the invitation with an open heart. The response is often surprisingly positive, allowing for a new understanding of the possibilities in the present moment, without being guided by the negative experiences of the past. This opens the possibility of intergenerational reconciliation (Framo, 1992). However, if this does not happen, the couple partner will have to deal with the rejection by the family, and the therapist can help the partner accept the reality and come to terms with it instead of holding out hope of going back and erasing the past. In doing so, even refusals become opportunities for people to develop acceptance, resilience, and strength. Then, the presence in the room of the other partner is very therapeutic and can encourage more benevolence and care in the couple relationship, reducing blame and conflict.

A shared, collective memory with multiple generations in the same room has a tremendously restorative potential and has a transformative effect on each person's individual growth, with positive reflections upon the entire family of origin and indirect effects on the couple's dynamics. The experience with the families of origin present is not an extra session, but it has a powerful transformative effect both at the individual level and in the couple relationship, and this tells us how therapeutic it is to engage each partner's families as part of couple therapy.

In the interviews conducted in our extensive follow-up research on how couples experienced their couple therapy (Andolfi et al., 2000), none of the participants reported feeling a sense of embarrassment or discomfort in sessions when the other partner's family was present. On the contrary, this presence during the session was seen as an important emotional support for a task perceived as difficult and painful. In addition, this led to greater understanding between them since the other partner would also have to go through the same experience with his or her family. These positive effects in co-presence were reported even though many couples had come to therapy due to their high-conflict relationship.

In sessions with the family of origin present, siblings may also be invited alongside parents. In some cases, we planned a second meeting for the siblings when we realized it was better to find a specific space to explore relationships in the sibling subsystem and go over some important growth experiences. Sometimes the invitation extended to siblings in a special session can be more challenging, especially if there have been rigid triangulations and favoritism toward one child over another in the past. Episodes of rivalry or long estrangement between adult siblings are often the result of distorted roles played since they were very young children, causing a painful emotional distance. When they occur, these sessions can help repair any relational distortion linked to rigid roles in the family and the difficulty of building or maintaining a generational alliance between siblings.

The case that follows shows very well the importance of siblings' sessions during couple therapy.

20.5 Case illustration: A hole in the stomach

Daniele's story is an example of how the death of his mother accentuated emotional distance from his siblings. Daniele is a man of about 40 years of age who is in a deep crisis with his partner. She complains he has always rolled himself up in a ball, being totally incapable of showing his deepest emotions, and how this threatens the relationship of the couple to the core. In the course of therapy, Daniele finds the courage to invite his sisters, with whom he has had a very cold and detached relationship, above all after the death of their mother, who was widowed for a long time and thus the emotional center for her children. His sisters see each other with their families and offer mutual support, but Daniele has cut himself off from the past, and he no longer considers them a reference point in his adult life, notwithstanding the fact that as a child he was cared for and loved by both of them. His sisters know nothing of his relationship problems and do not see him, much less his partner and their little girl, also because they live in different cities.

The arrival of the sisters to the session allows them to enter deeply into mourning for the loss of their mother, which Daniele has never discussed, since he never wanted to speak about the death of his mother, either with family or friends and colleagues. In fact, he even refused to attend the funeral and does not even know where his mother was laid to rest. After a long period of silence, Daniele finally manages to open up and speak of the "hole in his stomach" that he has felt for years, which he says is linked to the death of his mother. A mother who, it is disclosed, had a privileged relationship with him, as the only son and the youngest child. Daniele listens for some time to his sisters who, upon the therapist's invitation, speak of their mother's funeral, the emotion of everyone present, and the pain they and other family members felt because of his absence. With tears streaming, his sisters state that they lost not only their mother but also a brother who they always loved and cared for in every way when he was little. Emotion takes over and the three hug each other in a deep and liberating gesture. The session concludes with the suggestion that Daniele go together with his sisters to the place where their mother is buried, so as to repair a painful emotional fracture for all of them. Daniele's partner is present and participates in a discreet way in this magic moment of reconciliation, while being emotionally involved. In the sessions that follow, she states how much Daniele has changed after the meeting with his sisters: "He doesn't seem the same person anymore, now he speaks to me!"

20.6 The presence of children in the session

Children are the most precious thing and the strongest bond between two partners, especially when both wanted to have and raise children together. Although engaging members of the family of origin in a session can be a complicated task, causing strong reluctance in the couple, it is generally easier to request the presence of the children to help the therapist get to know the family better. However, parents might express some concern, fearing the children could get involved in their couple dynamics. They may therefore manifest a protective attitude toward the children, especially if they are still very young, and when asked to invite them, their answers sometimes are as follows: "They have nothing to do with our problems"; "We have always kept them out of our arguments"; "We have always behaved properly in front of the children and never got them involved."

Parents are even more reluctant to accept the therapist's request when they are in the process of separation and the children have somehow been involved in the couple's hostility and been forced to take one or the other's side. Guilt and embarrassment following judgmental children, especially teenagers, may prevail and be an obstacle to exposing themselves to more negative comments from the children and teens. For all of these reasons, it is important to establish the right timing and reach complete agreement between both partners, but, above all, to create an atmosphere of trust between the couple and the therapist. Once in the session, the mere presence of children changes the emotional climate entirely, and a context open to play and creativity is naturally created. We usually discover more positive relational qualities in each partner in a one-hour session with the children than in the course of several couple meetings. Men who are stiff-looking and rigid and are always on the alert during couple therapy turn into loving fathers lying on the floor and playing with their children. Sad and silent women regain their smile and lovingly caress their children.

We have always wondered, and sometimes verbalized it in couple therapy sessions, why parents try to give their very best to their children, even at times of severe psychological distress, reserving the "worst part" of themselves for the couple. Couples can play and feel much lighter with their children, while in their relationship with each other they amplify blame, criticism, and competition and lose the lightness and ability to discover and say positive things about each other. It is as if the responsibilities and struggles of adulthood overload the couple's space, splitting the partners from a We identity to a "You versus Me" identity, and the other partner is perceived more as an antagonist than a partner.

We have written about how important it is to move from a sole focus on protection to respect for children in many of our works (Andolfi, 2017; Andolfi & Mascellani, 2021; Andolfi et al., 2022). Respect is about listening to and appreciating the child's verbal and nonverbal language and communications. Children speak through words as much as through their body language (gestures, way of sitting, spontaneous expressive movements), the expression in their eyes, voice tone and pace, and their metaphors. Furthermore, perinatal research tells us that children develop a natural sense of care and protection for their own parents from the moment they are born. This caring attitude becomes much stronger in crisis situations, such as when their parents are in conflict or when a separation threat looms. All of this urges us to make the best use of children's endless resources during therapy. Sometimes we give the child a "magic wand" and ask him to wave it in the air and perform a "magic trick" to bring harmony back to the family. This is how we voice the hope for change and desire to end hostile or violent behavior between the parents/partners. Observing the children's capacity for imagination and their parents' emotional reactions when taking part in a creative game is truly amazing. With young children, we sometimes create a fairy tale that has a general script, beginning with these words, "Once upon a time, there was a happy family . . ." The parents and children then have to go on and describe what happened to make everyone sad or angry, and to find out at the very end that you can move in a different direction and allow everyone to go back to "living happily ever after." Through a fairy tale, parents break free of the burden of rigid and defensive positions and convey implicit messages of change to each other as a couple, to the children, and to the therapist.

In other cases, drawings can be used as a projective tool, asking children to draw the main figures in the family and the world surrounding them. The drawing will usually show how the children view family relationships. One child drew two small islands and a boat he used to go from one island to another to visit the "inhabitants of the two islands." Another child drew two small houses with a bridge to go from one to the other, thus voicing their concrete concern of parental separation but having a positive vision of a boat or a bridge "holding together" the two sides. By using their imagination, the different moods of each family member can be expressed. For example, anger may be expressed by drawing an erupting volcano or anxiety as a snake coiling around all the family members. Finally, we can ask the child's parents how much they see themselves reflected in the images created by their children. The drawing could be hung up in the kitchen so that everyone may reflect on how to avoid the volcanic eruption and how to keep the snake at arm's length.

The stance of teenagers who are invited to a special session with their parents is less playful and more challenging. However, behind dismissive or provocative attitudes typical of the age, again there is a genuine desire to help the family in distress, as well as the need to expose inauthentic and defensive behaviors of parents seeking new forms of relationship.

20.7 The presence of friends in the session

Friends represent the most important social network we all grow up in, creating lasting and important relationships from early childhood through late adulthood and old age. Friendships are chosen and renewed over time, although generally the most genuine and helpful friends are those with whom we have shared our experiences in the childhood, teen, and young adult stages of growth. We can share common experiences and parallel developmental processes with your friends, from early school age, to becoming a couple, to childbearing, midlife, and old age. Friends are an outstanding resource in the couple's relational life and growth, but it is striking to notice how little has been written in international literature about engaging friends in couple therapy.

Russell Haber was the first to stress the importance of friends in family therapy, in our edited book *Using Consultants in Family Therapy* (Andolfi & Haber, 1995). I was inspired by his ideas and clinical experience to introduce friends as special resources in couple therapy. The presence of friends in the therapy room facilitates a change in the quality and topics of the session, switching from the couple's private matters to their social bonds. Friends are special witnesses to each partner's development and can offer their life experiences and friendship as active resources in the continuation of couple therapy.

Those couples who have gone through immigration and painful departure from their countries of origin and from their families can invite friends living nearby who have experienced similar displacement issues. The counseling session can be extremely positive for the couple, who can retrace together with friends some of the steps of their departure from the same origins and adjustment to the new world, drawing strength and a sense of solidarity (Andolfi, 2004).

20.8 From the intergenerational dimension to the rediscovery of us in the couple

When couples in crisis come to therapy, their "we-ness" is greatly weakened, as if the partners were locked away in their own subjective description of reality, where all the negative things come from the other. "She doesn't listen to me, he prevaricates, she interrupts me, he doesn't see my suffering, she criticizes everything I do, he thinks I'm not worth anything" are just some of the many complaints coming from each partner during the session. These expressions seem to represent a cry of pain and express feelings of deep loneliness. At the same time, they appear to be a way to give up one's own personal agency.

In this respect, meeting with the family of origin, children, and friends can produce very positive results in regaining and strengthening each person's individuality, with indirect effects on the couple's relationship and ability to manage conflicts. One of the most important results is undoubtedly the greater solidarity within the couple who had approached therapy in a state of open conflict. It is as if personal risk-taking in the meeting with the family of origin or the presence of one's children had unexpectedly produced greater authenticity and a sense of mutual benevolence. This closeness is also often felt through affectionate gestures and looks of encouragement and mirroring of each other's stories.

A great deal of information about events in life or losses is not new to each partner and may even have been the subject of discussion, exchange, or even argument between the partners. What is new is the collaborative setting in which each partner's family narrative develops. Each partner, by remembering his/her own experiences of abandonment, grief, and suffering in a session that includes the "privileged witnesses and participants" of their development – meaning parents, siblings, uncles or aunts, or their own children, or friends – gains a greater understanding of "who I am" and of "who I am" in the couple relationship. This includes becoming more aware of the boundaries between himself/herself and others, especially the partner, and of his or her different roots, such that each partner has greater clarity about their respective sense of self, their "Me," their "Us" and "We" as a couple, and their respective intergenerational ties that largely formulated their "Me" and how they engage in being an "Us." The goal of intergenerational couple therapy is to focus on a broader system of relationships, of roots and resources, showing couples in crisis the right path to regaining respect, trust, and intimacy.

It is now a matter of embarking on a path for two and, with the help of the therapist, to rediscover one's authenticity and give up problematic "couple games" that make one feel bad but are much less challenging and, in a way, more emotionally comfortable and safe than having to answer essential questions about oneself such as, "Who am I? What do I want in life? Who do I really want to share my life with?" It is no coincidence that at this stage of therapy feelings of deep depression may prevail over previous aggressive behavior toward the other. Now is the time to come to terms with one's personal void and with that feeling of *self-deception*, which seems to have produced even more significant damage on each person's personality than the suffering experienced in an unhappy relationship (Andolfi & Mascellani, 2021; Andolfi et al., 2000). Self-betrayal is far more painful than the many deceptions/lies acted out by the other partner over the years. Becoming aware of these self-deceptions, as much as it may hurt, allows one to rediscover the value of respect, which is first subjective (an internal sensibility) and immediately after can turn into an explicit relational resource to be shared by the couple in their life. In practice, you cannot expect the other to respect you if you lack self-respect in the first place, nor does respect from the other greatly improve one's state of self-disrespect. Thanks to therapy, the two partners will go back to trusting each other and experiment with new, less predictable, and stereotypical roles and behaviors – a relationship now marked by play, creativity, and lightness. In other words, they will rediscover their childlike side that allows them to surprise each other and makes room for tenderness. If, as Schnarch (1997) reminds us, sexuality is the deepest form of dialogue in couple intimacy, its signs can be found in the looks, in the smile, in the physical closeness, and in the overall feeling of complicity and affection of the couple.

20.9 Conclusion: Essential ingredients of successful intergenerational couple therapy

This path toward a true renewal of couple relationship life is not always feasible for several reasons. Research on the effectiveness of intergenerational couple therapy (Andolfi et al., 2000) – and all subsequent clinical and methodological insights developed by the Clinical Service of the Family Therapy Academy in Rome – provide us with several relevant indicators for achieving satisfactory results in intergenerational couple therapy. We will be summarizing in the following sections the most important ones reported very clearly by couples who have discontinued or ended treatment.

20.9.1 Joint motivation

Achieving joint motivation seems to be a priority and is essential. It is rare for a couple to come to therapy with a clear agreement on the definition of the problem for which intervention is sought. Partners' therapy expectations and goals can also be contradictory. The most frequent way that couples initially come to treatment, in both heterosexual and same-sex couples, involves a "strong" partner taking the lead and a "weak" partner following or being drawn into therapy. Should both agree to seek couple therapy, their goals may be very different: One partner may want to "fix the marriage," while the other wants help to "separate with dignity" – what William Doherty and colleagues calls "mixed-agenda couples" (Doherty et al., 2015). Or perhaps one partner is coming to the session concerned about what might happen to the children after separation, or because their lawyer said they should come as a sign of good faith in a divorce process.

The therapist's task is to work with patience, empathy, and creativity towards a mediation that allows both partners' requests and issues of top concern to be accepted, addressed, and resolved (when they are not diametrically opposed, as in the case of mixed-agenda couples); or to transform the spouse who is reluctant to start therapy into an enthusiastic participant (as in the case of Laura and Luca); or to help mixed-agenda couples decide whether the relationship can be saved or should end.

20.9.2 Timing of the invitation to sessions of family of origin, children, or friends

Our research clearly shows that getting the timing of the extended family's invitation to the session wrong can be a serious mistake and can jeopardize the entire progress of therapy. Many disruptions in the therapeutic process were the consequence of having anticipated the right timing when a solid therapeutic alliance had not yet been built, and the two partners had not yet fully understood the meaning and purpose of this cry for help sent out to their family members. The work on the "symbolic family" (the families as described by each partner) allowed us to work first on family presences as if they were real and on metaphoric language, so as to prepare the groundwork for the next step.

20.9.3 Being in relational pain to avoid existential pain

The phrase "to suffer in order not to suffer," coined by Silvia Soccorsi many years ago (Soccorsi et al., 1987), perfectly describes the painful situations in which people prefer to stay idle, sometimes for years, rather than face the deeper pain that is at the origin of their discomfort. This often happens in couples who prefer to stay together amid quarrels and fights even for years in the hidden fear that separation corresponds to the total loss of their existential references. Suffering and touching the depths of emptiness and loneliness allows you to enter the deep dimension of one's own suffering and break the old entanglements of the couple and present oneself in a new way in the relationship (Roustang, 2004). A good therapist must be able to foster and attune to this condition of "being in pain" without rushing to help the couple out of it.

20.10 A final note: The healing value of the therapist's human experience and genuineness in therapy

This chapter describes the essence of multigenerational couple therapy, according to the Andolfi method. At the core of this approach is the emotional presence of the therapist, using his or her professional and personal life experiences to fully resonate and understand couples' challenges as well as their potential for change. If we ask our clients to break free from their self-deception and finally become authentic with themselves and their partners, we therapists must shed our professional uniform and be equally authentic so as to empathetically tune into areas of deep suffering that couples in distress have brought to therapy, and to help them rediscover the essence of love (Yalom, 2017; Minuchin, 2017; Andolfi, 2022).

References

Andolfi, M. (Ed.). (1999). *La coppia in crisi*. Raffaello Cortina Editore.
Andolfi, M. (Ed.). (2004). *Famiglie immigrate e psicoterapia transculturale*. Franco Angeli.
Andolfi, M. (2017). *Multigenerational family therapy-tools and resources for the therapist*. Routledge.
Andolfi, M. (2022). *The gift of truth*. Accademia Press.
Andolfi, M. (2024). The bottom-up approach in multigenerational family therapy: The child as the family guide. *Journal of Marital and Family Therapy*, *50*(4), 1026–1037. https://doi.org/10.1111/jmft.12730
Andolfi, M., Angelo, C., & D'Atena, P. (2000). *La terapia narrata dalla famiglia*. Raffaello Cortina.
Andolfi, M., & Haber, R. (Eds.). (1995). *Please help me with this family: Using consultants as resources in family therapy*. Routledge.
Andolfi, M., & Mascellani, A. (2021). *Intergenerational couple therapy*. Accademia Press.
Andolfi, M., Mascellani, A., & Salerno, A. (Eds.). (2022). *La magia del bambino in terapia familiare*. Accademia Press.
Bartholomey, K., & Horowitz, L. (1991). Attachment style among young adults. *Journal of Personality and Social Psychology*, *61*(2), 226–244. https://doi.org/10.1037//0022–3514.61.2.226
Baucom, D. H., & Epstein, N. D. (1990). *Cognitive-behavioral marital therapy*. Brunner/Mazel.
Boszormenyi-Nagy, I., & Spark, G. (1973). *Invisible loyalties*. Harper & Row.
Bowen, M. (1978). *Family therapy in clinical practice*. Jason Aronson.
Dattilio, F. M. (2010). *Cognitive-behavioral therapy with couples and families*. Guilford Press.
Doherty, W. J., Harris, S. M., & Wilde, J. L. (2015). Discernment counseling for "mixed-agenda" couples. *Journal of Marital and Family Therapy*, *42*, 246–255. https://doi.org/10.1111/jmft.12132
Fraenkel, P. (2017). Integration in couple and family therapy. In J. Lebow, A. Chambers, & D. Breunlin (Eds.), *Encyclopedia of couple and family therapy* (Vol. 3, pp. 1501–1506). Springer.
Fraenkel, P. (2022). Therapeutic palette integrative couple therapy. In J. L. Lebow & D. K. Snyder (Eds.), *Clinical handbook of couple therapy* (6th ed., pp. 339–361). Guilford Press.
Framo, J. (1992). *Family of origin therapy*. Brunner/Mazel.
Gottman, J. S., & Gottman, J. (2015). *Ten principles for doing effective couple therapy*. Norton.
Gurman, A., & Fraenkel, P. (2002). The history of couple therapy: A millennial review. *Family Process*, *41*, 199–260. https://doi.org/10.1111/j.1545–5300.2002.41204.x
Johnson, S. M. (2020). *The practice of emotionally focused couple therapy. Creating connections*. Brunner/Mazel.
Lebow, J. (1997). The integrative revolution in couple and family therapy. *Family Process*, *36*, 1–17. https://doi.org/10.1111/j.1545-5300.1997.00001.x

Lebow, J. L. (1987). Integrative family therapy: An overview of major issues. *Psychotherapy*, *40*, 584–594. https://doi.org/10.1037/h0085756
Minuchin, S. (2017). Saldavor Minuchin at 95 reflects on his life. *The Psychotherapy Networker*, *1*, 1–4.
Pinsof, W. M. (1995). *Integrated problem-centered therapy: A synthesis of family, individual, and biological therapies*. Basic Books.
Roustang, F. (2004). Che fare delle proprie sofferenze. *Terapia Famiiare*, *76*, 5–18.
Scheinkman, M. (2008). The multi-level approach: A roadmap for couples therapy. *Family Process*, *47*, 197–213. https://doi.org/10.1111/j.1545–5300.2008.00248.x
Schnarch, D. M. (1997). *Passionate marriage. Keeping love & intimacy alive in committed relationships*. Norton & Co.
Sharff, D. E., & Sharff, J. (2003). *Psychoanalitic couple therapy: Foundation of theory and practice*. Karnac Books.
Soccorsi, S., Lombardi, F., & Paglia, P. R. (1987). Capturing death: Families and children recovering from oncological diseases. *Family Systems Medicine*, *5*(1), 191–205. https://doi.org/10.1037/h0089710
Williamson, D. S. (1982). *The intimacy paradox*. Guilford Press.
Yalom, I. D. (2017). *Becoming myself: A psychiatrist's memoir*. Basic Books.

21

FAMILIES CREATED FROM THE HEART

Natividad Perez Alvarez and Carmen Calatayud Lliso

21.1 Introduction

Infertility is considered by the World Health Organization (WHO) to be a chronic disease of the male or female reproductive system and is defined as the inability to achieve pregnancy after 12 months or more of regular, unprotected sexual intercourse (WHO, 2023).

Most people plan to have their own biological children as part of their life project. Difficulty having them turns out to be one of the most stressful situations to face as a couple. This chapter provides information on the medical procedures involved in fertilization, the impact of fertility issues and treatment on the couple, and a wide range of psychological interventions to aid in handling these stressors and, hopefully, to attain the goal of pregnancy and childbirth.

In recent decades, the increasingly relevant role of women in in the workplace and other roles outside the home often means that they do not consider having children until they have achieved personal, social, economic, and work stability, which usually happens in their thirties. Unfortunately, this is the age at which their ability to fertilize decreases, and they experience greater difficulty achieving pregnancy. In fact, currently, 15% of couples of childbearing ages have fertility problems (WHO, 2023).

Women ask themselves, "Why don't I get pregnant, but my friends do?" Other questions accompanied by anxiety, regret, and guilt in partners include: "Has my lifestyle affected the quality of my semen? Have I missed my time? Do I have a genetic problem that could affect my offspring? Do I have an anatomical problem that prevents me from conceiving?" Women could come to think that because they had an abortion, this affects their ability to conceive.

The first step is to be aware that there is an issue and to put yourself in the hands of experts to diagnose and potentially treat the problem. However, diagnostic procedures and treatments frequently represent a source of stress for most couples (Aimagambetova et al., 2020), and stress itself can also negatively influence reproductive capacity, as occurs in the case of at least 5% of infertility problems of unknown origin.

21.2 Medical procedures of fertility treatment and their effects on patients

This section will focus on the medical procedures and psychological impact of these procedures in in vitro fertilization. Later in the chapter, we discuss procedures and associated psychological response and challenges in donor egg fertilization.

DOI: 10.4324/9781003536765-25

In the first phase of diagnosis, patients undergo medical visits, blood draws, semen analysis, genetic tests, ultrasounds, medications, decision-making, and scheduled sexual relations. All of these procedures create a feeling of loss of control over numerous aspects of couple partners' lives, including their bodies, their daily and weekly schedules (due to numerous medical appointments that disrupt their workdays), and their sexual relationship. Regarding the impact of fertility procedures on the couple's sexual relationship, they often result in decreased frequency of sexual relations and the loss of spontaneity that is replaced by scheduling sex during fertile periods (Starc et al., 2022; Wischmann et al., 2014; Piva et al., 2014). These stressors result in anxiety and a feeling of loss of control, which may translate into a variety of psychosomatic symptoms in both members of the couple (Ramiro-Cortijo et al., 2021; Zhang et al., 2022). Therefore, it is suggested that couples undergoing assisted reproduction (AR) techniques obtain psychological support before, during, and after treatment.

In the first phase of AR treatment, the woman must inject herself with medication every day to encourage the development of follicles containing the eggs (oocytes) in the ovaries. This lasts for about 11–12 days, which usually causes abdominal discomfort, swelling, and heaviness, and is often accompanied by anxiety and stress, since the woman administers the injections herself.

During this period, ultrasounds and blood draws are performed depending on the response to the medication, so the patient must go to the clinic on the day and time indicated, which can cause disruption to her daily life. Once the ovaries are ready to ovulate, she will have to inject herself with a final medication that will be responsible for the eggs to finish maturing and can be extracted to inseminate them with the sperm of her partner or donor. To do this, she must be very punctual with the injection since the extraction must be carried out in the operating room 36 hours later, and outside of this time window, it would not be possible to extract the eggs. It has been found that the anxiety levels of women at the time of oocyte retrieval and embryo transfer are like those of women undergoing serious gynecological surgical techniques (Lemmens et al., 2004).

The couple's concerns do not end here, since they are waiting for the news about how many oocytes have been recovered and how many are mature and suitable for insemination. If there are no mature oocytes, the process ends here for this cycle. On the day of ovarian puncture for follicular aspiration and oocyte retrieval, the man is asked to produce a semen sample to prepare it in the laboratory, where the sperm that will be used to inseminate the oocytes are selected. At this time, the man is under a lot of stress because it is now up to him to collect the semen sample, and sometimes, men become blocked and are not able to ejaculate to produce semen. If this happens, the oocytes must be frozen and the rest of the process canceled.

Assuming the requisite procedures have occurred, and the mature oocytes have been inseminated, they are placed in incubators with special conditions of temperature, oxygen, and humidity necessary for the correct development of the future embryos. The next day, the number of oocytes fertilized correctly is checked, as these will be the ones that will continue in cultivation for embryonic development. If there is no fertilization or the fertilization is abnormal, this is where the process ends for this cycle. This embryonic cultivation lasts for five days, during which there will be nonviable embryos. As a result, the patient sees their chances diminish without being able to do anything. This is because not all embryos will reach the blastocyst stage (last stage of embryo development), nor are all blastocysts destined to give rise to a live-born child.

After this fifth day, the embryo to be transferred to the woman's uterus is chosen and the rest of the suitable blastocysts will be frozen for later attempts, as long as these embryos have correctly reached the end of their in vitro development. However, it may be that the transfer is not carried out, not because there are no embryos available but because they need to be analyzed chromosomally/genetically before transferring them to the uterus to avoid a genetic or chromosomal disease. To do this, a group of cells from the trophectoderm of the blastocyst (outermost layer of cells of the blastocyst, which will later give rise to the placenta) is biopsied and analyzed to determine which are suitable or not for transfer in a future cycle. This result can take up to four weeks, during which time patients suffer uncertainty and anxiety.

On the day of the transfer, patients are simultaneously excited, nervous, and concerned that everything goes well. The woman undergoes further blood tests to monitor all hormonal parameters, and contact between staff and the patients is maintained with her partner until two weeks later, when the pregnancy test will be performed.

During those 15 days after the embryo transfer, the patients may feel stomach discomfort, breast swelling, slight blood losses, or simply feel nothing. Each of these symptoms, whether by their presence or total absence of changes, causes them anguish and fear.

On the day of the pregnancy test, with nerves on edge, the couple awaits the result. If it is positive: joy, laughter, hugs, although also caution and fear in case it does not go well. If negative: sadness, tears, frustration, anger – and the weight of deciding whether to continue, starting again, or give up. The entire treatment team must create a positive and supportive environment for the patients, and we must prepare ourselves with tools to deal with failure in the best possible way (Gameiro et al., 2015).

Sometimes, deciding to abandon treatment is more difficult than continuing it, and patients must be aware of the limits of their treatment. It is the responsibility of the therapeutic team to provide them with comprehensive advice on the different future options and new treatment perspectives after having reviewed and assessed the case holistically. In all cases, the work of the psychologist is essential to help patients manage this deficiency disease of infertility, in the best possible way.

21.3 Psychological interventions in assisted reproduction

Psychological help for patients who receive AR techniques is a fundamental part of the treatment, since for them it represents a life crisis that deeply affects their life project – a crisis that shares a category with severe depression due to a major illness or the loss of a loved one. This kind of help is necessary even when they have achieved their dream of becoming parents, because they face new challenges, such as wanting to share with their children how they were conceived, which can cause anxiety, since the subject is difficult to address. Tools such as the children's story, "Families Created from the Heart" (Pérez Álvarez, 2020), are a great way of explaining AR to little ones, facilitating communication between the child and the parents and other key adults in their support network. As Cyrulnik (2002) wrote, "making a child be born is not enough, it must be brought into the world" (p. 50). This statement highlights the importance of not limiting attention only to the biological process of conception and birth, but also extending it to the psychological dimension during upbringing and in the child's relationship with the parents.

Despite the incessant increase in the need for this service, AR remains largely unspoken, as many users experience it as a stigma and/or punishment for not being able to have children naturally and needing medical assistance, leading them to hide their reality, with the consequent pain and suffering. Louise Brown (born 1978), the first baby born after in vitro fertilization, on her 41st birthday said: "It is sad that In Vitro Fertilization remains a taboo subject" (Sánchez, 2020). Unfortunately, even today, the fear of being stigmatized still outweighs the real benefits that an infertile couple can achieve by openly sharing this fact. Even if they encounter someone they know at the clinic, they do not want them to know they are seeking fertility treatments, and the medical team takes care of protecting and preserving their privacy, just as the patients wish.

The duration of fertility treatment can deteriorate the emotional well-being of the woman and the couple, since the process itself can become very stressful, bringing them close to the limits of their coping ability, which has a great impact on the quality of life and relationship. Therefore, if the couple's relationship is not solid, the stress of undergoing fertility treatment can lead them to abandon the process and, sometimes, to break up the relationship. On the other hand, if the couple is solid, these challenges can make them unite even more. For this reason, psychological interventions to strengthen couples' coping ability are helpful.

For several years now, family diversity has become normalized, and access to AR treatments has allowed fulfilling the desire of motherhood that previously seemed unattainable. For example, lesbian motherhood was until recently an oxymoron, and now it is a reality.

These family structures are not homogeneous, but they share key characteristics, such as high motivation and involvement, along with the potential for overprotection due to the strong desire for children. Nonetheless, there is evidence of adjustment in terms of normality parameters, similar emotional bonds, social integration, and psychosexual development (Arranz Freijó & Oliva Delgado, 2010). For children born to homosexual couples, their well-being is greatly influenced by the quality of the relationship with the parents, the adequacy and security of the parents in terms of their ability to provide a stable and nurturing environment, and the satisfaction and stability of the parents' relationship, as well as their social relationships (Siegel & Perrin, 2013).

Although heterosexual couples predominate, some of them are blended families; an increasing number of single women and lesbian couples are turning to AR to achieve pregnancy. However, gay couples or single men cannot benefit from it in some countries including Spain, since surrogacy is not permitted.

21.4 Typical activities and therapy approaches of mental health professionals in fertility treatment

My (NPA) duties as a clinical psychologist at the CREA Valencia Assisted Reproduction Medical Center include:

- Individual, couple, family psychotherapy, and social support networking;
- Support groups for patients who have had embryo transfer or insemination (partner or donor) after finishing treatment and are waiting for the result of the beta test (a test, either blood or urine, that measures the levels of the hormone HCG to confirm pregnancy) when it's known whether there is a viable pregnancy or not;
- Telephone care and follow-ups in the interval between embryo transfer until the result is known, as well as support on the day of receiving the news, especially if it's a negative result;
- Intervention in situations of crisis and grief, for repeated miscarriages, gestational loss, and if they cannot have children at all;
- Conducting psychological evaluations to select gamete donors;
- Staff training, including training in psychophysical self-regulation techniques, communication-assertiveness techniques, and patient care for the CREA multidisciplinary team.

We attempt to involve both partners in the couple, but the reality is that women often come to the clinic alone. This occurs for a variety of reasons: medical appointments being incompatible with the partner's work schedules, not being able or not wanting to ask for time off from work for this purpose, women believing that it is more their responsibility, either because it is their body that is going to carry the pregnancy or because their partner is not involved and is not viewing it as their responsibility to help the woman with her disappointment if the procedures are unsuccessful. If the man comes (and it is always recommended that they come together for couples therapy), it is often with a resistant attitude and/or rejection of attending a psychological session or appointment. However, once involved, men typically express satisfaction with the process and their role, and both partners realize the importance of being together to better learn to cope with this path. He gets excited and responsive because, although he felt the obligation and responsibility to support his partner, he didn't know how to do it himself, leading him to suppress his emotions and withdraw from his female partner, leading her to feel misunderstood and alone in the complicated situation, and in this circular manner, resulting in conflict.

Clinical interventions are conducted in individual, couple, and family therapies and in post-transfer group support sessions. At CREA we advocate an integrative, multi-theoretical approach, and utilize systemic relational psychotherapy, Andolfi's multigenerational couple therapy (2017), the psychobiological couple approach model (PACT) by Stan Tatkin (2012, 2016), and polyvagal theory by Stephen Porges (2018).

Some patients are resistant to having sessions with the psychologist, protecting themselves from addressing their frustration and pain, with medical help being their only objective. Therefore, we need to understand their reluctance to address psychological/relational issues and gradually introduce the idea of receiving emotional help to complement the medical treatment, fostering "strength in unity" among the couple, the medical team, and the psychologist.

Our objective is to initiate a reorganization of relationships that is more functional, and to achieve this goal, to learn their history and beliefs related to their fertility journey, including their views on pregnancy and AR, and to improve communication skills. We wish to help them manage the emotional roller coaster that is endemic to the AR fertilization process – the feelings of disappointment, sadness, anger, hope, as well as excitement and joy. We give them guidance and tools that provide greater emotional and relationship security, and especially, guidance for the male partner to support the female partner. As was noted earlier, there is usually a decrease in desire, or in some cases sexual dysfunction, since sex stops being associated with pleasure due to instrumentalization of the body with the objective of procreation. Therefore, a frequent therapeutic focus is exploring the couple's sexual intimacy and trying to reactivate and revitalize it.

All of these therapeutic foci create a joint narrative of positive coping (Andolfi, 2017). Additionally, we explore the ways in which each partner's families of origin can provide support. We accomplish this by constructing the family genogram of three generations (Andolfi, 2017). The genogram pictorializes who is on their side, whom they can trust, the types of family and social interactions they experience, and to help them create boundaries. In some instances, it is possible to have the families come to sessions, but in others the empty chair technique is used. Through this therapeutic process, the couple is forced to face their families' emotions and expectations, and the different meanings attributed to the couple's fertility struggles and treatment (Andolfi, 2017). In some cases, the couple chooses to isolate themselves from family and friends for emotional protection, which can create relief but also loneliness and incomprehension. The chance of better emotional adjustment to fertility issues is greater if there is family and social support.

In addition to working on traditional foci of emotional adjustment, communication skills, and family support, we address couple partners' ability to self-regulate and co-regulate negative arousal on a more physiological level. According to Porges' polyvagal theory (2018), processing information leads to a variety of physiologically mediated arousal and emotional states. We want to help patients learn how the autonomic nervous system (ANS) works and teach them how to move from a stress response to an emotional state of well-being, to better connection with oneself and others in a manner that allows for bonding, and to improved mood.

In brief, the ANS collects information from neuroception (detection without awareness) of safety, danger, and threat to life. We show them Siegel's window of tolerance (2009), which clearly describes how the sympathetic "fight or flight" state of high and sustained nervous system activation wears them down, leading them to the dorsovagal parasympathetic or "freeze" state of arousal, associated with emotional blockage and interpersonal disconnection and isolation. Moving out from this fear response to a state of emotional well-being is more challenging than from sympathetic arousal, and so we teach patients how to recognize signs of the onset of "freeze" to help them prevent it from further taking over the body and mind, and how to quickly move out of this "freeze" state.

For example, when receiving bad news, the impact can lead to this dorsovagal state, associated with rigid posture and facial expression, and restricted, flattened emotions. The body becomes cold and pale; the person exhibits a blank stare, looking as if in a still photo; and there is no receptivity or connection with the other, due to a block than prevents the information from being received. They cannot readily process further information, as they are in a "shutdown," overwhelmed state of arousal. Dorsovagal parasympathetic activation is often compared to a threatened animal who "plays dead" in order to avoid fatal attack from a predator. Therapeutically speaking, if they are in a medical appointment, the healthcare professional can detect the signs of distress and help them by not offering more upsetting information, softening their own expression and tone of voice to become soothing and to decrease the patient's sense of threat and fear. If it is a couple's appointment, the doctor can encourage partners to engage in soothing physical contact and mindful breathing, all to help them move into a parasympathetic ventrovagal, calm state of safety and well-being. The healthcare professional also encourages healthy, calming, pleasurable activities such as walking, relaxation, singing, dancing, doing crafts, all to maintain a state of parasympathetic ventrovagal activation, which also helps the couple to enhance a positive, supportive connection and open expression of feelings.

According to Stan Tatkin's PACT model (2012, 2016), I work with the evolutionary patterns of growth and maturation, and the regulation of arousal, which involves two nervous systems and two different psychologies, those of the couple's members. Several types of emotional regulation are essential for understanding how individuals and couples manage their emotional states. Self-regulation refers to a person's ability to regulate their emotions autonomously, without being with another person, while regulation of self occurs during an interaction in critical situations, involving skills such as frustration tolerance and self-control. External regulation involves the professional modeling strategies that the patient will learn and use in interactive regulation, which occurs when couples balance arousal in real time, usually nonverbally and with true mutuality, supporting each other in emotional regulation. Finally, dysregulation occurs when a person is outside their window of tolerance (Siegel, 2009) or social interaction window (Porges, 2001), either through overstimulation (hyperactivation) or understimulation (hypoactivation). Bowlby's attachment theory (1998) explains how early attachment experiences impact emotional regulation throughout life, identifying secure, ambivalent, and disorganized attachment styles.

The objectives in drawing from all these therapeutic theories and practices is to provide patients with psychological knowledge and understanding; to create a state of security for them; to provide therapeutic spaces to express and share their fears, difficulties, anguish, and guilt; and to identify problematic patterns and dynamics in the relationship and avoid the repetition of dysfunctional interactional patterns. Therapy fosters effective communication and an overall enhanced, positive relationship that allows the couple to meet the challenges and uncertainties of fertility treatment with love, curiosity, and courage, so that they can best make vital decisions that will affect them for the rest of their lives. Although the starting point of therapy is around attempts to have a child, along the way they engage in important personal and relational growth.

21.5 The process of engagement: Steps in offering psychological treatment

One of the first contacts we have with patients is when we call to invite them to the post-transfer group support, and if they cannot attend, we speak to them over the phone. If we have had previous contact, their voice usually has a cheerful tone, since they are familiar with the therapist's voice. They are grateful for our interest in knowing how they are doing, since if they do not have a medical emergency, they go from having daily contact with the clinic to 15 days of silence and endless waiting until the day they receive their results. Other women initiate contact with our psychological services only after they have had a negative result. These women need help to face the next treatment, because emotionally they feel discouraged and very negative.

With all women, the basic work of the therapist is to listen to them describe their difficulties and their sense of not knowing what to do to overcome their hard moments. This empathic attention helps them feel that they are not alone and gives them strength and encouragement to continue. More specifically, many women describe fertility treatment as quite difficult, and sometimes they express a feeling of not understanding why these challenges are happening to them, feeling that "I don't deserve this hardship." Those women who are used to being in a high degree of control of their lives suffer from having to delegate control to the medical team. We validate and normalize their sense of uncertainty, concern, and anxiety, since they are anxious and eager to obtain a positive result that will end their emotional suffering. We encourage them to express their doubts and fears, and we reflect their feelings back to them in a manner that is organized and reassuring.

It is very helpful to frame the situation in terms of illusion and reality: illusion as the driving force, the thing that gets them moving towards their goal, and it is essential to balance it with reality. Our nature is very complex, and both "yes" and "no" are part of the process. By accepting this, we stop fighting against it. It is there whether you like it or not, and while there is respect, there is no fear. This acceptance allows for greater resilience against the consequences of stress and enhances the ability to focus on the positive. It enables the creation of a shared project, a reality that many people cannot access or have to abandon due to economic difficulties or medical limitations. We focus them on the present, since everything else (including the arrival of the baby) belongs to the future that is to come, and to help them not to exclude from their lives everything that is not focused on this goal.

Although therapeutic interventions are targeted at addressing emotional, psychological, and behavioral issues, they may also influence a woman's ability to get pregnant. The functions that our body performs, including those associated with reproduction, require energy. Psychotherapeutic interventions may help release and redirect energy from psychological symptoms to bodily systems involved in successful fertilization.

Along with the other techniques mentioned, we also do a relaxation intervention with guided visualization, which helps reduce stress associated with the fertilization process. These relaxation and visualization exercises are intended to help women change their attitudes and increase their morale and self-confidence. One visualization exercise leads women to verbalize, "When I visualize myself with my baby, I feel good things." This exercise can help address concerns about accepting a baby conceived through donor eggs, by neutralizing the belief that they won't be able to accept or bond with a child conceived through donation.

With women who have had a negative result, we give them space to express their pain. While they recover before the next treatment, we encourage them to take advantage of that time to reconnect with pleasurable emotions by enjoying recreational activities, exercise, yoga, and sports. This can help them recover their physical condition, especially since the hormones of the treatment usually cause fluid retention and weight gain. Focusing on taking care of what they have – their work, health, partner, and children if they already have them – and allowing themselves to recover their life outside of treatment, can help restore their self-confidence and spirit for the next attempt, so that they do not face it pessimistically. We want to bolster women's healthiest psychological self so that they do not isolate themselves from their partner, family, friends, and other supports. It is easy for women who've received a negative result to magnify the fear that the negative result will be repeated, and therefore, rejecting the possibility of getting excited to protect themselves from great disappointment. The goal of therapeutic interventions is to help the women bounce back resiliently from a negative result and to attain their best possible physical and emotional condition, with their batteries recharged for trying again.

Another unfortunate occurrence for women in reproductive assistance is a pregnancy loss, sometimes occurring at an advanced stage. Although loss of a pregnancy can occur both in natural and assisted reproduction, when the pregnancy comes about through assisted reproduction it often takes on even greater emotional magnitude, plunging the person into a state of devastation, since the loss of the child itself is combined with the wear and tear of treatment that has been involved in achieving that much-desired pregnancy. In these cases, feelings of guilt, wondering if they could have done something different to avoid it (although in most cases it is beyond their control), and anxiety and fear about trying again are all possible. The loss of self-esteem and great worry about being incapable of gestating and carrying a pregnancy may dominate the bereft woman's thoughts and feelings. She may also isolate herself if she feels that her pain and loss are not understood – for instance, by a partner who tries to help her by discounting the seriousness and emotional gravity of the loss. A split in how each partner views the lost pregnancy can create conflict and disconnection. In such instances, we advise the couple to perform a ritual that includes saying goodbye to their baby.

21.5.1 Case illustration: Maria and Jose

Maria, a 42-year-old woman, and Jose, a 46-year-old man, are a middle-class working couple of Caucasian descent. After receiving a diagnosis of idiopathic factor (infertility due to unknown causes) and two years of unsuccessful treatments, the couple was at the limit of their emotional and economic resources. She presented as extremely nervous, and the husband was absent from medical appointments and largely uninvolved in their relationship, as he was constantly traveling for work reasons. The doctor repeatedly encouraged her to have a session with me (NPA), but she always put up objections: For instance, because of her time constraints (both of them work), because "I am like this and I am not going to change," because therapy could not possibly remove her emotional suffering, and because her husband would not attend. Finally, I scheduled the session on a Saturday (not being my usual workday) to demonstrate my sincere concern and interest in helping them. The couple had decided that this would be their last AR treatment, so I suggested that they had nothing to lose and everything to gain, and that I might be able to help them identify aspects of their emotional life and relationship that could improve.

In the session, she was in a state of excessive sympathetic nervous system activation, showing clear signs of physical and emotional exhaustion, constant agitation, and shallow breathing. Her husband adopted a fixed, rigid posture, shifting his body away from her, not making eye contact. She, on the other hand, leaned towards him, asking him to nod in agreement with her comments, but he remained absorbed, disconnected from what was happening, almost dissociated. She verbalized that she was happy that something had brought them back together in the same room, given their usual disconnection, but he did not respond.

My first intervention was to help her calm down, in order to enable her to be receptive to further assistance. Despite her initial resistance, I continued to modulate my voice, making it deeper, and matched my breathing to hers. I then modeled abdominal breathing for her, gradually guiding her to shift her own breath to the abdominal area, which would help regulate it more effectively. Her husband did not spontaneously get involved, so I asked him to collaborate by putting his hand on her lower abdomen. Spontaneously, she put hers on top of his, giving herself the opportunity to surrender and close her eyes, progressively lowering her breathing to the abdomen. Although skeptical, the husband got involved. Gradually, he seemed to shift from skepticism to pleasure, as he learned how they could regulate each other's arousal through their coordinated breathing.

I then introduced the technique of the genogram, which I used to clarify how disengaged they were and where she gained any sort of support. The genogram showed how, in his absence, she turned to her support figures. This led to a dialogue between them about deep feelings of mutual abandonment.

She asked for a reorganization of their work schedules, as their long working hours were preventing them from spending quality time together, which directly influenced the sense of abandonment. They engaged in a productive, well-regulated conversation about how they could each do their part to welcome their longed-for baby. By the end of the session, there was significant change in both partners. Her voice was calm and her timbre more natural, and he was finally attentive to his wife, with a look of affection and interest in how she felt. Their shared reward was reconnecting as a couple, achieving the pregnancy, and welcoming their baby.

21.6 The emotional challenges of pregnancy through donor egg

Genetic grief is one of the most emotionally painful circumstances, when the woman or man must accept that their genetic material (eggs, sperm) is not of sufficient quality to give life. If the insufficiency is with her eggs, the woman often feels guilty for not having started earlier, as aging leads to a decrease in oocyte quality. Although reproductive medicine now provides the opportunity to have a child through gamete donation, some patients are reluctant to engage in this process. Some do not choose it for moral reasons, and they stop their AR process at that point. However, most patients faced with this situation decide to engage in the process of using donor eggs or sperm, depending on their specific fertility challenges. While the use of donor eggs is more common in cases of diminished ovarian reserve or poor egg quality, donor sperm may also be an option when male factor infertility is present. These options are often pursued by those who do not consider adoption a suitable alternative for their family-building goals. Thoughtful decision-making is essential when choosing to pursue fertility treatments. Single women and female homosexual couples often engage in this reflective process beforehand, which allows them to approach the fertility journey with greater enjoyment and emotional readiness.

If a woman or couple indicates interest in possibly pursing donor egg or donor sperm fertilization, they are offered a session with the psychologist (me/NPA in our clinic), to explain to them that they need to adjust their hopes and expectations about how they can possibly become pregnant. The therapist helps the couple say goodbye to and mourn about that hoped-for biological child. The therapist does not minimize the impact of moving to donation, but instead normalizes their feelings about it, and helps the couple see it as a means to an end, even if not the originally desired approach to having a baby in which the genetic material is fully their own. Distressed couples in this situation usually move to a place of improved connection with one another, as well as shared gratitude towards the donor, which allows them to have a sense of peace and do the process well. Although they initially attach great importance to not being able to use their own gametes, they gain comfort knowing that the woman's uterus is the nest where their embryo will grow.

If the couple decides to continue with the egg donor procedure, they typically get excited about the next stages. The clinic selects the most compatible donor by genotype and phenotype, looking for a donor who most resembles the recipient. Donors are young and healthy people, who in order to carry out the act of donation (which is anonymous by law), have to undergo medical, genetic, and psychological tests, and may or may not be found suitable. A structured interview and one of these clinical questionnaires are carried out: Clinical Analysis Questionnaire (CAQ; Krug, 1986), Millon Multiaxial Clinical Inventory (MCMI; Millon, 2011), FertiQol International Infertility Quality of Life Questionnaire, and the DERA Emotional Maladjustment/Adaptive Resources Questionnaire in Infertility. These tools help assess the patient's emotional state, psychological resources, and overall quality of life, as well as to rule out any underlying psychopathologies in potential donors that could interfere with the fertility process, ensuring the selection of suitable candidates for the donation.

In terms of the reasons why women choose to donate, most of them are motivated by altruism, often stemming from knowing someone who has had difficulty having children. Some are also blood and organ donors, so they are already inclined towards providing medical/biological assistance. They receive a monetary reward for the inconvenience that donation causes. Donating eggs requires going to the clinic for almost 15 days to be given hormonal medication, moderating their physical activity, going through an operating room procedure with sedation and through an ovarian puncture, extracting the eggs, and recovering for at least two days. This is exactly the same process that a woman goes through who needs to have her own eggs extracted.

21.6.1 Case illustration: Isabella

Isabella, a 35-year-old Caucasian and middle-class working woman, performed the process alone. When she underwent the medical examination, it was detected that her eggs could not gestate, so she resorted to double donation (egg and sperm donation). She had a beautiful baby girl, and two years later, she wanted to repeat the experience, asking for the same female donor, not knowing if that would be possible. The clinic called the donor, explaining the case to her, but the donor said that at that time, a family situation made it impossible for her to donate. However, she said that if the recipient could wait a few months, she would agree to donate again. She did so, and Isabella had a second beautiful daughter. She came to talk to me after giving birth, saying that she wished to express her gratitude to the donor. Due to anonymity, I came up with the idea of recording her voice to convey her exact words, and what she said to the donor was this:

> I have been offered the opportunity to say thank you, and I want to thank you personally, first of all because I have been able to become a mother thanks to your generous act of donation. At first you just donated, and I received. In this second time I asked for you to please be the donor again, and you accepted, and I achieved it, and it was a generous act, which for me, apart from offering me to create my own family, says a lot to me about you as a person. I can only tell you that I am immensely grateful, and that I wish the world were made of wonderful people like you! Thank you very much.

She was grateful to do so, and expressing her gratitude brought her peace. Through informed consent, she authorized the clinic to share her story with other patients who may need it, as well as with professionals. Her hope was that her voice, shared in the first person, could help others understand how such a painful situation can be transformed into something so precious. If wanting to have a child is an act of love, then having one through AR and gamete donation is a double act of love.

21.6.2 Case illustration: Ana and Juan

A concern that parents who had a child through donor egg usually have is whether they should inform their children of their biological origin. Ana, 46 years old, requested an individual session as she has a two-month-old baby with Juan, 48 years old. They are a middle-class working couple of Caucasian descent. They live abroad and have been together for four years. He has two teenage children from a previous relationship, while she has no children from previous relationships.

At the beginning of their relationship, Ana expressed her desire to have a child with Juan, a wish he shared, but after a year, he told her that he didn't want to have children because his father had bipolar disorder, a condition he also developed after having his children, which made him feel guilty about the risk of passing it on. Juan had not shared this information with Ana before. Ana became very concerned, fearing that their future child could inherit the illness. It was then that they were informed about the option of double donation (egg and sperm donation), which took them some time to decide on. Now, with their 2-month-old baby, Ana observes how her partner has connected deeply with the baby and doesn't understand why he initially refused to have one. In the session, she was able to release her major concern, which allowed her to bond more closely with the baby.

The reason for her individual psychological consultation was that she feels that the donors are the true parents of her baby. She is also worried about harming the baby when she has to reveal the baby's origin in the future because, although she wants to tell him, she fears he may feel that he has been deceived. She is concerned that he will experience a sense of loss for having had the "natural and legitimate right to know his true parents" taken away from him.

However, during the session, she experienced genuine gratitude towards the donors and accepted that they had the legal right to remain anonymous. This allowed her to integrate them as a key component in the construction of her family values, freeing her from the burden of deceiving the baby. A single online session was held, during which she held the baby in her arms, lovingly checking to ensure he was still asleep and well. Whenever she did this, I lowered the volume of my voice or muted myself, and when she returned to connect with me, she would do so with a smile and show me the baby with pleasure.

During the creation of her genogram, she acknowledged that she lived abroad partly to distance herself from her mother, with whom she had not had a good relationship or emotional bond. Her mother would constantly lie to her and prioritize her own interests over Ana's (she is an only child). Her alcoholic father passed away in an accident many years ago. When delving further into her relationship with her mother, she said, "I'm tired of not being able to get rid of her," and "I've done therapy before, and she always comes up, even when I didn't want her to." She only sees her mother's protagonism, with her continually placing her own needs above Ana's.

To protect herself, Ana has decided to distance herself from her mother and does not want to talk to her. I pointed out that humans tend to repeat the patterns of our ancestors and that, in order to heal that relationship and live authentically, it is necessary to work on it and not run away (Andolfi, 2017). Revealing her son's origin would be an act of maturation and differentiation from her mother and a way to authorize herself to make her own decisions. She understood that this was the ideal course, without hostile ruptures, transforming that relational pattern, and allowing herself to do what she truly wants without anger. That is, establishing healthy boundaries with their families of origin so that their opinions do not interfere with the couple's decisions.

There is still work to be done, which she will address when she feels strong enough to confront it. In a subsequent contact, she commented on the serenity she felt after the session, experiencing deep peace from having been able to feel gratitude and raise her son without the ambivalence that had previously tormented her.

A large number of recipients are concerned because, by considering the genetic contribution of the donor, they tend to attribute an emotional bond that does not truly exist and assign the category of "real parent" to the donor. This raises many questions and leads to the projection that the child might reject them. Will my son/daughter accept me as their mother/father if they know that I am not completely that? For this reason, it is essential to recognize the donor's contribution, symbolizing the connection between two generations in that ritual, even if it is not a personal connection. This recognition allows for peace and the experience of parenthood, while also transmitting to the child respect for the donor, understanding the contribution of family diversity. If this issue is not addressed, the recipients remain trapped in a disturbing cycle, justifying that the desire to protect the child is the reason for keeping the donation a secret, and fearing that revealing it could damage the relationship, claiming that the best approach is to prevent the child from accidentally finding out.

The feeling of parenthood is essential for fully embracing the responsibilities of raising a child: comforting and supporting them during difficult moments, caring for their health, reading them bedtime stories, and accompanying them through every vital stage where the relationship and emotional bond are shaped.

Patients requiring gamete donation often struggle to accept this reality, with some exceptions, such as individuals who have overcome cancer. In these cases, the damage to their gametes caused by chemotherapy or radiotherapy, followed by recovery, turns genetic donation into an invaluable gift, enabling them to fulfill their dream of parenthood after facing the possibility of death.

During pregnancy, factors such as nutrition, physical activity, lifestyle, and other environmental elements influence the activation or deactivation of genes in the fetus – a phenomenon known as *epigenetics*. This genetic exchange helps the mother bond with her baby, even in cases involving gamete donation. Although certain behavioral traits have genetic foundations, the environment and relationships are crucial in transmitting values such as kindness, generosity, altruism, and of course language. These environmental and relational factors form the core of the parent-child bond and shared experience.

It is recommended that parents who have successfully undergone the egg donation procedure reveal their child's origin. This helps avoid the creation of family secrets that lead to hyper-inclusivity with those who share the situation and the exclusion of those who do not, causing suffering and emotional distance between generations, among siblings, and within the couple (Andolfi, 2017). The best time to make this revelation is between 3 and 8 years old, depending on the child's maturity. It is advisable to avoid waiting until adolescence, as it is the most critical developmental stage, and any sensitive information will be poorly received, rejected, and will generate dramatic thoughts. This may lead the teenager to wonder if it is because they are not loved enough, causing harm by accidentally and belatedly discovering their origin (Turner & Coyle, 2000).

On the other hand, young children love to be told stories and anecdotes, and to see photos and details about themselves, as they have no memories. The parents and other support figures can pass on those moments to them. This makes them feel that they were very present for them, providing a context of security and affection, which strengthens the bond. Knowing from a young age that they come from a donation as the only way to be conceived allows them to integrate this reality naturally. It becomes part of their identity, along with the understanding that they have resilient parents who achieved their desire to have them. That is their best legacy: unconditional love and staying strong during the journey to find them. "You emerged in the most beautiful place in my heart" (Pérez Álvarez, 2020).

21.7 Conclusion

This chapter highlights the importance of addressing the emotional and psychological aspects of AR, particularly when using donor gametes. Beyond the medical process, emotional support is essential to help patients cope with their fears, doubts, and feelings of loss. The psychological work aims to foster resilience and promote openness, helping parents integrate the donation into their family narrative naturally and without secrecy. Recognizing the donor's role with gratitude and respect allows parents to embrace their parental identity fully, building stronger emotional bonds with their child. Ultimately, transparency about the child's origins, combined with the unconditional love and commitment of resilient parents, contributes to a secure, trusting, and emotionally healthy family environment.

References

Aimagambetova, G., Issanov, A., Terzic, S., Bapayeva, G., Ukybassova, T., Baikoshkarova, S., Aldiyarova, A., Shauyen, F., & Terzic, M. (2020). The effect of psychological distress on IVF outcomes: Reality or speculations? *PLoS One*, *15*(12), e0242024. https://doi.org/10.1371/journal.pone.0242024

Andolfi, M. (2017). *Multi-generational Family Therapy. Tools and resources for the therapist*. Routledge.

Arranz Freijó, E., & Oliva Delgado, A. (2010). *Desarrollo psicológico en la nuevas estructuras familiares*. Ediciones Pirámide.

Bowlby, J. (1998). *El apego y la pérdida*. Ediciones Paidós (Original work published, Attachment and loss, 1982).
Cyrulnik, B. (2002). *Los patitos feos. La resiliencia: una infancia infeliz no determina la vida*. Gedisa.
Gameiro, S., Boivin, J., Dancet, E., de Klerk, C., Emery, M., Lewis-Jones, C., Thorn, P., Van de Broeck, U., Venetis, C., Verhaaaak, C. M., Wishmann, T., & Vermeulen, N. (2015). ESHRE guideline: Routine psychosocial care in infertility and medically assisted reproduction – a guide for infertility staff. *Human Reproduction*, *30*(11), 2476–2485. https://doi.org/10.1093/humrep/dev177
Krug, S. E. (1986). *CAQ: Cuestionario de análisis clínico*. Hogrefe TEA Ediciones.
Lemmens, G. M., Vervaeke, M., Enzlin, P., Bakelants, E., Vanderschueren, D., D'Hooghe, T., & Demyttenaere, K. (2004). Coping with infertility: A body-mind group intervention programme for infertile couples. *Human Reproduction*, *19*(8), 1917–1923. https://doi.org/10.1093/humrep/deh323
Millon, T. (2011). *Inventario Clínico Multiaxial de Millon-III (MCMI-III)*. Pearson Clinical.
Organización Mundial de la Salud (OMS). (s. f.). *Infertilidad*. https://bit.ly/3RtXHoQ
Pérez Álvarez, N. (2020). *Familias creadas desde el corazón. Cuento para entender a niños y niñas concebidos mediante tratamientos de fertilidad*. Editorial Sentir.
Piva, I., Lo Monte, G., Graziano, A., & Marci, R. (2014). A literature review on the relationship between infertility and sexual dysfunction: Does fun end with baby making? *The European Journal of Contraception & Reproductive Health Care*, *19*(4), 231–237. https://doi.org/10.3109/13625187.2014.919379
Porges, S. (2018). *La Teoría Polivagal: El poder transformador de sentirse seguro*. Editorial Eleftheria.
Porges, S. W. (2001). The polyvagal theory: Phylogenetic substrates of a social nervous system. *International Journal of Psychophysiology*, *42*(2), 123–146. https://doi.org/10.1016/S0167-8760(01)00162-3
Ramiro-Cortijo, D., Soto-Balbuena, C., & Rodríguez-Muñoz, M. F. (2021). Early association factor for depression symptoms in pregnancy: A comparison between Spanish women spontaneously gestation and with assisted reproduction techniques. *Journal of Clinical Medicine*, *10*(23), 5672. https://doi.org/10.3390/jcm10235672
Sánchez, N. (2020, March 7). *Louise Brown, la primera bebé probeta: "Es triste que la fecundación in vitro siga siendo un tema tabú."* El País. https://bit.ly/48lmiCM
Siegel, B., & Perrin, E. (2013). Promoting the well-being of children whose parents are gay or lesbian. *Pediatrics*, *4*, 703711. https://doi.org/10.1542/peds.2013-0377
Siegel, D. J. (2009). *Mindsight: The new science of personal transformation*. Scribe Publications.
Starc, A., Aljija, S., Jukić, T., Dahmane Gošnak, R., Rotim, A., & Pavan Jukić, D. (2022). Sexual function and in vitro fertilization. *Acta clinica Croatica*, *61*(4), 661–671. https://doi.org/10.20471/acc.2022.61.04.13
Tatkin, S. (2012). *Wired for love: How understanding your partner's brain and attachment style can help you defuse conflict and build a secure relationship*. New Harbinger Publications.
Tatkin, S. (2016). *Wired for dating: How understanding neurobiology and attachment style can help you find your ideal mate*. New Harbinger Publications.
Turner, A., & Coyle, A. (2000). What does it mean to be a donor offspring? The identity experiences of adults conceived by donor insemination and the implications for counselling and therapy. *Human Reproduction*, *15*(9), 2041–2051. https://doi.org/10.1093/humrep/15.9.2041
Wischmann, T., Schilling, K., Toth, B., Rösner, S., Strowitzki, T., Wohlfarth, K., & Kentenich, H. (2014). Sexuality, self-esteem and partnership quality in infertile women and men. *Geburtshilfe und Frauenheilkunde*, *74*(08), 759–763. https://doi.org/10.1055/s-0034–1368461
World Health Organization. (2023, April 4). *WHO warns that one in six people globally is affected by infertility*. World Health Organization. www.who.int/es/news/item/04-04-2023-1-in-6-people-globally-affected-by-infertility
Zhang, L., Shao, H., Huo, M., Chen, J., Tao, M., & Liu, Z. (2022). Prevalence and associated risk factors for anxiety and depression in infertile couples of ART treatment: A cross-sectional study. *BMC Psychiatry*, *22*(1), 1–9. https://doi.org/10.1186/s12888-022-04256-9

22
IMPACT TECHNIQUES IN SYSTEMIC THERAPY

Umberta Telfener

22.1 Introduction

I would like to state an opening premise: From a systemic perspective, it does not matter whether we see a couple, a family, or an individual alone. As professionals, we always consider complex human systems and construct multifaceted hypotheses that involve taking into account interactive relationships at least on a three-generational basis, whatever the number of people in the session. We always attempt to construct a process that involves the multigenerational core, even if only a few are in the room: We organize an evolutionary and generative process that includes us. We deal with relational, emotional, and mental processes. We operate in the realm of relationships, we offer collaborative practice and reflective enquiry, we participate in narratives, and we nurture dialogue.

Therapy is a creative, transdisciplinary, and transformative art dealing with coordinated and dynamic actions; it is a practice based on "doing together," which requires knowledge about the rules of change. It is a process in which we perform (we ask questions, we dialogue, make hypotheses, actively investigate) and make others perform (organize joint actions, do homework, and perform during sessions) in order to change the conditions of possibility (Bianciardi & Telfener, 2014).

Perturbing in therapy increasingly means "creating events," making things happen, proposing ourselves simultaneously as healers and as clinicians (urgency, trust, closeness are the characteristics we need to put into play). The hypotheses we make do not represent reality (we do not propose a mirroring or a representation of what is told) but rather construct a new universe that emerges from our capacity of connecting with the events that have been brought to us. At the same time, we connect with the *capta*[1] that have been neglected. Hypotheses must allow for a multiplication/invention of new narratives that make the discourse freer and allow the emergence of the emotions that are connected to them.

> One should not try to see whether an idea is right or true. Instead, one should look for another idea, elsewhere, in another field or in the same one, so that between the two ideas something can pass that is neither one nor the other.
>
> *(Deleuze, 1986, p. 15)*

The work we do is not a process to bring out the truth. We are pushed to enter unknown domains, to tolerate doubt, and to abandon control. We are driven to reflect and work on feedback. We build

DOI: 10.4324/9781003536765-26

trust not truth, which implies the relationship between knowledge and ignorance, both of which are inescapable (Telfener, 2011).

We form, we invent, we produce, we fabricate connections that are images of thought, entities that have a purpose. This takes place in a process that does not "represent" the outside world or the intrapsychic one, but rather constructs an event, the occurrence of an embedded, self-referential, and reflexive reality, a singularity that opens a gash in the usual script: the eruption of the new. It is an exchange, a mixing, something that lies between the two possibilities and outside of them.

That's why you don't just work together, you work in between, between old and new narratives, between emotions, between points of view, memories, experiences, intuitions. (When you realize this kind of multiplicity, you perform in a micro-political context, but that's another topic.) Psychotherapy makes everything happen in the here and now; without proposing a beginning or an end, one arrives in the middle of something – as Deleuze says (2003) – and one only creates in the middle, giving new directions or bifurcations to lines that pre-existed. The new is the criterion, and the new is always the unexpected that immediately becomes eternal and necessary. Again, an exchange, a mixture, something that lies between and outside.

How then do we, as professionals, create change? Novelty is the criterion, and the new is always the unexpected that becomes immediately necessary. We must listen, understand, and disrupt; we must dance together, amplifying trust in the choreography and in the mutual respect. We need to bring out a recursive process that involves everyone, avoiding the risk of blocking the system's ability to self-correct and buying into the point of view of those involved. For this we look for the repetitive pattern that happens over and over again (fractal effect and isomorphisms), believing in what we do and in evolution.

I would like to talk in this chapter about the creation of an ex-new space-time that highlights the problems and questions we are trapped in, rather than offering answers. I propose the creation of a new syntax through unusual assemblages, in order to excavate a foreign language within language, to bring out new connections. I will then talk about impact techniques that allow the use of imagination and intuition; they allow abstract concepts to become concrete, bend already known information, bring out emotions, and ignite curiosity. They push participants to be actors in action (a modality already suggested by Milton Erickson in times long past) as a powerful tool for building change. Not to mention the fact that they impose the necessary use of the body, ranging from asking clients to imagine, to the possibilities of involving the body (roleplaying, EMDR, voice dialogue, acting out stories), to action methods such as the use of transitional objects, to the therapist's putting herself at stake in the first person.[2]

I propose the creation of a new space-time that triggers problems and questions in which we get involved, rather than offering answers. Therefore, I do not propose to acquire new strategies, to invent new theories to read contexts and situations, but instead I propose new small performances at one's own discretion; I propose to reflect more and more on what we do together so as to build a generative and responsible process.

22.2 Active techniques in therapy

It is increasingly necessary in therapy to act out the thoughts that are brought in, to render them present, to make them concrete, in order to reflect on them. It seems that in this post-truth and information society, words fly by and become elusive even in therapy. These hyper-modern times are very verbal and psychologically contaminated. But words are not enough as disruptors; we need to perform and make clients perform, multiply possibilities, stimulate desires, suggest opportunities, provide new perspectives, desensitize fears, and try out alternative behaviors.

I would like to emphasize a premise to the use of active techniques: Systemics offers the lens to read the dynamics of life and of events, and it is the framework that organizes interactions, including clinical and institutional situations. It is the systemic perspective that provides the framework that organizes interventions. We have to respect our epistemological responsibility that refers to the task of reflecting not only on the ways of reasoning, on the inevitable prejudices and partial constructions, but also the need to reflect on the ideas and behaviors that emerge in the session so as to assess the consequences they produce on a social and interactive level.

Actions create systems of meaning. Emotions and shared actions become our primary focus: We make narratives emerge from the coordination of actions, emotions, and meanings. We act recursively, and we perform second-order processes. Acting and making clients act becomes indispensable to activate reflection, to maintain the therapeutic relationship, and to perturb in an effective mode. Active techniques allow us to create a common cybernetic brain: heads and hearts together, accessing emotions through doing, reflecting on implicit premises and on the unspoken, accessing pre-verbal memories, making distinctions, giving voice to instinctive actions, accepting/respecting complexity, becoming a participant observer, increasing/explaining the multiple postures of the practitioner. To be simultaneously inside, outside, and in a reflective positioning; to transform structure into process and allow new narratives; to change language; to bring out the relational dance, to identify it, to interrupt it, to seek its local coherence, to recover resources.

Active techniques allow us to expand perceptions, to open up to new ways of thinking, behaving, and feeling. They allow clarification of one's ideas, explaining nuances, promoting an observer positioning and a circular complex point of view, eliciting new ideas and feelings about past events, present relationships, and future possibilities. They can create the kind of openings towards self-healing that are normally promoted by systemic therapists through circular questions, future and reflective questions, and the therapeutic conversation. A lot to do.

I consider active techniques like the use of picture postcards that portray in images the common dance; the dialogue with the different selves as a way to give depth to each person; the use of masks; drawing; the use of space to represent and self-represent oneself; the map of the present state and the map of desires; the search for a metaphorical object; the construction of rituals to fortify and protect oneself; the use of transitional objects; the emotional map; the dramatization of the past or the future; the revisiting of the past. We put to work whatever possible invention comes to mind, which we enjoy and is utilized in an ethical, processual, and generative manner.

How are these techniques utilized? By engaging the users and simultaneously participating in the proposed activity, asking circular questions, and sharing hypotheses. Always by getting involved as clinicians and choosing in turn one or more objects that represent the people we are working with. By getting our hands dirty and offering our own point of view.

When a couple is in a session, we try to stimulate the partners to rethink and reconstruct the themes they have woven into their narratives of life together, not just the current accounts of their relationship. Taken together, these measures are likely to highlight and challenge many long-standing patterns that preclude mutual gratification, as argued by Chasin et al. (1989).

22.3 The use of transitional objects

22.3.1 Case illustration

We are in the third session of a couple. Both are actors (he is more famous and more mature), aged 34 and 47. They live together and recently seem to have lost the harmony that used to characterize them. Both declare that they do not know what is happening to them; they seem cooperative and willing to understand what is happening according to their specific attitude towards life: She as more proactive and generous, while he is more cynical and secretive. I decide to take immediate action and ask them to choose two or three objects from a large set of miniatures, objects that represent their story today. She comes back first: "I choose the little man with his mouth sewn shut because you can't talk in the house without him getting angry and criticizing me. I choose the spinning top because I never know how the day will go, which way it turns. Then there is a crow that looms and hovers" (Figure 22.1). He is full of pauses and doubts, but finally speaks: "I chose the three things I like least, that give me sadness, that I hate, that are repulsive: the routine worker who always does the same job, the noise, and the fake goodness of angels" (Figure 22.2). "But you had to choose something about our relationship!" she retorts, disappointed. "Ha, I didn't understand," he replies, pretending to be wrong.

Figure 22.1

Figure 22.2

I too am annoyed because I notice a difference in the attitude of the two: She is cooperative, whereas he seems to indirectly sabotage any reflection on their relationship. However, I will use the objects they have chosen to continue the investigation. "How do you react to the three 'dangers' your partner has pointed out?" I ask him. "What relationship characteristics do you identify in the objects chosen by him?" I ask her. He describes her as too diligent but lately critical, a woman who is not afraid to ask and always wants more. She describes him as a stranger who enters the house with annoyance, who treats her as an enemy, whereas before he was loving and complicit. Already in the first session the transitional objects have revealed a pattern and seem explicit: It emerges from their answers that she would like to relaunch and think about having a child together while he calls himself out and with his defensive behavior seems to ask for a break. The dynamic that seemed mysterious immediately unfolds before my eyes, with the two of them going back and forth with the miniatures collection to add items and explain themselves.

22.4 The use of postcards

Postcards are also a very useful tool in both training and therapy. For years, wherever I go, I buy images that I like and that have metaphorical meaning for me. I base my choices on my preferences, and I choose instinctively, without a predetermined criterion.

I use postcards in therapy to ask people to describe themselves and other members of the system and to represent together certain steps in their lives, such as the history of their relationship, the first meeting, and the onset of discomfort and misunderstandings. I use them with both adolescents and couples, as in the following example.

22.4.1 Case illustration

Rosa and Valerio are 34 and 40 years old, respectively. They met in 2008, broke off their relationship for a year (2010), and got married in 2015. They came to me in 2021 because of misunderstandings that led them to feel estranged. We were in the first session, and instead of doing the analysis of their request (Telfener, 2019) – which I will do in the second session – I followed my intuition to immediately engage them with a "game." Maybe because she is a colleague, or maybe because he immediately enters disqualifying the context ("Let's have this chat," he says with an almost disgusted face, entering the office), I feel like surprising them and go along with my intuition.

How would she describe the couple on the postcard she selected (Figure 22.3): "an old-fashioned, romantic couple that works by the rules of yesteryear. He gets easily distracted while I keep my gaze fixed on us and keep things going, I'm focused. He is afraid, he keeps his distance, and I respect that."

How would he describe the couple on his chosen postcard (Figure 22.4)? "A couple swimming in blue water, they love each other, the way they go together is romantic."

As the woman looks at his postcard, she adds: "They are alone, they are in a desolate land, and then they are in danger of drowning, they are not swimming calmly, both of them. They are trying to keep afloat. The sea is deep and there can be predators."

When the man looks at her postcard, he says: "This couple is watching a black-and-white movie, in fact he is a bit fed up but stays with her because they are going to a restaurant afterwards."

I add the way in which I would describe the couple, by choosing a postcard myself that represents their relationship (Figure 22.5): "Two ducklings, two animals of the same species who have unwittingly backed themselves into a corner and cannot get out."

I ask them both how they would like this couple to be. Valerio chooses a new postcard (Figure 22.6) and answers: "A romantic and erotic couple, cheerful, dreamy, convivial, playing and dancing, doing things they both enjoy."

Figure 22.3

Figure 22.4

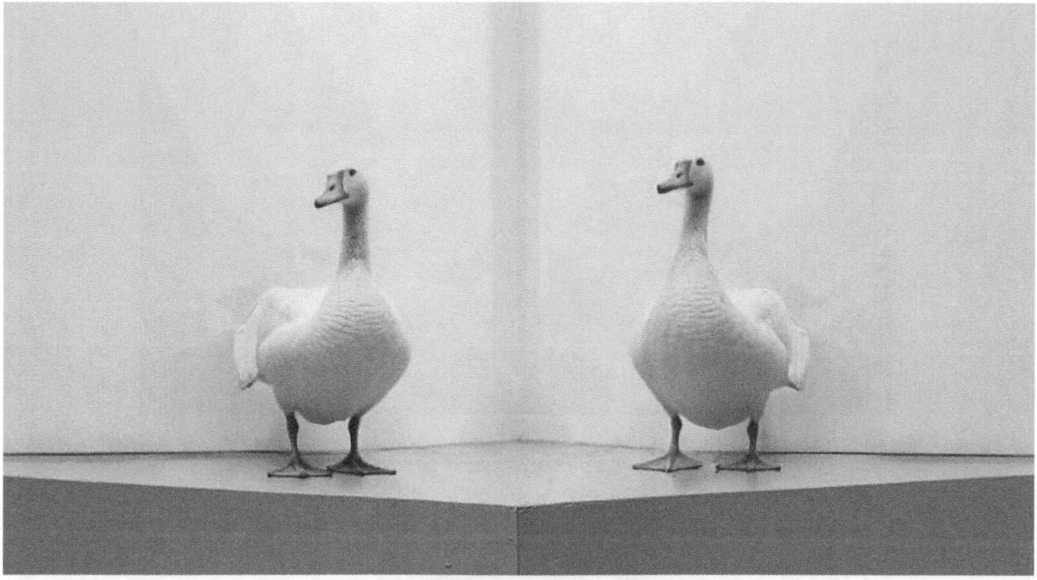

Figure 22.5

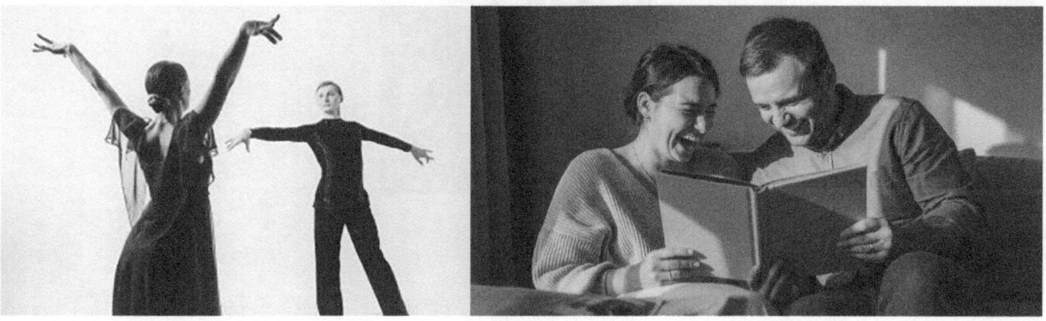

Figure 22.6

Rosa on her part follows (Figure 22.7): "Two people who do things together as equals, holding hands, looking in the same direction. They even go dancing together. Uh! We both chose a dancing card, we like Flamenco so much!!!"

For lack of space, I will not unravel the session. It is clear, however, that the material to work on is rich, dense, and full of cues; the script that moves each of them is quite vibrant. My hypothesis is that he has fewer expectations of the relationship than she does, that he is involved in a convivial way, whereas she seeks more. I hypothesize that they both pretend that their relationship is very good and that they never challenged it. One of them criticizes and the other resists and holds the bond: They seem to take turns. I later learn – revising with them the postcards of the first session – that they were not able to get pregnant, and that both feel this emptiness that weighs heavily.

Working with couples means looking for resources and not falling into the trap of believing that there is a persecutor and a victim. It implies recovering their intense and proactive moments and

Figure 22.7

recreating in the therapy room the generative emotionality that certainly brought them together, at least in the beginning.

It is obvious how the postcards, beyond the explanations that people give of them, offer the therapist immediate suggestions, show contradictions, propose hypotheses, reveal themes, indicate points of union and profound differences, trace one or more paths to follow in therapy, and open up many insights.

22.5 The emotional map

Emotions are the bridge between mind and body. They constitute a language that responds to a stimulus. Their recognition is a species-specific pre-linguistic human trait. I disagree with those who think that emotions have been neglected by systemic therapy. Boscolo and Cecchin's sessions included emotions, although it is true that it has now become necessary at times to "exaggerate" them in session so that our clients leave with the experience that something meaningful has happened. It has become more necessary to push people to amplify their emotionality, to make it corporeal and experience it in the here and now of the session, to make emotions demonstrative. However, our clients have just as much need to recognize, accept, and tame emotions, so that they do not overflow or wither away.

Emotions are a challenge, the door to decoding the world; they guide our lives, but they are also a means for our transformation. When they are confined and imprisoned, they become dangerous, and they make the person frozen, at risk of losing contact with him/herself. When set free, they fill like a river in a flood. If they are not managed, one risks wasting one's energy.

How to act out emotions in the session? It is necessary to ask what each of the people present is feeling and how the participants explain their feelings, how they connect them to other members of their nucleus, from whom they learned a certain recurring emotion, and with whom they share it usually. We constantly ask them to embody their emotions, to decode and awaken emotions, to emphasize them, to intensify them. I personally use images, body postures, transitional objects, and events that need to be expressed to create a rich emotional narrative.

To emphasize the relational sense of emotions that I consider interactive and dialogic processes linked to culture, I invented the use of a map of emotions that allows me to make emotions concrete, to objectivize them and link them to lived experiences, past and present. This map allows me to construct in the session emotional moments of active remembrance; it enhances nuances and stimulates clients to make connections.

22.5.1 Case illustration

Maria and Antonio are 53 and 54 years old, respectively. They have an 18-year-old son and both work happily. He is a public executive, and she an illustrator. However, they have been quarrelling fiercely for five years. After a therapy session that "woke her up," she stopped fitting in with the couple and started having a parallel life with her friends and openly and very loudly criticizing her partner "who is not as I wish him to be." He has become increasingly withdrawn from the relationship, coming home late and holing up in the bedroom reading "to defend myself from my wife's antagonism and rancor." Grocery shopping is their only joint activity. Sexuality languishes ("it's not how I want it," she says; "it involves too much negotiation," he says). The welfare of their "child" is the only common topic.

In the second session, I try to explore their emotions, and I am evaded by a series of words shouted by the woman against her partner. She utters violent and offensive insults, about which I cannot make any sense. I get up, take colored A4 sheets of paper, and ask each of them to write down their most frequent emotion towards the other. I ask this to clarify their personal reading of their emotions and to get the history of their feelings towards each other and the world. You will see in the continuing of the story that they will specify emotions more and more clearly, and they will redefine them and pass from generic ones (antagonism, resentment, withdrawal, and distrust) to more specific tones. They will also experience where they have learned these states of being and how the family of origin has had a say on their actual emotional state. At the end of the therapy process, they will even be able to put in the bin the old emotions they presented themselves with in therapy and suggest that they now feel curious towards the partner (the woman) and drawn to her (the man).

Maria writes "resentment," and Antonio "distrust" (Figure 22.8). I acknowledge that these are important emotions that they described and note that their interaction in the session showed them in action: distrust on the part of the husband who isolates himself, resentment on the part of the wife who accuses him and treats him blatantly badly. But they also seem to be interchangeable emotions: Distrust could be on the part of the woman, who has a fixed idea in her head and would like others to adapt to it; resentment could be felt also by the husband, who feels misunderstood and unheard. These are the two fundamental emotions in their relationship. I ask: Have they felt them all their lives, also in other relational situations? No. They agree that these feelings are a consequence of Maria's

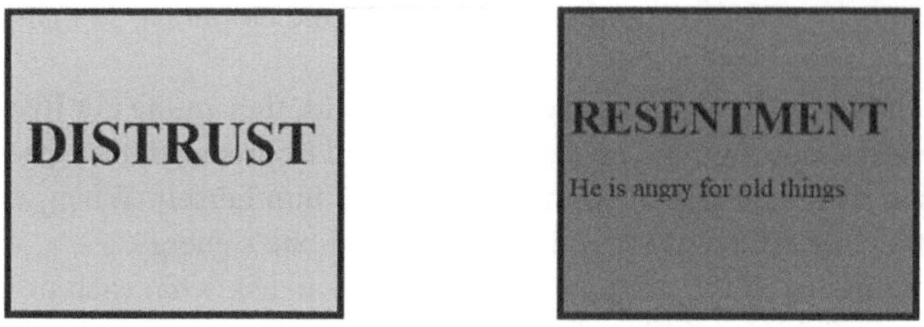

Figure 22.8

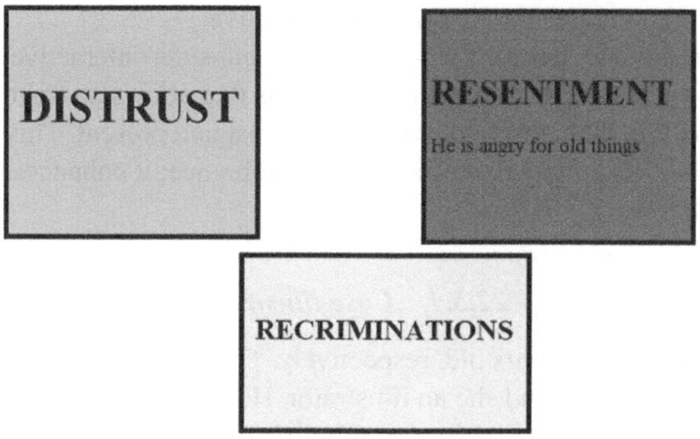

Figure 22.9

therapy, which led to her awakening and her "becoming a feminist." Her feelings are also due to her husband's lack of sexual interest in her, which triggers Maria's jealousy as she fantasizes about his possible sexual escapades. I ask each of them from whom they learned both resentment and mistrust; we wonder if it is a familiar theme and how much each of them has been emotionally literate since childhood to respond in these very recurrent modes.

They point out that they both recriminate. Antonio brings up things from ten years ago, and Maria constantly criticizes him because he is not what she would like him to be. It has been two years since the pandemic, during which they developed mutual anger, and anger triggers their respective recriminations. He specifies and corrects everything she does and says, whereas she recriminates based on her need to be adored, having created a film in her head of how he should respond to her. According to him, she always wants things to go as she imagines them, and she feels that what he offers is never enough for her. In circular fashion, she responds to this critique by remonstrating and makes scenes centered on jealousy. He justifies his lack of attention and then retires into a hole, licking his wounds. Each of them is quite familiar with one another's attitudes: recriminations, distrust, and resentment (Figure 22.9).

I ask each of them to place their feet on one of the sheets they personally wrote on the emotion they feel most often, resentment and distrust, in order to try and embody the emotion and remember some anecdotes that connect to it. I ask them to tell me their story in relation to the emotions we are investigating. We find out that his mother and brother are distrustful, that her father has always been suspicious and demanded that everyone in the family be suspicious too: closing the shutters, not letting the neighbors see or hear anything, not talking about personal things, doubting what others said.

Following providing their respective family-of-origin stories, the two look at each other and ask me, judge-like, to reason with them. I notice much complicity for the first time in the session, as two children that are playing a common game. As a result of their reflection on their pasts, they change their priorities regarding the emotions lived: anger governs their reciprocal behaviors. Anger is the dominant theme in both their families. They recall their respective experiences and need for anger in their original nucleus. In her family, her father "hated" her mother and wanted revenge for not having the courage to leave her. In his family, mother and brother felt special and different from everyone else – special but not recognized and therefore angry.

For a moment, the two agree on a shared common emotion, and a shiver of intensity runs through the therapy room. But as the session closes, she regrets and accuses him of not being the man of her dreams and he withdraws, shrugging his shoulders. They have come together in understanding some emotional similarities between their families – which could have resulted in mutual empathy and closeness, at least for the moment – but this threat of intimacy and letting their combative guard down scared them. They leave the session with an experimental task on my part: If anger gets defused by apologizing – as they have reported – I ask them to apologize even more than necessary. Whenever each of them feels misunderstood by the other, instead of accusing or recriminating, they should apologize for what they believe they have done to trigger the other's behavior.[3]

22.6 Using imagination and bringing out isomorphism

The concept of "isomorphism" in the clinical context is fundamental to systemic work and is utilized also across various theoretical orientations. It implies an assessment of a couple's or family's difficulties (or an individual's for that matter), utilizing what emerges from the relationship between each other and with us: which recurrent melodies, which outlines repeat themselves? It is, in simplest terms, the search for the relational patterns and the themes that occur recursively, in self-identical mode, among people dancing together. We can find similar repetitive patterns across generations, and in the relationships with us, even in what happens within our therapeutic context. Isomorphism refers to an interactional, to a key relational pattern that repeats itself across different specific contexts and circumstances. These patterns recur "unconsciously" within the observed system but need to become aware within the observing system that includes us. Identifying these patterns, through our embodied emotion and our hypothesis on what is happening, allows us to assume with more precision what is happening elsewhere. These patterns can become the target of therapeutic interventions, guided by the systemic premise that change implies modifying patterns around whatever is happening. Sheldrake (2009) and the "morphogenetic field" come to mind, a field in which we share an unconscious and we feel identical emotions or act in similar ways transversally to different contexts, behaviors, and emotions that can even surprise us.

I often find myself in supervision looking for emergent isomorphisms – similar patterns occurring across different contexts in the family/patient system, between the family or couple system and the therapeutic system (therapist plus family or couple), and between the organizing and clinical settings we inhabit. It almost seems that contexts organize repetitive patterns, maintained by unspoken premises, the origin of which one cannot initially understand.

22.6.1 Case illustration

I am conducting supervision at a dual-diagnostic therapeutic community outside Rome (addictions and psychiatric problems). I am working with the professionals in group. We have talked about the organization, and I noted a recurring emotion that leads to similar patterns. I hypothesize an isomorphism between (1) the dynamics among the professionals, (2) the problems they face in case management with patients, and (3) the feelings they share in their relationship with the management. I question myself and (4) look for the same pattern also with me. I turn to myself: What do I feel? I recall that arriving in the morning, I felt a lack of energy and was doubting what to do with them. I felt sort of discouraged, which is very emotionally near to dissatisfaction. Yes, dissatisfaction is the theme. The practitioners feel dissatisfied in their work, even if they actively cooperate with the management staff and are involved in decision making, being quite appreciated. The management staff, present at the supervision, also feels dissatisfied about the work of its professionals (nurses, psychologists, psychiatrists, social workers, counselors): The director feels a lack of recognition of his efforts to share responsibility with his staff. I felt a lack of energy, and the cases we are going to work on have some problems too.

I ask myself what is the source of this outspoken and lived dissatisfaction – is it theirs alone or does the dissatisfaction also belong to the client population they deal with, to the individual clients? Does it also belong to some hidden premises within the community's founding myth? How has this emotion discolored on them? We speak about it and realize that "dissatisfaction" is also a specific characteristic of the diagnostic category they "manage" as professionals: Addicts with psychiatric problems utilize dissatisfaction as a way of decoding their world. Have the professionals absorbed it, made it their own, and are they allowing themselves to bring it into supervision? Does it also derive from the dynamics between them and me? Has it to do with the relationship with me, their supervisor? The next question becomes: How much does this emotion belong to them, how much is embedded on the users, on the organization and on the supervision itself? How much is it endemic in their lives, and how much is it a symptom of this specific context? How many layers of dissatisfaction are involved in this narrative we are sharing? It becomes clear that the dissatisfaction is both personal and a function of that specific organization, and it also has a relational flavor in the encounter with the management and the clients.

After reflecting together at length, I ask them to do an exercise in pairs that will lead them to accentuate their frustration to examine it more openly, setting the stage for change. Without disclosing my intentions, I create a deliberate provocation to exacerbate the theme of "dissatisfaction" and their accompanying emotions, utilizing a neutral stimulus. I ask them to build a paper airplane in pairs, each holding their dominant hand behind their back.[4] The paper airplane must fly, so it needs to be built with all the right angles and attributes. Complaints, anger, despondency, as well as laughter and strange physical positionings emerge. Later, I discuss with them how they coped with this frustrating assignment. How did they mediate their discouragements? How did they manage to cooperate even in moments of difficulty? How did they access personal resources? I then open the conversation to the isomorphic challenges in working as a team with patients and among each other. We discuss what they valued in working with their colleagues on the paper airplane exercise, and which lessons they can learn from this exercise in order to transform their actual clinical and organizational frustration in working better together.

Once the exercise is over, and after a break, the second part of the day begins. They ask me to bring to everyone's attention a clinical situation that is difficult to handle on a daily basis. A 19-year-old girl, seemingly quite talented and socially competent (among other things, she is a budding singer who had some musical success before entering the community), constantly provokes both fellow patients and the staff and makes every interaction with her a battle for the definition and quality of the relationship. She is adept at putting professionals in check, provoking, and often ending up with a punishment. She behaves adequately only when she is the center of attention and when she is engaged in tasks of responsibility or in an intense relationship with one of the caregivers, who shows her esteem and trust. In unexceptional day-to-day interactions, she provokes and fails, it seems almost on purpose. They all know her, and each of them adds a few details that highlight the annoyance they each feel.

I ask them to construct a metaphor of the interaction with the girl through an image they find using their mobile phones and then showing it to all of us. One shows a picture of a roll of sandpaper, another an image of a grain of sand that has entered an eye, another an image of a bumpy path, and another of an obstacle course. It seems easy for each of them to construct an image and a metaphor that captures the quality of their interaction with the girl. I ask: How do these images resonate with what we have spoken about in the first part of the supervision? They feel amazed. "The body feelings are exactly the same," they comment. These images could apply to their description of their work together and to the actual relationship with the management. I choose not to meta-communicate on my hypothesis, on this similarity, but rather to let each of them draw their own conclusions: I trust them on their ability to elaborate a path of action.

Later in the afternoon, four exercises follow, one after another in order to amplify what happened until now. The first exercise involves them personally: "What meaning does the image, the visual metaphor they have brought up previously have for them?" How does it involve them personally? What significance does that image hold in their personal life story? How do they relate it to themselves, and how do they include it in their own life story?

The second exercise connects the climate of the therapeutic community to the individual professionals and their relationship with the clients. How does the image they each have put forward relate to their own experience in the community, and how do they think they can change this frustrating interaction? How can they personally break out of that frustrating script, to free themselves from a repetitive pattern?

The third concerns trying to hypothesize what led this girl to always have to sabotage the expectations of others and disappoint herself. I say, "Let's play at being scriptwriters who have to put into production an episode of a series about a girl like her. What do you think must have happened in her life for her to behave the way she does?" What premises and what needs drive her; what hiccups in life have led her to defend herself in this way, and how has an adaptive solution become a problem?

Finally, there is time for one last exercise: Everyone chooses together through voting the most significant image from those shared (the roll of sandpaper), and everyone writes a mini-story from that stimulus (Figure 22.10). It can be a personal story or not – short, intense, emotional, and with a

Figure 22.10

special meaning for each one of them. It is interesting how many take ownership of the image and make a connection to their own life story. Some find themselves accessing long-forgotten memories, while others connect the image for the first time to stimuli that were previously separated.

22.7 Conclusion

When teaching the systemic approach or supervising students, it is necessary that not everything goes through rational, purely cognitive, verbal channels of understanding. It is necessary that the imagination and the body are activated through the use of sculptures (we did not talk about them – I utilize them in any way possible), images, miniature figurines, colors, storytelling, analogic activities (like the paper airplane exercise), space, and other doors of connection. For example, members of a couple are often frightened of the stalemate they find themselves in, and they enact this fear by becoming bitter and vindictive enemies. They are anchored in their defensive behavior, each ready to react with little thought to the other's behavior. They are reluctant to make even small changes and to let go of the painful past, and to change the way they decode their common dance. They feel that they have been betrayed and that they are in the right. They therefore have difficulty venturing into alternative hypotheses about what is going on between them and what is truly missing in their relationship. Beneath the spitting waves of their rage often lie roiling currents of sadness, alienation, deep hurt and pain, and most of all, desperate loneliness.

Using action impact techniques not only allows for new, emotional, and relational experiences (both happy and sad), but invites them into new situations where they often find themselves in new and unpredictable configurations that amaze them and allow them to break out of the usual patterns. These techniques apply not only to couples but also to families and individuals, whose blocks and challenges are understood from a systemic, interactional perspective. Likewise, the same applies in supervision, as one of our aims is to deconstruct premises taken for granted and allow new experiences in a safe training setting, enabling each participant to step outside the box. In general, in systemic transformation, we are creating therapeutic circumstances and novel moments that allow people to experiment, to build new awareness, to connect the dots in a different manner, and to free themselves from old, dysfunctional patterns.

In this chapter, I have described some of the many impact techniques I routinely use with people who ask me for help. When do I do this? When words stagnate or seem too confused or chaotic, when I get bored or feel confused, when the dialogue does not seem sufficiently generative, and when I want to engage people emotionally. I use actions and images as tools to introduce energy into the session or the training space, to venture together into areas not explored before.

What follows? The emotional climate usually becomes warmer. Clients come to a greater understanding and experience cooperation in the session, which can then be enacted outside of the session. Seemingly pressing problems sometimes lose relevance, other times we find together in the middle of the storm. Clients and students, even colleagues, become more willing to acknowledge their own participation in maintaining the ongoing difficulties. In addition, those who attribute all problems to the other person "who will never change" find food for thought in shared dramatizations. Sometimes instead of a heightened awareness we see a diffusion of the problem, which, in my experience, can be just as generative. Sometimes the *insight* stimulated by new acting arrives the next day, allowing for creative, non-rational, sudden processing that catches people by surprise.

It always remains the responsibility of the clinician/trainer to choose how to intervene and to ensure that roles and individual dignities are respected. Even within an equal relationship, the asymmetry arising from our social mandate obliges the clinician to be able to explain why she is making one choice rather than another, to correct her strategy according to the feedback obtained (Telfener & Ticozzelli, 2023), and to take possible undesired outcomes into account (Bianciardi & Telfener,

2014). We respect our epistemological responsibility, which refers to the therapist's duty to reflect not only on her own way of thinking, on her own "prejudices," on implicit and explicit theories of reference, but also on the relationship, on those ideas that emerge in the session, in order to assess the consequences on a social and interactive level of the cognitive-emotional operations she performs with respect to the client and their significant system.

Notes

1 "Captures/capta" instead of "data" is critical psychiatrist R. D. Laing's proposed term, as he argues that they are not a priori data, but an observer chooses which ones to pull out of a background.
2 The author is a female and is representing the therapist as a "she."
3 In behavior therapy, this would be called "overcorrection"; in narrative therapy, strengthening the subordinated story; in structural couple therapy, a reframe, almost a paradoxical intervention, and certainly using the problem to strengthen their connection; and in intergenerational family therapy, differentiating from the similar stories of anger, blame, and mistrust. In the Milan model, it is not a technique but one of the possible lenses to read and enact what is happening.
4 This is a Theatre of the Oppressed exercise proposed to me by Olivier Malcor (2021).

References

Bianciardi, M., & Telfener, U. (2014). *Ricorsività in psicoterapia*. Bollati Boringhieri.

Chasin, R., Roth, S., & Bograd, M. (1989). Action methods in systemic therapy: Dramatizing ideal futures and reformed pasts with couples. *Family Process*, *28*, 121–136. https://doi.org/10.1111/j.1545-5300.1989.00121.x

Deleuze, G. (2003). *Che cos'è l'atto di creazione*. Cronopio (Original work published 1986).

Malcor, O. (2021). *Scripting violence, rehearsing change: Games and theatrical tools to work with perpetrators of gender-based violence*. European Network for the Work with Perpetrators of Domestic Violence. www.workwithperpetrators.eu/fileadmin/WWP

Sheldrake, R. (2009). *A new science of life*. Icon Books.

Telfener, U. (2011). *Apprendere I contesti. Strategie per entrare in nuovi ambiti di lavoro*. Raffaello Cortina.

Telfener, U. (2019, April). The analysis of the request as the main door to interventions. *Context, the Magazine of Family Therapy and Systemic Practice*, *162*, 28–30.

Telfener, U., & Ticozzelli, E. (2023). Strategizing the state of the art at the Milan School. *Family Process*, *62*(3), 1024–1039. https://doi.org/10.1111/famp.12900

23

FAMILY/COUPLE THERAPY THROUGH THE LENS OF INTIMATE PARTNER VIOLENCE

No limits or know your limits?

Elisa Agostinelli and Brian Sullivan

23.1 Introduction

Men's violence against women – particularly intimate partner violence and sexual violence – is a major public health and criminal justice problem, as well as being a major violation of women's human rights, across the world. In the past 25 years globally, ongoing domestic violence research, evidence-informed and community-based responses and interventions, developing practice wisdom, and listening to people's lived experience have added to safer and more accountable practice in terms of domestic violence intervention (Scott & Jenney, 2023).

Family systems theory is the underpinning theory of most couple and family therapy training. The focus is on understanding and unpacking functional problems on a complex systemic level rather than on the individual level – attention being paid to the couple or family dynamics as an interactive whole. Key concepts such as circularity, homeostasis, triangulation, and neutrality provide the clinician with hypotheses and insights about processes between and among people within the system, instead of just what is going on within them as individuals (Brown & James, 2014; Karakurt et al., 2013; Oka & Whiting, 2011). The problem with this language is that it infers complicity. It only takes one to abuse and bully. The other is the target, not the accomplice. This language can take responsibility for the violence away from the perpetrator and can lead to victim-blaming. Obviously, this is dangerously unhelpful.

From "family therapy has not served battered women well" (Kaufman, 1992, p. 233) to "under specific circumstances, conjoint couple therapy may be the appropriate intervention for IPV [intimate partner violence] if certain conditions are present, as determined by the clinician" (Hurless & Cottone, 2018, p. 327), the family therapy literature runs the full spectrum of contentions.

Most of the studies cited in this chapter acknowledged that not all violence is the same. Michael Johnson's work was most often cited in this matter (2006, 2008), where he identifies three kinds of violence: situational violence, resistive violence, and what he termed intimate terrorism. Generally, the family therapy literature endorses working with couples under strict conditions where situational violence is identified and safety for all is prioritized (Babcock, Armenti & Warford, 2017). Interestingly, Tutty's research, where she examined women's impressions of counselling for intimate partner violence (IPV), found that while most rate counseling as "quite a bit or very helpful," the exception was couple counseling (Tutty, 2023). Dissatisfaction with couples counseling was notable, with

DOI: 10.4324/9781003536765-27

women raising serious concerns that counselors did not understand IPV or, even more disturbingly, were siding with abusive men (Oka & Whiting, 2011).

Our thesis is that assessing situational violence as distinct from intimate terrorism can be much more complex and uncertain than one might think. This distinction requires a trained and expert eye to be performed accurately and a clear awareness of the potentially harmful unintended consequences (Lamb et al., 2022). To carry out this assessment safely and effectively, we must ask ourselves: Are family therapists and couple counselors routinely and sufficiently trained in risk assessment, and are they supervised by professionals proficient in domestic violence intervention to do this assessment safely and effectively? If not, then what risks involved in proceeding with family therapy or couple work are being overlooked or not even considered, to the detriment of victims' safety and the exoneration of perpetrators? We want to present what we (as domestic violence and trauma-informed practitioners) believe that couples counselors and family therapists need to understand and implement for working ethically, safely, and accountably, with couples where domestic violence may be suspected or disclosed. After all, doing no harm is embedded in the ethical codes of all helping professions (Prilleltensky et al., 1996).

Various terms are used to describe violence in couples and families, such as domestic violence, family violence, and spousal violence. In this chapter, we will be using the construct "intimate partner violence" (IPV) used by the World Health Organization (WHO) with the following definition:

> Intimate partner violence refers to behaviour within an intimate relationship that causes physical, sexual, or psychological harm, including acts of physical aggression, sexual coercion, psychological abuse and controlling behaviours. This definition covers violence by both current and former spouses and partners.
>
> *(cf. Violence Info – Intimate partner violence [who.int])*

While we are aware of the limitations of labeling, we will be specifically referring to heterosexual men's violence in intimate relationships with heterosexual women. Male partners will be interchangeably referred to as offenders, perpetrators, or abusers. Female partners will be generally referred to as victims or victim/survivors. This is not to say that this is the only context for IPV, but statistically it is the most prevalent and is the focus of our work. Lessons learned here may be transferable to other contexts, but that is another chapter.

With the widespread prevalence of heterosexual IPV, whether couples or family therapists are aware of it or not, they will be regularly working with violent offenders and their victimized and abused partners (Karakurt et al., 2013). Of course, clinicians should not only be aware but adequately trained to identify, respond, assess, and manage IPV offenders and work with victims, prioritizing safety always. Tutty (2023) identified several studies that document a general lack of domestic violence information and training in tertiary education for social work students, mental health professionals, and nursing students. It is far too easy for untrained professionals to collude with perpetrators and leave victims feeling blamed by them for the circumstances in which they find themselves. When the victim and her experience of abuse is doubted or unacknowledged, her feelings of worthlessness and helplessness can be reinforced. When practitioners respond inappropriately, the victim can feel at fault and often pathologized as the problem. She is the one *with* the problem, but she is *not* the problem. She is traumatized and trapped in a relationship with an abusive partner. Untrained and unsympathetic professionals can easily subvert the aim of supporting and advocating for the victim (Neale, 2018).

This lack of professional training seems to be common also in counseling and family therapy programs. There is an urgent need for couples and family therapists to understand the patterns, dynamics, and high-risk factors associated with IPV, the harmful effects on human physical/mental health and well-being, when family or couple therapy is contraindicated, because it is unsafe, and the unknown repercussions and unintended consequences are dangerous for the victim.

In 1999, Virginia Goldner so wisely stated: "We have to give up the illusory safe haven of neutrality and technique-centered professionalism. There is an urgent social need to bring psychologically informed moral discourses in the therapeutic realm" (p. 333). In this chapter, we want to include a "psychologically informed moral discourse" into family therapy practice, by outlining what we believe family therapists and couple counselors need to be aware of and implement if they are to practice ethically, safely, and accountably. We will be looking at (a) a shared understanding of male violence towards women and children, (b) high-risk factors we cannot ignore, (c) the ways men account for and describe their violence, (d) being an integrated practitioner within a coordinated community response, (e) recommendations for family therapists and couple counselors, and (f) recommendations for supervisors. Our space is limited, so the content will be basic, brief, and introductory.

23.2 Understanding IPV as a gendered crime

Although women can be violent, there are "dramatic differences in frequency, severity, and purpose of the violence" (Kimmel, 2002). Kimmel hypothesized that including assaults and homicides by ex-spouses and ex-partners, intimate partner homicide, and sexual assault, the gendered ratio of male-perpetrated violence to female-perpetrated violence would be closer to 4:1. Alternatively, violence that is instrumental in the establishment and maintenance of power and control – the more systematic, persistent, and injurious type of violence – is overwhelmingly perpetuated by men, with rates captured best by crime victimization studies and national statistics data. More than 90% of this violence is perpetrated by men. When sexual violence and violence by ex-spouses are considered, the evidence is overwhelming that gender asymmetry in domestic violence remains in full effect (Sardinha et al., 2022). Men are more violent than women, both inside the home and in the public sphere. The home is not a refuge from violence, and it is not a site where gender differences in the public sphere are somehow magically reversed. We must also be aware that the perpetrators of that violence – both in public and in private, at home or on the street, and whether the victim is male or female – are overwhelmingly men (Kimmel, 2002).

If we assume that all violence is gender symmetrical and situational, perpetrated at equal rates and equal harm, by men and women, we would be making a serious and risky mistake. Michael Kaufman spoke of the triad of men's violence: against women, against men, and against the self (2007). Women's violence tends to be largely resistive, reactive, or self-defensive (Nancarrow et al., 2020). While not denying violence in same-sex relationships, or women's use of force, we are stating that men's violence towards women is a major human rights issue in the world today (Violence against women [who.int]).

23.3 Men's intimate partner violence: Ill will or poor skill?

If the clinician believes a man's violence and abuse is the result of emotional regulation issues, communication, conflict resolution skills, or even deficiency in relational skills, emerging from his family of origin, then poor skills may be deemed the problem and skill-building and training may be the solution. However, if his violence and abuse is intentional, instrumental, purposeful, and strategic, chosen to gain power and control over his partner, then we are dealing with ill will. This is not only a moral problem but, importantly for all of us to understand, a criminal justice problem (Heyman et al.,

2023). This is not primarily a therapeutic issue under the remit of family therapy, but a wider societal problem that needs to be addressed by the community and the criminal justice system.

We are not asserting that men will not benefit from individual therapy. We are saying that therapy may be one part of case management, but never on its own, without the monitoring and supervision that a coordinated community response can provide, with its focus of victim safety and offender accountability. His counseling may include trauma counseling for his history of trauma, mental health counseling for any ongoing issues he may be dealing with, and group counseling with a men's domestic violence intervention group, which has been mandated by a court. We need to be aware that the offender can use conjoint therapy as a means of maintaining contact, and continuing his controlling and manipulation of her, under the guise of therapy, with a naïve and untrained therapist colluding with him.

It is our contention that men's violence towards women, in IPV, is not accidental, random, or isolated. It is a dynamic pattern of coercive control, intended to isolate, entrap, and harm her (Stark & Hester, 2019). His violence is learned behavior. It is behavior that works for him – it gets him what he wants, when he wants it, and how he wants it. And largely, he has gotten away with it with impunity. Violence is a core foundation of his masculine script and his relational script with women. Because of his belief system, his worldview, which supports and condones violence against women, family therapy is not the most effective way to address this safely and accountably (Kaufman, 1992). IPV (not situational violence) is another level of harm and risk. She is too exposed, unprotected, and at risk in this medium and mode of intervention.

23.4 How men talk about their violence

Male intimate partner abusers, when discussing their actions, tend to take control of the violence narrative. Many things are left unsaid (Hearn, 1998). Men's accounts of their violence and abuse are often "acts without agents" (Lamb, 1991). Typically, men will use denial, minimization, excuse-making, justification due to provocation, and outright blame. All of these are used to manage his image, tarnish hers, and avoid responsibility for his violence. Men will often diagnose their partner's mental health issues and disparage their character, personality, or weaknesses, all while diverting attention away from the critical issue of violence and abuse and the subsequent effects of that on her (Henning & Holdford, 2006).

Thus, when Goldner (1999) stated: "In violence work, couple treatment can create the condition for giving testimony and bearing witness, where the victim can speak her truth while her partner and the therapist suffer that truth in the act of listening" (p. 334), the repercussions of the victim's truth speaking upon returning home, far from the therapist's holding environment, or her reluctance to speak truth because if fear has taught her anything it is not to provoke him, do not appear to be considered. The victim will suffer that truth again and again in the act of her perpetrator's abuse. Goldner contended that "helping the man transcend his excuses and externalizations in order to acknowledge responsibility for violating and traumatizing his partner is an expression of a therapeutic commitment to him" (1999, p. 334).

This work is best left to men's domestic violence intervention programs that are linked to coordinated community responses where there are safety protocols and accountability processes, including the criminal justice system, not to isolated couple counselors who do not have the capacity to keep victims safe (Gondolf, 2012; Buzawa et al., 2017). Longer-term work with these men, with sufficient supervision and monitoring of their behaviors and beliefs, holding them to account, appropriate case management, with consequences for recidivism, ongoing risk assessment, and by trained facilitators of men's domestic violence intervention is called for here – not couple counseling or family therapy.

23.5 Coercive control

The construct of coercive control (Stark, 2007) reveals that IPV is much more than physical violence. Coercive control is constituted by tactics such as the gendered micro-regulation of everyday life, including when and what a partner can eat and drink, how they dress and style their hair, how they undertake household tasks, who they can spend time with, how they act around their family and friends, what they watch on television, how they drive, where they can go, what they can talk about, when and where they can sleep, how and when they have sex, and how they can spend their free time (Downes et al., 2019).

Coercive control is a deprivation of liberty and crime fueled by sexual jealousy and infidelity paranoia (Stark, 2007). It is a "course of conduct crime . . . similar to harassment rather than as an incident-specific assault" (Stark, 2009, p. 1515). It is not another type of IPV, but it is the atmosphere and environment that drives IPV. With this level of power and control over another person, the perpetrator may not need physical violence to achieve his ends. In the context of coercive control, the woman becomes a hostage more than a partner. She is isolated, intimidated, and entrapped. This is the environment she lives in and the atmosphere she breathes. A woman victim is deprived of her liberty, dignity, autonomy, and equality (Stark & Hester, 2019). Couples counseling or family therapy for the hostage and the hostage taker does not make sense and is never safe in this context.

23.6 High-risk factors: Assessment and management

Due to their manipulative ways, image management, and victim blaming, perpetrators of IPV skillfully work professionals into collusion. Collusion is a real risk in this work. It still confounds us that many domestic violence interveners and responders, including courts, can still underestimate the risk that these men pose. Without being alarmist or dramatic, we believe that abusers are high risk, some are higher risk, and there are those that are at the highest risk. Risk assessment, although an inexact science, can, with other sources of data, give us a better understanding of the likelihood of IPV recidivism and escalation. We do not have the space here to elaborate on risk assessment, but there are some key points to be made.

Any resistance to screening for IPV, particularly in organizational settings, must be overcome. IPV screening needs to be a component of any intake and psychosocial assessment of all couples beginning couples or family therapy. This kind of screening needs to be undertaken discreetly and sensitively, with privacy for both parties. This will likely increase the opportunities for women to disclose their experiences of abuse and access support. Second, women's advocacy services must be available and further developed.

High-risk factors, what we call the lethal Ss, include:

- separation (actual or pending)
- stalking
- sexual assault
- strangulation
- suicidality of the offender

Amongst others they are, taken together, indicators of extreme danger and even potential fatalities. These need to be assessed by experienced and well-trained professionals and responded to appropriately (Campbell et al., 2009). Ignoring these risk factors or being unaware of them can have catastrophic consequences for victims and families. These are dangerous patterns of behavior driven by coercive control that often precede domestic homicide (Myhill & Hohl, 2019). As such, these are serious criminal behaviors, not therapeutic matters.

For practitioners who are assessing whether to work with couples where you may suspect coercive control and abuse, risk assessment needs to be undertaken. Questions need to be asked before proceeding: What is the context of the couple's coming to therapy? What is the history of their relationship? What is the intention of each party? What has been the effect of being in this relationship for both? Who is afraid of whom? Who is in need of protection? What might be the deleterious impact on her of proceeding with couple therapy? Fear is an important determinant of abuse, and the emotional and physiological impact of fear can be devastating on the victim (Valliere, 2020).

A simple acronym we use in our training for this assessment is CHIEF – where we explore the context, history, intention, effects, and fear in the partners. The following questions may best be asked in case conferencing with your supervisor or referring agency or professional (and not with the couple in the same room ever). This is a kind of structured professional judgment approach to assess levels of risk and to identify who the aggressor is in the relationship. The shame, self-blame, and guilt a victim may experience are clear indicators that conjoint therapy should not proceed (Valliere, 2020). Alternatively, referrals to domestic violence services and men's domestic violence intervention programs may well be in order.

23.7 Recommendations for practitioners

The following recommendations are to support practitioners in understanding risk, safety, accountability, and unintended consequences of therapeutic work in IPV. Practitioners need to be reflective practitioners, especially when there may be a suspicion of working with a couple where there is an abuser and a victim (Thompson & Pascal, 2012; Martin, 2016).

- Sign up for domestic and family violence intervention training as a prioritized and ongoing component of your professional development.
- Learn how to undertake safe and sensitive interviewing that is IPV and trauma informed, with victim/survivors and with perpetrators of violence.
- Understand the importance and need of safety planning with her and the children.
- Understand and implement accountability policies and practices into your work with men who may be IPV offenders, to avoid exoneration of and collusion with him. This will focus on staff and client safety.
- Understanding that working with perpetrators can be unpredictable and volatile, with unintended consequences.
- Be an active member of your local coordinated community responses. Learn how to undertake risk identification, assessment, and management.
- Have police, women's shelter, women's domestic violence services, and men's domestic violence intervention program contacts available for you, your service, and your clients. Contact and consult with them as the needs arise.
- Know what you don't know about IPV and do something about that. We need to be humble enough to admit that "we don't know what we don't know," and sometimes what we think we know, may not be certain.
- Whatever we do or do not do with victim/survivors and offenders can have serious unintended consequences. We need to work in a critically reflective way so as to counter unintended consequences as far as possible.

23.8 Recommendations for supervisors

Therapists who are self-aware of their own values, family history of trauma and violence, and their mental and physical reactions during sessions can potentially be more capable in understanding and identifying IPV and the dynamics of power and control. Consequently, this increases the ability to ensure safety and stability within the chosen treatment modality. The role of the supervisor is to support the therapist in reflecting clearly on the relationship with their patient and to provide clarity on the dynamics of power and control, and the violence present in the couple and/or family system, to allow an informed decision on whether to continue with family therapy and/or couple intervention. When working with couple counselors and family therapists, supervisors always need to be cognizant of when this kind of therapeutic intervention is contraindicated. Supervision in the face of unpredictability and risk of further violence necessitates conversations including safety, doubt, and risk (Vetere & Sheehan, 2017). High-risk IPV cases are of this kind. Supervisors should be focused on the following:

- Ensure supervisees are practicing ethically, especially focusing on the principle of doing no harm. The best of therapeutic intentions can lead to unforeseen and dangerous outcomes for victim/survivors.
- Safety must be prioritized for clients and for staff.
- Reflective practice must be always asking safety and accountability questions.
- Ensure that organizational processes and policies hold offenders accountable, prioritize victim safety, are connected to a coordinated community response to IPV, and recognize the risk of unintended consequences.
- Consult with IPV specialists and women's advocates, if there is any suspicion of IPV or if it becomes apparent that there is IPV in couples and families on your caseload.
- Be connected to a coordinated community response to IPV in your community.
- Understand your role and responsibilities in information sharing in the coordinated community response.
- Understand the risk of vicarious trauma and working with supervisees to manage vicarious trauma. We pay a price for the stories we hear in IPV work.

23.9 Conclusion

As we have been alerted for more than 30 years now, couples counselors and family therapists who do not work with an IPV and trauma-informed lens are like "Red Cross workers visiting the P.O.W. camp asking, 'How are they treating you?' as the guards stand by. She is a prisoner; he is a guard; and we – the well-meaning helper – won't be there to ensure her safety after the visit" (Carlin, 1989, cited by Kaufman, 1992, p. 237). Training and education in responding to and interventions for IPV and domestic violence generally must be a mandatory requirement for all couples/family therapists if this work is going to be an ethical, safe, and accountable profession in the intervention space. Couple counsellors and family therapists must know their limits of competency and when Goldner's moral discourse and a criminal justice response needs to replace therapy in IPV cases (1999). Otherwise, family therapy will be risky business, and family therapists run the risk of offender-collusive practice, which is an always and escalating unsafe practice for victim/survivors. With high-risk offenders, where there is evidence of coercive control and high-risk markers for violence, our advice is not to proceed with caution but not to proceed at all with couple counseling or family therapy, at this time of elevated risk. Know your limits and know the risks.

References

Babcock, J. C., Armenti, N. A., & Warford, P. (2017). The trials and tribulations of testing couples-based interventions for intimate partner violence. *Partner Abuse*, *8*(1), 110–124. https://doi.org/10.1891/1946-6560.8.1.110

Brown, J., & James, K. (2014). Therapeutic responses to domestic violence in Australia: A history of controversies. *Australian and New Zealand Journal of Family Therapy*, *35*(2), 169–184. https://doi.org/10.1002/anzf.1053

Buzawa, E., Buzawa, C., & Stark, E. (2017). *Responding to domestic violence: The integration of criminal justice and human services* (5th ed.). Sage Publications.

Campbell, J., Webster, D., & Glass, N. (2009). The danger assessment: Validation of a lethality risk assessment instrument for intimate partner femicide. *Journal of Interpersonal Violence*, *24*, 4653–4674. https://doi.org/10.1177/0886260508317180

Downes, J., Kelly, L., & Westmarland, N. (2019). 'It's a work in progress': Men's accounts of gender and change in their use of coercive control. *Journal of Gender-Based Violence*, *3*(3), 267–282. https://doi.org/10.1332/239868019X15627570242850

Gondolf, E. W. (2012). *Batterer intervention systems: Issues, outcomes, and recommendations*. Sage Publications. https://doi.org/10.4135/9781452229263

Goldner, V. (1999). Morality and multiplicity: Perspectives on the treatment of violence in intimate life. *Journal of Marital and Family Therapy*, *25*(3), 325–336. https://doi.org/10.1111/j.1752-0606.1999.tb00251.x

Hearn, J. (1998). *The violences of men: How men talk about and how agencies respond to men's violence to women*. Sage Publications Ltd. https://doi.org/10.4135/9781446279069

Henning, K., & Holdford, R. (2006). Minimization, denial, and victim blaming by batterers: How much does the truth matter? *Criminal Justice and Behavior*, *33*(1), 110–130. https://doi.org/10.1177/0093854805282322

Heyman, R. E., Slep, A. M. S., Giresi, J., & Baucom, K. J. W. (2023). Revisiting "ill will versus poor skill": Relationship dissatisfaction, intimate partner violence, and observed "communication skills deficits." *Family Process*, *62*(3), 1233–1252. https://doi.org/10.1111/famp.12834

Hurless, N., & Cottone, R. R. (2018). Considerations of conjoint couples therapy in cases of intimate partner violence. *The Family Journal*, *26*(3), 324–329. https://doi.org/10.1177/1066480718795708

Johnson, M. (2006). Conflict and control: Gender symmetry and asymmetry in DV. *Violence Against Women*, *12*, 1003–1018. https://doi.org/10.1177/1077801206293328

Johnson, M. (2008). *A typology of DV intimate terrorism, violent resistance, and situational couple violence*. Northwestern University Press.

Karakurt, G., Dial, S., Korkow, H., Mansfield, T., & Banford, A. (2013). Experiences of marriage and family therapists working with intimate partner violence. *Journal of Family Psychotherapy*, *24*(1), 1–16. https://doi.org/10.1080/08975353.2013.762864

Kaufman, G., Jr. (1992). The mysterious disappearance of battered women in family therapists' offices: Male privilege colluding with male violence. *Journal of Marital and Family Therapy*, *18*(3), 233–243. https://doi.org/10.1111/j.1752-0606.1992.tb00936.x

Kaufman, M. (2007). The construction of masculinity and the triad of men's violence. In J. Schiffman, L. O'Toole, M. Edwards, & M. L. K. Edwards (Eds.), *Gender violence: Interdisciplinary perspectives* (pp. 33–55). New York University Press.

Kimmel, M. S. (2002). "Gender Symmetry" in domestic violence: A substantive and methodological research review. *Violence Against Women*, *8*(11), 1332–1363. https://doi.org/10.1177/107780102762478037

Lamb, K., Forsdike, K., Humphreys, C., & Hegarty, K. (2022). Drawing upon the evidence to develop a multiagency risk assessment and risk management framework for domestic violence. *Journal of Gender-Based Violence*, *6*(1), 173–208. https://doi.org/10.1332/239868021X16366281022699

Lamb, S. (1991). Acts without agents: An analysis of linguistic avoidance in journal articles on men who batter women. *American Journal of Orthopsychiatry*, *61*(2), 250–257. https://doi.org/10.1037/h0079243

Martin, S. P. (2016). Making practice inclusive in gender-based violence work. *International Journal of Human Rights in Healthcare*, *9*(3), 174–184. https://doi.org/10.1108/IJHRH-09-2015-0029

Myhill, A., & Hohl, K. (2019). The "Golden Thread": Coercive control and risk assessment for domestic violence. *Journal of Interpersonal Violence*, *34*(21–22), 4477–4497. https://doi.org.ezproxy.usq.edu.au/10.1177/0886260516675464

Nancarrow, H., Thomas, K., Ringland, V., & Modini, T. (2020). *Accurately identifying the "person most in need of protection" in domestic and family violence law (Research report, 23/2020)*. ANROWS.

Neale, J. (2018). Abused women's perceptions of professionals' responses: Valued support, or collusion with perpetrator? *Journal of Gender-Based Violence*, *2*(3), 411–427. https://doi.org/10.1332/239868018X15366982612051

Oka, M., & Whiting, J. B. (2011). Contemporary MFT theories and intimate partner violence: A review of systemic treatments. *Journal of Couple & Relationship Therapy, 10*(1), 34–52. https://doi.org/10.1080/15332691.2011.539173

Prilleltensky, I., Rossiter, A., & Walsh-Bowers, R. (1996). Preventing harm and promoting ethical discourse in the helping professions: Conceptual, research, analytical, and action frameworks. *Ethics & Behavior*, *6*(4), 287–306. https://doi.org/10.1207/s15327019eb0604_1

Sardinha, L., Maheu-Giroux, M., Stöckl, H., Meyer, S. R., & García-Moreno, C. (2022). Global, regional, and national prevalence estimates of physical or sexual, or both, intimate partner violence against women in 2018. *The Lancet (British Edition)*, *399*(10327), 803–813. https://doi.org/10.1016/S0140-6736(21)02664-7

Scott, K. L., & Jenney, A. (2023). Safe not soft: Trauma- and violence-informed practice with perpetrators as a means of increasing safety. *Journal of Aggression, Maltreatment & Trauma*, *32*(7–8), 1088–1107. https://doi.org/10.1080/10926771.2022.2052389

Stark, E. (2007). *Coercive control: How men entrap women in personal life*. Oxford University Press.

Stark, E. (2009). Rethinking coercive control. *Violence Against Women*, *15*, 1509–1525. 10.1177/1077801209347452.

Stark, E., & Hester, M. (2019). Coercive control: Update and review. *Violence Against Women*, *25*(1), 81–104. https://doi.org/10.1177/1077801218816191

Thompson, N., & Pascal, J. (2012). Developing critically reflective practice. *Reflective Practice*, *13*(2), 311–325. https://doi.org/10.1080/14623943.2012.657795

Tutty, L. M. (2023). "Looking back, the program kept me alive": Women's impression of counseling for intimate partner violence, women therapy. *Women & Therapy*, *47*(1), 129–155. https://doi.org/10.1080/02703149.2023.2167309

Valliere, V. N. (2020). *Understanding victims of interpersonal violence: A guide for investigators and prosecutors* (1st ed.). Routledge. https://doi.org/10.4324/9780367823245

Vetere, A., & Sheehan, J. (Eds.). (2017). *Supervision of family therapy and systemic practice*. Springer. https://doi.org/10.1111/1467–6427.12233

24

SERIOUS ILLNESS AND DISABILITY

Helping couples meet the challenges

John S. Rolland

Illness and disability are universal experiences in families. The variations in these experiences are when in our lives they will occur, under what conditions, how serious they will be, and how long they will last. What is perhaps most important is how the experience of serious health conditions will affect couple and family bonds and shared hopes and dreams. There is substantial evidence for the mutual influence of family and couple functioning, health, and physical illness (Gilliss et al., 2019; Hagedoorn et al., 2008) and the usefulness of couple and family-centered interventions with chronic health conditions (Hartmann et al., 2010; Martire et al., 2010; McDaniel et al., 2014; Shields et al., 2012). After a brief overview of a family systems-based model, some of the key challenges for couples are discussed (Rolland, 1994, 2018; Ruddy & McDaniel, 2015).

24.1 Family systems illness model

Most couples and families lack a psychosocial map for the challenges of serious health conditions. How can we organize this complex landscape in a manner that is helpful to families and clinical practice? The family systems illness (FSI) model (Rolland, 2016, 2018, 2019) provides a useful framework for assessment and treatment with families dealing with a range of serious and chronic illness and disability (see Rolland [2018] for useful resources, practice guidelines, and case examples). The FSI model is grounded in a strengths orientation, viewing family relationships as a potential resource and emphasizing possibilities for resilience and growth (Walsh, 2016). Seeing the family as the interactive focal point, this approach attends to the systemic interaction between an illness and family that evolves over time. The quality of "fit" between the psychosocial demands of a particular condition over time and the family style of functioning and resources is a prime determinant of successful versus dysfunctional coping and adaptation.

The FSI model focuses on three dimensions of experience: (1) a psychosocial typology of chronic conditions, (2) major time phases in their evolution, and (3) key family system components (see Figure 24.1) (Rolland, 2018). In addition to communication processes and organizational/structural patterns, particular emphasis includes family and individual life course development in relation to the time phases of a disorder, multigenerational legacies related to illness and loss, and belief systems (including influences of culture, ethnicity, race, spirituality, and gender).

DOI: 10.4324/9781003536765-28

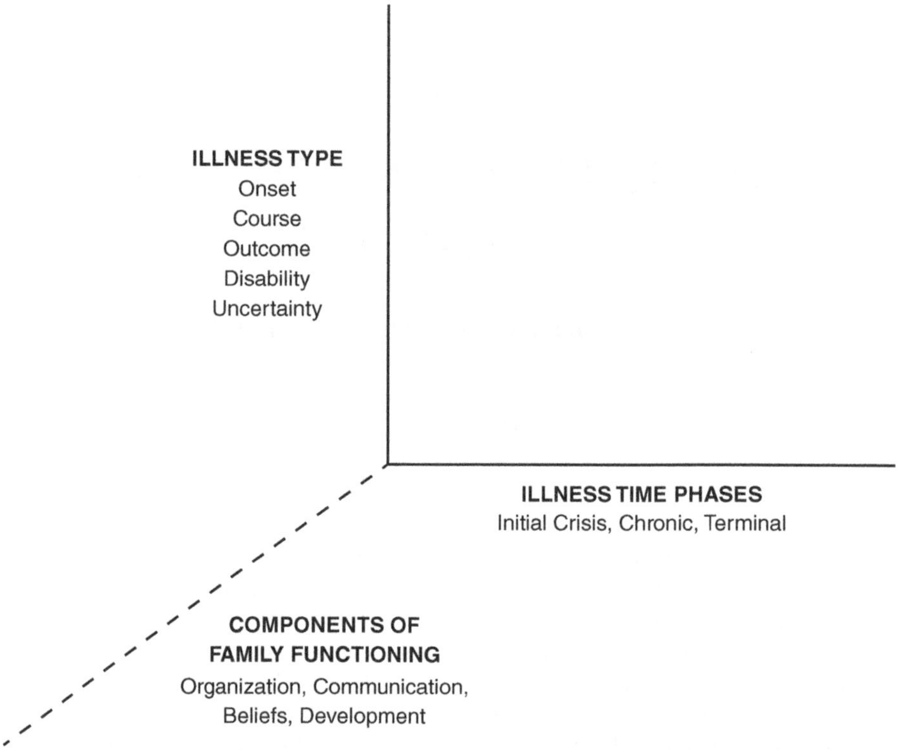

Figure 24.1

24.2 Psychosocial types of illness

Standard disease classification is based on purely biological criteria clustered to establish a medical diagnosis and treatment plan, rather than the psychosocial demands on patients and their families. I have proposed a different classification scheme that provides a better link between the biological and psychosocial worlds and thereby clarifies the relationship between chronic illness and the family. The goal of this typology is to define meaningful and useful categories with similar psychosocial demands for a wide array of chronic illnesses affecting individuals across the lifespan. Illness patterning can vary in terms of (a) onset (acute vs. gradual), (b) course (progressive vs. constant vs. relapsing), (c) outcome (fatal vs. life-shortening vs. non-fatal), (d) type and degree of disability, and (e) level of uncertainty about its trajectory (Rolland, 2018, 1990).

24.3 Illness time phases

Too often, discussions of coping or dealing with a major health condition approach illness and disability as static states and fail to address the evolution of illness processes over time. The concept of time phases provides a way for clinicians and families to think longitudinally and to understand chronic illnesses as ongoing processes with normative landmarks, transitions, and changing demands. Each phase poses psychosocial challenges and developmental issues that may require different strengths, attitudes, or changes for family adaptation. Core psychosocial themes in the natural history of chronic disease can be organized into three major phases: *initial crisis phase*, *chronic phase*, and *terminal phase*. Critical transition periods link the three time phases. These are times during which families reevaluate the appropriateness of their previous coping and adaptation methods in the face of new illness and disability-related challenges.

24.4 Multigenerational developmental lens

A multigenerational developmental framework encompasses salient prior illness experiences. It addresses the interweaving of major illness, family, and individual members' life course phases over time.

First, it is vital to understand what each partner brings from past multigenerational experiences with illness and disability (types of health condition) and major life stressors (e.g., poverty, divorce, migration). Key questions include: (1) How did the family organize itself? (2) What did each partner learn (strengths and vulnerabilities)? and (3) What are the learned differences among partners as they face the current health condition? Just as there can be stories of illness-related resilience in a partner's background, unresolved or traumatic illness experiences can compromise a partner's emotional response to a current health condition (Walsh, 2023). Second, it is essential to grasp where the initial crisis phase of the current illness or disability lands in both each partner's individual development and their family life cycle. A partner's heart attack would be particularly disruptive if it occurred when a couple is raising small children. Third, we need to have a framework to understand the ongoing interaction of the health condition with individual and family development as the illness evolves over time. The FSI model provides a conceptual lens for this process (Rolland, 2018, 2016).

Transition periods in either the illness, a family member's individual development, or family unit development are particularly important. For instance, consider a couple, living with one partner's diabetes, that want to start a family. They would need to shift their lens from a day-to-day living with diabetes to one that took account of diabetes over a roughly 20-year timeframe with the uncertainties of disease progression or genetic factors. For a transition into chronic illness, a diagnosis of multiple sclerosis in one partner could seriously compromise their ability to co-parent effectively. For the healthy partner, the resulting increase in parenting demands could coincide with caregiving for the ill spouse.

24.5 Health beliefs

When illness strikes, families strive to create meaning for the illness experience that promotes mastery. Clinicians' appreciative inquiry into beliefs is a powerful foundation for collaboration with patients and families (Rolland, 2018; Wright & Bell, 2009). As part of early consultations, particularly during the initial crisis phase, it is useful to inquire about key family beliefs that shape each partner's meaning-making, purpose, and coping strategies. This includes health beliefs about (a) normative illness experience; (b) ethnocultural, racial, and spiritual beliefs and dominant societal norms that may influence partners' values, concerns about health and illness, and their pathways in healing; this involves potential differing views about open communication, who is part of the caregiving system, and normative illness rituals (e.g., funeral, healing); (c) meanings attached to symptoms by a family, ethnic group, religion, or the wider culture, such as chronic pain; (d) mind-body relationship, mastery, control, and acceptance; (e) assumptions about what caused an illness and what can influence its course and outcome; (f) multigenerational factors that have shaped a family's health beliefs and response to illness; and (f) anticipated nodal points in individual, family, and illness development when health beliefs will likely be strained or may need to shift.

Inquiry regarding causal attributions that invoke blame or guilt are particularly important. For instance, blaming a spouse for one's heart attack ("your nagging gave me a heart attack") holds the spouse responsible for the heart attack and potentially a fatal recurrence. As in the following case vignette, sometimes such beliefs do not emerge until a crisis transition in an illness.

24.6 Case illustration

Lucy and Tom, a young couple, have one child, Susan, aged 5, who is terminally ill with leukemia. The pediatric oncologist has offered the parents a choice between an experimental treatment with a low probability of success or halting treatment. Tom's position is: "Let's stop; enough is enough." Lucy, on the other hand, felt: "We must continue; we can't let her die." The couple cannot reach an agreement, and the physician is immobilized. He requests a consultation for the couple. When asked: "How do you each try to explain or make sense of how your daughter got leukemia?", critical stories emerge. Tom basically sees it as bad luck. Lucy, however, has a very different belief. During her pregnancy with Susan, Lucy's father had a heart attack and died several months later from a second episode. This was a time period of great stress for Lucy, which she felt adversely affected Susan's intrauterine life. After Susan's birth by uncomplicated delivery, Lucy still mourned the loss of her father and felt that her grief affected the quality of her attachment with Susan and led to a hidden depression in her infant. Furthermore, Lucy had read research linking depression with a lowering of the effectiveness of the immune system, which could in turn decrease normal surveillance and clearing of cancer cells from the body. She believed this combination of factors caused her child's cancer and that if she had been a more competent mother, the disease never would have developed. Lucy said she had never told this story to anyone, including her husband, because no one had ever asked, and she was very ashamed. She had hoped for a cure, so that the whole issue could be resolved. She could not accept stopping treatment because, to her, it meant that Susan's death would then be her fault.

24.7 Summary of goals of relationally oriented consultation

- Emphasize that all family members are affected by the strains and challenges of living with a major illness and address the immediate emotional and practical needs of the patient and family members.
- Provide information about the illness and treatment and ways family members can be helpful.
- Provide family psychoeducation regarding a psychosocial understanding of the particular illness over time in relation to family expectations, offering practical management guidelines; this includes helping the family understand the illness in longitudinal and developmental terms: how different phases of the illness might affect plans and dreams for the patient, family members, and the family unit.
- Elicit history and information that may be vital to diagnosis and treatment decisions, including the family's multigenerational experience with illness and loss that may hinder or facilitate current coping and adaptation.
- Facilitate communication about the illness and treatment-related and caregiving issues and decisions.
- Understand the cultural and spiritual beliefs that guide the family; this is essential to fostering culturally sensitive collaborative care and helping the family make meaning of the illness experience.
- Identify high-risk, multi-stressed patients and families needing more intensive follow-up care.

- Educate the family about the usefulness of periodic family-centered consultations (psychosocial check-ups) and brief interventions at nodal points and transitions in the illness course and in the patient's, other family members' or family's development.

24.8 Helping couples meet the challenges

One of the most important marriage vows we make requires us to care for a partner "in sickness and in health," yet most of us celebrating a wedding have little idea what life together with an illness would mean. Chronic disorders can have devastating consequences for couples. To master the challenges, they must maintain a viable, balanced relationship while caring for an ill partner and coping with the uncertainties of planning and achieving normative life cycle goals despite the threat of loss. A partner's serious condition powerfully challenges couples' relationship rules and boundaries.

Couples' intimacy functions within a comfort zone that evolves over their life course. Their relationship processes determine whether this comfort zone allows intimacy to grow with the seasons of life or to become constricted and erode. Like other life challenges, illness and disability offer an opportunity for relationship growth and pose the risk of deterioration. Illness onset forcefully challenges the emotional and physical boundaries of a couple's relationship. The condition is an "uninvited guest" that must be incorporated into the couple's lives. Its psychosocial type determines the nature and demands of this "intruder" and how it will develop and make its presence felt over time. A severe disability, such as a spinal cord injury, always has an effect on a relationship. A relapsing condition (e.g., disc disease) does so intermittently. Cancers in remission may not require daily caregiving, but the undercurrent of threatened loss can nonetheless permeate the couples' lives.

24.9 My versus our shared challenge

Seeing the challenge of illness or disability from a shared "we" perspective is fundamental. Couples who engage in conjoint coping, exemplified by the use of the word "we" or "our" to describe an illness and its challenges, experience less psychological distress. Affirming a "we" perspective is perhaps the greatest preventive measure for all the other relationship imbalances. When illness strikes, defining the problem as the exclusive domain of the patient will inevitably distort a couple's relationship. Focus on the highly technical and medical aspects of the patient's condition around the initial diagnosis and crisis phase promotes framing the problem as the ill partner's, potentially marginalizing the other partner. Optimal couples' functioning depends largely on the willingness of both partners to challenge this fundamental assumption.

One woman described how her relationship with her husband, who had had amyotrophic lateral sclerosis (ALS), a serious, degenerative, neurological disorder, became more distant over the years. Finally, a marital crisis forced them to reconsider the basic beliefs that had been tacitly agreed upon in the initial crisis phase. She said:

> We never really acknowledged the fact that Bill had a terminal illness. We never talked about the fact that I would die someday too, maybe before him. Because we never discussed these key issues, our relationship became hopelessly unbalanced. He felt entitled, and I felt it was my role to satisfy his needs. Only when our relationship came to the brink of collapse did we deal with these assumptions, which had guided our behavior for so many years. We needed to contemplate death together to reestablish our intimacy. Our last year together was our closest. So many problems could have been avoided if only someone had guided us early on.

24.10 Communication challenges

A long-term health condition and threatened loss present powerful challenges to a couple's communication skills. Despite research that supports mutual sharing, couples coping with illness or disability often develop constrained communication in the mistaken desire to "protect" a loved one (Weingarten, 2013). The couple's comfort zone and patterns regarding openness will affect the functioning of the rest of the family system. Levels of personal disclosure that may have been functional before a disorder often become inadequate; discussions about living with threatened loss may represent new territory.

I suggest that a couple discuss important illness-related issues that include the following:

- Understanding the illness and its psychosocial demands over time
- Beliefs about who or what caused the disorder and what can affect its course
- How to live with uncertainty and threatened loss
- Personal and relationship priorities
- The roles of patient and caregiver
- How to maintain a balanced, mutual relationship
- Living wills and advance directives concerning a possible terminal phase

One couple facing the husband's terminal cancer found the quality of their relationship enormously enhanced by early discussions about limiting life-saving efforts in the terminal phase. It gave the husband a sense of control over his death that reduced unbearable uncertainties and enabled him to focus his energies on living. It reduced his wife's fears about having to make life-and-death decisions without knowing his true feelings. To foster a balanced position, I always suggest that both partners discuss their desires, such as about treatment in the terminal phase, and draw up a living will. While acknowledging the immediacy of the ill partner's situation, I try to minimize differences between the two partners along with the illusion that loss is a concern of the patient alone.

As part of my consultative work with couples, I propose that each partner make two lists of illness-related topics: (1) topics that they would like to discuss, but believe the partner would not, and (2) topics they thinks should be off limits and why. In the second step, the partners share their lists with each other either alone or in a consultation session. Typically, to their pleasant surprise, they discover a significant overlap in what they want to discuss. This exercise facilitates the next step of choosing specific previously restricted areas to discuss. Common reasons for keeping to oneself include tentativeness about exploring new territory, concerns about hurting the partner or worsening the condition, and fears that the relationship will not survive being open with each other in certain areas. If certain topics are going to be restricted, couples should consider the consequences and reach a mutual decision.

With progressive neurocognitive conditions (e.g., dementia), proactive early communication is particularly important. It maximizes the affected partner expressing their wishes and preferences early on before they may no longer be able to effectively communicate (Rolland, 2017).

24.11 Maintaining healthy boundaries with patient-caregiver roles

The imbalances inherent in the long-term caregiving and dependency needs of an ill partner can foster challenges concerning hierarchy, power, and reciprocity. A couple's expectations for shared, balanced role functions often become impossible to maintain when one partner has a significant disability. A new version of balance needs to be negotiated. Sustaining intimacy depends largely on establishing viable caregiving boundaries. Even the strongest relationships are strained by the discrepancies in shifts between two forms of relating: patient-caregiver and equal partners (non-illness aspects of their relationship). These boundaries may need to shift with the illness phase (as with progressive conditions like Alzheimer's disease) (Rolland, 2017) or periodic illness flares (e.g., multiple sclerosis or asthma).

It cannot be stressed enough that the long-term viability of a couple's relationship may depend on openly discussing and legitimizing both partners' needs. Facilitating this process early on promotes resilience and helps reduce the later emergence of ambivalence, escape fantasies, and survivor guilt. Because of gender-based socialization, women as healthy partners are more likely to accept limits on their own needs and development stoically and without question. With serious illness, couples adapt best when they can acknowledge different needs for separateness and togetherness. The healthy partner may need respite time and space apart from the demands of the illness. Sometimes, this includes maintaining an activity (e.g., hiking) that used to be a shared one that is no longer possible for the partner with disability. A healthy partner may minimize their own needs to protect the ill one from experiencing further emotional pain. This often leads to strong resentment and enormous strain on the overall relationship viability over the long haul of living with chronic conditions. Couples can strive to develop new interests and activities that are spared from a progressive physical disability, such as listening to music, or in the case of neurocognitive impairment taking walks together.

With dementia, the healthy spouse often is the first to recognize that their partner is "no longer the same person" and that they can no longer connect on a deeper level that was a vital aspect of their shared bond. With progressive dementia, clinicians can help the healthy spouse's often lonely, exhausting struggle to continue to revise their experience of intimacy, or help them redefine the relationship as a caregiving one, often with a sense of relief. We can affirm the healthy partner's experience and help them grieve these incremental losses (Rolland, 2017, 2018).

24.12 Sexuality

Chronic disorders can affect a couple's sexuality in a variety of ways (Sipski & Alexander, 1997). Yet, a discussion of the condition's possible effects on sexuality and inquiry about any actual impact on a couple's sexual intimacy is often lacking (Hughes et al., 2011; Scheinkman et al., 2022). Many times when I inquire about this, couples will state, "This is the first time we were asked." This is particularly true for older couples. As clinicians, when we don't ask, we reinforce the couple's hesitancy in bringing up any sexual difficulties. Unfortunately, this hesitancy fosters a barrier in communication between the healthcare provider and couple and inhibits healthy communication between partners. Couples need clear information about how a particular disease or disability can be expected to affect sexuality physiologically (disease and medical treatment effects) and psychosocially.

24.13 Conclusion

When facing the risks and burdens of chronic illness or disability, the most resilient couples can harness their experiences to improve their quality of life. Couples can achieve a healthy balance between accepting limits and promoting autonomy and connectedness.

A serious illness or brush with death provides an opportunity to confront catastrophic fears about loss. This can lead partners to develop a better appreciation and perspective on life, which results in clearer priorities and closer relationships (Walsh, 2016). Seizing opportunities can replace procrastination or passive waiting for the dreaded moment. Serious illness, by emphasizing life's fragility and preciousness, provides couples with an opportunity to heal unresolved issues and develop more close and caring relationships. For illnesses in a more advanced stage, clinicians should help couples emphasize the quality of life by defining goals that are more immediately attainable and that enrich patients' everyday lives.

Living well with the strains and uncertainties of illness can be a monumental challenge. The family systems illness model offers a way to address this challenge and makes the inevitable strains more manageable. Attending to the psychosocial demands of different kinds of conditions over time within a multigenerational, developmental, and belief system context can help provide a strength-based framework – a common language that facilitates collaborative, creative problem-solving and quality of life for couples facing illness, disability, and loss.

References

Gilliss, C. L., Pan, W., & Davis, L. L. (2019). Family involvement in adult chronic disease care: Reviewing the systematic reviews. *Journal of Family Nursing*, *25*(1), 3–27. https://doi.org/10.1177/1074840718822365

Hagedoorn, M., Sanderman, R., Bolks, H. N., Tuinstra, J., & Coyne, J. C. (2008). Distress in couples coping with cancer: A meta-analysis and critical review of role and gender effects. *Psychological Bulletin*, *134*(1), 1–30. https://doi.org/10.1037/0033–2909.134.1.1

Hartmann, M., Bazner, E., Wild, B., Eisler, I., & Herzog, W. (2010). Effects of interventions involving the family in the treatment of adult patients with chronic physical diseases: A meta-analysis. *Psychotherapeutics and Psychosomatics*, *79*, 136–148. https://doi.org/10.1159/000286958

Hughes, A., Hertlein, K., & Hagey, D. (2011). A MedFT-informed sex therapy for treating sexual problems associated with chronic illness. *Journal of Family Psychotherapy*, *22*, 114–127. https://doi.org/10.1080/08975353.2011.577689

Martire, L. M., Schulz, R., Helgeson, V. S., Small, B. J., & Saghafi, E. M. (2010). Review and meta-analysis of couple-oriented interventions for chronic illness. *Annals of Behavioral Medicine*, *40*(3), 325–342. https://doi.org/10.1007/s12160-010-9216-2

McDaniel, S., Doherty, W., & Hepworth, J. (2014). *Medical family therapy and integrated care* (2nd ed.). American Psychological Association Press.

Rolland, J. S. (1990). Anticipatory loss: A family systems developmental framework. *Family Process*, *29*(3), 229–244. https://doi.org/10.1111/j.1545–5300.1990.00229.x

Rolland, J. S. (1994). In sickness and in health: The impact of illness on couple's relationship. *Journal of Marital & Family Therapy*, *20*(4), 327–347. https://doi.org/10.1111/j.1752-0606.1994.tb00125.x

Rolland, J. S. (2016). Chronic illness and the life cycle. In M. McGoldrick, N. Garcia-Preto, & B. Carter (Eds.), *The expanding family life cycle: Individual, family, and social perspectives* (5th ed., pp. 430–454). Pearson.

Rolland, J. S. (2017). Neurocognitive impairment: Addressing couple and family challenges. *Family Process*, *56*(4), 799–818. https://doi.org/10.1111/famp.12316.

Rolland, J. S. (2018). *Helping couples and families navigate illness and disability: An integrated approach*. Guilford Press.

Rolland, J. S. (2019). The family, chronic illness, and disability: An integrated practice model. In B. Fiese, M. Celano, K. Deater-Deckard, E. Jouriles, & M. Whisman (Eds.), *APA Handbook of Contemporary Family Psychology* (Vol. 2). APA Publications. https://doi.org/10.1037/0000100-006

Ruddy, N., & McDaniel, S. H. (2015). Couple therapy and medical issues: Working with couples facing illness. In A. S. Gurman, J. Lebow, & D. Snyder (Eds.), *Clinical handbook of couple therapy* (5th ed.). Guilford Press.

Scheinkman, M., Iasenza, S., Ludwig, K., Cronin, T., Lemor, S., & Papp, P. (2022). Sexual intimacy and aging: An integrative framework to promote intimacy resilience in couple therapy. *Family Process*, *61*(1), 1–20. https://doi.org/10.1111/famp.12767

Shields, C., Finley, M., Chawla, N., & Meadors, P. (2012). Couple and family interventions in health problems. *Journal of Marital and Family Therapy*, *38*(1), 265–281. https://doi.org/10.1111/j.1752–0606.2011.00269.x

Sipski, M. L., & Alexander, C. J. (Eds.). (1997). *Sexual function in people with disability and chronic illness: A health professional's guide*. Aspen Pub.

Walsh, F. (2016). *Strengthening Family Resilience* (3rd ed.). Guilford.

Walsh, F. (2023). *Complex and traumatic loss: Fostering healing and resilience*. Guilford.

Weingarten, K. (2013). The "cruel radiance of what is": Helping couples live with chronic illness. *Family Process*, *52*, 83–101. https://doi.org/10.1111/famp.12017

Wright, L. M., & Bell, J. M. (2009). *Beliefs and illness: A model for healing*. 4th Floor Press.

25

CHILDREN AND PARENTS IN CONTEMPORARY FAMILIES

From boundary ambiguity to the construction of new belongings

Salvatore D'Amore

25.1 Introduction

Every transition (be it anticipated or unforeseen) in the life cycle of the family system has the effect of challenging the structural and symbolic organization of that system (Andolfi, 2015; Dupont, 2022; McGoldrick & Shibusawa, 2012). Events such as separation, divorce, reconstitution, migration, adoption, or a parent's coming-out are family transitions that demand significant adaptation on the part of both children and parents. This adjustment process can prove especially stressful, in line with the complexity of the personal and social contexts involved.

Unexpected family transitions may lead to relational losses, generating confusion, bewilderment, uncertainty, and loss of the affective meanings associated with previous family connections (D'Amore & Scarciotta, 2011; D'Amore et al., 2011). For example, a child undergoing parental separation and the subsequent formation of a stepfamily may feel overwhelmed by the extent of loss and the rapid pace of family change (Browning & Artelt, 2012; Papernow, 2013). In this scenario, the child's symptoms may function to decelerate the formation of a new family structure that appears to cater more to the parents' needs, rather than their own.

Estrangement from a parent, grandparent, extended family member, familiar place, or network of significant relationships (e.g., at school, among friends, in the neighborhood, in a sports group) may intensify children's emotional bond with the physically absent person or group. This may result in the heightened psychological presence of the significant other(s), despite their physical absence. The more restricted the child's physical access to the estranged figure(s), the more they will access them psychologically (Betz & Thorngren, 2006; Boss, 1983). This may result in persistent thoughts about the absent figure(s), accompanied by worry, fear, sadness, and sometimes anger. Consequently, the child must learn to navigate the contradiction between physical absence and psychological presence (Boss, 1999) to make sense of their experience of loss.

Relational losses may also alter family boundaries: a 7-year-old child might wonder if he still constitutes a family with his parents, despite no longer living together as a single unit. He may also question whether his father, who now has a child with his new partner, will continue to fulfill his paternal role, as before (Boss, 1977; Bullens & D'Amore, 2012). Will the new family system erase the previous one, or might it augment and potentially transform it? During the family reconstitution process, the same child may also ponder who now belongs to his family and who no longer does.

DOI: 10.4324/9781003536765-29

Sometimes children, unable to tolerate the ambiguity of loss and new family boundaries, idealize the pre-separation family and fail to acknowledge the difficulties that led to its separation. Such nostalgic embellishment may result in the dysfunctional past becoming more reassuring (because it is familiar) than the present (which seems devoid of a future), in which children may perceive adults as confused, clumsy, and occasionally lost.

Children in single-parent households may seek to include significant others (e.g., grandparents, uncles, cousins, teachers, friends) in their psychological family. Similarly, children born into queer families through the involvement of significant others (e.g., gamete donors, surrogates) must also navigate the question of who constitutes their psychological family (Carone, 2021).

In this chapter, we propose the ambiguous boundaries theory as a useful framework for understanding the emotional experiences of children across diverse family forms. In particular, we focus on queer families as a case study to explore the affective dynamics associated with ambiguous relational frontiers. Finally, we suggest approaches for family therapists working in this context.

25.2 The diverse family boundary ambiguity

Family boundaries are essential for defining and preserving the unique identity of a family system. The concept was first proposed by Minuchin (1974, 1985), referring to the rules that determine which individuals participate in family relationships and in what capacity. The concept continues to significantly influence the theory and practice of couple and family therapy.

Boss (2016, p. 37), a family therapist and researcher, enriched the family boundary concept by describing *boundary ambiguity* as a "state in which family members are uncertain about their perceptions about who is in or out of the family and who is performing what roles and tasks within the family system." Green and Mitchell (2008) also proposed a related concept of *relational ambiguity*, referring to the uncertainty involved in defining affective relationships for which roles and boundaries lack social support and acceptance.

Family boundary ambiguity can arise in situations of psychological or physical absence. Both forms of absence are likely to manifest in an unresolved or "frozen" sense of loss that is difficult to manage (Boss, 2016). In the classical concept of mourning, the psychic task is to detach from the lost object (Freud, 1917) in order to invest in something new. However, in the context of ambiguous loss, the "object" that must be mourned is the mourning itself (Boss & Carnes, 2012; D'Amore, 2015), so that individuals may come to accept and manage the paradoxical (physical/psychological) absence/presence. In this vein, Boss (1999, 2016) created and developed the ambiguous boundaries theory, emphasizing its significance for understanding family life cycle transitions. Through these changes, the family assumes a new, ambiguous nature that, if not effectively managed, can lead to stress and relational dysfunction.

The construction of new families involves not only identity loss but also the acquisition of new bonds and, at times, relational enrichment – particularly when the transition from the former family to the current one is managed in a functional manner that is attentive to the needs of both child and adult members. Thus, boundary ambiguity, while ubiquitous, is not necessarily problematic (Bullens & D'Amore, 2013). Rather, the impact of this ambiguity depends on its degree and intensity, as well as the psychic capacity of children and families to cope with physical absence.

When a family develops a clear narrative, alongside rituals and rules concerning boundaries, the boundaries become clearer and more defined. Conversely, when a family fails to articulate who is part of the family system, which members are physically absent, the extent of family members' participation in relationships, and the roles and functions of family members, ambiguous boundaries emerge. This ambiguity creates confusion about who is inside or outside the family and affects family identity (i.e., external recognition as a family), particularly in cultural, religious, and sociopolitical contexts in which the new family formation lacks normative models. Ambiguity can lead to stress and psychological rigidity, while also lowering resilience, purpose, mastery, flexibility, and adequacy. In extreme situations, it may generate immobility, loss of hope, and psychological suffering. This perspective aligns with Boss's (2012) notion of resilience as the capacity to tolerate ambiguity in family roles and boundaries.

25.3 Relationship ambiguity and boundaries in queer families

Although relational ambiguity is a typical stressor across all types of couples and families (Green & Mitchell, 2008), its effects may be amplified for those based on queer relationships. In many sociopolitical and religious contexts, queer families and couplings are not considered valid psychological systems. This makes the construction and management of their boundaries a particularly complex process. Due to heterosexist and heteronormative prejudices, queer couples and families may struggle to be recognized. Their legitimacy is often questioned, and their existence may be attacked, both directly and indirectly. Moreover, the lack of socially valued and accessible models for queer couples and families adds to their uncertainty around which family script to follow in their boundary negotiations.

Coleman and Ganong (2022) note that, while queer families experience the same boundary ambiguity dynamics as families headed by opposite-sex partners (resulting from, e.g., separation or divorce), they also face unique boundary-related challenges, arising from discrimination and inadequate social support. In queer families, the experience of relational ambiguity is likely to extend beyond the immediate family and also include wider systems of affective and instrumental support (e.g., families of choice). Additionally, in some queer families, one or both adults may have a child from a previous relationship, resulting in situations where only one adult has a biological or legal connection to the child. Thus, within the same family, there may be parents and children who are biologically/legally related or unrelated. Moreover, some parents and children may be physically absent though psychologically present, and some parents may not be recognized as valid parents in their own right, due to their queerness. Finally, some parents in queer families may not be recognized as "important," because they lack biological or genetic ties, or gestational or legal adoption links to their children. These parents may feel transparent or ignored, as if they do not exist in the family. For this reason, queer families present an interesting case of ambiguous boundary management.

25.4 Boundary ambiguity in queer families

25.4.1 Case illustration

Jenny (aged 41 years) and Charlotte (aged 36 years), both French, have been a couple for ten years. Together, they are raising Irma (aged 7 years). Irma was born in Belgium with the help of in vitro fertilization (IVF) and an anonymous donor. Charlotte is Irma's biological parent. Jenny and Charlotte are now seeking therapy because their family and relationship are in crisis. According to Jenny, the parental asymmetry caused by Charlotte's biological connection to Irma has become unbearable.

Since childhood, Charlotte always wished to have a child, while Jenny did not. Charlotte expressed her parental aspirations early on in her relationship with Jenny, who, despite not sharing this wish, decided to support her. After Irma's birth, Jenny, contrary to her expectations, became very involved in child care and increasingly claimed a co-parenting role. This shift caused significant tension within the couple.

Jenny now feels invisible and unacknowledged within the family, as well as in her family of origin, because she is not Irma's biological parent. Irma enjoys a privileged and at times fusion-like relationship with Charlotte, but she greatly appreciates Jenny, who has always taken good care of her. However, Irma does not call Jenny "Mom," as Jenny would like.

Irma draws a picture of her family that highlights ambiguous family boundaries. The picture shows a little girl straddling her mother's shoulders, with both mother and daughter depicted as happy. Irma explains that there is another "mother" in the family, but she is absent from the drawing because she has "gone on a trip." By omitting Jenny, Irma has excluded her from her psychological family, even though Jenny is actually present in Irma's real life.

Irma does not want Jenny to accompany her to school, because she does not consider Jenny her "mom." Even Irma's teachers refer to Jenny as her mother's "friend" and prefer to communicate important matters only to Charlotte. Jenny, who is becoming increasingly dissatisfied and angry, is threatening to separate from Charlotte. Charlotte, on her part, feels inadequate due to her perceived failure to reassure Irma. Simultaneously, she feels powerless in the face of Jenny, whom she struggles to recognize as a co-parent, despite appreciating her as a partner. Irma, who seems aware of the couple's crisis, has found a solution: at home, she calls Jenny by her name, but when alone she refers to her as "little mommy."

This case vividly illustrates a child's experience of ambiguous family boundaries in a queer family. In our clinical experience (D'Amore et al., 2022), we have identified seven systemic patterns of queer couples and families, concerning ambiguous boundaries.

25.4.2 Seven Patterns

The first pattern highlights the lack of clear and consistent sociocultural patterns of being and partnering within queer couples and families. Unlike heterosexual couples, who have the benefit of a traditional script with explicit and implicit rules (whether they choose to follow this script or not), there is no set way of being for queer couples and families. This lack of a model or script can lead to relational confusion and conflict. In therapy, tools such as the genogram and sociogram can reveal and activate intersystemic resources, strengthening queer individuals' sense of belonging to both the tri-generational family and the broader community and sociopolitical context. In more detail, these tools facilitate the deconstruction of tri-generational and sociocultural models of couple and family formation to make them more inclusive and respectful of differences.

Second, in queer couples, a coming-out differential (i.e., where one partner is out and the other is not) may affect relational and intimate boundaries. Where such a differential is present, the couple may exist in certain contexts but not in others, in order to protect the non-out partner. This situation refers to a second type of ambiguous loss (Boss, 1999), whereby the partner exists physically but not psychologically, because their true identity is hidden or denied. In therapy, it may be helpful to explore both the non-declared partner's "good reasons" for not coming out and the declared partner's experiences of frustration and helplessness in the face of this situation. If children are involved, the therapy should also explore their experiences of confusion and stress related to the parents' coming-out differential, in order to activate multiple resources.

Third, a lack of legal recognition of the non-biological parent may stiffen parental and family boundaries. Non-biological (or non-legal) parents may be rejected or excluded from various settings (e.g., their partner's family of origin, schools, medical environments, institutional settings) because they have no biological or legal connection to their children. Thus, they may suffer from rigid and exclusionary boundaries, which is likely to manifest in significant stress. Therapy with these parents should aim at enhancing the couple's recognition of the co-parenting role. Additionally, sessions with parents' families of origin may help increase overall consideration of the non-biological parent's role and functions in the family. Deconstructing the perceived primacy of the biological bond in child care and reinforcing co-parenting as a critical factor in growth may also be important.

Fourth, homonegativity (both internal and external) may also affect the boundaries of queer couples by attacking the couple and family identity. In some contexts, queer couples and families may make themselves "invisible" or use "dissimulation strategies" to defend themselves from this stigma. Importantly, therapy should aim at recognizing situations of homonegativity and their effects on children's and parents' thoughts, feelings, emotions, and relationships. Additionally, family therapy should facilitate open dialogue between children and parents about negative experiences. This is especially relevant, as children may be confronted with homonegative or heterosexist behaviors as early as kindergarten. Therapy aimed at recognizing homonegative sources, developing coping strategies, and maintaining open communication in the family may activate intersystem resources and foster greater resilience in queer families.

Fifth, ethnicity, culture, and religion may significantly contribute to boundary ambiguity in queer families, influencing the quality of relational functioning. In some countries and cultures, establishing a same-sex relationship or having children with a same-sex partner are considered unconscionable or sinful acts, or symptoms of disease. Consequently, when interacting with their countries of origin and the cultural and religious patterns and codes of those countries, queer couples and families may cease to psychologically "exist." Fears of losing familial love and respect or the support of religious communities may compel queer parents to hide the true nature of their relationships and family formation processes. Therapists working with these parents should support their development of coping skills to manage this ambiguity and build intersectional identities capable of integrating diverse aspects.

Sixth, the use of assisted reproduction (e.g., IVF with an anonymous donor, adoption, gestational surrogacy) may exacerbate boundary ambiguity in queer families by introducing complex relational dynamics. Intended parents (couples or single parents) must navigate new relationships with gamete donors and gestational carriers who may be physically absent but psychologically present. Later on, both children and parents must decide who to include within the family boundaries. For example, a child of queer parents may ask: Is the surrogate my mother? Is the donor my father? Who is part of my family? Therapy should support queer families in asking these questions and potentially broadening the family boundary to include significant others. Adoption of a circular family model may help children feel more integrated into an affective system that values diversity beyond the biological frontier.

The seventh and final pattern describes the impact of single parenthood on boundary ambiguity. Traditional family models define a biparental family unit composed of parents of different genders. Thus, a single parent (be they queer or not) may face societal expectations to be paired with an opposite-sexed partner with whom they will raise a child. Failure to enact this model may trigger social references to a supposedly absent "father" or "mother," which may generate significant discomfort and stress. Therapy should facilitate single parents' efforts to socialize their family and reduce boundary ambiguity, to better support their children.

25.5 Conclusions

New families often break with previous family, cultural, social, and religious traditions. As a result, they may experience loss, ambiguous boundaries, and stress due to the lack of inclusive socio-cultural models that respect their couple and family diversity. Drawing on Boss (2016) and Dahl and Boss (2020) regarding therapeutic work with loss and ambiguous boundaries, we propose the following strategies for therapeutic work with these families.

First, therapists should support families in increasing their capacity to manage and cope with external and internalized negative stigma, by both strengthening existing resources and finding and developing new ones. With respect to internalized stigma, therapeutic work should assist families in reconstructing the process through which negative representations have been internalized, while also helping them disconnect from these representations.

Second, therapists should help queer families reconstruct a new couple and family identity that integrates past and present. Specifically, the therapy should support the family in creating its own definition of family (i.e., who is part of it, who is not), including family roles and functions. In doing so, it should help families value and achieve flexibility and sharing in the exercise of couple and parental roles. Finally, the therapy may aim at the creation of new symbols and rituals to define and maintain the psychic space of the new family (Imber-Black & Roberts, 1992).

Third, therapists should support queer families in their efforts to accept and embrace the paradox of simultaneous presence/absence in the family and emotional and affective ambivalence. Viewing emotional dissonance as a resource, rather than a problem, may help queer couples and families navigate critical phases more easily, increase their tolerance, and find solutions based on dialogue and compromise.

To facilitate this work, the concept of loss and ambiguous boundaries should be integrated into the training of family psychologists and psychotherapists. Working on themselves, future therapists may find it valuable to reconstruct the map of loss and ambiguous frontiers within their own families of origin. Have they been able to construct alternative meanings for the ambiguities they experienced? Have they been able to handle ambiguity, seeing it as a resource, rather than a problem? Are they curious and tolerant of the ambiguities experienced by others? Can they identify ways in which gender role representations were constructed within their original family and sociopolitical contexts, and how these representations continue to influence their gender and sexual identities?

If therapists can see ambiguity as an opportunity to generate new questions, integrate different perspectives, and create new horizons for growth, the therapeutic context can become a welcoming place for clients of diverse identities.

References

Andolfi, M. (2015). *La terapia familiare multigenerazionale, Strumenti e risorse del terapeuta*. Raffaello Cortina.

Betz, G., & Thorngren, J. M. (2006). Ambiguous loss and the family grieving process. *The Family Journal, 14*(4), 359–365. https://doi.org/10.1177/1066480706290052

Boss, P. (1977). A clarification of the concept of psychological father presence in families experiencing ambiguity of boundary. *Journal of Marriage and the Family*, 141–151. https://doi.org/10.2307/351070

Boss, P. (1983). Family separation and boundary ambiguity. *International Journal of Mass Emergencies & Disasters, 1*(1), 63–72. https://doi.org/10.1177/028072708300100103

Boss, P. (1999). *Ambiguous loss: Learning to live with unresolved grief.* Harvard University Press.

Boss, P. (2012). Resilience as tolerance for ambiguity. In D. S. Becvar (Ed.), *Handbook of family resilience* (pp. 285–297). Springer.

Boss, P. (2016). *Loss, trauma and resilience*. W.W. Norton & Company.

Boss, P., & Carnes, D. (2012). The myth of closure. *Family Process, 51*(4), 456–469. https://doi.org/10.1111/famp.12005

Browning, S., & Artelt, E. (2012). *Stepfamily therapy: A 10-step clinical approach*. American Psychological Association. https://doi.org/10.1080/08975353.2011.551099

Bullens, Q., & D'Amore, S. (2012). Papa n'est pas mort: Clinique des séparations et perspectives de spéciation des familles divorçantes. *Thérapie Familiale, 33*, 123–136. https://doi.org/10.3917/tf.122.0123

Bullens, Q., & D'Amore, S. (2013). Pertes et reconstructions identitaires au sein des familles monoparentales et recomposées: La question des spécificités processuelles. *Thérapie Familiale, 34*, 355–369. https://doi.org/10.3917/tf.133.0355

Carone, N. (2021). *Le famiglie omogenitoriali. Teorie, clinica e ricerca*. Raffaello Cortina.

Coleman, M., & Ganong, L. (2022). Boundary ambiguity: A focus on stepfamilies, queer families, families with adolescent children, and multigenerational families: Research. In S. Browning, & B. van Eeden-Moorefield (Eds.), *Treating contemporary families: Toward a more inclusive clinical practice* (pp. 157–186). American Psychological Association. https://doi.org/10.1037/0000280-007

Dahl, C. M., & Boss, P. (2020). Ambiguous loss: Theory-based guidelines for therapy with individuals, families, and communities. *The Handbook of Systemic Family Therapy, 4*, 127–151.

D'Amore, S. (2015). Le deuil du deuil: Transitions critiques, pertes et nouvelles identités du familial. *Thérapie Familiale*, *36*, 29–39. https://doi.org/10.3917/tf.151.0029

D'Amore, S., Browning, S., DiNardo, D., & Methikalam, B. (2022). Boundary ambiguity: A focus on stepfamilies, queer families, families with adolescent children, and multigenerational families: Clinical applications. In S. Browning & B. van Eeden-Moorefield (Eds.), Treating contemporary families: Toward a more inclusive clinical practice (pp. 157–186). American Psychological Association. https://doi.org/10.1037/0000280-007

D'Amore, S., Gresse, K., & Pauss, V. (2011). Pertes et ressources dans la construction des nouvelles familles: Le cas des familles recomposées. *Thérapie Familiale*, *32*, 111–128. https://doi.org/10.3917/tf.111.0111

D' Amore, S., & Scarciotta, L. (2011). Los(t)s in transitions: How diverse families are grieving and struggling to achieve a new identity. *Journal of Family Psychotherapy, 22*(1), 46–55.

Dupont, S. (2022). Le cycle de vie familial: Un concept essentiel pour appréhender les familles contemporaines. In S. Dupont (Ed.), *Le cycle de vie des familles contemporaines* (pp. 21–39). Érès. https://doi.org/10.3917/eres.dupon.2022.01.0021

Freud, S. (1917). Trauer und melancholie. *Internationale Zeitschrift für Ärztliche Psychoanalyse*, *4*(6), 288–301.

Green, R. J., & Mitchell, V. (2008). Gay and lesbian couples in therapy: Minority stress, relational ambiguity, and families of choice. In A. S. Gurman (Ed.), *Clinical handbook of couple therapy* (pp. 662–680). Guilford Press.

Imber-Black, E., & Roberts, J. (1992). *Rituals for our times: Celebrating, healing, and changing our lives and our relationships*. Harper Collins.

McGoldrick, M., & Shibusawa, T. (2012). The family life cycle. In F. Walsh (Ed.), Normal family processes: Growing diversity and complexity (4th ed., pp. 375–398). Guilford Press.

Minuchin, P. (1985). Families and individual development: Provocations from the field of family therapy. *Child Development*, 289–302.

Minuchin, S. (1974). *Families & family therapy*. Harvard University Press.

Papernow, P. L. (2013). *Surviving and thriving in stepfamily relationships: What works and what doesn't*. Routledge.

PART 4

Trauma, loss, and resilience

The healing power of the extended family and community

26

CHANGING THE SUBJECT

From system to culture to the event

Vincenzo Di Nicola and John Farnsworth

26.1 Introduction: "All the systemic therapists have become philosophers"

In his Preface to *Reason and Violence* by British anti-psychiatrists R. D. Laing and David Cooper, French philosopher Jean-Paul Sartre (1964) wrote:

> I am convinced that your efforts will bring us closer to the day when psychiatry will, at last, become a truly *human* psychiatry.

"Changing the subject" addresses a predicament, a crisis. In response, we propose a new model, one drawn from philosophy and new to clinical work. The crisis we address is profound: a crisis of the subject, an individual and collective crisis, one that may involve a rupture of politics and of values where, afterwards, a way of living may be radically altered. In the language of philosopher Alain Badiou (Badiou & Tarby, 2013), it is an *evental site*: an uncertain moment of rupture with unforeseeable outcomes. Writing under the shadow of the war in Israel-Gaza and the Russian invasion of Ukraine, we can only reflect on how apt such a phrase is. Under these conditions, people daily face the liminal, the uncertain, the impossible: extreme experiences of human predicament. Others, elsewhere, suffer different forms of predicament: experiences of mental illness, relational distress, and social suffering.

Nothing is closer to the work of a therapist across all our clinical professions than change, however disturbing and distressing. With our combined decades of experience, however, we want to address change from the perspective of philosophy. When Vincenzo told Italian systemic family therapist Matteo Selvini about his doctorate in philosophy, he replied: "All the systemic therapists have become philosophers" (personal communication, 2012). Systems theorists and therapists, in fact, have always been philosophical, including Matteo's mother and Vincenzo's teacher, Mara Selvini Palazzoli. Palazzoli's work with the Milan Team of systemic family therapy was grounded in the philosophy of Whitehead and Russell, Ashby's cybernetics, and von Bertalanffy's general systems theory, as their ground-breaking volume *Paradox and Counterparadox* attests (Selvini Palazzoli et al., 1978).

As philosophers talking to therapists, we want to change the subject. Like the title of Vincenzo's first book, *A Stranger in the Family* (Di Nicola, 1997, 1998), "changing the subject" is a polysemous phrase with multiple meanings. "Change" concerns both theorists and therapists, while "subject"

DOI: 10.4324/9781003536765-31

refers ambiguously to both the subject as a frame of reference as well as to persons as subjects of therapy. To change the subject is a full response to a predicament, a crisis.

We understand, as practicing clinicians, how many theories compete to describe and address such predicaments. This cacophony of voices is joined by the crisis of psychiatry: a profession unsure whether it is a social science, a part of the humanities, or a branch of medicine or neuroscience (Di Nicola, 2021; Di Nicola & Stoyanov, 2021; Dhar & Di Nicola 2021; Stohlman-Vanderveen & Di Nicola, 2021). This chapter proposes a model of profound change in response. Following Badiou (Badiou & Tarby, 2013), we describe this as evental therapy. It identifies three gaps in relational theory and therapy, offers a potentially comprehensive response on many levels (individuals, families, culture, and society) and, by way of a case vignette, illustrates how such a model operates in practice.

26.2 Overview: Systems – culture – event

Three words guide us through the issues we will cover in family psychotherapy, sociocultural studies, and philosophy: *systems – culture – event.* We will unpack them in seven parts, starting with four questions to change the subject of what therapy can be about:

1. Why do we still call them *family dynamics* (rather than systemic properties)?
2. Why do we still call them *mental disorders* (rather than relational distress)?
3. Why do we still call them *systems* (rather than family cultures)?
4. *Three gaps* in relational theory and therapy (why do we still talk about change rather than event)?
5. *Predicament* and its aliases (rupture, crisis, evental site)
6. *The event* (the conditions for real change)
7. Antonella's story: *evental analysis and therapy*

26.2.1 Why do we still call them family dynamics?

Family therapy "changed the subject" by changing the frame of therapy, placing the individual in a family context, invoking *systems theory*. French philosopher Jean-Luc Nancy (2000) stated this beautifully, arguing that to be means "being with," that the individual's "I" does not take priority over the collective "we," and that existence is "co-existence."

Family therapy sees the individual as part of a family and the family as a *system.* Family therapy led to the crystallization of relational theory and therapy, in which the family is "the crucible of experience" (Di Nicola, 1985a). *Result:* Family therapy places the child in the context of the family and calls that a *system.* Yet, family therapy does not take its own theory seriously enough and still refers to family dynamics. If systems theory and family therapy have supplanted psychodynamic psychotherapy (Freud coined this word, inspired by *thermodynamics*), then we should call them *systemic properties* with their *interactions and relations*.

26.2.2 Why do we still call them mental disorders?

According to systems theory, an individual's symptoms are an expression of *relational dysfunction* and *systemic misalignments. Result:* Family therapy places the symptom in the context of the system and calls that *relational distress.* If individual symptoms are an expression of systemic dysfunction and relational distress, why does family therapy still call them mental disorders and not *relational disorders*?

26.2.3 Why do we still call them systems?

Cultural family therapy changed the subject by placing the family itself in the larger context of culture. *Result:* Cultural family therapy places the family in cultural context and calls that the family's culture. Cultural family therapy basically asks: Why do we still call them systems? (Di Nicola, 1985a, 1997, 1998, 2004). Systems theory expanded psychodynamic theory by adding interactions and relationships, changing the language of therapy (Di Nicola, 1993). By taking anthropology and cultural psychiatry seriously in family therapy, cultural family therapy expands systems theory and speaks to the deeper notion of culture (Di Nicola, 1985b). Accordingly, we should speak about each family's culture as an expression of a larger culture in which it is embedded and for which it becomes the vehicle of expression and transmission. These approaches "changed the subject" of our work – both the *identified patient* and the family *system* or *culture*.

26.2.4 Three gaps in relational theory and therapy

Now, we propose to "change the subject" again, identifying *three gaps* in relational theory and therapy: a *theory of the subject* (how we define persons), a *theory of therapy* (how to conduct therapy), and most important, a *theory of change* (how change or innovation occurs) (Di Nicola & Stoyanov, 2021). Although we have many competing theories of these tasks, there is no consensus among theorists and therapists in any "psy" discipline, from psychology to psychiatry to psychotherapy. To address these gaps, we invoke the *event* as a new model, based on the philosophy of Alain Badiou (Badiou, 2009; Badiou & Tarby, 2013).

26.2.5 Predicament and its aliases

Predicaments are unstable and unpredictable human situations that have a moral charge to them (Di Nicola, 1997). "Moral" here means that they cannot simply be reduced to the *facts* of the situation: There is a *value* attached to or at risk in a predicament. As Canadian singer-songwriter Leonard Cohen (1994) puts it in a song, "There is a crack in everything. That's how the light gets in." Furthermore, predicaments cannot be reduced to psychological distress, psychiatric disorders, or even relational problems; nonetheless, *as human problems*, mental illness, relational distress, and social suffering are also predicaments. When it persists, a predicament becomes a rupture or breach, inducing a crisis.

Faced with a *predicament* (a rupture leading to a crisis), two potential outcomes arise: *trauma or event* – things open up or they close down (Di Nicola, 1996, 2012, 2017, 2018b). We will examine another alias for predicaments: In Badiou's theory of the event, the place where they occur is an *evental site*. Now, against the longstanding "relativism" of the social sciences where nothing is absolute and the newer "spectrum" approach to psychiatric disorders in *DSM-5* where mental and relational phenomena are conceived dimensionally on a spectrum of severity, this approach to trauma and event is *categorical*. It's an event or it's nothing; if you are traumatized, it means that essential aspects of your life shut down. So, while predicaments are saturated in complexity and subjectivity, considerations of partial or contextual truths, and the nuances of what might have been and what could still be, their rupture yields a breakthrough or a breakdown. It is not surprising then that such a rupture, leading to trauma or event, draws a line, dividing life into "before" and "after" (Cook et al., 2005; Di Nicola, 2012, 2017).

Robert Jay Lifton (2012), an American trauma psychiatrist, echoes Amichai's poem, "Open Closed Open," to note that survivors of disasters and genocides may open out, porous and permeable to novation, or close down, emptied and evacuated, in a desubjectivized, traumatized state.

26.2.6 The event

By drawing a clear line, marking a "before" and an "after," the event changes a *world* – as an individual (*subject*), a family (*system, culture*), or an entire community (*the world*). Thus, the event speaks to the very definition of *being* – beyond attitudes, behavior, cognitions, and emotions – to what *being-in-the-world* means.

The event cannot be chosen, determined, or created: it simply happens. If you must believe in some reigning principle, believe in a radical *contingency*, pure chance. This evacuates all such popular notions as "things that are meant to be" to comfort us, a "dark fate" or "bright destiny" that awaits us, and a "guiding hand" or "guardian angel" that directs or protects us. Now, philosophy calls the place where it happens an *evental site*. The reason this is so appealing to systems theorists is that it is a near-alias for what cultural family therapy (Di Nicola, 1997, 1998) calls a *predicament*; Sartre wrote about *situations* in his novels and plays and in his existential philosophy. In fact, it's what makes his work so accessible (Blakewell, 2016), and clinically, you may encounter it as a *crisis*.

We can locate and name the elements of an *evental site*. It's like identifying stressors or understanding the social determinants of health (CSDH, 2008) and adverse childhood experiences (Felitti & Anda, 2010). In the clinic, it is still somewhat surprising that people do not easily connect such stressors with their current predicament (evental theory explains that as *pseudo-event*, our term for "resilience"). Nonetheless, the potential event that arises from the evental site is not an element of the site – not among the predisposing, precipitating, prolonging, or protective factors of their predicament or situation. The event is something different, something new; Badiou calls this process *novation* in French – let's call it *innovation* (Badiou & Tarby, 2013).

What does this mean? Event is neither determined nor predictable. It is not something that is "there"; it cannot be, as philosopher Richard Rorty (1989) said of social solidarity, "found waiting." It is something that emerges from the things that are there and are occurring in a life. Relational theory and therapy are congruent with the great Neapolitan thinker, Giambattista Vico (1668–1744), the founder of constructivist epistemology, who wrote: *Verum esse ipsum factum*, "What is true is precisely what is made" (Vico, 1710/2015).

Consequently, we cannot tell in advance. As clinicians, we can only rely on systemic thinking, relational engagement, and close fidelity to the subject's circumstances to enhance the prospect of innovation. If people in therapy, in daily life, or in politics decide that what was cooking there all along is just fine and don't want something new, that's an option. However, it isn't an event, it isn't novel, and – *it isn't change*. Psychoanalysis calls that "resistance" or a "flight into health." Systems theory calls that "homeostasis." Popular psychology calls that "resilience." And evental analysis calls that a *pseudo-event*.

Why is resilience a pseudo-event in our model? As Didier Fassin and Richard Rechtman (2009) documented in their critical study of trauma, resilience is a way of explaining gaps in trauma theory since not everyone succumbs to incidents that are potentially traumatizing. Resilience can be a denial of trauma. Yet wide-eyed optimism won't protect us from its impacts. In *Candide*, Voltaire's satire of the crisis in European worldview following the devastating earthquake in Lisbon in 1755, Professor Pangloss reassures us that, "All is for the best in the best of all possible worlds."

In the logic of scientific research, findings are tested against truth in a four-by-four "truth table" (see Figure 26.1).

We may adapt this to illustrate how evental theory defines true versus pseudo-trauma and event (see Figure 26.2).

A predicament (represented by the entire area of the table in Figure 26.2) may lead to a rupture and hence set the stage for a *true event* or *true trauma*. Things open up or shut down. Now, we may also postulate both *pseudo-trauma* and *pseudo-event* when such a rupture does NOT occur. The concept

Research

True Positive	False Positive
False Negative	True Negative

Figure 26.1

Predicament

True Event *rupture*	Pseudo Event *no rupture*
Pseudo Trauma *no rupture*	True Trauma *rupture*

Figure 26.2

of resilience implies no such break but rather continuity of experience. If there is no break or rupture, then there is no trauma, but there is also no possibility of an event. Hence, no change occurs since nothing new arises.

The three conditions for the event are (1) *being there* to witness the event, (2) *naming* the event, and (3) *fidelity* to the event, which radically changes the subject by identifying with the event. These conditions radically change the subject who identifies with the event. We may go so far as to say, following Badiou (2009), that the event makes the subject. So, to update Sartre (2007) philosophically: *The event precedes the subject*. In a now-famous lecture in 1946, Sartre coined the phrase that became the cornerstone of his existentialism: "Existence precedes essence." What he meant is that being alive comes before any given quality or meaning given to life. Now, what we are saying, inspired by Badiou, is that before you can find meaning and grounding to your life, you must experience an event.

26.3 Contexts, traditions, histories

Evental therapy is a radical therapy: As a practice, it emerges from numerous earlier investigations, debates, and conditions. Here, we outline three that inform it:

- The long investigations of trauma psychiatry and their deep links to philosophical thought; it provides evental therapy with the *coupling of trauma/event* (Di Nicola, 2018b).
- The significance of social and cultural psychiatry, particularly the work of family therapies with their traditions of slow, relational engagement.
- Lastly, the specific thought of Badiou: the symmetry between the event as an opening and trauma as a rupture; the symmetry shapes and informs evental work, complemented by the importance of his truth conditions (Di Nicola, 2017).

In *The Empire of Trauma*, Didier Fassin and Richard Rechtman (2009, p. 6), two French physician-anthropologists, argue that "trauma *is the new language of the event*." This language they see as a conjunction of three emergent fields: "psychiatric victimology, humanitarian psychiatry, and the psychotraumatology of exile." In the process, trauma has long moved beyond psychiatric diagnosis to become "embedded in everyday usage" (2009, p. 6). Not only has it become ubiquitous but, with its transformation, the language of trauma invents new subjects and new conditions. We discern *two trauma communities* – a clinical one and a cultural one (Di Nicola, 2018b). The cultural or literary community assumes the mantle of scientific authority from the clinical community (though undermining its clinical claims) while the clinical community expands its reach through the cultural one in both scholarly journals and social media. This point is taken up forcefully by British literary lion Will Self (2021, p. 24):

> I shall be advancing the heretical notion that trauma as we now understand it is not a timeless phenomenon that has affected people in different cultures and at different times in much the same way, but is to a hitherto unacknowledged extent a function of modernity in all its shocking suddenness.

Self (2021, p. 24) grounds this modern phenomenon in "the ubiquity of traumatogenic technologies in our societies: those of specularity and acceleration, which render us simultaneously unreflective and frenetic."

The reconfiguration of a field of psychiatry as a trauma psychiatry is situated, however, within a rich philosophical archaeology. This relates not simply to Michel Foucault's (1964) early work on madness but through commentaries by Adorno, Lyotard, Agamben, and Badiou. For example, Italian philosopher Giorgio Agamben (2004) describes the modern state, post-Holocaust, as "as a kind of desubjectivation machine" (Smith, 2004). Trauma becomes an apparatus. Desubjectivation involves what Agamben (2007) calls "the destruction of experience" so that, as Jean-François Lyotard observes, "experience becomes nameless" (Hartmann, 2002, p. 1). This destructive apparatus, whether it governs child abuse and other "trauma machines" (Agamben, 2007), has to be dismantled and rendered inoperative. Without it, the predicament (where rupture occurs) shuts down the possibility for states of exception (evental sites) and reduces lives to trauma that cannot be spoken.

In this context, the coupling of trauma/event becomes profound: It is the effort of clinician and subject to name, to transform what has been destroyed. This archaeology allows us to discern from these thinkers' work the components of an evental therapy: the relationships between rupture (predicament, state of exception, evental site), trauma (the destruction of experience, of the very possibility of experience), and event (contingent, unpredictable, undecidable).

These new long, powerful dialogues within phenomenology, psychology, and psychiatry also explore how trauma arises not simply as an individual experience but as distributed phenomena. As Fassin and Rechtman (2009) detail in their ethnography, distributed trauma arise across space and time. As contemporary phenomena, trauma are the sequelae of terrorist attacks, political repression, torture, economic exploitation, and geological or climate disaster. Across time, it is distributed through the long centuries of mental illness and incarceration or the global experience of colonial psychiatric institutions (Di Nicola, 2018b; Farnsworth, 2022, 2024). It is in these contexts that evental therapy is radical: It moves far beyond an individualizing psychology to a subject who may be political, mass, or individual. In such circumstances, the subject is not bounded by the skin of the individual but is defined as a distributed/relational subject.

This philosophical archaeology also enables us to identify the practices of an evental therapy: those that are repeatedly contextual, relational, dialogic (Di Nicola, 2011). In response to Badiou's ontology, one becomes a subject through a tripartite process of recognizing, naming, and being faithful to an event (Di Nicola, 1997, 1998). To do so requires the patient work of contextual, relational, dialogic engagement. Let us also note that, particularly in the world of digital media and collective, online worlds, such subjects are not bounded by the skin of the individual but can be defined as distributed/relational subjects (Farnsworth, 2022).

In these settings, "contextual, relational, dialogic" are quite specific. They mean an individual situated in a community (or a world in Badiou's terms). "Relational" involves encounters: exchanges among subjects in their worlds. "Dialogic" involves encounters and exchanges in the form of language and discourse (Di Nicola, 2018b, p. 36). Commonly, this takes place through the practice of *slow thought* (Di Nicola, 2018a). Relational, dialogic processes are, by their nature, slow; they take time.

"Contextual, relational, dialogic" equally describes the work of social psychiatry and with families across cultures. It is particularly salient to grasp how a social self and its troubles demand recognition and articulation, not just in the Global North but also in the Global South, by employing "southern epistemologies," as Portuguese jurist-sociologist Boaventura de Sousa Santos puts it (2016).

26.4 Case illustration

26.4.1 Antonella: "A stranger in the family"

Recalling the story of Antonella (Di Nicola, 1997, 2021), an Italian immigrant to Canada referred by an Italian family therapist, we conduct an *evental analysis* to examine her *lifeworld* (*Lebenswelt* in German), her search for meaning and identity. Through *evental therapy* (individual, couple, and family meetings), we *bear witness* to the event of her life. Reaching beyond the human world to become a dog breeder, Antonella resolves her ambivalent attachments to become – "at last," as Sartre (1964) said – a *genuinely human subject* with an identity and a purpose in life. Her transformation illustrates the wisdom of British historian Theodore Zeldin's (1994) conclusion that humanity is "a family that has hardly met."

Claudio Angelo is a psychiatrist and family therapist in Alto Adige who referred a young woman in her twenties with symptoms of an eating disorder as she was moving to Canada. "Antonella" was a foundling in Milan, adopted by a middle-class Milanese family. Feeling that she looked vaguely "Asian," she had always felt like a "stranger in the family." Antonella's story was so striking that it became a metaphor for cultural family therapy, inspiring the title of Di Nicola's book (1997, 1998), which he revisited at the Advanced Studies Seminar at Oxford in 2019 (Di Nicola, 2021). Here, we want to focus on her traumas and a possible event.

Her adoptive family also "adopted" the myth of her foreign origins. As a foundling child, her story was profiled in the local papers and, with her supposed Asian looks, her family adopted the myth that her father was an Asian man, perhaps Japanese, who had had a child with a local woman who then abandoned it. Antonio Ferreira's (1964) insightful work on *family myths* is crucial here because myths fill in the gaps where reality is wanting. Furthermore, Antonella played along with her assigned role of a stranger in the family. Even before meeting her family, what was striking about Antonella was the drama of her story. The way she lived and related it was strikingly theatrical, and there was an "as if" quality to her that pioneering psychoanalyst Helene Deutsch (1934) had described to explain women's ability to identify with others, but at the price of "depersonalization" so that they come across as "outwardly normal" but somehow "inauthentic." Relational therapy constructs all of these notions in relational terms originating in early and ongoing family patterns. Together, her adoption as a "foreigner" and her role as a "stranger in the family" undermined the possibility of integrating into her adoptive family and identifying as an Italian. As one of Wajdi Mouawad's (2009) characters complains in his play *Scorched*: "Childhood is a knife planted in your throat. You don't remove it easily."

Antonella's early life may be construed as a failure (abandoned as a foundling, followed by a failure of attachment) and a redirection (given the identity of a foreigner). In philosophical terms, we may call this a *negation* (Di Nicola, 2012; Di Nicola & Stoyanov, 2021). Negations are not merely negative. We reframe the anti-psychiatry movement as "psychiatry against itself," in which each of four leading anti-psychiatrists (Franco Basaglia, Frantz Fanon, Jacques Lacan, and R. D. Laing) negated some aspect of the theory or practice of psychiatry, opening new vistas (Di Nicola, 2012; Di Nicola & Stoyanov, 2021). As painful as it was, the negation of Antonella's identity as an Italian in the country of her birth also created the conditions for her to follow other identifications. Her predicament in her adoptive family led to a crisis in the family. When the opportunity presented itself, she undertook an adventure with an older Canadian man: she entered an evental site. Let's recall – the event cannot be determined or counted among the elements of an evental site. And indeed, her Canadian adventure turns out to be a pseudo-event. Marrying an older Canadian was at best a kind of barter – she got away from her adoptive family, and he got an exotic young companion. They had a "companionate marriage," but it was charmless and lacked any real intimacy, emotional or sexual. Just as she barely knew her adoptive family, Antonella and her husband remained "intimate strangers." The notion of the therapist as director of the family drama (Andolfi & Angelo, 1981) was never more apt than with Antonella's story where – at a distance at least – everyone seemed to be adrift, needing direction. Before we turn to the family sessions, let's do an evental analysis of Antonella's predicament.

26.4.2 Evental analysis

Evental analysis examines a lifeworld. An evental analysis of Antonella's lifeworld recognizes key experiences and names their salience in *evental theory*:

- "*A stranger in the family*" – adoption, estrangement, search for identity, meaning (*evental site*)
- "*The Canadian adventure*" – romantic encounter, falling in love with the idea of Canada, idealized partner (*pseudo event*)
- "*Marital malocclusion*" – no real "contract" for a mutual, intimate relationship; just abstract idealizations that soon descended into conflict (*pseudo trauma*)
- "*Killing me softly*" – in both her adoptive family and her marriage, issues of ambivalent attachment mixed with vague allegations of violence, brusquely followed by denials and self-criticism (*trauma*)
- "*It's a dog's life*" – discovers a love of dogs that is "overdetermined" as Freud said – husky dogs represented Canada and the pure northern frontier; are loyal, dependent, and responsive; she becomes a dog breeder, which gives her a sense of purpose, affection, and by going to dog shows, offers her a social life, essentially for the first time (*event*). The French symbolist poet Arthur Rimbaud (1871/1929) famously proclaimed: *Je est un autre* ("I is another"). In Antonella's world, her identification was displaced not only to another person but also to another species (*event*).

26.4.3 Evental therapy

Evental therapy helps people recognize that they are in a place where something new may arise, leading to change. Antonella's evental therapy included individual, couple, and family meetings. The guiding principles were to work on her *trauma story* (Mollica, 2006) and to bear witness to a possible event of her life. Across many meetings, ranging from practical matters to therapeutic sessions, the critical experiences were the sessions with Antonella's family when they came to Canada, invited by the family therapist.

In the first family session with Antonella's parents and their younger biological daughter, the parents launched into a plaintive sharing of their travails, punctuated by equal parts guilt, regrets, and accusations of their ungrateful adoptive daughter. As Harvard trauma specialist Richard Mollica

(2006) says, the trauma story is a story that must be told. We bear witness to suffering and trauma. What we add to this appealingly simple directive is critical: *it's a story that must be told to someone else*, in a *relational dialogue*, face to face. What makes a dialogue relational? When the relation is part of the dialogue. This is inspired by Mikhail Bakhtin's *dialogism* and has nourished the "narrative turn" in diverse therapeutic schools. Mollica (2006, p. 60) cautions, however, that, "Survivors must be allowed to tell their stories in their own way." We must be "enthusiastic and sensitive listeners" and "never be intrusive" (Mollica, 2006, p. 60). And we know that it is working when new information is released or brought into the relationship. Towards the end of the first session, the parents hinted at the real problems in their family: the explosive behavior of their biological daughter (we'll call her "Circe" for her mercurial temperament), who was unpredictably violent towards her mother. A few days later, they asked for an urgent session to deal with a new episode of violence. The mother arrived with many large bruises over her face, neck, and what was visible of her chest. Circe's violence towards her biological mother unmasked the real trauma, undoing a family myth, and liberating Antonella.

Evental therapy capsule:

- Life is an open work; contingent (random), not predetermined.
  - The event accounts for how new things arise (innovation) out of a predicament (evental site), offering us a philosophically grounded theory of change.
- The event, as part of a grounding ontology or theory of being, is a theory of the subject. Persons become *subjects*, meaning they are "subject to the truth" of the event.
- The event eschews the clinical language of symptoms.
- Evental theory establishes a typology of subjects, and evental analysis identifies them for therapeutic purposes (see Badiou & Tarby, 2013; Di Nicola, 2012, 2018b).
- Evental therapy recognizes when people are in an evental site and prepares them for the event.

26.5 Summary: From the threshold to the event

This chapter posed four questions about the evolution of relational therapy and introduced the event as a way to re-vision change and to propose a new theory and therapy based on the event. Echoing the binary *trauma/event*, evental therapy also reconfigures the history of relational therapy into two phases, *threshold/event* (Andolfi & Di Nicola, 2014; Di Nicola, 2016):

"On the threshold." The work we do with children and their families across cultures as migrants and refugees, and with other marginalized populations, recognizes them as living "on the threshold." Cultural family therapy strives to help them across the threshold (Di Nicola, 1997, 1998).

"The event." Evental therapy asks: What happens when they arrive? Will they wrestle forever with the moral dilemmas and existential dramas of living in a *predicament*, caught "betwixt and between," as anthropologist Victor Turner (1969) wrote about liminal states, neither completely out of their old worlds nor well adapted in their new ones? This is Sisyphus, rolling his boulder up a hill forever, advancing only to restart. This is "symptom relief," taking a painkiller for a migraine you know will relapse. It comes in two extremes of therapy: the "quick fix" of behavior therapy versus the "asymptote" of interminable psychoanalysis. As Freud (1937) quipped, the analysis is over when the analysand realizes it could go on forever. But it would take an event for that realization to occur – not more therapy.

The stakes are mighty and consequential, including the *intergenerational transmission of trauma* where everything becomes a repetition of the past, with no possibility of change or of becoming genuine subjects. In Kafka's (1994) parable, "Before the Law," a man seeks the law at a doorway but in spite of a long wait, giving up everything he has to gain admittance, he is told as he is about to die that the doorway will now close. This is nihilism, "learned helplessness," despair – refusing to seek help because the system is callous, the side effects are unpleasant, or therapists are imperfect people. Again, evental analysis reveals two extremes – to keep knocking your head against a door that never opens to prove that you're untreatable and unworthy, or to knock on every other door you find to prove that the world is incompetent or uncaring. Neither extreme will open the conditions for an event. A critical innovation of evental theory is a new language that permits the rejection of *pseudo-events* ("resilience"), where nothing changes as in Antonella's emigration and marriage, and *pseudo-traumas* (vicissitudes of life), such as her marital dissatisfaction and conflicts, along with a more exacting definition of *trauma* and a more exhilarating embrace of *event.* With Antonella, the trauma turned out to be the hidden and unavowed violence of her sister and its unjust displacement onto herself while the event of becoming a dog breeder was totally unpredictable from her predicament and completely new in her life.

And yet, the same predicament may become an *evental site* out of which a genuine *event* occurs that changes everything: the birth of a wished-for child, the completion of a poem, solving a mathematical theorem, the founding of a new political movement. Each event represents one of Badiou's (2009) four conditions of philosophy: *love, art (poetry), science (mathematics), and politics*. Each one, if it fulfills the three conditions of an event, is accompanied by the embrace of a new identity and the conviction of being authentic and faithful (subjectivation).

Evental analysis and therapy cannot make these things happen, much less guarantee them. Neither can any other form of therapy. Yet, in no philosophy or therapy can this happen passively and without a combination of contingency (or chance) and commitment (or fidelity). What we *can* do is to prepare people for the possibility of an event so that they recognize it when it comes their way; we can encourage them to find the courage to name an event in their lives; and we can accompany and support them to be faithful to the event of their lives and allow that fidelity to the truth to make them a genuine subject, subject to the truth of their event.

References

Agamben, G. (2004). *The open: Man and animal*. Stanford University Press.
Agamben, G. (2007). *Infancy and history: On the destruction of experience*. Verso.
Amichai, Y. (2000). *Open closed open: Poems*. Houghton Mifflin Harcourt.
Andolfi, M., & Angelo, C. (1981). The therapist as director of the family drama. *Journal of Marital and Family Therapy*, 7(3), 255–264. https://doi.org/10.1111/J.1752–0606.1981.TB01377.X
Andolfi, M., & Di Nicola, V. (2014). Dove sta andando la terapia familiare nel mondo? Un dialogo relazionale fra Vincenzo Di Nicola e Maurizio Andolfi. *Terapia Familiare, 106*, 93–111. https://doi.org/10.3280/TF2014–106004
Badiou, A. (2009). *Theory of the subject*. Continuum.
Badiou, A., & Tarby, F. (2013). *Philosophy and the event*. Polity Press.
Blakewell, S. (2016). *At the existential café*. Other Press/Oxford University Press.
Cohen, L. (1994). Anthem. In *Stranger music: Selected poems and songs*. Vintage.
Cook, A., Spinazzola, J., Ford, J., Lanktree, C., Blaustein, M., Cloitre, M., DeRosa, R., Hubbard, R., Kagan, R., Liautaud, J., Mallah, K., Olafson, E., & van der Kolk, B. (2005). Complex trauma in children and adolescents. *Psychiatric Annals, 35*(5), 390–398. https://doi.org/10.3928/00485713-20050501-05
CSDH. (2008). *Closing the gap in a generation: Health equity through action on the social determinants of health. Final report of the Commission on Social Determinants of Health*. World Health Organization.
De Sousa Santos, B. (2016). *Epistemologies of the south: Justice against epistemicide*. Routledge.
Deutsch, H. (1934). On a type of pseudoaffectivity ("As if"). *Internationale zeitschrift für psychoanalyse, 20*, 323–335.

Dhar, A., & Di Nicola, V. (2021, December 22). The crisis in psychiatry and the slow way back: Interview with Vincenzo Di Nicola. Spotlight interview: Rethinking mental health. *Mad in America: Science, Psychiatry and Social Justice*. www.madinamerica.com/2021/12/crisis-psychiatry-way-back-interview-vincenzo-di-nicola

Di Nicola, V. (1985a). Family therapy and transcultural psychiatry: An emerging synthesis. I. The conceptual basis. *Transcultural Psychiatric Research Review*, *22*(3), 151–180. https://doi.org/10.1177/136346158502200301

Di Nicola, V. (1985b). Family therapy and transcultural psychiatry: An emerging synthesis. II. Portability and culture change. *Transcultural Psychiatric Research Review*, *22*(2), 81–113. https://doi.org/10.1177/136346158502200301

Di Nicola, V. F. (1993). The postmodern language of therapy: At the nexus of culture and therapy. *Journal of Systemic Therapies*, *12*(1), 49–62. https://doi.org/10.1521/jsyt.1993.12.1.49

Di Nicola, V. F. (1996). Ethnocultural aspects of PTSD and related disorders among children and adolescents. In A. J. Marsella, M. J. Friedman, E. T. Gerrity, & R. M. Scurfield (Eds.), *Ethnocultural aspects of posttraumatic stress disorder: Issues, research, and clinical applications* (pp. 389–414). American Psychological Association. https://doi.org/10.1037/10555-015

Di Nicola, V. (1997). *A stranger in the family: Culture, families and therapy*. W.W. Norton.

Di Nicola, V. (1998). *Um estranho na família: Cultura, famílias e terapia*. Editora Artes Medicas Sul.

Di Nicola, V. (2004). Famiglie sulla soglia. Città invisibili, identità invisibili. In Andolfi, M. (Ed.), *Famiglie immigrate e psicoterapia transculturale* (pp. 34–47). FrancoAngeli.

Di Nicola, V. (2011). States of exception, states of dissociation: Cyranoids, zombies and liminal people. In *Letters to a young therapist: Relational Practices for the coming community* (pp. 149–162). Atropos Press.

Di Nicola, V. (2012). *Trauma and event: A philosophical archaeology* (Doctoral dissertation). European Graduate School.

Di Nicola, V. (2016, April 9). *From threshold to event: The implementation of cultural family therapy*. Day of Theoretical Lessons, Academy of Family Psychotherapy, Seraphicum Theological Faculty S. Bonaventura.

Di Nicola, V. (2017, November 23). Badiou, the event, and psychiatry, part 1: Trauma and event. *Blog of the American Philosophical Association*. https://blog.apaonline.org/2017/11/23/badiou-the-event-and-psychiatry-part-1-trauma-and-event

Di Nicola, V. (2018a, February 17). Take your time: Seven pillars of a slow thought manifesto. *Aeon*. https://aeon.co/essays/take-your-time-the-seven-pillars-of-a-slow-thought-manifesto

Di Nicola, V. (2018b). Two trauma communities: A philosophical archaeology of cultural and clinical trauma theories. In P. T. Capretto & E. Boynton (Eds.), *Trauma and transcendence: Limits in theory and prospects in thinking* (pp. 17–52). Fordham University Press.

Di Nicola, V. (2021). Antonella – A stranger in the family: A case study of eating disorders across cultures. In D. S. Stoyanov, C. W. Van Staden, G. Wong, M. Stanghellini, & K. W. M. Fulford (Eds.), *International perspectives in values-based mental health practice: Case studies and commentaries* (pp. 27–35). Springer International.

Di Nicola, V., & Stoyanov, D. (2021). *Psychiatry in crisis: At the crossroads of social science, the humanities, and neuroscience*. Springer Nature.

Farnsworth, J. (2022). Mediated psychotherapy, transitional space and cybernetic capitalism. *Ata: Journal of Psychotherapy Aotearoa New Zealand*, *26*(1), 53–71. https://doi.org/10.9791/ajpanz.2022.04

Farnsworth, J. (2024). What is the unconscious? *Ata: Journal of Psychotherapy Aotearoa New Zealand*, *27*(1), 13–30. https://doi.org/10.24135/ajpanz.2024.02

Fassin, D., & Rechtman, R. (2009). *The empire of trauma: An inquiry into the condition of victimhood*. Princeton University Press.

Felitti, V. J., & Anda, R. F. (2010). The relationship of adverse childhood experiences to adult medical disease, psychiatric disorders and sexual behavior: Implications for health care. In R. A. Lanius, E. Vermetten, & C. Pain (Eds.), *The impact of early trauma on health and disease: The hidden epidemic* (pp. 77–87.). Cambridge University Press.

Ferreira, A. J. (1964). Family myths: The covert rules of the relationship. *Confinia Psychiatrica*, *8*, 15–20.

Foucault, M. (1964). *Madness and civilization: A history of insanity in the age of reason* (R. Howard, Trans.). Tavistock.

Freud, S. (1937). Analysis terminable and interminable. *The International Journal of Psychoanalysis*, *18*, 373–405.

Hartmann, G. H. (2002). *The longest shadow: In the aftermath of the holocaust*. Indiana University Press.

Kafka, F. (1994). *The trial*. Penguin.

Lifton, R. J. (2012, May 13). Witness to an extreme century. *165th Annual Meeting of the American Psychiatric Association*.

Mollica, R. F. (2006). *Healing invisible wounds: Paths to hope and recovery in a violent world.* Harcourt International.

Mouawad, W. (2009). *Scorched.* Playwrights Canada Press.

Nancy, J.-L. (2000). *Being singular plural.* Stanford University Press.

Rimbaud, A. (1929). *Correspondance: Lettre du voyant, à Paul Demeny, 15 mai 1871. Text prepared by Roger Gilbert-Lecomte* (pp. 51–63). Éditions des Cahiers libres (Original work published 1871).

Rorty, R. (1989). *Contingency, irony, and solidarity.* Cambridge University Press.

Sartre, J.-P. (1964). Foreword. In R. D. Laing & D. Cooper (Eds.), *Reason and violence – A decade of Sartre's philosophy, 1950–1960.* Tavistock Publications.

Sartre, J.-P. (2007). *Existentialism is a humanism* (J. Kulka, Ed.). Yale University Press.

Self, W. (2021, November 22). A posthumous shock: How everything became trauma. *Harper's Magazine*, 23–34. https://harpers.org/archive/2021/12/a-posthumous-shock-trauma-studies-modernity-how-everything-became-trauma

Selvini, M. (n.d.). Pers. Comm.

Selvini Palazzoli, M., Boscolo, L., Cecchin, G., & Prata, G. (1978). *Paradox and counterparadox: A new model in the therapy of the family in schizophrenic transaction.* Jason Aronson.

Smith, J. (2004). "I am sure that you are more pessimistic than I am . . .": An interview with Giorgio Agamben. *Rethinking Marxism*, 115–124. https://doi.org/10.1080//0893569041000167618б

Stohlman-Vanderveen, M., & Di Nicola, V. (2021, October 8). The crisis of psychiatry is a crisis of being: An interview with Vincenzo Di Nicola. Recently Published Book Spotlight. *Blog of the American Philosophical Association.* https://blog.apaonline.org/2021/10/08/the-crisis-of-psychiatry-is-a-crisis-of-being-an-interview-with-vincenzo-di-nicola/

Turner, V. (1969). *The ritual process: Structure and anti-structure.* Aldine.

Vico, G. (2015). *On the most ancient wisdom of the Italians: Unearthed from the origins of the Latin language: Including the disputation with the Giornale de' letterati d'Italia.* Cornell University Press (Original work published 1710).

Zeldin, T. (1994). *An intimate history of humanity.* Penguin.

27

LOSS AND RESILIENCE THROUGH TURBULENT TIMES

Meaning-making, hope, and transformation

Froma Walsh

27.1 Introduction

We are all living through turbulent times. The experience of profound loss is widespread, from the tragic deaths and upheaval wrought by the COVID-19 pandemic to the collective trauma of environmental disasters, war, and displacement. Children and families have lost precious loved ones; livelihoods and ways of living have been upended. Many families struggle with ongoing multi-stress conditions and deep anxiety about the future. There is an urgent need to address complex and traumatic losses in families, yet most mental health services are individually based and deficit focused. The isolating constraints of the pandemic heightened our awareness that in overcoming adversity, human resilience is relationally based. Supportive family processes and sociocultural resources are essential to heal from losses, adapt to ongoing challenges, and regain the ability to thrive. Vitally important are family beliefs and practices that foster meaning-making, reorient hope, and provide transcendent values that offer spiritual moorings and inspire new purpose, creativity, and positive growth.

27.2 Resilience-oriented systemic practice approach

In the mental health field, the predominant therapeutic approaches with trauma and grief have been individually based, deficit oriented, and symptom focused. Manualized treatment models are inattentive to the family impact or to relational and contextual influences in recovery. The DSM/ICD psychiatric diagnosis of Prolonged Grief Disorder determines grief to be "abnormal" vs. "normal," based on a checklist of symptoms that persist more than a year. The diagnosis, with an arbitrary timeline, fails to consider cultural, family, and individual differences and pathologizes normal distress in highly abnormal and extreme situations of traumatic loss.

A resilience-oriented systemic approach with profound loss is collaborative, strengths-based, and contextual. We attend to individual grief *and* to family processes and sociocultural influences that can constrain or facilitate healing and resilience. In brief or more intensive therapeutic work, we may hold or combine sessions with individuals, couples, and families. In circumstances of widespread trauma, we facilitate family group and community-wide meetings to build mutual support and collaborative efforts in recovering from loss and in positive adaptation.

DOI: 10.4324/9781003536765-32

27.2.1 Facilitating grief processes: Research-informed practice

This systemic practice approach is grounded in current research-based understandings of loss, grief, and adaptive processes:

1. There is no "right way" to grieve. *"Normal grief" may entail varied reactions in diverse cultures and within families*, with gender, age, and individual differences.
2. *Grief involves a tangled web of emotions that ebb and flow over time*. Recovery processes do not follow a timetable or progressive stages; they involve adaptation, not resolution. Attention oscillates between grief and emerging life challenges. Grief gradually eases in intensity, yet it commonly resurfaces, and it may last a lifetime, as with the tragic death of a child. Healing and resilience are forged *through* grief – not by getting over it.
3. *Death ends a life but not the relationship*. Rather than detaching, adaptive mourning involves *continuing bonds*, transforming them from physical presence to spiritual connections, memories, shared stories, and deeds to remember and honor the deceased and all that was lost. Therapists can be helpful in healing old relational wounds; it is never too late.

27.2.2 Fostering healing and resilience in response to traumatic loss

The concept of resilience – the capacity to overcome adversity – is most often focused on individual strengths and images of invulnerability and self-reliance. As leading resilience research has recognized, resilience involves dynamic, multi-level systemic processes in the mutual, ongoing interaction of individual, family, community, and sociocultural influences (Masten, 2019). Vulnerability is inherent in the human condition; our resilience is nurtured by supportive relational bonds and our interdependence with others in our wider world. In responding to traumatic loss, therapists can best support healing and resilience by strengthening family processes and mobilizing supportive resources (Walsh, 2016).

A faulty view of resilience is the expectation to "keep positive" and "bounce back." With traumatic losses, the bereaved can't just "bounce back to normal." Their world has changed. Their grief is invalidated when others urge them to "get over it," "cheer up," and "move on." With multi-stress conditions, suffering, struggle, and setbacks are expectable over time. Resilience involves struggling well: working through, learning from, and growing stronger through a painful grieving and recovery process. It may require reorienting a future life vision. Over time, the pain of losses – and resilient responses – are gradually integrated into the chapters of life passage as the bereaved regain the ability to thrive.

27.3 Addressing traumatic losses in families

Traumatic loss experiences can wound the mind, body, spirit, and relationships and impact future life prospects. Some loss events are so highly stressful that most people would find them traumatic, such as a violent death, murder, or suicide, or collective experiences of widespread disasters or war. Although some persons are more vulnerable, none are immune to suffering in extreme situations.

27.3.1 The family impact of traumatic loss

A basic systems premise is that a significant loss impacts the whole family; in turn, how the family deals with the loss influences the adaptation (or maladaptation) of all members, their relationships, and the family unit. Family cohesion can be shattered, leaving each member to cope without relational support. One child may be withdrawn, depressed, or anxious, while another sibling may externalize distress in problematic behavior, and yet another may seem to be unaffected, cheerfully supporting an overwhelmed parent. A symptomatic child may be referred for therapy when the whole family is suffering and needing help.

27.3.2 Case illustration

Many months after the mother's death to cancer, Zoe, 18, away at college, was crying uncontrollably and unable to study; individual grief counseling was unhelpful. At home, her brother, Greg, age 12, was isolated in his room, immersed in video games. Her sister Denise, 16, kept cheerfully attentive to their widowed father, who was preoccupied with his demanding job.

The father and daughters came for a family consultation session. Zoe sat across the room, near the door; Denise sat close to the father. I offered my condolences for their loss and asked them how our session might be helpful. The father looked at Zoe, who replied, "I can't stop crying." I asked them, "Have you all shared your tears with each other?" Zoe responded: "I feel like I have all the tears for everyone. My brother's checked out. My sister's acting like the little mother, taking care of our father – and Dad [turning to him]: You act like you don't even care that Mom died!" I asked, "Would it help if your dad could share his tears?" She nodded vigorously, "Yes, yes!" As Denise reached out to pat her father's arm, I asked for her thoughts. "I worry that he loved my mother so much, he could fall apart or just disappear and we would lose him, too. So, I try to keep his spirits up." Turning to their father, I asked how this terrible loss has been for him. He replied, "It's all too much to bear, so I try to keep strong for my kids and just keep functioning." I acknowledged their pain and concerns. Noting the son's absence, I observed how hard it is to grieve such a huge loss alone and how beneficial their mutual support could be in their healing process. The father nodded, adding, "I didn't realize how much they need me to help them get through this – and how much we all need each other."

A tragic loss shakes the foundation of family life. Individual distress stems not only from grief, but also from disruptions in the family structure and emotional field, affecting marital, sibling, and intergenerational bonds. Emotional shock waves reverberate throughout relational networks, immediately and long after a death in far-ranging patterns of interaction and mutual influence (Walsh & McGoldrick, 2004; Walsh, 2023). Beyond family borders, social, educational, workplace, legal, and community systems impact bereavement and recovery processes. A lack of emotional and practical support or multi-stress obstacles in rebuilding lives, such as financial security, can complicate adaptation.

Although all losses may be painful to bear, traumatic death circumstances tend to complicate recovery. A *sudden death* is shocking, without time to prepare or say goodbyes. *Ambiguous losses* are agonizing, as in the cognitive declines with dementias, or in the uncertain fate of a loved one who is missing (Boss, 2017). When losses are *unacknowledged, minimized, or stigmatized* by others, the bereaved are isolated and denied their right to grieve. *Violent deaths*, in tragic accidents or in homicide, suicide, or substance use, are unbearable losses, with common recriminations of blame, shame, guilt, and remorse lasting years. In *catastrophic events* and *collective trauma*, prolonged suffering and struggle are widespread. A *pile-up of multiple losses and other stressors* can overload family functioning and interfere with grief. (See Walsh [2023] for practice principles and guidelines in helping families who are struggling with traumatic loss situations and complicated grief.)

27.4 Responding to collective trauma and loss

In this section, I focus attention on the pervasive losses families are experiencing as we emerge from the pandemic and face unprecedented political, economic, societal, and global upheaval. In extreme climate-related disasters and in war and displacement, families and communities are reeling from devastating losses and face long-term challenges. They will need our help.

27.4.1 Pandemic-related losses

In the grim statistics of Covid-related deaths, we may lose sight of the suffering of children and families who lost precious loved ones. The sudden crisis, hospitalization, and extreme suffering before death were excruciating experiences for patients and their families. Social distancing restrictions isolated them in their suffering and limited funeral rites and community support.

27.4.2 Case illustration

Amara, an immigrant in her forties, requested telehealth therapy. She was in unrelenting anguish since her mother's death, in her country of origin, from complications of Covid. As the eldest sibling, she had primary responsibility for her widowed mother, who was in homecare for a heart condition. Before the pandemic, Amara had visited frequently to oversee her care and to cook her mother's favorite dishes. As pandemic travel restrictions persisted, she felt increasingly guilty that she couldn't tend to her mother's needs. Late one night, Amara received a call from the physician: Her mother was in a life-threatening medical crisis – he and her brother needed her to decide if she should be hospitalized. This was an agonizing dilemma, as the local hospital had many Covid patients, posing risk of contagion. Alarmed by the mother's medical crisis, Amara told them to take her to the hospital. There, she contracted the virus and rapidly declined, requiring a ventilator over many weeks. Amara worried constantly, feeling helpless at a distance. The medical ordeal was too much for her mother's heart, which failed just as she was recovering. Unable to join her family in funeral ceremonies, Amara was isolated in unbearable grief and withdrew from her husband, who was increasingly impatient for her to "return to normal."

As we explored the many facets of Amara's suffering, she said that the worst was blaming herself for the death by making "the bad decision." I acknowledged her excruciating dilemma from afar. I suggested that she call the doctor to review the situation and gain his perspective. In their conversation, he acknowledged his own sense of urgency for hospital care, but also his hesitation. Yet, he said, either way, it was not possible for Amara to be there to attend to her, through no fault of her own. He told her he had long admired her devotion to her mother and knew the mother had valued her loving care before Covid intervened. "Her death is not your fault – it is this pandemic that took her life and has wreaked havoc on all our lives. We are all in mourning."

Since the death, Amara and her brother had been estranged. I encouraged her to have a video call with him. She was nervous, believing that he blamed her for the death. But in seeing her troubled face on the screen, he confessed his own inner turmoil and sense of guilt for not keeping their mother safe in the hospital. They began weekly contact, consoling one another, and reminiscing about their childhood family life. They set up a memorial website, inviting stories and photos to honor their mother, and held a Zoom gathering to celebrate her life. While Amara had occasional days of deep yearning for her beloved mother, she gradually re-engaged in her current life. A virtual couples' session increased her husband's understanding and support.

The pandemic has profoundly affected all aspects of life, as livelihoods and ways of living were upended. We talk about the "new normal," yet the future is precarious. Living with recurrent losses, disruptions, and uncertainty is extremely challenging, generating high anxiety. Cascading disruptions continue to impact families and communities in workplace, educational, and economic functioning. Children and adolescents struggle with losses in social and educational development. The emotional, relational, and functional toll has exacerbated difficulties for low-income and marginalized families, facing financial, housing, and food insecurity, and for persons with pre-existing health and mental health struggles. The demand has surged for both adult and youth mental health services. In the US there has been an alarming increase in depression, suicide, and addiction-related deaths. With most services individually focused, there is an urgent need for a family-focused approach.

Many families suppressed their pain to manage job or childrearing demands. As one bereaved mother said, "I had no time for tears." Many people, exhausted by the long ordeal, have "put the pandemic behind them," focusing on postponed plans and pleasures. "No one wants to see our sadness," said one woman, isolated in her grief after losing her husband to Covid. Some may seek our help much later, with reverberations of loss in their lives and relationships.

27.4.3 Loss and resilience in environmental disasters

Environmental disasters, such as earthquakes, floods, drought, and wildfires, are becoming more frequent and intense with climate change. When a community suffers a major disaster, the multiple losses, dislocations, and adaptational challenges are overwhelming. As one mother said, "It's a cascade of sorrows." In one community destroyed by wildfire, survivors faced daunting challenges to rebuild their homes and community structures, with a looming threat of future fires. Their deep personal connections and the resilient response of neighbors and strangers to help each another sparked their spirit and determination: "My family's life is here." "A house is just a structure: Your home is the people." "We're all family!" (Walsh, 2023).

The sense of rootedness in family and community life can sustain efforts to rise above tragic loss (Masten & Narayan, 2012). Helping professionals foster healing and resilience by understanding the impact of the loss situation, their immediate and long-term recovery challenges, and the values and deep connections that matter to them. Multifamily groups and community forums can mobilize extended kin, social, and practical support in efforts to restore lives. More than surviving, resilience involves learning from a tragedy to rebound stronger, addressing future needs to thrive.

In widespread destruction and rising death toll, as in the 2023 earthquakes in Turkey and Morocco, we find sparks of human resilience in heroic efforts by community members, digging through the rubble, to save every precious life possible. Yet, survivors can be tormented by guilt and remorse when loved ones could not be saved. Inaccessibility of essential aid and governmental failures in prevention, rescue, and recovery can fuel anger and a sense of injustice.

Families are often called the bedrock of a society; yet when disaster strikes, the lack of resources renders them vulnerable. Too often, those most affected – and neglected – are those who are marginalized and with limited means. For disaster preparedness and recovery, emergency coordination, communication, and follow-through are crucial. Prevention and post-disaster planning for sustainable communities must prioritize policies and practices to support resilience in families.

27.4.4 Traumatic loss in war and conflict regions

Loss is a central issue for families in war-torn regions. Ambiguous loss (Boss, 2017), with uncertainty if a missing loved one is dead or alive, is agonizing for loved ones. When a body is not recovered or identified, mourning processes are commonly blocked. Family conflict can ensue between members holding hope of survival and those wanting closure, to go on with life.

International humanitarian aid groups caution mental health professionals to avoid over-diagnosis of post-traumatic stress disorder (PTSD), pathologizing normal distress in extreme conditions. Losses are overwhelming in the vast human toll, destruction, and displacement wrought by war. In refugee resettlement services, attention understandably focuses on adaptational priorities. Trauma and loss experiences are commonly suppressed. Counselors need to attend with compassion to the painful losses of loved ones who perished and to kin, community, and cultural resources left behind. We can encourage ways to sustain connections with migration, as Falicov (2007) urges, "from a broken heart to living with two hearts."

Ethnic/racial/religious minorities and marginalized communities too often suffer poverty, war, and conflict across decades and generations. Reverberations of complex trauma, violence, and despair can fracture relational bonds and hinder child development. There is an urgent need for culturally appropriate, family-focused services. Resilience-oriented systemic approaches aim to foster: (1) the experience of being valued and supported; (2) a meaningful vision of the future, with reasonable hope of a life worth living; and (3) active agency (versus helplessness), through mutual support and collaborative efforts to create a viable future (Landau, 2007; Saul, 2013; Walsh, 2007, 2023). Families and communities have shown that they could endure the worst forms of suffering and grief and yet, with time and great effort, rebuild and grow stronger.

Families and their communities are intertwined in the impact of catastrophic events and in the mobilization of their resilience. In our intervention approaches, it is essential to attend to the losses suffered and to support individual, interpersonal, and broader systemic efforts in rebuilding lives. Through crisis, trauma, and suffering, a creative process can arise from the synergy of members supporting each other and working toward a common purpose. Resilience-oriented systemic approaches help families and communities expand their vision of what is possible not only to survive but also to regain their spirit to thrive.

27.5 Strengthening family healing and resilience

Traumatic loss situations, grief responses, and adaptation processes are varied and complex. In a resilience-oriented systemic perspective, we attend not only to individual grief but also to family processes and larger contextual influences that constrain or facilitate healing and positive adaptation. In helping survivors who are struggling, we explore the impact of the loss in their relational system and the family approach and response, in preparedness, immediate coping strategies, and long-term adaptive efforts. We explore both the circumstances of loss and the matrix of meanings it holds for individuals, their bonds, and their life aspirations. We seek to understand influences that contribute to suffering and to draw out and increase strengths and resources that can contribute to healing and resilience.

The research-informed Walsh Family Resilience Framework (Walsh, 2016) can be usefully applied, supporting key transactional processes in three domains of family functioning: belief systems, organizational resources, and communication processes. Here, I focus on belief systems, because they are shaken by traumatic loss and are vital for healing and resilience: (1) meaning-making of the loss and adaptational challenges; (2) regaining a hopeful outlook; and (3) tapping transcendent values and practices for inspiration, transformation, and growth.

27.5.1 Meaning-making

When tragic events occur, we construct and share narrative attempts to make sense of our experience. Meaning-making is socially constructed: nurtured, sustained, and altered through dynamic transactional processes in significant relational systems (Neimeyer et al., 2014). In families, these processes involve shared attempts to make sense of a death and loss, put it in perspective to make it more bearable, and gradually integrate it into life passage. Traumatic loss situations can shatter core assumptions about our world and our place in it, as well as our sense of normalcy, predictability, and security (Janoff-Bulman, 1992). Coming to terms with a "senseless" death, as in a random killing or an incomprehensible suicide, can be especially painful, with prolonged rumination common.

Still, meaning can be forged in response to tragedy. Meaning reconstruction promotes healing. Coming to terms with loss involves finding ways to weave the experience coherently into the fabric of individual and relational life passage. Clinicians can support efforts to comprehend the loss – including its lingering questions and its future implications – and gradually to place it in some meaningful perspective that fits coherently with their life experience and aspirations. Therapists should be cautious not to ascribe meaning to clients' unique experience: Our therapeutic role is not to *provide* meaning but to facilitate their meaning-making process (Frankl, 1946, 2006).

27.5.2 A positive outlook: Reorienting hope

Resilience is most often forged through suffering and struggle. *Hope* is most essential in times of deepest despair, fueling energies and efforts to cope and adapt. Weingarten (2010) stresses the importance of practicing reasonable hope and, as necessary, reorienting what is hoped for. Active agency in *mastering the possible* is crucial for resilience: focusing on what can be done, accepting what can't be changed, and tolerating uncertainty. In the wake of loss, families cannot bring a loved one back to life or change the circumstances of a death – nor can clinicians. Yet we can support the bereaved in their anguish, with compassion for their lost hopes and dreams, and encourage their efforts to find meaning and purpose in their lives going forward.

27.5.3 Transcendent values and practices

Transcendent values and practices help families surmount personal tragedy by expanding perspective from immediate suffering to view it in larger context of life passage and our common humanity. With death and loss, spiritual or existential matters commonly come to the fore. It's important to explore faith concerns (such as sin and punishment) that contribute to distress and to identify spiritual resources, fitting clients' orientation, that might support their healing and resilience. Spiritual nourishment may be found within and outside organized religion: through deep faith and/or congregational support, contemplative practices, and in connectedness with nature or in the expressive arts.

Beyond coping and adaptation, the suffering and struggle in adaptation to loss can yield both personal and relational transformation and growth in families, as studies of post-traumatic growth have found for individuals (Tedeschi et al., 2018). Catastrophic events can awaken us to what really matters in life and inspire us to reorder our priorities. Many develop new insights and abilities, reappraising and redirecting life pursuits. Enhanced compassion prompts initiative in caring actions to benefit others in need. In my practice, many families have forged new purpose in community service or in social action to prevent tragic deaths or address harmful conditions. A loss can heighten appreciation of surviving loved ones and spark efforts to repair grievances. Family stories and role models of courage, tenacity, and ingenuity in dealing with other adversity can offer inspiration in facing challenges.

27.6 Attending to death and loss: Our compassionate engagement

Helping professionals work with many situations of suffering, yet we are often uneasy in approaching death and loss. There is no safe boundary between professionals and our patients/clients: we, the helpers, are all vulnerable, facing anxieties for our own lives and for the loss of loved ones and significant relationships. This is especially challenging as we all face loss, or the threat of loss, in our own lives and the turbulent world around us.

As therapists, we may be unsure what to say or do in situations of complex and traumatic loss. We may feel overwhelmed and helpless. Brief solution-focused approaches seem inadequate: Death is not a problem to solve, and we can't bring back deceased loved ones or shattered lives. Words of cheer and platitudes offered by others ("At least . . ." or "Count your blessings") can minimize and invalidate deep suffering. How can we best help families in distress to grieve and adapt to losses and disruptions, to navigate the challenges ahead, and to go forward to live and love fully?

Over decades, studies comparing therapeutic approaches find that our therapeutic engagement matters more than specific models and techniques. As family therapy pioneers Virginia Satir and Harry Aponte emphasized, we bring ourselves – our relational selves – to all our therapeutic work. Our personal and family experience of loss can constrain our response – or, with recognition and reflection, can enhance our ability to engage compassionately with those who are struggling and to foster their healing and resilience (Walsh, 2023).

Our work is guided by courageous engagement with those who have suffered traumatic losses. We cannot heal all the wounds, but we can create a safe haven where individuals, families, and community members are able to share deep pain and renewed strivings. Of value is our compassionate witnessing of their suffering and struggle and our admiration for their courage and perseverance. When we shift focus from symptoms to strengths and potential, people tap unexpected competencies and resources and can build on them. We can rekindle their hopes and dreams and support their best efforts. We can encourage their mutual support and active strategies to overcome their challenges. In helping families cope and adapt to their losses, we also support their positive strivings, enabling them to go forward to live and love fully beyond loss. Our response to tragedy can embody the humanity that binds us all together.

References

Boss, P. (2017). Families of the missing: Psychosocial effect and therapeutic approaches. *International Review of the Red Cross*, *99*(2), 519–534. https://doi.org/10.1017/S1816383118000140

Falicov, C. (2007). Working with transnational immigrants: Expanding meanings of family, community, and culture. *Family Process*, *46*, 157–172. https://doi.org/10.1111/j.1545–5300.2007.00201.x

Frankl, V. (1946). *Ein Psychologe erlebt das Konzentrationslager*. Kösel Verlag.

Frankl, V. (2006). *Man's Search for Meaning*. Beacon Press.

Janoff-Bulman, R. (1992). *Shattered assumptions: Towards a new psychology of trauma*. Free Press.

Landau, J. (2007). Enhancing resilience: Families and communities as agents for change. *Family Process*, *46*(3), 351–365. https://doi.org/10.1111/j.1545–5300.2007.00216.x

Masten, A. S. (2019). Resilience from a developmental systems perspective. *World Psychiatry*. https://doi.org/10.1002/wps.20591

Masten, A. S., & Narayan, A. J. (2012). Child development in the context of disaster, war and terrorism: Pathways of risk and resilience. *Annual Review of Psychology*, *63*, 227–257. https://doi.org/10.1146/annurev-psych-120710–100356

Neimeyer, R., Klass, D., & Dennis, M. (2014). A social constructionist account of grief: Loss and the narration of meaning. *Death Studies*, *38*, 485–498. https://doi.org/10.1080/07481187.2014.913454

Saul, J. (2013). *Collective Trauma, collective healing: Promoting community resilience in the aftermath of disaster*. Routledge.

Tedeschi, R. G., Shakespeare-Finch, J., Kanako, T., & Calhoun, L. (2018). *Posttraumatic growth: Theory, research, and applications*. Routledge. https://doi.org/10.1002/anzf.1199

Walsh, F. (2007). Traumatic loss and major disasters: Strengthening family and community resilience. *Family Process*, *46*, 207–227. https://doi.org/10.1111/j.1545–5300.2007.00205.x

Walsh, F. (2016). *Strengthening family resilience* (3rd ed.). Guilford Press.

Walsh, F. (2023). *Complex and traumatic loss: Fostering healing and resilience*. Guilford Press.

Walsh, F., & McGoldrick, M. (2004). *Living beyond loss: Death in the family* (2nd ed.). Norton.

Weingarten, K. (2010). Reasonable hope: Construct, clinical applications, and supports. *Family Process*, *49*, 5–25. https://doi.org/10.1111/j.1545–5300.2010.01305.x

28

RESIGNIFICATION

The gift of elaboration and processing a traumatic experience

Shulamit Graber

28.1 Introduction

Threats and trauma are present in an abundant form in society. In the last ten years, the interest in the response of fellow human beings when facing situations that threaten their lives and their consequences has increased. The literature written about post-traumatic stress disorder (PTSD) from perspectives such as behavioral, cognitive, emotional, interpersonal, and neurobiological have increased the effectiveness of treatment models so that we may understand how a person is able to survive situations that threaten their life and how they are able to recover from those experiences. Examples of these traumatic experiences could be from domestic violence or family violence from a partner, or even natural disasters or universal ones.

When one lives a "limit" experience that places us in front of an *ambiguous loss* (Boss, 1999), for example, of liberty, dignity, or some mental faculty, or even a *real loss* including death, the body registers physical, mental, and emotional sensations that somehow, and independently to the course that the event or experience takes, there is left a "scar"; that imprinted "scar" should be removed and resignified to achieve accommodation internally with the possibility to convert it into a growth experience.

Trauma signifies a break; surely their life will be "before and after." From that the importance of reinventing oneself, finding new significance and connections, help integrate trauma into one's own story. The above approach permits a gradual decrease in feelings of helplessness, vulnerability, and hopelessness with respect to the associated difficulties, which would cushion the sensation of which some traumatic experience is lived, from having to "survive" that stress. In this process, some individuals report changes on a personal level, which have been concentrated on improving their quality of life and in the incorporation of self-care behaviors, feeling more strengthened from the experience.

Working with traumatic experiences allows for change to the sensations felt by the affected person, from being a victim of trauma and being "pursued" because of this, to a new sensation in which it is possible to learn from the past, confronting the demands of the present and protecting oneself in the future with new expectations and with a new sense of confidence in oneself. From here the key or rather the objective would be: How to convert a traumatic experience into a possibility for growth? Growing from a crisis, converting a difficult situation or a traumatic one into an opportunity for personal change: post-traumatic growth vs. post-traumatic stress.

DOI: 10.4324/9781003536765-33

28.2 How do we react to trauma?

By nature, human beings try to avoid pain at all costs. We are seekers of pleasure, but paradoxically that pain, a product of traumatic experience, is where the possibility exists to find growth and transformation. During a traumatic event, one is confronting emotions and fears they could have never imagined. In a natural disaster, people face multiple types of loss including death, and in the case of domestic violence living with fear of being beaten or mistreated continuously. Two questions are evident in these types of traumatic experiences: Will I be able to survive what I am going through? And, in any case, how will this change my life from this point forward?

There is a popular saying: "Time heals all wounds." I think the contrary: We must not leave a painful experience in the hands of time. The only form to heal a wound and keep moving forward with your life, including a better version of one's self, is to be bold enough to work on the experience. However, to achieve that we must let those emotions that were "blocked" or "frozen," for a brief period of time, while we found ourselves in "survival mode." Perhaps a couple of weeks after the event, or even three months later, these blocked or frozen emotions may be weighing on our consciousness, or they may remerge from our interiority, to give a touch of emotion to what was lived through. That is to say, to be able to bring to the present all the past emotions even though they are or were some of the most intense and painful.

Meanwhile, let us continue to detail the experience to be able to work on it from greater angles and possible perspectives, while the final result consists of accommodating it into a "comfortable place" in our interiority, where it would be a more efficient result. Remembering that life is not lived with an eraser, "what we live, we live," but what we can do is make ourselves responsible for what we choose to do with what we have lived.

Processing, accommodating, and resignifying the traumatic experience is the responsibility of the person who lived it. Remember that if you are not at peace with yourself, you will be a person at war with the whole world. The Buddha said, "You could have everything, but if you do not have inner peace, you have nothing." Eckhart Tolle (2003) elaborated:

> If you had not suffered the way you suffered you would not have depth like a human being, or humility, or compassion. Suffering opens the shell of the ego, but there comes a time when it has fulfilled its purpose. Suffering is necessary until you realize that it no longer is needed.

We will always be more than just what we live; a circumstance or event cannot encompass the totality of our identity. If so, if that is what defines us, we can forget about who we are. Remember: "You are not what happened to you."

Albert Einstein said, "We must achieve the cyclist's equilibrium, by pedaling." This is trying to say that we only live one life, and in that one, all the events that we come across should fit; we cannot hold ourselves back because of any of them, because life does not stop, the bicycle keeps running, and it requires our constant and continuous pedaling: "We do not stop to resolve, we resolve while we live."

It is because of this belief that my goal today consists of transmitting this to my patients; this idea of personal compromise with our own personal history, since only 10% is what happens to us and the other 90% is what we do with what happened to us.

28.3 Geometry of change: Processing traumatic experiences

Together with this model, it is explained how one can transcend a life crisis or one of trauma. I call this project: "From chaos to order," given that a traumatic experience deconstructs to the point that we run the risk of falling into a state of confusion, consuming our identity. This is applicable to any kind of traumatic experience, from natural disasters to domestic violence and other forms of abuse. And always remember to invite family members who wish to participate or who wish to accompany in the process those who have directly or indirectly lived that traumatic experience with the firm conviction that familial systems always support alternative histories or diverse perspectives. The steps of the model are as follows:

1. Elaboration
2. Resignification
3. Incorporation
4. Transformation

28.4 Elaboration

Elaboration goes through two different subphases: *normalization* and *narration*. Normalization refers to the re-establishment of a sense of security and the reorganization of everyday life; this is perceived as a necessary condition so one can first elaborate and then process traumatic memories. We need to make sure that the consultant has some strength or content in their being, which consists of the possibility of containing strong emotions, and is also a form of showing other people how to "touch base." It is a way of saying, "I can get out of the survival mode." The *narration of the event* refers to the ability to talk about oneself, which is directed by a therapist to mark the difference between what you have already told friends and family and what you will now talk about in the therapy process.

I remember when I was working with a group of colleagues in the town of Tultepec in the state of México when there was an explosion of rockets and fireworks in the main market of the town, a real "massive catastrophe." Various people lost not only loved ones but also their homes; therefore, the priority for them was to see how they could give a dignified burial ceremony for their family members who had passed away instead of looking for a place to live. The first thing is to cover security and the basic demands of their everyday life, so as therapists, at this stage, our function is primarily to become a companion or guide, because the person who lived the traumatic experience can be paralyzed or without clarity or proper strength to stabilize their lives.

Another necessary ingredient is that they have a certain self-regulation ability, which depends on how serious their trauma was. It is important to suggest to them to be more socially connected, using networks from family, from their work, or friends, and for them to try to do "a little more than what they are already capable of doing" to strengthen themselves and be able to cope better with their trauma.

Trying from the start with their social anxieties is a form of exemplifying how we will work with trauma. It is a less intense process, but it is a similar form to the path we shall take with self-work dealing with the traumatic experience, so we start working with the anxieties and affairs that paralyze us from day to day, everyday moments in life.

Let us remember that the survival mode is a mechanism that regulates the functioning of a human being when they perceive an existential danger. Human beings are – for the majority – programmed for survival. Efficient reactions when facing a threat are essential to surviving. The classic model of human response when facing a threat consists of three phases: (1) recognizing the threat, (2) evaluating the danger and its risks, and (3) evaluating and deploying adaptive resources. Any extreme threat seems to create a culturally different response to daily stress.

The evaluation of a threatening situation is instinctive for life, and the consequent behavioral responses are almost immediate. The experience while being aware of fear is revoked by the demands of acute threat to one's life, substituting cerebral functions of the highest level for instinctive functions through the most primitive parts of the brain: "Free will versus survival."

Under threat, the functioning of the neurophysiological system of an organism is restructured to free up energy in favor of immediate action. The objective of instinctive reactions is to cope with danger and re-establish security. There are many parts of the nervous system involved in how we respond to a threat. Our attention is stretched to detect the source of the danger and to evaluate its impact: the emotional consciousness decreases, and the behavioral responses are quick, swift, and focused on the objective. People frequently do not feel like "themselves" during times like these. Let us call this process "fragmentation" since it refers to a disassociation that occurs when it comes across a trauma: There is no other option other than to be in survival mode, which is to say, "you don't feel until you feel safe" until you are "safe," relaxed, and free of danger, because let us remember that during that trauma we are disconnected from any kind of emotion or feelings. This is known as *structural dissociation* because the interior fragments between the doing, the thinking, and on the other hand, the feeling.

During trauma, sensations are not relevant; everything is put on "pause," and we start to feel when "feelings" have already passed. It seems obvious, but it is not. This explains why on some occasions there are some who continuously like having limited experiences because they stop feeling: like adolescents. *Fragmentation* is the key to understanding survival, and it refers to an improper division of the personality that is found "at the heart of disorders related to traumas." Disassociation is, clearly, one of the processes that occur during serious threats. During an event that is perceived as threatening, any one of these three reactions can be activated: fight, flight, paralysis. Once the danger has moved away, the division of the personality should be re-evaluated.

We could give an infinite number of examples: cases of war, natural disasters, assaults. The survivors generally have this hue that permits them to react with a certain assertiveness and cognitive ability, precisely thanks to the process of fragmentation. This also explains what happens at the end of traumatic experiences that we ourselves don't even know "how we could cope with the experience," or "how was it that we were able to do this or that." It's not until the closest people in our lives begin to ask us "How were you able to . . . ?" that we enter into our consciousness what we did, of what we were capable of, and more so what could have possibly happened to us.

These reflections are provoked by the questions asked to us by our friends and family, about everything that we were capable of doing or sorting out. These are what break the process of fragmentation, and it is when we begin to feel that we start to feel nostalgia, fear, depression, hypersensitivity, and to explore what we lived from another angle, from another perspective, even up to questioning ourselves as to how we were capable of this or that – and simultaneously we scare ourselves by what we were actually capable of doing. In many cases, it is here where the real PTSD starts, just when "the emotions and feelings lower our consciousness." There also exist triggers that can wake up those same feelings, or moments of silence, or apparent relaxation, like when we find ourselves in the middle of an experience or of a success, where these same feelings emerge, as "non-wakeful states of being." However, it is important to understand the big difference between flashbacks and memory. Flashbacks are like if one were to be living it again, and memory is a memory. Therefore, in the work with trauma, it is important to detect and above all else differentiate between both, considering the oscillatory movement between "wanting to forget and not forgetting," it is not PTSD but "functioning normally or healthy." It is the expected, the coming and going, like a logical but necessary movement.

The important thing to know is that PTSD manifests more as a propensity for fragmentation, and from here the importance of taking into account this phenomenon before moving on to the phase of narrating the experience, where it is required to have a certain capacity to auto-regulate oneself emotionally to be able to talk and work through what we've lived, and we must be prepared to welcome a more detailed history with the traumatic experience.

Lastly, it is important to take into account the paradox of trauma: When the more you ask someone who has lived through a strong crisis or a trauma how they feel, "they feel less," and if you ask questions about details from the experience, without emotions, they feel more (through the details). When you want to understand how someone feels, it is better to ask them what happened, letting them know you care about what happened and you want to hear them out; contrary to questions like "How did you feel?" or "What are you feeling?" generally they answer with ideas or thoughts. Once as therapists we have managed to achieve coming across these phases of normalization and fragmentation with our patients, we will be prepared to hear about the narration of the experience.

28.4.1 Narration

Narrating what happened is very important, but the form in which you do it is even more important. It is because of this that during the therapy process, retelling the history of the traumatic experience should be a different form from what was already told and retold by the patient to their friends and family, now that from this moment the important reprocessing of what was lived begins. We remember that we are constructing reality with our own internal speeches; as a result, what we tell ourselves about what we have lived creates a type of "self-fulfilling prophecies." We can consider narration like a diagnostic interview because we wish to see what they are willing to answer; in a way, it shows us what they can talk about. Listening to their narration, we can observe how they are elaborating. We can detect and evaluate if they know the entire history, and for that, we must be curious. It is like standing on someone else's shoulders and looking at their story from there.

28.5 Resignification

The resignification process goes through two phases: *making sense* (from "Why?" to "For what purpose?") and *false justice*.

28.5.1 Making sense

What does not make sense to us becomes very difficult to process and resignify. Human beings move "by sense," meaning we want to say what we consider making sense, we are able to assimilate, but what does not, we tend to throw it away; this occurs not only in trauma but also in any event in everyday life. How do we make sense of something we consider nonsense? How do we find an explanation that leaves us at peace and satisfied with an experience that breaks all logical schemes and is also cruel and painful? My response is always the same: still, we should try to find some meaning.

How do we find meaning for a natural disaster? How do you search for meaning in an episode of familial violence where liberty is suspended? How was I able to achieve an escape from that existential maze? It was not until, in a moment of calmness, I asked: If what I lived had a "What for?," what could it be? And this was my response: Learning how to connect with my intuition and internal signs gave me clues that this relationship was not functioning anymore and that violence was becoming a pattern in my relationship. However, extended conversations with friends and family were more valid voices challenging my belief system that said a woman had to stay, despite everything, to endure everything.

Breaking pre-existing belief systems, above all else, was possible due to the transmission of generational guidelines, now that I had a daughter who didn't want to live with the violence of a mother who wouldn't reveal her true self, just as my mother had done to me. I wanted to stop that pattern, and that's when the "What for?" became clear in my life.

In any of these experiences, we are left with the persistent question, "Why me?" and we can't find the answer, "For what reason?" We become stagnant in a state of victimization, and if we still fail to find the meaning to our life experiences, it becomes very difficult to resignify or integrate what was lived from being "nonsense," then we run the risk of living life accompanied by pain, eternal claims, and a hint of bitterness.

If we think about why we had to live through this or that, it is to say, it already happened this way, so for what possible reason did I have to go through this in my life? What did it contribute to my life? Did I have a moment where I learned something important? Searching for these answers, which is not easy, puts us in the waiting room to find meaning to experiences we lived. This is the first step in post-traumatic growth now that we allow ourselves to ask: How do we transcend from this experience? If I could change my life or my reality, how would I go about it? How do I visualize myself after this moment?

28.5.2 False justice

Another very important point that does not allow us to advance is the theory of false justice, or universal justice, which we usually live by. This theory hypothetically states: "bad things happen to bad people" and that good things happen to good people, since they are worthy of happiness, harmony, and blessings. This is not true, and all the traumatic events that disregard any sense of elementary logic highlight this. Unfortunately, life is uncertain, and all of us can be exposed to any and everything. As Amado Nervo (1920) used to say, "The sky is blue, the ocean is salted, and life is uncertain." Added to this the popular belief that things happen only to others and not to oneself, meaning, "It doesn't happen to you, until it happens."

Many theories state that things are not possible until they happen to you, but once this occurs, other theories explain the probability of those things occurring in your life. In the book *The Black Swan*, Nassim Taleb (2007) explains the impact of the highly improbable, like finding a black swan; on the contrary, the logic changes, then it becomes a probable thing, and in that instant millions of other explanations arise for the probability of their discovery to be more affordable. The same occurs with universal disasters, human misfortunes, or in any kind of case dealing with violence.

When we live through difficult or critical moments, these thoughts about what is fair or not invade our mind, because the important thing is to listen to all the ideas and beliefs our patients and their families have in relation to the theme of justice, to be able to help them understand where those ideas come from and how they have gestated inside each and every one of them. Do they originate due to religion? Do they come from family legacies? Were they personal beliefs that up until that day were functional?

28.6 Incorporation

The most important element of narrating a traumatic event is the finale. The finale is what organizes the chaos. The finale allows you to recognize that the threat was left in the past and that today "I'm safe." Incorporation goes through two phases: beliefs and meanings.

28.6.1 Beliefs

Certain beliefs or thoughts can on occasion block the incorporation internally of the experience, but we must work on them through interventions directed on "deconstructing" the rigid part or to investigate what internal discourses flow inside the patient about their life, their past, or about the event or the traumatic event, that to a certain extent impedes on their healthy advance.

In the case of the woman who had lived through a severe case of domestic violence and she would tell herself that if she had left it would have put her in danger but staying there was also putting her in danger, and the guilt of destroying something with her exit the idea of a family being united "that stays together despite everything," the question then becomes: What good is it to have these kinds of thoughts or decrees now? The most likely answer is that the risk that would have been run was so severe due to the level of violence reached that the beliefs of having a happy family were probably causing the woman to not leave her situation, and upon staying in that kind of thought process was not allowing her to advance in her process. Therefore, we must forget about that "logic" and move on to asking questions that connect emotions and alternative possibilities. We can ask them questions such as: If everything were possible, how would you want to feel? Is it necessary and/or useful to feel fear?

Let us remember that our beliefs originate from our thoughts, which in turn originate from our emotions and finally our actions. We can also ask: This is something you could not do before and now you can, so what does it mean to you to be able to do it? What does that say about you? This question attempts to give a distinct meaning to what the patient has to say about the experience, resignifying it.

It is important for the patient to recognize that they were able to achieve this new significance to the event, not the therapist, and every small step that helps them continue moving forward in the life that they want or choose for themselves is a magnificent step.

This is coping with meaning.

28.6.2 Meaning

Meaning deals with how to change the narrative or the final history of what we have lived, to facilitate the accommodation in our inner self. It would first be worth it to clarify the following: What is the difference between an experience and something lived through? Living through something, as the name suggests, is something we go through, whereas an experience is something that goes through the nuance of meaning. With this I am referring to the way we give our experience significance determines our quality of life. This form would also depend on our history, systems of beliefs, thoughts, whether they be rational, religious, or spiritual, and finally the process of self-elaboration. Therefore, facing similar experiences could be different depending on their meaning. The final objective of working with trauma is the goal of resignification of the traumatic experience, which is going to be relevant to seal the process of incorporation.

28.6.3 The core of meaning

If the work we have been doing was like an onion, which we've been peeling away layer after layer until we reached the core, then this would be the core of meaning; in other words, the most painful, what the traumatic experience meant to them, remembering that as there is no communal suffering or pain, there are no communal meanings. Precisely reaching this nodal point is what gives us the possibility of incorporating experience.

Using the same case of the woman who suffered from domestic violence, most people would say that the biggest fear or the center of meaning for the experience was fear – fear of never seeing her kids again, fear that harm would come to her physically, fear that she would be raped, etc. Nonetheless, after working through her experience, she discovered that what traumatized her the most was the idea of freedom, and what it meant for her to be free. Knowing that she was not free, the belief she had in freedom to which she had lived for a large part of her life was false, or at least questionable, since they could snatch it away at any moment. This is why it is important to discover the core of meaning for everyone, carefully, not only to incorporate the meaning of what we lived through, but as a prelude to transforming from the experience, which implies growth and transcends apart from that lived moment.

28.7 Transformation

Transformation includes the following phases: window of life or of tolerance and the new reality/a new universe. Transformation refers to the possibility of reconstruction both internal and external. Inwards, putting the experience in a safe and reliable place, and outward, moving us to "believe in something" apart from what we have lived.

28.7.1 Window of life

If we were to set up an electrocardiogram, everything we've lived through along with the rest of our life would fit – what we've tolerated and what we haven't, the high points, the low points, the plateaus or the relevant harmonious moments, etc. – so we could see that our lives have high peaks, flat plateaus, and very low points. We can imagine our lived experience providing a window on our lives. The high peaks that stick out the window are the difficult moments that we have lived through, not necessarily traumatic experiences but rather conflicts, crises, and moments that were out of our hands. They also speak upon certain maniac tendencies. The very low spikes are "low" moments, such as depression and sadness, that are unresolved and are drowning us.

All of these moments that go to the center of our window are the things that we have been able to tolerate or manage in a somewhat stable form, how life usually is: moments of equilibrium, harmony, difficulties, and crisis, but in some we have had the tools to sort out the issue. On some occasions, the simple fear of thinking about the event and that it might get out of our control causes us to get out of our window of life; therefore, in my intense therapeutic work, I attempt to show my patients how to "widen" the window of their life. By this method they become more tolerant, they learn to self-regulate, to live in equilibrium and harmony, and therefore, the major part of their life becomes situated in the middle zone, or more or less in the center of their window, without too many peaks – whether they be high or low ones.

Various authors consider that there are two paths when talking about dealing with experiences: (1) actually working with the protruding peaks from the window, whether they are high or low, or else (2) widening the window of each individual so that those peaks are seen as minor and are not disparaging. According to my experience, my therapeutic challenge is to work both at the same time, both the peaks that protrude in any direction, how to "enlarge the window" so that more events are seen as tolerable; in this way, the event in which they seek my consultation acquires a broader meaning that is not solely reduced to working with a painful or traumatic experience, but to configure or reconfigure an entire life, becoming a clearer form in which they are able to face future events apart from that moment. Emotional self-regulation is a crucial part in this process since the way we manage our emotions is directly proportional to our equilibrium and harmony that we manage to conquer in our lives.

28.7.2 New reality/new universe

Once you have gone through this therapeutic journey with traumatic experience, it is necessary to return to our reality and observe it. Am I where I want to be? Would I make a change in my universe? Which one or what would these changes be? It is now when checking the orbits or areas in our lives, as well as our bonds or emotional relationships, this would prove to be very useful.

Each orbit is composed of fundamental areas that we rarely question or reflect about how we feel about them. In the same way, the people who surround us occupy some place in these orbits, whether close or distant, which should be questioned and reviewed. It usually happens that we have people very close to us, which today is more than we would like them to be, so changing their orbit would be prudent; or there are people who are in one of the last orbits and we would like them to be closer.

The same thing happens with events, moments lived, or areas that make up our life: will they all be in their corresponding orbit? This is an opportunity to move where we choose to do so, remembering that any life crisis – just like traumatic experience – is an opportunity to put into perspective any aspect of our lives; in this way, pain, suffering, and the experience all acquire a meaning: converting our post-traumatic stress into post-traumatic growth.

This is what you are, this is what we are. A universe with an infinite number of possibilities.

28.8 Conclusions

The most important thing for me is that you take some kind of action in your life and recognize that some crisis or traumatic experience (which we have all had) that you have experienced throughout your life is "stagnant," "paralyzed," or just there, nothing more. The time has come to question your universe and your reality, and it is always a good time to do so; make the movements and changes that you want to make in your life. Remember that you should not wait for a crisis, a trauma, or a strong event to change. It is a choice, a wise decision that is made at any time, every day.

What life do I choose to have from today? What would I have to do to conquer it? There are stories that can change your life, and I have witnessed with this work on trauma how pain and suffering were transformed into growth. Surprising events can lead a life down unexpected paths, sometimes happy and others not so much, through experiences that at first seemed to end tragically, events that at one time were perceived as dramatic situations that plunged a life into the depths of doubt and despair, occasions on which it was difficult to believe and maintain hope. But all of these stories and situations, with time and inner work, found a meaning, a purpose in their lives.

Thanks to my personal work, based on my own experience of kidnapping and working with thousands of patients during more than 16 years of experience in PTSD therapy, I have been able to build my own method to help in this journey "from chaos to order" in our lives. Today, it is clear to me that trauma is never healed in isolation. The healing process always occurs in the loving presence of someone else. And what better than the family, so including most of the members, whether or not they are involved in the experience, but with the will to accompany and heal, is a way in which an entire multigenerational system can benefit.

The most important element in the recovery from a traumatic event is the restoration of the sense of security: external security and internal security. Without these two elements, there is no recovery. *Because it is not what happens to you but what you do with what happens to you.*

References

Boss, P. (1999). *Ambiguous loss: Learning to live with unresolved grief.* Harvard University Press.

Nervo, A. (1920). *La amada immóvil, Versos a una muerta*. Biblioteca Nueva.

Taleb, N. N. (2007). *The black swan: The impact of the highly improbable*. Random House.

Tolle, E. (2003). *Stillness speaks*. New World Library.

29

REMEMBERING HELPS US FORGET

Antonello D'Elia

Silence meant absence and absence meant remembering.[1]

29.1 Introduction

The concept of trauma has long had immense cultural resonance, to the point of becoming not only an explanatory framework but also a lens through which to interpret a wide range of human experiences. These experiences range from the consequences of wars, disasters, physical and psychological violence, and abuse to more commonplace events of everyday life, such as parent-child dynamics, separations, divorces, and challenging interactions with partners, teachers, or peers.

This wide-ranging applicability has fostered the development of a comprehensive paradigm that transcends the expertise of psychologists and psychiatrists, influencing social, anthropological, and cultural spheres. For example, in literature, cinema, and media, the recurring and sometimes pervasive use of the term *trauma* appears to have become indispensable for understanding events and people. The term has become an indisputable reference point for describing facts and situations, and has become objectified as an inherent aspect of reality rather than an operational concept (Williams, 2009). Today, it seems impossible to describe a person who has lived through a profoundly painful and violent experience without referring to a "trauma" that he or she has experienced. This trauma is often viewed as a defining event that has long-term lingering consequences, which will probably be passed on to future generations as if by fate. As Daniele Giglioli (not coincidentally a literary critic) writes, "It has become a founding, structuring, identity element" (Giglioli, 2011). In the fields of psychology and psychiatry, post-traumatic stress disorder (PTSD), which is closely tied to the concept of trauma, has become a cornerstone of diagnosis and the basis for treatments designed to resolve them. The concept of trauma has further expanded to include a sequence of phenomena linked to explicitly traumatic experiences, including victimization, intergenerational psychic transmission, and, on other levels, the proliferation of individual psychiatric diagnoses, therapies, and a burgeoning educational market for trauma treatment (Young, 1997; Rosen, 2004; van der Kolk, 2014).

The history of psychic trauma lies beyond the scope of this chapter. Instead, we refer readers to significant works that trace its development, beginning with the emergence of Freudian psychoanalysis in the early 20th century and extending to contemporary cognitive science and neuroscience. This

DOI: 10.4324/9781003536765-34

body of literature also includes extensive studies on the Shoa and recent body of studies of PTSD (Leys, 2000; Mucci, 2008).

What follows is an account of an intervention conducted using various methods to support a social group in distress after experiencing painful events. As a psychiatrist and family therapist, I continue to reflect on this experience, grappling with the complexities and challenges posed by traumatic events, the limitations of the concept of trauma itself, and its application in designing interventions aimed at transformation and healing.

29.2 A huge housing complex in the middle of nowhere: Listening to the silence

The story begins in the late 1990s, when the community mental health center where I worked acquired premises in a building situated in a peripheral area of Rome. Drawing on prior experience working in a working-class urban neighborhood in another city, I obtained permission to establish an institutional space with two psychologist colleagues and three nurses. I had previously listened to several residents of the building and was struck by the consistency with which they referenced to the building in their life stories. They described it not merely as the setting [or backdrop] for their suffering, including crises, illnesses, and the deaths of relatives and friends, but as a disturbing presence in their lives. The site in question is not merely a building but a massive public housing complex constructed in the early 1980s on the outskirts of Rome, at what was then the city's far southwestern edge.

The name of the building is Corviale: a 998-meter-long structure with nine floors, flanked by two "minor" buildings – one of equal length but only three floors high, and the other a four-story building, measuring "just" 200 meters in length (Figure 29.1). This immense "housing machine" accommodates more than 4,000 residents – or more accurately, tenants – since the publicly owned complex operates as a single condominium with five primary access staircases. At the time it opened, the surrounding area was predominantly an open countryside, with no nearby connections to the rest of the city and an absence of shops or essential services. Corviale was a product of the urban planning utopias of its era, conceived in a location entirely devoid of any historical pre-existence. Beginning in 1982, the "big box" began to gradually fill with residents, a process delayed not so much by the need to complete construction but by the necessity of restoring apartments that had already been finished but had, in the meantime, been illegally occupied and vandalized. Residents arrived in waves until the building reached full occupancy. Many came from the historic center of Rome or other neighborhoods, particularly from peripheral settlements where shantytowns and illegal dwellings had emerged – some had even lived beneath the arches of ancient Roman aqueducts in the city's outskirts. These illegal dwellings had arisen as a result of massive urbanization of the capital and the shortage of adequate housing and social policies. Some families, evicted from their homes, had been living on the streets.

This situation confronted us with the dynamics of migration and accompanying challenges – conflict, as well as cultural, social, and political impacts. The people who moved to Corviale, all Roman citizens, had not traveled far geographically but experienced a different kind of displacement: an urban migration. Their relocation was as forced as the assignment of public housing to homeless families, bringing together individuals who shared a common fate in an unfamiliar and collectively imposed setting.

When we arrived, more than 20 years had passed since the events surrounding Corviale's initial opening to occupants, yet the stories we heard made it seem as though they had occurred only recently. Before opening a psychiatric service in such a heavily stigmatized area – an emblem of delinquency and neglect, synonymous with the "sick" peripheries of the nation and burdened by the prejudices associated with mental illness, stigma, and social exclusion – we recognized the need to approach the community with caution and respect. Our first step was to listen and attempt to understand the

Figure 29.1

emerging health needs of the residents. We organized and participated in public meetings with residents and their associations, and engaged in discussions with local and municipal politicians. We also met with local institutional and community-based organizations, including municipal social services, the police, the neighborhood library, family counseling center, senior center, the parish church, the boxing gym, and a community of street priests who were established in the building. After a year of "participatory planning" (Farina, 2012) and making ourselves known to the community, we opened a direct-access, non-bureaucratic listening center. This center enabled us to continue gathering stories, which not only highlighted pressing current issues but also exposed the lingering scars of the past: evictions, housing crises, poverty, and isolation. Residents shared experiences of lost status, economic security, and full citizenship, as well as severed familial and community ties caused by their relocation. These narratives were filled with regret, pain, and a deep sense of nostalgia for what had been left behind.

The environment the new residents encountered was deeply hostile: the apartments already required repairs, the elevators – essential for navigating the nine floors – were frequently out of service, and the corridors, stretching the entire length of the building, were dark and foreboding. These dimly lit passageways became fertile ground for fantasies of crime or the acting out of transgressive behaviors. The building's inner spaces, spanning a full kilometer, even served as an unofficial motorcycle racing track. From the physical environment, our attention shifted to the personal and family stories: tales of fear, humiliation, violence, vandalism, petty and serious crimes, drug use, arrests, overdoses, and deaths from AIDS. These grim narratives painted a picture of marginalization in an abandoned suburb, compounded by the oppressive confinement of a single, massive structure housing approximately 5,000 residents.

There had been protests, roadblocks, and bonfires as residents demanded public transportation, building maintenance, safety measures, grocery stores, and the attention from institutions that had long neglected them. It was a "heroic" era of collective struggle. Meanwhile, the adolescents who had arrived with their families were growing up in an environment steeped in deviance, petty crime, and substance abuse. These behaviors unfolded in plain view, within the confined space of the architectural giant, bordered by two roads and characterized by stifling separation that suppressed potential for growth. An entire generation of young people received little attention from their parents and families, many of whom were overwhelmed by their own struggles. Left to fend for themselves, most wandered aimlessly, trying to fill the void with drugs, delinquency, and dangerous behaviors. For them, this was a desperate and unprotected entry into adulthood, akin to throwing themselves into the void without a parachute or safety net. This void was their urban suburb – a place abandoned to social marginalization and petty crime, where they became spectators or victims, decimated by overdoses, AIDS, and incarceration. The youth's struggles also manifested in a high incidence of behavioral and psychiatric disorders, becoming a significant concern for the Department of Mental Health.

Over the years, the "Serpentone" (the big snake), as the building was nicknamed, had undergone significant changes. Petty crime was now under control, daily violence had disappeared, and connections to the city were available. Our arrival coincided with a "pacified" phase in its history. What remained were resentment, grief, nostalgia, and the emotions that emerged from the stories of the parents, their children, and even the children's children – the new adolescents. These feelings were so vivid that they demanded our attention.

Despite these changes, both real and figurative deaths continued to cast a shadow over the building, marking it as a place of suffering and persistent unease. The conflicts between roles and generations often devolved into futile struggles where mutual violence became a distorted mechanism for establishing distance and differentiation. Many parents carried a heavy sense of educational failure, burdened by the guilt for having brought their families into such an environment. Family networks had weakened due to their physical separation from relatives' former homes, while relational isolation and sadness became entrenched states of mind for many.

Equally significant was the confrontation with "otherness." In many places, the "Other" is identified as the foreigner, the Roma, the Black person, or the Southerner, facilitating – albeit through defensive projection mechanisms – a reinforced identity defined "against." However, when the "Other" resides "within" the community and is indistinguishable from the "Same," the resulting hardship can be deeply unsettling, shaking the very foundation of the relational pact (Portelli, Bonomo, Sotgia et al., 2006). In this case, the "Others" were the residents themselves – all of them – collectively stigmatized by outsiders as strangers and dangerous. This external labeling not only mirrored but also intensified an internalized self-perception within the community, creating a destructive feedback loop. The burden of this internalized stigma, continually reinforced by external judgment, fueled a pervasive and corrosive process that deeply eroded the social fabric of the building.

> *From a distance, we saw a huge black spot – perhaps it looked darker because it was a rainy day. There was nothing but mud, ruined houses, destruction everywhere, and abandoned structures. It was impossible to imagine that this could be considered residential housing for civilians.*
>
> *When I first came here, I thought, "Oh God! What is this? Mamma mia! It looks like a cemetery." It was raining, and when it rains here, everything becomes so gloomy – everything turns gray. All you can see are the lights, and they look like graveyard lanterns. I thought, "Oh*

God! How awful!" I swore I'd never want to live here. But then fate stepped in – and when it did, what could I do?

The first impact was traumatic. I was only 10 years old and got a fever for two days. When I realized I had to come back here, I felt physically sick. It was hard, and I ended up having a terrible nervous breakdown.

In my stairwell, there were seven deaths – young people. Seven. They say you can escape drugs . . . sure, if you're dead! And all of them were young. Imagine – in one family alone, five children died.

Dozens and dozens of friends lost – to drugs, acid, heroin. Some died in those motorcycle races in the big parking lot. The low wall at the end of the lot basically became a memorial, covered with bouquets, photos, and inscriptions. Someone I knew – some friend or acquaintance – was gone because of tragic stories of drugs, loneliness, and marginalization. People who decided to end their lives. It makes you feel like a survivor, but it's a bitter kind of survival.

We were completely abandoned; there was nothing here. We were victims of an unjust eviction.

On one hand, I hate Corviale – I want to leave. But to hate something often means, in a strange way, that you also love it. And I do love Corviale, in a way. As I said, there's this need to show others that Corviale doesn't just produce garbage. It can also produce good people – even great people.

Mom, the problem was that you were afraid when I was a kid – that I'd get hooked, that I'd start smoking joints. Just say it, right? You need to say it. You have to say these things!

29.3 Trauma or injury

What were those people really telling us? When a 12-year-old boy spoke of love and hate, what did he mean? This was a child born into a family whose grandfather had brought them to Corviale following an eviction while they had been living outdoors under the colonnades of St. Peter's Basilica. And what were the things the mother of that psychiatric patient finally had to say, encouraged by her son to open up and speak to us?

In the intimacy of these conversations, every word seemed saturated with the weight of the past. Meanwhile, within the social fabric of that immense Roman building, home to 5,000 residents, an unsettling silence prevailed. The atmosphere felt suspended in time, briefly animated each day by students leaving school, only to settle back into a tense, heavy calm. It was as though the air itself carried the weight of fears, humiliations, and the echoes of violent and premature deaths. Could Minuchin's *Families of the Slums* (Minuchin et al. 1967) and Andolfi's "South Bronx" (Andolfi, 1997) help us understand and help Corviale?

The persistent repetition of shared memories, the overwhelming return to events from a past that seemed never to have passed, and the personal pains mirrored in a collective memory of suffering within families, all resonated deeply with the concept of trauma. In psychiatric practice, trauma is often understood as the lingering trace of past violence that remains active in the present, explored through its psychic underpinnings (Leys, 2000) or its material basis embedded in the brain (van der Kolk et al., 1996). However, what we faced here was a collective dimension of damage that resisted materialist interpretations. These harms were deeply tied to historical and social events – shared experiences of suffering that had become the individual heritage of each person. Traditional individual or relational diagnoses failed to capture the complexities of what we were witnessing and hearing. Applying diagnostic labels to people's suffering seemed not only inadequate but reductive – especially when the environment played such a decisive role. In fact, doing so might even be considered unethical (Losi, 2020). By "damage," we refer to the conditions that obstruct, delay, or undermine the process of overcoming loss through socialization, and the collective or individual processing of suffering and fear. These conditions encouraged defensive responses such as isolation, emotional encapsulation, denial, and the concealment of pain – responses that were fostered, induced, or even incentivized by the surrounding environmental circumstances. In our practice, those who came to our center received attention, direct responses to varying degrees, and, when necessary, guided referrals to other services better equipped to address their specific needs. Yet what struck us most was the physical, sensory experience of an unexpected and pervasive silence that hung over the scene of this immense, overcrowded phalanstery. This silence was profoundly unsettling.

The critique of the individualistic and ahistorical construct of PTSD (Young, 1997) served as a caution against reducing historically situated suffering to a simplistic diagnosis. Seeking a descriptive rather than categorical terminology (Migone, 2013), we aimed to avoid the medical-biological and individualistic naturalization of psychological and psychic phenomena that were clearly rooted in a specific social and relational context (Caruth, 1995; Fassin & Rechtman, 2009). We also found it inappropriate to frame the building as a breeding ground for vaguely defined "personality disorders," a diagnostic construct that, while widespread, remains tenuous. In the face of historical realities, we need not always metaphorize symptoms to uncover the imprints of past events within them (Beneduce, 2013). When discussing references, we prefer the term "injury," specifically "moral injury," which emphasizes moral "damage" while avoiding the term "wound," to maintain a clear distinction from biomedical definitions (cf. above). The concept of moral injury, as used by some authors, incorporates moral and social evaluations alongside medical and psychological perspectives. This approach seems more fitting to describe the complex interplay of emotions and interactional dynamics that ultimately formed a psychological bond among the inhabitants (Papadopoulos, 2020).

29.4 Urban migration and its consequences

We also asked ourselves what it meant to be a community. Was merely being forced by circumstance to live in the same place enough to form one? The residents embodied what Max Weber might call a "collectivity of fate" but not a "community of fate." Circumstances had brought them together in a single location, but history had not allowed for the creation of a relational fabric – a shared sense of purpose, collaborative projects, or the exchange of material and symbolic elements that could transform memories into a unifying bond. At best, one might describe it as a "failed community." In the past, there had been mobilizations to address the lack of essential services, absences rooted in institutional neglect, which had monopolized the residents' energy and attention (Campanella, 1995). However, these efforts, while collective in nature, had not succeeded in fostering a deeper sense of solidarity or shared identity. There had been something resembling a fleeting moment of community, centered around collective demands for improvement. The residents had briefly united around shared grievances, channeling their anger against a common enemy – the unjust institutions. They protested by setting garbage on fire, blocking roads, and disrupting traffic. However, this brief unity was not enough to establish a lasting foundation for the future. Once the shared struggle ended, residents retreated into individual or family isolation, and only a few fragile interpersonal connections remained from that "heroic" era. This prompted us to examine the individual and collective dynamics within the residents' community and to hypothesize why a more developed form of social cohesion had failed to emerge. Instead, the residents seemed trapped in a nostalgic suspension, longing for a past when they did not feel alone, when shared suffering had been at the forefront and had briefly fueled a sense of belonging. This confirmed that a community is never an inherent reality but rather a possibility (Basaglia, 1974) – the painstaking result of deliberately and patiently constructing relational, emotional, and value-based networks. None of this had been able to take root in Corviale.

How, then, should we interpret these painful individual and collective experiences? We had already acknowledged the inadequacy of applying trauma diagnoses at the individual level, but we also felt a certain hesitation in using the same categories employed for forced displacement – such as those applied to entire populations uprooted by wars, internal conflicts, or natural disasters (e.g., IDPs, internally displaced persons) – to the urban phenomena of a large city. After all, we reminded ourselves, these residents had simply been provided with housing they previously lacked and could not have otherwise afforded. And yet, the experiences of uprooting, accompanied by a deeply humiliating aftermath, were alive and vivid. They told stories of individuals and families fractured, of unresolved and crystallized losses, often exacerbated by external events marked by threats, fear, and exposure to violence. These narratives revealed that a form of urban forced migration did, in fact, exist. When these experiences transcended the boundaries of individual or family stories, they deserved recognition, validation, and a place in the broader conversation about displacement and suffering.

The question remained open as to why some young people repeated the narratives of their fathers and grandfathers. They spoke of events they had only heard about – events that had often occurred before they were even born. They, too, were "prisoners of memory," albeit someone else's memory, and like everyone else, they bore the consequences of a projection onto a visible, collective harm of personal or familial pain that, in some way, had marked their lives. We had to grapple with the issue of private memory and public memory, a subject of great significance (Huyssen, 2003), especially in the dominant view of trauma as a "pathology of memory." This perspective posits that an event exceeding the capacity for representation and symbolization echoes in a return of memory, making it present again later, even long after the event occurred – the enigma of the dual temporality of trauma described by Freud. We were faced with individual memory, reinforced by collective memory, which was embraced by all, regardless of age, as a reservoir of fragments of identity. In the trauma paradigm, intergenerational transmission is an almost inevitable outcome (van der Kolk, 2014). However, such a direct connection was overly mechanical and failed to account for the individual stories we had heard – stories that were all similar yet each unique, specific to that person, to that family. Once again, rendering trauma "objective," naturalizing it, and detaching it from its historical context was misleading.

Trauma cannot be the central category for addressing the broader discourse on memory, because

> trauma as a psychic phenomenon is located on the threshold between remembering and forgetting. . . . But trauma cannot be the central category in addressing the larger memory discourse. It has been all too tempting to some to think of trauma as the hidden core of all memory. But . . . to collapse memory into trauma . . . would unduly confine our understanding of memory, marking it too exclusively in terms of pain, suffering, and loss. It would deny human agency and lock us into compulsive repetition. Memory, whether individual or generational, political or public, is always more than only the prison house of the past.
>
> *(Huyssen, 2003, p. 8)*

Approaching history solely through the lens of trauma does little to illuminate the multiple political layers inherent in the discourse on memory. The problem arises when trauma is simplistically transposed into the realm of history, even though it is difficult to avoid invoking the term when individuals, groups, and nations grapple with the violence they have endured (Beneduce, 2010). We were confronting both individual harm – possibly even cumulative trauma (Khan, 1964) – and a collective phenomenon that, even more so than personal harm, demanded consideration of its historical, social, and political dimensions. The harm we observed spanned a gradient of experiences: personal histories of past loss, displacement to an isolated periphery, the painful events of everyday life, the suffering and deaths of the next generation, the challenges of living in an overwhelming and isolating building, the pervasive sense of abandonment by institutions, the scorn of other city residents, the shame of living in such a stigmatized environment, and countless other "offenses." No single term could adequately encompass this multifaceted reality. Moving beyond traditional psychoanalytic frameworks (though not dismissing them) and cognitivist models, we sought guidance in anthropological perspectives. Following Beneduce, we adopted trauma as a "hinge concept," a term that connects "the dimensions of the unconscious and those of history, between individual conflicts and collective dramas, between private experiences and cultural meanings" (Beneduce, 2010, p. 25). Rather than viewing trauma as a timeless phenomenon, we recognized in its repetitive nature "an unresolved experience rooted in history" (Huyssen, 2003, p. 175).

This approach allowed us to contextualize the suffering within a broader historical and cultural framework, linking personal pain to collective narratives. Equally significant was the reflection on loss and mourning. In this context, the diagnostic framework for complicated grief in the *Diagnostic and Statistical Manual of Mental Disorders* provided little assistance in addressing the fixed memories and relentless repetition of certain recollections. The theme of mourning emerged prominently, not only because an entire generation had been decimated by drugs and AIDS, but also because the place itself was imbued with a sense of dark power – a "curse" believed to be responsible for many deaths. This belief even led to the fabrication of a story about the suicide of the architect who designed the "Serpentone," creating a myth of fateful nemesis. Consider, for instance, the recurring imagery in residents' statements, where themes of gloomy darkness and associations with cemeteries frequently surfaced. The chain of losses was deeply intertwined with the chain of grief – emotional and affective ruptures, hidden shame, untold secrets, and unresolved traumas. These were the things left unsaid, for which there seemed to be no adequate words. "You need to say these things!" was the son's heartfelt plea to his mother (Andolfi & D'Elia, 2007).

29.5 A documentary film for a new beginning

These premises laid the groundwork for an intervention designed to have both a collective and emotional impact – an action that would not stand in isolation but instead would be integrated into an ongoing process. The hypothesis was that the repetitive suspension and pervasive silence were manifestations of unspoken truths – a convergence of concealed grief and social humiliation. The ambitious goal was to begin breaking this silence by introducing words and publicly validating a shared history, adopting a non-clinical approach to address the collective suffering. We envisioned a multi-level, phased intervention. To begin, we presented a project to urban planners at the Department for Peripheries of the Municipality of Rome. The plan involved filming interviews to capture personal testimonies, editing them into a documentary, and screening it publicly in Corviale, specifically in the council chamber of the municipal office located there. This screening would serve as the starting point for a series of follow-up meetings with residents, fostering collective reflection and dialogue. Upon securing a modest amount of funding, we expanded the working group. Alongside the two psychologist colleagues and three nurses – an invaluable source of professional expertise, humanity, and cultural insight – we included a director, two screenwriters, and a production secretary, forming an unconventional team for a mental health center. It was clear to everyone that the intervention needed to address structural issues, acknowledging the material and economic realities faced by the residents. At the same time, it was equally evident that previous efforts in this regard, though not insignificant (albeit delayed), needed to be complemented by a focus on relational, symbolic, and emotional dimensions. Without this, the pervasive "silence" would persist. We understood that the social and political dimensions could not be replaced by a clinical approach and that multiple levels of intervention had to be integrated.

Through the film, we aimed to harness the emotional power of images combined with words – a medium uniquely effective in capturing the repetitive nature of individual private stories while transforming them into a shared collective narrative. This was the story of familial and personal episodes of pain, resilience, and change. Together, these narratives could form the foundation of a new community identity – one no longer stuck in time, but moving forward.

Communities often come together in moments of struggle but tend to dissolve in the diminished tension of everyday life, as happened in the "building." Without an awareness of a shared destiny, events, violence, and grief are treated as isolated occurrences, excluding the possibility of solidarity and hindering the collective capacity to foster relational changes and draw on interpersonal resources (Castelli & Sbattella, 2003). By comparing the experiences of multiple generations, we identified distinct differences. The "pioneers" – the parents who first arrived in Corviale – were weighed down by familial responsibilities, the harsh living conditions imposed by the building, and the guilt they felt for the consequences their families endured. Their children, now in their forties or fifties, had survived a lost adolescence, marked by the deaths of friends and neighbors, and had each developed their own strategies for enduring fear and pain. The youngest generation – the children of these survivors – represented a third wave. They had inherited not only the pain of the first and second generations but also the mythology of the earlier struggles. These struggles, now perceived as mythical, timeless, and disconnected from their historical roots, had become an identity-forming narrative to which this generation clung.

At a distance from the damaging events, the most vulnerable are often those in their developmental stages, while adults, preoccupied with material concerns, remain focused on providing for their families and managing the demands of survival. In this struggle, they frequently fail to recognize or address the needs and fears of their children.

The act of bearing witness, as a form of emotionally charged remembrance, grants the witness the role of a social therapist. However, verbalizing events does not automatically transform them into symbolic terms, and an overuse of words can be just as much a defensive mechanism as silence (Levi, 1988). To move beyond the confines of mythical memory (Andolfi & Angelo, 1989), that memory needed to be transformed into history – anchored, contextualized, and made accessible for reflection and growth. The stereotyped repetitiveness of the stories revealed a duality in the residents: their public persona – assertive, resentful, and demanding reparations – contrasted sharply with their private, grief-stricken, and melancholic selves. People often "performed" the role of the resident offended by institutions, introducing a theme that was more moral in nature than psychological or mental (Fassin & Rechtman, 2009). It was crucial to avoid reducing the residents to mere victims by affirming their public identity while neglecting their need to process experiences privately. Thus, our narrative approach began with the public sphere to create an entry point into the private.

We approached mourning as a transformative process rather than a restorative one (Andolfi & D'Elia, 2007). Revisiting dramatic events, even after significant time had passed, offered an opportunity for reconstruction. The collective processing of grief allowed for breaking the pact of silence that "blocks, through multiple projections, both personal and collective memory" (Castelli & Sbattella, 2003, p. 173). Throughout, we maintained expressive rigor, consciously avoiding any sensationalization of pain, instead fostering an environment for meaningful reflection and emotional engagement.

We wanted to stimulate community resilience, enhance social cohesion, build a collective narrative, and affirm the traumatic experiences of the residents: "Those events happened, they were serious and painful, and now everyone knows it" (Landau & Saul, 2004).

Memory becomes collective when it is embraced and validated by institutions (De Luna, 2011). By organizing a public screening, we created a ritual – a form of social celebration. For us, this was also an act of justice: restoring dignity and meaning to the emotions and experiences that had surfaced, shaping them into a shared narrative through a "fictional" product. This medium unified different levels of experience and fragments of personal stories within a common framework (Castelli &

Sbattella, 2003, pp. 146–147). During the screening, many participants who had shared their interviews appeared visibly nervous, standing up and sitting down in a peculiar restlessness. It wasn't until the discussion afterward that they seemed to regain their composure, resuming their public roles as resentful protesters. In these public personas, they appeared more comfortable, distanced from the raw, intimate pain that had been exposed on the screen. This shift suggested that they felt more at ease in their familiar roles of collective indignation than in the vulnerability of their private suffering, now brought into public view. Institutional representatives, who had funded the project, expressed genuine regret for the failures of the past, without pretension or hypocrisy. The screening was followed by public meetings, additional viewings, and lively debates. Copies of the DVD, deposited in the Corviale library, were in high demand, borrowed so frequently that reservations became necessary. It seemed that the private and intimate act of viewing the film at home was more tolerable for many than the shared experience of a public screening (D'Elia, 2008, 2010).

29.6 Conclusion

Questioning the trauma model allowed us to recover the temporal dimension of human experience, along with the personal and relational capacities that had existed before, and those that had developed after, the harmful events (Walsh, 2006; Papadopoulos, 2002). To address the silence of Corviale, we had to rethink the conceptual and practical tools of psychiatry and psychotherapy, seeking ways to engage meaningfully with people who had endured humiliation, powerlessness, and the concealment of their pain – experiences that no diagnostic category can fully encapsulate. If traumatic repetition represents a constrained and blocked temporality, the practice of memory – realized by creating a shared object – was intended to counteract this process of "detemporalization." Emotions, like memory, can evolve over time rather than remaining frozen in the past. By tapping into community resources, these emotions can be reactivated and redefined within a historical and social context. To achieve this, it was essential to differentiate between the model of early psychic trauma and that of extreme adult experiences (Mucci, 2008, p. 135), while broadening the focus from the individual to the collective. Collective trauma, which inevitably breeds distrust and resentment, is fundamentally a social wound. As Palestinian psychiatrist Samah Jabr (2021, p. 47) observes, collective trauma "harms the integrity of the social fabric, its ability to produce collective bonds, trust, and shared visions of the world." Frozen memory, in this sense, perpetuates pain and suffering more intensely than the harmful events themselves.

A social approach that prioritizes the developmental, relational, and intergenerational dimensions offers a meaningful alternative to the medicalization and psychologization of suffering. These individualized models, whether psychiatric or psychotherapeutic, systematically overlook the collective aspects of human experience. When a theoretical construct like trauma acquires generalized and standardized meanings, interpretations, diagnoses, and care practices – almost by inertia – it loses its epistemic power. Its effectiveness risks being diluted into rigid, automatic patterns of thought, techniques, and protocols that often produce outcomes far removed from the original intentions of those applying it. The experience in Corviale provided a foundation for subsequent large-scale social interventions I undertook in other contexts, using different tools (such as in the Idroscalo of Ostia and with suffering residents on an island in Lazio). These interventions shared a critical reassessment of the concept of therapy and a reevaluation of transformative practices that were non-technical, non-focused, and respectful of the voices and needs of individuals. These practices aimed to be more equitable, less directed toward predefined changes, and instead centered on activating resources that encouraged movement in unpredictable and organic directions. The aim is always to navigate between the social and personal dimensions, passing through the familial (Andolfi, 2017), to bring individual differences to the surface against a shared historical and biographical background. Remembering helps to forget.

Note

1 Merril Block, S. (2008). *The story of forgetting*. Random House.

References

Andolfi, M. (1997). Dov'è il South Bronx? La marginalità come strategia dell'esclusione. *Terapia Familiare, 54*, 11–19.
Andolfi, M. (2017). *Multi-generational family therapy. Tools and resources for the therapist*. Routledge.
Andolfi, M., Angelo, C., & de Nichilo, M. (1989). *The myth of Atlas. Families and the therapeutic story*. Brunner-Routledge.
Andolfi, M., & D'Elia, A. (Eds.). (2007). *Le perdite e le risorse della famiglia*. Raffaello Cortina.
Basaglia, F. (1982). L'utopia della realtà. In F. Basaglia (Ed.), *Scritti II 1968–1980* (pp. 339–348). Einaudi (Original work published 1974).
Beneduce, R. (2010). *Archeologie del trauma. Un'antropologia del sottosuolo*. Laterza.
Beneduce, R. (2013). Illusioni e violenza della diagnosi in psichiatria. *Aut Aut, 357*, 187–211.
Campanella, N. (1995). *Roma: Nuovo Corviale. Miti, utopie, valutazioni*. Bulzoni.
Caruth, C. (Ed.). (1995). *Trauma. Explorations in memory*. The Johns Hopkins University Press.
Castelli, C., & Sbattella, F. (2003). *Psicologia dei disastri*. Carocci.
D'Elia, A. (Producer). (2008). *Il Silenzio di Corviale*. [Documentary Film] 42'. Comune di Roma.
D'Elia, A. (2010). Storie di palazzo. Migrazione urbana e narrazioni collettive. *[Conference presentation] Terapeuti e narratori nell'arcipelago dell'identità.*
De Luna, G. (2011). *La Repubblica del dolore. Le memorie di un'Italia divisa*. Feltrinelli.
Farina, F. (2012). *Ricerca sociale e progettazione partecipata*. Bonanno.
Fassin, D., & Rechtman, R. (2009). *The empire of trauma: An inquiry into the condition of victimhood*. Princeton University Press.
Giglioli, D. (2011). *Senza trauma*. Quodlibet.
Huyssen, A. (2003). *Present Pasts. Urban palimpsests and the politics of memory*. Stanford University Press.
Jabr, S. (2021). *Sumud. Resistere all'oppressione*. Sensibili alle foglie.
Khan, M. M. R. (1974). Ego – Distortion, cumulative trauma and the role of reconstruction in the analytic situation. In M. M. R. Khan (Ed.), *The privacy of the Self*. Hogarth Press (Original work published 1964).
Landau, J., & Saul, J. (2004). Facilitating family and community resilience in response to major disaster. In F. Walsh & M. McGoldrick (Eds.), *Living Beyond Loss* (2nd ed., pp. 285–309). Norton.
Levi, P. (1988). *The drowned and the saved*. Simon & Shuster.
Leys, R. (2000). *Trauma. A Genealogy*. University of Chicago Press.
Losi, N. (2020). *Critica del trauma*. Quodlibet.
Migone, P. (2013). La diagnosi descrittiva in psichiatria: luci e ombre. *Scienze dell'interazione, 1*(2), 14–39.
Minuchin, S., Montalvo, B., Guerney, B. G., Rosman, B. L., & Schumer, F. (1967). *Families of the slums*. Basic Books.
Mucci, C. (2008). *Il dolore estremo. Il trauma da Freud alla Shoah*. Borla.
Papadopoulos, R. (2002). *Therapeutic care for refugees. No place like home*. Karnac.
Papadopoulos, R. (2020). *Moral injury and beyond. Understanding human anguish and healing traumatic wounds*. Routledge.
Portelli, A., Bonomo, B., Sotgia, A., & Viccaro, U. (2006). *Città di parole. Storia orale da una periferia romana*. Donzelli.
Rosen, G. M. (Ed.). (2004). *Posttraumatic stress disorder. Issues and controversies*. Wiley.
Van der Kolk, B. (2014). *The body keeps the score: Mind, brain and body in the healing of trauma*. Viking Press.
Van der Kolk, B., McFarlane, A. C., & Weisaeth, L. (Eds.). (1996). *Traumatic stress. The effects of overwhelming experience on mind, body, and society*. The Guilford Press.
Walsh, F. (2006). *Strengthening family resilience* (2nd ed.). The Guilford Press.
Williams, R. (Ed.). (2009). *Trauma e relazioni. Le prospettive scientifiche e cliniche contemporanee*. Raffaello Cortina.
Young, A. (1997). *The harmony of illusions. Inventing post-traumatic stress disorder*. Princeton University Press.

30

YOUNG CHILDREN REMEMBER

The family as a resource in the treatment of pre-verbal childhood trauma

Arianne Struik and Raffaella Salvo

30.1 Introduction

Despite the common belief that young children do not remember, infants and toddlers (0–4 years) can suffer intensely from multiple traumatizing situations such as accidents, invasive medical procedures, prematurity, separation from parents, suffocation, domestic violence, and sexual, physical, or emotional abuse or neglect. The impact of traumatic experiences on the young child is significant but too often unrecognized. When childhood trauma goes untreated, it can have devastating and prolonged effects on the child's development and on the family dynamic. Quoting Winnicott (1960/1965), we can state that a child does not exist without the mother (parent), and consequently the traumatic experiences of the young child are expressed not only in infantile symptoms but also in relational ones.

Eye movement desensitization and reprocessing (EMDR) therapy is an individual, evidence-based treatment of a child's traumatic memories using bilateral distracting stimuli. In this way, traumatic memories lose vividness and their emotional content, alleviating the child's post-traumatic symptoms. This chapter describes the use of EMDR with pre-verbal trauma in children aged 0–4 years and their parents. The brief relational parent-child EMDR therapy protocol (Struik, 2019; Struik & Salvo, 2023 July 6–8; Went, 2014, 2018; Went et al., 2024) takes into account key factors from intersubjective theory of infant and young child development (Siegel et al., 2021; Stern, 1985; Tronik & Beeghly, 2011) and the guiding principles of dyadic and relational therapeutic interventions developed within the field of infant mental health (Baradon et al., 2017; Fraiberg et al., 1975; Lieberman & Van Horn, 2008; Went, 2014, 2018; Went et al., 2024). The aim of this family treatment is to free the child, the parents, and their relationships from the "impact of unprocessed traumatic memories that can create deficits in affective co-regulation and emergent sense of self and other," as well as somatization, affective/cognitive distortions, and relational blockages between the child and his/her parents. This helps the child and family to resume individual and relational growth, otherwise blocked by the trauma.

30.2 The concept of mental health of the newborn and young child

The international *Zero to Three* association defines infant and early childhood mental health as the child's ability to (1) experience, regulate, and express a range of emotions; (2) form intimate and secure emotional relationships; and (3) explore the environment (ZERO TO THREE, 2001). These

DOI: 10.4324/9781003536765-35

capacities are fully developed within a sensitive parental environment that is attuned to the child's needs and within a social context that respects the family, community, and cultural expectations and values of the family unit. The field of infant and young child mental health considers infancy as the developmental period from conception to the child's fifth birthday, in contrast to the pediatric definition of infancy, which runs from birth to the first year of life (Zeanah, 2018).

30.3 Definition of traumatizing event

According to the *Diagnostic and Statistical Manual of Mental Disorders*, 5th ed.; DSM-5-TR (American Psychiatric Association, 2022), a traumatizing event in children under the age of 6 years may consist of the direct experience of a death threat, severe injury(s), or sexual violence, as well as directly witnessing, or becoming aware of, traumatizing events that occurred to a family member or attachment figure. As a result, infants and young children may experience high levels of emotional, psychological, and physical distress that may temporarily disrupt their ability to function normally in daily life and impact their mental health.

30.4 Impact of pre-verbal trauma in the newborn and young child

Many people mistakenly believe that children do not notice or remember traumatizing events. In reality, any situation or event in a family that may impact older children and adults can also have an impact on infants. Some common reactions to trauma in infants/toddlers may include:

- unusually high levels of distress upon separation from the parent or primary caregiver
- a kind of "frozen vigilance," whereby the child may look "shocked"
- the impression of being numb and not showing their emotions or appearing to be somewhat "cut off" from what is happening around them
- loss of playful and engaging behavior, such as smiling and laughter
- loss of the ability to eat
- avoidance of eye contact
- restlessness and much more difficult to calm down
- a regression in physical abilities, such as sitting, crawling, or walking, and appearing clumsier (Better Health, 2022, September 20)

When an infant suffers perinatal trauma, it can be difficult to understand its impact, and sometimes it is only after psychotherapeutic treatment that parents recognize that the child's behavioral and affective reactions, which they believe to be part of his or her temperament, may have been post-traumatic symptoms.

Trauma can severely impair important aspects of a child's development occurring before the age of 3 years old. These may include the relationship and bonding with parents, as well as development in the areas of language, mobility, physical and social skills, and emotion management. In addition, trauma-specific symptoms such as flashbacks, avoidance behavior, reduced joy and pleasure response, and an elevated state of alertness (arousal) may persist over time if the child is not helped to process the pre-verbal traumatic memory. When young children are exposed to traumatizing or stressful events, they may manifest difficulties in one or more of the following areas: sleep, crying, feeding, toileting, relationship, expression, stress tolerance, and regulation of emotions and mood, as well as developmental delays or regression. Because the infant's/toddler's brain is still maturing and the child has not developed verbal language, pre-verbal memories, consisting mostly of sensory and emotional information, are stored in implicit memory (Gaensbauer, 2002; Siegel, 2015) and are therefore not accessible for regular EMDR therapy (Went et al., 2024).

30.5 Standard EMDR therapy protocol

Traumatic memories can be processed with EMDR therapy, and randomized control trials have shown the effectiveness of EMDR therapy on children with post-traumatic stress disorder (PTSD) from the age of four (Olivier et al., 2021; Rodenburg et al., 2009). EMDR therapy is based on the adaptive information processing (AIP) model (Shapiro, 2001), which describes how memories related to negative events and experiences are maladaptively stored in neural networks and the information stored in such unprocessed memories underlies post-traumatic clinical symptoms. The AIP model emphasizes the body's intrinsic capacity to integrate traumatizing and stressful events, and change is brought about by associative processes (Solomon & Shapiro, 2012). The standard EMDR protocol (Shapiro, 2001) involves eight phases: history-taking (Phase 1), preparation for treatment with installation of positive resources (Phase 2), and the assessment phase (Phase 3), in which the child selects a target image from the traumatic memory and identifies cognitions, the emotions, stress levels, and body sensations. In the desensitization phase (Phase 4), the child focuses on the target image while focusing simultaneously on associations and bilateral stimulation, which can be ocular, i.e., by asking the patient to move their eyes by following the therapist's fingers, or through tapping, which the therapist performs on the patient's hands, or acoustic, through listening to alternating sounds through earphones/headphones. After the target image is no longer distressing, a positive belief is instilled (Phase 5), followed by a body scan to assess residual negative body sensations (Phase 6), optional installation of a future template to reduce fear and avoidance of future situations or events, and concluding with a positive ending in which the child is helped to focus on the positive aspects of him/herself, learned during therapy (Phase 7). The next session begins with a re-evaluation of the previously processed target image (Phase 8).

30.6 EMDR therapy with young children with pre-verbal trauma

The standard EMDR therapy protocol cannot be used with young children (usually under the age of 4) because they cannot identify and describe their memories. Many years ago, Joan Lovett developed the storytelling method (Lovett, 1999, 2015), in which the therapist reads with the parents a preconstructed story to the child to activate and process the child's traumatic memories. This story is built around the following elements: the child's current situation, the child's strengths and resilience, aspects of the child that the family values, a description of the traumatizing event experienced by the child, a difficult/tricky aspect of the child's life, and a solution to the current problem, enriched with psycho-educational aspects and positive beliefs. During the reading of the story, the therapist offers continuous bilateral stimulation to the child (Lovett, 2015). The storytelling method is based on the AIP model (Shapiro, 2001) and was developed through empirical and experimental applications. Variants of the storytelling protocol are used widely with good clinical results, and several case and pilot studies have been published (Adler-Tapia & Settle, 2017; Gomez, 2013; Rathore, 2018; Swimm, 2018; Went et al., 2024; Wesselmann et al., 2018), and de Roos et al. (2025) found preliminary evidence for the safety, feasibility, and efficacy. However, to date, research to explain the method and its mechanisms is limited.

Went (2014) and (Went et al., 2024) developed the relational parent-child EMDR therapy protocol – an alternative procedure that integrates the infant mental health principles and research in the field of memory and EMDR therapy.

30.7 Infant mental health principles applied to EMDR therapy of the young child

The application of EMDR therapy in the under-4 child should reflect the core principles of infant mental health and maintain a relational focus, like any other mental health intervention for this age group (Baradon et al., 2017; Fraiberg et al., 1975; Lieberman & Van Horn, 2008; Went, 2014). As argued by Winnicott (1960/1965), when he stated "there is no child without the mother," infants and parents are mutually connected, and infants cannot be considered separately from their relational context (Zeanah, 2018). Infants' and young children's well-being and sense of security are closely linked to the sensitivity and responsiveness of their attachment figures to whom young children turn to seek comfort and protection, especially when frightened or emotionally fragile (Bowlby, 1969). Infants and toddlers may be exposed to potentially traumatizing events, beyond parental control (or sometimes at the hands of the parents themselves), and such events may have a simultaneous impact on the child and parent (Cicchetti & Lynch, 1993).

When exposed to traumatizing events, infants or young children may change their perception of the parent who in their eyes did not protect them, or was absent, powerless, or dangerous. At the same time, the parent may also be traumatized by the same event and change their internal representations of themselves and the child. All of this can have an impact on the parent-child relationship and their capacity for affective co-regulation (Winnicott, 1960/1965). The parent's perception of the traumatizing event and the effect of that event on the child can have an impact on the child's post-traumatic response as well as on the symptomatology and, conversely, the child's symptomatology contributes to the parent's perception and representation of the event itself (Stuber & Shemesh, 2006). Parents may, for example, perceive the child as fragile, frightened, but also fearful and disgusting, and they may perceive themselves as powerless and unable to offer protection. This in turn may trigger reactions of overprotection, distancing, and/or stress in the parent that will have an impact on the interaction with the child. Trauma can affect the attachment relationship through its impact on the mutual interactions and behaviors of the dyad/triad. It follows that EMDR therapy for children under the age of 4 must focus on both the child and the parent, as well as their interaction as a mechanism of change (Lieberman et al., 2011).

The therapist's role in EMDR therapy work with young children and parents is not limited to facilitating the processing of the traumatic memory. Parents need support and guidance because often, after a traumatic experience, they find themselves bewildered and confused when faced with their child's emotional and behavioral reactions. Parents feel that their parenting strategies are not working, and their confidence in themselves and their relationship with the child may weaken. Sometimes, the trauma experienced by the child may resurface unprocessed traumas of the parent and possibly related to the parenting history (e.g., premature birth, postpartum medical complications, etc.). The therapist has the delicate task of helping parents to understand the child's experience, reactions, and needs as well as their own reaction and the effect this has on the interaction with the child. Furthermore, parents often need guidance and scaffolding to make sense of the child's changes during and after treatment, so that they can empathize with the child and rebuild confidence in their own parenting skills.

30.8 The relational parent-child EMDR therapy protocol (0–4 years)

This EMDR protocol focuses on the representation of the trauma of the child and parent, as well as the effect their representations have on their interaction. As the young child cannot describe their own internal representations of the traumatic memory, the parents assist the child by offering a narrative storyline of the traumatic experience, which will activate their own memory networks as well as those of the child. As with the standard EMDR protocol, the child's and parent's responses to the narrative storyline remain the focus of treatment (trauma processing), while the narrative becomes the vehicle for activating the traumatic memory. Relational EMDR therapy is aimed at facilitating the processing of the traumatic representations, supporting parent-child interaction, and supporting the family dyad/triad in adapting to changes resulting from the treatment. In this way, parents regain confidence in their parenting skills and parent-child interaction improves.

The relational EMDR therapy protocol consists generally of one or two preparatory sessions with the parents (Phase 1–2), optional additional EMDR therapy for the parent, three or four parent-child EMDR sessions (Phase 3–8), telephone or e-mail support for the parent between sessions, and an optional interaction support session without EMDR (based on play as an additional source of expression and trauma processing) for the child and parents.

The protocol is used with young children who present post-traumatic symptoms and developmental delays attributable to exposure to adversity and traumatizing/stressful events in the early stages of development. This modified protocol can also be used for children over the age of 4 or for children and adults with an intellectual disability.

30.9 Case illustration: Tommy

30.9.1 History taking and problem identification

Tommy is a 3 ½-year-old boy who lives with both parents and his 2-year-old sister. His parents describe him as frightened, anxious, and always looking for reassurance. They also report that Tommy does not play much with other children and often seems lost in his own world. The parents believe that Tommy has been like this since he had a very painful episode of constipation when he was about 2 ½ years old.

The mother reports that while she was breastfeeding the baby, Tommy was playing in the other room. The mother reports that, suddenly, Tommy started crying, complaining that he had a tummy ache. The mother tried to console him by talking to him and asking him to come to the room where she was with the little sister, but Tommy did not come. Meanwhile, the crying had become inconsolable. As soon as the mother was able to put the little one down, she ran into Tommy's room, who by then was rolling around on the carpet, curled up on himself, pale and sweaty. The mother remembers that the crying at that point was wailing and that she had absolutely no idea how to help him. She was aware that Tommy had not had a bowel movement for a few days and suspected that he was constipated. After consulting the pediatrician by telephone, the mother realized that it could be intestinal obstruction and took Tommy to the emergency room. By then Tommy had stopped crying, and his mother says it was as if he was no longer there. She talked to him, but he had a blank look on his face. The doctors did a rectal examination and treated Tommy with laxative medication and monitored him until he was able to relieve himself. Since then, Tommy has been holding stools and is often constipated to the point that his rectum is constantly dilated, he has lost his appetite, and has frequent episodes of secondary encopresis.

30.9.2 Assessing and understanding the impact of trauma on the family

The parents report that Tommy does not seem to have conscious memories of the precipitating event as he does not talk about it and does not use symbolic play to represent what happened to him. The parents report that before the triggering episode Tommy was a confident, sociable, and independent child. During the first interview, both parents agree that Tommy now seems like a different child and that they find it hard to recognize their first-born child in him.

Currently, Tommy avoids going to the toilet and holds his feces for multiple days to the point of experiencing frequent soiling accidents. Tommy has also developed a persistent interest in feces and is often asking his parents for explanations on how food transforms into feces.

He has become withdrawn and quite socially isolated. He is reportedly anxious, fearful of new situations, and clingy and has stopped going for sleepovers with his friends. His sleep is disturbed, and the parents report he has weekly nightmares.

The mother seems to empathize with Tommy and to understand the connection between his avoidance towards going to the toilet and the toileting issues and the painful and traumatic experience. Further, she thinks that Tommy's recent clinginess and anxieties might be linked to the traumatic experience. She reports feeling guilty towards Tommy because, during the painful episode, she was caring for her newborn baby and could not help Tommy or comfort him. She says she felt helpless then and still feels helpless and sad about Tommy's transformation from outgoing and independent to insecure and withdrawn. She describes the feeling of losing "her Tommy."

The mother also reports that Tommy's difficulties are putting a strain on the family as moments of intense tension arise in the couple. The father believes that Tommy is simply lazy and should be firmly pushed to use the toilet, while the mother finds herself justifying Tommy and his avoidance of the toilet because she too feels anxious and fears that Tommy will suffer as he did that time. The parents say that no one talks about the triggering episode in the house because everyone fears this will make things worse and make Tommy even more afraid.

The father seems to minimize the traumatic impact of the painful experience and seems to perceive Tommy as unmotivated and attention-seeking. He also reports feeling disgusted whenever Tommy has an episode of encopresis and thinks it is time for Tommy to forget and stop "being difficult."

The assessment phase also includes a joint session with Tommy and the parents to observe the triad's relational style, their communication mode, the child's global functioning, and the triad's ability to play. It emerges that Tommy's play is inhibited and not very exploratory. Tommy tends to interact mainly with his mother, who is attentive and present, although emotionally switched off. He addresses his father rarely and hesitantly. Interactions between them appear stunted and detached. It appears from the assessment that Tommy meets criteria for PTSD as per DSM-5-TR (American Psychiatric Association, 2022) and DC: 0–5 (ZERO TO THREE, 2016). The focus of therapy should be on processing the trauma related to the constipation episode, as well as the impact of the trauma's consequences on Tommy's relationship with his parents and especially with his father.

30.9.3 Preparation for EMDR therapy: The narrative

In preparation, the parents are asked to describe the narrative of the traumatizing event from Tommy's point of view and in the third person. Parents are supported to describe the sensory elements as well as the factual elements, Tommy's behavioral responses, and the possible emotions he experienced. For example, instead of just saying "Tommy was scared," they should describe how, while the doctors were examining him, Tommy's eyes were wide open, his body seemed to be without strength, and he did not move. The therapist revises the narrative and assists the parents in making it sensorially and emotionally pregnant to maximize the opportunity to activate the traumatic memories of Tommy and his parents.

The therapist provides psychoeducation to the parents about the method, the procedure, and possible reactions to the treatment, to prepare them for Tommy's possible initial distress and strong reaction once exposed to the story. Information on the post-traumatic response and the effect of exposure to the stimulus and subsequent desensitization is provided, not only with respect to the child but also to oneself. It is explained to the parents how the parent often develops a post-traumatic response to the event and tries to avoid triggering situations or might begin to accommodate the child's wishes to avoid certain activities due to their own traumatic experience. For instance, Tommy's mother reported feeling anxious whenever she sees Tommy rubbing his tummy, as this is how Tommy started to show his discomfort at the time of the constipation accident. She also reported delaying taking Tommy to the toilet and trying to delegate the task to dad or the grandparents because she finds it unbearable to see Tommy experiencing any pain.

30.9.4 Application of the relational EMDR therapy protocol and shared play

In the first desensitization session, the mother talks about the narrative while the father holds Tommy on his lap and the therapist gently touches Tommy's knees alternately. Tommy listens motionless and seems "frozen" while the mother seems cautious and hesitant to proceed. The therapist describes the triad's behavioral responses and mentalizes the affective states by saying that everyone seems very scared and frozen in listening to what happened to Tommy's tummy. Particular attention is paid to the exchange between Tommy and the mother and the latter's fear of re-traumatizing Tommy in talking about what happened. It is verbalized how since the incident, Tommy is often frightened and how his mother tries to protect him. Once the story is over, Tommy suddenly asks his mother to accompany him to the bathroom as he needs "to poo." The parents are stunned. The session ends with a moment of shared play between Tommy and Mum in which both appear hesitant and unsure of how to play together. Tommy explores the games timidly and does not create a play theme. The affective tone is flat and no fun is perceived. The father entertains himself with toys and plays in parallel to the mother-child dyad. The therapist verbalizes how difficult it is to play and have fun all together and how lost and lonely everyone seems.

In the second session, a few days after the first, Tommy decides to assist the therapist in helping his mother. While his father describes the narrative, Tommy moves his fingers in front of his mother's eyes, wearing mittens with puppets on his fingers. In doing so, Tommy's eyes and body move bilaterally in synchrony with Mum's eye movement, and the therapist does not provide tapping on his knees. The therapist points out how Tommy has now taken charge and is helping mum and himself by moving his fingers and body to get rid of the unpleasant memories attached to the narrative. The affective tone is higher, and the dyad appears energized and synchronous. At the end, Tommy and Mum play together. This time the game is richer on a symbolic level. Tommy leads the game, and the mother follows. The father remains peripheral. Tommy decides to be the doctor who visits Mum and gives her medicine to make her better. Tommy says that Mum is afraid of doctors but that he knows how to help her. The therapist emphasizes how Tommy seems to be feeling stronger now and can be in charge, just like the doctors. Tommy's care and concerns towards mum are also verbalized. The father interacts more actively than the previous time and decides to be Tommy's assistant in helping Mum. The therapist points out how the atmosphere is more cheerful and how the family appears more united and playful.

30.9.5 Follow-up

The parents keep in touch by e-mail for the entire month following the treatment through weekly communications and report that Tommy is more cheerful and less anxious. They also report that Tommy now goes to the toilet on his own and has regular bowel movements.

There have been no more episodes of encopresis. The mother says she feels optimistic and confident. Both parents say that the atmosphere in the home is more relaxed. Two months after the EMDR intervention, the pediatric physiotherapist who worked with Tommy to help him with his incontinence writes that Tommy has made tremendous progress, considering the severity of his symptoms and his physical state. She also reports that Tommy has regained bowel motility and that his appetite has markedly improved.

30.10 Conclusions

This clinical case illustrates how even a single traumatizing event can have a negative impact on a child's developmental trajectory as well as on the family relational dynamic. The clinical case exemplifies the treatment of post-traumatic stress disorder (PTSD) through the application of the parent-child relational EMDR protocol and illustrates the potential of this protocol to provide timely relief from post-traumatic symptoms for young children (0–4 years) and their parents. As symptoms improve and trauma is metabolized, the child-parent dyad/triad(s) regains synchrony. Child and parents reunite on an affective level, reconnect, and rediscover each other. This in turn promotes the affective and relational well-being of the child and his or her family.

References

Adler-Tapia, R., & Settle, C. (2017). *EMDR and the art of psychotherapy with children: Infants to adolescents* (2nd ed.). Springer Publishing Company.

American Psychiatric Association. (2022). *Diagnostic and statistical manual of mental disorders* (5th ed., text rev. ed.). https://doi.org/10.1176/appi.books.9780890425787

Baradon, T., Biseo, M., Broughton, C., James, J., & Joyce, A. (2017). *The practice of psychoanalityc parent-infant psychotherapy. Claiming the baby*. Routledge.

Better Health. (2022, September 20). *Trauma and children 0–2 years*. https://doi.org/www.betterhealth.vic.gov.au/trauma-and-children-0-2-years-italian#bhc-content

Bowlby, J. (1969). *Attachment and loss*. Basic Books.

Cicchetti, D., & Lynch, M. (1993). Toward an ecological/transactional model of community violence and child maltreatment: Consequences for children's development. *Psychiatry*, *56*(1), 96–118. https://doi.org/10.1080/00332747.1993.11024624

de Roos, C., Offermans, J., Bouwmeester, S., Lindauer, R., & Scheper, F. (2025). Preliminary efficacy of eye movement desensitization and reprocessing for children aged 1.5–8 years with PTSD: A multiple baseline experimental design (N = 19). *European Journal of Psychotraumatology*, *16*(1), 2447654. https://doi.org/10.1080/20008066.2024.2447654

Fraiberg, S., Adelson, E., & Shapiro, V. (1975). Ghosts in the nursery. A psychoanalytic approach to the problems of impaired infant-mother relationships. *Journal of the American Academy of Child & Adolescent Psychiatry*, *14*(3), 387–421. https://doi.org/10.1016/s0002–7138(09)61442–4

Gaensbauer, T. J. (2002). Rrepresentations of trauma in infancy: Clinical and theoretical implications for the understanding of early memory. *Infant Mental Health Journal*, *23*(3), 259–277. https://doi.org/10.1002/imhj.10020

Gomez, A. M. (2013). *EMDR Therapy and adjunct approaches with children. Complex trauma, attachment and dissociation*. Springer Publishing Company.

Lieberman, A. F., Chu, A., Van Horn, P., & Harris, W. W. (2011). Trauma in early childhood: Empirical evidence and clinical implications. *Development and Psychopathology*, *23*(2), 397–410. https://doi.org/10.1017/s0954579411000137

Lieberman, A. F., & Van Horn, P. (2008). *Psychotherapy with infants and young children: Repairing the effects of stress and trauma on early attachment*. Guilford Press.

Lovett, J. (1999). *Small wonders: Healing childhood trauma with EMDR*. The Free Press.

Lovett, J. (2015). *Trauma-attachment. Modifying EMDR to help children resolve trauma and develop loving relationships*. Routledge.

Olivier, E., de Roos, C., & Bexkens, A. (2021). Eye movement desensitization and reprocessing in young children (ages 4–8) with posttraumatic stress disorder: A multiple-baseline evaluation. *Child Psychiatry & Human Development*, *53*(6), 1397–1404. https://doi.org/10.1007/s10578-021-01237-z

Rathore, H. E. (2018). Trust and attunement-focused EMDR with a child. *Journal of EMDR Practice and Research*, *12*(4), 255–268. https://doi.org/10.1891/1933-3196.12.4.255

Rodenburg, R., Benjamin, A., de Roos, C., Meijer, A. M., & Stams, G. J. (2009). Efficacy of EMDR in children: A meta-analysis. *Clinical Psychology Review*, *29*(7), 599–606. https://doi.org/10.1016/j.cpr.2009.06.008

Shapiro, F. (2001). *Eye movement desensitization and reprocessing: Basic principles, protocols, and procedures* (2nd ed.). Guildford Press.

Siegel, D. J. (2015). *The developing mind. How relationships and the brain interact to shape who we are*. The Guilford Press.
Siegel, D. J., Schore, A. N., & Cozolino, L. (2021). *Interpersonal neurobiology and clinical practice*. WW Norton & Company.
Solomon, R., & Shapiro, F. (2012). EMDR therapy and adaptive information processing: The development of resilience and coherence. In *Individual trauma: Recovering from deep wounds and exploring the potential for renewal* (pp. 281–302). Nova Science Publishers.
Stern, D. (1985). *The interpersonal world of the infant: A view from psychoanalysis and developmental psychology*. Routledge.
Struik, A. (2019). *Treating chronically traumatized children: The sleeping dogs method* (2nd ed.). Routledge.
Struik, A., & Salvo, R. (2023, July 6–8). *Young children remember: Family as a resource in the treatment of preverbal childhood trauma: The parent-child relational EMDR protocol family therapy*. The Road That Connects Individual and Social Resources.
Stuber, M. L., & Shemesh, E. (2006). Post-traumatic stress response to life-threatening illnesses in children and their parents. *Child and Adolescent Psychiatric Clinics of North America*, *15*(3), 597–609. https://doi.org/10.1016/j.chc.2006.02.006
Swimm, L. L. (2018). EMDR intervention for a 17-month-old child to treat attachment trauma: Clinical case presentation. *Journal of EMDR Practice and Research*, *12*(4), 269–281. https://doi.org/10.1891/1933-3196.12.4.269
Tronik, E., & Beeghly, M. (2011). Infants' meaning making and the development of mental health problems. *The American Psychologist*, *66*(2), 107–119. https://doi.org/10.1037/a0021631
Went, M. A. T. (2014). Ouder-kind-trauma-therapie. *GZ-Psychologie*, *2*, 18–24.
Went, M. A. T. (2018). Ouder kind trauma therapie Hoe werkt dat nou bij baby's? *Tijdschrift voor Kinder-en Jeugdpsychotherapie*, *54*(1), 76–93.
Went, M., Struik, A., Möller, E., Zijlstra, B. J. H., Dumoulin, A., van Haaften, G., & Rodenburg, R. (2024). Parent-child EMDR therapy for children aged 0–4 years: Protocol, pilot-data, and case study. *European Journal of Trauma & Dissociation*, *8*(4). https://doi.org/10.1016/j.ejtd.2024.100475
Wesselmann, D., Armstrong, S., Schweitzer, C., Davidson, M., & Potter, A. (2018). An integrative EMDR and family therapy model for treating attachment trauma in children: A case series. *Journal of EMDR Practice and Research*, *12*(4), 196–207. https://doi.org/10.1891/1933-3196.12.4.196
Winnicott, D. W. (1965). The theory of the parent-infant relationship. In *The maturational processes and the facilitating environment* (pp. 37–55). International Universities Press (Original work published 1960).
Zeanah, C. (2018). *Handbook of infant mental health* (4th ed.). Guilford Press.
ZERO TO THREE. (2016). *DC:0–5TM: Diagnostic classification of mental health and developmental disorders of infancy and early childhood*. Author.
ZERO TO THREE Infant Mental Health Task Force Steering Committee. (2001). *Definition of Infant Mental Health*. National Centre for Clinical Infants Programs.

PART 5

Cultural diversity, migration, and social discrimination

31
MALAYSIA
A multicultural mosaic shaped by historical transformations

Bawany Chinapan and Wai Eng Ding

31.1 Introduction

Situated in Southeast Asia, Malaysia spans diverse regions across the Malay Peninsula and Borneo, sharing borders with Thailand, Indonesia, Singapore, and Brunei. Renowned for its scenic beaches, expansive rainforests, and a rich cultural mosaic shaped by Malay, Chinese, Indian, and European influences, including the unique contributions of Sabahans and Sarawakians, Malaysia's population stands at 34.1 million (Department of Statistics Malaysia, 2025).

The country's societal fabric is intricately woven with diverse ethnicities, each steadfastly preserving their distinct religious practices, customs, and ways of life. The religious landscape reflects a Muslim majority (60.4%), alongside Buddhists (19.2%), Christians (9.1%), Hindus (6.3%), followers of Confucianism, Taoism, and other traditional Chinese religions (2.6%), individuals identifying with other or unidentified faiths (1.5%), and those embracing a secular stance (0.8%) (Commisceo Global Consulting Ltd., 2020). Given this rich tapestry of cultures, understanding Malaysia's multicultural dynamics necessitates a historical perspective (Andaya & Andaya, 1984).

This chapter will delve into two key aspects: (1) exploring the historical underpinnings embedded in cultural norms, and (2) a case illustrating the impact of strict parenting and filial piety within Malaysia's patriarchal culture.

31.2 A brief history of Malaysia

Before colonial powers arrived 500 years ago, the Malay Archipelago was a cultural melting pot, incorporating indigenous (Malay and *Orang Asli*) and non-indigenous (Chinese, Indian, Arab) communities. Malays, referred to as *Bumiputera* or the "Son of the Soil," have historically constituted the predominant indigenous ethnic group on the Peninsula, contributing significantly to its societal fabric. According to Al-Attas (1965, pp. 171–189), many Southeast Asian coastal and riverine societies, including the 15th-century Malacca Sultanate, exhibited a pluralistic nature or witnessed increased pluralism without significant social upheaval. The Malay society's historical interactions with Hindu-Buddhism and Islam showcased an open and adaptive culture. Indian influences are evident in political structures and social customs, indicating a willingness to assimilate external ideas (Wang, 2001).

DOI: 10.4324/9781003536765-37

However, conflicts arose with the advent of Western colonialism in Malaysia, which was then known as Malaya. The unfolding of historical events, notably with the advent of Western colonialism commencing in the 16th century and intensifying with British colonial influence from the latter half of the 19th century, resulted in a profound metamorphosis of the Malay Peninsula. The erstwhile homogeneous societal fabric underwent a marked transition toward heterogeneity. In the field of Southeast Asian studies, the term "plural society," coined by Furnivall (1956) more than seven decades ago, stands out as a central and enduring concept. British colonial influence introduced a plural society, emphasizing ethnicity and segregating labor along ethnic lines, particularly with Malays in the unwaged peasant sector and non-Malays (Chinese and Indians collectively) in the waged capitalist sector (Furnivall, 1956). This deliberate division aimed to limit interactions between ethnic groups, thereby hindering the maintenance of a cohesive societal structure. The historical context of colonial-era Malaysia exemplifies the manifestation of such a plural society.

The Japanese occupation during World War II exacerbated inter-ethnic tensions as Malay policemen were enlisted to combat the Chinese-dominated Malayan People's Anti-Japanese Army, pitting different ethnic communities against each other (Abd Wahid, 1970). After the war, the granting of independence in 1957 was based on a power-sharing arrangement within the WWII Euro-American Alliance, characterized by a politics of difference. This emphasized the political supremacy of Malays and the economic dominance of non-Malays, especially the Chinese – a dynamic that persists to the present day.

Malaysian diversity, marked by diverging dynamics, saw notable tension in the May 1969 ethnic unrest in Kuala Lumpur. However, persistent contestation and tension endured, impacting ethno-religious relations (Embong, 2002). The 1969 inter-ethnic violence, mainly between Malays and Chinese, was attributed to factors such as economic inequality (Henderson et al., 1977). In response, the state initiated affirmative action programs like the New Economic Policy (NEP), favoring the Malay ethnic group across various domains (Noor & Leong, 2013). Instituted post-independence, these policies aimed at poverty eradication and avoiding ethnic-based economic roles, emphasizing a commitment to socioeconomic equity (Jesrina et al., 2022). Recent migrants, primarily of Indonesian origin, play a consequential role in shaping Malaysian current historical trajectories (Embong, 2000).

31.3 The psychosocial terrain of Malaysia

The history of Malaysian society, its development from a colony to independent status, and its shift from plural to multicultural status, where diversity was managed towards assimilation, are all significant in appreciating not only the nation at a specific time of its growth but even more so the psyche of its people (Mydin, 2009). Today, Malaysians of all ethnic cultural groups (mainly Malays, Chinese, and Indians) prioritize collectivism, consistent with broader Asian cultural norms favoring communal interests over individualism. Collectivists perceive the self as intricately intertwined with the social environment, thereby embracing an interdependent perspective of the self (Markus & Kitayama, 1991; Triandis, 1999).

The extended family holds greater societal importance than the nuclear family, emphasizing values such as cooperation, helpfulness, obedience, and interdependence. These principles are instilled during childhood through daily activities and rituals (Kling, 1995; Krishnan, 2004). Family members are expected to maintain these values, recognizing the impact of individual actions on the entire familial system. Malaysian communication tends towards indirectness, with limited expression of emotions. Malaysians are often characterized as belonging to a "high-ambiguity-tolerant culture," demonstrating resilience in the face of unknown situations (DeVito, 2008, p. 39). Despite their high levels of tolerance and diplomatic skills (Shanmuganath, 2003), societal values underscore the importance of etiquette and formality within Malaysian culture. Employing the appropriate form of address is crucial to prevent unfavorable perceptions of the speaker and to mitigate potential misunderstandings during interactions (Othman, 2006).

Central to the societal fabric is the family unit, revered as the cornerstone of the social structure. There are the profound cultural values of unity, loyalty, and deference to elders, positioning families as crucial sources of both emotional and financial sustenance for individual members. Address forms serve as a means to express politeness between conversational participants, reflecting a commendable etiquette highly esteemed in a Malay culture (Sabran & Syam, 1984). Particularly in a Malay family, kinship terms are often used as a form of address with the family, relatives, and older close family members to show respect. A form of address refers to a word or phrase employed in both spoken and written communication to directly mention or refer to an individual. It serves the purpose of establishing the relationship's placement on the dimension of social closeness-distance, thereby structuring the relationship between the speaker and the listener in everyday interactions (Moain, 1987).

As an example, a kin term is added before the name such as *pakcik* Ali (uncle Ali) or *kakak* Ani (sister Ani) as an indication of respect towards the person's rank or age. In Malay society, the eldest child is denoted as *sulung*, the middle child is referred to as *tengah*, and the youngest child is called *bongsu*. Through the use of these reference terms – *sulung*, *tengah*, and *bongsu* – the Malay family has developed a form of address that indicates the number of children in the family or the birth order of the children. For example, terms like *yong*, *along*, *abang long*, and *kak long* are used to address the eldest child, while the youngest, *bongsu*, may sometimes be addressed as *usu*, *busu*, or *adik*. These terms of kinship are particular to Malay families (Mansor, 2018). In Mansor's study (2018), the results showed an overwhelming propensity to use kin terms as a sign of respect when speaking to other relatives. This occurs without exception with older adults, such as parents and grandparents. Although relatives' age and status are factors, gender plays no role in determining degree of respect and indication of position in the family relational hierarchy. Members of the family are anticipated to uphold and preserve familial values, as the actions of an individual reverberate throughout the entire family system, and saving face is deemed important.

As a collectivist society where power distribution is based on factors such as age, generation, and gender, patriarchy is a prevalent feature in Malay families, including among Chinese, and Indians in Malaysia. Traditionally, the role of decision maker within a family was typically held by the eldest male, reflecting this patriarchal structure. However, the widespread influence of modernization and global media may have posed challenges to the entrenched dominance of patriarchy in Malaysian culture (Ibrahim & Osman, 2022).

Contemporary Malaysian families exhibit other notable changes compared to a few decades ago. There is increased affluence and improved lifestyles (Ng, 2003). The nuclear family is gaining emphasis, with factors such as education, employment, and migration playing pivotal roles in shaping new family structures. Many migrations within the country from rural to urban settings may not have the support of the extended family, meaning the nuclear unit becomes the sole or main source of support and the focus of meaningful relationships among members.

Despite some shifts in family organization and practices, the tradition of filial piety remains a central value and practice in Malaysian family life across diverse ethnicities. Filial piety, defined as a set of norms, values, and practices regarding children's behaviors toward parents, has been a moral foundation for Chinese intergenerational relations for centuries. It is rooted in ancient spiritual traditions of ancestor worship, which underpin Chinese society. The philosopher Confucius refined filial obligations to prioritize family, virtue, and social order. His principles still shape the Chinese social structure. Confucius pointed out two ethical requirements of filial piety: prioritize close relationships and show deference to elders (Wei, 2023; Bedford & Yeh, 2021). These practices foster strong bonds and a sense of unity among family members. This interconnectedness extends beyond the immediate family, contributing to broader social harmony, as Confucius emphasized respect for authority and hierarchical structures in the broader society. Filial piety provides children with a stable sense of belonging, identity, and value in the family. In return, the expectation for adult children to care for their aging parents includes emotional, financial, and physical assistance. Filial piety forms the bedrock of Malaysian Chinese cultural identity, anchoring communities to their traditions and values across generations. In particular, the Malaysian Chinese uphold strong family bonds, particularly in parenting (Hossain, 2014).

Although there are commonalities in family life across different Malaysian ethnic groups, there are also differences. For instance, among Malaysian Indians practicing Hinduism, children are viewed as carrying predisposed *samskaras* (Hossain, 2014). "Samskaras" is a Sanskrit word referring to rites of passage that mark a person's life from conception to cremation. Childhood is considered a carefree period, with mothers playing a key role in caring for family members. Fathers manage economic and social responsibilities, and rituals like *kannyadaan* – which means giving away of the bride to the groom's family in marriage – reflect social and spiritual duties. In traditional Hindu society, once a daughter is married, she is considered to be under the care and responsibility of her husband's family. An integral aspect of this transition is the practice of *kannyadaan*, a significant ritual during a Hindu wedding.

In both Chinese and Indian cultures, sons, particularly eldest sons, are often privileged due to the expectation that they will assume the responsibility of caring for their aging parents. Conversely, a daughter in a Chinese family, once having married and left her family of origin, is expected to serve her husband and his family, similar to Indian culture. The Laws of Manu are an ancient sacred law that describes a set of obligations or dharma in Indian culture that influence this patriarchal family structure, emphasizing men's authority, whereas the wife typically serves her husband, children, and in-laws, who play an ancillary decision-making role. Mothers are expected to embrace domesticity, purity, and a submissive role within the family. The concept of *shravan kumar* in Hindu means a dutiful and respectful son who cares for his aging parents. This practice is similar to the concept of filial piety in Chinese culture, where a son is expected to dutifully care for his parents, thereby preserving traditional values and customs.

Malaysian Malay families are influenced by Islamic customs and local practices known as *adat* (Hossain, 2014). *Adat* refers to teachings that emphasize the collaborative role of both parents in raising children, while also instilling important moral values such as respect, humility, and loyalty.

In traditional settings, joint family systems and polygyny are common, but in modern urban families, these practices are less prevalent due to factors such as women's education, a smaller nuclear family size, and women's involvement in the workforce. Young educated families move away to the cities for work opportunities and away from their extended families. Urbanization has contributed to the shift in traditional gender roles, with more educated young fathers taking an active role in child-rearing, particularly in dual-career families without the support of extended family.

Many young Malaysian couples, regardless of ethnicity, face similar challenges living in the city away from their extended families. For instance, as families move from rural to more expensive urban areas and from living in a house to living in an apartment, the adult children who now have their own children may simply not have room for the elderly parents. Parents live in their hometown, and some young couples commute weekly to care for their parents.

Despite its positive contributions, filial piety can also negatively influence individuals and societies. The pressure on children to meet the expectations of filial piety can lead to stress and anxiety, particularly if they find themselves unable to fulfill perceived obligations, especially care for elderly parents. Interpersonal conflicts may emerge when individual adult children's aspirations clash with the expectations dictated by filial piety, potentially straining family relationships. Additionally, tensions between generations may surface, especially if younger members and females seek greater autonomy and independence, challenging the traditional patriarchal authority structure.

31.4 Case illustration

This case will illustrate the impact of generational trauma transmitted by adhering to strict parenting and high expectations in a Malaysian Chinese family through the lens of multigenerational family therapy. Pei Li and Ken Ming's parents instilled values of kindness, filial piety, hard work, thriftiness, and scholastic achievements. Although this family holds a profound sense of filial piety, they grapple with challenges in cultivating closeness owing to the impact of generational trauma, especially from the wife, Pei Li's family of origin. She also struggled to accept the gender biases in wealth inheritance coming from patriarchal traditions within her own family. Her brothers got a share of the inheritance, and the girls were given very much less. Ken Ming, the husband, being the most educated male, had to care for his siblings and parents' well-being.

31.5 Navigating the storms: A journey of healing and transformation

Ken Ming and Pei Li are a couple of three decades who engaged in tumultuous storms in their marriage. Their numerous arguments centered on managing career and family responsibilities, with the added challenge of raising a special needs child. Their marital challenges, flavored by anger and anxiety, were like those experienced in prior generations. Ken Ming and Pei Li, professionals in their mid-fifties in Kuala Lumpur, have three daughters. Sue Li is in her early thirties and recently got married. Ju Li and Joo Li are twins in their late twenties. Joo Li was diagnosed as having learning disabilities due to multiple seizures since the age of two. Joo Li, an adult with special needs characterized by pervasive learning difficulties and illness, has been a source of stress for the family throughout the children's growing years due to her recurrent epileptic episodes. She still suffers with seizures in adulthood and is on medication. Ju Li, her twin, who lives in another country due to work, joined sessions via Zoom. She flew down to Kuala Lumpur for four family sessions out of ten sessions. The girls felt that explosive anger and high anxiety run in the family, and they get triggered easily when together without someone losing their temper. The family sought therapy at the initiative of Sue Li, the eldest girl, to mend the relationship with her parents, especially her mother, and to promote overall family healing and connectedness.

31.6 Shared motivation

All family members have been seeing therapists for individual work. Sue Li, the eldest daughter, initiated family therapy in the belief that it would help heal their family's intergenerational trauma, ensuring that it not be passed down to the next generation, as she and her spouse want to start a family of their own. A shared motivation was clear from the first session, as each felt they would benefit from family therapy. In the initial sessions, the therapist listened with respect, curiosity, and empathy and gave space for each of them to be heard. These sessions allowed the therapist to join with the family and gain their trust (Andolfi, 2017).

31.7 Surviving trauma through therapy

Intergenerational trauma permeated the family through the maternal lineage, leaving an indelible mark on Pei Li and her daughters. Pei Li's mother, who had to survive a harsh upbringing in an imbalanced gender system favoring males, is a strong yet very angry woman. She wished her children to adhere to good moral values and etiquette, be respectful to their parents and elderly, do well, and be successful in life.

Pei Li, entangled in the complex dynamics of her upbringing within a patriarchal system, emotional abuse by her step-grandmother and step-aunts towards her family during her childhood, and a conflictual relationship with her mother, yearned for her daughters to acknowledge the pain she carried. Andolfian family therapy used a multigenerational lens to identify patterns in three generations (Andolfi, 2017). Pei Li's family dynamics revealed a submissive father and an obstinate, critical, forceful, and invalidating mother, yet both her parents were submissive to emotional abuse, leading to a perpetual cycle of familial acquiescence.

Ken Ming shared his own childhood trauma. His family was poor and his parents needed to work very hard to provide for many children. Growing up was hard and children needed to fend for themselves. His parents were absent emotionally; his mother was highly anxious, with a father who was harsh and punitive. Ken's parents provided for basic needs because life was hard, and children needed to obey and not misbehave. He related one incident in which his punitive father tied him up in a gunny sack and threatened to throw him into a river if he did not obey. Ken grew up to be independent but disengaged with his family members. He was taught to be responsible for caring for the needs of the family, yet emotionally distant.

The seeds of discord within Ken Ming and Pei Li's families were sown during Pei Li and Ken Ming's early years as parents. Stressed and overwhelmed, they found themselves caught between two generations – striving to meet the demands of being good children to their parents, as dictated by filial piety and patriarchy, while also navigating the challenges of being parents. Andolfi and Mascellani (2013) referred to them as sandwiched couples.

Pei Li's displays of anger and insensitivity towards her children mirrored the similar experiences in her upbringing and subjected their children to punitive measures, leaving scars. Schechter et al. (2011) reported that maternal distress significantly mediates the relationship between a mother's history of abuse and her invalidating parenting practices. Emotional abuse in childhood can shape one's self-perception, often leading to difficulties in emotional regulation in adulthood (McWilliam & Klohnen, 2014) and impairing adult relational dynamics, including trust and emotional regulation within relationships (DiLillo & Damashek, 2007). Frequent disagreements between Ken Ming and Pei Li left a mark on Sue Li and Ju Li's disposition. Ju Li, sometimes neglected by the parents and tasked with caring for her special needs twin, Joo Li, developed into a short-fused, anxious individual as an adult. With the parents often preoccupied by their careers and because the twins shared a bedroom, went to the same school, and grew up spending more time together, Ju Li became the parentified child to her twin sister. She recalled many traumatic moments during Joo Li's epileptic episodes, and how she was left to care for her. Ken Ming's anxiety about Joo Li's illness exacerbated the family dynamics, surfacing more prominently in later years with his developing immune disorder, so that he took on early retirement.

Children, especially girls growing up in three-generational families, were not seen nor heard. Yet, when they become adults, they need to maintain strong ties and invisible loyalties with the family of origin. They need to conform to social norms as obedient children, yet they learned to take charge, to suck it up, and to be in control to manage anxiety. The cycle of punitive parenting caused trauma, yet it also produced seemingly successful adults who met societal expectations of a successful family, although they remain emotionally broken and in need of healing.

31.8 Voices of pain

Genogram was utilized as a tool to describe the relational context of the family, enlarging some significant life events in the developmental history and family life cycle to be made more explicit. This graphic representation of the family development was useful as it was dealt with in family sessions through the family's verbal description, which helped illustrate the family emotional system (Andolfi, 2017).

Using temporal jumps as a therapeutic intervention helped to explore the intergenerational aspects of the family. Pei Li's traumatic childhood is repeated, as she became her mother to her daughters by placing high expectations and strict rules to obey, followed by punishments, which was supported by Ken Ming coming from strict parenting as well. The intensity of hurt and pain of unheard childhood voices and trauma of the daughters reverberated in the initial sessions. Each daughter needed to be heard, as each felt dismissed by their parents, which permeated throughout the maternal generations, whereby voiceless angry children became dismissed angry adults. Intergenerational questions, asking Pei Li about her mother at Sue Li's younger age, helped raise awareness of the family plots (Andolfi, 2017). Utilizing intergenerational questions was helpful in reconnecting similar experiences between the past and present generations within this nuclear family.

31.9 Space to hold pain

In each therapy session, Pei Li navigated a tumultuous sea of emotions, experiencing overwhelming sadness, frustration, and tears as she heard the voices of her children narrating their childhood experiences. Despite the challenges, Pei Li displayed tenacity in facing and embracing the pain she had inadvertently inflicted on her children. The wrath of dismissal had a heavy penalty.

Enactments of the relational pain were given space. Revisiting the family's developmental history paved the way to stitch broken emotional wounds, and Sue Li was used as the guide to bridge two generations followed by the sisters. As the girls felt heard, they gave more listening ears to their parents and their pain growing up. Sue Li was guided to enact a family sculpture of one childhood experience. This was recreated in a safe space to voice her deep pain as a child, which paved the way for intergenerational reconciliation. She also did a sculpture of the future family she envisioned. It further opened doors to deep exploration of all members for a sense of connection and belongingness.

Blame has been a common language to show who is strong and the other is wrong (Satir, 1972) among the females here. Pei Li, born out of a patriarchal system, needed to fight and prove her worth. She did so with a heavy price, holding a lot of anger and hurt but keeping a calm face, emanating control. A language of the heart was introduced, replacing the language of the head, as Sue Li demonstrated the need to be loved and belong in the sculpture. Each of the girls had their voices heard by their mom, dad, and the therapist witnessing pain, hurt, and anger. Anger has caused so much distancing and isolation. The realization dawned upon Pei Li that her own voice had never been truly heard or comforted by her own mother. Tears united daughters and mother in the therapeutic space held by Ken Ming as the only male figure in this nuclear family. Touch and hugs within the members of the family happened with ease during the therapeutic encounters.

The family therapy sessions became a transformative space (Andolfi, 2017) for Sue Li, Ju Li, and Joo Li to voice their pain and confront the impact of their strict upbringing. It was an experiential process for all as they embraced and comforted each other witnessed by the therapist. The journey involved acknowledging past hurt and trauma, fostering healthy communication, and establishing new boundaries and therapeutic tasks as a family. The sibling subsystem was activated in the process of family therapy, where the girls connected and formed a deeper bond with each other. The aftermath revealed signs of healing, with Sue Li and Ju Li working towards rebuilding relationships with their parents, and Ken Ming and Joo Li learning to let go of their dependence on each other and better manage their anxiety. Ken Ming and Pei Li's bond is closer, and they spend more time together as a couple.

31.10 Patriarchal ideology

In linking the case of Pei Li and Ken Ming to the theory of multigenerational family therapy, we can understand how family dynamics and cultural traditions shape their experiences and emotional responses across generations. Pei Li's disillusionment with her parents' adherence to patriarchal traditions, especially their decision to favor their sons in inheritance, may not be something she wants to conform with because she feels it is unfair. Taking the "I position" in acknowledging her disgruntlement and sadness, she braved herself to express her voice to her father and felt much relief because her father listened to her pain. Her work on self-differentiation of self (Bowen, 1978) has begun. She is aware that he may not change, but she felt relieved by expressing her voice to him. The conquest of personal authority (Williamson, 1991; as cited in Andolfi, 2017, pp. 13) and not depending emotionally on her family of origin will take time for her to be on an egalitarian position with her parents. She realizes that she can learn to work on herself and pave the way for her adult daughters as they are also working toward their autonomy and personal authority. As a highly educated career woman, Pei Li acknowledged that the healing journey was an ongoing process with the support of Ken Ming. She grappled with the loss of trust in her parents, who were bound by cultural obligations, because of the deeply ingrained patriarchal tradition. The ongoing detriangulation process with her mother unfolded, and now with the support of her nuclear family.

Through the process of therapy, Ken Ming felt more compassion toward his parents and their hardship in his growing years. Although being the youngest son and more successful, he is expected to support his extended family on money problems and healthcare issues. His siblings expect him to pay for nursing expenses for his frail parents as he is more educated and successful. Ken Ming still struggles to stand up to his brothers, who avoid patriarchal obligation, giving financial burden as a reason. Being a filial son, he feels it is his duty to contribute to care for his ailing parents. The male in his family, regardless of sibling position, has a duty of care for their parents.

The patriarchal system and concept of filial piety is akin to what Boszormenyi-Nagy and Spark (1973) state about existential debts by children to their parents, whereby family members internalize and obey unexpressed rules present in the family system and develop loyalties that are transmitted through the generations. Andolfi (2017) concurs that relationship within a family is influenced by loyalties and respect for the multigenerational narratives and its mandates (p. 13).

31.11 On follow-up post-therapy progress: Celebrating resilience and transformation

On follow-up, Sue Li showed notable calmness, signaling positive changes, and stated that she engaged in meeting her parents often. Pei Li and Sue Li actively rebuilt their mother-daughter relationship through activities like yoga. Sue Li's support extended to Joo Li during a family holiday, and plans were made for them to join weekly yoga classes. The sibling subsystem was strengthened, as Sue Li is now calmer and takes Joo Li on sister-bonding activities. The relationship between Ju Li and Sue Li is much closer, and they keep tabs on expanding resources to help Joo Li. The sisters are close and look out for each other and have frequent conversations. The parents/couple subsystem is also strengthened. Positive developments emerged during an overseas visit with Ju Li, when Sue Li expressed much joy and Ju Li (the parentified child) felt supported by her parents. Joo Li's anxiety lessened as Ken Ming embraced newfound enthusiasm, sharing hobbies with Pei Li. Focusing on work and retirement savings, Pei Li aimed for a balanced life, breaking free from invisible loyalties, embracing authoritative filial piety, acknowledging equality, and celebrating women's progress despite historical and developmental challenges.

31.12 Post-therapy

Pei Li and Ken Ming's family journey reflects resilience and healing within the complexities of intergenerational family dynamics, where mom struggles within the patriarchal system of her own family of origin. Pei Li visits her ailing mother and cares for her father with a new perspective. The transformative power of therapy has paved the way for rebuilding relationships, fostering understanding, and embracing personal growth. The celebration lies not only in acknowledging the pain but also in the determination to create a new narrative marked by love, acceptance, and genuine connection.

The strong influence of filial piety persists across different cultures and ethnic backgrounds, even though the case illustrated one example. It is subtle and yet loud. Filial piety in Malaysian culture, while promoting family unity and support for the elderly, also brings challenges such as rigid traditions, gender role expectations, parental pressure, and generational tensions. Balancing these aspects is crucial to adapt cultural values to evolving societal norms. Recognizing individual freedom alongside traditions fosters a more flexible and inclusive cultural framework. Deeply rooted in Malaysian culture, filial piety influences family structures, mental well-being, and intergenerational relationships, remaining a significant force amid societal changes, shaping family values, elder care practices, and public policy considerations.

In conclusion, Malaysia's multicultural journey, shaped by historical forces from pre-colonial pluralism to patriarchal structures to contemporary challenges, highlights a delicate balance. The enduring influence of filial piety, amidst modernization, defines Malaysia's path: embracing positive cultural values while adapting to evolving societal norms, reflecting growth, resilience, and celebration of its rich heritage.

References

Abd Wahid, Z. A. (1970). Japanese occupation and nationalisms. In Z. A. Abd Wahid (Ed.), *Glimpses of Malaysian history* (pp. 93–98). Dewan Bahasa dan Pustaka.

Al-Attas, S. N. (1965). Islamic culture in Malaysia. In T. Alisjahbana, X. S. T. Nayagam, & G. Wang (Eds.), *The cultural problems of Malaysia in the context of Southeast Asia* (pp. 124–131). The Malaysian Society of Orientalists.

Andaya, B. W., & Andaya, L. Y. (1984). *A history of Malaysia*. Macmillan International Higher Education.

Andolfi, M. (2017). *Multi-generational family therapy: Tools and resources for the therapist*. Routledge.

Andolfi, M., & Mascellani, A. (2013). *Intergenerational couple therapy*. Accademia Press.

Bedford, O., & Yeh, K. H. (2021). Evolution of the conceptualization of filial piety in the global context: From skin to skeleton. *Frontiers in Psychology*, *12*, 1–14. https://doi.org/10.3389/fpsyg.2021.570547

Boszormenyi-Nagy, I., & Spark, G. M. (1973). *Invisible loyalties: Reciprocity in intergenerational family therapy*. Harper & Row.

Bowen, M. (1978). *Family Therapy in Clinical Practice*. Jason Aronson.

Commisceo Global Consulting Ltd. (2020). *Malaysia-culture, etiquette, and business practices: Facts and statistics*. www.commisceo-global.com/resources/country-guides/malaysia-guide

Department of Statistics Malaysia. (2025, January 20). *Demographic*. www.dosm.gov.my

DeVito, J. A. (2008). *The interpersonal communication book* (12th ed.). Pearson Education.

DiLillo, D., & Damashek, A. L. (2007). Childhood emotional abuse and its impact on adult relational functioning. *Journal of Family Violence*, *22*(5), 241–252. https://doi.org/10.1007/s10896-007-9111-9

Embong, A. R. (2000, August 18). *The culture and practice of pluralism in post-independence Malaysia*. IKMAS Working Paper Series No. 18 (pp. 9–39). Institute of Malaysian and International Studies, Universiti Kebangsaan Malaysia. National University of Malaysia Press.

Embong, A. R. (2002). Malaysia as a multicultural society. *Macalester International*, *12*(10), 37–58. http://digitalcommons.macalester.edu/macintl/vol12/iss1/10

Furnivall, J. S. (1956). *Colonial policy and practice*. New York University Press.

Henderson, J. W., Vreeland, N., Dana, G. B., Hurwitz, G. B., Just, P., Moeller, P. W., & Shinn, R. S. (1977). *Area handbook for Malaysia*. American University, Foreign Area Studies.

Hossain, Z. (2014). Parental beliefs and fathers' and mothers' roles in Malaysian families. In H. Selin (Ed.), *Parenting across cultures: Childrearing, motherhood and fatherhood in non-western cultures* (pp. 77–90). https://doi.org/10.1007/978-94-007-7503-9_7

Ibrahim, A., & Osman, R. (2022). *Patriarchalism, literalism, and androcentrism on the rise in Malaysia*. ISEAS – Yusof Ishak Institute. Retrieved from www.iseas.edu.sg/wp-content/uploads/2022/05/ISEAS_Perspective_2022_56.pdf

Jesrina, A. X., Ponamalar, N., & Lee, K. Y. (2022). Disparity in the progress of ethnic Indian enterprises: A study on transgenerational succession in Malaysia. *Ethnicity*, *23*(2), 249–261. https://doi.org/10.1080/14631369.2020.1796586

Kling, Z. (1995). The Malay family: Beliefs and realities. *Journal of Comparative Family Studies*, *26*(1), 43–67. https://doi.org/10.3138/jcfs.26.1.43

Krishnan, U. D. (2004). *Parent-adolescent conflict and adolescent functioning in a collectivist, ethnically heterogeneous culture: Malaysia* (Doctoral dissertation, Ohio State University). OhioLINK Electronic Theses and Dissertations Center. https://etd.ohiolink.edu/

Mansor, N. S. (2018). Addressing family members in the Malay culture: Practices of "young-adult" university students. *Lenguas Modernas*, *51*, 63–76. https://doi.org/10.5354/0719-650X.2018.51912

Markus, H. R., & Kitayama, S. (1991). Culture and the self: Implications for cognition, emotion, and motivation. *Psychological Review*, *98*(2), 224–253.

McWilliams, L. A., & Klohnen, E. C. (2014). The long-term impact of childhood emotional abuse on adulthood: The mediating role of self-compassion. *Journal of Clinical Psychology*, *70*(11), 1035–1047. https://doi.org/10.1002/jclp.22259

Moain, A. J. (1987). Sistem sapaan dalam Bahasa Melayu: Satu analisis sosiolinguistik. *Jurnal Dewan Bahasa*, *37*(8), 717–721.

Mydin, R. M. (2009). Multiculturalism and the politics of expression: An appraisal. *European Journal of Social Science*, *5*(2), 43–63.

Ng, K. S. (2003). Family therapy in Malaysia. In K. S. Ng (Ed.), *Global perspectives in family therapy: Development, practice, and trends* (pp. 31–38). Brunner-Routledge.

Noor, M. N., & Leong, C. H. (2013). Multiculturalism in Malaysia and Singapore: Contesting models. *International Journal of Intercultural Relations*, *37*(6), 714–726. https://doi.org/10.1016/j.ijintrel.2013.09.009

Othman, Z. (2006). *Bentuk sapaan untuk pengajaran bahasa* [Form of address for language instructors] (Unpublished master's thesis, Universiti Pendidikan Sultan Idris). UPSI Digital Repository (UDRep).

Sabran, R., & Syam, R. (1984). *Kajian Bahasa untuk pelatih maktab perguruan*. Fajar Bakti Sdn. Bhd.

Satir, V. (1972). *People making*. Science and Behavior Books.

Schechter, D. S., Willheim, E., Hinojosa, C., Scholfield-Kleinman, K., Turner, J. B., McCaw, J., Zeanah, C. H., & Myers, M. M. (2011). Intergenerational transmission of abusive parenting: Role of prospective maternal distress and family violence. *Journal of the American Academy of Child & Adolescent Psychiatry*, *50*(3), 241–249. https://doi.org/10.1016/j.jaac.2010.11.004

Shanmuganath, T. (2003). The influence of culture on compliments responses. In T. Shanmuganath (Ed.), *Issues in language and cognition: Selected papers from the International Conference on Language and Cognition* (pp. 127–142). University of Malaya Press.

Triandis, H. C. (1999). Cross-cultural psychology. *Asian Journal of Social Psychology*, *2*(1), 127–143. https://doi.org/10.1111/1467-839X.00029

Wang, G. (2001). Continuities in Island Southeast Asia. In K. S. Jomo (Ed.), *Reinventing Malaysia: Reflections on its Past and Future*. National University of Malaysia Press.

Wei, Q. (2023). The positive and negative effects of Chinese filial piety. *Journal of Education, Humanities and Social Sciences*, *8*(2), 563–568. https://doi.org/10.54097/ehss.v8i.4310

Williamson, D. W. (1991). *The intimacy paradox*. Guilford Press.

32

MIGRATION IN SEVEN WORDS

An inspirational tool for thinking about family therapy

Ivy Daure

32.1 Introduction

Migration can be broadly defined as any voluntary or involuntary movement of people from one country to another, with the intention of living and settling there for a certain period of time. It can be an uncertain, temporary, or permanent time, since departure from the country of origin brings with it the prospect of possible, improbable, real, imagined, or fantasized return.

In this sense, migration encompasses many reasons, circumstances, and motives for movement from one country to another: exile, chosen mobility, expatriation, refugee status, economic migration, so-called intellectual migration for educational reasons, the movement of unaccompanied foreign minors (UFMs), and any movement that involves a journey outside the country of origin. Migration comes with emotional investments, losses, ruptures, discoveries, encounters, and the questioning of one's culture of origin through interculturation.

Consequently, it is difficult to define this movement, as it is so singular and unique depending on the individual and his or her history, context, and story. We will therefore try to shed light on the undefined, from the point of view of Eric Cattelain,[1] linguist and professor at the University of Bordeaux – France, who suggests seven words to help discern the various key issues, which are so complex that they cannot be described definitively. Here we will essentially conduct an original exercise around the word "migration."

Cattelain provides an interesting tool that allows us to think about migration in terms of these seven units of analysis or seven variables: time, space, communication, knowledge, economy, power, and society. Together, they give us a new perspective on the complexity of migration. The exercise presented here is based on my several years of work on migration issues and providing support to people from other countries and their families. In a different vein, but closely related, Célia Falicov (2005) in the US had already proposed a reading on communication, power, the economy of emotions, and intergenerational relations in a migratory context.

Thinking about migration from a dynamic perspective will help the therapist to place it in the therapeutic context and in a treatment perspective: Broadening the point of view and thinking about other possibilities becomes a facilitating factor in making migration a therapeutic lever.

Although all of the vignettes about therapy patients are of individuals, rather than families, the perspective I bring to this discussion and therapy practice with migrants is decidedly contextual and systemic, and is thus relevant for this handbook.

DOI: 10.4324/9781003536765-38

32.2 Time

People have always moved. The traveler's drive is at work in this need for elsewhere, for discovery beyond boundaries, and curiosity about others.

At the level of the individual, the body, and the psyche, we might ask whether there is a time to travel, a time to migrate, an age of travel. From a clinical perspective, we also have three times: the time of preparation for the trip, the time of travel, and the time of arrival in the host country. Three moments to be investigated from a clinical point of view in order to draw up a picture of the motivations and context of migration, very useful for thinking about the way in which each person experiences his or her migration. We would tend to think, inspired by observation, that it is easier for an adult to deal with the dangers of migration. However, unaccompanied minors undertake the migratory journey in large numbers and at younger and younger ages, and a very large number of them are women; 48% of the millions of migrants[2] in the world are women. In France, 41.3% of the total number of asylum seekers in 2020 were women (IOM – International Office for Migration).

The length of time required for the migration can vary dramatically. Some migratory journeys occur within a few hours, and some occur over a period of several months and years. The pace and period of time in which migration occurs can affect the speed and degree of adjustment or sense of "settling" in the host country. From the point of view of those migrating, the length of time needed to settle in a new country is often more gradual than is expected by non-migrating persons – either professionals in various roles that work with individuals and families who have migrated, or neighbors and other non-immigrant persons in the broader society who have lived for years (or their entire lives) in the host country. We often hear a kind of impatience from professionals who are also pressed to carry out the migration and social service procedures, and who sometimes feel that migrants take too long to learn the language, manage to settle socially and emotionally, understand how the government administration works, or even find a job. Or the person who has migrated may have unreasonable expectations of themselves and social and economic systems in terms of how quickly they can gain access to needed resources.

32.2.1 Case illustration

Amid is a young Nigerian boy who arrived in France at the age of 16 and was taken in by child protective services after a migratory journey that lasted nearly two years. France was the country of destination, but to get there he had to cross at least five countries, staying for longer or shorter periods, often with the feeling of being detained, of being prevented from continuing his journey to the country of destination. Forced to wait, to be patient, when Amid was finally picked up by the services that would finally accompany him to France, he had a sense of urgency. He says, "I have already lost a lot of time. I need to work. Why don't you give me a job?" The administrative constraints and timelines of the services are not satisfactory, he is in a hurry, and he feels that no one understands his needs. So, he rebels, coming into conflict with social workers who "prevent" him from working, earning money, and helping his family. Professionals find him demanding and unpleasant. A temporal impasse has been created, an impasse of urgency. Only by re-reading the young man's progress and renegotiating priorities were social workers able to understand Amid's reality.

When it comes to documents and authorizations to live and work in the host country, immigrants often express unhappiness about the long wait. Some put their lives on standby or feel they do. Life becomes an exercise in waiting for documents and authorizations, which often occupies all the emotional and cognitive space of a suspended life. Volunteering or learning the language of the host country while waiting for documents to clear feels psychologically impossible, even though it might be a good use of time and energy during this period.

Migration is a life cycle event that affects families over multiple generations. It involves multiple protagonists in a story that merges multiple histories beginning in the country of origin and continuing in the new country of residence. The voluntary or involuntary circumstances of departure get told and retold across generations, and that telling influences how the family builds an identity for today and tomorrow.

Migration does not have a fixed beginning and end; at different levels and in different ways, one never stops migrating. Even when a migrant feels fairly well settled in the new country, a particular context, event, or another aspect of life may remind them that they are not from "here" but from elsewhere, that they have left family behind, and that their identity includes aspects from "here" but also a little or a lot from elsewhere. Different time periods, spaces, and identities sometimes overlap, and the therapeutic space is perhaps the place where the various temporalities and experiences come together.

32.3 Space

Migrating means moving through different spaces, places, territories, and countries. Some migrations involve crossing different countries, discovering different languages, behaviors, and cultures. The experience is that of leaving one's intimate and familiar space, one's familial and socially recognized context with points of reference (we could say safe points of reference at least for some people) to go towards the unknown, the strange, the foreignness of a territory within which the subject does not know how to move because of unfamiliarity with codes, geography, and means of transportation. It is like being in a place that one is not yet part of, even though one is physically there. Distances between people are not clearly defined; once the physical boundaries between countries are crossed, cultural, relational, and communicative boundaries are discovered.

Through migration, some people discover the notion of the individual and intimacy, the need for security, distrust, and fears, leading to the need to have their own physical space, a room, a bed, a closet, a suitcase, a bag. These are all levers of therapeutic work. Invoking memories of the suitcase, the time of its preparation and its contents, are very useful ways for therapists to address, symbolically but also practically, the contents of the suitcase, in other words: history, heritage, and identity (Daure, 2023).

32.3.1 Case illustration

Fatou is a 32-year-old Somali woman with nine children from three different partners. She has been widowed twice, and her third husband and family take care of her children. Forced into marriage all three times, she faced the migratory journey alone. Having arrived at her destination, she applies for asylum, her plan being to obtain family reunification. The workers at the reception center where she lives are very intrigued by her behavior: she lives in shared housing and wants to lock everything up; she does not put food in the shared refrigerator because there is a risk of contaminating herself with other people's food; she keeps her suitcase locked, as well as the many bags she carries with her, never settling. She is suspicious of everyone and, by a mirror effect, perceives that people think she is strange. The other women in the apartment find her obnoxious and arrogant. Fatou needs to protect herself, so she protects her belongings; she feels subjected to the need to assert constant control of her things in a never-ending migratory journey and in a life in which everything escapes her. Through possession of her belongings, she attempts to construct a new identity as a woman. A space of identity that refers to property, certainly, but also to identity, to self, to a self that is not someone else. An existence. A place.

Place is related to the human need to connect one's existence to a territory, a physical, geographic space. Migration involves de-territorializing and re-territorializing oneself and seeking a place alone or with others. By migrating, one has lost a place within the family of origin and its physical places, and it is essential to find a way to build a new place here, which also helps build a new relationship to the places in the country of origin.

Information and communication technologies (ICTs) are revolutionizing migration today (Borcsa, 2023; Borcsa & Hille, 2022; Daure & Borcsa, 2020). Migration 20 years ago involved physical distance accompanied by a break with daily life. The slowness of letters and the exorbitant cost of phone calls made the distance even greater. Today, with the help of live video, migrants can participate in the daily lives of family members or their circle of friends back home, and even in important events such as weddings and funerals. In this way, there is an attempt to erase borders, like being here and there, an illusion of ubiquity that does not last over time, but probably has a function for everyone. "You are gone, but you are here. I'm gone, but I'm with you." And this can be heard in what people say, "Yesterday I saw my mother," who lives in Georgia, "last week we celebrated my uncle's birthday," who lives in Mali, "we were together, my sister and I," when we know that the sister lives in the United States. This makes things a bit special, since the people talking to the therapist live in France.

This all introduces the third theme, that of communication.

32.4 Communication

Communication among people from different countries has been facilitated by computers and cell phones, but these technologies have created new social needs, such as to show oneself in a better light to one's family back home and appear responsible and successful, when perhaps still struggling to survive. The individual thus may escape the social control that they lived under in the home country. This is often viewed as one of the advantages of migration, as it provides a form of freedom, a chance to be different and show oneself differently, and to establish relationships with others that are not guided by the conventions and social rules of the home country. Fatma says, "Here (in France) I can have a drink with a man without thinking of meeting someone from my family or someone who knows my family and being looked down upon."

Another interesting example is that of Aoa,[3] a woman who found it difficult to install Whatsapp on her phone. She resisted, or at least did not take the opportunities offered by those around her to install the application, which would allow her to have regular, even daily, contact with her family. It seemed that her reluctance to install the app was a form of self-protection by creating a communicational boundary between herself and her family back home. Indeed, another advantage of migration is that it creates relational and communicative boundaries that give people the sense of being able to live their lives as they see fit. It is clear that the diaspora of many people is a means of control over social/familial connections and regulation of degree of involvement with customs, behaviors, and social codes from their cultures of origin.

As another woman named Maryam[4] recounted, "I got on the bus wearing a tight dress, which did not fit. Before I got off the bus, a man said to me, 'Sister, are you Ivorian? Are you Muslim? Just like me. So I'm telling you it's not right to dress like that.'" There are several elements to this example: the man recognized her as Ivorian. He took the liberty of giving her instructions on how to dress. It is a reminder of the community's gaze, its presence, even when you don't expect it. It is not uncommon for people to avoid contact with their compatriots in an attempt to escape this scrutiny and thus feel more at home and free of culture-of-origin constraints in the country where they now live.

Another aspect concerns communication with the native population, which is often hampered by language problems. Difficulties in learning the language of the host country have an enormous impact on, among other things, the primary need for security, shelter, food, and financial resources. Barriers to these essential resources due to an inability to express oneself verbally is a source of great frustration and sometimes even despair and vulnerability. Social workers, when present, provide support, as do peer groups, who may also play a role in accessing information and administrative services, but they have little to offer in terms of the immigrant building relationships with neighbors, storekeepers, bank workers, police, and other members of the local population who speak only the dominant language.

The therapeutic space is a place that represents the host society; going to therapy alone or with family is not an option in all cultures, and is even an almost inaccessible option in some countries. Consulting a psychologist, psychiatrist, or therapist is therefore a step toward the culture of the country in which the immigrant now lives. It is therefore important for people to be able to express themselves easily, and this is not always possible given inadequate fluency in the dominant language. In some situations, an interpreter can play a crucial role. It is not uncommon for people who express themselves well in the language of their adopted country to want to express themselves in therapy in their native language, and we are seeing the emergence of online therapy with professionals who are not in the same country as the patient they are working with, but who speak the same native language. For more information on this topic, see Borcsa and Daure (2023).

32.5 Knowledge

In Europe, the word "migration" often evokes prejudices and stereotypes of migrants who crossed the Mediterranean on a makeshift raft. Migrants may also be expatriates, political refugees, intellectuals who come to work, students, and anyone who moves to a country other than their own for an extended period of time, as mentioned at the beginning of this chapter. The individual is inevitably faced with a lack of knowledge about the institutions, daily life practices and routines, laws, social etiquette and expectations about personal space during interactions with others, temporal issues such as the society's perspectives and practices regarding punctuality, and other aspects of culture. This can lead even an immigrant with much education and skill at negotiating their country-of-origin's procedures for living to feel utterly incompetent. A fellow psychologist said, "When I came to live in France, I became illiterate because I could not write in French. I made a lot of spelling mistakes, even for every word. It was difficult to accept that I was incompetent." Migration is a life experience in which people can feel disoriented due to seeing their professional, social, and relational skills undermined. This reality pushes the individual into a process that is not a linear progress in acquiring the knowledge needed to comprehend and operate in a wide range of settings, but rather, involves comings and goings in relation to the host culture, ambivalence about mastering this knowledge, and fluctuating between feelings of discouragement and blockage on the one hand and curiosity and desire for discovery on the other.

Learning is the key word of migration: learning to speak the language, learning to orient oneself in new constructed spaces, learning the social codes of relationships, of seduction and assertion, and of all the nuances of professional and nonprofessional relationships. Learning requires energy and desire (which can flag at times due to the load), and this transforms people and leads them to reexamine their original, familiar sets of knowledge. Learning requires emotional availability, some modicum or periods of serenity, and space and time to think.

Being a migrant can deprive the individual of work and make their existed occupational knowledge and skill irrelevant, as they may not be able to practice their original profession. This reality is even more evident when the immigrant seeks asylum, because in many countries such as France work is prohibited during the asylum process. This situation reinforces the sense of helplessness and frustration in the face of a wait that is often prolonged without clear limits (Daure, 2020).

32.5.1 Case illustration

Irina is a Ukrainian woman who was a school director in her country, but the war forced her to leave with her children and her partner. She speaks Russian, Ukrainian, and some English, but not French. Irina could work, but she cannot find employment up to her abilities and tries to do housework, but she cannot find any because of her poor command of French. Very depressed about the situation in her country, her family, and her professional reality, she often cries during sessions. Irina regularly talks about the sense of humiliation she feels at not being recognized for her abilities and her social downgrading. She mourns her losses and her experience of incompetence and inadequacy in a country that welcomes her but fails to include her based on her abilities and uniqueness.

In the context of asylum, there is an urgency to earn a living, to get out of waiting and invisibility, to get involved in the new country, to have a space in the new society, and, above all, the urgency to return to the world of people who are viewed as worthy and legitimized to live a better life than the one they had in their country of origin.

The knowledge that equips one to pursue a profession is acquired in the host country sometimes formally through university studies and other times informally through oral transmission. However, even though objectively qualified to work in this occupation, for a whole host of reasons the person may not be recognized by employers or governing/licensing bodies, resulting in a loss of identity and sense of legitimacy because of this rejection. Conversely, we can also observe specific culturally connoted skills that would not have been recognized as exceptional or unique in the country of origin since they are quite common, whereas in the host country they become "exotic," new, and valued knowledge: for example, martial arts, ballroom dance, cooking certain cuisines, or certain types of medical or holistic treatment, such as child massage. These skills give individuals status and recognition that they might not have in their country of origin, a *know-how* that projects them into a special position that reinforces their original identity and emphasizes their abilities. The theme of work is often present in therapy and condenses key elements such as legitimacy, place, recognition, status, and identity.

32.6 Economy

We often think that in many cases migration is motivated by economic reasons, especially when it comes to certain journeys, such as between Africa and Europe, or from South America to the United States. Our clinical observations lead us to believe that some migrations may indeed be motivated by economic considerations or the search for a better life. However, each migration is unique, and listening to so many people who have arrived from elsewhere, it is not uncommon to hear of reasons other than economic hardship, and that are more personal, more intimate, and more relational. Yes, migration is also a relational process, meaning in this context "motivated by or affecting relationships including to self-identity in the country of origin and/or the country of resettlement." Even when in practice it is accomplished by a person moving alone physically, there are relational, emotional, and socioeducational motivations that are more important migratory *drivers* than just economic survival or improvement needs. For instance, the women described in the vignettes so far all sought economic improvement but also a chance to escape restrictive sociocultural norms. As another example, parents may wish to pursue or to have their children able to pursue better or more varied educational opportunities than were available in the country of origin – irrespective of the greater income that education is likely to provide.

As psychologists, we are certainly less qualified to talk about economics than economists or other social scientists whose domain of expertise centers on this topic. However, given that economics is a topic often used by politicians to say what they want from a pro- or anti-migration perspective, it is important for mental and other health professionals to familiarize themselves with the fundamentals of economics as part of advocating for immigrant persons' rights to exist. However, we can argue that migration also serves the economic needs of the host country – for instance, at the lower end of the income/pay scale, migration provides workers to do certain jobs that citizens of the host country are unlikely to be willing to do (in the US, farming-related jobs such as picking strawberries and cotton, restaurant dishwasher, janitor, or hotel housekeeper). We must also consider the wealth of cultural, culinary, artistic, intellectual, and scientific contributions that migrants contribute to building and creating a society and to improving the country's economic standing and gross national product (GNP). Importantly, many migrating persons may not *arrive* with the knowledge or skills that later enable them to make these contributions, but rather, *acquire them* through dedicated hard educational effort.[5]

As for *the psychic economy*, it is in great demand during the different stages of the migration process, between preparing for the journey, making the migration odyssey, and adjusting to life in the host country. Truly, the psychic economy of the individual is being tested, and the typical immigrating person struggles to activate the life drives or instinct (Eros) over the death instinct (Thanatos), where the latter would be represented by giving up in the face of numerous challenges. The immigrant expends a great deal of energy in the act of traveling from home country to new country, in the pursuit of a better present and future for self and family members, and in the ongoing need to adapt, to reinvent oneself, and to hold the cultural and life-pragmatic differences. It is useful and accurate to reframe these many struggles as simultaneously requiring the expenditure of psychic energy, but also an opportunity to gather energy through the tension that comes from struggle and adaptation This energy, born of and sustained by the psychic tension necessary for change, is directed into learning and producing in the work economy. In simpler terms, immigrants bring with them and further develop through mastering challenges a certain quantum of psychospiritual energy that makes them "hard workers," and this benefits the society they now live in. In this perspective, arguments by conservative anti-immigrant politicians and citizens/voters that immigrants drain the host country's economy are inaccurate – immigrants are typically hardy workers who put their capacity for perseverance into work, whatever the type of work and socioeconomic level, and often with little or no complaining.

Having argued for the contribution immigrants make to the economics of the host societies, it's important as therapist advocates to remember that the economic and financial aspects are important for most migrants. In my opinion, there are three imperatives of migration and three foci that therapists working with them must keep front of mind: Immigrants, like longtime citizens, need (1) a secure physical and relational *place*; (2) they need to be *recognized and shown respect* for their hard work; and (3) they need to reap *financial success* for their efforts. Ignoring or, even worse, marginalizing immigrants while still profiting as a society from their diligent work is unfair and damaging psychologically to persons who simply and honestly have sought a better life than the one they lived in their country of origin – and that is a human right that transcends politics and policies (Borcsa & Daure, 2023).

32.6.1 Case illustration

Julie, a 25-year-old patient of Portuguese grandparents, proudly recounts how her illiterate grandparents left Portugal on foot and managed to build a house in France and another in Portugal – both with swimming pools – and who raised their three children now working in French administrative posts. Julie adds that her grandparents know everyone in their neighborhood and are highly regarded by their neighbors in France.

This sense of redemption and pride is very important to those who have migrated. It gives meaning to the journey and all the sacrifices involved. Feeling recognized, finding one's place, and garnering professional and family success answer the question about whether it was a good decision to migrate when they share their migration stories to succeeding generations. Was it a good choice? Was it worth it? These are questions that migrants ask themselves many times throughout their lives.

32.7 Power

The power of the dominant society and administration is a power that extends over the life and future of the migrant individual: over his or her right to territory to stay, to live, a dwelling, to the legitimacy of becoming an ordinary person and citizen in the host country, thereby emerging from marginalization and invisibility.

Migration today is the result of globalization, with 280 million people on the move around the world, according to the United Nations (Report La Cimade, 2022), a figure that is increasing but stable in relation to the world's population growth. Trying to control and counter migration by banning entry into countries is like fighting against the force of the waters. The best thing to do is to accompany it, guide and structure it in a manner that respects both the host country and immigrants, and experience the migrant population as a resource rather than a nuisance and drain on a country's resources.

Without knowing how best to proceed, governments face opposing positions on the reality of migration. In the confusion about which policy position to adopt, public opinion and populism (and government leaders who, at least in a democracy, obtain power through votes and political advocacy group) find a place of opportunity to propose the mistaken idea[6] that migrants are largely criminal opportunists set on invading the host country and transforming the dominant culture to fit the cultures they bring with them. The number of migrants in France, according to INSEE,

> in 2022, is 7.0 million, or 10.3 percent of the total population; 2.5 million migrants, or 35 percent, have acquired French citizenship. The foreign population living in France is 5.3 million, or 7.8 percent of the total population, of which 4.5 million are immigrants who have not acquired French nationality and 0.8 million people born in France of foreign nationality.[7]

These numbers indicate that we are far from the large replacement by foreigners that populist politicians in France, other European countries, and in the US talk about, appealing to the fears of citizens by claiming the risk of Europeans facing displacement of existing citizens and cultural disintegration. However, they fail to point out that immigration figures have been low and stable since 2012 and that there has been no increase in the migrant population compared to the native population, in contrast to right-wing fearmongers.

In fact, it is migrants who mostly experience marginalization and powerlessness. Racism, prejudice, and economic and housing insecurity create a power imbalance between the society and those who wish to exercise their human right to settle in a safer and more facilitative country. Many immigrants, especially people of color with limited financial means from the Global South (or also white persons escaping political violence and war trauma such as Ukrainians), experience humiliation, exploitation, and powerlessness. Treated this way, the migrants' dreams of a welcoming and safe society may end up crushed by these economic and social forces. These feelings may be passed on from generation to generation through the telling and retelling of the person's narrative of immigration. Aldo Naouri, a psychoanalytic pediatrician specializing in intrafamilial relationships, who was born in Libya and lives in France, says that under such oppressive power imbalances and social forces, we integrate through revenge or resentment. Although some may transform these negative, unfair experiences into fuel for a positive driving force, others may unfortunately be trapped in the negative and damaging cycle of revenge.

In light of all these challenges, the therapeutic space becomes a place of peace, of reconciliation, and appeasement, where people feel heard and recognized. However, without broader sociopolitical and economic shifts, it can be quite difficult for patients to sustain their regained positive identities and sense of being cared for by the sympathetic therapeutic community.

In contrast to the usual disempowerment migrants experience once in the host country, it is important for therapists working with migrants to honor and highlight the *personal power* that permeates the act of migrating and resettling. These stories are narratives of strength, resilience, courage, faith and hope, fortitude, self-confidence, and curiosity, among other powerful personal characteristics required to fulfill the dreams of success and the freedom to pursue a better life on foreign soil.

These personal characteristics, these human values displayed in action, are exactly what we hear from many women in the "reliance" support group that we facilitate. The support group is held at the Maison d'Ella, an association that works with women who are victims of violence. On Monday mornings, with two other female colleagues, I lead a support group for women from other countries.

32.7.1 Case illustration

Samia says that the migration journey freed her from the violence of her husband and in-laws. She feels stronger and freer. No one has power over her, and she makes life decisions for herself. She no longer wants to marry, and no man is present in her life. She avoids intimate relations or the prospect of remarrying because she fears that a man would threaten her freedom, the power she has gained over her life, and her place as a woman in French society.

As Samia's story and those of many others in the group have attested to, migration often represents an opportunity for autonomy and disengagement from family and social control, putting personal power in the hands of formerly oppressed women (Borcsa & Daure, 2023; Daure, 2010; Daure & Reveyrand-Coulon, 2017).

32.8 Society

The host society plays an important role for migrants in the quality of the relationships established with representatives of the host society. The degree to which they feel welcomed is important in establishing trust and collaboration and facilitating access to institutions.

Not all migrants are perceived in the same way, and social representations related to the country of origin influence how the person is viewed, with implicit or explicit biases. Being Mauritanian in Europe does not have the same reception as being Ukrainian or American, and this has a significant effect on the migrant's adjustment.

32.8.1 Case illustration

Nadine is an Argentinian woman who had a successful career in international law. In her case, Nadine explains that whenever she says she is a migrant, people correct her with "No, not you," and "You are not a migrant," even though she sees her migration as an asset, a resource that is a daily tool in her work with clients of different nationalities and in her everyday life. Nadine insists in an interview, "Okay, I'm not black, I'm not Arab. I didn't cross the Mediterranean on a makeshift boat, but I feel like a migrant. And this is a beautiful word that we need to rehabilitate."

Nadine's political and social engagement reveals the greatest challenge of migration, that of articulating the cultures of the country she lives in and the country of origin, languages, and codes. Living one's multiple cultural affiliations as a resource requires security and a positive experience in the host country. Somewhat paradoxically, it is probably easier to do this when one is *not* seen by locals as a migrant, with all the negative references that come with the word, even though the migrants facing the largest challenges in integrating their culture of origin with the culture of the host country (and possibly needing the greatest support and "enhanced welcoming") are those whose race, ethnicity, and often overall appearance and style of dress (for instance, a woman wearing a burka, sari, or African wrap dress) clearly mark them as "migrants" – even if they happen to have attained citizenship!

32.9 Interculturation or negotiation of allegiances

Interculturation is the inevitable process established through contact between the migrant and the native, since there is subjective influence in the encounter. Interculturation appeals to life experiences, encounters, and exchanges that occur in different contexts and periods and involve all those who move through the migrant's landscape. In other words, each time migration occurs, a unique transformative process takes place that continues throughout the migrant's life and that of his or her descendants.

In this context, what place will there be for the family, a small sample of society that transmits Culture with a capital C? Also, how do specific families with their unique cultures – members or composition, styles of communication, quality of marital relations and parent-child relations, family routines, and so on – adjust to a new societal setting? Other tensions occur when a family member leaves the family behind and migrates to a new land. The family member who migrated may fear or actually find their place in their families threatened. In some cases, migration is turned into a test of loyalty – both the continued loyalty of the migrant to her or his family (often displayed by regular dispatches of money or gifts), as well as the loyalty of the family left behind to the migrant member. Leaving loved ones, changing countries, living elsewhere, changing languages, and integrating into a new society all take place with the continued need to make their presence felt in the family despite their absence, to prove their loyalty, and to reaffirm their belonging in the family even while they seek to establish a new life in the new country. This may become particularly challenging if the migrant adult marries and has children with someone in the new country.

> Being loyal means adopting, in spite of ourselves, the same gestures, the same voice inflections, the same speech tics, the same behavioral demands. It means living in a city, a neighborhood, a street. It means taking root in a territory, a land where our ancestors are buried, where one place awaits us and another will await our children when the time comes.
>
> *(Balta, 2003)*

As noted earlier, sending money, clothing, foodstuffs, and sharing news of successes with the family "back home" all may demonstrate continued loyalty, which is so central to providing a valid reason for the migration. The migrant also demonstrates loyalty to the culture and society of origin and the family back home by preserving traditions and customs, and maintaining the language of origin.

32.10 Create an opening and never closing the door

Migration does not have a definitive endpoint. The physical migration may occur in a matter of hours, but the psychological and relational aspects of migration occur over a lifetime – in fact, often extending across succeeding generations. This chapter has hopefully provided a framework to broaden the way we read, look at, and think about migration.

Eric Cattelain's original proposal as a linguist was a fruitful opportunity to think about migration in terms of seven meaningful units of analysis. Seven words that tell a story, make connections with many other words, and describe migration in a systemic, dynamic, global, and contextual way. This is what systemic therapy is all about: Helping people tell their story by creating a link between them and the story being told, expanding points of view, logics, and readings. It is an experience of openness that invites us to reread the migration movement and, in a non-exhaustive way, to rethink it with singularity and originality. Analyzing the migratory event as an organizer of relationships opens new windows in the therapeutic space to help us think about "families with multiple horizons" (Moro, 2020).

Migration, like therapy, is a transformative experience not only for those directly involved, but also for the diverse systems of reference and belonging of which members are a part.

Notes

1 The "Dialogues of 21" originated from UNESCO's World Day for Cultural Diversity on May 21, 2021. In collaboration with UNESCO, Eric Cattelain created a forum for a wide range of professionals and people working in the field to discuss diversity in its broadest sense.

2 The term "migrant" is used here for brevity's sake in lieu of the longer but less totalizing description, "people who have migrated." People who have migrated are full and diverse human beings, and I do not mean to reduce them to one word – "migrant" – but it becomes unwieldy to repeatedly use the longer phrase.

3 Woman supported by the Maison d'Ella, an association that cares for women victims of violence. And Aoa is part of a Monday morning discussion group for women from other countries.

4 Woman also supported by the Maison d'Ella.

5 My American colleague Peter Fraenkel, co-editor of this book, tells me that his college, The City College of New York, is one of 11 campuses of The City University of New York, whose mission is to provide educational opportunities to thousands of first- and second-generation immigrant students, and that these students are usually the first in their families to attain a college degree. It is also noteworthy that there are more Nobel Prize winners from City College than from any other American university.

6 Mistaken at least from what is likely the majority view of most therapists and others who work with migrants.

7 www.insee.fr/fr/statistiques/3633212

References

Balta, F. (2003). Les expressions de la loyauté. *Générations*, *29*, 4–6.

Borcsa, M. (2023). Le famiglie globalizzate: Una lettura sistemica. In M. Borcsa & I. Daure (Eds.), *Mobilités et migrations. Repenser l'approche systémique à l'heure de la mondialisation* (pp. 13–21). ESF Sciences Humaines.

Borcsa, M., & Daure, I. (2023). *Mobilités, migrations: repenser l'approche systémique à l'heure de la mondialisation*. ESF. Sciences Humaines.

Borcsa, M., & Hille, J. (2022). Il Genogramma 4.0: famiglie globalizzate e relazioni virtuali. In I. Daure & M. Borcsa (Eds.), *Il Genogramma nella pratica sistemica contemporanea. Sviluppi e prospettive* (pp. 127–139). Franco Angeli.

Daure, I. (2010). *Familles entre deux cultures: Dynamiques relationnelles et prise en charge systémique*. Fabert.

Daure, I. (2020). L'approccio sistemico interculturale: Il migrante è il "bien-venu". *Le Journal des psychologues*, *375*(3), 26–30.

Daure, I. (2023). La valise comme métaphore. In M. Borcsa & I. Daure (Eds.), *Mobilités, migrations: Repenser l'approche systémique à l'heure de la mondialisation* (pp. 117–124). ESF Sciences Humaines.

Daure, I., & Borcsa, M. (2020). *Les génogrammes d'aujourd'hui: la clinique systémique en mouvement*. ESF Sciences Humaines.

Daure, I., & Reveyrand-Coulon, O. (2017). *Le migrant et sa famille: Défis interculturels en psychologie clinique*. ESF Sciences Humaines.

Falicov, C. J. (2005). Emotional transnationalism and family identities. *Family Process*, *44*, 399–406. https://doi.org/10.1111/j.1545-5300.2005.00068.x

Moro, M. R. (2020). *Guide de psychothérapie transculturelle: Soigner les enfants et les adolescents*. In Press.

Naouri, A. (2019). *Des bouts d'existence*. Éditions Odile Jacob.

Report La Cimade. (2022). www.lacimade.org/faq/les-migrations-internationales-faits-et-chiffres/

33
CULTURAL DIVERSITY AS A RESOURCE IN FAMILY THERAPY

Lorena Cavalieri

33.1 Introduction

The migration phenomenon concerns entire communities that are forced to move to search for better living conditions. It is a movement of peoples that has always existed and that in the modern era has clashed with the limits imposed by the more or less flexible welcoming policies of the wealthier countries, usually Western, to which these masses are directed. Although it is not an extraordinary event, it always assumes extreme relevance in political confrontations, often not as an event that needs to be understood and controlled but rather as a problem to be solved and, if possible, eliminated. Reality, on the other hand, shows us that every institution encounters foreign people, often not yet citizens, who access schools, hospitals, social services, judicial circuits, and psychiatric wards from which they expect answers and by which they will be served, or managed if necessary. Unfortunately, many institutional responses to migrated persons are unclear and ineffective or give rise to real cultural misunderstandings. People who immigrate carry their own cultural baggage, their own traditional and religious values, different if not totally opposite from those of the country of landing; even in the clinical field and in psychotherapy, we might ask whether the models we have learned are fitting and appropriate for that specific family unit we encounter in the therapy room.

Does it mean one really has to be an expert in so many different cultures to ensure effective clinical intervention? And is this the solution? Psychotherapy, which is known and practiced in Western countries, often does not focus enough on cultural diversity and on the different ways of dealing with family values, child-rearing, and care of the elderly, among many other aspects of family life. We have come a long way since the origins of family therapy and systemic theories in the US, and its worldwide diffusion has been exceptional. However, Western culture is still the one on which intervention is modeled, even with families from countries and cultural realities far from the Western ones.

33.2 Family models on which family therapy was built

Family therapy pioneer Murray Bowen based his theory of the family and on its intergenerational development by first observing relationship models within families with a schizophrenic member, then those of his own students' families, concluding that it was clear that all families were pretty much alike (Bowen, 1978). Of course, Bowen's observational "sample" was a particularly homogenous section of the American population – largely middle-class heterosexual white US citizens in

DOI: 10.4324/9781003536765-39

two-parent families, living in the geographic area in and around Washington, DC, where he was based at Georgetown University Medical Center. This majority racial and social class group was assumed to be the unquestioned "norm" upon which was based ideas of assessment and treatment of any family, irrespective of their racial, ethnic, class, education, sexual orientation, gender identity, and citizenship status. Other family therapy pioneers (with Salvador Minuchin somewhat an exception due to his early work with low-income inner-city African American families) assumed this demographic to be the norm from which their research, theories, and interventions were developed. Of course, with these theories being developed mostly in the US in the 1960s through the 1970s, the families studied shared a certain dominant version of Western culture that assumed certain relational structures, values, and child development norms, such as the focus on individualism and the belief in launching children in their late teens into independent living, rather than the collectivism and ongoing daily contact among multiple family generations that doesn't end when a child reaches 18 years of age, and that characterizes the majority of families and cultures outside the stereotypic West and Global North.

However, over time, family therapy has been practiced all over the world, and cultural contaminations have increased with migration flows involving the displacement of a great number of families from one continent to another, so that many different cultures coexist. In addition, as colleagues of various ethnic, racial, and cultural groups have gained voice and power in the field through publishing, presenting at conferences and leading training workshops, the assumptions, theoretical constructs, and interventions of early models have been challenged. One excellent example is the notion that families vary on the dimension of closeness, involvement, and connectedness, from one pole of "disengagement" to the other pole of "enmeshment." However, both poles had been assumed to be characteristic of dysfunctional families, such that the extreme closeness and involvement that characterizes many South Asian families, for instance, was automatically viewed as a sign of pathology.

With our growing awareness of the great diversity in family forms and cultures, when we meet in therapy with a family with a different cultural background from our own or from the majority reality we share, we now ask ourselves questions such as: Are we sure the family model we are using for an initial assessment is the right one for the family unit sitting in front of us? This is a question for every therapist and for every training institution for family therapists who meet families coming from other cultures. Going back to the pioneers of family therapy (Andolfi, 2014), some of them, together with their followers, had focused more on the therapeutic effects of the alliance or relationship between family and therapist (often now termed the *nonspecific factors of therapy*), others more on systemic diagnoses (for instance, the early obsession for many years with first- and second-order cybernetics, negative and positive feedback loops, and homeostatic mechanisms similar to self-guided machines and physiological systems) and techniques to disrupt systemic rigidity hypothesized to underlie a family member's psychiatric symptoms.

In both styles of intervention, something had changed in the field of mental health, and one could no longer assess a patient without assessing how symptoms functioned in the family. Despite this revolutionary change, the early theories omitted some important aspects, including both differences in power between men and women, and cultural diversity.

In short, family therapy has long suffered from the construction of theories and interventions forged on a model of a certain type of Western family applied without making the necessary transformations across cultures. Family therapy spread, exported as a psychological product to countries in South America, Africa, and Asia, without considering cultural realities such as multigenerational families living together, a different view about permeability of boundaries between subsystems and between the family and their social context, the focus on loyalty and filial piety in relation to one's family of origin, and the strength of religious and spiritual values – all quite different from the generic Western world where the ties between generations are less binding and strong (Lee & Cheng, 2018; Nwoye, 2004). Sluzki (1979) noted how in families belonging to certain cultures, where mutual dependence is equated with loyalty, any attempt to increase the independence of its members by the therapist can be seen as an attack on core family values.

Lau (1984) explained this very well in an article focused precisely on how much the cultural background can affect the work of family therapists working with diverse ethnic-cultural backgrounds. Psychotherapy practiced in Western countries often does not focus enough on cultural differences and on the different ways of understanding family values, child-rearing, and care of the elderly, which may differ for many from those of the majority society in which they and we are living. If I meet a family in Italy, in Australia, or in the US in therapy, I will most likely consider the Italian, or Anglo-Saxon, hence the Western family model, even if the family comes from a culturally traditional background in Ghana, Bolivia, or India. I will take for granted that the underlying family relationships in cultures very different from my own are based on the same rules and values of the country we live in, and subsequently I will ask questions based on these assumptions.

Can this trend be reversed? I believe so, by learning to listen but more importantly to use our eyes more during session and observe what is happening on an implicit, analogue level. Verbal language is often limited due to the lack of understanding of the language and can be compensated for by the eyes and gaze of the therapist, as Andolfi (2017) explains: His ability to observe the family movements was sharpened by a form of sensory deficiency due to his lack of knowledge of English in his early years of training in the United States. Another key aspect to reach out to families from cultures different from our own is the curiosity that helps us explore other worlds, other traditions, other ways of relating and communicating feelings and moods. Family therapists working cross-culturally must adopt more of an ethnographic stance *where we learn from the family* about how families are constructed, their rules and habits of interaction, and their relational meaning systems, rather than imposing a pre-made abstract theoretical frame in a "one-size-fits-all" manner.

33.3 The iceberg model in culturally attuned family therapy

A useful way to think about culture is to follow the iceberg model introduced by the American anthropologist Edward T. Hall (1990), who investigated proxemics. I always bear this model in mind when I work with mixed-culture couples. The model is based on the idea that one part of culture is more emergent, visible, and recognizable, and another is deeper and harder to access for those who do not belong. However, even a cultural "insider" is sometimes not fully aware of all the assumptions that characterize and structure a culture, because some aspects operate at an unconscious level or are expressed in automatic behaviors that are rarely subjected to self-reflection. When the family I'm working with belongs to a culture different from mine, and does not belong to the culture of the place they are presently living in, I wonder how that submerged part has interacted or has influenced the process of integrating into a new culture. More visible aspects guide us while thinking about the differences, including physical appearance, the way people dress, some explicit religious practices and beliefs references, the foods they eat, the way they speak, including the paralinguistics of speech (tempo, volume, pitch, accent, intensity), and the facial expressions they use to express themselves in their mother tongue or the language they learned later in their country of residence. Then there are those cultural aspects that emerge after a second, third, or further encounter and that govern the choices, routines, and the quality of interpersonal relationships in their lives. These are norms, beliefs, expectations, social rules, rules of descent, gender roles, and roles defined by age, social class, occupation, kinship: All come into play in relational and social life either explicitly or implicitly. These are the relational modes and styles one adopts, patterns learned and "sedimented" through experience into the very ground or basis of their existence and movements through the world. They are patterns of how one relates with one's subordinates and superiors, with intimates, acquaintances, neighbors, institutional and government officials, strangers. At an even deeper and less conscious level is the context of the society one has grown up in and the core values absorbed. These values may be quite different or even opposed to the prevailing values of the society one now lives in, such as in the competition/cooperation or individualism/collectivism binomials. Concepts such as time, fairness, equity, justice, beauty, honesty, love and affection, and so on may also be differentially endorsed or expressed in the family's culture of origin versus in their current country of residence to which they migrated.

For instance, a colleague (Peter Fraenkel) tells of living in Nairobi, Kenya, early in his career and being asked by a local counseling center to teach an introductory course in couple therapy. He reasoned that a good start would be to teach them a reflective listening style of couple communication (wherein each partner gets a chance to speak and to listen and repeat back what they heard), but quickly, the women in the class began to shake their heads. Asked by Peter why, they declared that in many more traditional couples, "the woman cannot talk back or she will be beaten." This form of couple communication, created and researched in the West, assumes a basic level of equity of voice and power between men and women, a value not endorsed in many Kenyan couples whose referenced values are drawn from strictly patriarchal tribal cultures. Cultural identity is a very broad concept that is not only about ethnic identity (Beneduce, 1998). It is also constructed and modified by being exposed to diverse cultures as well as traumatic life experiences or events such as wars or exile. Cultural identity is like a set of different aspects binding an individual to a significant group, allowing him/her to belong to and identify with this group, through direct or indirect experiences passed down through generations as well as modified by powerful events and exposure to other ways of living (Cavalieri, 2004).

Culture is like the plot of a narrative on which family events are positioned, and together they shape the history of that unique family. Moreover, it is not motionless and intact, but a process that is co-constructed and modified in the relationship with the others depending on life experiences and time passages. This becomes even more relevant when migration leads to living longer or shorter periods that are more or less forced in another country, even if you maintain a strong attachment to your own cultural codes. It is important to consider the cultural background related to events and experiences in life: Culture is constantly evolving, but to better understand a family, it is important to know the family of origin.

33.4 From diagnosis to cultural knowledge

At this point in the field of mental health, it is generally understood that the diagnostic process must be influenced by an understanding of the patient's culture: One cannot simply apply a diagnosis without taking cultural facts into account. The list of diagnoses in the DSM-5 and ICD-10 are based in culture, in what the cultures of professionals who create diagnoses consider well-being and illness, and in the notion that the individual person should be the receiver of a diagnosis as opposed to a family or even a social context. As any beginning student in a mental health discipline learns (or should learn) in graduate or medical school, diagnoses are words meant to summarize a list of behaviors (criteria) considered maladaptive and pathological; diagnoses are not discovered in people but rather are constructed *about* people, and those constructions are culturally determined. Depression, anxiety, and borderline personality disorder cannot be found inside the body like a tumor; they are not *in* the body, but rather, are about patterns of the person's behavior, feelings, and emotions.

The best way to conduct the process of assessment and diagnosis is as a relational tool in which the professional seeks to understand the meaning a type of distress has in the history of that person and that family, at what stages of the life cycle and in what social and cultural context he/she is living at that precise moment, and what their relationship is with their cultural context. This diagnostic process is useful in setting up the therapeutic process. On the one hand, we have how the problem is interpreted and a diagnosis made by the professional, and on the other hand, how this problem is experienced by the family in front of us – and the former should be influenced greatly by the latter.

What often happens in families who have moved or migrated to another country is a kind of disconnect between the internal experiences and behaviors viewed as a mental health issue in the new country and the same behavior that would not have been experienced as such had it occurred in the country of origin. This disconnect produces a desire to change by means of the tools and help received from outside, as it is impossible to use the resources within the nuclear family to address a problem that would not be viewed as a problem in the family's culture/country of origin. Nor could resources be sought in the extended family, who is often still living in the country of origin and would not understand the need for change. In such cases, we should ask ourselves what is the purpose of bringing the family of origin into therapy. A culturally sensitive approach is to get opinions from the family of origin in the host country and the country of origin as to whether the behavior being diagnosed and targeted for treatment is indeed a problem at all, and if a problem, how would it be handled through the healing resources and beliefs in the origin culture. On the other hand, a behavior may become legitimately problematic in the country to which the family has relocated because of aspects of the new society that are not present in the country of origin. For instance, the family may come from a country and culture where a child's days at school are not as long and desk-bound as they are in the new country. Thus, the child's behavioral difficulties at school may be genuine but only exist because of the educational practices to which the child must fit in.

When migrating to a different country, the family's cultural identity goes through a series of adjustments. For individuals or families who are in the process of integrating in another context, the cultural element is the aspect that needs to be accommodated back into a new frame. Sometimes the frame is narrow, urgent, and restrictive – for instance, if a family comes from a culture in which corporal punishment is acceptable and are now living in a culture that forbids such forms of punishment, and the parent risks losing custody of the child if they continue such punishment. Sometimes the frame is wider, and the adjustments needed are less or nonexistent – for instance, a family may be able to procure the foodstuffs they need to maintain their traditional cuisine, and are certainly not legally mandated to stick to the types of food and dishes more common in the culture to which they have migrated.

However, for all individuals and families that have migrated, the question of whether and the degree to which they will need to adjust is inevitable. A therapist can provide helpful support as the family decides whether they will fully assimilate to the new culture, reject the new culture in part or in its entirety, or adopt a bicultural model in which they maintain aspects of their culture of origin and regular contact with family and friends "back home," and also adopt some aspects of the host culture (Falicov, 2007, 2016).

Given all the nuances and complexities of the practical and meaning-making cultural transformations that families who have migrated go through over years as they settle in a new land, what is the best approach for a therapist to learn about their cultural background and adjustments? The solution is to let yourself be guided by the family. The first important point in this process is to bear in mind that in order to create a meaningful therapeutic relationship, each culture present in the therapy room must be recognized and legitimized. Dialogue between cultures is only possible if the other's culture is legitimized – even if certain beliefs and practices are at variance with the therapist's own cultural premises. When building therapeutic bonds, giving space to this cultural element creates an immediate connection with the other.

How can this door be opened? When asked to point out their own country on the map, many families at first seem surprised by this request and display of the therapist's genuine, detailed interest. They then talk about their childhood homes, and just like tour guides, they take us with them into India, Africa, or Peru on a journey into their families and cultures. As I have had the chance to describe on multiple occasions (Andolfi et al., 2000; Cavalieri, 2004; Andolfi & Cavalieri, 2010), our learning process travels into and through their geographic and cultural identity, transforming their deeply held roots and reality – often not considered too important by members of the new country – into a truly concrete and visible one that further sparks our own imagination and curiosity. It is useful to ask them to write down a few words in their own language, pronounce these words, and then for us to try to repeat them together, so that even their most familiar sounds can become part of the construction of an important and emotionally involving experience such as therapy.

In other words, to get to know the culture of the family in front of us, we must enter this culture together with them and become curious about it with the stance of a respectful learner. The therapist's "I don't know position" proves useful to provide the family the relational space to express the emotional dimension of places, environments, contexts, events, family mandates and histories, and relational rules, all of which are otherwise exposed as diktats (Cavalieri, 2004; Cavalieri et al., 2018). Through the therapist deliberately assuming a *cultural handicap*, the family is allowed to take an authoritative role in exploring its own cultural reality. The therapeutic encounter thereby may become the first time since immigrating to a new land that the family feels themselves respected as competent experts on their own lives, rather than as constantly trying to master the rules, procedures, and meaning systems of the country to which they have immigrated. Family members, especially adults, are the true cultural experts; they have lived it, experienced it, and passed it on in part or in full to their children's generation.

Another way to shorten the distance between therapist and family and get to know families from cultures different than ours, especially in those cases in which the therapist has traveled extensively or has had some experiences in the family's home country, is what Andolfi (Andolfi, 2022) calls *transcultural self-disclosure*. Connecting with the family by talking about one's own experience in their home places and cultural contexts contributes to building the therapeutic alliance, and helps to reduce the emotional distance and hierarchy between immigrant families and the dominant culture of the new country (Andolfi, 2022).

33.5 The Garcia family and the myth of Llorona: Learning about magical, spiritual, and traditional thinking

Opening to magical and spiritual thinking that we Western-based therapists do not necessarily share is a basic part of the therapeutic relationship in cross-cultural work with many immigrant families. Once the therapist has sensed and shown interest in these beliefs, this can facilitate the family discussing them and their significance. Magical, spiritual thinking and beliefs related to a traditional culture, although not presented immediately in therapy, may represent a significant part of the experience of families who lived in traditional settings before migrating abroad and must adapt to the kind of rational, empirical thinking that dominates Western thinking. Sensing their existence, or catching nuances of the language spoken, can be the gateway to providing consent to the family to express their beliefs more openly in an atmosphere of respect and curiosity. The therapist can ask questions, foster symbolic associations, and allow something that has been part of the family members' lives to emerge without fear of judgment from those who do not understand because they do not belong.

The Garcia family consists of Carmen, the mother, and her teenage son Pablo. Carmen explains that she decided to migrate with her son shortly before he became old enough to start participating in guerrilla warfare, a reality of the rural area where they came from, and where her husband and the rest of the family had remained. According to Carmen, once Pablo arrived in Italy he "got in with the wrong crowd" and started taking drugs. His drug use scared Carmen, who had tried to keep her son away from it by taking him away from their home country. Pablo felt he had to play a more adult role, and considering the family's experience, this unfortunately implied making transgressive choices and falling into dangerous situations, just as would have likely happened in the home country. He kept his mother's thoughts occupied worrying about his drug use, and in doing so, distracted and to some extent protected her from the cognitive and emotional burden of worrying about many unresolved family situations. During the period of the therapy, Pablo became quite sick, vomiting and foaming at the mouth after taking drugs and alcohol to the point of losing consciousness, and also almost drowned in a nearby lake.

Exploring her family history during therapy, Carmen recounts a very serious event that happened when she was a child: her mother, due to her deep depression, tried to drown her in a lake.

The therapists explored the family's religious and spiritual beliefs as a possible source of help in times of difficulty. At first, Carmen hesitated to move towards a different level, from the medical-psychiatric model as a solution to a mental problem, sticking with this model and language as if she expected that she would have to agree on this view because it is more consistent with the Western, and therefore the therapist's, cultural context. But with encouragement and implied permission to talk about her native cultural beliefs, she shared the idea that a spirit had perhaps taken possession of her mother. This led to an interesting, nuanced narrative of explanation for her mother's state of mind that moved between the rational and spiritual worlds.

Therapist: You sometimes talk about the feeling that certain things have been passed down in your family from one generation to the next, of the way you deal with depression and insanity to the point that even your sister was afraid Pablo would become as sick as your grandmother. Does faith help in this? Can religion help?

Carmen/Mother: Yes, but depression is a health problem, you have to go to the doctor and take pills like you do for any other illness. . . . My mother took pills all her life . . . what she did to me . . . she was a bit mad, or maybe she had a spirit inside of her . . . I'm not sure. One day she was taken to see a woman who was throwing up black things, strange things, and the woman said she was cursed. Once we went on an outing to a lake and I . . . I don't really remember what happened . . . all I know is that at one point I was in the water and I was calling for help but mum didn't come! What if I had died in the water?

Here we see that Carmen shared her understanding of her mother's depression on the one hand as an illness that must be treated with medication, and on the other hand as a consequence of spirits living inside her body. The therapist latches onto this second dimension and associations to her knowledge of a traditional Colombian story about a female spirit. This started a lively exchange between the therapist, mother, and son, which led organically to the family's history of relationship to their traditional culture, hitherto shared only with family members belonging to the same culture and belief system.

Therapist: Your story reminded me of the story of La Llorona, do you know about this legend?

Mother: It is the spirit of a woman who killed her children and mourns her children, constantly seeking them.

Pablo: It's true, I've known the story since I was a kid, it scared me. I've read books, I've researched everything about La Llorona. The original story is that she drowned her children in the river and then committed suicide. God condemned her to wander like a spirit searching for her children and screaming.

Therapist: Did it remind you of Mum's story?

Pablo: No, no, what are you saying!

Therapist: (to Carmen) I thought it did! I was struck by the story of the lake where your mother wanted to leave you in the water and then the story of your son who had been sick, had lost consciousness, and was afraid of dying. There was a lake here, too, and it all happened shortly after you had shared your memory here in therapy.

Entering the world of the spirit and a belief that is not strictly rational encourages familiar mythical tales and magical practices to which the maternal grandmother had been subjected, which, according to Pablo's interpretation, and perhaps Carmen's, alongside other family events, may have played a role in the onset of his grandmother's mental illness.

Mother: My grandmother used to tell me that when my mother was very young she suffered from catalepsy and they thought she was dead, she was cold and stiff: she looked dead to them, they put her in a coffin and lit candles. My grandfather who lived out in the country went into the village, which was far away, to buy funeral clothes. The journey lasted a couple of days, and on his way back my mother gasped and sighed while all the people were mourning.

Pablo: When I was little, my grandmother told me that she had died for three days and then returned.

Therapist: Do you think there are spirits in this family?

Pablo: I don't know, maybe. . . .

Therapist to Mother: Do you look like your mother?

Mother: I don't know, but I seem to look more like my father.

Therapist: Have you ever thought you were not your mother's daughter?

Mother: All the time!

Therapist: You have always thought so?

Mother: Yes, my mother always used to say: you are not my own daughter.

In the same session in which magical and spiritual beliefs are accepted, therapists will form and share with mother and son an assessment using the language they used in talking about spirits.

Therapist: To recap, this spirit arrived when you were born and was angry with you. You said earlier that maybe the reason is because you are fragile; we disagree with that, in fact you are a very strong woman. You were a very strong child, putting up with the fear of being killed by your own mother means being strong. . . . We thought that when you, Pablo, were by the lake, it was as if you had found a way to perform an exorcism, because you were vomiting a lot and then you felt better. Then you felt calmer and less worried. Maybe something has changed since that day by the lake.

Mother: Yes, that day life gave him another chance.

Therapist: Maybe you both had it.

Mother: Sometimes I think that the spirit of my dead brother-in-law entered my son's body, this spirit did something and then left, because that day Pablo had another presence inside.

Therapist: I don't know what it was, I even thought it might be something from the distant past. The events of the lake happened after you told us the story about your childhood. Reliving those feelings liberated everyone from the spirits. It was like a response to pain, as if it had freed him from the spirits of the past. When emotions are very strong, either a spirit comes in or someone loses one's mind.

Mother: When my mother was little, she did not speak and they put a hummingbird inside her mouth and told her to bite hard. A boy caught a hummingbird – not easy to catch – put it into my mother's mouth who had her eyes closed, bit it hard and then the bird died.

Therapist: Pablo, do you know this story?

Pablo: But how could you ever put a live bird inside your mouth!

Mother: People say this bird makes a sound before it dies and a person will start to speak, and from that moment my mother started speaking.

Therapist: How old was your mum then?

Mother: She was young, she was about 4 years old.

Therapist: This story is complex, whether it is spirits or whether it is psychic suffering, maybe both are present. Pablo, when I asked you what happened to Grandma, you said maybe something happened to her as a child, maybe she suffered some kind of trauma, did I understand correctly?

Pablo: Yes!

Therapist: Actually killing a bird with your teeth can scare a child, wouldn't you be afraid? (Pablo nods)

Mother: I was thinking that my mother was not to blame. I was afraid, but it was as if another person possessed her. I never asked her: why did you want to hurt me? (Pablo puffs)

Therapist: You must be tired of listening to this story, but it is important that you talked about it. You have gone through many difficult situations in life; maybe what happened to your mother was locked up inside her. It must have been so scary and painful to see your own mother threatening to kill you that it is as if those emotions were frozen. Being able to talk about them thawed them and liberated them, maybe far too much, perhaps that day by the lake Pablo reenacted your experience as a child, he threw up like your grandmother when the exorcism was performed, he was afraid of the water like you were afraid of falling into the water as a child. So maybe talking about it at length was liberating for you and for your mum.

The therapist explores together with the family some Colombian beliefs about the myth of La Llorona, a tormented female spirit who wanders weeping in search of her own children she killed. This theme is close to the story of this mother, who felt her own mother as being dangerous and capable of putting her own life at risk. As noted earlier, the chance taken by the therapist to enter into this spiritual dimension and be guided by the family initiated Carmen's sharing of aspects of the family history such as curses, apparent deaths, and subsequent resurrections of a grandmother. This brought forward and into the therapeutic space memories of a reality alive inside them, but that she felt she could never discuss after migrating to Italy, aware that she would not be believed or understood here. Through the mother's childhood memories and by opening up to this spiritual dimension, memories are awakened, frozen emotions are released, and secrets are unveiled. This process liberated the next generation – Pablo – from having to take over the protective role that his mother had taken towards her mother, taking on dangerous roles that are far too serious and big for his age.

33.6 Conclusion

Building a therapeutic project with families is like assembling a jigsaw puzzle; we need to find the right pieces, put them together, and incorporate them into a story that makes sense and that provides healing. On the one hand, we need to put together the sometimes seemingly unconnected pieces of the family history. On the other hand, we will have to put together all of the pieces relating to the family's social network, first and foremost the care services that have become part of their lives, such as work, school, or judicial settings. All of this must be tied to a pattern formed by the families' culture of belonging and by the cultural influences of the country they are now living in. The encounter and the union of the two cultures often creates a third intermediate one. The storyline also creates a frame that encloses and holds everything together. Exploring this frame that keeps the parts together becomes our resource and guides us in therapy and in the collaborative co-construction of this puzzle, which will take shape and be the result of a shared design providing answers and finding new interpretations and new solutions to the moments of crisis that force families into therapy.

References

Andolfi, M. (2014). *I pionieri della terapia familiare*. Franco Angeli.

Andolfi, M. (2017). *Multigenerational family therapy*. Routledge (Original work published 2015). https://doi.org/10.4324/9781315545592

Andolfi, M. (2022). *The gift of truth. The inner journey of the therapist*. Accademia Press (Original work published 2021).

Andolfi, M., & Cavalieri, L. (2010). Familles immigrées et psychothérapie transculturelle. In S. D'Amore (Ed.), *Le nouvelles familles: Approches cliniques* (pp. 369–387). De Boeck.

Andolfi, M., Cavalieri, L., & Falcucci, M. (2000). La psicoterapia come processo transculturale. *Psicobiettivo – "Psicoterapie e società multietniche," 1*, 13–28.

Beneduce, R. (1998). *Frontiere dell'identità e della memoria*. Franco Angeli.

Bowen, M. (1978). *Family therapy in clinical practice*. Jason Aronson Publishers.

Cavalieri, L. (2004). Psicoterapie e immigrazione, due percorsi in una stanza. In M. Andolfi (Ed.), *Famiglie immigrate e psicoterapia transculturale*. Franco Angeli.

Cavalieri, L., Cimmino, C., & Russo, R. D. (2018). Costruire progetti terapeutici con le famiglie immigrate: La complessa ricostruzione di un puzzle. *Terapia Familiare, 116*, 75–97. https://doi.org/10.3280/TF2018–001005

Falicov, C. J. (2007). Working With transnational immigrants: Expanding meanings of family, community, and culture. *Family Process, 46*, 157–171. https://doi.org/10.1111/j.1545-5300.2007.00201.x

Falicov, C. J. (2016). The multiculturalism and diversity of families. In T. Sexton & J. L. Lebow (Eds.), *Handbook of family therapy* (pp. 66–85). Routledge.

Hall, E. T. (1990). *The hidden dimension*. Anchor Books/Doubleday.

Lau, A. (1984). Transcultural issues in family therapy. *Journal of Family Therapy, 6*, 91–112. https://doi.org/10.1046/j.1467-6427.1984.00638.x

Lee, W. Y., & Cheng, V. (2018). Eastern philosophy in couple and family therapy. In J. L. Lebow, A. L. Chambers, & D. C. Breunlin (Eds.), *Encyclopedia of couple and family therapy* (pp. 819–825). Springer.

Nwoye, A. (2004). The shattered microcosm: Imperatives for improved family therapy in Africa in the 21st century. *Contemporary Family Therapy, 26*, 143–164. https://doi.org/10.1023/B:COFT.0000031240.00980.88

Sluzki, C. E. (1979). Migration and family conflict. *Family Process, 18*, 379–390. https://doi.org/10.1111/j.1545-5300.1979.00379.x

34

EMPOWERING AND SUPPORTING JAPANESE FAMILIES

A gender perspective

Tazuko Shibusawa, Shinichi Nakamura, Takeyoshi Nozue, Noriko Odagiri, and Mami Onishi,

34.1 Introduction

Gender equality has long been a pressing issue in Japan, as highlighted by the 2023 World Economic Forum report, which ranks the country 118th out of 146 nations in terms of gender equality (World Economic Forum, 2024). Within the Organization for Economic Cooperation and Development (OECD), Japan exhibits the lowest proportion of women among masters' graduates and a considerable gender gap in labor force participation. Japanese women, who constitute less than half of public sector employment, face significant underrepresentation in public leadership positions, holding the smallest share of seats in the Diet. This pattern extends to the private sector, where women are also underrepresented among managers. The persistent gender pay gap in Japan reflects deep-rooted structural inequalities, including an uneven distribution of paid and unpaid work, differences in job roles and responsibilities within companies, and occupational and sectoral segregation with an undervaluation of traditionally female-dominated roles. Japanese women earn 22% less than their male counterparts for equivalent work. Japan's gender pay gap for full-time earners is among the widest within the OECD nations.

How does gender inequality affect families and family relationships? In this chapter, we discuss gender dynamics of Japanese families, examining how social and traditional cultural norms impact family relationships and the field of family therapy. We begin by addressing the repercussions of the recent pandemic on Japanese women and exploring the cultural origins of gender inequality. Subsequently, we highlight the challenges faced by families divided by divorce and share recent examples of initiatives by family therapists aimed at empowering and supporting such families. We conclude with a presentation of a couple therapy case to illustrate therapeutic work that integrates cultural and gender dynamics when working with Japanese couples.

34.2 The pandemic and Japanese families

The pandemic, impacting all segments of Japanese society, brought to light the detrimental consequences of pre-existing gender gaps (Shibusawa et al., 2021). In contrast to Euro-American nations, gender roles in Japanese families are more distinct, with women predominantly managing households and men perceived as the primary breadwinners. This division extends to the unequal distribution of domestic responsibilities, where women bear 80% of the housework. During the pandemic,

DOI: 10.4324/9781003536765-40

women faced the added challenges of balancing childcare, their professional duties, and household chores, often while also tending to husbands who worked from home and caring for elders.

Lockdowns and stay-at-home measures exacerbated domestic violence. Referred to as the "shadow pandemic," domestic violence affected women globally (UN Women, 2020). The increase in Japanese women who sought help for partner abuse prompted the government to provide additional 24-hour hotlines to assist them (Shibusawa et al., 2021).

The surge in remote work added difficulties for women, impacting their ability to maintain a healthy work-life balance and potentially hindering career development. Although 70% of Japanese women are employed, 54% of them work part-time. The economic downturn hit these women hard, particularly those in pandemic-affected sectors such as service, retail, and travel industries.

During the pandemic, suicide rates among Japanese women rose by 83%, highlighting the severe mental health consequences of the crisis. This impact on women underscores the urgent need for addressing and rectifying gender inequalities in Japanese society.

34.3 *Ie*: The traditional Japanese household system

Gender inequality and its impact on families in Japan are closely intertwined with the traditional family system known as the *ie*. The *ie* system was established in the 1870s following the abolishment of a feudal system that had ruled Japan for more than 600 years. Under this system, the household (*ie*) became a legal unit and granted the head of the household the right to control the activities of family members. The household was characterized by a patriarchal framework that prioritized family continuity through sons. Typically, the eldest son inherited the family estate and continued the family lineage, resulting in daughters often being excluded from inheritance, thereby suffering economic and social disadvantages. Within this system, whose effects are still felt, women are perceived as joining their husband's household and are expected to fulfill traditional roles, including the performance of domestic duties and looking after their husband's parents, husband, and children. The goals and needs of the household took precedence over the needs and desires of individual members. Deviating from these societal expectations could subject women to social stigma, a situation that is still evident in Japan.

Ie is rooted in the patriarchal belief that women are outsiders who have entered the family through marriage. One illustration is that to this day women are legally not allowed to retain their maiden name after marriage. Although the *ie* system officially ended as a legal institution after World War II in 1947, its influence has persisted in shaping attitudes towards family and society (Nakamura, 2011). Until recently, government policies mirrored the traditional family philosophy, viewing women as being primarily responsible for the family's well-being, especially in caring for elders and children.

Another manifestation of the patriarchal values that have presented a challenge is the income tax system, a significant factor in discouraging married women from pursuing full-time careers (The Tokyo Foundation for Policy Research, 2023). If a woman earns 1.03 million yen (approximately $6,600) or less per year, then her husband can claim a spousal tax deduction on his income tax, reducing his taxable income. If a married woman's income exceeds 1.03 million yen, then her husband's tax burden increases. As a result, many women limit their work hours to keep their income below 1.03 million yen. This creates a "tax wall" that discourages women from progressing in their careers.

Japan has one of the largest aging populations in the world. As of 2023, 29% of the population in Japan was 65 years and older (Ministry of Internal Affairs and Communications, 2023). However, it was only in the late 1990s that the government began to address the growing need for public geriatric care programs such as nursing homes, daycare centers, and home healthcare. Because of the rapidly aging population, there was an increase in bedridden elderly, and many women had to leave the workforce to care for the elderly. Furthermore, the aging of the population meant that women in their sixties, some of whom might require care, were becoming care providers for the elderly.

The increase in the aging population has been exacerbated by low birthrates. The total fertility rate among women is 1.26, which is significantly below the replacement rate of 2.3. Although Japan has incorporated comprehensive efforts to boost the fertility rate by increasing childcare facilities and encouraging family-friendly workplaces, the policies have fallen short of achieving a fertility rate that would mitigate the social and economic effects of population decline and aging.

34.4 Marriage and divorce

A decline in the popularity of marriage has also contributed to lower birthrates. Close to 41% of women in their thirties remain unmarried, and this can be attributed to the persistence of traditional domestic gender roles, and hardships which force women to strike a difficult balance between work and family. The cohort of women in their thirties and younger are reluctant to enter into these traditional gender roles. The current situation highlights the need for broader societal shifts to address gender inequality and support family structures.

Currently, the divorce rate in Japan stands at one out of three couples (33%). Not surprisingly, most single-parent households are headed by women, and their precarious financial situation also reflects sociocultural gender inequalities. Although most single mothers are employed, most take low-wage part-time work so that they have time to care for their children. There has also been a decrease in three-generational family structures, which results in lack of support and increased social isolation among single mothers.

At the same time, there has been an increase in people living alone, the result of people not marrying, marrying late, and aging. In the 1960s, 30% of Japanese lived in three-generational families – children, parents, and grandparents – but in 2020, only 7% lived in three-generational households. There are more single-person households (38%) than parent-child households (25%).

34.5 Couple therapy in Japan

The dissolution of marriage and other enduring, committed, intimate partnerships, be it through divorce or persistent conflict and distress, takes a significant toll on public health (Gurman & Fraenkel, 2002). Marital conflicts are linked with poor physical and mental health. Many couples, especially the younger generation in Japan, are open to couple therapy. Yet few therapists in Japan practice conjoint couple therapy.

In the United States, couple therapy developed before the advent of systemic family therapy and became a professional discipline in the 1940s (Broderick & Schrader, 1991). According to Gurman and Fraenkel (2002), in the United States couple therapy has been the primary clinical activity for family therapists for decades. On the other hand, couple therapy in Japan did not develop as a separate entity and was introduced as part of family systems therapy only in the 1980s. When therapists see couples, it is usually in the latter's roles as parents of their child who is the identified client. Consequently, therapy tends to focus on parenting rather than directly addressing the marital relationship.

Several factors contribute to the lack of availability of conjoint couple therapy in Japan. First, under the traditional family system, marriage has been seen as a union of families, not individuals. In contrast, in the Judeo-Christian context, marriage is viewed as a commitment between two individuals in the presence of God. Second, parent-child relationships take precedence over marital relationships in a culture that places priority on the continuity of family lineage (Nakamura, 2011). Under this system, partner selection based on individual choice and romantic attachments traditionally was rare.

The notion of romantic love in partner selection (love marriages) became more common after World War II. Since the mid-1960s, love marriages have surpassed the number of arranged marriages (Ministry of Health Labor and Welfare, 2015). However, this does not mean that love marriages hold the same expectations for marriage as in Euro-American cultures. For example, in the United States there is an expectation that romantic love will continue among partners after marriage and the birth of children. On the other hand, in Japan, romance is emphasized before marriage, but there is less emphasis on attempts to maintain romance and to keep the passion alive after marriage (Rothbaum et al., 2000). In fact, it is common for parents in Japan to sleep in the same room with their young children. It is interesting to note that in the Japanese media there is an assumption, unsupported by official data, that 40% of love marriages end in divorce, while only 10% of arranged marriages, including those facilitated through matchmaking services, end in divorce.

Sociocultural behaviors and values also affect interpersonal relationships. Researchers comparing Japanese and Euro-American relationships have noted differences between (1) individualism and collectivism, (2) emphasis on individual-centered values versus situation-centered values, and (3) independent versus interdependent conceptions of self (Rothbaum et al., 2000). These values and conceptions of self are embedded in ways that couple partners interact with each other. Thus, therapists in Japan need to adjust couple therapy practices that were developed in Euro-American cultures when applying them to their work in Japan. Therapists note that, in general, Japanese partners are initially more prone to accommodate their partners. Compared to Euro-American couples, Japanese couples are less prone to verbally assert and express their needs. Not knowing how to assert oneself leads to verbal, psychological, and physical abuse in both partners, creating a challenge in working with high-conflict couples (Nozue, 2015).

Therapists who do not understand gender inequalities can end up pathologizing female clients. There is a tendency for therapists to view couples in their family roles. Women are seen as mothers or wives, rather than as individuals with personal needs. When therapists are not aware of their own expectations about the way women should behave and act as mothers, they can become critical towards women who experience family conflict. Women in therapy who openly express negative emotions or are demanding towards their husbands can be viewed as being immature and selfish. It is important for therapists to be aware of how their own expectations towards gender roles affect the way they work with couples (Nakamura, 2011; Nozue & Iwai, 2004).

34.6 Working with divorced parents and children of divorce

Although many divorces involve children, the Japanese legal system does not assist in maintaining family connections once the divorce is legalized. This is because the Japanese court does not recognize joint custody. Child support, as a result, is not legally enforced. Women obtain child custody in most cases, and only 20% receive child support from their ex-husbands. Not surprisingly, the poverty rate among single mothers is 50%, the highest among developed nations.

Divorce can have long-term negative consequences on children. Decline in academic performance, behavioral changes such as acting out or withdrawal, loss of interest in social activity, difficulty adapting to changes, health problems, and loss of faith in marriage and family unit have been reported among children of divorced parents (Odagiri, 2020; Onishi, 2023).

Studies in the United States indicate that joint physical custody has better outcomes for child well-being. Children who have relationships with both parents have better physical health and fewer psychosomatic and stress-related problems.

Because joint custody is not recognized in Japan, the court does not facilitate parental visitations. In the traditional *ie* system, there were no expectations to maintain connections once a member left the family. Similarly, the court system does not recognize the importance for children to have their parents maintain connections once they are divorced (Odagiri, 2020). When the mother obtains custody in Japan, children lose their relationships not only with their fathers but also with other extended family members including grandparents. Social stigma towards divorce remains strong in Japan, which prevents people from openly talking about the divorce. In fact, some parents do not disclose the divorce to their children and provide excuses for the absence of the non-custodial parent (Fukumaru, 2023).

Research in the United States indicates that parental visitations are crucial in helping children recognize that they are loved by both parents. Having contact with the non-custodial parent also promotes individuation since the children do not become overly enmeshed with the custodial parent. Contact with the non-custodial parent also increases the chances for financial child support. Therefore, it is important for therapists to find ways to assist couples who divorce to maintain cordial, cooperative relationships for the sake of the children (Odagiri, 2020).

Some Japanese family therapists work with divorce attorneys to provide supervised parental visitations (Odagiri, 2020). Other therapists work with high-conflict divorce cases in which parents fight over custody. Therapists also support children whose parents have divorced by providing workshops for both children and parents. One such program is the Families in Transition program (FAIT), which has been adapted from the Families in Transition (FIT) program in the United States (Onishi, 2023). FIT in the United States is a court-mandated program that offers classes for parents to prevent children's anxiety, aggression, depression, and behavioral problems, while assisting children to develop social competencies, which are critical to children's adjustment following divorce (Brown et al., 1994). In the United States, the FIT program helps couples who are divorced collaborate as parents. In the absence of joint custody, the Japanese program focuses on assisting couples to learn how to maintain a cooperative relationship after the divorce (Fukumaru, 2023).

Many parents who have child custody seek assistance from their own parents by moving in with them or by receiving help for childcare. Therefore, the Japanese program works with grandparents to help them understand the unique needs of their grandchildren who are coping with the aftermath of the divorce. The FAIT program also offers support groups for children and adolescents to help children adjust to their parents' divorce. The program provides groups to encourage children to talk about their experiences of divorce, to understand that there are multiple forms of families, and to understand that they are not the cause of the divorce (Onishi, 2023). Another important aspect of the program is based on a multisystemic approach, which takes into consideration the child's involvement in school and other institutions. Therapists offer educational workshops for teachers and social service providers so that they can understand the effects of divorce on the children (Onishi, 2023).

34.7 Case illustration: Couple therapy addressing intimate partner violence

Nearly one in three women worldwide have experienced physical and/or sexual violence by an intimate partner (UN Women, 2024). In Japan, a 2020 government report found that approximately one in four women and one in five men have experienced violence from their spouse, with about one in ten women reporting repeated victimization (Gender Equity Bureau Cabinet Office (2002). In this chapter, we present a couple therapy case addressing intimate partner violence, with Shinichi Nakamura, the second author, serving as the therapist.

34.7.1 The couple

Mari, 25, was referred to therapy by a women's support center after seeking help for issues with her husband, Hiro, 27. She reached out because she was concerned about her own behavior towards him. During a recent argument, she became upset and attempted to harm Hiro with a kitchen knife. The couple met five years earlier through a mutual friend and married two years later. Hiro was initially drawn to Mari's free-spirited, cheerful personality and storytelling skills, while Mari appreciated Hiro's quiet and attentive nature. Although Hiro stated that their occasional arguments during courtship never turned physically violent, Mari recalled several incidents when he displayed aggressive behavior. She was shocked when he physically assaulted an intoxicated man who had bothered him on the street. More concerningly, during their wedding preparations, Hiro slapped Mari in public after a meeting with a banquet hall consultant, accusing her of disrespecting his opinions in front of the staff.

After their marriage, the couple chose to live near Hiro's workplace to shorten his commute, despite significantly extending Mari's. The added travel time, combined with household chores, left Mari exhausted. When Hiro casually suggested she quit her job, she grew angry. Determined to maintain her career, she insisted on working. Tensions escalated when Hiro began complaining about his long hours, making dismissive remarks like, "I work harder, so I'm more important." Heated arguments followed, culminating in physical violence. During one altercation, Hiro struck and kicked Mari, leaving her with injuries that took three weeks to heal. From then on, she feared for her safety whenever he raised his voice. Anticipating an attack, she would grab a kitchen knife for protection. Hiro, feeling threatened, would try to take it from her, leading to physical struggles and further injuries on both sides. Eventually, Mari quit her full-time job and switched to part-time work to focus on household responsibilities. However, this only worsened their relationship, as Hiro grew even more dismissive of her. Their arguments continued, and Mari sank into depression.

34.7.2 Assessment and contract

Mari and Hiro attended the intake session together. Hiro maintained a stiff smile and remained mostly silent, while Mari frequently cried and exhibited facial tics, which she said had begun after their marriage. During the interview, she tearfully expressed her desire for a divorce. Speaking in a low voice, Hiro stated that he was firmly against separating and wanted to work on their problems. Mari agreed to therapy but stated that she would seek a divorce if therapy did not work.

When working with couples experiencing intimate partner violence, therapists must first assess the nature and severity of the abuse to determine whether therapy is appropriate (Keilholtz & Spencer, 2022). The therapist must also establish a safety plan for the victim and evaluate the offender's motivation to change. During the intake session, it became evident that Hiro was the primary aggressor. To assess his self-awareness, the therapist asked him about his physiological responses to anger. Hiro identified physical symptoms such as a rapid heartbeat, clenched fists, and restless legs, as well as subjective feelings of irritation and surges of rage. The therapist then introduced "time-out" strategies to help him de-escalate. Hiro agreed to remove himself from tense situations by taking a one-hour walk to cool down, promising to inform Mari of his whereabouts before returning home.

The therapist also worked with Mari to develop a safety plan in case Hiro became violent. She agreed to stay near the front door, call for help loudly, or contact the police if she sensed danger. She also committed to avoiding the use of kitchen knives for self-defense.

In cases of life-threatening intimate partner violence among heterosexual couples, the female partner often appears expressionless during intake sessions. However, Mari displayed anger and openly argued with Hiro in front of the therapist. Hiro's apparent sincerity in seeking reconciliation and his willingness to follow the therapist's advice warranted continuing therapy. In family therapy involving children, shared concerns about the child can help unite families. However, couples therapy carries a higher risk of dropout and, in some cases, the sessions can escalate violence. To ensure commitment and structure, the therapist had the couple agree to attend ten sessions.

During the intake session, several issues became apparent. Despite being in his late twenties, Hiro held traditional expectations of Mari, expecting her to handle all household chores. He resented her exhaustion from work, as it interfered with her domestic responsibilities. Although Mari was a designer, he did not value her career. This attitude was further reinforced by Japan's tax system, which as mentioned earlier incentivizes households to reduce tax payments by limiting wives to part-time work.

34.7.3 The couple therapy process

34.7.3.1 Initial sessions

After the intake session, the couple took a short two-night trip and reported having no arguments. When asked why, Mari said, "I felt reassured knowing my husband had started counseling," adding that it also felt safer knowing violence was not an option for resolving conflicts. They mentioned spending more time together than most couples, similar to their dating period when they went out nearly every day. Hiro enjoyed sharing a double bed, but his uninterest in sex made Mari uneasy. As she shared these concerns, Hiro appeared embarrassed and tried to control the conversation. However, Mari's facial expression seemed brighter, and her facial tics had lessened. Mari also complained that Hiro was clingy, wanting to bathe with her and even following her to the kitchen and bathroom. Yet, he would suddenly withdraw when she expressed emotions like anxiety. She noted that he could not support her emotionally, stating, "Maybe I'm more like his mother." The therapist observed that Hiro's distress when apart from Mari resembled separation anxiety in toddlers.

34.7.3.2 The genogram

During the initial sessions, the therapist reviewed the couple's genogram. It became evident that Hiro's family history included men who were physically violent toward their wives. His father was reserved, domineering, and at times destructive, breaking furniture during outbursts. As a result, Hiro's understanding of manhood was shaped by violence and the need to control women. Hiro's mother, preoccupied with his younger brother, who had a disability, had little time for Hiro. This left him longing for affection but unable to express his needs. In contrast, Mari's parents had a more equal partnership and demonstrated adaptive problem-solving skills. However, Mari's father was strict with her and would hit her whenever she talked back.

Exploring their family histories and how those influenced their current conflicts seemed to ease the couple's emotional turmoil. Even Hiro, typically reserved in sessions, showed interest in the genogram and spoke more openly about his family relationships than usual. Their marital expectations revealed a deep-rooted dynamic: Hiro sought emotional support from Mari, longing for the affection he lacked in childhood. Meanwhile, Mari wanted Hiro to be gentle and accepting – something she had not experienced from her strict father. Hiro had an idealized image of a mother who would offer unconditional acceptance, while Mari sought an understanding husband, compensating for the emotional distance she had felt from her father.

In Euro-American cultures, the self is typically viewed as an independent entity, defined by internal attributes such as personality traits, motives, goals, and attitudes. Individuals in these cultures rely on these internal attributes to guide their actions and exert influence over others and their surroundings. In contrast, many non-Western societies, including Japan, emphasize an interdependent view of the self, where identity is shaped by social roles and relationships within one's in-group. Japanese couples often perceive themselves less as individuals within a partnership and more as family members fulfilling specific roles. Hiro saw himself primarily as a husband and expected Mari to meet his emotional needs. Mari wanted to pursue her career, but felt that she had to prioritize her role as a wife.

34.7.3.3 Trial separation

During the fourth session, Mari recounted a painful incident in which a close friend harshly criticized her over the phone, leaving her deeply hurt. In tears, she called Hiro for support. He had promised to come home early but did not, citing work obligations. The following week, he broke another promise about returning home on time. Late one night, overwhelmed by distress, Mari took an overdose of cold medicine in front of Hiro. She was rushed to the hospital by ambulance, where her stomach was pumped. Through tears, she said, *"I wanted to die. He says he's busy with work and won't listen to me."* Hiro appeared frozen in shock. Mari also revealed past incidents of violence but admitted, *"He doesn't have anyone else who understands him but me. I couldn't leave him because he'd be lost without me. But today, I want to try living apart for a while."* She proposed a temporary separation, and the therapist supported the idea. Mari decided to move in with her parents. Hiro looked bewildered and distressed. Before concluding the session, the therapist advised them to reach out in case of any emergencies or crises.

Mari's statement, *"He'd be lost without me,"* is a common sentiment among women in abusive relationships. They tend to over-function in relationships and feel responsible for their partner's well-being. At the same time, Mari demonstrated strength by choosing temporary separation. The therapist supported this decision, believing that the ability to live independently could be key to improving their marital relationship. Therapy sessions continued after the couple began living apart. Mari reported that Hiro called her daily in tears, saying, *"Alcohol makes me feel even lonelier,"* and sobbing, *"I won't be violent tonight; please come back."* As Mari shared this, Hiro listened anxiously. Mari observed, *"Hiro is deeply afraid of showing his weaknesses to others."* However, she also noted, *"I think Hiro is slowly starting to understand that we are separate individuals."* Hiro agreed, admitting, *"I relied on her too much and couldn't make decisions for myself."* Mari also acknowledged that Hiro no longer lost his temper as easily. She expressed a willingness to try living together again but made it clear that if it didn't work out, she would proceed with divorce.

34.7.3.4 Living together again

After a month of separation, Mari decided to move back in with Hiro. The therapist supported her decision and conducted a safety assessment with Hiro. There were no incidents of violence. Mari found a part-time job close to their home and appeared cheerful and relaxed. While occasional arguments occurred, there was no violence or sense of danger. To ease her loneliness while waiting for Hiro to return from work, they adopted a cat. Unexpectedly, Hiro became very attached to it, and they both laughed about how much the cat adored him. Hiro reported that whenever he felt agitated, he went outside for a walk to cool down. For the first time, Hiro openly expressed his emotions during sessions. Both Mari and Hiro seemed relieved to have found a more stable life together. Mari noted that they had become less emotionally dependent on each other and more comfortable with maintaining some distance. Reflecting on their growth over the past months, she remarked on how much they had changed, and Hiro nodded quietly. He shared that he had made a conscious effort to avoid saying hurtful things and that his clinginess had significantly lessened.

During their last session, when asked for feedback, Mari laughed and said,

> *At first, neither of us had the capacity to understand each other. But the therapist helped us listen. In the beginning, Hiro didn't talk much, but I realized he was listening. Slowly, he started expressing his opinions too. He's someone who doesn't open up easily, not even to his parents. I think he talked more here than anywhere else.*

Hiro blushed and smiled. The following year, in their New Year's card to the therapist, they shared that they were doing well and that Mari was pregnant.

34.7.3.5 Epilogue

Three years after giving birth to her son, Mari reached out to the therapist to request an individual session. During their meeting, she shared that she had divorced Hiro and was now raising her son as a single mother. Mari appeared happy and confident in her decision. Although the violence had stopped, she felt that Hiro's struggles with anger management remained an issue, ultimately leading to her decision to divorce. She expressed gratitude to the therapist, saying his support had helped her view her relationship with Hiro more objectively. Mari also noted that she had been able to tolerate Hiro's separation anxiety throughout the divorce process and had been able to manage her own feelings of guilt about leaving him.

34.7.4 Reflections on the case

At the outset, the therapist was skeptical about Hiro's ability to change his violent behavior. However, Hiro's strong attachment to Mari ultimately made this transformation possible. Mari's resilience was particularly striking – she endured a month-long separation, during which she only communicated with Hiro by phone. This period became a turning point, allowing both partners to engage in deep self-reflection, leading to profound changes in their relationship.

The therapist was able to provide a safe space for Hiro and Mari to work through their conflicts. His ability to create this environment was shaped by his own in-depth family-of-origin work, which helped him understand the constraints of traditional values on contemporary Japanese families. His perspective was further enriched through participating in international case conferences and consultations with non-Japanese family therapists, which helped him develop an outsider's view of Japanese family dynamics. Additionally, his study of feminist family therapy and gender-sensitive approaches deepened his awareness of how societal gender inequities and power imbalances affect couples.

34.8 Conclusion

This chapter focused on Japanese families from a gender perspective and discussed how traditional gender inequality continues to affect Japanese society, including individuals, couples, and families. Family therapists need to recognize the effects of gender inequality on families and work with families so that no one is forced to sacrifice their needs and personhood for the sake of their family. It is also important for family therapists to recognize their unconscious biases and become aware of their attitudes towards families. As stated in the Assisi Manifesto, family therapists "need to acknowledge the interconnectedness of individuals, families, communities, and societies, and incorporate family therapy as a vehicle for accessing resilience and healing" (Andolfi & The International Faculty, 2023).

References

Andolfi, M., & The International Faculty. (2023). *The Assisi Manifesto*. www.accademiapsico.it/the-assisi-manifesto/

Broderick, C. B., & Schrader, S. S. (1991). The history of professional marriage and family therapy. In A. S. Gurman & D. P. Kniskern (Eds.), *Handbook of family therapy* (pp. 3–40). Brunner/Mazel.

Brown, J. H., Portes, P., Cambron, M. L., Zimmerman, D., Rickert, V., & Bissmeyer, C. (1994). Families in transition: A court-mandated divorce adjustment program for parents and children. *Juvenile and Family Court Journal*, *14*(1), 27–32. https://doi.org/10.1111/j.1755-6988.1994.tb00932.x

Fukumaru, Y. (2023) The FAIT program. In Y. Fukumaru (Ed.), *FAIT: Psychoeducational program to support parents and children experiencing divorce* (pp. 19–30). Shinyo Publishers. (In Japanese)

Gender Equity Bureau Cabinet Office. (2002). *Information on spousal violence*. Retrieved November 10, 2023, from www.gender.go.jp/policy/no_violence/e-vaw/chousa/r02_boryoku_cyousa.html

Gurman, A., & Fraenkel, P. (2002). The history of family therapy: A millennial review. *Family Process*, *41*(2), 199–260. https://doi.org/10.1111/j.1545-5300.2002.41204.x

Keilholtz, B. M., & Spencer, C. M. (2022). Couples therapy and intimate partner violence: Considerations, assessment, and treatment modalities. *Practice Innovations*, *7*(2), 124–137. https://doi.org/10.1037/pri0000176

Ministry of Health Labor and Welfare. (2015). *Changing statistics between love and arranged marriages*. Retrieved November 10, 2023, from www.mhlw.go.jp/wp/hakusyo/kousei/15/backdata/01-01-03-009.html

Ministry of Internal Affairs and Communications. (2023). *Statistics of the aging population*. Retrieved November 10, 2023, from www.stat.go.jp/data/topics/pdf/topics138.pdf. (in Japanese)

Nakamura, S. (2011). *The practice of marital and family therapy*. Kongo Shuppan. (in Japanese)

Nozue, T. (2015). *Assertion for couples*. Kaneko Shobo. (in Japanese)

Nozue, T., & Iwai, M. (2004). Gender issues in couple communication. In Japanese Association of Family Psychology (Ed.), *Family communication* (pp. 112–125). Kaneko Shobo. (in Japanese)

Odagiri, N. (2020). Child-centered parental visitations. In N. Odagiri & R. Noda (Eds.), *Divorce and parental visitations* (pp. v–xvi). Kongo Shuppan. (in Japanese)

OECD. (2023). *Joining forces for gender equality: What is holding us back*? Country Note. www.oecd.org/japan/Gender2023-JPN-En.pdf

Onishi, M. (2023). Listening to children's voices. In Y. Fukumaru (Ed.), *FAIT: Psychoeducational program to support parents and children experiencing divorce* (pp 103–138). Shinyosha. (in Japanese)

Rothbaum, F., Pott, M., Azuma, H., Miyake, K., & Weisz, J. (2000). The development of close relationships in Japan and the United States: Paths of symbiotic harmony and generative tension. *Child Development*, *71*(5), 1121–1142. https://doi.org/10.1111/1467–8624.00214

Shibusawa, T., Ishii, C., Nakamura, S., Tamura, T., & Watanabe, T. (2021). COVID-19 and Japanese families. *Australian and New Zealand Journal of Family Therapy*, *42*(1), 58–69. https://doi.org/10.1002/anzf.1438

The Tokyo Foundation for Policy Research. (2023). *Making work pay for Japanese women: Toward a smarter approach to tax and social security reform*. Retrieved September 15, 2024, from www.tokyofoundation.org/research/detail.php?id=946

UN Women. (2020). *Violence against women and girls: The shadow pandemic*. Retrieved November 10, 2023, from www.unwomen.org/en/news/stories/2020/4/statement-ed-phumzile-violence-against-women-during-pandemic

UN Women. (2024). *Facts and figures: Ending violence against women*. Retrieved December 20, 2024, from www.unwomen.org/en/articles/facts-and-figures/facts-and-figures-ending-violence-against-women

World Economic Forum. (2024). *Global gender gap report: Insight report 2024*. https://www3.weforum.org/docs/WEF_GGGR_2024.pdf

35

THE INVENTIVENESS OF LOSS NARRATIVES OF TRAUMA AND RESILIENCE AMONG PALESTINIAN REFUGEES FORCIBLY DISPLACED IN ISRAEL

Mustafa Qossoqsi

35.1 My private Nakbah

I come from a family bearing the indelible mark of the Nakbah and its consequent immeasurable losses. My very surname, Qossoqsi, is a scar, a trace of a lost place of origin. The once-existing place, Qossqoss, now exists only as an often misspelled and mispronounced surname – a symbolic wounded representation of a vanished site, whose existence is conveyed through narratives and post-memories (Hirsch, 2012), persisting despite its physical disappearance. This place was taken from my family 24 years before the Nakbah of 1948 when my family was expelled from their village between Haifa and the Valley of Ibn Amer (Emek Yizrael in Hebrew). Their land, cunningly purchased by Zionist organizations, was used, like other parts of historic Palestine, to serve as a homeland for Jews fleeing European anti-Semitism. The name I carry, Qossoqsi, signifies a "present absence" resisting oblivion and continuing to vivify the memory of Qossqoss. The Israeli colonial bureaucracy coined the term "present absentees" to describe Palestinians who were absent from their homes during the 1948 war but remained within the borders of the emerging state of Israel or were forced to leave and later returned. Their homes and lands were subsequently confiscated, rendering them refugees or internally displaced persons. From fleeing to Lebanon to precarious journeys seeking safe refuge, our family has lived through the profound impact of war and the Nakbah lasting more than 100 years in various forms, with the latest and perhaps most devastating war on Gaza in 2023–2025. Revisiting the intergenerational experiences of my family, while following with pain and horror the massacre of Palestinians, I am struck by the emotional pervasiveness of the Nakbah in our lives, deaths, and individual and family identities, on our perceived presents and futures.

35.2 The Nakbah

The Nakbah, literally "the immense catastrophe," is the Palestinian term indicating the geographical, political, and social undoing of Palestine, with the 1948 war as its canonical moment of deflagration. The Nakbah is an apocalyptic event in recent Palestinian history but is primarily the inexorable unfolding of a dispossession project that some historians trace back to 1881 with the start of colonization of Palestine by European Jews (Litvak, 2009; Said, 1979). The Nakbah has been and continues to

DOI: 10.4324/9781003536765-41

be characterized by a multifaceted traumatic layering of violent injustices: ethnic cleansing (Pappè, 2007), mass expulsion of 750,000 Palestinians (70% of the Palestinian people are refugees, including internally displaced Palestinians in Israel), destruction of more than 500 Palestinian villages (Abu Sitta, 2001), loss of homes, lands, and properties, forced displacement, dispossession, uninterrupted land confiscations, institutional racism, apartheid, and numerous other colonial practices culminating in the International Court of Justice at The Hague's request for Israel to respond to allegations of violating its obligations under the United Nations Convention on Genocide in the context of its war against Palestinians in Gaza (ICJ, 2024). These injustices have generated and continue to generate an experience of intergenerational trauma and collective memory that shapes the identity and experiences of Palestinians today and fuels their cultural resilience and their struggle for freedom and self-determination.

35.3 Palestinian refugees

According to BADIL (2022), an estimated 9.17 million of the 14 million Palestinians worldwide (65.5%) are forcibly displaced persons. Among them, there are approximately 8.36 million Palestinian refugees and 812,000 internally displaced persons (IDPs). The displaced Palestinian population includes a total of 7 million who became refugees in 1948 and their descendants (a figure that includes the 5.8 million Palestinian refugees registered and eligible for UNRWA assistance), 1.33 million refugees of 1967 and their descendants, 439,171 Palestinians forcibly displaced in 1948 Palestine/Israel, and 372,793 Palestinians forcibly displaced in the Occupied Palestinian Territories (OPT) in 1967 and their descendants, plus an unknown number of Palestinians who are neither 1948 nor 1967 refugees. About 38.3% of the displaced Palestinian population registered with the United Nations Relief and Works Agency (UNRWA) is registered in Jordan, 26.2% in the Gaza Strip, 16.9% in the West Bank, 10.2% in Syria, and 8.5% in Lebanon.

35.4 Palestinian citizens of Israel

The Palestinian population of Israel includes more than 1.5 million people, or 20% of Israel's population, and constitutes a minority group in its own country according to international human rights law (Adalah, 2019). For 18 years (1948–1966), military administration was imposed on the indigenous Palestinian minority of about 156,000 people remaining within the borders of the nascent state of Israel, with restrictive and all-encompassing measures of "thorough surveillance" (Sa'di, 2013). A powerful and relentless military and bureaucratic machine was put in place to minimize the number and survival capacity of Palestinians reduced to "citizen strangers" (Robinson, 2013). Palestinians faced "a rather elaborate system of control and oppression" (Pappe, 2011, p. 48) whose democratic margins will increasingly be thin and fragile. Although legally citizens under Israeli law, Palestinians in Israel are subject to continuous violations of their citizenship rights, with draconian and undemocratic laws denying them collective rights, as in the case of the "nation-state law" (2018), or the law sanctioning the institutional commemoration of the Nakbah (2011), and about 200 other discriminatory laws that penetrate and harass every aspect of their life (Adalah, 2017).

35.5 Marginality and epistemic coloniality

Affected by countless losses, dispersion, and political isolation, Palestinians in Israel have focused on survival while their psychosocial experience remained for many decades silenced and unexplored (Lentin, 2013). Various forms of "institutional trauma" (Thompson, 2021) inflicted on Palestinians within Israel have been compounded by epistemic violence that for many years has obscured and even forgotten them (Pappe, 2011), not only as real people but as intelligible moral and psychosocial beings (Jayyusi, 2007). Although many authors refer to the Nakbah as a volatile reality presenting psychosocial threats and mental health risks (Litvak, 2009), only recently have more psychological studies, conducted mainly by Palestinian scholars from Israel, addressed this issue (Abu El Hija, 2018; Ghnadre-Naser, 2016; Shalhoub-Kevorkian, 2019; Qossoqsi, 2010, 2017, 2020). Their double marginality in Israeli society has translated into limited academic interest in their psychosocial experiences, amplified by the extensive and deep research on the psychosocial effects of the Holocaust on survivors and their descendants.

The epistemic coloniality of knowledge production by Israeli academic centers on Palestinians in Israel and reproduces a distorted or absent representation of Palestinian subjectivity similar to that found in Western academia (Sayigh, 2013).

Consequently, the decolonization of research (Smith, 2012) on the Nakbah in Palestinian refugee communities (Al-Hardan, 2013) is an epistemological urgency that calls for a "critical awareness that knowledge produced about Palestinian refugees is a diffraction of the world's coloniality" (Al-Hardan, 2013, p. 69).

Although most psychological studies have focused on the experimentation and validation of the Western model of trauma and resilience, little is still known about the meaning of these constructs in other cultures, especially in the context of forced displacement due to war and political violence in general. As suggested by various authors, Western approaches to trauma and resilience tend to systematically overlook aspects related to cultural and community factors varying among populations. The Nakbah represents a unique case of both historical and continuous intergenerational trauma. At the same time, its intergenerational resilience traits deserve to be studied, considering the criticized hegemony of the trauma discourse in the West (Afuape, 2011; Fassin & Rechtman, 2009; Papadopoulos, 2007, 2021).

35.6 Intergenerational trauma

Intergenerational trauma is transmitted through generations via mechanisms of identification, dissociation, and mutation of social, cognitive, and family processes (Andolfi, 2017; Danieli, 1998). Studies on intergenerational trauma have generally adopted a narrow trauma-focused perspective, ignoring the examination of transmission aspects and factors that reduce the possibility of transmitting stress (Dekel & Goldblatt, 2008). An entire field of research has emerged in recent years, with a particular focus on indigenous populations exposed to various situations of chronic or ongoing traumatic stress and on intergenerational traumatization where children are directly or indirectly affected by the continuing effect of the original trauma experienced by a parent or other family member (Duran et al., 1998; Fast & Collin-Vezina, 2010).

Multigenerational transmission models have been developed by Atkinson in Australia (2008) and Blanco in South America (Levine & Kline, 2007). Both models describe a multigenerational cycle linking colonization and forced displacement of indigenous populations with high rates of family violence, alcoholism, drug abuse, and mental illness. The intergenerational transmission of resilience and trauma in the family is governed by biological, psychological, social, cultural, and political factors (Alexander, 2012; Danieli, 1998; Denham, 2008). Significantly, the forced displacement of Palestinian families in Israel due to the Nakbah, along with other burdensome related experiences, constitutes an intergenerational adversity sustained by interconnected personal, family, social, and political narratives.

35.7 Intergenerational resilience

Recent contributions (Fassin & Rechtman, 2009; Papadopoulos, 2007, 2021) challenge the concept of historical trauma and its confused conceptualization that tends to exclude individual and collective resilience reactions to historical trauma. These contributions emphasize that individual and collective strengths expressed in the face of historical and current injustices, inequalities, and poverties are generally diminished and underestimated. The theory of "adversity grid" (Papadopoulos, 2007, 2021) seems to offer a very useful socio-constructionist systemic model for investigating and disentangling individual, family, and social reactions to collective adversity or trauma of involuntary displacement. Applied with theoretical efficacy to intervention contexts concerning the experience and care of refugees, it proposes a distinction between resilience, defined as a neutral reaction to adversity, and positive reaction, or adversity-activated development (AAD). A third category covers three possible negative effects: ordinary human suffering (OHS), distressful psychological reaction (DPR), and psychiatric disorder (PD), mainly post-traumatic stress disorder (PTSD).

35.8 Trauma and resilience narratives

The present research contributes to the understanding of the experiences of internally displaced Palestinian families in Israel. The use of a qualitative methodology, combining constructivist grounded theory (Charmaz, 2006) and interpretative phenomenological analysis (IPA) (Smith & Osborn, 2003), has allowed uncovering of intergenerational dynamics and narratives (Andolfi, 2017) of resilience and trauma. The analysis of retrospective and current narratives of three generations of internally displaced Palestinian families in Israel in relation to the Nakbah has revealed a theory of "complex intergenerational resilience" (Qossoqsi, 2017). The concept of "complex intergenerational resilience," understood as the multifaceted response and adaptation of subsequent generations to trauma or collective adversity, is mapped using Papadopoulos's "adversity grid" model (Papadopoulos, 2007, 2021). This model allows categorizing the phenomenon of intergenerational reactions to the Nakbah into two main dimensions of resilience, three dimensions of adversity-activated development (AAD), and two dimensions of trauma.

35.8.1 AAD dimensions

1. *The compass of return*: pragmatic nostalgia, management of ambivalence, overcoming static aspect of existence, future-oriented attitude to life, origin rituals, recognition, quest for justice, stability, political activism, self-cohesiveness, overcoming frozenness, hope, stability, intergenerational cooperation
2. *Heightened awareness of cultural identity*: cultural identity, challenging the Zionist discourse, community heritage, cultural activities, political activities, pride, poetry of resistance, art, books, celebrating heritage, belonging, pride, acting upon values, collective rights
3. *Inventiveness of loss*: survival, creativity, the struggling "we," speaking truth to power, rebuilding life, management of ambivalence, political activism, self-confidence, courage, disconnecting from traditional limits related to typically rural life and opening up to the world, imagination, freedom

35.8.2 Resilience dimensions

1. *Land and place attachment*: poetic of place, identity, intimate knowledge of land, mythologizing, naming places, belonging, memories, caring, origin rituals
2. *Social relatedness*: solidarity, empathy, familiarity, security, equality, communal love, identity, happiness, cooperation, sense of home, common fate, commitment to collective cause, sense of community, pride

35.8.3 Trauma dimensions

1. *Ambiguous loss*: multiple losses, injustice, devastating event, split, trauma of belonging, fear, denial, suspension, deep sense of precariousness and uncertainty, idealizing and infantilizing of place, existential restlessness, anger, sense of betrayal, disillusionment, comparisons between pre- and post-Nakbah, numbness
2. *Carrying the intergenerational anxiety*: silence, shame, blame, anger, self-silencing, regression, desperation, heartache, loneliness, disappointments, frozenness, extreme family distress, pessimism, weakened intergenerational hierarchy, family disunity of the resulting in sense of loneliness of the older generation, a life ruptured, physical illness, painful memories, silenced women, in-group discrimination, suspicion

35.9 The Nakbah and Palestinian families

The analysis revealed that the emergent theory is strongly influenced by family, social, and cultural identity. Historically and psychosocially contextualizing the interrelationship between involuntary displacement, resilience, and vulnerability (Papadopoulos, 2007, 2021; Werner, 2012) allowed unveiling a multigenerational family circular processes (Andolfi, 2017; Bowen, 1978) of resilience related to involuntary displacement in the context of Nakbah and other past and present repressive colonial practices. The complexity is reflected in a dialectical balance inclined towards resilience and changing over time between pre-displacement and post-displacement resilience dimensions and trauma-related vulnerability and suffering dimensions. The theory expands Papadopoulos's "adversity grid" model (Papadopoulos, 2021) by emphasizing its intergenerational validity and applicability to indigenous populations exposed to historical trauma and subject to attacks on their survival and cultural diversity (Samson, 2003, 2008, 2013).

An integrated, unsilenced, and intergenerationally negotiated account of family experiences and post-memories (Hirsch, 2012) seems to enhance the entire "intergenerational self" of its members and the family identity as a resilient system (Walsh, 2003). The present study supports research findings on resilience and trauma in the context of involuntary displacement and political violence, suggesting overlaps with dimensions present in the literature such as place attachment, intensified sense of cultural identity, social connectedness, and ambiguous loss. Two resilience dimensions introduced in this research seem to be less considered in the literature: the compass of return and the inventiveness of loss. The compass of return refers to the energizing nature of the unresolved tension between the two poles of the concept of home, the retrospective and the prospective: home as a place of origin and a place to aspire to return to (Papadopoulos, 2021). The guiding idea of returning to original places is also stabilizing for the sense of identity in a threatening world, self-cohesion and collective cohesion, control over unpredictability and chaos throughout our lives, humanity (Papadopoulos, 2007), social justice (Ungar, 2008), and recognition (Thomas et al., 2011). Inventiveness of loss, on the other hand, highlights the creativity of survival and vitality exemplified by the iconic Palestinian novel *The Secret Life of Saeed: The Pessoptimist* (Habibi, 2003), presenting an AAD dimension (Papadopoulos, 2006) that challenges limits and goes beyond the known threshold towards new, unknown transformative and non-dichotomous perceptions of self, relationships, and the meaning of life (Frankl, 1963).

The inventiveness of loss underscores the profound impact of involuntary displacement on individuals and families, encompassing the loss of home, family ties, personal dreams, and a familiar world. Although the loss is pervasive and painful, it also generates growth, renewal, and a revaluation of personal and collective identities. The experience of loss mobilizes the collective capacity for political action, stimulating activism and cultural empowerment. Dislocation becomes a catalyst for exploring the unknown, overcoming cultural boundaries, and embracing knowledge and modernity, as reflected in the words of a second-generation participant in my research (Qossoqsi, 2017):

> On one hand, families were torn apart; on the other, we moved from that small, closed place to the outside world . . . we were left without land and home . . . we only had ourselves, we had to rebuild ourselves . . . study, work, move forward . . . you had to leave the rural world and reach the modern world . . . to study . . . to explore . . . not to be confined to a single place . . . you could reach places that previous generations couldn't reach.

The experience of "ambiguous loss" and the associated emotions seem to be channeled into an exploration of the unknown outside world and future unexplored territories, going beyond cultural limits and familial intergenerational hierarchical boundaries and authority (Williamson, 1982).

The intergenerational narrative reflects a dialectical approach to loss, integrating both nostalgic disorientation (Papadopoulos, 2007) and the meaning of survival and creativity. It highlights the resilience and strength of Palestinians in rebuilding themselves and their cause, challenging oppression and asserting their rights. Subsequent generations show increasing courage, boldly speaking truth to power and disrupting the dominant narrative. Engagement in resistance and resilience is a form of intergenerational code. Narratives of intergenerational transmission of family resilience do not exclude or minimize negative responses and vulnerabilities to forced displacement related to the war but emphasize and expose a more balanced perception and interpretation of events and identity personally and collectively (Denham, 2008).

35.10 Research summary

The research thus far underscores the need highlighted in the scientific literature (Bonanno, 2005; Duran & Duran, 1995; Papadopoulos, 2007, 2021; Ungar, 2008) to study the intergenerational psychosocial effects of colonial hegemony on natives more deeply and less dichotomously. "Narratives do not need to include only 'traumatized' (passive, speechless, horror-struck) victims in dialectical relation to colonialists, but can themselves be both stories of and vehicles for adaptation and strength" (Crawford, 2014, p. 357). Particularly interesting is the intergenerational dynamic involving Nakbah-related involuntary displacement. An intergenerationally developed ability to discuss, negotiate, and contain differences and narrative nuances seems to provide displaced families with a balancing function. The second generation is absorbed by the fusion anxieties and silences of the first generation, while the third generation appears more differentiated (Andolfi, 2017; Bowen, 1978) in terms of managing the post-memories of previous generations and demands for uncritical invisible loyalties (Andolfi, 2017; Boszormenyi-Nagy & Spark, 1984; Bowen, 1978). The first generation confers moral authority while the third generation introduces energy and creativity. The sense of generational continuity within the community takes shape, keeping in mind that "studies that seek to understand the relation between memory and identity within this community must be more attentive to the fact that different generations should, and do, have distinct relations to the past" (Allan, 2005, p. 53). Family-level differentiation can also be implemented at the social level in displaced Palestinian communities that tend to reinforce fusion. On a more general note, questioning the disabling and victimizing "trauma discourse" (Summerfield, 2001) and the "politics of trauma" (Kaplan, 2005) in the context of refugees and colonized should not divert attention from the real sufferings and vulnerabilities of internally displaced, refugees, colonized, and marginalized people in the name of socially irresponsible "resilience politics" (Drury, 2012).

35.11 Case illustration

Aram, a young student, has been struggling for many years with a devastating trauma and with a very complex relationship with his unemotional narcissistic father. In one session, he speaks about a growing sense of suffocation he has been experiencing recently. He then reveals a family secret regarding his late paternal grandmother. His grandmother, who later was diagnosed with schizophrenia, was the victim of a horrific colonial crime. While resisting the Israeli army forces confiscating her land in Galilee in the 1950s, she was, at some point, tied by her hair to a military vehicle and dragged for about 200 meters until one of the village dignitaries intervened and saved her from a certain dragging death – but not from a precipitated madness. She was hospitalized for many years, away from her young children. At a certain point, her younger son, Aram's father, transferred her to his home, where Aram used to take care of her from the time when he was a young child.

The story was mostly untold in the family, but its deep intimate destructive waves seem to have since overwhelmed the intergenerational family dynamic, resulting in blocked individual and family processes and wounded intimate family relations. The colonial act of confiscating the land was literally and psychologically inscribed and engraved in the family body and psyche: violating the land and the body, both home to the essential humanity of the family. The humiliating bodily violence, with its sexual degrading connotations all put on public display, was to be intergenerationally translated into an enduring legacy of trauma, relational frozenness, and existential breathlessness. Aram's own trauma experience will be multiplied by the intergenerational trauma. His fragility painfully infused with the intergenerational sense of shame and rage speaks about the intimate ways the collective disaster is experienced, metabolized, or dissociated by the individual. The sense of suffocation experienced by Aram cannot be disconnected from the intergenerational and very present sense of suffocation of the whole family, and the struggle in inhaling and exhaling the breath needed to share this story. His frustrated love and individuation needs seem to be drifted and distorted by the traumatic family history, resulting in a dragging psychological death. The term *confiscation* resonates with suffocation. Presenting Nakbah-informed trauma into the therapeutic discourse shed a new light on the madness of this family and on the suffering of Aram, while enabling him to start a movement of differentiation and disentanglement from the family traumatic emotional process and to rediscover and recover elements of family resilience.

35.12 Conclusion

As a clinical psychologist, family therapist, and researcher, I observe the intergenerational effects and responses to the Nakbah in various clinical situations. These effects can be deeply traumatic, but it is important to recognize that they are not exclusively negative. Alongside traumatic elements, we often see a revitalized and enriched subjectivity emerge. The Nakbah, understood as colonial trauma, permeates every aspect of the psychosocial life of Palestinians. Its impact is evident in couple relationships, parenting skills, experiences of depression and anxiety, a pervasive sense of insecurity and uncertainty, and a lasting sense of alienation and ambiguous loss. It also reflects in cases of domestic and community violence, as well as symbolic violence inflicted by institutions, both explicitly and implicitly. Palestinian psychotherapists are called to develop their clinical and therapeutic approaches to tune into the various voices and body languages of the Nakbah in the lives of their patients and families. Colonial madness, as Fanon (2008) teaches us, is a political form of madness, and political systems can suffer from mental disorders. Understanding this allows us to appreciate the complexity and depth of the struggle for freedom. Being truly free means resisting and transcending the limitations imposed by such madness, recognizing that madness itself can be the result of the limitations on our freedom.

Various factors and variables should be questioned if we want to analyze the intergenerational psychosocial impact of the Nakbah-related forced displacement on surviving Palestinian families within Israel, including personal history, relational and social context, power, gender, experience conceptualization, and others (Danieli, 1998; Papadopoulos, 2007, 2021). Although loss is very present in the intergenerational narratives of internally displaced Palestinian families in all its painful nuances, it is also associated with affirmative content of growth, renewal, and positively revised perceptions of the personal and collective intergenerational self (Bonanno, 2004). "One possesses one's own homeland only when one loses it" (Sharabi, 1991, p. 15). The intergenerational "emotional community" (Rosenwein, 2006) of internally displaced families has transformed "cultural mourning" (Eisenbruch, 1991) into cultural revitalization (Samson, 2013), and the moral state of "we who suffer and mourn" into "we who struggle and are empowered by loss" (Charmaz, 1999), moving from passive victimization (Fassin & Rechtman, 2009) to assertive and proactive adaptation (Papadopoulos, 2002).

Loss is signified and reinterpreted as a mobilizer of collective political agency and complex political victimization (Bouris, 2007), and expressed in political activism and cultural empowerment. "Resilience necessarily involves movement" (Boss, 2006, p. 83). The intergenerational narratives of loss have triggered a movement from a state of social confinement to an inevitable force, from a simple and self-isolated existence to an exploratory mode of life embracing knowledge and modernity. Displacement narratives diverge and converge as they are passed down from one generation to the next. While first-generation narratives may be influenced by biases of objectivity, memory, and forgetfulness, subsequent generations are shaped by the dominant narratives within their families and communities. However, there is a circularity in intergenerational family dynamics, with subsequent generations questioning family silences and integrating them into new perspectives. Collective adversity narratives, including the Nakbah, focus on issues of loss, fragmented identities, memories, and places. However, they also include healing, cultural identity, resistance, and reconciliation. The intergenerational interaction between past, present, and future brings to light various concepts and domains that contribute to the understanding of the psychosocial effects of the Nakbah-related internal forced displacement.

The Nakbah is often discussed within a historical trauma discourse, emphasizing victimization. However, a qualitative exploration of Nakbah narratives reveals the complexity, diversity, and fluidity of the intergenerational experience (Qossoqsi, 2010, 2017). The systemic constructionist "adversity grid" model, context-aware and culturally sensitive, provides a more comprehensive understanding than the pathologizing and universalizing historical trauma model. Qualitative research methods are valuable for capturing the multiplicity of voices and lived experiences in marginalized communities. Publication of case histories featuring in-depth exploration of these themes would also contribute to greater awareness and refinement of clinical skill in witnessing and working with these forms of trauma. There is no better example in our world, including presently, of how the "political becomes personal," as war and oppressive governmental policies wreak havoc and lasting pain on families and their members. The intergenerational conversation about the Nakbah among involuntarily displaced Palestinian families involves not only verbal communication but also visual representations, spatial interactions, and shared rituals. This model suggests that intergenerational resilience is a complex interplay of reactions, adaptations, growth, and narratives constructed through the tension between trauma and survival. By understanding and recognizing these dimensions, we can provide more holistic support to communities grappling with intergenerational trauma and resilience.

References

Abu El Hija, A. (2018). *Intergenerational transmission of parental Nakba-related trauma experiences among Palestinians living in Israel* (Doctoral dissertation, University of Konstanz). Konstanz University Publications. https://kops.uni-konstanz.de/entities/publication/7e766046-6c0c-45a3-a8f1-2714f15b8216

Abu Sitta, S. (2001). *From refugees to citizens at home*. Palestine Land Society and The Palestinian Return Centre. www.plands.org/en/books-reports/books/from-refugees-to-citizens-at-home

Adalah. (2017). *Palestinian citizens of Israel: A primer*. www.adalah.org/en/content/view/7771

Adalah. (2019). *Palestinian citizens of Israel: A primer*. www.adalah.org/en/content/view/9271

Afuape, T. (2011). *Power, resistance and liberation in therapy with survivors of trauma: To have our hearts broken*. Routledge.

Alexander, J. C. (2012). *Trauma: A social theory*. Polity Press.

Al-Hardan, A. (2013). Decolonizing research on Palestinians: Towards critical epistemologies and research practices. *Qualitative Inquiry*, *20*(1), 61–71. https://doi.org/10.1177/1077800413508534

Allan, D. (2005). Mythologizing Al-Nakba: Narratives, collective identity, and cultural practice among Palestinian refugees in Lebanon. *Oral History: Re-presenting the Past*, *33*(1), 47–56. www.jstor.org/stable/40179820

Andolfi, M. (2017). *Multi-generational family therapy: Tools and resources for the therapist*. Routledge.

Atkinson, C. L. (2008). *The violence continuum: Australian aboriginal male violence and generational post-traumatic stress* (Publication No. 28907724) [Doctoral dissertation, Charles Darwin University]. ProQuest Dissertations & Theses Global. https://doi.org/10.25913/5ea23b0cbbd5d

BADIL Resource Center for Palestinian Residency & Refugee Rights. (2022). *Survey of Palestinian refugees and internally displaced persons, 2019–2021* (Vol. X, N. Al-Azza, Ed.). Al-Ayyam Printing, Press. www.badil.org/cached_uploads/view/2022/10/31/survey2021-eng-1667209836.pdf

Bonanno, G. A. (2004). Loss, trauma, and human resilience: Have we underestimated the human capacity to thrive after extremely aversive events? *American Psychologist*, *59*(1), 20–28. https://doi.org/10.1037/0003-066X.59.1.20

Bonanno, G. A. (2005). Resilience in the face of potential trauma. *Current Directions in Psychological Science*, *14*(3), 135–138. https://doi.org/10.1111/j.0963-7214.2005.00347.x

Boss, P. (2006). *Loss, trauma, and resilience: Therapeutic work with ambiguous loss*. W. W. Norton & Company.

Boszormenyi-Nagy, I., & Spark, G. (1984). *Invisible loyalties: Reciprocity in intergenerational family therapy* (2nd ed.). Brunner/Mazel (Original work published 1973).

Bouris, E. (2007). *Complex political victims*. Kumarian Press, Inc.

Bowen, M. (1978). *Family therapy in clinical practice*. Aronson.

Charmaz, K. (1999). Stories of suffering: Subjective tales and research narratives. *Qualitative Health Research*, *9*, 362–382. https://doi.org/10.1177/104973239900900306

Charmaz, K. (2006). *Constructing grounded theory: A practical guide through qualitative analysis*. Sage Publications.

Crawford, A. (2014). "The trauma experienced by generations past having an effect in their descendants": Narrative and historical trauma among Inuit in Nunavut, Canada. *Transcultural Psychiatry*, *51*(3), 339–369. https://doi.org/10.1177/1363461512467161

Danieli, Y. (1998). *International handbook of multigenerational legacies of trauma*. Plenum Press.

Dekel, R., & Goldblatt, H. (2008). Is there intergenerational transmission of trauma? The case of combat veterans' children. *American Journal of Orthopsychiatry*, *78*(3), 281–289. https://doi.org/10.1037/a0013955

Denham, A. R. (2008). Rethinking historical trauma: Narratives of resilience. *Transcultural Psychiatry*, *45*(3), 391–414. https://doi.org/10.1177/1363461508094673

Drury, J. (2012). Collective resilience in mass emergencies and disasters: A social identity model. In J. Jetten, C. Haslam, & S. A. Haslam (Eds.), *The social cure: Identity, health and well-being* (1st ed., pp. 195–215). Psychology Press. https://doi.org/10.4324/9780203813195

Duran, E., & Duran, B. (1995). *Native American postcolonial psychology*. State University of New York Press.

Duran, E., Duran, B., Brave Heart, M. Y. B., & Yellow Horse-Davis, S. Y. (1998). Healing the American Indian soul wound. In Y. Danieli (Ed.), *International handbook of multigenerational legacies of trauma* (pp. 341–354). Plenum Press.

Eisenbruch, M. (1991). From post-traumatic stress disorder to cultural bereavement: Diagnosis of Southeast Asian refugees. *Social Science & Medicine*, *33*(6), 673–680. https://doi.org/10.1016/0277-9536(91)90021-4

Fanon, F. (2008). *Black skin, white masks*. Grove Press (Original work published 1967).

Fassin, D., & Rechtman, R. (2009). *The empire of trauma: An inquiry into the condition of victimhood*. Princeton University Press.

Fast, E., & Collin-Vezina, D. (2010). Historical trauma, race-based trauma, and resilience of Indigenous peoples: A literature review. *The First Peoples Child & Family Review*, *5*(1), 126–136. http://journals.sfu.ca/fpcfr/index.php/FPCFR/article/view/181/150

Frankl, V. E. (1963). *Man's search for meaning*. Pocket Books.

Ghnadre-Naser, S., & Somer, E. (2016). "The wound is still open": The Nakba experience among internally displaced Palestinians in Israel. *International Journal of Migration, Health and Social Care, 12*(4), 238–251. https://doi.org/10.1108/IJMHSC-07-2015-0024

Habibi, E. (2003). *The secret life of Saeed: The pessoptimist.* Interlink Books.

Hirsch, M. (2012). *The generation of postmemory: Writing and visual culture after the Holocaust.* Columbia University Press.

International Court of Justice. (2024, January 26). *Application of the convention on the prevention and punishment of the crime of genocide in the Gaza strip (South Africa v. Israel).* www.icj-cij.org/node/203447

Jayyusi, L. (2007). The Palestinian exodus and the Arab role in the Nakba. In A. Sa'di & L. Abu-Lughod (Eds.), *Nakba: Palestine, 1948, and the claims of memory* (pp. 1–14). Columbia University Press.

Kaplan, E. A. (2005). *Trauma culture: The politics of terror and loss in media and literature.* Rutgers University Press.

Lentin, R. (2013). Melancholia, Nakba co-memory and the politics of return. In *Co-memory and melancholia: Israelis memorialising the Palestinian Nakba* (pp. 153–172). Manchester University Press. https://doi.org/10.7765/9781847793225.00012

Levine, P., & Kline, M. (2007). *Trauma through a child's eyes.* North Atlantic Books.

Litvak, M. (2009). *Palestinian collective memory and national identity.* Palgrave Macmillan.

Papadopoulos, R. K. (2002). *Therapeutic care for refugees: No place like home.* Karnac Books Ltd.

Papadopoulos, R. K. (2006). *Refugees and psychological trauma: Psychosocial perspectives.* The National Children's Bureau. www.ncb.org.uk/media/963817/arc_1_10refandpsych.pdf

Papadopoulos, R. K. (2007). Refugees, trauma, and adversity-activated development. *European Journal of Psychotherapy and Counselling, 9*(3), 301–312. https://doi.org/10.1080/13642530701496930

Papadopoulos, R. K. (2021). *Involuntary dislocation: Home, trauma, resilience, and adversity-activated development.* Routledge.

Pappè, I. (2007). Review of "The Ethnic Cleansing of Palestine." *Journal of Genocide Research, 9*(4), 675–681. https://doi.org/10.1080/14623520701644465

Pappe, I. (2011). *The forgotten Palestinians: A history of the Palestinians in Israel.* Yale University Press.

Qossoqsi, M. (2010). The narrative of the Nakbah and the politics of trauma. *Jadal, 3*(7). https://mada-research.org/post/1131

Qossoqsi, M. (2017). *Intergenerational psychosocial effects of Nakbah on internally displaced Palestinians in Israel: Narratives of trauma and resilience* (Doctoral dissertation, University of Essex). University of Essex Repository. https://repository.essex.ac.uk/20433/1/PhD%20Dissertation%20Mustafa%20Qossoqsi.pdf

Qossoqsi, M. (2020, August 22). *Notes on an intimate disaster: Nakbah in the clinic and beyond* [Lecture, Episode 10]. Café Palestine, UK Palestine Mental Health Network. https://ukpalmhn.com/cafe-palestine/cafe-palestine-index/cafe-palestine-10/

Robinson, S. (2013). *Citizen strangers: Palestinians and the birth of Israel's liberal settler state.* Stanford University Press.

Rosenwein, B. H. (2006). *Emotional communities in the early Middle Ages.* Cornell University Press.

Sa'di, A. (2013). *Thorough surveillance: The genesis of Israeli policies of population management, surveillance, and political control towards the Palestinian minority.* Manchester University Press.

Said, E. (1979). *The question of Palestine.* Times Books.

Samson, C. (2003). *A way of life that does not exist: Canada and the extinguishment of the Innu.* Iser Books.

Samson, C. (2008). A colonial double-bind: Social and historical contexts of Innu mental health. In L. J. Kirmayer & G. Valaskakis (Eds.), *Healing traditions: The mental health of Aboriginal peoples in Canada* (pp. 195–244). University of British Columbia Press.

Samson, C. (2013). *A world you do not know: Settler societies, indigenous peoples and the attack on cultural diversity.* University of London Press. https://library.oapen.org/handle/20.500.12657/86303

Sayigh, R. (2013). On the exclusion of the Palestinians from the "trauma genre." *Journal of Palestine Studies, 43*(1), 51–60. https://doi.org/10.1525/jps.2013.43.1.51

Shalhoub-Kevorkian, N. (2019). *Incarcerated childhood and the politics of unchilding.* Cambridge University Press.

Sharabi, H. (1991). Introduction. In Jaffa Research Center, *Jaffa, the perfume of a city* (p. 15). Dar Al-Fata Al-'Arabi.

Smith, J., & Osborn, M. (2003). Interpretive phenomenological analysis. In J. A. Smith (Ed.), *Qualitative psychology: A practical guide to research methods* (pp. 51–80). Sage Publications.

Smith, L. T. (2012). *Decolonizing methodologies: Research and indigenous peoples* (2nd ed.). Zed Books.

Summerfield, D. (2001). The invention of post-traumatic stress disorder and the social usefulness of a psychiatric category. *BMJ*, *322*(7278), 95–98. https://doi.org/10.1136/bmj.322.7278.95
Thomas, F. C., Roberts, B., Luitel, N. P., Upadhaya, N., & Tol, W. A. (2011). Resilience of refugees displaced in the developing world: A qualitative analysis of strengths and struggles of urban refugees in Nepal. *Conflict and Health*, *5*(20), 1–11. https://doi.org/10.1186/1752-1505-5-20
Thompson, L. (2021). Toward a feminist psychological theory of "institutional trauma." *Psychology of Women Quarterly*, *31*(1), 1–13. https://doi.org/10.1177/0959353520968374
Ungar, M. (2008). Resilience across cultures. *British Journal of Social Work*, *38*(2), 218–235. https://doi.org/10.1093/bjsw/bcl343
Walsh, F. (2003). Family resilience: A framework for clinical practice. *Family Process*, *42*(1), 1–18. https://doi.org/10.1111/j.1545-5300.2003.00001.x
Werner, E. E. (2012). Children and war: Risk, resilience, and recovery. *Development and Psychopathology*, *24*(2), 553–558. https://doi.org/10.1017/S0954579412000156
Williamson, D. S. (1982). Personal authority in family experience via termination of the intergenerational hierarchical boundary: Part III – Personal authority defined, and the power of play in the change process. *Journal of Marital and Family Therapy*, *8*(3), 309–323. https://doi.org/10.1111/j.1752-0606.1982.tb01454.x

36

INTERETHNIC MARRIAGES AND FAMILY DYNAMICS IN SENEGAL

Geneviève Platteau and Fatou Waly Diop

36.1 Introduction

This chapter discusses the growing trend of intercultural marriage in Senegal. In Senegal, marriage remains influenced by ethnic, religious, and social status differences. Historically, unions were arranged to preserve social status and strengthen inter-family alliances, as described in Abdoulaye Bara Diop's ground-breaking research (1981). Traditional family influences on marriage remain significant, particularly regarding caste and ethnic considerations. However, in contemporary Senegal, young people's identities are increasingly built on the one hand through identification with their peers and on the other through the more traditional process of identification with their parents and other elders. Identification with peers, especially in urban areas, means exchange of worldwide social media, encouragement to pursue higher education and achieve greater financial independence. This contributes to shifting social norms. As a result, there are tensions between tradition and modernity, with young people faced with multiple, sometimes contradictory allegiances within the family unit and in the broader sociocultural sphere, and a gap between traditional ideal cultural models and contemporary models of behavior.

One result of these changes in young adult development is that interethnic marriages are becoming more common, especially in urban areas. Along with the factors already listed, the increased connections between persons from different cultural groups is facilitated by using humor ("joking relationships") between people of different ethnicities, which ease tensions between groups. However, religious diversity can create challenges, particularly regarding rituals, child upbringing, and social pressures. The caste system still impacts matrimonial choices, with family elders often opposing unions that could alter their lineage's social standing.

Although some couples defy familial constraints, others wait for traditional societal attitudes to shift before making choices not approved of in those traditions. Marriage in Senegal thus reflects the ongoing struggle between historic, cultural heritage and rapidly changing models of how potential partners come together and go on to marriage.

Whereas in traditional Senegalese marriages (between members of the same ethnicity and social caste) bonding is largely of a filial or family nature (extended family to extended family within the ethnic group), bi-cultural marriages are characterized by *affiliation* between two people across different ethnic groups. This affiliation is largely driven by attraction, not by determination to preserve the collective family line. The attraction is often based on partners' perceptions of their differences,

DOI: 10.4324/9781003536765-42

including a sense of the other as "exotic" or mysterious. Although in all couples, there is a tension or balance between belonging to the marital relationship and preserving and growing a sense of personal, individual identity, given the immediately perceived, physiognomic differences as well as other differences based on distinct cultures, more emphasis may be placed on establishing and sustaining a strong romantic bond. This contrasts with many Western Anglo couples, where the emphasis is on differentiation, with personal identity taking precedence over belonging to the marital unit (Maalouf, 2000).

36.2 Intercultural families

Culture provides an essential source of personal and group identity, and the beliefs, customs, and rituals in one's culture are often strongly protected and held to represent absolute truths about the world. In the best-case scenario, partners from differing cultures do not seek to erase or invalidate each other's cultures. Instead, they adopt a stance of respectful curiosity and even excitement when presented with the unknown and mysterious about their partner. In turn, on a deeply personal, idiographic level, the explorations, both-and combinations, and cultural interweaving that occur in intercultural couples and families represent and drive social change, one family at a time. Partners (and their children) in intercultural couples inhabit a "double existence": double cultural belonging, double loyalty, double identity, double recognition by others. This is both a resource that provides them with openness and a broader view of the way the world might be conceived, and at the same time, an area of possible fragility, a tug-of-war where choices among cultural practices can seem challenging or even impossible.

The partners in the couple function between filiation (loyalty to one's own culture and family) and affiliation (adoption of the other's culture and values). Young people can be torn between the beliefs of their parents' country of origin and those of the country where they live, i.e., between tradition and modernity, or even between different cultural beliefs of their and their partner's ethnic and religious groups within the same country.

In addition to the effects of modernization in the increase of intercultural marriage, choosing a partner who is visibly different from oneself may be an attempt to draw a clear line between the birth family and the couple. In other words, choosing a partner from outside one's culture can serve as a way of increasing a partner's differentiation from their family and culture of origin. As Platteau writes (2012), "We know that, paradoxically, we choose the 'different' to find similarities, when it is precisely in the 'similar' that we are looking for something different" (p. 252).

36.3 Challenges of being an intercultural couple

All newly married couples need to establish each partner's roles and the ways in which power is held and distributed between partners. Partners from differing cultures may come with different traditional expectations as to whether power and hierarchy will be organized in a patriarchal and matriarchal fashion. Partners need to understand the cultural roots of each other's gender/power expectations. Where there are different expectations, partners need to find compromises so that each one finds his place and recognizes his partner's place and function. These challenges emerge most clearly when children are born. Hopefully, the couple negotiates them in a respectful way.

36.3.1 Case illustration: The N. Family

This family came to therapy to address the symptoms of their eldest daughter Aida, aged 13. This intercultural couple consisted of a white Belgian wife/mother and a black Senegalese husband/father. The mother and their two daughters had been living in Senegal for a year. The father was living mostly in Belgium, where he had an important job. Even if the couple's choice was to move full-time back to Senegal, the father did not want to risk leaving his job without finding an equivalent position in Senegal.

His birth family lived in Dakar and, like any good African son, he regularly sent money to his family. He was previously married to a Belgian woman, who was 18 years older than him, and they had a son who was currently 24 years old. They separated after 15 years of marriage.

The husband/father left Senegal as soon as he came of age to study, as he could no longer tolerate certain aspects of his country's functioning. However, he was sent to boarding school at a young age at a very harsh institution. He had two brothers and two sisters who live in Senegal. He described his father as narcissistic and violent. The husband/father was extremely close and loyal to his mother, again like any good Senegalese son.

The wife/mother was Belgian but had lived in Congo until she was 6 years old. Then, during a period of turmoil in that country, her parents sent her back to Belgium to live with her paternal grandparents, and she never returned to Congo or another African country before meeting her husband in Belgium. As a child, she felt abandoned by her parents.

The husband/father described himself as a "citizen of the world," but he felt closer to Belgian customs than Senegalese ones, with which he no longer identified, given the corruption prevalent in the country. The mother/wife complained about not having enough alone time with her husband. For him, the notion of being "just the two of them" did not resonate. These differences in valuing couple time versus time for work were revealed to stem in large part from the partners' cultural differences, filtered also through gender. Upon exploration, the husband/father revealed that his great emphasis on career and financial status over time with his wife and children reflected cultural codes and expectations for men in Senegalese culture. The wife/mother's father and grandfather also worked hard, and both her mother and grandmother often felt left alone. She was attracted to her husband because he, like her father and grandfather, had a strong work ethic (also important in Belgian culture), but she wanted more attention and time from him than her mother and grandmother had received from their spouses.

In one session, we conducted an exercise/exploration of emotional closeness and distance among family members. Each family member in turn showed the distance they felt from the other. A very close relationship between each dyad was observed, except between Aida and her mother. Aida distanced herself greatly from her mother. She said, "Since my sister was born, I feel rejected. I am like an adopted child." Surprised at Aida's physical demonstration and verbalization of felt emotional distance from her, the mother countered by disagreeing, saying that "No, she holds a *central* place." We comment to the parents, and indirectly to Aida, "OK, but is it perhaps because of her symptoms that Aida occupies this central place?" The parents and Aida became quietly reflective and later said that this session was important in helping them understand the parents' contribution to Aida's problematic behavior.

We also noted the strong intergenerational theme between the mother's sense of being abandoned by her parents when she was sent to Belgium and Aida's sense of being displaced in the strength of the mother's attention when her sister was born. The mother was surprised and intrigued by this therapeutic suggestion, and it led her to explain to her daughters the history of her life in Senegal and then being sent to her grandparents in Belgium against her will.

The family therapy also revealed other issues with cultural underpinnings and helped the couple negotiate compromises where there had been conflict. Many of these issues centered on parenting. For instance, and perhaps against some stereotypes held by some Anglo readers about European versus African parents, the mother was more demanding and the father laxer about homework and other duties. On the other hand, whereas the father strongly emphasized the need to suppress sadness and fear, the mother encouraged the children to express their emotions. For example, when Aida cried, the father would say, "tears serve no purpose," and the mother would say, "let your emotions out."

Interestingly, the wife/mother most wished to settle permanently in Senegal, noting "I was born here, it is my true home!" As noted earlier, the husband/father had strong negative feelings about some aspects of the culture and especially about the politics in Senegal and was more comfortable with Belgian culture. The two girls took their CEB exams in Belgium and passed them, and the parents decided to return the whole family to live in Belgium, for at least a year. Two months after the start of the school year, the father obtained an interesting job opportunity in Senegal. We encouraged them to stay and finish the school year in Belgium, after which they moved to Senegal permanently.

36.3.2 Case illustration: The Cis family

This Belgian mother came with her 15-year-old son Ibrahim because he was misbehaving so much that she said, "I can't deal with him anymore." The family lived in Senegal.

Ibrahim had a 9-year-old sister from the same father and another sister, 2 months old, from another father. The mother lives alone with her three children. At the time of the first divorce from a Malian father, Ibrahim was 7 years old. The father went back to live in Mali. The mother was granted sole custody. The father was given the opportunity to take his children on holiday for two months a year, which he never did.

During the first session, Ibrahim expressed hatred towards his mother. He resented her for marrying this second Senegalese husband. He observed that this man had emotional problems and was using drugs. As soon as the traditional marriage took place, this man had unbearable fits of jealousy. The mother left that husband when she was five months pregnant, but Ibrahim remained upset about his mother having brought such a man into his life.

Her son also resented her for coming to live in Senegal (she lived and worked in Belgium for a short time), depriving him of his dreams of being a basketball player, which he could have pursued in Belgium. He resented her for following the philosophy of a small religious cult and taking him and his sisters with her to spend weekends at cult gatherings. Ibrahim felt that the cult members mattered more to his mother than he did. He said he would like to go to boarding school (in Senegal), then move to Belgium, and live with his maternal grandmother and other relatives, who understood him well.

Given the tension between Ibrahim and his mother, we suggested seeing Ibrahim alone. After seeing him alone, we saw his brother and sister, the grandmother and Ibrahim, the mother alone, and finally the mother and her three children. In our individual session, Ibrahim immediately said that he exaggerated his negative feelings towards his mother in the previous session. He said he was angry and felt betrayed by her, but that he loved her. He loved his school and his friends in Senegal, but he hoped to return to Belgium to fulfill his dream of being a basketball player. We had a few more sessions with Ibrahim to give him a chance to express his feelings and be heard. He became more emotionally regulated over the weeks, and his mother reported great improvement in his behavior.

In the next full family session, the mother was touched when we told her that her children worried about her. Ibrahim said something he had first revealed to us in the last individual session – that he saw her as a victim. He said he wanted to protect her and, at the same time, he resented her for marrying such a problematic man and for seeming to struggle so much with life as a mother.

We observed aloud that Ibrahim had matured over the sessions and was more measured in his words. His mother and his sister agreed. He says that he doesn't like going to the cult meetings, but that it has "probably" spiritually benefited him, and that perhaps later he will thank his mother.

We hypothesized aloud that through his "problem behaviors" that were labeled as symptoms, Ibrahim, a mixed-race child, might be trying to find his place as the man in the family, as is typical in Senegal for first-born sons. In Senegal, that son does take on the role of the "little husband" and protects his mother. Ibrahim was proud when one of us mentioned that he immediately detected that his mother's second husband had problems and was not suitable for her.

36.4 Historical heritage and social structure

36.4.1 Borders in the Senegalese family

Some borders are tacit, such as those of affiliation to "castes" and those of polygamy. For instance, marriage is initially sealed between two people, but most Senegalese men sign the choice to engage in "polygamy" in the civil marriage act. When they choose to take a second wife (sometimes under the influence of their mother), they only inform the previous wife when the marriage is consecrated. The borders between ethnicities are more explicit, and even if it is advisable to marry someone from one's own ethnic group, there is greater social and religious tolerance where difference is accepted.

36.4.2 Ethnic, religious, and social diversity in marriage in Senegal

In Senegal, ethnic, religious, and social differences remain deeply embedded in the culture, despite being increasingly challenged by modernization. These disparities also generate tensions, particularly in the domain of marriage. Senegalese society has long been characterized by a hierarchical system that structures ethnic groups and castes, which continues to exert a strong influence on marital choices today. Marriage was not merely the union of two individuals but rather that of two families, and sometimes even two lineages bound by strategic alliances aimed at ensuring the transmission of heritage and cultural values. In this context, unions were often arranged to guarantee social homogeneity and maintain group cohesion. This organization is based on a collective perception of marriage as a social act, where matters of honor and respectability take precedence over individual feelings.

Senegalese sociologist Abdoulaye Bara Diop, in his work *La Société Wolof: Tradition et Changement* (1981), highlights this reality by explaining that endogamous marriages were a means for families to perpetuate their social status and reinforce their influence through strategic alliances. According to him, these marriages ensured the continuity of social norms and the transmission of community values. Another Senegalese sociologist, Djiby Diakhaté (in Barro, 2018), emphasizes the considerable influence of family in the choice of a spouse, which remains a predominant factor even in urban settings. He indicates that although modernization and education tend to shift mentalities, they do not always suffice to dismantle centuries of codified social practices and entrenched prejudices.

Following this logic, the choice of a spouse was primarily influenced by the family, particularly the mother of the future husband, who favored a wife from the same ethnic group or caste. This adhered to the tradition that the daughter-in-law should care for her mother-in-law and integrate seamlessly into her new environment. This custom remains particularly strong in certain communities, such as the Wolof, Peul, and Serer, where roles and responsibilities are defined from childhood. Although this structure may appear rigid, it was justified by a desire to preserve cultural heritage and stabilize social relations within the community.

Cheikh Anta Diop, in his foundational work *Nations Nègres et Culture* (1955), explores the historical foundations of African societies, demonstrating how traditional structures have evolved over time. His later work, *Civilisation ou Barbarie* (1981), underscores the importance of African cultural roots in resisting external influences – an idea that resonates with the persistence of caste-based matrimonial customs in Senegal.

36.5 Interethnic marriage and *Cousinage à Plaisanterie* in Senegal

In Senegal, interethnic marriage is a social reality that reflects the country's openness and cultural diversity. With more than a dozen ethnic groups coexisting for centuries, unions between Wolof, Peul, Serer, Mandingue, Diola, and other ethnic groups have become increasingly common, particularly in urban centers where social diversity is more pronounced. These marriages promote integration and strengthen the social fabric by facilitating cultural blending and reducing ethnic tensions. However, beyond the societal benefits they bring, such unions may also pose challenges linked to differences in customs, languages, and sometimes religious practices.

In this context, *cousinage à plaisanterie* (joking relationships) play a fundamental role in facilitating coexistence and defusing potential tensions between ethnic groups. This practice is based on codified relationships of teasing and banter between certain ethnic groups or family lineages, creating an atmosphere of conviviality and goodwill. For example, such interactions are commonly observed between the Serer and the Toucouleur, or between the Wolof and the Peul. When an interethnic marriage takes place, *cousinage à plaisanterie* can serve as a unifying factor, fostering fraternity between the families of both spouses, easing communication, and reinforcing family cohesion.

This tradition helps establish cordial relations and facilitates the integration of new members into their in-laws' family while fostering an environment of tolerance and mutual openness. Moreover, it plays a role in educating children born from such unions by instilling in them values of respect and cultural diversity, thereby broadening their worldview. More broadly, it becomes a tool for conflict resolution, as it helps alleviate tensions through humor and lighthearted dialogue.

36.6 Challenges of religious diversity

Although interethnic marriages are generally well accepted in Senegal, religious diversity can sometimes pose significant challenges within couples and extended families. Differences in religious practices, particularly concerning rites, prayers, or religious celebrations, may lead to disagreements if one partner expects the other to actively participate in their spiritual traditions. This issue becomes especially sensitive when it comes to transmitting religion to children, as families may have specific expectations in this regard.

Family and societal pressures also play a crucial role in managing interfaith marriages. In a society where religion holds a central place, some families may express reservations about unions that do not align with their cultural and spiritual expectations. Such influences can generate tensions and conflicts, particularly when parents attempt to impose their views on their children.

Another major challenge lies in the celebration of key rites such as marriage, funerals, or other religious ceremonies that mark the couple's life. Divergent beliefs can complicate the organization of these events, sometimes leading to misunderstandings or frustrations. Additionally, a lack of mutual understanding may arise if one spouse does not make an effort to learn about the other's religion, which can create feelings of rejection or disrespect.

Furthermore, certain religious differences may give rise to conflicts of values, particularly concerning gender roles, parenting, or lifestyle choices. These divergences can become points of contention within the relationship, especially if they affect fundamental aspects of marriage and family life. In some cases, interfaith couples also face discrimination from society, religious institutions, or even their close social circles, adding further pressure to their relationship.

Despite these challenges, many couples manage to overcome these obstacles through dialogue, adaptability, and mutual understanding. The key to a successful interethnic and interfaith marriage lies in the partners' ability to respect and value their differences while finding common ground that allows them to build a harmonious and fulfilling relationship.

36.7 The weight of castes in matrimonial unions

Historically, Senegalese society was organized into a strict hierarchy composed of various socio-professional categories. At the top, the *geer* (nobles) enjoyed a privileged status and held positions of power, followed by the *gewel* (griots) – the guardians of the country's historical and cultural memory, then the *laobe* (carpenters), the *ñeeño* (blacksmiths), and finally the *jaam* (descendants of slaves), who were considered inferior within this social structure. Though rooted in ancestral traditions, this stratification continues to influence perceptions of marriage.

This organization has long reinforced matrimonial discrimination, with *geer* families avoiding unions with individuals from so-called lower castes to preserve their prestige. These distinctions become particularly evident during marriage ceremonies, where noble families offer substantial dowries, while families from lower castes are often relegated to roles in entertainment, craftsmanship, or service. Many marriage proposals fail due to parental opposition to "blood mixing," as families seek to maintain the "purity" of their lineage and perpetuate traditional alliances.

Sociologist Djiby Diakhaté (in Barro, 2018) highlights that the preservation of castes is part of a broader resistance to change, with families fearing the dilution of their social and cultural identity. Thus, despite growing discourse on equality and social evolution, many young people continue to encounter these barriers when attempting to formalize a union perceived as transgressive.

Amadou Hampâté Bâ, in *Amkoullel, l'enfant peul* (1991), offers a rich autobiographical account of oral tradition and family values in African societies, shedding light on how these factors continue to shape social interactions, including marriage. His book *Vie et enseignement de Tierno Bokar* also explores themes of wisdom, social cohesion, and respect for traditions, which remain central to matrimonial choices in Senegal.

36.8 Towards a relaxation of social norms

As Senegalese society evolves, caste-based constraints on marital choices remain a major social issue. Between respect for tradition and the pursuit of individual freedom, younger generations navigate between family expectations and aspirations for a marriage based on love and compatibility rather than social or ethnic criteria. The intergenerational transmission of traditional values clashes with emerging social models, creating a duality between modernity and adherence to customs. Marriage, as an institution, thus remains a reflection of the tensions between past and present, between conformity and emancipation, in a society undergoing constant transformation.

36.9 Conclusions

Implicit disagreements in education, or separations, are frequently revealed by the symptoms of young people. Their multiple affiliations give them multiple reference points. Is there a choice of culture for the child? Probably in an irrational way. Indeed, the recognition of a culture is transmitted and anchored within oneself through the attachment bond. We are in the logic of ambiguity much more than in that of ambivalence, in an almost impossible choice, a form of indecisiveness in the logic of ambiguity, where there is no room for compromise formation (Ndiaye, 1993). Through their symptoms, young people show an attempt to break free from their ambivalence . . . between tradition and modernity.

The process of cultural differentiation goes much deeper because it touches on cultural heritage; love does not always triumph over the prejudices and misunderstandings that are part of the heritage each of us carries, whether as an asset or a burden. On the one hand, this cultural transmission unconsciously binds us to loyalties, family values, and beliefs, but on the other hand, this integrated baggage either secures us or makes us insecure, while the culture of the other, even if it attracts us, disturbs us or limits us to what we know too well.

In mixed families consulting in Senegal, white women have idealized Africa and are discovering other codes that they try to adopt but that pose some problems for them, especially in their relationship to their spouse (e.g., the unspoken). They appreciate the group culture, the "we are together" mentality, which is so unfamiliar in the West.

In mixed families living in Europe, most of the time, the foreign spouse has already chosen and accepted European codes, which seems to make them more comfortable.

In our experience, it seems that the mixed families who consult in Belgium are more likely to have marital problems, masking the problems linked to cultural differences, whereas the families who consult in Senegal are more likely to have cultural differences, sometimes leading to symmetrical struggles and misunderstandings that were unsuspected at the outset, masking the marital problems. The child awakens old affiliations and a certain repressed nostalgia. Isn't our work the co-construction of a bond chiseled with mutual recognition? (Métraux, 2011).

References

Anta Diop, C. (1955). *Nations nègres et culture: Analyse approfondie de l'histoire et des traditions Africaines*. Presence Africaine.

Anta Diop, C. (1981). *Civilisation ou barbarie*. Presence Africaine.

Bara Diop, A. (1981). La société wolof. Tradition et changement. Karthala Ed.

Barro, M. (2018). *Une jeunesse pour la relève*. L'Harmattan.

Hampaté, B. A. (1991). *Amkoullel, l'enfant peul – Récit autobiographique sur la tradition orale et les valeurs familiales Africaines*. Les Ateliers d'ACTES SUD.

Maalouf, A. (2000). *In the name of identity: Violence and the need to belong*. Penguin Books (Original work published 1998).

Métraux, J. C. (2011). *La migration comme métaphore*. La Dispute.

Ndiaye, S. (1993). *Islam et mariage traditionnel wolof au Sénégal*. Université Cheikh Anta Diop de Dakar.

Platteau, G. (2012). Mixed couples, the adoption of two cultures? *Cahiers critiques de thérapie familiale et des pratiques de réseaux*, *49*(2), 241–258. https://doi.org/10.3917/ctf.049.0241

37

INTRODUCING CLIMATE CHANGE IN MENTAL HEALTH PRACTICE

Olga Garcia Falceto, Enrique Falceto de Barros, and Luisa Falceto de Barros

37.1 Introduction

Each person we receive in a mental health clinic brings with him/her the complexity and the resources of his/her family and community. Each one of us, psychiatrists, psychologists, and other mental health professionals, also brings along to the therapeutic encounter our personal positive qualities and difficulties. As health professionals, we are trained in a specific scientific knowledge leading to certain actions. Still, worldwide there is often little or no space to learn about the professional's own personal shortcomings and resources, which is an essential issue, since our professional main instrument is the use we make of personal resources (Andolfi, 2022).

This chapter emphasizes that the qualities developed by family therapists to work with complex human systems are of great importance in times of climate change. It introduces information that is still scarce about the impact of climate change on mental health, emphasizing the role of air pollution as a main driver of both direct brain injury and global warming. We aim to provide beginning maps to include greening strategies into the therapy room, focusing on personal and professional changes needed and highly emphasizing the need to develop large supportive networks to face the multiple and difficult tasks brought by climate change.

37.2 Mental health while Earth's climate is changing

What are the known effects of global warming and other Anthropocene Epoch phenomena on general health and mental health in particular? (Rao, 2022; Heinz & Brandt, 2024).

The Anthropocene Epoch is the name given to the large impact humans' economic development has caused on Earth, starting with the Industrial Revolution and accelerating since the 1980s. Air pollution is one of its consequences. Almost nine million people die every year from direct consequences of air pollution, such as cardiorespiratory events and cancer (Lelieveld et al., 2023). The World Health Organization (WHO) compares pollution's impact to that of tobacco. Air pollution is directly linked to coal and petroleum burning that also provoke most of the global warming effects, leading to climate change.

For example, we know as mental health workers that a major precipitant of psychopathology is unresolved mourning (Szuhany et al., 2021); what do these mortality figures imply as psychopathological consequences? On the other hand, it is known that global warming will probably increase the

DOI: 10.4324/9781003536765-43

frequency of pandemics, and we must remember that the COVID-19 deaths during the pandemic are estimated to be 14.83 million excess deaths, rather than the reported 5.42 million for the period (Msemburi et al., 2023). The COVID-19 pandemic eruption was likely influenced by deforestation and climate warming. It is estimated that the prevalence of mental illness is increasing globally, associated with the effects of the COVID-19 pandemic (Nochaiwong et al., 2021; King et al., 2022), but this increase seems to be also linked to air pollution and climate change. There is emerging evidence that air pollution causes dementia, depression, and anxiety, with increased risk for children, adolescents, old people, and other vulnerable populations (Bhui et al., 2023; Hernandez Carballo et al., 2022). It is likely that air pollution was also associated with an increased risk of death by COVID-19 (Wu et al., 2020). Two recent articles bring additional scary information. One of the studies is from the US and the other is from China. Both are population studies that show a strong association between the increase of PM2.5 levels and suicide. In the US 2023 study, a 13% increase in PM2.5 from forest fires was associated with a 2% increase in suicide rates in rural areas that already had a high incidence of suicide (Molitor et al., 2023). The Chinese study, including all of the country, found that a one standard deviation (SD) increase in PM2.5 was associated with a 25% increase in weekly suicides, as an immediate effect, leading the authors to conclude that there is a neurobiological impact of air pollution particles on emotional regulation and impulsivity. They also mentioned the effect of the Chinese Air Pollution Control Plan, which resulted in a decrease in suicide rates across the country (Zhang et al., 2024).

Heat waves, which are becoming increasingly common, with 2024 being globally the warmest year on record, are directly associated with cardiovascular deaths, anxiety, depression, and interpersonal violence (Ebi et al., 2021). It is important to remember that the use of psychiatric medication makes body heat regulation more difficult, so our medicated psychiatric patients are more at risk than others (Martin-Latry et al., 2007).

Floods, the most frequent climate disaster globally, cause drowning in cities and devastation in rural areas. Droughts and floods cause hunger. Both are responsible for migrations, which result in family and community dislocation and disorganization, with severe consequences to mental health, affecting present and future generations (Batista et al., 2024). The increased temperatures and landscape disruptions increase infectious diseases with negative influence in mental health (Charlson et al., 2021). Other health impacts, such as those on the respiratory and cardiac systems, cancer, and others, are strongly associated with air pollution and pesticides, yielding established negative consequences on mental health as well.

There are other health consequences of the natural resources overexploitation we still know little about. For instance, we are only starting to understand the impact on human health of the immense amount of plastic garbage, a novelty created by humans. What we already know is that microplastic is associated with cancer risk, endocrine disruption, and heart attacks. It has recently been found in human tissues, including in the brain, human placenta, and maternal breast milk (Ragusa et al., 2021; Lee et al., 2023; Campen et al., 2024).

37.3 What consequences may this have for the human species?

Infants are especially susceptible to environmental toxicity. Their developing organs will very likely be affected by the ingestion of nanoplastics. Beyond the organic risk that is not well defined, we can hypothesize that it will have psychological consequences as nursing is at the center of human psyche and relational formation. The mother-father-baby relationship builds the basis of personal identity. Figure 37.1, from author OGF's doctoral thesis of 20 years ago, illustrates it (Falceto et al., 2004). The triad is surrounded and supported by their family and community, which includes the healthcare team. The human psyche is formed by biological factors and interpersonal relations. These

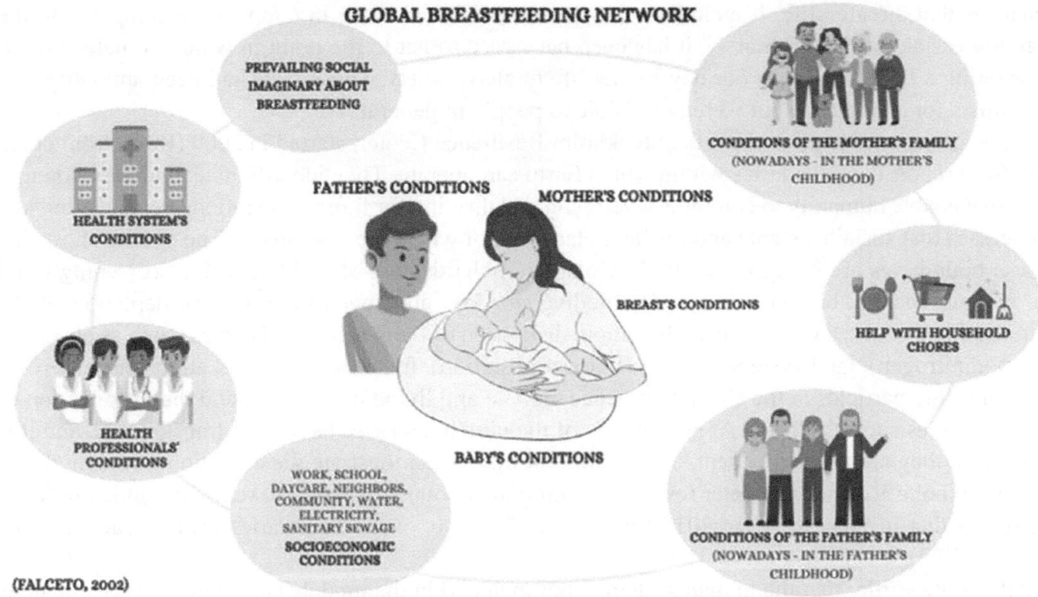

Figure 37.1

processes have obviously been interfered with through the centuries, in the beginning of the 20th century by the introduction of industrialized milk, with Occidental mothers being informed that it was the "best option for babies." Now we know that on top of this misleading message, taking power away from women and interfering in the biological/psychological nursing process there is a present threat. Recently, traces of plastic have been found in breast milk, with detrimental consequences still to be studied, although nanoplastic is known to be carcinogenic and affect hormonal functions. What can the impact on mental health be, as well? What are the symbolic consequences to the mother-child dyad of "poisoning" mother's milk? If the feeling of safety is essential for healthy development, where can we find/offer safety nowadays?

37.4 Introducing climate change consciousness and action in clinical practice

Health practitioners are faced at present with the urgent challenge of how to introduce climate change consciousness and action into clinical practice. Each clinician will need to become familiar with the unfortunate everyday facts that come up in the media and have the task of looking for evidence-based information to be sure that they are not "fake news." In recent years, there are many articles demonstrating the effects of air pollution and climate change–related disasters on mental health. Unfortunately, there is still scarce material on how to include these facts clinically.

Anyway, it is urgent to introduce the concept of what is called the Anthropocene Epoch. Clinicians must, judiciously, make its discussion a part of increasing clients' systemic awareness. The Anthropocene Epoch is a geologic term that describes the most recent period in Earth's history when human activity is responsible for producing the most significant changes on the planet's surface, climate, and ecosystems. It is extremely rare in Earth's history that a single species so rapidly reshaped the planet's climate and other conditions that have been making life livable. The excessive use of fossil fuels to run industry and pesticides to facilitate agriculture has triggered a cascade of environmental changes that threaten life. It includes a 1.5-degree Celsius increase in temperature compared to the pre-industrial era. Unfortunately, it has been necessary to get to the point in which climate is demonstrating a huge change in our day-to-day life to alert society. Those facts had been announced by scientists for a long time but were not visible to people in general.

One group of scientists, from the Stockholm Resilience Center, started in 2009 (Rockström et al., 2009) to report the boundaries within which Earth can operate. They identify nine planetary boundaries that enable humanity to continue developing and thriving for future generations, representing key processes that sustain a stable and resilient planet, all of which are interlinked. The studies show that these boundaries are being increasingly violated (Richardson et al., 2023), with a worsening trend in climate change, biosphere integrity (biodiversity loss and species extinction), depletion of the stratospheric ozone layer, ocean acidification, disruption of biogeochemical cycles (such as phosphorus and nitrogen), land-system changes (like deforestation), freshwater overuse, atmospheric aerosol loading (tiny particles in the air that influence climate and living organisms), and the introduction of novel entities such as plastic. At present, six of the nine boundaries have been transgressed, and it is clear that they are interdependent. Three different figures demonstrate the evolution of the model of the Stockholm Resilience Center towards defining nine boundaries that make life possible on Earth. It shows that in 2009 three, in 2015 four, and in 2023 six of the boundaries were already crossed (Figure 37.2).

It is noteworthy that the human system is not included in the model. The authors suggest that, as humans are indeed a natural system that is also developing dystopically, and to make clear that humanity is part of the "natural" interdependent process, a tenth planetary boundary could be included, describing the socioeconomic human organization that is exploiting nature's resources beyond its capacity to regenerate. The economist Raworth (2017) provides an interesting map of the economic limits within which it is safe for humans to develop with equity as a central value. A transdisciplinary panel with mental health specialists, sociologists, economists, and others should delve into this aspect of planetary imbalance.

Planetary health is an emerging transdisciplinary field that can guide clinicians to include climate change in their work. It emphasizes the intrinsic connection between humans and nature, being that humans are part of nature, and provides a new perspective on health. Planetary health states that a healthy human system needs to seek the highest possible level of health and well-being for all,

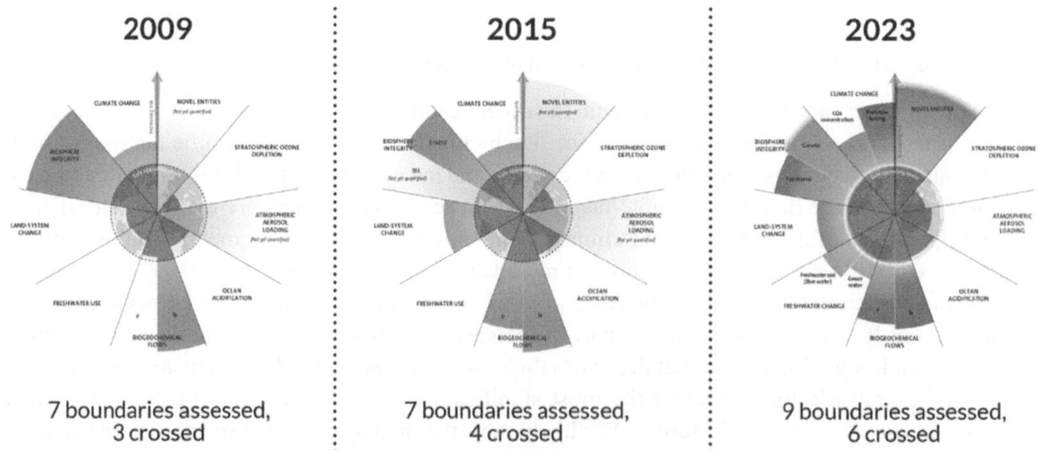

Figure 37.2

with international equity, working on balancing the management of human political, economic, and social systems with Earth's natural systems, which define the limits within which humanity can thrive (Myers et al., 2021).

As each clinician must find their own way of relating to this complex world, the authors will describe their own pathways, which are limited, but steady and developing.

OGF's pathway started about ten years ago (Falceto & Falceto de Barros, 2023). EFB, my son, introduced me to the Brazilian group that works with the Lancet Countdown, the British-led international effort to improve awareness of global warming consequences on human health. With the same group, I participate now in the Brazilian Program of Ambassadors of Planetary Health, which mentors university students from all over Brazil to learn and act on planetary health issues.

This group launched in October 2021 The São Paulo Declaration on Planetary Health (Myers et al., 2021) during one of the Planetary Health Alliance annual meetings, an international network now based at Johns Hopkins University in Baltimore, Maryland, US. It reads:

> This great transition demands a rapid shift in how we produce and consume food, energy, and manufactured goods; requires rethinking the way we design and live in the world's cities; and insists we heal our relationship with nature and to each other. Such a paradigm shift requires participation of every sector, every community, and every individual.

These principles are at the base of what systems-oriented psychotherapy must aim at.

In our clinical work with families, we start by doing a systemic diagnosis and therapeutic plan, and we identify who needs to participate to facilitate change, bringing to the sessions as many family members (and others) as needed or as possible. Goals for therapy are defined along with the family. Do planetary issues come up? Although ubiquitous, ecological determinants of health probably do not emerge explicitly in the clinic, except in special circumstances, mainly in disasters. But many common concerns families bring into therapy are related to their "family carbon footprint" and climate change: how they feed themselves, how they commute, how they treat each other and the environment, how they spend their leisure time, how they consume.

The question "shouldn't we bring associations with the planetary problems into the sessions?" seems to have an obvious answer, as we start to know that there is a climate emergency in course and that our planet is our big house, and there is no Planet B to go to. Furthermore, don't we all "become family" if we live in the same house? Bringing climate change into the therapeutic room seems quite reasonable although counterintuitive. It may sound like adding more problems to those already present in the room. But, if we want our children to have a future, facing these difficulties at all levels of our lives seems mandatory.

37.5 Some maps to help us in the therapy room

There are at least three well-studied health prescriptions associated with the co-benefit of environmental improvement: (1) use the car as little as possible, walk and bike when you can (Brand et al., 2021), and you will decrease your cardiovascular risk and others; (2) forest bathing is very effective for anxiety and depression (Kotera et al., 2022); and (3) change your food management, eat as little red meat as you can (Vatn et al., 2022), due to the high carbon-footprint of its production, plus buy fresh vegetables and cereals from close by (to decrease the carbon print) and from known producers that do not use pesticides.

As family therapists, we add that our clinical experience shows that most family dynamics related to power and gender are very evident at the table. So, discussing family eating patterns presents a great opportunity to work on changing family relationship patterns. There is another encompassing issue: Our civilization must rethink its level of consumerism as we are depleting Earth's reserves with no chance of renewal. We could add, based on recent literature, that we must rethink our relationship with plastics use at all levels: food packaging, clothing, toys, etc.

EFB has developed a method of introducing climate change in his family and community medicine practice in a rural area in South Brazil, using routinely "one minute" of the consultation to talk about the relationship of symptoms and therapeutics with climate change. He argues that the primary care provider is a systems health practitioner that can introduce knowledge and change using the concepts of planetary health care. As everything in human health is interrelated with nature, if the clinician maintains this in mind he will find the links to present it to his patient (Falceto de Barros et al., 2022b). This is probably true also for systems-oriented psychotherapists. Of note, the very concept of "One Minute for the Planet" was inspired by the book *10 Minutes for the Family* (Asen et al., 2004) intended for primary care practitioners, taking opportunistic moments for appropriate second- and third-order thinking treatments.

Another author (LFB), a family and group therapist working in a city on the border between Brazil and Uruguay, seeing patients from both countries, develops methods of eco-psychology, running groups inside nature and finding them very effective in motivating people to change lifestyle and interpersonal relationships. Lately, she has been rescuing art, always a fundamental aspect of her life, in a different way, with the intention of sensibilization on the urgent environmental need for action and, of course, the development of healthier human bonds.

Recently, OGF is working with a group of eco-psychologists that report much more effectiveness with severe depression doing psychotherapy inside nature. They also make events with groups at the margins of the city lake, collecting plastics and other garbage, at the same time that they build personal, collective, and environmental awareness. We are starting to network internationally with similar groups of practice.

There are no "one size fits all" or "ready made" answers on how to introduce climate change in our clinical work. The idea is that change in human attitudes towards a simpler and harmonious way of life is so urgent that we must use judicious opportunities to bring the issue of climate crisis to clinical work.

37.6 Networking to build actions

We are inspired by Fridays for Future, the youth movement, on how to become more of an activist. We hope that, as the future is theirs, they will be able to develop more real power of intervention.

We are constantly and actively trying to find where we can be more efficient. It is important to find where we can fit. OGF and EFB are part of a local movement of physicians, called Medicine in Alert (https://medicinaemalerta.com.br/en/home/), which has been offering information about human health problems related to climate change, and more specifically about air pollution, to a large social movement in our home state. It was part of the big social movement effort to stop the building of an open pit coal mine, at a distance of only 16 km from our city, to be started in 2018. It would be the largest in South America. Luckily, with the great effort of a large social movement, the project was stopped by the justice system in 2022. A rare and inspiring eco-social victory in our country. But we must remain alert! We think that the entrepreneurs will try again.

We all follow on the news the disasters associated with global warming and how they are on the increase. Most of the time, though, we think: "What can I do?", "How do I include this knowledge in my life, in my work?", "Are we on time?".

We must train ourselves to not panic, be patient, and look for opportunities. And we must build solidarity networks, as we hope it is becoming clear in this text. Our personal change started with the help of our family, but maintaining it requires belonging to larger groups.

Working with families, we need to take into account the recent findings published in an article about the prevalence of eco-anxiety in young people around the world, in December 2021 (Hickman et al., 2021). The authors used Kantar Platform to send a questionnaire to thousands of youngsters, financed by AVAAZ. Ten thousand 16- to 25-year-old people responded. The results are worrisome or, on the other hand, may introduce hope: 59% are very worried with the climate crisis; 45% say that the worries affect their daily functioning; and there is a generalized feeling of betrayal by the governments – betrayal by the authorities, meaning their grown-ups. If anxiety affects functioning for a large period, should we consider eco-anxiety a disorder? The authors don't think so, because we consider that it is a sign of good reality testing (Falceto de Barros et al., 2022a).

We are living in a very complex age – the Anthropocene Epoch. No wonder young people are perplexed and enraged. Humans have been able to better their/our life on the planet in unprecedented ways by increasing the human life span, decreasing poverty, and decreasing child mortality. In the process, though, humans have become ultra-consumerists and have depleted and poisoned Earth resources in also unprecedented ways, increasing carbon dioxide emissions, acidifying the oceans, using excessive amounts of energy and water sources, destroying forests, and poisoning the soil with pesticides. The biosphere integrity boundary is in severe danger (Hurley & Tittensor, 2020).

It is also very important to emphasize that those countries that are poorer and have contributed less to the warming process are those that suffer the larger consequences. We need to develop equity policies in mitigation. Equity is different from equality. Poorer countries need more resources and assistance to face their problems, and the resources should come from the richest countries (Whitmee et al., 2015).

These actions cannot be done individually, so networking is essential. There are many local and international groups at work. It is our task to look for them. One of the most important globally, the Planetary Health Alliance, based in the US at Johns Hopkins University, recently offered a road-map for action (https://drive.google.com/file/d/1ZFUFo09NkJJRpOl5Y5cLmV_HoA_4msRe/view PHAM, 2024).

37.7 Is mental illness a cause of climate mutation?

As already said, the impact of climate change in mental health is still not sufficiently recognized. What to say of thinking about how human mental health is associated with the causation of the global climate crisis or mutation as the French philosopher Latour (2017) suggested, being that we are approaching that which was the Paris agreement top of 1.5 degrees Celsius increase in the global temperature? (IPCC, 2018).

Who is responsible for these events? It is not difficult to identify human greed as the responsible party. It is the cause of the hyper-exploitation of nature, especially the greed of the richest people and companies in the world. As Gandhi said, "*Earth* provides enough to satisfy every man's needs, but not every man's *greed*." Some humans' omnipotence causes the use of natural resources beyond the possibility of recovery. This obviously comes along with the exploitation of other submissive human beings that are simultaneously "trained" for hyper-consumerism.

This is old news, although not ventilated enough. The new scenario is that nowadays those are suicidal behaviors because nobody can flee Earth's air pollution or global warming. So, we have omnipotence and submission, two primitive complementary ill behaviors at the base of how global warming started and continues to increase. Those behaviors are associated with our submission to a hyper-consumerist society. These automatic attitudes are associated with society's "addiction" to fossil fuels, which is closely related to a hyper-consumerist lifestyle, quite prevalent especially in the so-called developed world.

If we identify addiction patterns, shouldn't we consider the transtheoretical model of drug addiction treatment to guide our thinking about remedies? It seems that socially we are still in the

Figure 37.3

precontemplative stage (Figure 37.3). The questions are: How can we help our patients and society go beyond this stage? How can we introduce in the clinic ways to develop consciousness, prepare new behaviors, act differently, and maintain the gains towards a better balance with nature? (Prochaska et al., 1992). Is this a reasonable goal towards which systems psychotherapists can work?

37.8 Levels of systemic mental health work to mitigate climate mutation

How can we work from within the contemporary reality of climate change? What can we do? It seems so overwhelming that the tendency is to try to deny the facts or not to perceive them altogether, and/or, in acknowledging them, finding the task so impossible that we give up.

Maybe the concept of levels of thinking that comes from cybernetics can help us understand our reactions. Third-order thinking has introduced the idea that when patients and therapists are part of the same fieldwork, both are affected by its organization with relationships becoming more entangled, complex, interdependent, and less easily interpretable. Clarifying, we could say, for example, that the usual clinical situation of medicating a patient can be described with first-order thinking, although if one looks closer to that action we see that it is influenced by the quality of the patient-doctor relationship, meaning second-order thinking as the physician becomes part of the field of action. Third-order thinking needs to be also introduced in that situation to explain what happens when there is scarcity of medications, for example, and doctors and patients are frustrated by the environmental situation with the doctor sometimes having to choose who to treat and not to treat. But, in this case, the person most clearly affected is the patient and, ideally, the physician should introduce that complexity as a theme in the consultation (McDowell et al., 2019).

An even more difficult situation happens when both patient and doctor are in a similar vulnerable environment, like during a flood. Both are in danger. How can the clinician think and act clearly? Clinicians are trained to be in charge. It is very hard to think during situations in which control is lost. But, unfortunately, this is what the climate crisis presents us with. Are we as mental health professionals sufficiently trained to face uncertainty and vulnerability? There are antidotes, like what happened during recent severe floods in South Brazil with incredible amounts of solidarity at work and in neighborhoods during the crisis that helped clinicians to persevere and be efficient at work.

We must be prepared to work in uncertain situations with a patient-centered and family approach, developing culturally sensitive community resources. Making sure the care is accessible, comprehensive, continuous, and coordinated, because it needs to be multidisciplinary. Planetary health must be the larger systemic framework (Falceto de Barros et al., 2022b).

Mental health workers must learn to identify evidence of climate change in their environment and the psychiatric signs and symptoms associated with them. The constant goal is to educate ourselves and our patients and community about risks. In the process, strategies as to how to contribute towards their mitigation will come up. To prepare ourselves to do this, we have personal work to do: some reading and changes in our personal lifestyle. We must be careful, though, not to create a culture of individual culpability, as it is individually improbable to escape the trap of the dyad omnipotence and submission, which induces our hyper-consumerism.

Once we realize the urgency of the facts, we need to start working at all levels, from the individual patient to our teaching institutions, the local and national mental health system and beyond, including the socioeconomical system as a whole. What a task! Do we have energy and power for that? For sure we have some power: Some of us have economically and politically influential patients, and most of us have a good influence in our communities. Those of us who have experience with grassroots activism, know that with a good balance, activism can bring a sense of belonging and joy to activists.

If we develop the knowledge, skills, and attitudes to apply One Minute for the Planet, we can become competent and effective system-changers, as we simultaneously uncover resources, to overcome seemingly insurmountable challenges. We are familiar with this, as it happens during psychotherapeutic work with individuals, families, and communities. The process promotes networking and creates support structures, bringing possibilities of transformation. Even happiness can be promoted in the process. There are interesting articles about this process in the reconstruction work in New Orleans, after the Katrina hurricane: There is the description of human solidarity and community resilience being developed (Raker et al., 2020).

Another field where transformation is necessary is the organization of the healthcare system. It has been calculated that if the international health system was a country, it would have the fifth worst carbon footprint globally (Sherman et al., 2020). As part of it, there are estimates that overtreatment and overmedicalization are the third highest cause of death in the United States (Sunshine et al., 2019). It is estimated that only 20% of human health well-being is provided by the health system. Community and personal health is mostly associated with socioeconomic and environmental determinants (Kruk et al., 2018). This makes it evident that many medical interventions need to be downsized and that the health system needs to become greener (Falceto de Barros et al., 2022b).

37.9 Systems family therapists in action

Humans are natural and social beings that develop inside families and communities. For thousands of years there has been a stable global climate to develop into. Mental symptoms usually start as a maladaptation to the present life situation, a result of family and its network inability to adjust to needed changes, often due to transgenerational invisible loyalties and/or traumas that seem impossible to overcome. When there is economic scarcity, with poor feeding, housing, lack of education, and health resources, everything becomes even more difficult. Conflictual and/or abusive interpersonal patterns of relationship develop. It is known that psychiatric symptoms can also be caused by adverse drugs or substances, but nowadays there is the addition of air pollution and other climate change phenomena likely causing direct damage to the brain.

Preserving human mental health in such an environment is difficult, but as systems-oriented therapists we have good roadmaps to offer to the health system to help its adaptation and change. We daily experience in clinical practice how the improved and more equitable human relational systems we help develop with our clients bring them new resources, creativity, and transformation. We are facilitators of human development. This knowledge must be passed on to healthcare systems.

We must and can influence our present mental healthcare system to develop a larger systemic diagnosis of patients presenting symptoms, including third-order thinking, with an evaluation of the carbon footprint involved. Interventions need the participation of the family and, ideally, the community resources. Once a psychotherapeutic systems approach is set in motion, including family members and close others, of different generations, usually unexpected personal and group resources come to light. Much suffering is saved, the same for financial resources, personal and public. Medication may be used but, usually, is less necessary.

In a world undergoing a climate mutation, originated by the way humans exploit natural resources looking for profit, wealth, and endless comfort, due to confusion about what is happiness, health, and being modern, the mental health professionals must decide what is indeed healthy and sustainable behavior and act accordingly to it. Indigenous cultures around the world have experiences that can inspire us, like the Brazilian author Krenak (2020). He maintains that the present climate crisis is rooted in society's concept of "humanity" as something that exists apart from Earth itself, unlike the indigenous people that see rivers and trees as their "brothers." We must reflect about how the human perception of itself dissociated from nature may be a serious unrecognized mental illness most of us, who live in cities, are suffering from.

In summary, systems-oriented clinicians must advocate for greater harmony between humans and Nature at every level, both as professionals and citizens. A family systems approach to physical and mental health can identify powerful natural healing resources while making health systems greener, more efficient, and less costly.

References

Andolfi, M. (2022). *The gift of truth, the inner journey of the therapist*. Accademia Press.

Asen, E., Tonson, D., Tonson, P., & Young, V. (2004). *Ten minutes for the family*. Routledge.

Batista, C., Knipper, M., Sedas, A. C., Farante, S. V., Wainstock, D., Borjas-Cavero, D. B., Araya, K. R., España, J. C. A., & Yglesias-Gonzãlez, M. (2024). Climate change, migration, and health: Perspectives from Latin America and the Caribbean. *The Lancet Regional Health – Americas*, *40*, 100926. https://doi.org/10.1016/j.lana.2024.100926

Bhui, K., Newbury, J. B., Latham, R. M., Ucci, M., Nasir, Z. A., Turner, B., O'Leary, C., Fisher, H. L., Marczylo, E., Douglas, P., Stansfeld, S., Jackson, S. K., Tyrrel, S., Rzhetsky, A., Kinnersley, R., Kumar, P., Duchaine, C., & Coulon, F. (2023). Air quality and mental health: Evidence, challenges and future directions. *BJPsych Open*, *9*(4), e120. https://doi.org/10.1192/bjo.2023.507

Brand, C., Dons, E., Anaya-Boig, E., Avila-Palencia, I., Clark, A., de Nazelle, A., Gascon, M., Gaupp-Berghausen, M., Gerike, R., Götschi, T., & Iacorossi, F. (2021). The climate change mitigation effects of daily active travel in cities: Transportation research part D. *Transport and Environment*, *93*(4), 102764. https://doi.org/10.1016/j.trd.2021.102764

Campen, M., Nihart, A., Garcia, M., Liu, R., Olewine, M., Castillo, E., Bleske, B., Scott, J., Howard, T., Gonzalez-Estrella, J., Adolphi, N., Gallego, D., & Hayek, E. E. (2024). Bioaccumulation of microplastics in decedent human brains assessed by pyrolysis gas chromatography-mass spectrometry. *Research Square [Preprint]*, *6*, rs.3.rs-4345687. https://doi.org/10.21203/rs.3.rs-4345687/v1

Charlson, F., Ali, S., Benmarhnia, T., Pearl, M., Massazza, A., Augustinavicius, J., & Scott, J. G. (2021, April 23). Climate change and mental health: A scoping review. *International Journal of Environmental Research and Public Health*, *18*(9), 4486. https://doi.org/10.3390/ijerph18094486

Ebi, K. L., Capon, A., Berry, P., Broderick, C., Dear, R., Havenith, G., Honda, Y., Kovats, R. S., Ma, W., Malik, A., Morris, N. B., Nybo, L., Seneviratne, S. I., Vanos, J., & Jay, O. (2021). Hot weather and heat extremes: Health risks. *The Lancet*, 398(10301), 698–708. https://doi.org/10.1016/S0140-6736(21)01208-3

Falceto de Barros, E., Falceto, O. G., Zandavalli, R. B., & Souza, D. O. (2022a). Eco-anxiety: A new disease or a "new normal"? *Trends in Psychiatry and Psychotherapy*, *46*, e20220543. https://doi.org/10.47626/2237-6089-2022-0543

Falceto de Barros, E., Souza de Camargo, T., Tetelbom, S., Abelsohn, A., & de Souza, D. O. (2022b). Planetary health action framework: A case study: GRASSROOTS. *International Health Trends and Perspectives*, *2*(3), 106–123. https://doi.org/10.32920/ihtp.v2i3.1700

Falceto, O. G., & Falceto de Barros, E. (2023). From individual psychiatry to planetary health care: A personal account of a Brazilian social psychiatrist. *World Social Psychiatry*, *5*(1), 29–35. https://doi.org/10.4103/wsp.wsp_11_23

Falceto, O. G., Giugliani, E., & Fernandes, C. L. (2004). Influence of parental mental health on early termination of breastfeeding: A case-control study. *Journal of the American Board of Family Medicine*, *17*(3), 173–183. https://doi.org/10.3122/jabfm.17.3.173

Heinz, A., & Brandt, L. (2024, June 14). Climate change and mental health: Direct, indirect, and intersectional effects. *The Lancet Regional Health-Europe*, *43*, 100969. https://doi.org/10.1016/j.lanepe.2024.100969

Hernandez Carballo, I., Bakola, M., & Stuckler, D. (2022). The impact of air pollution on COVID-19 incidence, severity, and mortality: A systematic review of studies in Europe and North America. *Environmental Research*, *215*(Pt 1), 114155. https://doi.org/10.1016/j.envres.2022.114155

Hickman, C., Marks, E., Pihkala, P., Clayton, S., Lewandowski, R. E., Mayall, E. E., Wray, B., Mellor, C., & Van Susteren, L. (2021). Climate anxiety in children and young people and their beliefs about government responses to climate change: A global survey. *Lancet Planet Health*, *5*(12), 863–873. https://doi.org/10.1016/S2542-5196(21)00278-3

Hurley, E., & Tittensor, D. P. (2020). The uptake of the biosphere integrity planetary boundary concept into national and international environmental policy. *Global Ecology and Conservation*, *22*(2), e01029. https://doi.org/10.1016/j.gecco.2020.e01029

IPCC. (2018). *Global warming of 1.5°C: An IPCC special report on the impacts of global warming of 1.5°C above pre-industrial levels and related global greenhouse gas emission pathways, in the context of strengthening the global response to the threat of climate change, sustainable development, and efforts to eradicate poverty* (V. Masson-Delmotte, P. Zhai, H.-O. Pörtner, D. Roberts, J. Skea, P. R. Shukla, A. Pirani, W. Moufouma-Okia, C. Péan, R. Pidcock, S. Connors, J. B. R. Matthews, Y. Chen, X. Zhou, M. I. Gomis, E. Lonnoy, T. Maycock, M. Tignor, & T. Waterfield, Eds., p. 616). Cambridge University Press. https://doi.org/10.1017/9781009157940; www.ipcc.ch/sr15/

King, J. D., Zhang, S., & Cohen, A. (2022). Air pollution and mental health: Associations, mechanisms and methods. *Current Opinion in Psychiatry*, *35*(3), 192–199. https://doi.org/10.1097/YCO.0000000000000771

Kotera, Y., Richardson, M., & Sheffield, D. (2022). Effects of Shinrin-Yoku (forest bathing) and nature therapy on mental health: A systematic review and meta-analysis. *International Journal of Mental Health and Addiction*, *20*, 337–361. https://doi.org/10.13140/RG.2.2.12423.21920

Krenak, A. (2020). *Ideas to postpone the end of the world*. Anansi International.

Kruk, M. E., Gage, A. D., Arsenault, C., Jordan, K., Leslie, H. H., Roder-DeWan, S., Adeyi, O., Barker, P., Daelmans, B., Doubova, S. V., & English, M. (2018). High-quality health systems in the sustainable development goals era: Time for a revolution. *Lancet Global Health*, *6*(11), e1196–e1252. https://doi.org/10.1016/S2214-109X(18)30386-3

Latour, B. (2017). *Down to earth, politics in the new climatic regime*. Polity Press.

Lee, Y., Cho, J., Sohn, J., & Kim, C. (2023). Health effects of microplastic exposures: Current issues and perspectives in South Korea. *Yonsei Medical Journal*, *64*(5), 301–308. https://doi.org/10.3349/ymj.2023.0048

Lelieveld, J., Haines, A., Burnett, R., Tonne, C., Klingmüller, K., Münzel, T., & Pozzer, A. (2023). Air pollution deaths attributable to fossil fuels: Observational and modeling study. *BMJ*, *383*, e077784. https://doi.org/10.1136/bmj-2023-077784

Martin-Latry, K., Goumy, M. P., Latry, P., Gabinski, C., Bégaud, B., Faure, I., & Verdoux, H. (2007). Psychotropic drugs use and risk of heat-related hospitalisation. *European Psychiatry*, *22*(6), 335–338. https://doi.org/10.1016/j.eurpsy.2007.03.007. PMID: 17513091.

McDowell, T., Knudson-Martin, C., & Bermudez, J. M. (2019). Third-order thinking in family therapy: Addressing social justice across family therapy practice. *Family Process*, *58*(1), 9–22. https://doi.org/10.1111/famp.12383

Medicina em Alerta. https://medicinaemalerta.com.br/en/home/

Molitor, D., Mullins, J., & White, C. (2023). Air pollution and suicide in rural and urban America: Evidence from wildfire smoke. *Proceedings of the National Academy of Sciences*, *120*(38), e2221621120. https://doi.org/10.1073/pnas.222162112

Msemburi, W., Karlinsky, A., Knutson, V., Aleshin-Guendel, S., Chatterji, S., & Wakefield, J. (2023). The WHO estimates of excess mortality associated with the COVID-19 pandemic. *Nature*, *613*(7942), 130–137. https://doi.org/10.1038/s41586-022-05522-2

Myers, S. S., Pivor, J. I., & Saraiva, A. M. (2021). The São Paulo declaration on planetary health. *Lancet*, *398*(10308), 1299. https://doi.org/10.1016/S0140-6736(21)02181-4

Nochaiwong, S., Ruengorn, C., Thavorn, K., Hutton, B., Awiphan, R., Phosuya, C., Ruanta, Y., Wongpakaran, N., & Wongpakaran, T. (2021). Global prevalence of mental health issues among the general population during the coronavirus disease-2019 pandemic: A systematic review and meta-analysis. *Scientific Reports*, *11*(1), 10173. https://doi.org/10.1038/s41598-021-89700-8

Planetary Health Alliance Org. (PHAM). (2024). *Planetary health roadmap and action plan*. https://drive.google.com/file/d/1ZFUFo09NkJJRpOl5Y5cLmV_HoA_4msRe/view

Prochaska, J. O., DiClemente, C. C., & Norcross, J. C. (1992). In search of how people change: Applications to addictive behaviors. *American Psychologist*, *47*(9), 1102–1114. https://doi.org/10.1037//0003-066x.47.9.1102

Ragusa, A., Svelato, A., Santacroce, C., Catalano, P., Notarstefano, V., Carnevali, O., Papa, F., Rongioletti, M. C. A., Baiocco, F., Draghi, S., D'Amore, E., Rinaldo, D., Matta, M., & Giorgini, E. (2021). Plasticenta: First evidence of microplastics in human placenta. *Environment International, 146*, 106274. https://doi.org/10.1016/j.envint.2020.106274

Raker, E. J., Arcaya, M. C., Lowe, S. R., Zacher, M., Rhodes, J., & Waters, M. C. (2020). Mitigating health disparities after natural disasters: Lessons from the RISK project. *Health Affairs*, *39*(12), 2128–2135. https://doi.org/10.1377/hlthaff.2020.01161

Rao, M. (2022). Mental health impacts of the climate crisis: The urgent need for action. *International Review of Psychiatry*, *34*(5), 439–440. https://doi.org/10.1016/j.trd.2021.102764

Raworth, K. (2017). A doughnut for the anthropocene: Humanity's compass in the 21st century. *The Lancet Planetary Health*, *1*(2), e48–e49. https://doi.org/10.1016/S2542-5196(17)30028-1

Richardson, K., Steffen, W., Lucht, W., Bendtsen, J., Cornell, S. E., Donges, J. F., Drüke, M., Fetzer, I., Bala, G., Von Bloh, W., & Feulner, G. (2023). Earth beyond six of nine planetary boundaries. *Science Advances*, *9*(37), eadh2458. https://doi.org/10.1126/sciadv.adh2458

Rockström, J., Steffen, W., Noone, K., Persson, A., Chapin, S., Lambin, E. F., Lenton, T. M., Scheffer, M., Folke, C., Schellnhuber, H. J., & Nykvist, B. (2009). A safe operating space for humanity. *Nature*, *461*, 472–475. https://doi.org/10.1038/461472a

Sherman, J. D., Thiel, C. L., MacNeill, A., Eckelman, M. J., Dubrow, R., Hopf, H., Lagasse, R., Bialowitz, J., Costello, A., Forbes, M., & Stancliffe, R. (2020). The green print: Advancement of environmental sustainability in healthcare. *Resources, Conservation and Recycling*, *161*. https://doi.org/10.1016/j.resconrec.2020.104882

Sunshine, J. E., Meo, N., Kassebaum, N. J., Collison, M. L., Mokdad, A. H., & Naghavi, M. (2019). Association of adverse effects of medical treatment with mortality in the United States: A secondary analysis of the global burden of diseases, injuries, and risk factors study. *JAMA Network Open*, *2*(1), e187041. https://doi.org/10.1001/jamanetworkopen.2018.7041

Szuhany, K. L., Malgaroli, M., Miron, C. D., & Simon, N. M. (2021) Prolonged grief disorder: Course, diagnosis, assessment, and treatment. *Focus (American Psychiatric Publishing*, *19*(2), 161–172. https://doi.org/10.1176/appi.focus.20200052

Vatn, A., Aasen, M., Thøgersen, J., Dunlap, R. E., Fisher, D. A., Hellevik, O., & Stern, P. (2022). What role do climate considerations play in consumption of red meat in Norway? *Global Environmental Change*, *73*, 102490. https://doi.org/10.1016/j.gloenvcha.2022.102490

Whitmee, S., Haines, A., Beyrer, C., Boltz, F., Capon, A. G., de Souza Dias, B. F., Ezeh, A., Frumkin, H., Gong, P., Head, P., Horton, R., Mace, G. M., Marten, R., Myers, S. S., Nishtar, S., Osofsky, S. A., Pattanayak, S. K., Pongsiri, M. J., Romanelli, C., . . . Yach, D. (2015). Safeguarding human health in the anthropocene epoch: Report of The Rockefeller foundation-lancet commission on planetary health. *Lancet*, *386*, 1973–2028. https://doi.org/10.1016/S0140-6736(15)60901-1

Wu, X., Nethery, R. C., Sabath, B. M., Braun, D., & Dominici, F. (2020). Exposure to air pollution and COVID-19 mortality in the United States: A nationwide cross-sectional study. *medRxiv*, *7*. https://doi.org/10.1101/2020.04.05.20054502

Zhang, P., Carleton, T., Lin, L., & Zhou, M. (2024). Estimating the role of air quality improvements in the decline of suicide rates in China. *Nature Sustainability*, *7*, 260–269.

INDEX

Note: Numbers in *italics* indicate figures and page numbers in **bold** indicate tables on the corresponding page. References following "n" refer to notes.